THE OUTLINE BIBLE

The
Outline
Bible

HAROLD L.
WILLMINGTON

Tyndale House Publishers, Inc.
WHEATON, ILLINOIS

Library of Congress Cataloging-in-Publication Data

Willmington, H. L.
  The Outline Bible / Harold L. Willmington.
    p. cm.
    ISBN 0-8423-3701-6 (hc. : alk. paper) — ISBN 0-8423-3702-4 (sc : alk.paper)
    1. Bible—Outlines, syllabi, etc. I. Title.
  BS592.W55 2000
  220'.02'02—dc21   99-048752

Printed in the United States of America

06   05   04   03   02   01   00   99
8   7   6   5   4   3   2   1

Table of Contents

Introduction

The Outline Bible is a tool for making the content of the Bible easy and enjoyable to learn—and remember! This handy resource organizes every single verse of the Bible into an easy-to-remember outline format. Each of the major levels of the outlines uses a literary device—such as alliteration, rhyme, etc.—to help the point stick in your mind and heart, and the unique formatting for each level helps you easily recognize it on the page.

This exhaustive resource is perfect for teachers, pastors, and others who want to present Scripture in a way that people will remember and enjoy. It's also great for private study, offering a rich treasure for anyone interested in an organized and memorable overview of any passage of Scripture.

The books of the Bible appear in canonical order, and each book includes at least one (and usually several) outline. At the head of each outline is a brief summary of the information covered under that outline. References have been provided at almost every level so that the reader can easily and instantly recognize all the verses covered under that point.

May God bless you as you read his Word, and may he use this resource to help bring to remembrance all that he teaches you through it.

PART ONE

Pentateuch

Genesis

PART ONE : THE PRELIMINARIES (1–11)
This first part of Genesis describes four great happenings: the creation of
the universe, the fall of humanity, the universal flood, and the Tower of
Babel.

SECTION OUTLINE ONE (GENESIS 1–2)
This section describes the creation of all things.

I. GOD'S WORKING SCHEDULE (1:1–2:19)
   A. **First day: creation of light** (1:3-5): "Then God said, 'Let there be
      light.'" He then divides the light from the darkness.
   B. **Second day: creation of space and water** (1:6-8): He separates
      the atmospheric, upper water from the earthly, lower water.
   C. **Third day: creation of plant life** (1:9-13): First he separates the
      water from the land. The earth then brings forth green grass,
      plants, trees, and vegetation of every kind.
   D. **Fourth day: creation of sun, moon, and stars** (1:14-19)
   E. **Fifth day: creation of fish and fowl** (1:20-23)
   F. **Sixth day: creation of land animals and people** (1:24-31; 2:7-20)
      1. *The brute creatures: livestock and all wild beasts* (1:24-25)
      2. *The blessed creature, who is given two things:*
         a. The image of God (1:26-27)
         b. The instructions from God (1:26-31; 2:15-19)
            (1) People are to rule over all nature (1:26, 28),
            (2) to fill the earth with their own kind (1:28),
            (3) to cultivate and care for their beautiful home, the
                  Garden of Eden (2:15),
            (4) to eat from any tree except the tree of the knowledge of
                  good and evil (2:16-17),
            (5) and to provide names for all the other creatures
                  (2:19-20).
   G. **Seventh day: God rests** (2:1-6): His creative work is complete
      and is pronounced good. God blesses and sets apart the seventh
      day.

II. God's Wedding Schedule (2:20-25)
   A. **The making of Eve** (2:20-22): Eve, the first woman, is formed from the flesh and bone of Adam's side.
   B. **The marriage of Eve** (2:23-25): Eve is returned to Adam's side. "This explains why a man leaves his father and mother and is joined to his wife, and the two are united into one." This marks history's first marriage.

SECTION OUTLINE TWO (GENESIS 3–5)
This section describes the corruption of all things.

I. The Transgression of Adam (3:1-24)
   A. **Adam's disobedience** (3:1-6)
      1. *The treachery* (3:1-5)
         a. Satan begins by casting doubt on God's Word (3:1-3): "Did God really say you must not eat any of the fruit in the garden?"
         b. Satan concludes by denying God's Word (3:4-5): "'You won't die!' the serpent hissed. . . . 'You will become just like God, knowing everything, both good and evil.'"
      2. *The tragedy* (3:6): Both Eve and Adam disobey God and eat of the forbidden tree.
   B. **Adam's deceit** (3:7-8): He attempts to cover his nakedness by making clothes from fig leaves. He then hides among the trees.
   C. **Adam's despair** (3:9-11): He acknowledges his fear and nakedness before God.
   D. **Adam's defense** (3:12-19): Adam blames Eve, but Eve blames the serpent.
   E. **Adam's discipline** (3:14-19): God sets up his divine court in Eden and imposes the following sentences:
      1. *Upon the serpent* (3:14-15): to be the most cursed of all creatures and to crawl on its belly, eating dust. Also, his head will be crushed by the offspring of the woman.
      2. *Upon the woman* (3:16): to suffer pain in childbirth and to be ruled by her husband.
      3. *Upon the man* (3:17-19): to endure wearisome labor as he grows food from unproductive soil and to eventually die physically.
      4. *Upon nature* (3:18): to be infested with thorns and thistles.
   F. **Adam's deliverance** (3:15, 20-21)
      1. *The promise* (3:15): Someday a Savior will defeat Satan, the serpent!
      2. *The provision* (3:20-21): After Adam names his wife Eve, God clothes both of them with animal skins.

G. Adam's dismissal (3:22-24)

1. *The grace* (3:22-23): God removes them from the garden so that they cannot eat of the tree of life and live forever in their sin.
2. *The guards* (3:24): God stations angelic beings with flaming swords at the eastern entrance of Eden to keep Adam and Eve out.

II. THE TESTIMONY OF ABEL (4:1-26)

A. Abel, the godly son (4:1-2, 4): He is a shepherd who obediently offers an animal sacrifice to God.

B. Cain, the godless son (4:3-26)

1. *The apostate* (4:3): He offers God a bloodless offering.
2. *The angered* (4:5-7): God refuses Cain's offering but urges him to offer an acceptable one.
3. *The assassin* (4:8-16)
   a. Cain's crime (4:8): In a fit of rage and envy, Cain kills Abel.
   b. Cain's curse (4:9-12): He becomes a vagrant and a wanderer on the earth.
   c. Cain's complaint (4:13-16): He worries that whoever finds him will kill him! To prevent this, God puts a mark on Cain to warn those who might try to kill him. Cain then marries someone who is probably one of his sisters.
4. *The architect* (4:17-24)
   a. The talented society founded by Cain (4:17-22): Cain builds history's first city. His descendants are the original tent dwellers and herdsmen. They also are the first musicians and metalworkers.
   b. The treacherous society founded by Cain (4:23-24): They practice polygamy and are given over to violence.

C. Seth, the granted son (4:25-26): Eve gives birth to a third son, Seth, whom God grants to take the place of the murdered Abel.

III. THE TRANSLATION OF ENOCH (5:1-32)

A. The first patriarchs living before the Flood (5:1-17): There are six, from Adam to Jared, each living more than nine hundred years.

B. The favored patriarch living before the Flood (5:18-24): Enoch

1. *Enoch's relationship with God* (5:18-22): He walks with God!
2. *Enoch's removal by God* (5:23-24): He is taken to heaven without dying!

C. The final patriarchs living before the Flood (5:25-32): There are four, from Enoch to Noah. One of them, Methuselah, lives for 969 years, making him recorded history's oldest human being! Another, Noah, fathers three sons: Shem, Ham, and Japheth.

SECTION OUTLINE THREE (GENESIS 6–10)
This section describes the condemnation of all things.

I. THE PREPARATION FOR THE FLOOD (6:1-22)
   A. **God's grief** (6:1-7): He sees nothing but human wickedness of every kind, everywhere, at all times.
   B. **God's grace** (6:8-10): Noah, because of his righteous living, finds favor in the sight of God.
   C. **God's guidance** (6:11-22)
      1. *Destruction! (what God will do)* (6:11-13): He is going to destroy all life upon the earth—except for Noah and his family—through a flood.
      2. *Construction! (what Noah will do)* (6:14-22): He is to construct a wooden boat that is 450 feet long, 75 feet wide, and 45 feet high. Upon completion, Noah is to bring his family inside, along with at least one male and one female of every animal.

II. THE PROTECTION DURING THE FLOOD (7:1-24)
   A. **The occupants inside the ark** (7:1-9, 13-16): They include Noah, his wife, their three sons and their wives, plus a pair of all animals and seven pairs of clean animals.
   B. **The ordeal outside the ark** (7:10-12, 17-24): The underground waters burst forth, and torrential rain falls from heaven for forty days, covering the highest mountains and drowning all human and animal life.

III. THE PARTICULARS FOLLOWING THE FLOOD (8:1–10:32)
   A. **Noah's security** (8:1-5): "But God remembered Noah."
   B. **Noah's search** (8:6-12)
      1. *The unsuccessful attempt by the raven* (8:6-7): It cannot find dry ground.
      2. *The successful attempt by the dove* (8:8-12): After one earlier attempt, the dove finds dry ground, returning with a freshly plucked olive leaf in its beak.
   C. **Noah's surveillance** (8:13-14): Noah removes the ark's covering and surveys the new world after the Flood!
   D. **Noah's summons** (8:15-19): God orders Noah, his family, and all the animals to leave the ark.
   E. **Noah's sacrifice** (8:20-22): He builds an altar and sacrifices on it animals approved by God for that purpose.
   F. **Noah's sign (from God)** (9:1-17)
      1. *Concerning the animals of the earth* (9:1-10): They will fear people and provide food for them, but their blood is not to be consumed.
      2. *Concerning the rainbow in the sky* (9:11-17): It will serve as a sign of God's promise that he will never destroy the earth by water again.

G. Noah's shame (9:18-29)
1. *The failure* (9:18-24): Noah becomes drunk with wine and exposes himself.
2. *The foretelling* (9:25-29): Noah curses Canaan and his descendants and blesses Shem and Japheth and their descendants.

H. Noah's sons (10:1-32)
1. *Japheth* (10:2-5): a list of his descendants, including Gomer, Magog, Tubal, and Meshech
2. *Ham* (10:6-20): a list of his descendants, including Canaan and Nimrod
3. *Shem* (10:21-32): a list of his descendants, including Peleg (who may have lived during the tower of Babel dispersion). He was the ancestor of Terah (the father of Abram) and Abram and Sarai

SECTION OUTLINE FOUR (GENESIS 11:1-32)
This section describes the confusion of all things.

I. THE SIN (11:1-4): All human beings attempt to unify themselves for their own glory.

II. THE SENTENCE (11:5-9): God scatters them by confusing their language at the tower of Babel.

III. THE SETTLEMENT (11:10-32): A history is given of Shem's descendants. Shem is the ancestor of Abraham.

PART TWO : THE PATRIARCHS (12–50)
This second part of Genesis describes four great heroes: Abraham, Isaac, Jacob, and Joseph.

SECTION OUTLINE FIVE (GENESIS 12:1–25:18)
This section covers the life of Abraham.

I. THE CONVERSION AND CALLING OF ABRAM (12:1-5)
A. The place (12:1): Ur of the Chaldeans (see Genesis 11:31).
B. The promises (12:2-3): Abram will found a great nation; and God will bless him, make his name great, and cause him to bless others. Those who bless Abram will be blessed; those who curse him will be cursed. Everyone on earth will be blessed through him. This takes place through Jesus Christ, a descendant of Abram.
C. The pilgrimage (12:4-5): Abram travels from Ur to Haran and from Haran to Canaan.

II. THE CANAAN OF ABRAM (12:6-9)
   A. Abram at Shechem (12:6-7): The Lord promises to give Canaan
   to Abram, and Abram builds an altar there.
   B. Abram at Bethel (12:8-9): Abram builds another altar.

III. THE CARNALITY OF ABRAM (FIRST OCCASION) (12:10-20)
   A. The famine (12:10): Abram goes from Canaan to Egypt to escape
   a famine.
   B. The falsehood (12:11-13): Afraid for his life, Abram tells Sarai to
   pretend she is his sister.
   C. The favor (12:14-16): Pharaoh rewards Abram with riches for
   Sarai's sake, probably intending to marry her.
   D. The frustration (12:17): God plagues Pharaoh and his household
   for his plans to marry Sarai.
   E. The fury (12:18-20): Pharaoh rebukes Abram for his deceit and
   sends him and Sarai away.

IV. THE CONDESCENSION OF ABRAM (13:1-18)
   A. The arrival (13:1-4): Abram arrives at Bethel and worships God
   again.
   B. The argument (13:5-7): The herdsmen of Abram and Lot (his
   nephew) have a dispute over grazing rights.
   C. The agreement (13:8-13)
      1. *The terms* (13:8-9): Abram allows Lot to select his own land.
      2. *The tragedy* (13:10-13): Lot foolishly chooses land close to the
      morally perverted city of Sodom.
   D. The assurance (13:14-18): After Lot's departure, God again
   promises to make Abram's descendants as numerous as the dust
   of the earth and to give them the land of Canaan.

V. THE COURAGE OF ABRAM (14:1-16)
   A. The villains (14:1-11)
      1. *The rebellion* (14:1-4): Five Canaanite city-states rebel against
      Kedorlaomer of Elam.
      2. *The retaliation* (14:5-11): Kedorlaomer and his allies defeat the
      armies of the five city-states, plunder their cities, and carry
      many people away as slaves.
   B. The victim (14:12): Lot, now living in Sodom, is taken away as a
   slave.
   C. The victory (14:13-16)
      1. *Abram's army* (14:13-14): Upon learning of Lot's capture,
      Abram and his 318 trained servants ride out to rescue Lot.
      2. *Abram's attack* (14:15): Abram divides his men and initiates a
      surprise attack at night.
      3. *Abram's achievements* (14:16): Kedorlaomer is defeated, and
      Lot is rescued.

VI. THE COMMUNION OF ABRAM (14:17-24)
   A. The godly and priestly king of Salem (14:17-20): As he is return-

ing from battle to his home in Hebron, Abram meets Melchize-
dek, who blesses him. Abram offers him a tenth of all the goods
he has recovered from Kedorlaomer.
  B. **The godless and perverted king of Sodom** (14:21-24): In stark
     contrast, Abram refuses to have any fellowship with Bera, king of
     wicked Sodom.
VII. THE COVENANT WITH ABRAM (15:1-21)
  A. **Abram's faulty assumption** (15:1-3): Abram complains that upon
     his death all his goods will be passed on to Eliezer, one of his
     servants from Damascus. Eliezer will then become the heir to the
     covenant.
  B. **God's faithful assurance** (15:4-21)
     1. *The revelation* (15:4-5): God tells Abram that the promised
        heir will be Abram's own son and that Abram's descendants
        will be as numerous as the stars in the heavens!
     2. *The response* (15:6): "And Abram believed the LORD, and the
        LORD declared him righteous because of his faith."
     3. *The ratification* (15:7-17)
        a. The details (15:7-11): God ratifies his promise to Abram
           with a covenant sealed by blood.
        b. The dream (15:12): At sunset Abram falls into a deep sleep
           and sees troubling visions.
        c. The destiny (of Israel) (15:13-16): God speaks to Abram in
           his sleep, telling him his descendants will be enslaved for
           four hundred years. God also tells him that the oppressors
           will be punished, and that Abram's descendants will be set
           free and depart with great riches.
        d. The descent (of God himself) (15:17): A smoking firepot
           and a flaming torch, probably symbolizing God himself,
           pass between the dead animals of the blood covenant.
     4. *The real estate* (15:18-21): God reveals to Abram the
        boundaries of the Promised Land, from the border of Egypt to
        the Euphrates River.
VIII. THE COMPROMISE BY ABRAM (16:1-16)
  A. **The rationale for his compromise** (16:1-3)
     1. *The problem* (16:1): Sarai is still unable to bear a son.
     2. *The plan* (16:1-3): Sarai convinces Abram to marry Hagar, her
        servant, in order to have a son through her.
  B. **The results of his compromise** (16:4-16)
     1. *Hagar's marriage to Abram* (16:4): After Hagar conceives, she
        begins to look down upon Sarai.
     2. *Hagar's mistreatment by Sarai* (16:5-6): After suffering harsh
        treatment from the frustrated Sarai, Hagar flees into the desert.
     3. *Hagar's meeting with the Lord* (16:7-14)
        a. The Lord advises her (16:7-9): The angel of the Lord comes

to her by a well and tells her, "Return to [Sarai] and submit to her authority."

    b. The Lord assures her (16:10-14): The angel of the Lord tells Hagar that she will have innumerable descendants through her unborn son, who will be called Ishmael ("God hears").

  4. *Hagar's mothering of Ishmael* (16:15-16): She gives birth to Ishmael when Abram is eighty-six years old.

IX. THE CIRCUMCISION OF ABRAHAM (17:1-27)

  A. God and Abram (17:1-14)

    1. *Abram's new title* (17:1-8): God changes Abram's name from Abram ("exalted father") to Abraham ("father of many").

    2. *Abraham's new task* (17:9-14)

      a. The particulars (17:9-13): As a sign of the covenant, he is to circumcise himself, all males in his camp, and all baby boys eight days after their birth.

      b. The penalty (17:14): Those who refuse to be circumcised are to be cut off from the Israelites.

  B. God and Sarai (17:15-19)

    1. *The renaming of Sarai* (17:15): God changes her name from Sarai to Sarah ("princess").

    2. *The reassuring of Sarah* (17:16-19): God promises that this barren woman will indeed become the mother of nations.

  C. God and Ishmael (17:20-27)

    1. *Revealing the future of Ishmael* (17:20-22): God tells Abraham that Ishmael will become the ancestor of twelve princes and a great nation.

    2. *Removing the flesh of Ishmael* (17:23-27): At age ninety-nine, Abraham circumcises himself, the thirteen-year-old Ishmael, and all the men in his camp.

X. THE COMPASSION OF ABRAHAM (18:1–19:38)

  A. The tremendous news (18:1-15)

    1. *The reception by Abraham* (18:1-8)

      a. Meeting with his heavenly visitors (18:1-3): The Lord himself and two angels visit Abraham near Hebron.

      b. Ministering to his heavenly visitors (18:4-8): Abraham prepares a meal of veal, cheese curds, milk, and bread for his visitors.

    2. *The reaction of Sarah* (18:9-15)

      a. The details (18:9-10): In her tent Sarah overhears the Lord's promise concerning the birth of Isaac.

      b. The doubts (18:11-12): Sarah laughs in unbelief.

      c. The declaration (18:13-14): "Is anything too hard for the LORD? . . . Sarah will have a son."

      d. The denial (18:15): In fear, Sarah denies that she laughed in unbelief.

B. The tragic news (18:16–19:38)
1. *The indictment against Sodom* (18:16-22)
    a. Abraham's faithfulness (18:16-19): God determines to tell Abraham about his plan for the city of Sodom, since Abraham has been chosen to be the father of a righteous people.
    b. Sodom's filthiness (18:20-22): The Lord tells Abraham about the wickedness of Sodom.
2. *The intercession for Sodom* (18:23-33)
    a. Pleading for fifty (18:23-26): Abraham asks if the Lord will spare the city for the sake of fifty righteous people found there. The Lord answers yes.
    b. Pleading for forty-five (18:27-28): For forty-five? Yes.
    c. Pleading for forty (18:29): For forty? Yes.
    d. Pleading for thirty (18:30): For thirty? Yes.
    e. Pleading for twenty (18:31): For twenty? Yes.
    f. Pleading for ten (18:32-33): For ten? Yes.
3. *The incineration of Sodom* (19:1-38)
    a. Predestruction events (19:1-14)
        (1) Lot and the angels (19:1-3): Two angels visit Lot, and he invites them to spend the night in his home.
        (2) Lot and the Sodomites (19:4-11): The men of Sodom demand that Lot hand over the two angels so that they can sexually molest them.
        (3) Lot and his family (19:12-14): In vain Lot warns his daughters' fiancés to flee the city.
    b. Destruction events (19:15-29)
        (1) The firmness (19:15-17): Reluctant to leave, Lot and his family are led out of the doomed city by the angels.
        (2) The fear (19:18-22): Lot begs that they be allowed to live in Zoar, a small village near Sodom.
        (3) The fury (19:23-25): The fiery wrath of God falls upon Sodom and other wicked cities of the plain.
        (4) The fatality (19:26): Looking back to the burning Sodom, Lot's wife becomes a pillar of salt.
        (5) The firestorm (19:27-29): From a distance of over twenty miles Abraham sees smoke rising from the destruction of Sodom and Gomorrah.
    c. Post-destruction events (19:30-38)
        (1) The supposition of two sisters (19:30-31): Lot's daughters fear they will never marry and raise children.
        (2) The sins of two sisters (19:32-36): They get their father drunk and sleep with him in order to become pregnant.
        (3) The sons of two sisters (19:37-38): Moab, father of the Moabites, is born to Lot's older daughter, and Ben-ammi, father of the Ammonites, to Lot's younger daughter.

XI. THE CARNALITY OF ABRAHAM (SECOND OCCASION) (20:1-18)
   A. Abraham and Abimelech: round one—deceiving (20:1-8)
   1. *The deception* (20:1-2): Again, fearing for his life, Abraham introduces Sarah as his sister.
   2. *The dream* (20:3-8)
      a. God informs Abimelech (20:3-6): In a dream God warns Abimelech that Sarah is married.
      b. God instructs Abimelech (20:7-8): God tells Abimelech to return Sarah to Abraham and promises that the patriarch will then pray for him.
   B. Abraham and Abimelech: round two—defending (20:9-13)
   1. *The painful question (asked of Abraham)* (20:9-10): "Why have you done this to us?"
   2. *The pitiful answer (given by Abraham)* (20:11-13): Abraham says he feared that Abimelech would have killed him to marry Sarah.
   C. Abraham and Abimelech: round three—delivering (20:14-18): Abimelech returns Sarah and compensates Abraham for his trouble. Abraham prays for Abimelech, and God lifts the curse he has placed upon Abimelech's household.

XII. THE CELEBRATION OF ABRAHAM (21:1-21; 25:12-18)
   A. The fulfillment (21:1-7)
   1. *The nature of the fulfillment* (21:1-2): Sarah gives birth to the heir of the covenant!
   2. *The name for the fulfillment* (21:3-7): He is named Isaac, meaning "laughter," because everyone who hears of this will laugh.
   B. The feast (21:8): The purpose is to celebrate Isaac's weaning.
   C. The flouting (21:9): Sarah sees Ishmael mocking Isaac.
   D. The fury (21:10-11): Sarah demands that Abraham order Hagar and Ishmael to leave the camp.
   E. The farewell (21:12-14): After Abraham is reassured by God that Hagar will be provided for, he sends her away with a supply of food and water.
   F. The fear (21:15-16): In the wilderness Hagar fears both of them will soon die of exposure.
   G. The faithfulness (21:17-21; 25:12-18)
   1. *The deliverance and development of Ishmael* (21:17-21): God provides food and water for Ishmael in the wilderness and later guides him into adulthood.
   2. *The descendants of Ishmael* (25:12-18): Just as God had foretold, Ishmael fathers twelve sons.

XIII. THE CONTRACT BY ABRAHAM (21:22-34)
   A. The persons (21:22): Abimelech and his commander, Phicol, come to make a treaty with Abraham.
   B. The plan (21:23-24): Neither Abimelech nor Abraham will harm each other.

C. **The problem** (21:25-26): Abraham complains that Abimelech's servants have taken away one of his wells. Abimelech says he knew nothing about it.
D. **The pact** (21:27-30): A special peaceful covenant between the two men is ratified as Abraham gives Abimelech some sheep and oxen.
E. **The place** (21:31-34): This is done at Beersheba ("well of the oath").

XIV. THE COMMAND TO ABRAHAM (22:1-24)
A. **Abraham's sorrow** (22:1-8)
   1. *The order* (22:1-2): God commands Abraham to sacrifice his son Isaac as a burnt offering.
   2. *The obedience* (22:3): Along with Isaac and two servants, Abraham heads out for the land of Moriah.
   3. *The ordeal* (22:4-8)
      a. Isaac's question (22:7): "Father? . . . Where is the lamb for the sacrifice?"
      b. Abraham's answer (22:8): "God will provide a lamb, my son."
B. **Isaac's submission** (22:9-10): He allows Abraham to bind him on the altar.
C. **God's substitute** (22:11-24)
   1. *The nature of Abraham's offering* (22:11-13): He is commanded to offer up a nearby ram instead of Isaac.
   2. *The name of Abraham's God* (22:14): Abraham calls that place "Yahweh Yir'eh" ("The LORD Will Provide").
   3. *The number of Abraham's descendants* (22:15-19): The angel of the Lord again promises Abraham that his descendants will be as numerous as the stars of the sky and the sand on the seashore.
   4. *The news concerning Abraham's family* (22:20-24): Abraham learns that his brother Nahor has had eight sons. One of them is Bethuel, who will become the father of Rebekah (Isaac's wife).

XV. THE CAVE OF ABRAHAM (23:1-20)
A. **Abraham's tears** (23:1-2): He weeps for Sarah, who died at age 127.
B. **Abraham's testimony** (23:3-13): He describes himself as a stranger and sojourner in Canaan and asks Ephron the Hittite if he may buy the cave of Machpelah that he might bury Sarah in it.
C. **Abraham's transaction** (23:14-20)
   1. *The price* (23:14-16): four hundred shekels of silver
   2. *The place* (23:17-20): the cave of Machpelah, located in Hebron

XVI. THE COMMISSION BY ABRAHAM (24:1-67)
A. **The plan** (24:1-4): Abraham instructs his servant (probably Eliezer) to find a wife for Isaac from Abraham's native land of Mesopotamia.
B. **The problem** (24:5-6): Even if Eliezer cannot find a willing bride there, he is not to take Isaac there to live.

C. The promises (24:7-9)
1. *God's promise to Abraham* (24:7-8): Abraham remembers the Lord's promise concerning the land of Canaan.
2. *The servant's promise to Abraham* (24:9): He will do exactly as Abraham has instructed.

D. The preparation (24:10): The servant loads ten camels with gifts and departs.

E. The prayer (24:11-21)
1. *The request* (24:11-14): The servant asks the Lord to cause the woman chosen as Isaac's bride to volunteer to provide water for him and his camels.
2. *The results* (24:15-21): Even as the servant is praying, Rebekah appears upon the scene and fulfills the sign.

F. The presents (24:22-33)
1. *Rebekah and the servant* (24:22-28): The servant gives Rebekah some gold jewelry.
2. *Laban and the servant* (24:29-33): Rebekah's brother invites the servant into his home.

G. The proposal (24:34-58)
1. *The overview by the servant* (24:34-48)
   a. The servant's conversation with Abraham (24:34-41): The servant recounts to Laban the mission Abraham has given to him.
   b. The servant's conversation with God (24:42-44): The servant recounts how God has answered his prayer.
   c. The servant's conversation with Rebekah (24:45-48): The servant recounts his initial meeting with Rebekah.
2. *The offer by the servant* (24:49-56): He gives Rebekah more costly jewelry and clothing and invites her to accompany him back to Canaan to marry Isaac.

H. The persuasion (24:57-60): "Are you willing to go with this man?" And [Rebekah] replied, "Yes, I will go."

I. The pilgrimage (24:61): Abraham's servant and Rebekah and her servants leave Mesopotamia for Canaan.

J. The presentation (24:62-67): Isaac is walking through a field when he meets his new bride. They marry and provide each other with love and comfort.

XVII. THE CLOSING YEARS OF ABRAHAM (25:1-11)

A. Abraham's family (25:1-4)
1. *Abraham's last spouse* (25:1): Abraham marries his third wife, Keturah.
2. *Abraham's last sons* (25:2-4): Keturah bears him six sons, including Midian.

B. Abraham's fortune (25:5-6): He passes on his wealth to his sons, giving the greatest part to Isaac.

C. Abraham's farewell (25:7-11): He dies at the age of 175.

I. ISAAC AND REBEKAH (25:19–26:16)
   A. **Isaac's devotion to Rebekah** (25:20-34)
      1. *The request* (25:19-22): He prays that Rebekah will conceive a child.
      2. *The results* (25:23-34): God answers Isaac's prayer in double measure!
         a. The birth of the twins (25:24-26): Esau is born first, followed quickly by Jacob.
         b. The birthright and the twins (25:27-34): Upon reaching manhood, Esau sells his birthright for a bowl of stew.
   B. **Isaac's deception concerning Rebekah** (26:1-16)
      1. *God's direction* (26:1-5): During a famine, God forbids Isaac from going to Egypt, but allows him to enter Philistia.
      2. *Isaac's deceit* (26:6-7): As his father had previously done, Isaac lies to Abimelech (the Philistine king) about his wife, claiming she is his sister.
      3. *Abimelech's detection* (26:8-16): Upon seeing Isaac caressing Rebekah, Abimelech rebukes Isaac for deceiving him. In spite of this, God continues to bless Isaac.

II. ISAAC AND THE PEOPLE OF GERAR (26:17-22): An argument erupts concerning the ownership of some wells.

III. ISAAC AND GOD (26:23-25): In a dream, the Lord appears to Isaac and confirms the covenant he made with Isaac's father, Abraham.

IV. ISAAC AND THREE PHILISTINE LEADERS (26:26-33): Realizing God's blessing upon Isaac, the Philistines propose a peace treaty with him. Isaac accepts and celebrates with a great feast.

V. ISAAC AND HIS SONS (26:34–28:9; 36:1-43)
   A. **The pain** (26:34-35): Esau marries two Hittite women, who make life miserable for Isaac and Rebekah.
   B. **The preparations** (27:1-4): Believing that death is near, Isaac instructs Esau to hunt some wild game and prepare a meal for him. Isaac promises to bless Esau following this meal.
   C. **The plot** (27:5-29)
      1. *Conceived by Rebekah* (27:5-17): Overhearing this conversation, Rebekah prepares a similar meal, disguises Jacob to resemble Esau, and sends him in to Isaac.
      2. *Carried out by Jacob* (27:18-29)
         a. The reluctance of Isaac (27:18-23): At first Isaac is confused, saying, "The voice is Jacob's, but the hands are Esau's."
         b. The reassurance by Jacob (27:24-29): Jacob convinces Isaac that he is indeed Esau and receives his father's blessing.

D. The perplexity (27:30-33): As Jacob exits, Esau enters, ready to be blessed.
E. The plea (27:34-38): Weeping in sheer anger and frustration, Esau says: "O my father, bless me, too!"
F. The prophecy (27:39-40): Isaac predicts that Esau and his descendants will live by the sword and serve his brother for a time.
G. The prejudice (27:41): Esau vows to kill Jacob following the death of their father.
H. The parting (27:42–28:5)
1. *Rebekah's words to Jacob* (27:42-46): She urges him to escape Esau's wrath by going to her hometown of Haran in Mesopotamia.
2. *Isaac's words to Jacob* (28:1-5): Isaac tells Jacob to go to Haran and choose a bride from his mother's relatives.
I. The perception (of Esau) (28:6-9): Realizing that his Canaanite wives are a source of grief to his parents, Esau marries Mahalath, daughter of Ishmael (Abraham's son through Hagar).
J. The people (of Esau) (36:1-43): This chapter is a list of Esau's descendants.

SECTION OUTLINE SEVEN (GENESIS 28:10–35, 37–38)
This section covers the life of Jacob.

I. THE TRAVELER (28:10-22)
A. Jacob's vision (28:10-15)
1. *He sees the angels of God* (28:10-12): During a dream at Bethel, Jacob sees angels ascending and descending upon a stairway reaching from earth to heaven.
2. *He sees the God of the angels* (28:13-15): The Lord is standing at the top of the stairway and reaffirms to Jacob the covenant he established with Abraham.
B. Jacob's vow (28:16-22): Upon waking, Jacob promises to serve God, but only if God protects him and provides for him.

II. THE LOVER (29:1-30)
A. Jacob's love for Rachel (29:1-17)
1. *First meeting with Rachel* (29:1-12): Jacob meets Rachel by a well and rolls away a huge stone from its entrance so she can water her father's sheep. Her father is Laban, Jacob's uncle.
2. *First meeting with Laban* (29:13-17): Jacob and Laban meet each other and decide that Jacob should work for Laban.
B. Jacob's labor for Rachel (29:18-30)
1. *The diligence of Jacob* (29:18-21): Jacob asks to marry Rachel in exchange for seven years of work for Laban.
2. *The deception of Laban* (29:22-30): On the eve of the

wedding, Laban secretly substitutes Leah for Rachel, forcing
Jacob to work yet another seven years.

III. THE FAMILY MAN (29:28–30:24; 35:16-18, 23-26)
    A. Jacob's four wives (29:28-30; 30:1-4, 9)
        1. *Leah* (29:28): Jacob's first wife
        2. *Rachel* (29:30): Jacob's second wife
        3. *Bilhah* (29:29; 30:1-4): Rachel's servant
        4. *Zilpah* (30:9): Leah's servant
    B. Jacob's twelve sons (29:31–30:24; 35:16-18, 23-26)
        1. *Reuben* (29:31-32): Leah's first son
        2. *Simeon* (29:33): Leah's second son
        3. *Levi* (29:34): Leah's third son
        4. *Judah* (29:35): Leah's fourth son
        5. *Dan* (30:5-6): Bilhah's first son
        6. *Naphtali* (30:7-8): Bilhah's second son
        7. *Gad* (30:9-11): Zilpah's first son
        8. *Asher* (30:12-13): Zilpah's second son
        9. *Issachar* (30:14-18): Leah's fifth son
      10. *Zebulun* (30:19-20): Leah's sixth son
      11. *Joseph* (30:22-24): Rachel's first son
      12. *Benjamin* (35:16-18): Rachel's second son
    C. Jacob's one daughter, Dinah (through Leah) (30:21)

IV. THE EMPLOYEE (30:25–31:55)
    A. The specification (30:25-43): Jacob agrees to continue working
    for Laban under certain conditions.
        1. *The request* (30:25-34): Jacob asks that he be allowed to keep
        all the speckled and spotted animals from the flock.
        2. *The results* (30:35-43): Jacob becomes a very wealthy man!
    B. The separation (31:1-55): Jacob finally decides to leave Laban.
        1. *The reasons for the separation* (31:1-3, 13-16)
          a. Laban's resentment (31:1-2): Laban's sons turn his heart
          against his son-in-law, whom they envy.
          b. God's revelation (31:3, 13): The Lord tells Jacob, "Return to
          the land of your father and grandfather." So Jacob returns to
          Bethel.
          c. Rachel and Leah's reassurance (31:14-16): Jacob's wives
          encourage him to follow what God tells him to do.
        2. *The review prompting the separation* (31:4-13): Jacob feels
        Laban has deceived him, changing his wages on ten occasions
        (see 31:7, 41).
        3. *The reunion following the separation* (31:17-55)
          a. Frustration! (31:17-23): Laban learns that Jacob and his
          entire camp have left without informing him and evidently
          have stolen the family idols.
          b. Revelation! (31:24-25): During his ride to overtake Jacob,
          Laban is warned by God not to harm him.

       c. Confrontation! (31:26-30): Laban asks, "Why did you slip away secretly? . . . Why have you stolen my household gods?"

       d. Explanation! (31:31-42): Jacob replies that Laban's dishonesty caused him to leave. He says that he left secretly because of fear, but insists that he did not steal Laban's gods.

       e. Representation! (31:43-55): Both men agree to an uneasy truce, building a pile of stones to serve as a visible reminder.

V. THE WRESTLER (32:1–33:16)

  A. Jacob's communion with God (32:1-32)

    1. *The presence* (32:1-2): As Jacob and his family continue on their way, angels come and meet them.

    2. *The plan* (32:3-5): Upon learning that Esau is nearby, a frightened Jacob sends messengers to his brother, promising him great riches.

    3. *The panic* (32:6-8): The messengers return with some terrifying news: Esau is coming with four hundred men to meet Jacob.

    4. *The prayer* (32:9-12): Jacob "reminds" God of the covenant he established with Abraham and cries out for help.

    5. *The payment* (32:13-21): He attempts to bribe Esau by sending him great herds and flocks of goats, rams, camels, cattle, and donkeys.

    6. *The power struggle* (32:22-32)

       a. The travail (32:22-26): As Jacob is waiting alone by the Jabbok River during the night, a man comes and wrestles with him until dawn.

       b. The triumph (32:27-29): Jacob maintains the upper hand, and God changes his name from Jacob (meaning, "the deceiver") to Israel ("one who struggles with God").

       c. The testimony (32:30-32): Jacob calls the place Peniel, meaning "face of God." Following this event, he will (literally) never walk the same again!

  B. Jacob's reunion with Esau (33:1-16)

    1. *Jacob presents himself to Esau* (33:1-4): Jacob bows seven times as he approaches Esau. To Jacob's immense relief, Esau embraces and kisses him! Soon both are weeping for joy.

    2. *Jacob presents his family to Esau* (33:5-7)

    3. *Jacob presents his flocks to Esau* (33:8-16)

VI. THE OBEDIENT PATRIARCH (33:17-20; 35:1-7, 9-15)

  A. The returns (as ordered by God) (33:17-20; 35:1)

    1. *To Shechem* (33:17-20): Here Jacob buys a field and builds an altar, calling it El-Elohe-Israel, meaning "God, the God of Israel."

      2. *To Bethel* (35:1): At God's command, Jacob returns to Bethel, where he first saw the dream of the stairway to heaven.

B. The revival (35:2-7): Jacob collects and buries all the idols in his camp, ordering each person to "wash yourselves, and put on clean clothing." Following this, Jacob builds an altar and calls it El-bethel, meaning "the God of the house of God."

C. The revelation (35:9-15): God again confirms to Jacob the covenant he established with Abraham.

VII. THE BROKEN-HEARTED (34:1-31; 35:8, 16-29; 37:1-36; 38:1-30)

  A. The funerals (35:8, 16-20, 27-29)

    1. *The death of Deborah* (35:8): She had been Rebekah's former nurse.

    2. *The death of Rachel* (35:16-20): Rachel dies while giving birth to Benjamin and is buried along the way to Bethlehem.

    3. *The death of Isaac* (35:27-29): Both Jacob and Esau return to Hebron and bury their 180-year-old father.

  B. The failures (the sins of Jacob's children) (34:1-31; 35:21-26; 37:1-36; 38:1-30)

    1. *Murder, on the part of Simeon and Levi* (34:1-31): After Dinah is raped by Shechem, a local Canaanite prince, several events take place.

      a. The suggestion (34:3-12): Hamor, father of Shechem, meets with Jacob, proposing close relationships between both peoples, beginning with the marriage between Dinah and Shechem.

      b. The subtlety (34:13-24): Pretending to agree with this suggestion (but inwardly abhoring it), the brothers insist that Hamor and his men must first be circumcised.

      c. The slaughter (34:25-29): On the third day, when the men of the town are helpless because of their wounds from circumcision, Simeon and Levi walk into their camp and slaughter them!

      d. The scandal (34:30-31): Jacob rebukes his sons for causing his name to "stink" among the other Canaanites in the land, fearing that some might seek revenge.

    2. *Adultery, on the part of Reuben* (35:21-22): Reuben sleeps with Bilhah, Jacob's concubine and Rachel's former servant.

    3. *Sexual immorality and hypocrisy, on the part of Judah* (38:1-30)

      a. Judah's Canaanite wife (38:1-5): Judah fathers three sons by her: Er, Onan, and Shelah.

      b. Judah's choice (38:6-10): Judah chooses a woman named Tamar to be Er's wife. But Er dies before fathering any children, leaving Onan to raise up a family for him through Tamar. But Onan also dies without fathering any children.

      c. Judah's contract (38:11-13): Judah promises Tamar that Shelah, his youngest son, will someday take her as his wife.

    d. Judah's carnality (38:14-23): Later, realizing this promise has not been kept, Tamar disguises herself as a prostitute and entices Judah to sleep with her.

    e. Judah's condemnation (of Tamar) (38:24-25): Three months later, Judah learns of Tamar's pregnancy and orders her to be burned. Tamar, however, quickly produces irrefutable evidence that the father of her unborn child is none other than Judah himself!

    f. Judah's confession (38:26-30): A red-faced Judah acknowledges, "She is more in the right than I am."

4. *Deceit and treachery, on the part of Jacob's ten sons* (37:1-36): These brothers, jealous of their father's special affection for Joseph, sell their younger brother into Egyptian slavery.

SECTION OUTLINE EIGHT (GENESIS 37, 39–50)
This section covers the life of Joseph.

I. JOSEPH, THE FAVORED SON (37:1-35)
  A. Loved by his father (37:3)
  B. Loathed by his brothers (37:1-35)
    1. *The reasons for their hatred* (37:1-11)
      a. The devotion he enjoys (37:1-4): "Now Jacob loved Joseph more than any of his other children because Joseph had been born to him in his old age. So one day he gave Joseph a special gift—a beautiful robe."
      b. The dreams he experiences (37:5-11): Joseph has two dreams that symbolically portray his brothers bowing down before him.
    2. *The results of their hatred* (37:12-35)
      a. The trip (37:12-17): Jacob sends Joseph to check on the ten brothers. Joseph catches up with them at Dothan.
      b. The treachery (37:18-27): The brothers, still angry over Joseph's dreams and favored status with their father, plan to kill Joseph. But Reuben convinces them to throw him alive into a pit.
      c. The transaction (37:28-30): The brothers decide to sell Joseph to a band of Ishmaelite traders for twenty pieces of silver.
      d. The trickery (37:31-35): The brothers deceive Jacob into believing that Joseph has been killed and eaten by a wild animal.

II. JOSEPH, THE FAITHFUL STEWARD (37:36; 39:1-20)
  A. Joseph's service (37:36; 39:1-6): Joseph becomes a faithful and highly effective servant in the house of Potiphar, captain of Pharaoh's palace guard.

B. Joseph's self-control (39:7-20)

1. *The request* (39:7): Potiphar's wife attempts to seduce Joseph.
2. *The refusal* (39:8-12): He refuses her advances repeatedly, even running from the house on one occasion, leaving his shirt behind.
3. *The revenge* (39:13-20): Joseph is falsely accused of attempted rape and thrown into prison!

III. JOSEPH, THE FORGOTTEN SLAVE (39:21–40:23)

A. Joseph and the jailer (39:21-23): Joseph gains favor with the jailer, who places him in charge of the entire prison!

B. Joseph and the prisoners (40:1-23)

1. *The characters* (40:1-4): Pharaoh's chief cup-bearer and chief baker anger him, and he throws them into prison. Joseph is assigned to take care of them.
2. *The confusion* (40:5-8): Both the cup-bearer and the baker have dreams that they cannot understand.
3. *The clarification* (40:9-19): Joseph interprets both dreams.
   a. The cup-bearer's dream (40:9-15): Pharaoh will release and restore him in three days.
   b. The baker's dream (40:16-19): He will be executed in three days!
4. *The conclusion* (40:20-23): Both prophecies come true at the end of three days. The cup-bearer, however, promptly forgets Joseph.

IV. JOSEPH, THE FAMED STATESMAN (41:1-57)

A. The dreams of Pharaoh (41:1-36)

1. *The revelation* (41:1-8): Pharaoh has two dreams.
   a. First dream (41:1-4): He sees seven thin cows devouring seven fat cows.
   b. Second dream (41:5-8): He sees seven thin heads of grain devouring seven healthy ones.
2. *The remembrance* (41:9-13): After no one is able to interpret Pharaoh's dreams, the cup-bearer suddenly remembers that Joseph was able to interpret his dream.
3. *The review* (41:14-24): Joseph is brought from prison to hear the king relate his two mysterious dreams.
4. *The rendering* (41:25-32): God reveals to Joseph that Pharaoh's dreams are foretelling the events of the next fourteen years. The first seven years will witness abundant crops, while the next seven will see only famine.
5. *The recommendation* (41:33-36): Joseph suggests that someone be appointed to store up food supplies during the good years to prepare for the bad ones.

B. The decrees of Pharaoh (41:37-57)

1. *Joseph's promotion* (41:37-46): Pharaoh appoints Joseph to

oversee the storage of grain, placing him in charge of the entire government in Egypt.

2. *Joseph's program* (41:47-57): Joseph stores massive amounts of grain in nearby cities. So when the famine comes, "people from surrounding lands also [come] to Egypt to buy grain from Joseph."

V. JOSEPH, THE FORGIVING SAINT (42:1–48:22)

  A. Joseph and his brothers (42:1–45:28)

    1. *The unknown brother* (42:1–44:34)

      a. First trip of Jacob's sons to Egypt (42:1-38)

        (1) The reason (42:1-6): Jacob tells his ten oldest sons, "I have heard there is grain in Egypt. Go down and buy some for us before we all starve to death."

        (2) The recognition (42:7-8): Joseph recognizes his brothers, but they do not recognize him.

        (3) The rebuke (42:9-14): Attempting to make them squirm, Joseph accuses his brothers of being spies, which they deny.

        (4) The requirement (42:15-20): Joseph demands that his brothers return home and bring back Benjamin, the youngest brother. Simeon is kept as a guarantee that they will return.

        (5) The remorse (42:21-23): The guilt-stricken brothers conclude that God is punishing them for selling Joseph into slavery.

        (6) The restraint (42:24): Upon hearing this, Joseph leaves the room so that he does not reveal his true identity as he weeps.

        (7) The return (42:25-28): The nine brothers arrive in Canaan with their food. As they unpack, they are astounded to discover in their bags the money they had used to buy the food!

        (8) The review (42:29-38): Jacob's sons tell him all about their first trip, including how "the man" (Joseph) has requested that Benjamin accompany them on their return journey. Jacob refuses.

      b. Second trip of Jacob's sons to Egypt (43:1–44:34)

        (1) The promise (43:1-14): After Judah guarantees Benjamin's safety, a reluctant Jacob finally agrees to let Benjamin go.

        (2) The preparation (43:15-17): Upon arriving, Joseph sends the brothers to his home, where food is being prepared for them.

        (3) The panic (43:18-25): The manager of Joseph's household reassures the frightened brothers that his master means them no harm. Simeon is now released and joins them.

(4) The presentation (43:26-30): Joseph enters and is "introduced" to Benjamin.

(5) The placing (43:31-34): To his brothers' amazement, Joseph seats them at the banquet table in the order of their ages.

(6) The plot (44:1-17): Joseph orders that his own silver cup be secretly placed in Benjamin's sack. Shortly after leaving the city, the brothers are stopped and searched. To the brothers' horror, the cup is found in Benjamin's sack, and he is arrested.

(7) The plea (44:18-34): Judah begs Joseph to release Benjamin, offering to be imprisoned in his place.

2. *The unveiled brother* (45:1-28)

   a. The climax (45:1-4): Unable to hold back any longer, a tearful Joseph reveals his true identity to his astonished brothers!

   b. The consolation (45:5-8): Joseph tells his brothers that God has allowed everything to happen as it did so that he might save people from starvation during the famine.

   c. The counsel (45:9-15): Joseph tells his brothers to go home and tell their father to pack up and move to Egypt.

   d. The command (45:16-24): Pharaoh says the same to the brothers.

   e. The confirmation (45:25-28): Upon seeing the wealth brought back by his sons, Jacob believes their report about Joseph.

B. **Joseph and his father** (46:1–47:31)

   1. *Jacob's trip to Egypt* (46:1-27)

      a. The promise of God (46:1-7): God directs Jacob to move to Egypt, promising to care for him there.

      b. The people of God (46:8-27): Jacob and his entire family, seventy in all, move to Egypt.

   2. *Jacob's time in Egypt* (46:28–47:31)

      a. The meetings (46:28–47:10)

         (1) Between Jacob and Joseph (46:28-30): Father and son meet and embrace in Goshen.

         (2) Between Jacob and Pharaoh (46:31–47:10): Pharaoh gives the best of the land to Jacob and his family.

      b. The ministry (47:11-31): Joseph carefully attends to the needs of his father, Jacob.

         (1) The provision (47:11-12): Joseph personally sees to it that his family has all the food they need.

         (2) The promise (47:27-31): Joseph promises his father, Jacob, that he will bury him beside his ancestors in the Promised Land, not in Egypt.

C. **Joseph and the Egyptians** (47:13-26): The continuing famine eventually forces all the Egyptians (except for the priests) to sell their land to Pharaoh for food. Joseph then redistributes the land and establishes a law requiring one-fifth of all crops to be given to Pharaoh.

D. Joseph and his sons (48:1-22)

1. *Jacob adopts Joseph's sons* (48:1-7): Manasseh and Ephraim now enjoy the same status as Jacob's other twelve sons.
2. *Jacob anoints Joseph's sons* (48:8-22): Ignoring Joseph's initial objections, Jacob bestows the greater blessing on Ephraim, the younger son, instead of on Manasseh, the firstborn.

VI. JOSEPH, THE FRUITFUL TREE (49:1–50:26)

A. The blessing of Jacob (49:1-27): Each of the Jacob's sons receives a blessing from him.

1. *Reuben* (49:3-4): He is as unruly as the stormy sea and is demoted because of his immorality.
2. *Simeon and Levi* (49:5-7): They are violent men given to anger and cruelty, so their descendants will be scattered throughout Israel.
3. *Judah* (49:8-12): He will be praised by his brothers and will defeat his enemies. The scepter (royal line) will not depart from him "until the coming of the one to whom it belongs."
4. *Zebulun* (49:13): He will live by the seashore and become a harbor for ships.
5. *Issachar* (49:14-15): He will work with animals and till the land.
6. *Dan* (49:16-18): He will be like a snake beside the road.
7. *Gad* (49:19): He will defend himself against all enemies.
8. *Asher* (49:20): He will produce rich food fit for kings.
9. *Naphtali* (49:21): He will be as free as a deer.
10. *Joseph* (49:22-26): He will be like a fruitful tree beside a fountain, blessing others. He has been persecuted, but he has been strengthened by God. He will be blessed by God and will be a prince among his brothers.
10. *Benjamin* (49:27): He will devour his enemies like a hungry wolf.

B. The body of Jacob (49:28–50:26)

1. *The request* (49:28-33): Again Jacob requests to be buried with his ancestors in the cave of Machpelah at Hebron. Then he dies.
2. *The return* (50:1-14): Following a 70-day period of mourning, the twelve brothers carry their father's embalmed body to Hebron.
3. *The reassurance* (50:15-21): After the brothers return to Egypt, Joseph tries to calm their fears that he will seek revenge. He tells them, "God turned into good what you meant for evil."
4. *The remaining years* (50:22-26): Joseph lives to see the third generation of Ephraim's children and dies at age 110.

Exodus, Leviticus, Numbers, Deuteronomy

P A R T   O N E : GOD'S DELIVERANCE OF ISRAEL—THE PREVIEW
(EXODUS 1)
The first part of the book of Exodus sets the scene for God's deliverance
of his chosen people, Israel, from slavery in Egypt.

SECTION OUTLINE ONE (EXODUS 1)
Israel is being persecuted by an Egyptian pharaoh, probably Thutmose I.

I. THE REASONS FOR PERSECUTION (Ex. 1:1-10)
   A. Fruitfulness (Ex. 1:1-7): Beginning with 70 individuals, the
   nation of Israel multiplies so quickly that they soon fill the
   land.
   B. Fear (Ex. 1:8-10): Such growth causes Pharaoh great concern,
   since the Israelites might join others and attack Egypt.

II. THE RESULTING PERSECUTION (Ex. 1:11-22)
   A. Pharaoh's building decree (Ex. 1:11-14): To lessen the threat
   from Israel's growing strength, Pharaoh enslaves the Israelites,
   forcing them to build two storage cities, Pithom and Rameses.
   In spite of persecution, Israel continues to multiply.
   B. Pharaoh's bloody decree (Ex. 1:15-22)
   1. *His order to the midwives* (Ex. 1:15-21): In his continuing
      efforts to curb Israel's strength, Pharaoh tells the Hebrew
      midwives to kill all Israelite male babies at birth. "But because
      the midwives feared God, they refused to obey the king and
      allowed the boys to live."
   2. *His order to the masses* (Ex. 1:22): Finally, Pharaoh orders
      his people to throw all Israelite male babies into the Nile
      River.

PART TWO : GOD'S DELIVERANCE OF ISRAEL—THE OVERVIEW (EX. 2—NUM. 36)
This lengthy section covers the life and mission of Moses. We see him as the prince of Egypt, the shepherd of Midian, and the lawgiver of Israel.

SECTION OUTLINE TWO (EXODUS 2:1-15)
This section details Moses' early years and his role as the prince of Egypt.

I. THE BABY IN THE BASKET (Ex. 2:1-10)
   A. **Moses and his parents** (Ex. 2:1-3): Moses is born to a Levite couple, Amram and Jochebed (see Ex. 6:20). After hiding him from Pharaoh for three months, they place Moses in a small basket and set it along the bank of the Nile River.
   B. **Moses and the princess** (Ex. 2:4-10)
      1. *Rescuing Moses* (Ex. 2:4-6): Pharaoh's daughter discovers the baby Moses and has compassion for him.
      2. *Raising Moses* (Ex. 2:7-10): Moses' sister, Miriam, has been watching the princess and suggests to her that a young Hebrew mother be found to nurse the baby. The princess agrees, and Miriam gets her mother so she can nurse her own child! Moses is named and raised by Pharaoh's daughter.

II. THE MAN IN THE MIDDLE (Ex. 2:11-15)
   A. **The helpless slave** (Ex. 2:11-12): Moses kills an Egyptian who is brutally beating a Hebrew slave.
   B. **The hostile slave** (Ex. 2:13-15): The next day Moses rebukes a Hebrew slave who is mistreating a fellow Hebrew. But the man turns the tables on Moses, asking, "Do you plan to kill me as you killed that Egyptian yesterday?" Realizing that his deed had become known, Moses flees to Midian.

SECTION OUTLINE THREE (EXODUS 2:16–4:31)
This section recounts Moses' years as the shepherd of Midian.

I. THE MARRIAGE OF MOSES (Ex. 2:16-22)
   A. **He assists a Midianite girl at a well** (Ex. 2:16-20): Moses drives away some unfriendly shepherds, allowing some women to water their flocks.
   B. **He accepts a Midianite girl as his wife** (Ex. 2:21-22): Moses marries Zipporah, one of the women he helped at the well, and fathers two sons, Gershom (Ex. 2:22) and Eliezer (Ex. 18:4).

II. THE MISSION OF MOSES (Ex. 2:23–3:10)
   A. **Israel's misery** (Ex. 2:23-25): Egypt's persecution of Israel

intensifies. God hears their cries and remembers his covenant with Abraham.

B. Moses' mystery (Ex. 3:1-3): He sees a bush engulfed in flames, but it is not consumed by the fire.

C. God's message (Ex. 3:4-10)
1. *Take your shoes off!* (Ex. 3:4-9)
   a. The why of the matter (Ex. 3:5): "You are standing on holy ground."
   b. The what of the matter (Ex. 3:7-8): The Lord says he has heard the Israelites' cries and will deliver them.
2. *Put your shoes on!* (Ex. 3:10): The Lord tells Moses that he has chosen him to deliver his people.

III. THE MISGIVINGS OF MOSES (Ex. 3:11–4:23)
A. The protests (Ex. 3:11-15; 4:10-17)
1. *First objection* (Ex. 3:11-12)
   a. Moses says that he is not important enough to appear before Pharaoh.
   b. The Lord tells Moses that he will be with him and will bring him back to Mount Sinai.
2. *Second objection* (Ex. 3:13-15)
   a. Moses complains that he holds no authority.
   b. The Lord tells Moses that he, the "I Am," is his authority.
3. *Third objection* (Ex. 4:1-5)
   a. Moses insists that the people will not believe him.
   b. The Lord turns Moses' staff into a snake and tells him that the people will believe him when they see this.
4. *Fourth objection* (Ex. 4:10-17)
   a. Moses complains that he is not a good speaker.
   b. The Lord tells Moses that Aaron, his brother, will be his spokesman.

B. The prophecies (Ex. 3:16-22)
1. *Israel will be brought out of Egypt and into Canaan* (Ex. 3:16-17).
2. *Israel's leaders will believe Moses* (Ex. 3:18).
3. *Pharaoh will oppose Moses* (Ex. 3:19).
4. *Egypt will suffer God's judgment* (Ex. 3:20).
5. *Israel will receive riches from Egypt* (Ex. 3:21-22).

C. The proofs (Ex. 4:2-9)
1. *First proof* (Ex. 4:2-5): Moses' rod turns into a snake.
2. *Second proof* (Ex. 4:6-8): Moses' hand becomes leprous.
3. *Third proof* (Ex. 4:9): The Nile River waters will later become blood.

D. The permission (Ex. 4:10-18): God allows Moses' older brother, Aaron, to accompany Moses as spokesman. Moses receives permission from his father-in-law to leave.

E. The preparation (Ex. 4:19-20): Moses says good-bye to his father-in-law.

F. The plan (Ex. 4:21-23): God will help the hand of Moses (in performing miracles) but will harden the heart of Pharaoh!

IV. THE MISTAKE OF MOSES (Ex. 4:24-26): For some reason Moses carelessly neglected, or perhaps even refused, to circumcise his firstborn son, Gershom.
   A. The anger of God (Ex. 4:24): This carelessness almost costs Moses his life!
   B. The act of Zipporah (Ex. 4:25-26): Realizing the danger, Zipporah quickly circumcises their son.

V. THE MEETINGS OF MOSES (Ex. 4:27-31)
   A. Moses meets with his brother Aaron (Ex. 4:27-28): Moses now tells Aaron the details of their mission.
   B. Moses meets with the elders of Israel (Ex. 4:29-31): Upon hearing Aaron's message and seeing Moses' miracles, the elders believe them and worship God.

SECTION OUTLINE FOUR (EXODUS 5–17)
This section details Moses' role and experiences as the lawgiver of Israel.

I. LIBERATING THE PEOPLE OF GOD (Ex. 5:1–13:22)
   A. The problems (Ex. 5:1-23)
      1. *From Pharaoh* (Ex. 5:1-14)
         a. Pharaoh insults the God of Israel (Ex. 5:1-3)
            (1) Moses to Pharaoh: "This is what the LORD, the God of Israel, says: 'Let my people go.'"
            (2) Pharaoh to Moses: "I don't know the LORD, and I will not let Israel go."
         b. Pharaoh increases the burdens of Israel (Ex. 5:4-14): He forces them to gather their own straw to make bricks.
      2. *From the people* (Ex. 5:15-23): Upon learning the reason for their additional burdens, the Jewish elders become angry with Moses and Aaron. Moses, in turn, complains to God.
   B. The promise (Ex. 6:1-30)
      1. *The nature (of the promise)* (Ex. 6:1-13): Moses is reassured that the God of Abraham, Isaac, and Jacob—the Lord himself—will indeed deliver them from Egypt and lead them into the Promised Land!
      2. *The names* (Ex. 6:14-30): These verses record the families of Reuben, Simeon, and Levi (the ancestor of Moses and Aaron).
   C. The prophet (Ex. 7:1-2): Aaron is appointed by God to serve as a prophet and spokesman for Moses.
   D. The power (Ex. 7:3-7): God will soon pour out his divine wrath upon the land of Egypt!
   E. The preliminaries (Ex. 7:8-13): When Moses and Aaron confront

Pharaoh again, Pharaoh demands that they demonstrate the power of their God. So Aaron throws down his staff, which turns into a snake. Pharaoh's magicians do the same, but Aaron's snake swallows up their snakes.

F. The plagues (Ex. 7:14–10:29; 11:1, 4-10): Because Pharaoh refuses to listen, the Lord begins a series of 10 plagues on Egypt. After each plague, the Lord gives Pharaoh opportunity to change his mind, but Pharaoh continually refuses.

1. *Blood* (Ex. 7:14-25): Moses strikes the Nile with his staff, causing its waters to change into blood. Soon all water in Egypt is polluted in similar fashion.

2. *Frogs* (Ex. 8:1-15): A plague of frogs covers every square foot of the land. Pharaoh begs Moses to remove them, promising Israel's deliverance, but then refuses after the frogs disappear.

3. *Gnats* (Ex. 8:16-19): Aaron strikes the dust, and gnats suddenly infest the entire nation. Pharaoh's magicians advise him to release Israel, but he again refuses.

4. *Flies* (Ex. 8:20-32): Egypt is filled with great swarms of flies, but none appear in the land of Goshen, where the Israelites live. Again Pharaoh promises to set Israel free but refuses when the flies are gone.

5. *Plague on livestock* (Ex. 9:1-7): All Egyptian livestock suddenly become sick and begin to die, but not one Israelite animal is affected.

6. *Boils* (Ex. 9:8-12): After Moses tosses soot from a furnace into the air, festering boils break out on people and animals.

7. *Hail and lightning* (Ex. 9:13-35): Before this plague, God tells Moses and Pharaoh the purpose of the plagues: "that you might see my power and that my fame might spread throughout the earth." Some Egyptians heed God's warning and bring their livestock in from the fields for protection from the fearful lightning and hail. Pharaoh tells Moses that he will let his people go but changes his mind after the plague stops.

8. *Locusts* (Ex. 10:1-20): Pharaoh agrees to allow only the men of Israel to go worship the Lord. Moses rejects this offer, and the Lord sends a strong east wind that blows in the worst locust plague in Egyptian history! Pharoah repents, the Lord removes the locusts, and then Pharaoh changes his mind yet again.

9. *Darkness* (Ex. 10:21-29): The Lord sends a deep, terrifying darkness over all of Egypt for three days. Pharaoh agrees to let the people go, but the flocks must stay. Moses refuses.

10. *Death of firstborn sons* (Ex. 11:1, 4-10): The Lord tells Moses that this plague will result in Israel's freedom.

G. The preparation (Ex. 12:1-11, 14-28): Each Israelite family is instructed to slay a lamb on the fourteenth of the first month of the Hebrew calendar (in the spring). Its blood must be sprinkled on the door frame of the home.

H. The protection (Ex. 12:12-13): The Lord warns the people that he will "kill all the firstborn sons and firstborn male animals in the land of Egypt." But he reassures them that "when I see the blood, I will pass over you," sparing the firstborn of the home from death.

I. The panic (Ex. 12:29-33): Following the death of his firstborn on the fourteenth of the month, Pharaoh summons Moses and commands him to lead Israel out of Egypt.

J. The presents (Ex. 11:2-3; 12:34-36): The frightened Egyptians give the departing Israelites clothing and costly gifts of silver and gold.

K. The parting (Ex. 12:37-39): Some 600,000 men (some of whom were not Israelites), along with their wives and children, leave Egypt that night.

L. The period of time (Ex. 12:40-41): Israel has been in Egypt for the past 430 years.

M. The Passover festival (Ex. 12:42-51): Foreigners are forbidden to eat the Passover lamb unless they are circumcised. No bone of the Passover lamb is to be broken.

N. The parents and children (Ex. 13:1-16): All firstborn Israelite sons are to be dedicated to God. Upon reaching the Promised Land, the Israelites are to observe the Passover feast yearly, and parents are to tell their children of God's faithfulness in bringing them out of Egypt.

O. The pillar of cloud and fire (Ex. 13:17-22): God leads his people to the Promised Land on a longer route through the wilderness and toward the Red Sea. A pillar of cloud leads them by day, and a pillar of fire leads them by night.

II. LEADING THE PEOPLE OF GOD FROM EGYPT TO MOUNT SINAI (Ex. 14:1–17:16)

A. Phase one: Israel at the Red Sea (Ex. 14:1-18)

1. *The decision of Pharaoh: Follow up!* (Ex. 14:1-9): Regretting his decision to free Israel, Pharaoh orders the Egyptian army, including 600 chariots, to capture the Israelites by the Red Sea.

2. *The despair of the people: Give up!* (Ex. 14:10-12): In great fear and anger the Israelites cry out to Moses, "Our Egyptian slavery was far better than dying out here in the wilderness!"

3. *The declaration of Moses: Look up!* (Ex. 14:13-14): Moses reassures them, "Don't be afraid. Just stand where you are and watch the LORD rescue you."

4. *The decree of God: Lift up!* (Ex. 14:15-18): Moses is told to raise his staff over the Red Sea, dividing the waters and allowing Israel to walk across on dry ground.

B. Phase two: Israel crosses the Red Sea (Ex. 14:19–15:21)

1. *The protecting* (Ex. 14:19-20): The pillar of cloud moves between the Egyptians and the Israelites. At night it becomes a

pillar of fire once again, resulting in darkness for the Egyptians but glorious light for the Israelites.

2. *The parting* (Ex. 14:21-22): A strong east wind blows and parts the Red Sea, forming walls of water on each side.

3. *The perishing* (Ex. 14:23-31): Attempting to pursue the Israelites across the dry path, the Egyptians drown when Moses lifts his hand, causing the waters to collapse on them.

4. *The praising* (Ex. 15:1-21): A great victory celebration is held on the eastern banks of the Red Sea. Moses and his sister, Miriam, lead the nation in singing, music, and dancing.

C. **Phase three: Israel at Marah** (Ex. 15:22-26)

1. *The problem* (Ex. 15:22-24): After traveling three days without finding water, the people discover the oasis at Marah has only bitter and undrinkable water.

2. *The purification* (Ex. 15:25): The Lord tells Moses to throw a tree in the water and it will become clear and cold.

3. *The promise* (Ex. 15:26): Obeying God will result in divine protection from the diseases he inflicted upon the Egyptians.

D. **Phase four: Israel at Elim** (Ex. 15:27): This oasis has 12 springs and 70 palm trees.

E. **Phase five: Israel in the Sin Desert** (Ex. 16:1-36)

1. *A special diet* (Ex. 16:1-22, 31-36): In spite of the Israelites' constant complaining, the Lord sends them quail to eat in the evening and provides a daily supply of bread ("manna") from heaven.

2. *A special day* (Ex. 16:23-30): Moses tells the people to keep the Sabbath, a weekly day of rest.

F. **Phase six: Israel at Rephidim** (Ex. 17:1-16)

1. *The rock struck open by Moses* (Ex. 17:1-7): At a place called Rephidim, the thirsty and rebellious Israelites threaten to kill Moses. At God's command, Moses strikes a rock there, which supernaturally gushes forth with cold, clear water!

2. *The foe struck down by Moses* (Ex. 17:8-16): Joshua leads the Israelite army to victory over the fierce Amalekites as Moses prays for them from a nearby hill. Aaron and Hur assist Moses as he holds up his staff during the battle.

SECTION OUTLINE FIVE (EXODUS 18:1–NUMBERS 10:10)
The nation travels to Mount Sinai and remains there for eleven months and five days. Three significant events transpire during this time: the constitution of Israel, the prostitution of Israel, and the restitution of Israel.

I. THE CONSTITUTION OF ISRAEL (MOSES AND THE LAW OF GOD): the requirements for fellowship (Ex. 18:1–31:18)

A. **The circumstances preceding the constitution** (Ex. 18:1–19:25)

1. *The welcome of Moses* (Ex. 18:1-12): Moses is met by his wife, Zipporah; his sons, Gershom and Eliezer; and his father-in-law, Jethro. He relates how God has led the nation out of Egypt!
2. *The wisdom of Jethro* (Ex. 18:13-27): Jethro suggests that Moses appoint capable men to serve as judges regarding the various disputes among the people.
3. *The wonders of God* (Ex. 19:1-25)
    a. God's words from Mount Sinai (Ex. 19:1-15): While Israel is camped at the base of Mount Sinai, Moses climbs the mountain and is instructed to inform the people that the Lord himself will visit them in the form of a thick cloud at the end of three days. Thus, all the people must purify themselves for this meeting.
    b. God's works on Mount Sinai (Ex. 19:16-25): The Lord appears, accompanied by thunder, lightning, and a loud blast from a ram's horn. Mount Sinai is suddenly covered with smoke. Moses and Aaron ascend the mountain to meet with God.
B. **The contents of the constitution** (Ex. 20:1—Lev. 20:27)
    1. *The moral code: The Ten Commandments* (Ex. 20:1-26; 24:1-18; 31:18)
        a. The requirements (Ex. 20:1-17; 31:18)
            (1) "Do not worship any other gods besides me" (Ex. 20:3).
            (2) "Do not make idols of any kind" (Ex. 20:4).
            (3) "Do not misuse the name of the LORD your God" (Ex. 20:7).
            (4) "Remember to observe the Sabbath day by keeping it holy" (Ex. 20:8).
            (5) "Honor your father and mother" (Ex. 20:12).
            (6) "Do not murder" (Ex. 20:13).
            (7) "Do not commit adultery" (Ex. 20:14).
            (8) "Do not steal" (Ex. 20:15).
            (9) "Do not testify falsely" (Ex. 20:16).
            (10) "Do not covet" (Ex. 20:17).
        b. The reaction (Ex. 20:18-23): Moses reassures the frightened crowd that God's purpose in appearing is to impress upon them his awesome power.
        c. The ratification (Ex. 20:24-26; 24:1-8): As instructed, Moses builds an altar with 12 pillars representing the 12 tribes. He then ratifies God's covenant with Israel by sprinkling animal blood on the altar.
        d. The radiance (Ex. 24:9-18): Moses, Aaron, Nadab and Abihu (Aaron's sons), and 70 Israelite elders are allowed to see God on Mount Sinai. "Under his feet there seemed to be a pavement of brilliant sapphire, as clear as the heav-

ens." After this, Moses ascends the mountain alone, where he spends the next 40 days.

2. *The social code (community laws):* Following is an alphabetical listing of the topics these laws address.

   a. Blasphemy (Ex. 22:28; Lev. 19:12; 20:9): The punishment for speaking against God, against rulers, or against parents is death.

   b. Blessing (conditions for it) (Lev. 26:3-13): Obedience to God assures Israel of fruitful crops, victory over their enemies, and the very presence of God among them!

   c. Blood (Ex. 23:18; Lev. 17:10-16; 19:26): No blood sacrifice is to be offered along with anything containing yeast. The eating or drinking of blood is strictly prohibited, for "the life of any creature is in its blood."

   d. Childbirth and ceremonial cleansing (Lev. 12:1-8): A mother will be ceremonially unclean for 41 days following the birth of a son and for 80 days following the birth of a daughter. Upon offering a lamb and some birds, the mother's time of defilement will be over.

   e. Dedication of persons and things (Lev. 27:1-29): These "persons" fall into four categories: those from 20 to 60, from 5 to 20, from one month to 5 years, and over 60. The "things" include animals, homes, and fields.

   f. Diet (Lev. 11:1-47; 20:25): These creatures are permitted as a source of food: all animals that have cloven hooves and chew their cud, fish with fins and scales, insects that jump, and clean birds.

   g. Disfiguring oneself (Lev. 19:27-28): The Israelites are not to shave certain sections of their head, to cut themselves, or to wear tattoos, because pagans do these things.

   h. Disobedience (Lev. 26:14-46): If the Israelites disobey God's laws, they will experience punishments: sudden terror, wasting diseases, defeat by their enemies, famines, attacks by wild animals, destruction of their cities, and exile. But true repentance will bring restoration.

   i. Elderly (Lev. 19:32): Israel is to give due honor and show great respect to the elderly.

   j. Fathers and daughters (Ex. 21:7-11): There are laws concerning work contracts and weddings.

   k. God's angel (Ex. 23:20-23): If the Israelites obey this angel, God will assure them victory over all their enemies. Many people today believe this angel was Christ himself.

   l. Handicapped people (Lev. 19:14): The deaf are not to be cursed nor the blind taken advantage of.

   m. Hatred (Lev. 19:17-18): The Israelites are forbidden to hate, to bear a grudge, or to seek vengeance against others. People are to love their neighbors as themselves.

n. Helping one's enemy (Ex. 23:4-5): An enemy's ox or donkey that has strayed away must be returned. Assistance must be rendered to an enemy's donkey that is struggling under its load.

o. Holiness (Ex. 22:31; Lev. 19:1-3; 20:7, 26): The bottom line is: "You must be holy because I, the LORD your God, am holy." This involves many things, including respecting one's parents and observing the Sabbath.

p. Idolatry (Ex. 22:20; 23:13, 24; Lev. 18:24-30; 19:4; 20:1-5; 26:1): Israel is forbidden even to speak the names of pagan gods, and worshiping them warrants death by stoning.

q. Land (Ex. 23:10-11; Lev. 19:23-25): There are various laws governing the planting, eating, and dedication of crops.

r. Leprosy (Lev. 13:1-59; 14:1-57; Num. 5:1-4): There are instructions regarding leprosy, including its recognition, its effect on ceremonial cleanness, and the sacrifices to be offered for it.

s. Lying (Ex. 23:1-3, 6-7; Lev. 19:11, 16): The Israelites are prohibited from slandering others and lying, even to help a poor person.

t. Marriage (Ex. 22:16-17): There are laws concerning the payment of dowries.

u. Masters and slaves (Ex. 21:1-6): There are laws concerning slaves and their families. Some of these laws address the release of slaves or the actions to be taken if slaves choose to remain with their masters.

v. Obedience (Ex. 23:25-33; Lev. 20:22-24): God will reward the Israelites' obedience by providing them with abundant food, long lives, and victory over their enemies. They will also be spared from diseases, miscarriages, and barrenness.

w. Punishment for harming others (Ex. 21:12-36; 22:1-15, 21-24; Lev. 24:17-22): Those who commit willful murder, engage in slave-trading, or curse one's parents must be put to death. All victims must receive payment from the guilty, and there are severe punishments for those who exploit widows and orphans. In essence, the punishment is to fit the crime, demanding eye for eye, tooth for tooth, hand for hand, foot for foot.

x. Poor (Ex. 22:25-27; Lev. 19:9-10): The clothes of the poor cannot be kept as pledge for repayment. Farmers are to leave behind some of the grain in the fields and the grapes on the vine so that the poor can collect them.

y. Redemption of land (Lev. 25:24-55): There are special laws regarding slaves who are Israelites. In the jubilee year (occurring every 50 years), land must be returned to its original owner, and Israelite slaves must be set free.

z. Righteous actions (Lev. 19:15, 35-37): Judges are commanded to render just decisions. Everybody must use accurate measurements.

aa. Separation of cattle, seed, and clothing (Lev. 19:19): The Israelites are not to mix two kinds of these things. They are not to plow with two kinds of animals, to plant two kinds of seed in the same field, or to use two kinds of fabric woven in an article of clothing.

bb. Sexual discharges (Lev. 15:1-33): Instructions are given regarding a man's seminal discharge and a woman's menstrual flow.

cc. Sexual impurities: Punishments are imposed for various sexual sins.
   (1) Adultery (Lev. 18:20; 19:20-22; 20:10, 14)
   (2) Bestiality (Ex. 22:19; Lev. 18:23; 20:15-16)
   (3) Homosexuality (Lev. 18:22; 20:13)
   (4) Incest (Lev. 18:1-18; 20:11-12, 17, 19-21)
   (5) Prostitution (Lev. 19:29)
   (6) Relations during menstruation (Lev. 18:19; 20:18)

dd. Stealing (Ex. 23:8; Lev. 19:13): All kinds of stealing are prohibited, including theft, taking of bribes, and cheating workers out of their wages.

ee. Tithe (Ex. 22:29-30; 23:19; Lev. 27:30-34): Ten percent of Israel's crops and livestock are to be given to God.

ff. Treatment of foreigners (Ex. 23:9; Lev. 19:33-34): Israelites are not to oppress or take advantage of foreigners. They should love them as they love themselves.

gg. Witchcraft (Ex. 22:18; Lev. 18:21; 19:31; 20:6, 27): Sorcerers are to be put to death.

3. *The spiritual code (laws dealing with worship, feasts, sacrifices, the priesthood, etc.):* For a fuller discussion of the spiritual code, see the section under subhead C, "The Restitution of Israel (Moses and the Tabernacle)."

II. THE PROSTITUTION OF ISRAEL (MOSES AND THE GOLD CALF): the ruination of fellowship (Ex. 32:1-35; 33:1-23; 34:1-35)

A. The grief (Ex. 32:1-35; 33:1-6)

1. *The perversion* Israel (Ex. 32:1-8): While Moses was on Mount Sinai, the people pressured Aaron into constructing a gold calf image. Then they worshiped it and indulged themselves in pagan revelry.

2. *The prayers* Israel (Ex. 32:9-14, 30-34): Moses pleads for the people before God, reminding him of his covenant with Abraham. So God does not destroy Israel.

3. *The punishment* Israel (Ex. 32:15-29, 35): Moses descends the mountain and sees the idolatry and immorality among the Israelites. He breaks the tablets containing the Ten Commandments, melts down and grinds the gold calf into powder, mixes it with water, and forces the people to drink it. Moses

rebukes Aaron and orders the Levites to kill 3,000 of the primary troublemakers.

    4. *The promise* Israel (Ex. 33:1-6): God will send an angel to drive out Israel's enemies, but God will not go with them.

B. The glory (Ex. 33:7-23; 34:1-35)

    1. *The grace of God* (Ex. 33:7-17): God himself meets with Moses at the entrance of the Tent of Meeting and speaks to him as one friend to another. At Moses' request, God agrees to continue with Israel on their journey.

    2. *The grandeur of God* (Ex. 33:18-23; 34:5-9, 18-35): Moses is allowed to see God's glory while standing in the cleft of the rock, and it causes Moses' face to glow.

    3. *The guarantee of God* (Ex. 34:1-4, 10-17): God writes the Ten Commandments on two tablets once again and promises to drive Israel's enemies out of the land of Canaan.

III. THE RESTITUTION OF ISRAEL (MOSES AND THE TABERNACLE): the restoration of fellowship

    A. The statistics concerning the Tabernacle (Ex. 25:9; 26:30): God gives Moses exact details for building the Tabernacle.

        1. *Its gifts* (Ex. 25:1-8; 35:4-29; 36:5-7; Num. 7:1-89): God gives Moses a list of acceptable gifts for the Tabernacle: gold, silver, fine linen, etc. He also describes the proper kind of giver: "Everyone who wants to may bring me an offering." Numbers 7 describes the gifts presented by the 12 leaders of the tribes during a 12-day period of time.

        2. *Its materials* (Ex. 26:1; 27:10; 30:18; 35:7): The Tabernacle is to be constructed from silver, bronze, fine linen, and animal skins.

        3. *Its craftsmen* (Ex. 31:1-11; 35:30-35; 36:1-4): Bezalel from the tribe of Judah and Oholiab from the tribe of Dan are appointed to supervise the building of the Tabernacle.

        4. *Its court* (Ex. 27:9-15, 18; 38:9-17): The Tabernacle is to be 150 feet long, 75 feet wide, and $7^{1}/_{2}$ feet high.

        5. *Its entrance* (Ex. 27:16-19; 38:18-20): The Tabernacle is to be covered by a curtain that is thirty feet wide.

        6. *Its curtains* (Ex. 26:1-13; 36:8-18)

          a. The linen curtains (Ex. 26:1-6; 36:8-13)

          b. The goat-hair curtains (Ex. 26:7-13; 36:14-18)

        7. *Its coverings of ram skins* (Ex. 26:14; 36:19)

        8. *Its boards and sockets* (Ex. 26:15-29; 36:20-34): There are to be 48 boards for the tent itself, each 15 feet high by $2^{1}/_{4}$ feet wide.

        9. *Its incense and scented oils* (Ex. 30:22-29, 34-38; 37:29): Incense and scented oils for the Tabernacle are to be made by mixing together ingredients such as pure frankincense, liquid myrrh, fragrant cinnamon, and olive oil.

      10. *Its bronze altar* (Ex. 27:1-8; 38:1-7): The bronze altar is to be

made of acacia wood covered with bronze, 7½ feet wide by 4½ feet high, with a horn on each corner.

11. *Its bronze washbasin* (Ex. 30:17-21; 38:8): This washbasin is to be filled with water and used for ceremonial cleansing. Its pedestal is to be covered with mirrors.

12. *Its table* (Ex. 25:23-30; 37:10-16; Lev. 24:5-9): This table is to be made of acacia wood overlaid with gold. It is to be 3 feet long, 1½ feet wide, and 2¼ feet high. Twelve loaves of the Bread of the Presence are to be placed on this table each Sabbath day.

13. *Its lampstand* (Ex. 25:31-40; 27:20-21; 37:17-24; Lev. 24:1-4; Num. 8:1-4): This is to be made of pure hammered gold with six branches and a center stem, and it is to be kept lit continually.

14. *Its incense altar* (Ex. 30:1-10; 37:25-28): This altar is to be made of acacia wood overlaid with gold. It is to be 1½ feet square and 3 feet high and is to be placed in front of the curtain of the Most Holy Place.

15. *Its Ark of the Covenant* (Ex. 25:10-22; 26:34; 37:1-9): This chest is to be made of acacia wood overlaid with gold. It is to be 3¾ feet long, 2¼ feet wide, and 2¼ feet high. The lid, called the place of atonement, is to be made of solid gold. Two gold cherubim with outstretched wings are to be attached to the top of the lid.

16. *Its inner curtain* (Ex. 26:31-33; 36:35-36): It is to be made of purple, blue, and scarlet fine linen and is to separate the Holy Place from the Most Holy Place.

17. *Its outer curtain* (Ex. 26:36-37; 36:37-38): It is to be similar to the inner curtain and is to separate the outer court from the Holy Place.

18. *Its sanctuary tax* (Ex. 30:11-16): Half a shekel (one fifth of an ounce) of silver is to be given by all males 20 years old and older.

19. *Its cost* (Ex. 38:21-31): 2,200 pounds of gold, 7,545 pounds of silver, and 5,310 pounds of bronze are collected from the people.

20. *Its completion* (Ex. 39:32–40:33): "The Israelites had done everything just as the LORD had commanded Moses. . . . Moses inspected all their work and blessed them." The Tabernacle is then set up on the first day of the year, one year after the Israelites have been delivered from Egypt.

21. *Its glory* (Ex. 40:34-38): "Then the cloud covered the Tabernacle, and the glorious presence of the LORD filled it. Moses was no longer able to enter the Tabernacle."

B. The stewards (priests) overseeing the Tabernacle

1. *The garments for the high priest* (Ex. 28:1-5): God instructs Moses to begin fashioning Aaron's priestly clothing.

      a. The ephod (Ex. 28:6-14; 39:1-7): This is to be made of multicolored threads of fine linen. It is to consist of front and back pieces joined at the shoulders. The names of Israel's 12 tribes are to be inscribed on two onyx stones.

      b. The chestpiece (Ex. 28:15-30; 39:8-21): This pouch made of fine linen is to be nine inches square. Twelve precious stones representing the 12 tribes of Israel are to be mounted on it in four rows. The Urim and Thummim are to be inserted into the pocket of the chestpiece, but it is not certain what the exact origin and function of these stones are. Somehow they are used to determine God's will.

      c. The robe of the ephod (Ex. 28:31-35; 39:22-26): This robe is to be made of blue cloth with gold bells attached to the hem.

      d. The gold medallion (Ex. 28:36-38; 39:30-31): This medallion is to be made of pure gold and engraved with "SET APART AS HOLY TO THE LORD." It is to be fastened to the front of Aaron's turban.

2. *The garments for the other priests* (Ex. 28:39-43; 29:29-30; 39:27-29): The other priests are to be given tunics, sashes, and headdresses.

3. *The food for the priests* (Ex. 29:31-34): Some of the priests' food comes from the sacrifices made at the Tabernacle.

4. *The offerings for the priests* (Ex. 29:35-46)

      a. Sin offering (Ex. 29:36-37): A young bull is to be sacrificed to ordain the priests to their office.

      b. Burnt offering (Ex. 29:38-46): A yearling lamb is to be sacrificed every morning and evening.

5. *The dedication and anointing of the priests* (Ex. 29:1-28; 30:30-33; Lev. 8:1-36)

      a. As ordered by God (Ex. 29:1-28; 30:30-33): A young bull and two rams are to be killed, and bread without yeast is to be offered. Blood is to be put on the tip of the right earlobe, right thumb, and big toe of the right foot of the priests.

      b. As obeyed by Moses (Lev. 8:1-36): Moses dedicates Aaron and his sons in the manner prescribed by God.

6. *The regulations for the priests* (Lev. 21:1-24; 22:1-16)

      a. Concerning defilement (Lev. 21:1-4, 10-12; 22:1-16): Instructions are given regarding ceremonial uncleanness due to contact with a corpse, an unclean animal, a bodily discharge, etc.

      b. Concerning disfiguring (Lev. 21:5-6): The priests are prohibited from shaving their heads, trimming their beards, and cutting themselves.

      c. Concerning domestic life (Lev. 21:7-9, 13-15): A priest

cannot marry a prostitute or a divorced woman. The high priest's wife must be a virgin from the tribe of Levi.

d. Concerning defects (Lev. 21:16-24): A person may not offer sacrifices if he is a dwarf or is blind, lame, or humpbacked, or has suffered damage to various parts of the body.

7. *The beginning of the priestly ministry* (Lev. 9:1-24): After offering up the prescribed sacrifices, Aaron "raise[s] his hands toward the people and blesse[s] them. . . . Fire blaze[s] forth from the LORD's presence and consume[s] the burnt offering and the fat on the altar."

C. The sacrifices in the Tabernacle

1. *The correct way to sacrifice* (Lev. 17:1-9; 22:17-33)
2. *The burnt offering* (Lev. 1:1-17; 6:8-13)
3. *The grain offering* (Lev. 2:1-16; 6:14-23)
4. *The peace offering* (Lev. 3:1-17; 7:11-38; 19:5-8)
5. *The sin offering* (Lev. 4:1-35; 6:24-30)
6. *The guilt offering* (Lev. 5:1-19; 6:1-7; 7:1-10)
7. *The offering for the firstborn* (Ex. 34:19-20)

D. The special days of the Tabernacle (Ex. 23:14-17; 31:12-17; 34:18, 21-26; 35:1-3; Lev. 16:1-34; 19:30; 23:1-44; 25:1-24; 26:2)

1. *The Sabbath day* (Ex. 31:12-17; 34:21; 35:1-3; Lev. 19:30; 23:1-3; 26:2): Israel is commanded to rest on the seventh day and keep it holy. Those who desecrate it are to be put to death. The Sabbath is intended to remind Israel of two things (Ex. 31:17):

a. God created the world in six days and then rested.

b. God has a special relationship with Israel.

2. *The Sabbath year* (Lev. 25:1-7): Israel is to let the land rest from cultivation every seventh year.

3. *The Year of Jubilee* (Lev. 25:8-24): Every fiftieth year all public and private debts are to be cancelled and all land returned to the original owners.

4. *The Passover* (Lev. 23:4-5): This festival occurs on the fourteenth day of the first month. It celebrates Israel's deliverance from slavery in Egypt after the angel of the Lord passed over the homes marked with blood on the doorposts.

5. *The Festival of Unleavened Bread* (Ex. 34:18; Lev. 23:6-8): This festival begins on the fifteenth day of the first month. For seven days no bread made with yeast is to be eaten. All Israelite males are required to be present at the Tabernacle during this festival.

6. *The Festival of Firstfruits* (Lev. 23:9-14): During this festival, the Israelites are to offer a portion of their first crops of the harvest as well as a year-old lamb with no physical defects. All males are required to be present at the Tabernacle during this festival.

7. *The Festival of Harvest* (Lev. 23:15-22): This festival follows
the Festival of Firstfruits by seven weeks. An offering of bread
is made, and several animals are to be sacrificed.
8. *The Festival of Trumpets* (Lev. 23:23-25): This day of rest
occurs on the first day of the seventh month and is celebrated
by the blowing of trumpets.
9. *The Day of Atonement* (Lev. 16:1-34; 23:26-32): All of Israel is
to fast on the tenth day of the seventh month in contemplation
and sorrow for sin. On this day, atonement will be made by
the high priest for the Most Holy Place and the rest of the
Tabernacle, as well as for the sins of the people.
10. *The Festival of Shelters* (Lev. 23:33-44): Beginning on the
fifteenth day of the seventh month, families are to live in shelters made of tree branches to commemorate Israel's wanderings in the wilderness after their deliverance from Egypt. All
Israelite males are to be present at the Tabernacle during this
festival.

E. The survey for the Tabernacle
1. *The census of the regular tribes* (Num. 1:1-46; 2:1-34)
a. The figures (Num. 1:1-46)
(1) The names of the tribal leaders (Num. 1:1-16): The
leaders of each of Israel's tribes (minus Levi) are
recorded.
(2) The number of the tribal laity (Num. 1:17-46): The
grand total (minus the Levites) of all males at least
20 years old is 603,550. The largest tribe is Judah
(74,600), and the smallest, Manasseh (32,200).
b. The field positions (Num. 2:1-34): Each tribe is assigned
a place to set up camp in relation to the Tabernacle.
(1) East side (Num. 2:1-9): Judah (leader), Issachar, and
Zebulun
(2) South side (Num. 2:10-17): Reuben (leader), Simeon,
and Gad
(3) West side (Num. 2:18-24): Ephraim (leader), Manasseh,
and Benjamin
(4) North side (Num. 2:25-34): Dan (leader), Asher, and
Naphtali
2. *The census of the religious tribe* (Levi)
a. The facts (Num. 1:47-54; 3:1-17, 38-51; 8:5-26): The
Levites are not to be included in the regular census, for
God has especially adopted them and made them supervi-
sors over the Tabernacle. All male Levites one month old
and older are to be counted. They are to begin serving at
the Tabernacle at age 25 and must retire at age 50.
b. The figures (Num. 3:18-24, 27-30, 33-35)
(1) Gershonite clan (Num. 3:21-24): 7,500 males
(2) Kohathite clan (Num. 3:27-30): 8,600 males

(3) Merarite clan (Num. 3:33-35): 6,200 males
  c. The field assignments (Num. 3:25-26, 31-32, 36-37; 4:1-49)
    (1) Gershonites (Num. 3:25-26; 4:21-28, 38-41): They are to camp on the west side of the Tabernacle and are responsible for its curtains and coverings.
    (2) Kohathites (Num. 3:31-32; 4:1-20, 34-37): They are to camp on the south side of the Tabernacle and are responsible for its furniture (the Ark, the lampstand, etc.).
    (3) Merarites (Num. 3:36-37; 4:29-33, 42-49): They are to camp on the north side of the Tabernacle and are responsible for its crossbars, posts, frames, etc.
F. **The standard procedures of the Tabernacle** (Num. 5:5-31; 9:1-14)
  1. *Regarding unfaithfulness* (Num. 5:5-31)
    a. Jealousy removed (Num. 5:11-31): If a husband is suspicious that his wife has been unfaithful, a priest must pronounce a curse over a jar of water and make the woman drink it. If she is guilty, she will become infertile.
    b. Justice restored (Num. 5:5-10): Those who wrong others are to make restitution to those they have wronged.
  2. *Regarding uncleanness* (Num. 9:1-14): A second Passover is established for those who cannot participate in the first due to ceremonial uncleanness. Instructions are also given concerning foreigners and those who disregard Passover.
G. **The separated (Nazirites) of the Tabernacle** (Num. 6:1-21): Nazirites, who have dedicated themselves totally to God, are required to observe three vows:
  1. *Abstain from anything that comes from the grapevine* (Num. 6:3-4).
  2. *Abstain from cutting their hair* (Num. 6:5).
  3. *Completely avoid going near a dead body* (Num. 6:6-7).
H. **The supplication (prayer) to be uttered from the Tabernacle** (Num. 6:22-27): Aaron and his sons, the priests, are instructed to pronounce this blessing over the people of Israel: "May the LORD bless you and protect you. May the LORD smile on you and be gracious to you. May the LORD show you his favor and give you his peace."
I. **The support for the Tabernacle** (Num. 7:1-89): The gifts presented by the leaders of Israel's twelve tribes are recorded.
  1. *Day one* (Num. 7:12-17): Judah's offering
  2. *Day two* (Num. 7:18-23): Issachar's offering
  3. *Day three* (Num. 7:24-29): Zebulun's offering
  4. *Day four* (Num. 7:30-35): Reuben's offering
  5. *Day five* (Num. 7:36-41): Simeon's offering
  6. *Day six* (Num. 7:42-47): Gad's offering

      7. *Day seven* (Num. 7:48-53): Ephraim's offering
      8. *Day eight* (Num. 7:54-59): Manasseh's offering
      9. *Day nine* (Num. 7:60-65): Benjamin's offering
     10. *Day ten* (Num. 7:66-71): Dan's offering
     11. *Day eleven* (Num. 7:72-77): Asher's offering
     12. *Day twelve* (Num. 7:78-83): Naphtali's offering

J. The shekinah of the Tabernacle (Num. 9:15-23): When the Tabernacle is set up, the Lord's presence (sometimes called the "shekinah") hovers over it as a cloud by day and as fire by night. When it moves, the people follow; when it stops, the people stop.

K. The silver trumpets of the Tabernacle (Num. 10:1-10): Two silver trumpets are to be fashioned for instructing the people. When both are blown, all the people are to assemble at the entrance of the Tabernacle. When only one is blown, only the tribal leaders are to respond.

L. The sons of Aaron at the Tabernacle (Lev. 10:1-20)

    1. *Nadab and Abihu: the misconduct* (Lev. 10:1-11): After offering unholy fire upon the altar (perhaps while drunk), Nadab and Abihu are consumed by a fire sent by the Lord.

    2. *Eleazar and Ithamar: the misunderstanding* (Lev. 10:12-20): Eleazar and Ithamar do not follow the instructions Moses has given them regarding the sin offering. This angers Moses, but Aaron's explanation of their actions satisfies him.

M. The slander against the God of the Tabernacle (Lev. 24:10-16, 23): A man with an Israelite mother and an Egyptian father blasphemes the Lord. The Lord instructs the Israelites to stone him to death, even though his father is not an Israelite.

SECTION OUTLINE SIX (NUMBERS 10:11–12:16)
This outline describes the experiences of the Israelites as they travel from Mount Sinai to Kadesh-barnea.

I. THE SIGNAL FROM THE SKY (Num. 10:11-12): "One day in midspring [on the twentieth day of the second month], during the second year after Israel's departure from Egypt, the cloud lifted from the Tabernacle," signaling that it was time once again for the Israelites to move.

II. THE STRIKING OF THE TENTS (Num. 10:13-28): The twelve tribes follow the pillar of cloud.

III. THE SOLICITATION BY MOSES (Num. 10:29-32): Moses attempts to secure the services of his brother-in-law as a guide through the wilderness.

IV. THE SECURITY IN THE CLOUD (Num. 10:33-36): Each time the Ark is lifted up to follow the cloud, Moses says, "Arise, O LORD, and let your enemies be scattered! Let them flee before you!" Each time the cloud stops and the Ark is set down, Moses says, "Return, O LORD, to the countless thousands of Israel!"

V. THE SINS ALONG THE WAY (Num. 11–12)

A. **The defiance and punishment of Israel** (Num. 11:1-9, 31-35)

1. *First occasion* (Num. 11:1-3): Fire falls upon some of the Israelites for complaining bitterly against God at a place that is later called Taberah.

2. *Second occasion* (Num. 11:4-9, 31-35): Some of the foreigners accompanying Israel begin to complain, "We remember all the fish we used to eat for free in Egypt. And we had all the cucumbers, melons, leeks, onions, and garlic that we wanted. But now our appetites are gone, and day after day we have nothing to eat but this manna!" God sends quail for them to eat, but he also punishes them with a plague.

B. **The despair of Moses** (Num. 11:10-30)

1. *The reason for his complaint* (Num. 11:10-15): Moses tells God that the burden of leading a rebellious people is too heavy to bear and he prefers death instead!

2. *The results of his complaint* (Num. 11:16-30)

a. The seventy in general (Num. 11:16-25): God instructs Moses to summon 70 leaders to the Tabernacle. There God anoints 70 Israelite elders with his Spirit to assist Moses in leading the people. The leaders prophesy at this time, but that is the only time this happens to them.

b. The two in particular (Num. 11:26-30): Two of these elders, Eldad and Medad, are absent when the others meet together, but they begin prophesying in the camp. Moses tells Joshua not to stop them, saying, "I wish that all the LORD's people were prophets, and that the LORD would put his Spirit upon them all!"

C. **The disrespect of Miriam and Aaron** (Num. 12:1-16)

1. *The reasons for their disrespect* (Num. 12:1-3): Miriam and Aaron (Moses' sister and brother) criticize Moses for two reasons:

a. He has married a Cushite woman.

b. He has been given greater authority over the Israelites.

2. *The results of their disrespect* (Num. 12:4-16): God sternly rebukes Miriam and Aaron. Miriam is struck with leprosy. Aaron begs Moses to pray for their sister, so her leprosy is healed.

SECTION OUTLINE SEVEN (NUMBERS 13–14)
The Israelites camp at Kadesh-barnea and send scouts into the Promised Land.

I. THE PENETRATION BY THE SCOUTS (Num. 13:1-25)
  A. **The names of the men** (Num. 13:1-16): Twelve men are chosen to scout out the land of Canaan, the Promised Land. Among them are Caleb from the tribe of Judah and Joshua from the tribe of Ephraim.
  B. **The nature of the mission** (Num. 13:17-25): Moses instructs the scouts to do two things:
    1. *find out what the inhabitants are like* (Num. 13:17-19) and
    2. *bring back samples of the crops grown in the land* (Num. 13:20-25).

II. THE LAMENTATION BY THE PEOPLE (Num. 13:26-33–14:10)
  A. **The report of the scouts** (Num. 13:26-33; 14:6-10)
    1. *The faithless report of the ten* (Num. 13:26-33): "The people living there are powerful, and their cities and towns are fortified and very large. . . .We even saw giants there, the descendants of Anak. We felt like grasshoppers next to them, and that's what we looked like to them!"
    2. *The faithful report of the two* (Num. 14:6-10): "The land we explored is a wonderful land! And if the LORD is pleased with us, he will bring us safely into that land and give it to us. . . . Do not rebel against the LORD, and don't be afraid of the people of the land. . . . They have no protection, but the LORD is with us!"
  B. **The reaction of the crowd** (Num. 14:1-5): Upon hearing the report of the ten scouts, the people become worried and make plans to return to Egypt.

III. THE SUPPLICATION (PRAYER) BY THE PROPHET (Num. 14:11-21)
  A. **The proposition** (Num. 14:11-12): The Lord becomes angry with the Israelites and says to Moses, "I will disown them and destroy them with a plague. Then I will make you into a nation far greater and mightier than they are!"
  B. **The plea** (Num. 14:13-19): Moses begs the Lord to pardon Israel, lest the pagans say, "The LORD was not able to bring them into the land he swore to give them, so he killed them in the wilderness."
  C. **The pardon** (Num. 14:20-21): The Lord forgives his people, although there will still be consequences.

IV. THE CONDEMNATION BY THE LORD (Num. 14:22-45)
  A. **The punishment** (Num. 14:22-38): The Lord spares the people of Israel from complete destruction as a nation, but they will still be punished: No one 20 years old or older (with the exceptionss of

Caleb and Joshua) will enter the Promised Land. They will wander in the wilderness for the next 40 years until all of them die and a new generation is born. The 10 faithless scouts die immediately from a plague.

B. **The presumption** (Num. 14:39-45): The fickle crowd now decide they want to enter the Promised Land after all, but they are completely routed by their enemies.

SECTION OUTLINE EIGHT   (NUMBERS 15–36)
The Israelites travel from Kadesh-barnea to the eastern bank of the Jordan River.

I. THE TESTIMONY (Num. 15:37-41): God commands the people of Israel to make tassels and attach them to the corners of their garments with blue cord. The tassels will remind them that they are to be holy just as the Lord is holy.

II. THE TABERNACLE INSTRUCTIONS
   A. **Concerning the offerings** (Num. 15:1-31; 28:1-31; 29:1-40)
      1. *The sacrifices* (Num. 15:1-13, 17-21; 28:1-31; 29:1-40): An overview of the various details to be followed regarding sacrifices.
      2. *The strangers* (Num. 15:14-16): Rules concerning foreigners and sacrifices.
      3. *The sins* (Num. 15:22-31)
         a. Sins of ignorance (Num. 15:22-29): The course of action to be taken for unintentional sin.
         b. Sins of intention (Num. 15:30-31): The course of action to be taken for intentional sin.
   B. **Concerning the Levites** (Num. 18:1-32): Details relating to their duties and privileges.
   C. **Concerning vows** (Num. 30:1-16): Rules governing the making, fulfilling, and nullifying of vows.

III. THE TROUBLEMAKERS
   A. **The profaner of the Sabbath** (Num. 15:32-36): A man is stoned to death for disobeying God's law by gathering wood on the Sabbath.
   B. **The presumptuous Korah** (Num. 16:1-50)
      1. *Korah's accusation* (Num. 16:1-3, 13-14): Korah and a group of rebellious Israelites accuse Moses of the following:
         a. he is a dictator;
         b. he has brought the Israelites into the wilderness to kill them;
         c. he has been unable to bring them into the Promised Land.
      2. *Moses' answer* (Num. 16:4-12, 15-30)
         a. To the rebels (Num. 16:4-12, 15-22): Moses tells the rebels

to show up the next day at the Tabernacle entrance with their incense burners. Then the Lord will show them who is holy and set apart for him.

    b. To the rest (Num. 16:23-30): Moses warns the people to stay clear of the troublemakers if they want to continue living.

3. *The Lord's anger* (Num. 16:31-50)

    a. At the ringleaders (Num. 16:31-40): The very ground where they are standing opens up and swallows them alive! Fire blazes from the Lord and burns up Korah's followers who are offering incense.

    b. At the rest (Num. 16:41-50)

       (1) The rebellion (Num. 16:41-42): The next morning people confront Moses and Aaron, saying, "You two have killed the LORD's people!"

       (2) The response (Num. 16:43-46): The Lord sends a plague on the people to destroy them.

       (3) The rescue (Num. 16: 47-50): Aaron burns incense and makes atonement for the people in order to stop the plague. Before it stops, 14,700 Israelites die.

C. The people of Edom (Num. 20:14-22): The Israelites ask the Edomites if they can pass through their land quickly and peacefully. The Edomites refuse, despite the fact that they are descended from Jacob's twin brother, Esau.

D. The prophet Balaam (Num. 22:1–24:25): King Balak of Moab sees that the Israelites are numerous and powerful, so he begins to fear for his kingdom. He sends for a prophet named Balaam to come and curse the Israelites.

1. *Balaam's foolishness* (Num. 22:1-41)

    a. The warning from God (Num. 22:1-21): God forbids Balaam to accept a bribe from King Balak of Moab to curse Israel. However, God does permit the prophet to accompany Balak's messengers to Moab.

    b. The wrath of God (Num. 22:22-27): En route, Balaam's donkey is frightened by something Balaam cannot see—God's angel standing in the road with a drawn sword! Unaware of this, the angry prophet beats his seemingly unruly animal.

    c. The witnesses for God (Num. 22:28-34): Balaam is rebuked by his donkey, who complains about its undeserved beating! Now Balaam sees the angel, who then rebukes him for coming.

    d. The words from God (Num. 22:35-41): In essence, Balaam is warned to speak only what God tells him to. Upon arriving in Moab, the prophet relates all this to Balak.

2. *Balaam's frustration* (Num. 23:1–24:25): Five times Balaam stands over the people of Israel and is unable to curse them.

   a. First occasion (Num. 23:1-12): "How can I curse those
      whom God has not cursed? . . . I see a people who live by
      themselves, set apart from other nations. Who can count
      Jacob's descendants, as numerous as dust?"
   b. Second occasion (Num. 23:13-24): "God is not a man, that
      he should lie. . . . I received a command to bless. . . . No
      misfortune is in sight for Jacob. . . . God has brought them
      out of Egypt. . . . No curse can touch Jacob. . . . These
      people rise up like a lioness."
   c. Third occasion (Num. 23:25–24:9): "How beautiful are
      your tents, O Jacob . . . . [You are] like fruitful gardens by
      the riverside. . . . [You are] like cedars beside the
      waters. . . . [Your] kingdom will be exalted. . . . Blessed is
      everyone who blesses you, O Israel."
   d. Fourth occasion (Num. 24:10-19): "I see him, but not in the
      present time. I perceive him, but far in the distant future. A
      star will rise from Jacob; a scepter will emerge from Israel.
      It will crush the foreheads of Moab's people."
   e. Fifth occasion (Num. 24:20-25): Balaam predicts divine
      judgment on Moab and other pagan nations: "Alas, who
      can survive when God does this?"

IV. THE TRAGEDY (Num. 20:2-13)
   A. **The disbelief of Israel** (Num. 20:2-6): When the Israelites run out
      of water, they blame Moses and lament the fact that they are not
      back in Egypt.
   B. **The directive of God** (Num. 20:7-8): The Lord tells Moses to
      assemble the people and command a rock to give them water.
   C. **The disobedience of Moses** (Num. 20:9-13): After the rebellious
      people are assembled, Moses' anger causes him to cry out,
      "Must we bring you water from this rock?" He disobeys the
      Lord's command and strikes the rock twice. The water still
      comes out, but Moses pays a sad price for his disobedience:
      he cannot lead the people into the Promised Land.

V. THE TRIUMPHS (Num. 21:1-4, 21-35; 31:1-54): The Lord gives Israel
   several victories on their way to the promised land.
   A. **Over the king of Arad** (Num. 21:1-4): The Canaanite king of
      Arad attacks the Israelites and takes some of them as prisoners.
      But the Israelites counterattack, and God gives them total victory.
   B. **Over King Sihon** (Num. 21:21-32): King Sihon of the Amorites
      refuses the Israelites' peaceful request for passage and attacks
      them, but he suffers total destruction.
   C. **Over King Og** (Num. 21:33-35): This giant warrior king of
      Bashan (Deut. 3:11) is killed by the Israelites, along with his sons
      and his entire army.
   D. **Over five Midianite kings** (Num. 31:1-54)
      1. *The battle* (Num. 31:1-12): Twelve thousand crack Israelite

soldiers (1,000 from each tribe) are chosen to battle the Midianites. All five Midianite kings are killed, along with the prophet Balaam.

2. *The bungling* (Num. 31:13-24): Moses is angry with the army officers for sparing some Midianite women who had previously sexually seduced many Israelite men.

3. *The booty* (Num. 31:25-54): At God's command, half of the war spoils are kept by the soldiers and half are given to the people. This includes 675,000 sheep, 72,000 cattle, 61,000 donkeys, and 32,000 young girls.

VI. THE TRANSITIONS (Num. 20:1, 23-29; 27:12-23)

   A. Two deaths (Num. 20:1, 23-25, 28-29)

      1. *Miriam, Moses' sister* (Num. 20:1): Miriam dies and is buried in the wilderness of Zin, near Kadesh.

      2. *Aaron, Moses' brother* (Num. 20:23-25, 28-29)

         a. The preparation for his death (Num. 20:23-25): Moses is commanded to take Aaron and Eleazar (Aaron's son) up on Mount Hor and there transfer the clothing (and office) of Israel's high priest from father to son.

         b. The place of his death (Num. 20:28-29): Aaron dies and is buried on Mount Hor. The people then mourn for Aaron for 30 days.

   B. Two designations (Num. 20:26-28; 27:12-23)

      1. *Eleazar succeeds Aaron* (Num. 20:26-28): Eleazar now becomes Israel's second high priest.

      2. *Joshua succeeds Moses* (Num. 27:12-23)

         a. The command (Num. 27:12-14): Moses is to climb a mountain and view the Promised Land, for he must soon die.

         b. The ceremony (Num. 27:15-23): Joshua is appointed as Israel's new leader. In a public ceremony Moses lays hands on Joshua and passes the torch of leadership to him.

VII. THE TRANSGRESSIONS (Num. 25:1-18)

   A. The sin of the crowd (Num. 25:1-5, 9)

      1. *Their perversion* (Num. 25:1-3): Shortly after the Balaam incident, many Israelite men engage in sexual immorality with Moabite women. Then they commit idolatry by bowing to their pagan gods.

      2. *Their punishment* (Num. 25:4-5, 9): All involved are executed, resulting in the deaths of 24,000 people.

   B. The sin of a couple (Num. 25:6-8, 10-18)

      1. *Their perversion* (Num. 25:6, 14-15): Despite the punishment that has just occurred, an Israelite man brings a Midianite woman into the camp in full view of Moses.

      2. *Their punishment* (Num. 25:7-8, 10-13, 16-18): In righteous

indignation, Phinehas, son of Eleazar, enters the couple's tent and kills them with his spear.

VIII. THE TABULATIONS (SECOND CENSUS) (Num. 26:1-65): "Take a census of all the men of Israel who are 20 years old or older, to find out how many of each family are of military age."
   A. **The reason for the census** (Num. 26:52-56): The amount of land allotted is determined by the size of the tribe.
   B. **The results of the census** (Num. 26:5-51, 57-62)
      1. *Reuben* (Num. 26:5-11): 43,730
      2. *Simeon* (Num. 26:12-14): 22,200
      3. *Gad* (Num. 26:15-18): 40,500
      4. *Judah* (Num. 26:19-22): 76,500
      5. *Issachar* (Num. 26:23-25): 64,300
      6. *Zebulun* (Num. 26:26-27): 60,500
      7. *Manasseh* (Num. 26:28-34): 52,700
      8. *Ephraim* (Num. 26:35-37): 32,500
      9. *Benjamin* (Num. 26:38-41): 45,600
      10. *Dan* (Num. 26:42-43): 64,400
      11. *Asher* (Num. 26:44-47): 53,400
      12. *Naphtali* (Num. 26:48-50): 45,400
      13. *Levi* (Num. 26:57-62): 23,000
      14. *Total (not counting the tribe of Levi)* (Num. 26:51): 601,730

IX. THE TRAVELS (Num. 21:10-20; 33:1-49)
   A. **A partial listing of Israel's stops** (Num. 21:10-20): Nine stops are recorded. During one stop Israel sings praise to God for providing their water.
   B. **A perfect (complete) listing of Israel's stops** (Num. 33:1-49): Many geographical locations are listed, beginning with Rameses in Egypt to the plains of Moab just east of the Jordan River.

X. THE TYPES (Num. 17:1-13; 19:1-22; 21:4-9; 32:1-42; 35:6-34): Many scholars see symbolic representations, or "types," in many of the images found in the book of Numbers.
   A. **Types of Christ** (Num. 17:1-13; 19:1-22; 21:5-9; 35:6-34)
      1. *The death of Christ* (Num. 19:1-22; 21:5-9)
         a. The red heifer (Num. 19:1-22): A blemish-free red heifer is to be killed and its blood sprinkled seven times toward the Tabernacle. The carcass is then to be burned, mixed with cedarwood, hyssop, and scarlet thread. The ashes are to be used for purification.
         b. The brass serpent (Num. 21:5-9): Poisonous snakes are sent to punish rebellious Israel. In response to the people's prayer for forgiveness, God instructs Moses: "Make a replica of a poisonous snake and attach it to the top of a pole. Those who are bitten will live if they simply look at it!"
      2. *The resurrection of Christ* (Num. 17:1-13): Aaron's rod has also been seen as a type of Christ's resurrection.

a. God's message (Num. 17:1-5): Responding to a challenge to Aaron's leadership, God orders Aaron and each of Israel's tribal leaders to place their staffs in the Tabernacle.

b. God's miracle (Num. 17:6-13): The next day only Aaron's staff has budded, is blossoming, and has ripe almonds hanging from it!

3. *The security in Christ* (Num. 35:6-34): Six cities, three on the west of the Jordan River and three on the east, are designated as refuges for those who have accidentally killed someone. These people can safely enter and be protected from any of the victim's relatives who seek revenge.

B. A type of worldly believer (Num. 32:1-42): The three tribes east of the Jordan River have been compared to worldly believers today.

1. *The request* (Num. 32:1-5): The tribes of Reuben and Gad, and the half-tribe of Manasseh seek permission from Moses to live on the eastern side of the Jordan River.

2. *The reprimand* (Num. 32:6-15): Moses asks, "Do you mean you want to stay back here while your brothers go across and do all the fighting? . . . Are you trying to discourage the rest of the people of Israel from going across to the land the LORD has given them?"

3. *The reassurance* (Num. 32:16-32): The 2 tribes solemnly promise to fully support the other 9 1/2 tribes in conquering Canaan.

4. *The results* (Num. 32:33-42): Moses grants their request.

XI. THE TERRITORY (Num. 33:50–35:5)

A. Purging the land (Num. 33:50-56): Israel is commanded to invade Canaan, drive out its inhabitants, destroy the idols, and settle the land.

B. Partitioning the land (Num. 34:1–35:5)

1. *Areas assigned to the regular tribes* (Num. 34:1-29): The borders of the Promised Land are Kadesh-barnea in the south, the Mediterranean Sea in the west, Mount Hor in the north, and the Jordan River in the east. The 2 1/2 tribes will live just east of the Jordan River.

2. *Areas assigned to the religious tribe* (Num. 35:1-5): The tribe of Levi is to be given 48 cities throughout the land.

XII. THE TENACITY (Num. 27:1-11; 36:1-13)

A. The request (Num. 27:1-11): Inasmuch as their dead father had no sons, the five daughters of Zelophehad request that they be allowed to inherit his land. The Lord instructs Moses to grant this request, but with one qualification.

B. The restriction (Num. 36:1-13): In order to inherit the land, the daughters must marry men within their tribe of Manasseh, which they do.

PART THREE : GOD'S DELIVERANCE OF ISRAEL—THE
REVIEW (Deuteronomy 1–34)
This part covers the section of Deuteronomy consisting mostly of four
sermons that review and summarize the history and laws of Israel.
Moses delivers these sermons to the Israelites as they are about to enter
the Promised Land.

SECTION OUTLINE NINE (DEUTERONOMY 1–4)
Moses delivers his first sermon to the Israelites.

I. AN OVERVIEW OF ISRAEL AT MOUNT SINAI (Deut. 1:1-18)
   A. **The area promised by the Lord** (Deut. 1:7-8): The Lord gives the
   Israelites all the land from the Negev to the Euphrates River.
   B. **The administrators picked by Moses** (Deut. 1:9-18): Moses
   recounts the selection of the 70 elders (see Num. 11:14-17).

II. AN OVERVIEW OF ISRAEL AT KADESH-BARNEA (Deut. 1:19-46)
   A. **The route of the spies** (Deut. 1:19-25): See Num. 13:1-17.
   B. **The rebellion of the crowd** (Deut. 1:26-33): See Num. 14:1-4.
   C. **The retribution by the Lord** (Deut. 1:34-46): See Num. 14:26-38.

III. AN OVERVIEW OF ISRAEL EN ROUTE TO THE JORDAN RIVER (Deut.
   2:1–3:29): Moses recounts how the Lord finally said to him "You
   have been wandering around in this hill country long enough; turn
   northward."
   A. **The three friends (peaceful nations)** (Deut. 2:4-23): Moses
   reviews how the Lord commanded the Israelites not to seize the
   land of three nations.
   1. *Seir* (Deut. 2:4-8): "Don't bother them, for I have given them
   all the hill country around Mount Seir as their property, and I
   will not give you any of their land."
   2. *Moab* (Deut. 2:9-15): "Do not bother the Moabites, the
   descendants of Lot, or start a war with them. I have given
   them Ar as their property, and I will not give you any of their
   land."
   3. *Ammon* (Deut. 2:16-23): "Do not bother the Ammonites, the
   descendants of Lot, or start a war with them. I have given the
   land of Ammon to them as their property, and I will not give
   you any of their land."
   B. **The two foes (enemy nations)** (Deut. 2:24–3:11): Moses reviews
   how the Lord commanded the Israelites to attack two other
   nations.
   1. *King Sihon of Heshbon* (Deut. 2:24-37): Moses reviews Israel's
   victory over this king.
   2. *King Og of Bashan* (Deut. 3:1-11): Moses reviews Israel's
   victory over this huge giant, whose iron bed measured 13 feet
   long by 6 feet wide!

C. The two favors (Deut. 3:12-29)

1. *The request of the 2½ tribes* (Deut. 3:12-22): Moses reviews how he granted the request of Reuben, Gad, and Manasseh to settle on the eastern side of the Jordan River.
2. *The request of Moses* (Deut. 3:23-29): Moses reviews how the Lord refused his request that he be allowed to enter the Promised Land.

IV. AN OVERVIEW OF ISRAEL'S RELATIONSHIP WITH THE LORD (Deut. 4:1-49)

A. The God of Israel (Deut. 4:1-19, 24, 31-40): Israel is commanded to worship God and God alone, to keep his laws, and to be careful not to add to or subtract from his laws.

B. The Israel of God (Deut. 4:20-23, 25-30): Israel is commanded to remember that they belong to the Lord and that they will be punished if they stray from him.

C. The law of Moses (Deut. 4:41-49): Some final instructions are given by Moses, and the law that follows in the next several chapters is introduced.

SECTION OUTLINE TEN (DEUTERONOMY 5–26)
Moses delivers his second sermon to the Israelites.

I. CONCERNING THE MORAL LAW: Moses reviews and expands upon the laws the Lord had given the Israelites regarding morality.

A. The covenant (Deut. 5:1-5): Moses reviews the covenant God made with Israel at Mount Sinai (see Ex. 19:5).

B. The commandments (Deut. 5:6-22; 6:1-9, 20-25)

1. *The record* (Deut. 5:6-22; 6:1-5): Moses reviews the Ten Commandments as originally given in Exodus 20 with the addition of the "Hear, O Israel! The LORD is our God, the LORD alone. And you must love the LORD your God with all your heart, all your soul, and all your strength."
2. *The responsibilities* (Deut. 6:6-9, 20-25): Moses tells the people that they must teach the commandments to their children and remind them of their rescue from Egypt.

C. The chosen (nation) (Deut. 7:6-11; 9:1-6; 10:12-22): Moses reminds the Israelites that God's love for them is based on his grace, not their goodness. How is Israel to respond? "What does the LORD your God require of you? He requires you to fear him, to live according to his will, to love and worship him with all your heart and soul, and to obey the LORD's commands and laws that I am giving you today for your own good."

D. The circumstances (Deut. 5:23-33; 9:7–10:5)

1. *The reception of the law* (Deut. 5:23-33): Moses recounts how

the people responded to the Lord's awesome presence on Mount Sinai (see Ex. 19:9-25).

   2. *The rejection of the law* (Deut. 9:7-29): Moses recounts several occasions when the people rebelled against the Lord's commands.
      a. At Mount Sinai (Deut. 9:7-21): Here Israel worshiped the golden calf, which led Moses to smash the two stone tablets containing the Ten Commandments (see Ex. 32).
      b. In the wilderness (Deut. 9:22-29): At Taberah, Massah, and Kibroth-hattaavah, Israel refused to enter the Promised Land (see Num. 13–14).
   3. *The replacement of the law* (Deut. 10:1-5): Moses recounts how two new tablets containing the Ten Commandments were made to replace the tablets that were dashed to the ground.
   E. **The choices** (Deut. 10:6-9): Moses recounts the selection of Eleazar (Aaron's son) as high priest (see Num. 20:23-29) and of the tribe of Levi as ministers before the Lord (see Ex. 32:25-29).
   F. **The confidence** (Deut. 7:12-24; 11:22-32): Moses assures the Israelites that obedience to the Lord's commands brings blessing, wealth, health, and victory over enemies.
   G. **The caution** (Deut. 6:10-19; 7:1-5, 25-26; 8:11-20; 11:16-17): Moses warns the Israelites to fear the Lord, to worship and obey him only, and to remember his faithfulness. He also directs them to destroy their enemies and the pagan idols of the land.
   H. **The country** (Deut. 8:7-10; 11:8-15): Moses tells the people that Canaan is a land of abundant water and lush lands of wheat, barley, vines, figs, pomegranates, olives, and honey. The land also contains rich stores of iron and copper.
   I. **The compassion** (Deut. 8:1-6; 10:10-11; 11:1-7): Moses recalls the Lord's great faithfulness and compassion toward the Israelites during their wilderness wanderings.

II. CONCERNING THE SOCIAL LAW: Moses reviews and expands on the laws that the Lord had given the Israelites regarding society. Following is an alphabetical topical list of these laws.
   A. **Animals** (Deut. 22:6-7; 25:4): Don't take a mother bird from its nest. Don't muzzle an ox while it is treading out the grain.
   B. **Building** (Deut. 22:8): Every new house must have a guardrail around the roof to prevent someone from falling.
   C. **Clothing** (Deut. 22:5, 11-12): Clothing is not to be made from both linen and wool. Women are forbidden to wear men's clothing, and men are forbidden to wear women's clothing. The Israelites are to wear tassels on the four corners of their cloaks.
   D. **Dietary laws** (Deut. 14:3-21; 15:19-20, 22-23): The Israelites are to regard certain animals as clean and others as unclean. They are not to eat the unclean animals.

  E. Divorce (Deut. 24:1-4): There are rules governing both divorce and remarriage.

  F. Domestic situations (Deut. 21:10-17; 22:13-30; 24:5; 25:5-12)

   1. *Captive wife* (Deut. 21:10-14): There are rules regarding the treatment and rights of a captive woman who is taken as a wife.

   2. *Multiple wives* (Deut. 21:15-17): There are rules governing how an inheritance is to be divided among the children of multiple wives.

   3. *Suspect wife* (Deut. 22:13-30): There are rules governing various issues related to sexual purity and faithfulness.

   4. *New wife* (Deut. 24:5): A man is not to be drafted during his first year of marriage, so he can be home with his new wife.

   5. *Widowed wife* (Deut. 25:5-10): The brother of a deceased man must agree to care for his brother's widow or be disgraced in the community.

   6. *Inappropriate wife* (Deut. 25:11-12): She will be punished for wrongly aiding her husband in a fight with another man.

  G. Guilt (Deut. 24:16): Parents should not be put to death for the sins of their children, or children for the sins of their parents.

  H. Honesty (Deut. 25:13-16): Always use accurate scales.

  I. Hygiene (Deut. 23:9-14): There are rules governing personal sanitation.

  J. Idolatry (Deut. 13:1–14:2; 16:21-22; 17:2-7; 18:9-14, 20-22): The practice of idolatry is strictly forbidden.

   1. *The prophets* (Deut. 13:1-18; 18:20-22): Prophets who encourage people to worship pagan gods are to be stoned to death.

   2. *The perversions* (Deut. 14:1-2; 16:21-22; 17:2-7; 18:9-14): The Israelites are forbidden to engage in pagan and idolatrous practices.

  K. Inquests (Deut. 21:1-9): If a murder victim is found and the crime cannot be solved, the leaders of the nearest city are to sacrifice a young cow and pray: "Our hands did not shed this blood, nor did we see it happen. O LORD, forgive your people Israel whom you have redeemed. Do not charge your people Israel with the guilt of murdering an innocent person."

  L. Judges (Deut. 16:18-20; 17:8-13; 19:15-21; 25:1-3): Various laws are given to ensure just verdicts and punishments.

  M. Juvenile delinquency (Deut. 21:18-23): A stubborn and rebellious son who constantly refuses to obey his parents must be stoned to death.

  N. Kings (Deut. 17:14-20): Five rules are given concerning Israel's future kings:

   1. *He must be an Israelite and not a foreigner* (Deut. 17:15).

   2. *He must not acquire great numbers of horses* (Deut. 17:16).

   3. *He must not take many wives* (Deut. 17:17).

4. *He must not accumulate large amounts of silver and gold* (Deut. 17:17).

5. *He must read and obey the law of God daily* (Deut. 17:19-20).

O. **Laborers** (Deut. 24:14-15): Never take advantage of poor laborers. Pay them their wages each day before sunset.

P. **Landmarks** (Deut. 19:14): Do not move your neighbor's boundary stone.

Q. **Leprosy** (Deut. 24:8-9): Israel was to carefully observe the instructions concerning leprosy (see Lev. 13–14). They were also to remember how God cursed Miriam with leprosy (see Num. 12:1-15).

R. **Neighbors** (Deut. 22:1-4; 23:24-25): If you see someone's ox or sheep wandering away, return it. You may eat of the fruit from someone's vineyard or grainfield, but do not abuse this privilege.

S. **Planting** (Deut. 22:9-10): Don't plant two kinds of seed in your vineyard. Don't plow with an ox and donkey yoked together.

T. **Pledges** (Deut. 24:6, 10-13, 17-18): There are rules governing what may be received as security for a loan.

U. **Prostitution** (Deut. 23:17-18): Both male and female prostitution is forbidden.

V. **Retribution** (Deut. 25:17-19): The Israelites are commanded to wipe out the Amalekites for their cruel acts against them.

W. **Servants** (Deut. 15:12-18; 23:15-16; 24:7): There are various rules governing the treatment of servants.

X. **Tithes** (Deut. 14:22-29; 26:12-15): All Israelites are to tithe their crops each year, bringing the revenue to the Tabernacle. They also are expected to help support the Levites, foreigners, widows, and orphans living in their town or city.

Y. **Usury** (Deut. 23:19-20): One can charge interest to a foreigner but not to a fellow Israelite.

Z. **Vows** (Deut. 23:21-23): Vows to the Lord must be promptly fulfilled, although it is not a sin to refrain from making a vow.

AA. **Warfare** (Deut. 20:1-20): Instructions are given regarding the preparation for and practice of warfare. Four types of individuals are exempted from going to battle:

1. *one who has just built a new home* (Deut. 20:5);

2. *one who has just planted a vineyard* (Deut. 20:6);

3. *one who has just become engaged* (Deut. 20:7);

4. *one who is terrified* (Deut. 20:8).

BB. **Welfare** (Deut. 24:19-22): Leave a portion of your crops behind for foreigners, widows, and orphans to glean.

III. CONCERNING THE RELIGIOUS LAW: Moses reviews and expands upon the laws that the Lord had given the Israelites regarding religious and ceremonial practices. Following is an alphabetical topical list of these laws.

A. **Central sanctuary** (Deut. 12:1-32; 23:1-8): Laws are given regarding the Tabernacle.

   1. *The place* (Deut. 12:1-32): "You must seek the LORD your God
      at the place he himself will choose from among all the tribes
      for his name to be honored. There you will bring to the LORD
      your burnt offerings, your sacrifices, your tithes, your special
      gifts, your offerings to fulfill a vow, your freewill offerings, and
      your offerings of the firstborn animals of your flocks and
      herds." The final, permanent location for the Tabernacle is
      later revealed to be Jerusalem.
   2. *The prohibitions* (Deut. 23:1-8): Four kinds of individuals are
      prohibited from entering the Tabernacle:
      a. An emasculated person (Deut. 23:1)
      b. A person of illegitimate birth (Deut. 23:2)
      c. An Ammonite (Deut. 23:3)
      d. A Moabite (Deut. 23:3)
B. **Cities of refuge** (Deut. 19:1-13): Moses reviews the purpose for
   these cities (see Num. 35:9-34).
C. **Festivals** (Deut. 16:1-17; 26:1-11)
   1. *The overview* (Deut. 16:1-15; 26:1-11): Various instructions
      are given regard the following festivals:
      a. Passover/Festival of Unleavened Bread (Deut. 16:1-8) (see
         also Lev. 23:5-8)
      b. Festival of Harvest (Deut. 16:9-12) (see also Lev. 23:15-22)
      c. Festival of Shelters (Deut. 16:13-15) (see also Lev.
         23:33-43)
      d. Festival of Firstfruits (Deut. 26:1-11) (see also Lev. 23:9-14)
   2. *The obligations* (Deut. 16:16-17): All Israelite men are
      required to attend the following three festivals each year:
      a. Passover/Festival of Unleavened Bread
      b. Festival of Harvest
      c. Festival of Shelters
D. **The prophet** (Deut. 18:15-19): Moses tells the people that the
   Lord will send them a prophet who will speak for him and whom
   everyone must obey. The New Testament makes it clear that
   Jesus was the ultimate fulfillment of this promise (see John 6:14).
E. **Israel** (Deut. 26:16-19): Moses reviews Israel's responsibilities
   before the Lord. They are to obey his commandments and be a
   holy people. In return, the Lord will elevate them above all the
   other nations.
F. **Levites** (Deut. 18:1-8): Moses reviews the Levites' privileges and
   responsibilities.
G. **Offerings** (Deut. 15:21; 17:1): No lame, blind, sick, or blemished
   animal will be accepted by God as a sacrifice.
H. **Sabbath year** (Deut. 15:1-15): All debts are to be canceled at the
   end of every seventh year. All slaves who are Israelites are to be
   released at the end of every seventh year as well.

I. THE COMMAND TO BUILD (Deut. 27:1-8): Israel is to construct an altar on Mount Ebal and write the laws of God on it.

II. THE COMMAND TO BROADCAST (Deut. 27:9–28:68): Six tribes (Simeon, Levi, Judah, Issachar, Joseph, and Benjamin) are to stand on Mount Gerizim and proclaim a blessing over the Israelites (for obeying the law). Then the other six tribes (Reuben, Gad, Asher, Zebulun, Dan, and Naphtali) are to stand on Mount Ebal and proclaim a curse (for disobeying the law).

A. The curses for disobedience (Deut. 27:14-26; 28:15-68)

1. *The reasons* (Deut. 27:14-26): The Levites are to proclaim a curse on the following people:
   a. those who make idols (Deut. 27:15)
   b. those who despise their parents (Deut. 27:16)
   c. those who move boundary markers (Deut. 27:17)
   d. those who lead the blind astray (Deut. 27:18)
   e. those who are unjust to foreigners, orphans, or widows (Deut. 27:19)
   f. those who commit incest of various sorts (Deut. 27:20, 22-23)
   g. those who practice bestiality (Deut. 27:21)
   h. those who commit murder or accept payment to do so (Deut. 27:24-25)
   i. those who do not obey the law (Deut. 27:26)

2. *The results* (Deut. 28:15-68): If the people do not obey the laws that the Lord gives them, they will experience curses.
   a. Destruction in the land (Deut. 28:15-24, 26-31, 33-35, 38-48): Disobedience will result in diseases, plagues, famine, drought, dust storms, defeat in war, infertility, constant fear and frustration, and the enslavement of their children.
   b. Dispersion from the land (Deut. 28:25, 32, 36-37, 48-68): Disobedience will also cause the Israelites to be surrounded by their enemies, reduced to cannibalism, removed from the land, enslaved, and dispersed among the nations. They will become a proverb and an object of horror and mockery among the nations, and they will find no rest there. The Lord will cause them to tremble and despair. They will live in constant fear, with no reason to believe that they will survive.

B. The blessings for obedience (Deut. 28:1-14): If the Israelites heed God's laws, they will experience blessings in their towns and in the country. They will have many children, ample crops, and large flocks and herds. They will have victory in war and lend to many nations, borrowing from none. They will be the head and not the tail.

SECTION OUTLINE TWELVE (DEUTERONOMY 29–30)
Moses delivers his fourth and final sermon to the Israelites as they are about to enter the Promised Land.

I. THE COVENANT (Deut. 29:1-29): Moses reminds the Israelites of the Lord's covenant with them and urges them to obey its laws so that they will not experience its curses.

II. THE CHANGE (Deut. 30:1-10): Moses tells the people that the Lord will change their hearts while they are in captivity, and they will love the Lord wholeheartedly. The Lord will then gather them together once again and restore them to their land. He will bless them and make them more prosperous than ever.

III. THE CHOICE (Deut. 30:11-20): "Today I have given you the choice between life and death, between blessings and curses. I call on heaven and earth to witness the choice you make. Oh, that you would choose life, that you and your descendants might live! Choose to love the LORD your God and to obey him and commit yourself to him, for he is your life."

SECTION OUTLINE THIRTEEN (DEUTERONOMY 31–34)
Moses gives his parting instructions and prepares to pass on the responsibilities of leadership to Joshua. Moses dies on Mount Nebo.

I. THE SETTING APART (Deut. 31:1-8, 14-15, 23): Before all the people, Moses commissions Joshua as their new leader, commanding him to be courageous, for he "will lead these people into the land that the LORD swore to give their ancestors."

II. THE SCRIPTURES (Deut. 31:9-13, 24-27): Moses finishes writing the law and instructs the Israelites to read it every seventh year at the Festival of Shelters. This is so the people will always know the law, and it will stand as a witness against their sins.

III. THE SONG (Deut. 31:16-22, 28-30; 32:1-47)
   A. **The crisis** (Deut. 31:16-22, 28-30)
      1. *The Lord tells Moses* (Deut. 31:16-22): The Lord reveals that his people will eventually rebel against him after Moses' death and that he will severely punish them for their sins.
      2. *Moses tells Israel* (Deut. 31:28-30): "I know that after my death you will become utterly corrupt and will turn from the path I have commanded you to follow. In the days to come,

disaster will come down on you, for you will make the LORD
very angry by doing what is evil in his sight."
B. The contents (Deut. 32:1-43)
    1. *The greatness of God* (Deut. 32:1-4, 39-42): The Lord is
Israel's perfect, just, and faithful Rock! He is the only God,
able to kill and to give life, to wound and to heal.
    2. *The grace of God* (Deut. 32:5-14, 43): "Jacob is [the Lord's]
special possession. He found them in a desert land, in an
empty, howling wasteland. He surrounded them and watched
over them; he guarded them as his most precious possession."
    3. *The grief of God* (Deut. 32:15-38)
      a. What Israel has done (Deut. 32:15-18, 28-29): They have
rejected and abandoned God for the gods of the pagan
nations.
      b. What the Lord will do (Deut. 32:19-27, 30-38): The Lord
will hide his face from them, bring calamities upon them,
and scatter them among the nations. He will bless the Gentiles.
C. The challenge (Deut. 32:44-47): Moses commands the Israelites:
"Take to heart all the words I have given you today. Pass them
on as a command to your children so they will obey every word
of this law. These instructions are not mere words—they are your
life! By obeying them you will enjoy a long life in the land you
are crossing the Jordan River to occupy."

IV. THE SUMMONS (Deut. 32:48-52): God instructs Moses to climb
Mount Nebo and gaze westward upon the Promised Land before he
dies there on the mountain.

V. THE SUMMATION (Deut. 33:1-29): Moses blesses each of the tribes
before he dies, summarizing what will happen to each of them in
the future.
A. Reuben (Deut. 33:6): "Let the tribe of Reuben live and not die
out, even though their tribe is small."
B. Judah (Deut. 33:7): "Give them strength to defend their cause;
help them against their enemies!"
C. Levi (Deut. 33:8-11): "Now let them teach your regulations to
Jacob. . . . They will present incense before you and offer whole
burnt offerings on the altar."
D. Benjamin (Deut. 33:12): "The people of Benjamin are loved by
the LORD and live in safety beside him."
E. Joseph (Ephraim and Manasseh) (Deut. 33:13-17): "May their
land be blessed by the LORD with the choice gift of rain from the
heavens . . . with the finest crops of the ancient mountains."
F. Zebulun (Deut. 33:18-19): "May the people of Zebulun prosper
in their expeditions abroad."
G. Issachar (Deut. 33:18-19): "May the people of Issachar prosper
at home in their tents."

    H. Gad (Deut. 33:20-21): "Blessed is the one who enlarges Gad's territory!"

    I. Dan (Deut. 33:22): "Dan is a lion's cub, leaping out from Bashan."

    J. Naphtali (Deut. 33:23): "You are rich in favor and full of the LORD's blessings; may you possess the west and the south."

    K. Asher (Deut. 33:24-25): "May he be esteemed by his brothers; may he bathe his feet in olive oil. May the bolts of your gates be of iron and bronze; may your strength match the length of your days!"

VI. THE SIGHT (Deut. 34:1-4): On Mount Nebo the Lord shows Moses the entire Promised Land.

VII. THE SEPARATION (Deut. 34:5-9): Moses dies on Mount Nebo.

    A. The location of his grave (Deut. 34:5-6): "[Moses] was buried in a valley near Beth-peor in Moab, but to this day no one knows the exact place."

    B. The length of his life (Deut. 34:7): "Moses was 120 years old when he died, yet his eyesight was clear, and he was as strong as ever."

    C. The lamentation over his death (Deut. 34:8): "The people of Israel mourned thirty days for Moses on the plains of Moab, until the customary period of mourning was over."

    D. The leader in his place (Deut. 34:9): Joshua son of Nun officially assumes the leadership role that had belonged to Moses.

VIII. THE SAINT (Deut. 34:10-12): "There has never been another prophet like Moses, whom the LORD knew face to face."

PART TWO

History

Joshua

SECTION OUTLINE ONE (JOSHUA 1–2)
Joshua assumes command of Israel and sends two scouts into the Promised Land.

I. THE MESSENGER (1:1-18)
   A. **The Lord's message to Joshua** (1:1-9): After the death of Moses, the Lord encourages Joshua in his new role.
      1. *The Lord's words concerning Israel's borders* (1:1-6): He establishes the boundaries of the Promised Land.
      2. *The Lord's words concerning Israel's book* (1:7-9): Israel must read and heed the Book of the Law.
   B. **Joshua's message to the people** (1:10-18)
      1. *Joshua's message to the leaders* (1:10-11): Joshua tells the leaders to get ready, for in three days they are going to move out.
      2. *Joshua's message to the 2¹/₂ tribes* (1:12-18): These tribes were Reuben, Gad, and the half-tribe of Manasseh.
         a. Joshua's reminder (1:12-15): Joshua recalls the tribes' promise to assist the 9¹/₂ tribes in conquering Canaan before settling on the east side of the Jordan River.
         b. The tribes' reassurance (1:16-18): They reaffirm their promise to assist the other tribes.

II. THE MISSION (2:1-24): Joshua assigns two spies to a special task.
   A. **The spies' trip** (2:1-22): They enter Jericho to spy out the city.
      1. *Rahab's assistance to Israel's spies* (2:1-7): The two men take refuge in the home of a prostitute who has come to fear the Lord.
         a. The spies' danger (2:2-3): The king of Jericho dispatches men to Rahab's house to arrest the spies.
         b. The spies' deliverance (2:4-7): Rahab deceives the king's men into believing the spies had already left.
      2. *Rahab's assurance from Israel's spies* (2:8-21)
         a. Rahab's petition (2:8-13): She asks that she and her family be spared when the Israelites capture Jericho.
         b. The spies' promise (2:14-21): The spies agree to spare Rahab's family.

B. The spies' testimony (2:22-24): Upon returning to camp, the spies reassure the Israelites that God will indeed deliver Jericho into their hands.

SECTION OUTLINE TWO (JOSHUA 3–5)

Joshua leads Israel across the Jordan after God dries up the river. Memorial stones are set up, all Israelite males are circumcised, and the people observe the first Passover in the Promised Land.

I. THE PREPARATION FOR CROSSING (3:1-6, 8-13)
   A. Joshua's commands to the people (3:1-5, 12):
      1. *Follow the Ark of the Covenant to the Jordan River* (3:3-4).
      2. *Purify yourselves* (3:5).
      3. *Choose 12 men (one from each tribe) for a special task* (3:12).
   B. Joshua's commands to the priests (3:6, 8-11, 13):
      1. *Carry the Ark to the river* (3:6).
      2. *Stand in the river* (3:8).
      3. *Expect the water to separate* (3:13).

II. THE PROMISE OF VICTORY (3:7): God assures Joshua of his presence and his power.

III. THE PASSAGE OF ISRAEL (3:14-17; 4:12-19)
   A. How they cross over (3:15-17)
      1. *The priests stand in the water* (3:15).
      2. *The water separates, allowing the people to cross over* (3:16).
   B. Where they cross over (3:16): They cross just opposite the city of Jericho.
   C. Who first crosses over (4:12-13): The 2¹/₂ tribes (Reuben, Gad, and Manasseh) lead the other tribes across the river.
   D. When they cross over (4:15-19): On the tenth day of the first month (about late March) of the Hebrew calendar.

IV. THE PILES OF STONES (4:1-11, 20-24): Joshua builds two stone memorials commemorating the Israelites' crossing of the Jordan.
   A. First pile (4:1-8, 20-24)
      1. *God's order* (4:1-5): One man from each of the 12 tribes is chosen to take a stone from the riverbed. On the west bank of the Jordan, the men pile the 12 stones.
      2. *God's objective* (4:6-8, 20-24): The stones are to serve as a memorial to later generations that the Lord separated the Jordan River for the Israelites to cross.
   B. Second pile (4:9-11): Joshua builds this monument, also of 12 stones, in the middle of the riverbed where the priests stood.

V. THE PLACE OF ENCAMPMENT (4:19): The Israelites' first camp in Canaan is in Gilgal, near Jericho.

VI. THE PROMOTION OF JOSHUA (4:14): God now exalts Joshua in the eyes of Israel, just as he promised.

VII. THE PANIC OF THE HEATHEN (5:1): The Amorites and Canaanites are paralyzed with fear after learning of the Jordan river crossing!

VIII. THE PURIFICATION OF THE PEOPLE (5:2-9): God instructs the circumcision of the entire male population.

IX. THE PASSOVER OF THE LAMB (5:10): Israel observes Passover for the first time in the Promised Land.

X. THE PROVISIONS FROM THE LAND (5:11-12): The manna now ceases to appear, but Israel is able to live off the abundant crops of Canaan.

XI. THE PRESENCE OF THE LORD (5:13-15): Joshua is confronted by the commander of the Lord's army. Many scholars believe this was the pre-incarnate Christ.

SECTION OUTLINE THREE (JOSHUA 6–8)

In this central campaign, Joshua leads Israel to victory at Jericho, but he encounters defeat at Ai before Achan's sin is discovered and removed. After the blessings and curses of the law are read as Moses had commanded (Deut. 27:2-8), the central part of the land is secure.

I. THE TWO CITIES (6:1–8:29): The Israelites attack two cities, Jericho and Ai, during the central campaign.

A. **Jericho** (6:1-27): This strongly fortified city is the Israelites' first military encounter in Canaan.

1. *The commands* (6:1-11): The Israelites are given specific instructions for conquering Jericho.

a. Action during the first six days (6:1-4): For six days, the Israelites are to walk around the city once a day, led by seven priests blowing rams' horns.

b. Action during the final day (6:4-11): On the seventh day, the Israelites are to walk around the city seven times; at a given signal, they are to give a mighty shout. The walls will then collapse!

2. *The conquest* (6:12-21): The Israelites follow the Lord's commands, and the walls fall down, allowing them to take the city.

3. *The clemency* (6:22-25): As previously agreed, Rahab and her entire family are spared.

4. *The curse* (6:26-27): Joshua places a curse on anyone

attempting to rebuild Jericho. The builder's oldest son will die
when the foundation is laid, and his youngest son will die
when the gates are set up.
B. Ai (7:1–8:29)
   1. *Ai defeats Israel* (7:1-26): The Israelites' second military
   encounter in Canaan is with the people of Ai.
      a. The sin (7:1): Achan disobeys God's command and takes
      some of the spoils from Jericho for himself.
      b. The setback (7:2-5): Israel is totally routed in their attempt
      to capture Ai.
      c. The supplication (7:6-9): In great anguish Joshua complains
      to the Lord concerning Israel's defeat.
      d. The solution (7:10-15): The Lord responds to Joshua by tell-
      ing him two things regarding their defeat.
         (1) The cause (7:10-12): Someone in the camp has both
         stolen and lied.
         (2) The cure (7:13-15): The Lord tells Joshua to find the
         sinner and destroy him.
      e. The search (7:16-23): The Lord gives Joshua specific
      instructions for determining who the guilty person is.
         (1) The method (7:16-17): The Lord points out the tribe to
         which the guilty person belongs; then he points out the
         clan, then the family, and finally the person himself.
         (2) The man (7:18-23): Achan is found to be the guilty
         person.
      f. The stoning (7:24-26): Achan and his guilty family mem-
      bers are stoned and their bodies burned.
   2. *Israel defeats Ai* (8:1-29).
      a. The encouragement (8:1-2): The Lord now gives Joshua a
      new plan to defeat Ai. He instructs him to set an ambush
      behind the city.
      b. The execution (8:3-29): Joshua carries out the Lord's
      instructions and captures Ai.
         (1) He sets an ambush (8:3-9, 12);
         (2) he stages an attack (8:10-11, 13-14);
         (3) he pretends to retreat (8:15-17);
         (4) he signals to the men in ambush (8:18-20); and
         (5) he captures the city (8:21-29).

II. THE TWO MOUNTAINS (8:30-35): After Joshua conquers Jericho and
Ai, he carries out Moses' parting instructions.
   A. The altar (8:30-32): Joshua builds an altar on Mount Ebal and
   copies the law of God onto the stones.
   B. The announcement (8:33-35): At the foot of Mount Ebal half of
   the Israelites read the blessings for keeping the law, and at the
   foot of Mount Gerizim the other half read the curses for disobeying the law. Then Joshua reads the entire Book of the Law to the
   people.

SECTION OUTLINE FOUR (JOSHUA 9–12)
Israel is deceived by the Gibeonites. Israel defeats five Amorite kings after the Lord miraculously extends the day of the battle. Then they defeat the rest of the southern cities and move north to defeat the cities there, securing both regions.

I. THE SOUTHERN CAMPAIGN (9:1–10:43)
   A. **The deception** (9:1-27): Israel is deceived into making a treaty with the Gibeonites.
      1. *The characters* (9:1-13): While the Israelites camp at Gilgal, some nearby Gibeonite ambassadors arrive, wearing worn-out clothes and claiming they are from a distant land.
      2. *The cause* (9:14-15): Because the Israelites do not consult the Lord and do not realize that these people live nearby, they are tricked into signing a peace treaty with the Gibeonites.
      3. *The consequences* (9:16-27): Upon learning the truth, Israel is forced to employ the Gibeonites as woodchoppers and water carriers instead of driving them out as God commanded.
   B. **The destruction** (10:1-39): God empowers Israel to fight seven successful battles and gain control over all of southern Canaan.
      1. *The battle against the enemies of Gibeon* (10:1-14)
         a. The pagans (10:1-5): Adoni-zedek, king of Jerusalem, and four other kings determine to attack the Gibeonites for signing a peace treaty with Israel.
         b. The plea (10:6-7): The Gibeonites appeal to Joshua for military help.
         c. The promise (10:8): The Lord reassures Joshua of victory.
         d. The provision (10:9-14): The Lord gives the Israelites victory by sending a hailstorm upon their enemies. He also miraculously lengthens the day to ensure total victory.
      2. *The battle against Makkedah* (10:15-28)
      3. *The battle against Libnah* (10:29-30)
      4. *The battle against Lachish* (10:31-33)
      5. *The battle against Eglon* (10:34-35)
      6. *The battle against Hebron* (10:36-37)
      7. *The battle against Debir* (10:38-39)
   C. **The dimensions** (10:40-43): The total extent of Joshua's victories in the southern region is recounted.

II. THE NORTHERN CAMPAIGN (11:1-15)
   A. **The ringleaders** (11:1-5): King Jabin of Hazor joins forces with several other kings in northern Canaan to fight the Israelites.
   B. **The reassurance** (11:6): The Lord reassures Joshua that he need not worry, for the next day all his enemies will be dead.
   C. **The routing** (11:7-8): Joshua completely defeats all these kings.
   D. **The ravaging** (11:9-15): Joshua ravages the enemy cities, killing the people and capturing their goods.

III. THE OVERVIEW OF ALL CAMPAIGNS (11:16–12:24)
   A. The enemy land occupied (11:16-23)
   B. The enemy leaders overcome (12:1-24)

SECTION OUTLINE FIVE (JOSHUA 13–17)
The land is divided among the tribes. The land east of the Jordan is given to Reuben, Gad, and the half-tribe of Manasseh. The land west of the Jordan is divided among the remaining 9½ tribes.

I. THE PROMISE (13:1-7): The Lord promises to drive out the people that still remain in Canaan. He tells Joshua to divide up the land among the tribes.

II. THE PREVIOUS DECISIONS (13:8-33): Some of the tribes were already assigned their inheritance under Moses' leadership, and now they return to their land.
   A. Reuben (13:15-23): This tribe possesses the land east of the Jordan and just north of Moab.
   B. Gad (13:24-28): This tribe possesses the land east of the Jordan and just north of Reuben.
   C. East Manasseh (13:29-31): This half-tribe possesses the land east of the Jordan and just north of Gad.
   D. Levi (13:14, 32-33): No land is given to them, for the Lord himself is their inheritance.

III. THE PARTITIONING (14:1–17:18): Joshua divides the land west of the Jordan among the remaining 9½ tribes.
   A. The allotment (14:1-5): Land areas for the tribes are determined by casting lots, supervised by Joshua and the high priest Eleazar.
   B. The asking (14:6-12): Caleb requests that he be granted a portion of land for his family.
      1. *Caleb's reminder* (14:6-11)
         a. His faithfulness to the Lord (14:6-9): Caleb reviews what transpired with the scouts at Kadesh-barnea.
         b. The Lord's faithfulness to him (14:10-11): At 85 years old, Caleb is still as strong as ever!
      2. *Caleb's request* (14:12-15): Caleb asks Joshua to grant him the hill country occupied by giants so that he might drive them out! Joshua grants him this request.
   C. The area (15:1–17:13): The borders of the areas that belong to Judah, Ephraim, and West Manasseh land are described.
      1. *Judah* (15:1-63)
         a. Land given to the people (15:1-12, 20-63)
            (1) Their territory (15:1-12)
            (2) Their towns (15:20-63)
         b. Land given to the person (Caleb) (15:13-19): As promised, Joshua gives Caleb the hill country of Hebron.

      (1) Caleb the fighter (15:13-15): He succeeds in driving the giants from his land.

      (2) Caleb the father (15:16-19): As a reward for capturing Debir (or Kiriath-sepher), Caleb gives his daughter Acsah in marriage to her cousin Othniel and gives her some springs of water.

  2. *Ephraim* (16:5-10)
    a. Their territory (16:5-8)
    b. Their towns (16:9-10)
  3. *West Manasseh* (16:1-4; 17:1-13)
    a. Their ten parcels (17:1-6): Zelophehad's daughters remind Joshua of the Lord's promise to give them the land once allotted to their father. As a result, the half-tribe of Manasseh consists of 10 parcels of land (one for each of Manasseh's sons and one for each of Zelophehad's daughters) plus the regions of Gilead and Bashan.
    b. Their territory (17:7-10)
    c. Their towns (17:11-13)

D. The appeal (17:14-18):
  1. *The protest* (17:7-14): The half-tribes of Joseph (Ephraim and Manasseh) complain to Joshua that they need more land due to their large numbers of people.
  2. *The proposal* (17:15-18): Joshua enlarges their borders and tells them to drive out the Canaanites near them and occupy their land.

SECTION OUTLINE SIX (JOSHUA 18–19)
When the Tabernacle is moved from Gilgal to Shiloh, Joshua notices that seven tribes still have not taken possession of their allotted land. So he sends scouts to map out the land for them.

I. THE DELAY (18:1-3): After the Israelites set up the Tabernacle at Shiloh, Joshua asks why seven of Israel's tribes seemed reluctant to occupy the land.

II. THE DISPATCH (18:4-10): Joshua sends scouts to map out the land that is to be taken by these remaining tribes.

III. THE DIVISION (AGAIN) (18:10–19:51): Lots are cast once again to determine which tribe should claim each section of land.
  A. Benjamin (18:11-28)
    1. *Their territory* (18:11-20)
    2. *Their towns* (18:21-28)
  B. Simeon (19:1-9)
    1. *Their territory* (19:1, 9)
    2. *Their towns* (19:2-8)
  C. Zebulun (19:10-16)

1. *Their territory* (19:10-14)
2. *Their towns* (19:15-16)
D. Issachar (19:17-23)
   1. *Their territory* (19:17)
   2. *Their towns* (19:18-23)
E. Asher (19:24-31)
   1. *Their territory* (19:24)
   2. *Their towns* (19:25-31)
F. Naphtali (19:32-39)
   1. *Their territory* (19:32-34)
   2. *Their towns* (19:35-39)
G. Dan (19:40-48)
   1. *Their territory* (19:40, 47-48)
   1. *Their towns* (19:41-46)
H. Joshua (19:49-50): The Israelites give Joshua a special piece of land—any town he wants. He chooses Timnath-serah of Ephraim.

SECTION OUTLINE SEVEN (JOSHUA 20–22)
The six cities of refuge are appointed, and the Levites claim their cities. Joshua issues a call to faith to the eastern tribes. The conflict over the altar that the eastern tribes erected is resolved.

I. THE DESIGNATED CITIES (20:1–21:45)
  A. The six cities of refuge (20:1-9)
    1. *Why they exist* (20:1-6): To protect anyone who unintentionally kills another person.
    2. *Where they exist* (20:7-9): There are three cities east of the Jordan River and three west of the river.
  B. The 48 Levitical cities (21:1-45)
    1. *Where they are* (21:1-8): The Levites' towns are distributed among the tribes of Israel by casting lots.
     a. Thirteen towns are located in the tribes of Judah, Simeon, and Benjamin (21:4).
     b. Ten towns are located in the tribes of Ephraim, Dan, and the half-tribe of eastern Manasseh (21:5).
     c. Thirteen towns are located in the tribes of Isaachar, Asher, Naphtali, and the half-tribe of western Manasseh (21:6).
     d. Twelve towns are located in the tribes of Reuben, Gad, and Zebulun (21:7).
    2. *Which ones they are* (21:9-45): A list of all the Levitical towns is given.

II. THE DIVISIVE ALTAR (22:1-34): Now that the Promised Land has been divided among the tribes, Joshua sends the 2¹/₂ eastern tribes back to their land with a challenge.

A. **The contents of Joshua's challenge** (22:1-8)
   1. *His commendation* (22:1-3): Joshua praises the 2¹/₂ tribes for their obedience to God in helping their fellow Israelites on the west side of the Jordan.
   2. *His caution* (22:4-8): Joshua exhorts the tribes to continue their obedience after they return to the east side of the Jordan.
B. **The confusion following Joshua's challenge** (22:9-34)
   1. *The altar by the 2¹/₂ tribes* (22:9-10): The eastern tribes erect a large altar just before crossing the Jordan River.
   2. *The accusation by the 9¹/₂ tribes* (22:11-20)
      a. Mobilizing against their brothers (22:11-12): The 9¹/₂ tribes wrongly conclude that the altar is a pagan shrine; they muster an army at Shiloh and prepare for war against the eastern tribes!
      b. Meeting with their brothers (22:13-20): Before any fighting begins, a delegation led by Phinehas, the son of the high priest, meets with the 2¹/₂ tribes. They demand to know the reason for the eastern tribes' pagan act and warn them of God's swift and terrible punishment.
   3. *The answer by the 2¹/₂ tribes* (22:21-29): The eastern tribes explain to Phinehas that the altar is to serve as a memorial, reminding them and their descendants of the common faith and kinship they share with the other tribes.
   4. *The acceptance by the 9¹/₂ tribes* (22:30-34): The explanation of the altar's purpose satisfies the 9¹/₂ tribes, thus avoiding a civil war.

SECTION OUTLINE EIGHT (JOSHUA 23–24)
Joshua issues a call to faith, first to the leaders and then to the whole nation. The deaths of Joshua and Eleazar and the burial of Joseph's bones are recorded.

I. JOSHUA'S FAREWELL ADDRESS TO ISRAEL'S LEADERS (23:1-16)
   A. **What the Lord has done** (23:1-5, 9-10): Joshua reminds Israel's leaders that the Lord has given them victory over their enemies.
   B. **What Israel must do** (23:6-8, 11-16)
      1. *Joshua's words of wisdom* (23:6-8, 11):
         a. obey the Lord (23:6);
         b. do not associate with pagans (23:7);
         c. be faithful to the Lord (23:8).
      2. *Joshua's words of warning* (23:12-16): Joshua warns the leaders that disobedience will bring disaster.

II. JOSHUA'S FAREWELL ADDRESS TO ALL ISRAEL (24:1-33)
   A. **The details** (24:1-28)

1. *The summary* (24:1-24): Joshua again reviews God's faithfulness and goodness toward Israel.
   a. What the Lord has done (24:1-13)
      (1) In the days of Abraham (24:1-4)
      (2) In the days of Moses (24:5-10)
      (3) In the days of Joshua (24:11-13)
   b. What Israel must do (24:14-24): Joshua tells Israel that they must obey and serve the Lord, just as he and his family will do.
2. *The symbol* (24:25-28): Joshua sets up a large stone by the Tabernacle to remind the Israelites of their promise.

B. The deaths (24:29-31, 33)
   1. *Joshua* (24:29-31)
   2. *Eleazar* (24:33)

C. The displacement (24:32): Joseph's bones, which have been carried to Canaan from Egypt, are buried at Shechem.

Judges

SECTION OUTLINE ONE (JUDGES 1–2)
The conquest of Canaan continues, although the Israelites are unable to completely drive out the inhabitants there. A preview of Israel's apostasy and judgments is given.

I. THE CAMPAIGNS OF ISRAEL (1:1-36)
   A. **Military campaign of Judah** (1:1-20)
      1. *The merger of Simeon* (1:1-3): The men of Simeon's tribe agree to join forces with the men of Judah's tribe so they can conquer the land given to them.
      2. *The men of Judah* (1:4-9, 16-19): The men of Judah defeat the Canaanite king, Adoni-bezek, killing 10,000 of his troops. They capture Jerusalem, along with three important Philistine cities—Gaza, Ashkelon, and Ekron. They cannot defeat the enemies who have iron chariots.
      3. *The man of Judah (Caleb)* (1:10-15, 20): Caleb leads Judah to capture the cities of Hebron and Debir.
         a. The challenge (1:11-15): Caleb offers his daughter Acsah as a wife for the one who conquers the city. Othniel leads the attack and wins Acsah.
         b. The conquest (1:10, 20): Caleb conquers Hebron, driving out the inhabitants (who are descendants of the giant Anak).
   B. **Military campaign of Benjamin** (1:21): Even though Judah previously burned the city of Jerusalem, Benjamin is not able to drive out the Jebusites who live there.
   C. **Military campaign of Manasseh and Ephraim** (1:22-29): They defeat some of their enemies but allow them to stay in the land as slaves.
   D. **Military campaign of Zebulun** (1:30): They enslave their enemies, whom they are unable to drive out of the land.
   E. **Military campaign of Asher** (1:31-32): They are also unable to drive out their enemies.
   F. **Military campaign of Naphtali** (1:33): They are unable to drive out the enemies living in their land, but they enslave them.

G. Military campaign of Dan (1:34-36): The Amorites confine this tribe to the hill country, although the tribes of Manasseh and Ephraim enslave the Amorites later.

II. THE CASTIGATION OF ISRAEL (2:1-5): At a place called Bokim, the angel of the Lord sternly rebukes Israel for making treaties with the people living in Canaan and for failing to drive them out.

III. THE CORRUPTION OF ISRAEL (2:6-23)
   A. The root of the matter (2:6-10): Israel serves the Lord as long as Joshua lives, but when he dies, they fail to remember what the Lord has done for them.
   B. The fruit of the matter (2:11-23): Because they fail to remember the Lord's deeds, Israel experiences a series of five-step cycles.
      1. *Step one: sin* (Israel turns from the Lord.)
      2. *Step two: servitude* (The Lord allows Israel's enemies to oppress them.)
      3. *Step three: supplication* (Israel prays for forgiveness.)
      4. *Step four: salvation* (The Lord raises up a judge, or deliverer, to rescue them.)
      5. *Step five: sin* (The cycle begins again.)

SECTION OUTLINE TWO (JUDGES 3–5)
Israel intermarries with the Canaanites and worships their gods. The judgeships of Othniel, Ehud, Shamgar, and Deborah are recorded. Deborah sings her song of deliverance.

I. THE TEST (3:1-6)
   A. The facts (3:1-4): The Lord allows some of the pagan peoples to remain in Canaan so the faith and fighting skills of Israel's later generations can be exercised.
   B. The failure (3:5-6): The Israelites flunk the Lord's test by intermarrying with the pagans and worshiping their gods.

II. THE TROUBLES (3:7-31): The Israelites' sin brings punishment from the Lord, but in grace he repeatedly sends them leaders to rescue them.
   A. Othniel, the first deliverer (3:7-11)
      1. *Israel's sin* (3:7): The Israelites forget about the Lord and worship Baal and the Asherah poles.
      2. *Israel's servitude* (3:8): For eight years the Israelites are ruled by King Cushan-rishathaim of Aram-naharaim.
      3. *Israel's supplication* (3:9): In response to the Israelites' cries for help, the Lord raises up Othniel, Caleb's nephew, to rescue them.
      4. *Israel's salvation* (3:10-11): Othniel defeats King Cushan-rishathaim, and the land has peace for 40 years.

B. Ehud, the second deliverer (3:12-30)
1. *Israel's sin* (3:12): The Israelites do what is evil in the Lord's sight.
2. *Israel's servitude* (3:13-14): The Israelites are subject to the rule of King Eglon of Moab for 18 years.
3. *Israel's supplication* (3:15): The Israelites cry out to the Lord for help once again, and he raises up another deliverer for them.
4. *Israel's salvation* (3:15-30): Ehud, a left-hander from the tribe of Benjamin, is sent to deliver Israel's tax money to King Eglon.
   a. Ehud's trickery (3:16-25): After delivering the tax money to King Eglon, Ehud requests a private meeting with the king to tell him a secret message. The king sends his servants out of the room, and Ehud approaches the king as if to give him a message. Drawing his dagger with his left hand, he kills the monarch. Ehud locks the doors and escapes through the latrine.
   b. Ehud's trumpet (3:26-27): After escaping, Ehud sounds a call to arms and rallies an army.
   c. Ehud's triumph (3:28-30): Ehud and his men attack and conquer the Moabites, killing 10,000 warriors. The land is peaceful for 80 years.
C. Shamgar, the third deliverer (3:31): He kills 600 Philistines with an ox goad.
D. Deborah (and Barak), the fourth deliverer (4:1–5:31)
1. *Barak's command* (4:1-7): Through Deborah, the Lord chooses Barak to rescue the oppressed Israelites.
   a. The problem (4:1-3): Because of their sin, Israel is oppressed for 20 years by King Jabin of Hazor, a Canaanite.
   b. The prophet (4:4-5): The Lord speaks to a woman named Deborah, who has become a judge in Israel.
   c. The prophecy (4:6-7): Deborah informs Barak that he has been chosen to raise an army of 10,000 men to fight the enemy. She tells him that the Lord will give him victory over Sisera, the commander of King Jabin's army.
2. *Barak's conditions* (4:8-9)
   a. The help he required (4:8): Barak agrees to go, but only if Deborah goes with him.
   b. The honor he relinquished (4:9): Deborah agrees to go with Barak, but she warns him that because he requested her help, the credit for the victory will go to a woman instead of to him.
3. *Barak's coalition* (4:10-11): Warriors from the tribes of Zebulun, Naphtali, Ephraim, Benjamin, and Issachar quickly form Barak's army (see also 5:14-15).
4. *Barak's charge* (4:12-24): Barak and his forces engage Sisera and his army in battle.

a. The defeat of Sisera (4:12-16)
   (1) The places (4:12-13): The battle took place around Mount Tabor and the Kishon River.
   (2) The promise (4:14): Deborah tells Barak, "Get ready! Today the LORD will give you victory over Sisera, for the LORD is marching ahead of you."
   (3) The panic (4:15-16): When Barak attacks, the Lord causes Sisera and his forces to panic and flee; Sisera escapes.
b. The death of Sisera (4:17-24)
   (1) The woman (4:17-20): Jael, the wife of a man who is friendly with King Jabin, invites Sisera into her tent and helps him hide.
   (2) The weapon (4:21-24): After Sisera falls asleep, Jael drives a tent peg through his temple and kills him.
5. *Barak's celebration* (5:1-31): Following the battle, both Deborah and Barak sing a song of victory.
a. Before the battle (5:1-18, 23)
   (1) The coming of the Lord (5:1-5): Barak and Deborah speak of the greatness of the Lord when he comes to rescue Israel.
   (2) The cry of Israel (5:6-8): Barak and Deborah describe how bad things were for Israel before the victory.
   (3) The cooperation of Israel (5:9-18, 23): Barak and Deborah tell about those who joined them in their cause.
     (a) The tribes who responded (5:9-15, 18): Barak's forces included people from Zebulun, Naphtali, Ephraim, Benjamin, and Issachar.
     (b) The tribes who refused (5:16-17, 23): The people of Reuben, Dan, and Asher refused to join in the fight.
b. During the battle (5:19-22): Barak and Deborah recount how Sisera's forces fought against them, but the stars of heaven fought for Israel, and the Kishon River swept away the enemy.
c. After the battle (5:24-31)
   (1) The blessed woman (5:24-27): Barak and Deborah sing the praises of Jael.
   (2) The bewildered woman (5:28-31): Barak and Deborah describe Sisera's mother as she wonders why her son is so late in returning from battle.

SECTION OUTLINE THREE (JUDGES 6)
Midian oppresses Israel, so the Lord raises up Gideon, the fifth
deliverer. Gideon tears down the altar of Baal and calls together all
those who will fight for Israel. Then he uses a fleece to check whether
God has indeed called him to rescue Israel.

I. THE ANGUISH (6:1-10)
   A. **Israel's rebellion** (6:1): Once again the Israelites turn to idolatry
      and anger the Lord.
   B. **The Lord's retribution** (6:2-6): The Lord allows the cruel Midian-
      ites to oppress the Israelites for seven years.
   C. **The prophet's rebuke** (6:7-10): A prophet sternly reminds the
      people that sin has caused their suffering.

II. THE ANGEL (6:11-23): The angel of the Lord appears to a man
    named Gideon and tells him that he will rescue Israel from the
    Midianites.
   A. **The place** (6:11): The angel appears to Gideon under an oak tree
      at Ophrah, where Gideon is secretly threshing wheat in a
      winepress.
   B. **The protest** (6:12-13)
      1. *The greeting* (6:12): The angel greets Gideon: "Mighty hero,
         the LORD is with you!"
      2. *The grumbling* (6:13): Gideon replies, "Why has all this
         happened to us? And where are all the miracles our ancestors
         told us about?"
   C. **The promise** (6:14-16)
      1. *The command* (6:14): The angel tells Gideon, "Go with the
         strength you have and rescue Israel from the Midianites."
      2. *The cowering* (6:15): Gideon responds, "My clan is the
         weakest in the whole tribe of Manasseh, and I am the least in
         my entire family!"
      3. *The comfort* (6:16): But the angel of the Lord assures Gideon,
         "I will be with you. And you will destroy the Midianites as if
         you were fighting against one man."
   D. **The proof** (6:17-23): Gideon asks for a sign to be certain that he
      is to rescue Israel.
      1. *The meal* (6:17-19): Gideon goes home to prepare a meal for
         the angel.
      2. *The miracle* (6:20-23): When the angel touches the meal with
         his staff, fire flames up and consumes the food, convincing
         Gideon that the angel was sent from the Lord.

III. THE ALTARS (6:24-32): Gideon builds two altars to the Lord.
   A. **The first altar** (6:24): Gideon builds the first altar after the angel
      of the Lord appears to him and causes the meal to burn up. He
      names this altar "The LORD Is Peace."
   B. **The second altar** (6:25-32)

1. *The directive to Gideon* (6:25-27): The Lord tells Gideon to destroy his father's altar to Baal and construct an altar to the Lord in its place. Gideon does so under cover of darkness.
2. *The disgust with Gideon* (6:28-30): The morning after Gideon pulls down the altar, the people of Ophrah threaten to kill him.
3. *The defense of Gideon* (6:31-32): Gideon's father defends him, saying, "If Baal truly is a god, let him defend himself."

IV. THE ANOINTING (6:33-35): Soon after these events, the spirit of the Lord comes upon Gideon and empowers him to fight the Midianites.
   A. **The threat** (6:33): A vast army of Midianites and Amalekites unite to attack Israel.
   B. **The trumpet** (6:34-35): The Spirit of the Lord comes upon Gideon, and he blows a ram's horn to gather an army.

V. THE ASSURANCE (6:36-40): Gideon requests two signs from God to assure him of his calling to rescue Israel. God answers Gideon's request.
   A. **First sign** (6:36-38): Cause a certain fleece to be wet while the ground is dry.
   B. **Second sign** (6:39-40): Cause the fleece to be dry while the ground is wet.

SECTION OUTLINE FOUR (JUDGES 7–8)
The Lord reduces Gideon's army from 32,000 to 300 but causes them to defeat the Midianites through panic. The Israelites pursue the fleeing Midianites and punish two cities that refuse to help. Gideon refuses the offer of a crown but takes the Midianites' gold earrings.

I. THE ARMY (7:1-8)
   A. **The reduction** (7:1-6): The Lord tells Gideon that his army of 32,000 is too big and reduces it in two stages.
      1. *Due to panic* (7:1-3): Gideon sends 22,000 men home because they are fearful.
      2. *Due to posture* (7:4-6): Gideon sends 9,700 troops home because of the way they drink water.
   B. **The right number** (7:7-8): The army is now reduced to 300 soldiers—all that God needs to win!

II. THE ATTACK (7:9–8:21)
   A. **Before the battle** (7:9-18)
      1. *The sign* (7:9-15)
         a. The details (7:9-12): Because Gideon is still afraid to attack the Midianites, the Lord sends him to the enemy camp to give him assurance of victory.

     b. The dream (7:13-15): At the enemy camp, Gideon over-
hears one soldier tell another of a dream he had. The
dream shows that God will give Gideon victory over the
Midianites.

   2. *The strategy* (7:16-18): At Gideon's command his men are to
blow horns, hold up torches, and shout, "For the LORD and for
Gideon!"

B. During the battle (7:19-25)

   1. *The sound of victory* (7:19-22): The soldiers blow their
trumpets; the enemy panics, and they fight each other.

   2. *The summons to victory* (7:23-25): Gideon invites other
Israelite tribes to chase after the fleeing Midianites.

C. After the battle (8:1-21)

   1. *The criticism against Gideon* (8:1-4): The jealous men of
Ephraim complain that they had not been asked to fight
sooner.

   2. *The contempt for Gideon* (8:5-9): The cities of Succoth and
Peniel refuse to provide food for Gideon's hungry troops.

   3. *The capture by Gideon* (8:10-12, 18-21): Gideon captures the
two enemy leaders Zebah and Zalmunna.

     a. Their defeat (8:10-12)

     b. Their deaths (8:18-21)

   4. *The chastisement from Gideon* (8:13-17): The cities of Succoth
and Peniel are severely punished for refusing to help Gideon's
troops.

III. THE APOSTASY (8:22-33): Again Israel turns away from following the
Lord.

  A. The refusal of kingship (8:22-23): The grateful Israelites ask
Gideon to be their king, but he refuses.

  B. The return to idolatry (8:24-27, 33-35): Gideon takes some of the
gold earrings of the Midianites and makes a sacred ephod, which
then becomes an idol for Gideon and the rest of the Israelites.

  C. The rest of Gideon's life (8:28-32): The land is at peace for the
rest of Gideon's life (about 40 years). Gideon has many wives
and one concubine. He fathers many children before he dies and
is buried at Ophrah.

SECTION OUTLINE FIVE (JUDGES 9–12)
This outline covers the murderous reign and demise of Abimelech,
Gideon's son. Tola and Jair rule over Israel as judges. Israel sins again,
and the Lord refuses to raise up a new judge. The events of Jephthah's
life and judgeship are recorded, as well as the judgeships of Ibzan,
Elon, and Abdon.

I. THE APOSTATE SUCCESSOR OF GIDEON (9:1-57): Soon after Gideon's
death, his son Abimelech attempts to become Shechem's king.

A. Abimelech's destruction (9:1-6): In order to secure his reign, Abimelech murders all but one of his 70 half brothers.
B. Abimelech's denouncement (9:7-21)
   1. *The ridicule* (9:7-15): Jotham, the only surviving half brother, ridicules Abimelech by telling a parable of trees that want a king. In the story Abimelech is portrayed as a worthless thornbush.
   2. *The rebuke* (9:16-21): Jotham denounces the Israelites who have chosen Abimelech to rule over them.
C. Abimelech's difficulties (9:22-41)
   1. *Caused by God* (9:22-25): After three years, God stirs up trouble between Abimelech and the people of Shechem, who unsuccessfully attempt to ambush him.
   2. *Caused by Gaal* (9:26-41): Gaal, a leading citizen of Shechem, organizes a revolt against Abimelech.
D. Abimelech's depravity (9:42-49): Abimelech and his men ruthlessly slaughter the people of Shechem for rebelling against him.
E. Abimelech's death (9:50-57): Abimelech and his men then attack Thebez and trap some of the people in a tower. But a woman drops a millstone upon Abimelech's head and crushes his skull, so he begs his armor bearer to kill him so he does not die at the hands of a woman.

II. THE ANOINTED SUCCESSORS OF GIDEON (10–12): After Abimelech's death, the Lord raises up several more judges to lead Israel.
A. Tola, the sixth deliverer (10:1-2): For 23 years Tola, a man from the tribe of Issachar, reigns as Israel's judge.
B. Jair, the seventh deliverer (10:3-5): Tola dies, and a man named Jair from Gilead becomes Israel's judge for 22 years. His 30 sons ride 30 donkeys and own 30 towns throughout Gilead.
C. Jephthah, the eighth deliverer (10:6–12:7)
   1. *The setting for Jephthah's deeds* (10:6-18)
      a. Israel's sin (10:6): Again the nation turns from the Lord and practices idolatry.
      b. Israel's servitude (10:7-9): Because of Israel's sin, the Lord allows the Philistines and the Ammonites to oppress them for 18 years.
      c. Israel's supplication (10:10-18)
         (1) The rebuke (10:10-14): The Lord tells the people, "You have abandoned me and served other gods. So I will not rescue you anymore. Go and cry out to the gods you have chosen! Let them rescue you in your hour of distress!"
         (2) The revival (10:15-16): The Israelites repent of their sin and promise to serve only the Lord.
         (3) The resolution (10:17-18): The people determine to crown as king anyone who saves them from the Ammonite army that is preparing to attack.

2. *The story of Jephthah's deeds* (11:1–12:7)
   a. His vindication (11:1-29)
      (1) Jephthah, the scorned (11:1-3): Born out of wedlock to
          a prostitute, Jephthah is despised and driven out of his
          home in Gilead by his half brothers. He forms a large
          band of rebels.
      (2) Jephthah, the sought after (11:4-11): When Gilead is
          threatened by the Ammonites, the people ask Jephthah
          to be their commander and ruler, and he accepts.
      (3) Jephthah, the statesman (11:12-28)
          (a) The problem (11:12-13): Jephthah learns that the
              Ammonites are angry because they believe Israel
              stole land from them.
          (b) The peace attempts (11:14-28): To avoid a battle,
              Jephthah attempts to explain how the Israelites got
              the land. The Ammonites, however, are not satisfied.
      (4) Jephthah, the soldier (11:29): The Lord's Spirit comes
          upon Jephthah, and he leads an army against the
          Ammonites.
   b. His vow (11:30-31): Jephthah vows that if the Lord gives
      him victory over the Ammonites, upon returning, he will
      sacrifice as a burnt offering the first thing that comes out of
      his house to greet him.
   c. His victory (11:32-33): Jephthah and his men completely
      defeat the Ammonites.
   d. His vexation (11:34-40)
      (1) The father's anguish (11:34-35): Jephthah's only
          daughter is the first one to come out of the house to
          greet him. Jephthah tears his clothes in anguish.
      (2) The daughter's agreement (11:36-38): Jephthah's
          daughter tells him that he must keep his vow, but she
          asks for two months to lament the fact that she will
          never be married.
      (3) Israel's annual event (11:39-40): Jephthah keeps his
          vow. This tragedy becomes a yearly remembrance
          among the young women of Israel.
   e. His vengeance (12:1-7)
      (1) The rebuke against Jephthah (12:1-4): The people of
          Ephraim threaten Jephthah for not allowing them to
          share in his victory against the Ammonites. Though
          Jephthah explains that he did indeed invite them, they
          begin to insult the people of Gilead.
      (2) The retaliation by Jephthah (12:4-7): Jephthah is
          angered by the insults of the people of Ephraim, so he
          attacks them.
          (a) His triumph (12:4): Jephthah defeats the people of
              Ephraim.

(b) His testing (12:5-7): To identify the fugitives from Ephraim, Jephthah places a checkpoint at the Jordan River and forces all passersby to say, "Shibboleth." If the person cannot pronounce the word correctly, Jephthah's men know that he is an Ephraimite, and they kill him.

D. Ibzan, the ninth deliverer (12:8-10): Jephthah dies, and Ibzan becomes Israel's judge for seven years. He has 30 sons and 30 daughters.

E. Elon, the tenth deliverer (12:11-12): After Ibzan dies, Elon, a man from Zebulun, becomes Israel's judge for 10 years.

F. Abdon, the eleventh deliverer (12:13-15): Elon dies, and Abdon becomes Israel's judge for eight years. He has 40 sons and 30 grandsons.

SECTION OUTLINE SIX (JUDGES 13–16)
God raises up Samson to rescue Israel from the Philistines. Samson's exploits include killing 30 Philistines to pay off a wager he made regarding a riddle, slaying 1,000 Philistines with a donkey's jawbone, carrying away the city gates of Gaza, being tricked into capture by a woman named Delilah, and killing thousands of Philistines by pulling down their temple of Dagon.

I. SAMSON'S MISSION (13:1-25): After the Israelites sin once again and are oppressed by the Philistines, the angel of the Lord promises a son to Manoah and his wife. This son will rescue Israel from the Philistines.
  A. First visit by the angel of the Lord (13:1-8)
    1. *The revelation* (13:1-5): The angel of the Lord appears to Manoah's wife, who is unable to become pregnant, with this message.
      a. Her firstborn (13:1-3): Manoah's wife is told she will give birth to a son.
      b. His future (13:4-5): The child will be raised as a Nazirite; he is to be dedicated to the Lord and must abstain from alcohol and any forbidden food. He will rescue Israel from the Philistines, who have been oppressing Israel for 40 years.
    2. *The conversation* (13:6-7): Manoah's wife tells him of the angel's visit.
    3. *The supplication* (13:8): Manoah prays that the angel will return and give them more instructions about the child.
  B. Second visit by the angel of the Lord (13:9-25)
    1. *The repetition* (13:9-14): The angel appears again to Manoah's wife, who runs and tells her husband to come.

The angel repeats his instructions to raise the child as a Nazirite.

2. *The realization* (13:15-25): Manoah and his wife desire to honor the angel after his second appearance.

a. The sacrifice to the Lord (13:15-16): Manoah offers a young goat to the angel, who instructs him to offer it as a sacrifice to the Lord.

b. The secret of the Lord (13:17-18): The angel refuses to tell Manoah his name.

c. The sign by the Lord (13:19-23): While Manoah makes the sacrifice, the angel ascends in the fire blazing from the altar. Manoah realizes it was the angel of the Lord.

d. The son from the Lord (13:24-25): Samson is born. Soon he experiences the blessing and anointing of the Spirit of the Lord.

II. SAMSON'S MARRIAGE (14:1-4)

A. **Samson's order** (14:1-2): Samson notices a Philistine girl in Timnah and tells his parents to make arrangements for him to marry her.

B. **The parents' objection** (14:3): Samson's parents try to convince Samson to marry an Israelite girl. Samson says no.

C. **The Lord's ordination** (14:4): This marriage is part of the Lord's plan to free Israel from Philistine oppression.

III. SAMSON'S MIGHTY DEEDS (14:5–16:3)

A. **The ripping apart of the lion** (14:5-19): As Samson travels to Timnah, a lion attacks him, but he kills it with his bare hands. Later, Samson passes by the lion's carcass and notices that bees have made honey in it.

B. **The riddle of the honey** (14:10-20)

1. *The proposal* (14:10-14): Samson uses his experience with the lion to tell a riddle before his wedding day.

a. The companions (14:10-11): Before the wedding, Samson throws a party for 30 young men from Timnah.

b. The challenge (14:14): During the party, Samson gives the men a riddle: "From the one who eats came something to eat; out of the strong came something sweet."

c. The consequences (14:12-13): Samson says that he will give each of the men a plain robe and a fancy robe if they answer his riddle in seven days. If they cannot, they must each give him the same.

2. *The pressure* (14:15-18)

a. Upon Samson's wife (14:15): The men from Timnah threaten to kill both her and her father unless she tells them the answer to the riddle.

b. Upon Samson (14:16-18): Samson's wife pleads with him

to give her the answer. At last Samson does, and she
reveals the answer to the men of Timnah.
3. *The payment* (14:19): In order to pay off his wager, Samson
kills 30 men from Ashkelon, takes their clothing, and gives it
to the men of Timnah.
4. *The parting* (14:20): Samson becomes infuriated with his wife
because she has caused him to lose the wager, and he goes
home to live with his parents. So the bride's father gives her to
the man who had been Samson's best man.
C. **The ruin of the grain** (15:1-8)
1. *The foxes* (15:1-4): Discovering that his wife has been given to
another, Samson catches 300 foxes, ties their tails together in
pairs, and lights a torch fastened to each pair.
2. *The fiery fields* (15:5): The foxes run through the fields of the
Philistines, burning the grain to the ground!
3. *The fury* (15:6): The Philistines strike back by killing the
woman given away in marriage and her father.
D. **The rage of Samson** (15:7-8): In retaliation for the death of his
wife and her father, Samson kills many Philistines.
E. **The raid of the Philistines** (15:9-20): Continuing the cycle of retribution, the Philistines raid the town of Lehi in Judah.
1. *The binding of Samson* (15:9-13): Three thousand men from
Judah come to bind Samson with ropes and hand him over to
the Philistines, and he allows them to do so.
2. *The bloodletting by Samson* (15:14-20)
a. His power from God (15:14-17): When the Philistines
come to take Samson away, the Spirit of the Lord comes
upon him, causing him to easily snap the ropes around
him. Using a donkey's jawbone, he kills 1,000 Philistines.
b. His prayer to God (15:18-20): In terrible thirst, Samson
cries out for water, which God causes to gush up from the
ground!
F. **The removal of the gates** (16:1-3)
1. *The prostitute* (16:1): Samson visits a prostitute in the Philistine
city of Gaza.
2. *The plot* (16:2): When word of Samson's presence there
spreads, the men of Gaza plan to kill him when he leaves
through the city gates in the morning.
3. *The posts* (16:3): Samson leaves at midnight, however, lifting
the city gates and its posts right out of the ground and carrying
them to the top of a hill many miles away.
IV. SAMSON'S MISTRESS (16:4-19): Later Samson loves a woman named
Delilah.
A. **The bribe** (16:4-5): The Philistines offer Delilah a great deal of
silver to find out the secret of Samson's strength.
B. **The betrayal** (16:6-19)
1. *The fiction concerning his great strength* (16:6-15): On three

occasions Samson lies to Delilah about the source of his power.

2. *The facts concerning his great strength* (16:16-19): Finally, after much nagging by Delilah, Samson confesses that he is a Nazirite and that if his hair is ever cut, he will lose his strength. So Delilah lulls him to sleep in her lap and calls for someone to shave his hair off.

V. SAMSON'S MISERY (16:20-22): The Philistines capture Samson, gouge out his eyes, bind him in chains, and force him to grind grain in prison. But soon his hair begins to grow back.

VI. SAMSON'S MARTYRDOM (SELF-INFLICTED) (16:23-31)
   A. The derision by the Philistines (16:23-28)
      1. *The ridicule of Samson* (16:23-25): Samson is brought forth during a public celebration of the Philistine god Dagon.
      2. *The request by Samson* (16:26-28): Samson asks the Lord for strength that he might punish the Philistines one final time for blinding him.
   B. The destruction of the Philistines (16:29-31): Samson pushes on the two central pillars of the temple, bringing it crashing down. Samson kills more Philistines in this one act than in all his other deeds combined, but he dies also.

SECTION OUTLINE SEVEN (JUDGES 17–21)
Idolatry is initiated in Dan by a Levite who becomes a priest for a man named Micah. Another Levite starts a war between Benjamin and the other tribes to avenge the rape of his concubine. The outcome and aftermath of the war are recorded.

I. IDOLATRY IN DAN (17:1–18:31)
   A. The family practice of idolatry (17:1-13): Micah's family helps initiate idolatry in Dan.
      1. *Micah's dishonesty* (17:1-4): Micah confesses to stealing a large amount of silver from his mother and returns it. She uses the silver to make an idol.
      2. *Micah's desecration* (17:5-13): Micah makes a shrine for the idol and hires a Levite traveling from Bethlehem to become his personal priest.
   B. The formal practice of idolatry (18:1-31)
      1. *Dan's move* (18:1-26): Unable to drive out the Philistines in the southwest part of the Promised Land, the tribe of Dan looks for a new home in the north.
         a. The first visit (18:1-10): Dan sends five warriors to scout out new land, and for a night they stay in Micah's home. They ask the Levite priest there if they will have a successful journey.

b. The second visit (18:11-26): After experiencing victory over their enemies—as the Levite priest predicted—the tribe decides to take Micah's idols. They also persuade the priest to become the priest for their tribe, despite Micah's objections.
2. *Dan's mistake* (18:27-31): The tribe of Dan destroys and rebuilds the city of Laish, renaming it Dan. They worship idols in the city and appoint Jonathan, a descendant of Moses, as their priest.

II. IMMORALITY IN BENJAMIN (19:1-30): The concubine of a Levite living in Ephraim becomes the victim of sexual perverts.
   A. **The Levite and his concubine** (19:1-2): The Levite's concubine becomes unfaithful and returns to live with her father in Bethlehem.
   B. **The Levite and the concubine's father** (19:3-10): The Levite travels to Bethlehem and persuades his concubine to return after a pleasant four-day visit with her father.
   C. **The Levite and an old man** (19:11-21): After arriving at dusk at the Benjamite city of Gibeah, the couple accepts an invitation by an old man to spend the night at his home.
   D. **The Levite and some sexual perverts** (19:22-28): During their stay, many wicked men of the town surround the home of the old man and his guests.
      1. *Their demand* (19:22-24): The perverts demand that the Levite be sent out so they can have sex with him. The old man refuses, offering them his own virgin daughter and the concubine. They refuse his offer.
      2. *Their depravity* (19:25-28): The Levite sends out his concubine anyway, and the men rape her throughout the night. Finally they let her go, and she crawls back to the house and dies on the doorstep.
   E. **The Levite and the tribes of Israel** (19:29-30): The Levite carries his concubine's body back to Ephraim and cuts it into 12 pieces. He sends one piece to each of Israel's tribes, arousing the nation to punish such sexual perverts living in the land of Benjamin.

III. INDIGNATION FROM ISRAEL (20:1–21:25): The tribes of Israel respond with great anger over the terrible treatment of the Levite's concubine.
   A. **The origin of the war** (20:1-17): The leaders of the 10 tribes meet together in Mizpah to decide what must be done about the matter.
      1. *The report of the Levite* (20:1-7): The Levite reviews how sexual perverts murdered his concubine in the Benjamite city of Gibeah.
      2. *The resolve of the 10 tribes* (20:8-11): The leaders of the tribes resolve to attack Gibeah and execute the criminals as soon as possible.

3. *The refusal of Benjamin* (20:12-17): The people of Benjamin refuse to allow the tribes to attack Gibeah. Instead they come out to fight against the other tribes.

B. The overview of the war (20:18-48)

1. *The slaughter* (20:18-46)

   a. First battle (20:18-21): The Lord instructs the tribe of Judah to lead the fight, but the Benjamites kill 22,000 men from the other tribes.

   b. Second battle (20:22-25): The Lord directs the other tribes to continue fighting, but the Benjamites kill 18,000 experienced warriors from the other tribes.

   c. Third battle (20:26-45): After seeking direction from the Lord once again, the other tribes set up an ambush and defeat the warriors from Benjamin.

2. *The survivors* (20:46-48): The tribe of Benjamin loses 25,000 men, leaving only 600 alive after the third battle!

C. The outcome of the war (21:1-25)

1. *The sorrow* (21:1-7): The other tribes of Israel experience regret and grief over the apparent loss of an entire tribe. The problem is compounded because they have sworn not to allow their daughters to marry a Benjamite.

2. *The solution* (21:8-25)

   a. Sparing wives for the men (21:8-15): In order to find wives for the severely diminished tribe, Israel's leaders agree to give them all the virgins taken from Jabesh-gilead. This town had refused to appear at Mizpah when the issue of war with Benjamin was discussed. After raiding the town, they find only 400 virgins.

   b. Snatching wives for the men (21:16-25): The other 200 men of Benjamin are given permission to kidnap all the young virgins who participate in a festival at Shiloh.

Ruth

SECTION OUTLINE ONE (RUTH 1–4)

This outline covers the life of Ruth, a Moabite widow who trusts in the God of Israel and is rewarded with a new husband and child. Ruth becomes an ancestor of King David and, eventually, of the Messiah.

I. RUTH RENOUNCING (1:1-22)
   A. **The famine** (1:1-2): An Israelite family (Elimelech; his wife, Naomi; and their two sons) leave their home in Bethlehem to escape a famine and move to Moab.
   B. **The funerals** (1:3-5): Elimelech dies, and his sons marry Moabite women. Ten years later the sons die, and now Naomi and her daughters-in-law are widows.
   C. **The farewells** (1:6-15)
      1. *Naomi's decision* (1:6-7): Hearing that there is abundant food in Bethlehem, Naomi determines to return to her homeland. Both her daughters-in-law begin the journey with her.
      2. *Naomi's despair* (1:8-15): A bitter and broken Naomi gently urges her daughters-in-law, Orpah and Ruth, to return to Moab and begin new lives. Orpah does, but Ruth stays with Naomi.
   D. **The faith** (1:16-18): Ruth vows to accompany her mother-in-law and makes Naomi's God her God.
   E. **The frustration** (1:19-22): Arriving in Bethlehem, Naomi tells her old friends not to call her Naomi, meaning "pleasant," but to call her Mara, meaning "bitter."

II. RUTH REAPING (2:1-23)
   A. **The mission of Ruth** (2:1-2): Ruth volunteers to glean the leftover grain from the fields of some kindly farmer so she and Naomi have food to eat.
   B. **The meeting with Boaz** (2:3-17)
      1. *His encounter with Ruth* (2:3-13)
         a. The circumstances (2:3-7): As Ruth sets out to gather grain,

she selects a field belonging to a wealthy man named
Boaz. Boaz arrives and inquires about Ruth.

  b. The conversation (3:8-13): Boaz tells her to stay in his field
     and praises Ruth for her kindness to Naomi.

  2. *His encouragement to Ruth* (2:14-17)

     a. The invitation (2:14): Boaz invites Ruth to eat from the food
        he has provided for his harvesters.

     b. The instructions (2:15-17): Boaz instructs his workers to
        leave ample heads of barley in the field for Ruth!

C. **The marveling of Naomi** (2:18-23): Upon returning home,
   Ruth tells Naomi about Boaz's kindness. Naomi blesses
   Boaz and tells Ruth that he is a close relative (who can marry
   her).

III. RUTH RESTING (3:1-18)

  A. **The plan** (3:1-5): Desiring to provide a home for Ruth, Naomi
     gives Ruth instructions for presenting herself as a potential
     spouse for Boaz. She sends Ruth to find Boaz at the threshing
     floor. Ruth is to wait until Boaz finishes his meal and lies down,
     and then she is to lie at his feet.

  B. **The proposal** (3:6-9): In the middle of the night a startled Boaz
     awakes to find Ruth lying at his feet! She then asks him to per-
     form his duties as her family redeemer.

  C. **The problem** (3:10-13): Boaz explains to Ruth that there is
     another man more closely related to her than he is. If that rela-
     tive won't marry Ruth, he will.

  D. **The precaution** (3:14): Boaz requests that Ruth stay until dawn
     and secretly leave, lest her mission be misinterpreted by wit-
     nesses.

  E. **The provision** (3:15-17): Boaz sends Ruth home with six mea-
     sures of barley.

  F. **The persistence** (3:18): Naomi reassures Ruth that Boaz will
     not rest until he has followed through concerning her
     request.

IV. RUTH RECEIVING (4:1-22)

  A. **The summons** (4:1-6): At the town gate Boaz meets with the
     other family redeemer and 10 town leaders.

     1. *The rights of the family redeemer* (4:1-5): Boaz reminds the
        other family redeemer that he has first chance to buy
        Elimelech's land. The man is interested, but then Boaz adds
        that the buyer must also marry Ruth.

     2. *The refusal by the family redeemer* (4:6): The other family
        redeemer declines to buy the land since it would endanger his
        own estate.

  B. **The symbol** (4:7-12): The family redeemer offers Boaz the estate
     and validates the transaction by giving him his sandal.

C. The son (4:13-17)
    1. *The fruitfulness of Ruth* (4:13): Ruth becomes Boaz's wife, and she gives birth to a son.
    2. *The faithfulness of God* (4:14-17): The women in Bethlehem remind Naomi of the Lord's goodness to her!
D. The summary (4:18-22): In God's marvelous plan Boaz and Ruth become great-grandparents of King David!

1 Samuel

SECTION OUTLINE ONE (1 SAMUEL 1–2)

A barren woman named Hannah prays for a son and vows to give him back to the Lord if he answers her prayer. Samuel is born; she leaves him at the Tabernacle when he is old enough, where he helps Eli, the priest. Hannah praises the Lord. Eli has two wicked sons, who are judged for their sinful actions.

I. THE FAMILY OF HANNAH (1:1–2:11, 18-21, 26)
   A. **Her spouse** (1:1-2): Hannah is married to Elkanah.
   B. **Her sorrow** (1:3-8): Hannah is heartbroken because she does not have any children.
      1. *Reassurance by Elkanah* (1:4-5, 8): Elkanah tries to comfort Hannah, reminding her of his love and devotion to her.
      2. *Ridicule by Peninnah* (1:6-7): Elkanah's other wife, Peninnah, taunts Hannah because she has no children.
   C. **Her supplication** (1:9-18)
      1. *The promise* (1:9-11): Hannah visits the Tabernacle and prays that if the Lord will give her a son, she will give him back to the Lord.
      2. *The protest* (1:12-16)
         a. Eli's condemnation (1:12-14): When the priest Eli sees Hannah praying, he wrongly concludes that she is drunk.
         b. Hannah's clarification (1:15-16): Hannah quickly explains that she is praying to the Lord out of great anguish and sorrow.
      3. *The prayer* (1:17-18): Eli asks the Lord to grant Hannah's request. Hannah rejoices over Eli's prayer.
   D. **Her son** (1:19-28; 2:11, 18-20, 26): The Lord honors Hannah's request, and she gives birth to Samuel. Hannah dedicates Samuel to the Lord and leaves him at the Tabernacle after he is weaned. She visits Samuel yearly, making a coat for him each year and watching him grow.
   E. **Her song** (2:1-11): In this remarkable prayer, Hannah praises the Lord for his holiness, his omniscience, his sovereignty, his compassion, and his justice.

F. Her sons and daughters (2:21): The Lord blesses Hannah with three more sons and two daughters.

II. THE FAMILY OF ELI (2:12-17, 22-25, 27-36): Eli the priest has two wicked sons, Hophni and Phinehas.
    A. Their wickedness (2:12-17, 22)
        1. *They are guilty of impiety* (2:12, 17).
        2. *They are guilty of intimidation* (2:13-16).
        3. *They are guilty of immorality* (2:22).
    B. Their warning (2:23-25, 27-36)
        1. *From the parent* (2:23-25): Eli attempts to correct his rebellious sons, but it is too late.
        2. *From the prophet* (2:27-36): Finally a prophet warns Eli of the consequences of his family's behavior: They will no longer serve as priests, and Eli's two sons will die on the same day.

SECTION OUTLINE TWO (1 SAMUEL 3–5)
God calls Samuel to deliver a message of judgment against Eli's family. Israel fights the Philistines, the Ark of the Covenant is captured in battle, and Hophni and Phinehas are killed. Eli dies after hearing of the Ark's capture. The Ark is transported throughout Philistia and wreaks havoc in the land.

I. THE ANOINTED (3:1-21): Samuel has already been chosen by God to replace Eli as the spiritual leader of Israel.
    A. Samuel's message from the Lord (3:1-18): While Samuel is still a young boy, the Lord speaks to him about Eli.
        1. *Samuel receives the message* (3:1-14)
            a. Where he is (3:1-9): The Lord calls to Samuel one night as he is sleeping. At first Samuel thinks it is Eli calling him. Eli realizes it is the Lord and tells Samuel to listen.
            b. What he hears (3:10-14): The Lord tells Samuel that he will soon severely punish Eli and his two wicked sons.
        2. *Samuel repeats the message* (3:15-18): The next morning Samuel tells Eli everything the Lord said to him.
    B. Samuel's ministry for the Lord (3:19-21): Soon all Israel comes to recognize Samuel as a great prophet of the Lord.

II. THE ATTACKS (4:1-22): The Israelites engage in war with the Philistines.
    A. The defeats (4:1-11): The Israelites suffer two defeats by the Philistines.
        1. *First defeat* (4:1-9)
            a. The routing (4:1-2): The Philistines kill 4,000 Israelites in the first encounter.
            b. The rallying (4:3-9): The Ark of the Covenant is carried to the battlefield to encourage Israel and frighten the Philistines. But the Philistines stage a rally!

2. *Second defeat* (4:10-11): The Philistines kill 30,000 Israelites, including Eli's sons, Hophni and Phinehas, and capture the Ark of the Covenant.
   B. The despair (4:12-22)
   1. *Of Eli* (4:12-18)
      a. His anxiety (4:12-16): Eli sits near the gate of Shiloh, fearfully awaiting news of the battle and the Ark.
      b. His accident (4:17-18): Hearing of Israel's defeat, the death of his sons, and the capture of the Ark, Eli falls from his seat, breaks his neck, and dies!
   2. *Of Eli's daughter-in-law* (4:19-22)
      a. The tragic news (4:19-20): When Phinehas's pregnant wife hears that her husband and father-in-law are dead and the Ark has been captured, she goes into labor and dies in childbirth.
      b. The tragic name (4:21-22): Just before her death, Phinehas's wife names her infant son Ichabod, meaning "Where is the glory?"
III. THE ARK (5:1-12)
   A. In Ashdod (5:1-8)
   1. *The temple* (5:1-5): The Lord causes the Philistine idol Dagon to fall down before the Ark.
   2. *The tumors* (5:6-8): The people of Ashdod are afflicted with tumors because of the Ark's presence. So they send the Ark to the city of Gath.
   B. In Gath (5:9): The citizens there also suffer from an outbreak of tumors.
   C. In Ekron (5:10-12). When the people of Gath try to send the Ark to Ekron, tumors and great fear begin to sweep through Ekron.

SECTION OUTLINE THREE (1 SAMUEL 6–7)
The Philistines return the Ark to Israel with gifts. Samuel calls Israel to repentance, and Israel defeats the Philistines. Samuel continues his role as judge over Israel.

I. THE RETURN OF THE ARK (6:1-21)
   A. The treasure (6:1-6): After seven months of trouble over the Ark, the desperate Philistines are advised by their own priests to send the Ark back to Israel with a guilt offering of five gold tumors and five gold rats!
   B. The test (6:7-12): To determine whether their troubles were caused by the Ark or by coincidence, the Philistines devise a test. Two cows that have just given birth to calves are tied to a cart holding the Ark. If the cows don't cross the border, it was chance that caused the tumors. But if they cross into Israel, the Lord

caused the plagues. The cows carry the Ark to the Israelite town of Beth-shemesh.

C. **The thanksgiving** (6:13-18): The people of Beth-shemesh rejoice at the return of the Ark.

D. **The tragedy** (6:19-21): The Lord killed 70 men for looking inside the Ark, so the people of Beth-shemesh ask the people of Kiriath-jearim to come and take it away.

II. THE REVIVAL BROUGHT ABOUT BY THE ARK (7:1-17)

A. **The repentance** (7:1-6): After 20 years of spiritual decline, Samuel leads the people to repentance. The Israelites destroy their idols and worship only the Lord. Samuel becomes Israel's judge.

B. **The routing** (7:7-11): The Philistines attack the Israelites, but the Lord's mighty voice thunders from heaven, throwing the Philistines into confusion and allowing the Israelites to defeat them.

C. **The rock** (7:12): Samuel sets up a huge stone to remind the people of God's help and calls it Ebenezer, meaning "the stone of help."

D. **The respite** (7:13-14): The Philistines are forced to return much of the land they captured from Israel and do not invade them again for a long time.

E. **The routine** (7:15-17): Samuel travels throughout Israel for many years, serving as judge over the people.

SECTION OUTLINE FOUR (1 SAMUEL 8–11)

Samuel's sons are corrupt judges, so Israel asks for a king. Samuel warns the people about the problems a king will bring, but they insist. The Lord shows Samuel that Saul is to be Israel's first king. Samuel anoints Saul king and presents him to Israel. Saul leads Israel to victory over the Ammonites and is crowned king.

I. THE ASKING (8:1-22): Israel asks Samuel for a king.

A. **The logic** (8:1-5): The people request a king because Samuel is old, his sons are corrupt, and the surrounding nations have kings.

B. **The lamentation** (8:6-9): This request upsets Samuel, but the Lord assures him that the people are rejecting God, not him.

C. **The liabilities** (8:10-22): Samuel explains the consequences of allowing a king to rule over them.

1. *The review* (8:10-18): A king will force military service and slave labor upon their sons and daughters and impose heavy taxes on them.

2. *The refusal* (8:19-22): In spite of Samuel's warning, the people still demand a king!

II. THE ACQUISITION (9:1-27): Samuel acquires a king for Israel, a man named Saul.

A. **The person** (9:1-2): The Lord chooses Saul to become the first king of Israel. Saul is a tall, handsome man from the tribe of Benjamin.

B. The particulars (9:3-27)

1. *The mission of Saul* (9:3-13)

   a. The search (9:3-5): Saul is sent by his father to locate some donkeys that have strayed; he does not find them.

   b. The suggestion (9:6-13): One of Saul's servants advises him to ask a seer concerning the whereabouts of the lost donkeys.

2. *The message to Samuel* (9:14-16): In the meantime, the Lord tells Samuel that he is sending a man from the tribe of Benjamin to become Israel's first king.

3. *The meeting of both* (9:17-27): As Saul approaches Samuel to ask where the seer lives, the Lord tells Samuel that this is the man who will be king.

   a. Samuel's assurance (9:17-20): Samuel tells Saul that the missing donkeys have been found and that he is the focus of Israel's hopes!

   b. Saul's amazement (9:21): Saul finds this difficult to believe, pointing out that he comes from an unimportant family from Benjamin, Israel's smallest tribe.

   c. Saul's actions (9:22-27): Samuel prepares a meal for Saul and his servants and specially honors him. Later Samuel makes accommodations for Saul and sends him on his way.

III. THE ANOINTING (10:1-27): Just before Saul leaves, Samuel anoints him as the next king of Israel.

   A. The proof (10:1-9): Samuel anoints Saul and tells him that several signs will demonstrate that he has indeed been chosen as Israel's king. These signs are fulfilled after Saul leaves Samuel:

   1. *The message of two men* (10:2): Two men will tell Saul that the donkeys have been found and that his father is worried about him.

   2. *The meal of three men* (10:3-4): Three men will offer Saul two loaves of bread.

   3. *The music of some prophets* (10:5): Saul will meet some prophets coming down from a hill and playing music.

   4. *The ministry of the Spirit* (10:6): The Spirit of the Lord will come upon Saul and cause him to prophesy with the prophets.

   B. The proverb (10:10-12): Saul's prophetic experience so amazes his friends that they create a proverbial expression "Is Saul a prophet?"

   C. The placating (10:13-16): When Saul returns from his trip, his uncle asks him where he has been. Saul tells him that he went to see Samuel and that the donkeys have been found, but he does not mention being anointed king of Israel.

   D. The presentation (10:17-24): At Mizpah Samuel introduces Saul to the people as their king, although Saul must be brought out from his hiding place among the baggage!

E. The parchment (10:25): Samuel writes the king's responsibilities in a book and deposits it in the Tabernacle.

F. The positions (10:26-27): Some support Saul and become his constant companions; others oppose him and refuse to bring him gifts.

IV. THE AFFIRMATION (11:1-15): Through military victory and a second coronation, Saul's kingship is affirmed.

A. The crisis (11:1-11)

1. *The demand* (11:1-2): A cruel Ammonite king named Nahash surrounds the Israelite town of Jabesh-gilead. When the people ask for a peace treaty, he demands they allow him to gouge out the right eye of every citizen!
2. *The desperation* (11:3): The elders ask for seven days to see if they can find someone to rescue them.
3. *The decree* (11:4-10): Upon learning of this, a furious and Spirit-filled Saul sends out a call to arms and gathers an army to fight against Nahash.
4. *The deliverance* (11:11): Saul and his army destroy Nahash's forces and save Jabesh-gilead.

B. The confirmation (11:12-15): Saul has now proven his ability to reign and is reconfirmed as king by Samuel and the people at Gilgal.

SECTION OUTLINE FIVE (1 SAMUEL 12–13)

Samuel delivers his farewell address. Israel continues to battle the Philistines. When Saul usurps Samuel's position as priest and disobediently offers a burnt offering, the Lord punishes Saul by ending his dynasty.

I. SAMUEL'S FAREWELL SPEECH (12:1-25)

A. The contents (12:1-13): Samuel reviews the faithfulness that has been shown to Israel by himself and the Lord.

1. *Samuel's faithfulness* (12:1-5)
2. *The Lord's faithfulness* (12:6-13)

B. The choice (12:14-15)

1. *Obeying the Lord will bring good things.*
2. *Forsaking the Lord will bring punishment.*

C. The confirmation (12:16-25): The Lord displays his disapproval of the people's desire for a king by sending loud thunder and heavy rain. Samuel urges the people to sincerely worship the Lord only.

II. SAUL'S FOOLISH SIN (13:1-23)

A. Saul's wickedness (13:1-14)

1. *The panic* (13:1-7): Saul's son Jonathan and his army destroy the garrison of Philistines at Geba, so the enemy mobilizes its entire army of chariots, horsemen, and soldiers against Israel. Saul and his men tremble in fear at the sight!
   2. *The presumption* (13:8-9): To rally his frightened troops, Saul unlawfully assumes the role of priest and offers up the burnt offering.
   3. *The punishment* (13:10-14): Samuel arrives and rebukes Saul for his actions. He pronounces that the Lord will punish Saul by ending his dynasty.

B. **Israel's weakness** (13:15-23)
   1. *Lack of warriors* (13:15): Saul's army dwindles to only 600 men.
   2. *Lack of weapons* (13:16-23): There are no blacksmiths in all Israel, so the only soldiers who have a sword or spear are Saul and Jonathan!

SECTION OUTLINE SIX (1 SAMUEL 14–15)

Jonathan demonstrates great courage before the Philistines. Later he unknowingly disobeys an order from Saul. When Saul plans to have him executed, the people intercede and save his life. Saul disobeys Samuel's charge to kill all the Amalekites, so the Lord rejects him as king. Saul pleads for Samuel's forgiveness, but it is too late.

I. SAUL'S FOES (14:1-23): Saul camps outside Gibeah, but Jonathan and his armor bearer attack the enemy by themselves and initiate a great victory!
   A. **The strategy** (14:1-8): Jonathan and his armor bearer attempt to single-handedly defeat an entire Philistine garrison!
   B. **The success** (14:11-23)
      1. *The courage* (14:11-14): Jonathan and his armor bearer kill 20 Philistines while scaling a cliff!
      2. *The confusion* (14:15-23): The Lord sends an earthquake, throwing the Philistines into terrified panic.

II. SAUL'S FAST (14:24-46): To assure full revenge on his enemies, Saul had forced his men to vow that they would not eat anything that day, so they were worn out.
   A. **Its effect on his soldiers** (14:24-26, 31-35)
      1. *Weakness* (14:24-26): Saul's men are forced to fight on empty stomachs, so they become very weak and hungry.
      2. *Wickedness* (14:31-35): After the battle, the victorious but famished soldiers butcher the captured animals, eating the raw meat, blood and all, which is forbidden under the law of Moses. So Saul arranges for the animals to be properly drained of blood so the men can eat the meat.
   B. **Its effect on his son** (14:27-46)

1. *The sustenance* (14:27-30): Unaware of his father's command, Jonathan eats some honey.
2. *The search* (14:31-43): Because God does not answer Saul's prayer, Saul realizes that a sin has been committed. Jonathan is found guilty and confesses to eating the honey.
3. *The saving* (14:44-46): Saul intends to execute Jonathan for his deed, but the soldiers intervene and save Jonathan's life.

III. SAUL'S FERVOR (14:47-52): Now that Saul is securely in control of the throne, he vigorously attacks his enemies in every direction.

IV. SAUL'S FAILURE (15:1-35)
   A. **The rebellion** (15:1-9): The Lord commands Saul to attack and totally destroy the Amalekites and all their animals. Saul attacks and captures them, but he spares King Agag and some of the animals.
   B. **The revelation** (15:10-11): The Lord tells Samuel that he is sorry he ever made Saul king.
   C. **The rendezvous** (15:12-13): Saul and Samuel meet on the morning following the battle with King Agag.
   D. **The rebuke** (15:14-23): Samuel condemns Saul's disobedience, refusing to accept his miserable excuse that he saved the animals so he can sacrifice them to God. He tells Saul that the Lord has rejected him as king.
   E. **The remorse** (15:24-25): Saul admits his sin and begs Samuel to forgive him and give him another chance.
   F. **The replacement** (15:26-31): Samuel tells Saul his kingdom will be given to someone better than he.
   G. **The retribution** (15:32-35): Samuel carries out what should have been Saul's responsibility and kills Agag as repayment for all the violence he committed against Israel.

SECTION OUTLINE SEVEN (1 SAMUEL 16–17)
Samuel anoints young David to be king of Israel. David serves in Saul's court to soothe him with music. Goliath intimidates Israel and is slain by David.

I. DAVID THE CHOSEN (16:1-13)
   A. **The rejection of Jesse's older sons** (16:1-10)
      1. *Samuel's mission* (16:1-5): The Lord tells Samuel that he has selected someone to replace Saul as king. He directs Samuel to go to Bethlehem and anoint one of Jesse's sons as Israel's next king.
      2. *Samuel's meeting* (16:6-10): Jesse introduces each of his seven oldest sons to Samuel, but none of them meet the Lord's approval.
   B. **The selection of Jesse's youngest son** (16:11-13): The Lord tells

Samuel to anoint David, Jesse's youngest son. When he does so, the Spirit of the Lord comes upon David.

II. DAVID THE COURT MUSICIAN (16:14-23)
   A. **The misery of King Saul** (16:14-20)
      1. *A wicked spirit* (16:14): A tormenting spirit causes Saul to become depressed and fearful.
      2. *A wise suggestion* (16:15-20): Saul's servants encourage him to bring in a good musician who can soothe him with harp music. Saul agrees, and they send for David.
   B. **The ministry to King Saul** (16:21-23): David's music quickly brings relief to the troubled king.

III. DAVID THE COURAGEOUS (17:1-58): David kills the Philistine giant named Goliath and spurs the Israelites on to victory.
   A. **The aggravation** (17:1-11, 16)
      1. *The contention* (17:1-3): The Israelites and the Philistines face off for battle on opposites sides of the valley of Elah.
      2. *The champion* (17:4-7): Among the Philistines is a fierce fighter named Goliath, who is over nine feet tall!
      3. *The challenge* (17:8-11): Goliath defies Israel, demanding that they send out a soldier to fight him.
      4. *The chronology* (17:16): Goliath makes this challenge twice every day for 40 days.
   B. **The action** (17:12-15, 17-54)
      1. *The care package* (17:12-15, 17-19): David's father instructs him to carry food to three of his brothers in Saul's army.
      2. *The criticism* (17:20-30): When David arrives at the site of the impending battle, he is rebuked by his oldest brother for asking why Goliath is allowed to insult Israel's army.
      3. *The concern* (17:31-40)
         a. Saul's reservation (17:31-33): David volunteers to fight Goliath, but Saul is afraid that David will be no match for the Philistine giant.
         b. David's reassurance (17:34-37): David tells Saul that as a shepherd he killed lions and bears who threatened his sheep. He promises to do the same with Goliath! Saul agrees to let David fight.
         c. David's refusal (17:38-40): Saul offers David his own royal armor, but David refuses it, choosing to use his sling and stones instead.
      4. *The contempt* (17:41-47): Goliath taunts the Israelites and curses David by the names of his gods.
         a. Goliath's reviling (17:41-44): "Come over here, and I'll give your flesh to the birds and wild animals!"
         b. David's response (17:45-47): "Today the LORD will conquer you, and I will kill you and cut off your head."

5. *The clash* (17:48-51): David hurls a stone at Goliath and hits him in the forehead, causing him to fall down. David takes Goliath's sword and cuts off Goliath's head.
6. *The conquest* (17:51-54): When the Philistine army sees that Goliath is dead, they flee. The Israelites chase them and destroy them.
C. **The asking** (17:55-58): Saul desires to find out more about David, asking the young shepherd about his background and family.

SECTION OUTLINE EIGHT (1 SAMUEL 18–19)
As David gains prominence, Saul becomes jealous and makes several attempts to kill him. Saul gives his daughter Michal to David as a reward for killing 200 Philistines. Jonathan warns David of his father's plot to kill him. Michal saves David's life. Saul prophesies again.

I. THE FURY OF SAUL (18:1–19:17): Saul becomes jealous of David and tries to kill him.
A. **David's rise** (18:1-7): After David's victory over Goliath, David gains great favor in the eyes of others.
    1. *With the prince* (18:1-4): Jonathan, Saul's son, becomes David's closest and most beloved friend.
    2. *With the people* (18:5-7): After David's victory the people sing, "Saul has killed his thousands, and David his ten thousands!"
B. **Saul's rage** (18:8–19:17): David's popularity makes Saul angry and jealous. He attempts to kill David five times—all are unsuccessful.
    1. *First and second attempts* (18:10-16): Twice Saul hurls a spear at David as he plays his harp.
    2. *Third attempt* (18:17-30): Twice Saul offers one of his daughters in marriage to David if he proves himself by fighting the Philistines. Instead of being killed, David kills 200 Philistines and gains Michal as his bride.
    3. *Fourth attempt* (19:1-10)
        a. The truce (19:1-8): As a result of Jonathan's pleas, Saul promises to no longer seek David's death.
        b. The treachery (19:9-10): Soon a tormenting spirit comes upon Saul; he tries again to kill David with a spear!
    4. *Fifth attempt* (19:11-17)
        a. Saul's intention (19:11): Saul sends men to kill David when David leaves his house one morning.
        b. Michal's intervention (19:11-17): David's wife, Michal, tells David of the plot and helps him escape through a window. She places an idol in his bed to fool the men and gain more time for David to escape.

II. THE FLIGHT FROM SAUL (19:18-24)
  A. **David's message** (19:18): David goes to Ramah and tells Samuel how Saul is trying to kill him.
  B. **Saul's men** (19:19-24): Three times Saul sends men to arrest David, but each time the men are overcome by the Spirit of God and begin to prophesy. Finally Saul himself goes, and the same thing happens to him!

SECTION OUTLINE NINE (1 SAMUEL 20–21)
David and Jonathan make a covenant of loyalty before they sadly go their separate ways because of Saul's anger. David flees to the city of Nob, where he is fed holy bread by Ahimelech the priest. David then flees to Gath in Philistia and feigns madness to escape harm by the king there.

I. DAVID AND THE PRINCE (20:1-42): David finds Jonathan and tells him of Saul's determination to kill him. Jonathan devises a plan to find out if this is true and warn David.
  A. **The cause of David's fears** (20:1-23)
    1. *The problem* (20:1-11): In spite of Jonathan's attempts to reassure him, David is convinced that Saul is still trying to kill him.
    2. *The promise* (20:12-17): Jonathan promises to warn David about his father's plans, and both men make a sacred vow to be loyal to each other, whatever the cost.
    3. *The plan* (20:18-23): On the new moon festival David will hide in a field. The next day Jonathan will warn him by a prearranged signal. He will shoot arrows and tell a servant to go fetch them. If he tells the servant to go farther, David will know that Saul is planning to kill him.
  B. **The confirmation of David's fears** (20:24-42)
    1. *David's absence* (20:24-29): At the new moon festival Saul notices that David is not present at the meal. Jonathan makes up the excuse that David has gone to Bethlehem to take part in a family sacrifice.
    2. *Saul's anger* (20:30-34): A furious Saul not only states his intention to kill David but actually attempts to murder Jonathan for befriending him!
    3. *Jonathan's arrows* (20:35-42): In accordance with their plan, Jonathan shoots some arrows to warn David. So David meets with Jonathan one final time to affirm his loyalty and say good-bye before he leaves.

II. DAVID AND THE PRIEST (21:1-9): David goes to the city of Nob to see Ahimelech the priest.
   A. **The falsehood** (21:1-2): David tells the priest that Saul has sent him on a private mission.
   B. **The favor** (21:3-9): The priest provides David with holy bread and offers him Goliath's sword.

III. DAVID AND THE PAGAN (21:10-15): David seeks refuge from Saul in the Philistine city of Gath. He fears what the king of Gath might do to him, so he pretends to be insane.

SECTION OUTLINE TEN (1 SAMUEL 22–23)
David gathers his own army of 400 men. Saul orders the execution of 85 priests because he suspects them of helping David. Saul tries to capture David at Keilah and in the wilderness.

I. DAVID IN THE CAVE OF ADULLAM (22:1-5): David leaves Gath and hides in the cave of Adullam.
   A. **David's men** (22:1-2): While at the cave of Adullam, David assembles a personal army of 400 men. This band is formed from his relatives, those who are in trouble, in debt, or simply discontented.
   B. **David's move** (22:3-5): David leaves the cave for Mizpeh in Moab, but then the prophet Gad tells him to return to the land of Judah.

II. DAVID IN THE FOREST OF HERETH (22:5-23): While David is hiding in the forest of Hereth, Saul steps up pressure to find him.
   A. **The slaughter by Saul** (22:5-19): Because he suspects that Ahimelech and the other priests are helping David, Saul orders their execution.
      1. *The background for this slaughter* (22:5-17): King Saul puts pressure on his officers to find David, so Doeg the Edomite tells Saul about Ahimelech's dealings with David. So Saul orders the execution of the priest and his family.
      2. *The butcher of this slaughter* (22:17-19): After Saul's men refuse to carry out his orders, Doeg the Edomite kills 85 priests and their families.
   B. **The sorrow of David** (22:20-23): Abiathar, one of Ahimelech's sons, escapes and flees to David, who regrets causing the death of Abiathar's family.

III. DAVID IN THE TOWN OF KEILAH (23:1-12)
   A. **David's assistance** (23:1-5): At the Lord's command, David attacks and defeats the Philistines, who are stealing grain from the people of Keilah.
   B. **The Lord's answers** (23:6-12): Abiathar brings the ephod to

David, and David learns that the people of Keilah plan to turn him over to King Saul.

IV. DAVID IN THE HILL COUNTRY OF ZIPH (23:13-23): Before the people of Keilah can turn David over to King Saul, David and his men leave for the hill country of Ziph.
  A. **The chase** (23:13-15): Saul continues his murderous pursuit of David.
  B. **The covenant** (23:16-18): Jonathan finds David near Horesh and reaffirms their covenant of friendship. He recognizes that David will be the next king of Israel.
  C. **The conspiracy** (23:19-23): The men of Ziph volunteer to capture David and turn him over to Saul.

V. DAVID IN THE DESERT OF MAON (23:24-29): David flees farther into the wilderness to a great rock, but Saul continues to close in on him. Saul receives word that the Philistines are raiding Israel again, so he calls off his pursuit.

SECTION OUTLINE ELEVEN (1 SAMUEL 24–25)
David spares Saul's life at En-gedi, so the two men enter a treaty of nonaggression. Samuel dies. David is angered by a man named Nabal, but Nabal's wife, Abigail, intercedes for her husband. News of this causes Nabal to have a stroke, and he dies. David marries Abigail.

I. DAVID'S MERCY TOWARD SAUL (24:1-22): This is the first of two occasions when David could easily kill Saul but does not do so.
  A. **The resumption** (24:1-2): After routing the Philistines, Saul once again continues his relentless hunt for David.
  B. **The realization** (24:3-4): David's men, hiding in the cave, realize that there is an opportunity to kill Saul, who has entered the cave to relieve himself.
  C. **The restraint** (24:4-7): David does not kill Saul but cuts off a piece of Saul's robe without the king knowing it.
  D. **The rebuke** (24:8-15): After Saul leaves the cave, David calls out to him and bows low before him, showing him the piece of robe he cut off. David uses this to prove that he is not seeking Saul's harm, because he could have killed him if he had wanted to. David asks Saul why he continues to chase him.
  E. **The remorse** (24:16-19): Saul becomes ashamed and acknowledges that David is a better man than he.
  F. **The realization** (24:20-22): Saul also acknowledges that God has indeed chosen David to be king over Israel!

II. DAVID'S MARRIAGE TO ABIGAIL (25:1-44): Samuel soon dies, and David moves to the wilderness of Maon.
  A. **David and Nabal** (25:1-13)

1. *The request* (25:1-9): David asks a wealthy man named Nabal to repay past kindness toward him by giving David's men some provisions.
2. *The refusal* (25:10-12): Nabal sharply denies this request.
3. *The retaliation* (25:13): David becomes angry and plans to punish Nabal.
   B. **David and Abigail** (25:14-44)
   1. *The wise woman* (25:14-35): Nabal's servants tell his wife, Abigail, about the incident and warn her that David is coming.
      a. Her appeal to David (25:14-31): Abigail prepares a large supply of food and rides out to meet David, pleading with him not to kill her husband.
      b. Her acceptance by David (25:32-35): David thanks God for sending Abigail to him and agrees not to harm Nabal.
   2. *The widowed woman* (25:36-38): After a night of heavy drinking, Nabal is told by Abigail about the terrible danger he had been in; he suffers a stroke. Ten days later the Lord strikes him and he dies.
   3. *The wedded woman* (25:39-44): Following Nabal's death, David asks Abigail to become his wife, and she accepts.

SECTION OUTLINE TWELVE (1 SAMUEL 26–27)
David again spares Saul's life, and taking only his spear and jug, he flees to the Philistine city of Gath. Eventually David and his men take up residence in Ziklag for a year and four months.

I. DAVID FOREGOES (26:1-25): David chooses not to take advantage of a second opportunity to kill Saul.
   A. **The constraint** (26:1-11): David and Abishai sneak into Saul's camp late one night.
   1. *The request* (26:7-8): Abishai asks David's permission to kill the sleeping king with his own spear!
   2. *The refusal* (26:9-11): David refuses, saying that Saul is still God's anointed one.
   B. **The call** (26:12-16): David and Abishai leave, taking Saul's spear and water jug. From a safe distance, David wakes his enemies by shouting insults at Abner (Saul's general) for sleeping on the job!
   C. **The criticism** (26:17-20): David asks Saul why he continues to pursue him when David has not harmed him.
   D. **The confession** (26:21-25): Saul confesses that he has wronged David and tells him that he will no longer try to harm him.

II. DAVID FEIGNS (27:1-12)
   A. **David's doubt** (27:1-4): Fearing that Saul will still try to kill him, David moves from Judah to the land of the Philistines.
   B. **David's deceit** (27:5-12)

1. *The facts* (27:5-9): David and his men regularly raid the villages of pagan people living along the road to Egypt.
2. *The fiction* (27:10-12): David leads King Achish of the Philistines to believe that he is raiding Israelite villages.

SECTION OUTLINE THIRTEEN (1 SAMUEL 28–29)
Terrified of the Philistine army, Saul asks a spirit medium from Endor to summon Samuel's spirit from the dead. She does so, but Samuel's words are disturbing to Saul. The Philistines reject David's help in battle, so he and his men return to the land of the Philistines.

I. THE MEDIUM (28:1-25): Saul visits a spirit medium in the city of Endor.
   A. The reason (28:1-8)
   1. *Saul's desperation* (28:1-6): The Philistines are threatening to attack the Israelites. Samuel has died, so Saul no longer has anyone to counsel him. When he asks the Lord for answers, he is not given any response.
   2. *Saul's decision* (28:7): To allay his fears, Saul seeks help from a spirit medium.
   3. *Saul's disguise* (28:8): Before he goes to visit the medium, Saul dresses in ordinary clothes so he will not be recognized, for he has banned all mediums from Israel.
   B. The results (28:9-25)
   1. *The calling up of Samuel* (28:9-14): When the medium asks Saul whom he wants to speak with, he tells her to summon the spirit of Samuel.
      a. The medium's dread (28:12-13): The woman is fearful upon recognizing Saul and seeing Samuel come out of the earth!
      b. The medium's description (28:14): She describes Samuel as "an old man wrapped in a robe."
   2. *The condemnation by Samuel* (28:15-19)
      a. Samuel reviews Saul's terrible past (28:15-18): Samuel tells Saul that he has lost his kingdom to David because he failed to completely destroy the Amalekites.
      b. He previews Saul's tragic future (28:19): Samuel tells Saul that his army will be defeated by the Philistines and that he and his sons will be killed.
   3. *The cowering by Saul* (28:20-25): At Samuel's words, Saul falls on the ground, paralyzed with fright. Eventually the medium convinces him to eat something before he leaves.

II. THE MISTRUST (29:1-11)
   A. The desire (29:1-3): David volunteers to join with the Philistines in fighting against Saul's army.
   B. The denial (29:4-11): Some of the Philistine leaders mistrust

David, fearing he will turn against them during battle. So King
Achish sends David back to the land of the Philistines.

SECTION OUTLINE FOURTEEN (1 SAMUEL 30–31)
David finds that Ziklag has been destroyed by the Amalekites. He
pursues and defeats them, recovering all those who were captured by
them. The Philistines defeat the Israelites in battle, killing Saul and his
sons, including Jonathan.

I. DAVID'S VENGEANCE (30:1-31)
   A. The sorrow (30:1-8)
      1. *The destruction* (30:1-5): While David and his men are gone,
         the Amalekites destroy Ziklag and carry off its citizens,
         including David's two wives.
      2. *The distress* (30:6): David's men threaten to kill him for
         allowing this to happen.
      3. *The direction* (30:7-8): The Lord orders David to attack the
         enemy, assuring him of victory.
   B. The success (30:9-20): David mobilizes his men and attacks the
      Amalekites.
      1. *Two hundred exhausted men* (30:9-10): As David and his men
         cross Besor Brook, 200 of his men are too tired to continue;
         only 400 men press on to fight the Amalekites.
      2. *One Egyptian man* (30:11-16): David's men find an Egyptian
         slave who had been left behind by the Amalekites. The man
         agrees to take David to the Amalekites' camp.
      3. *Four hundred energized men* (30:17-20): David's men attack
         the camp and destroy the Amalekites, recovering all the
         captives and goods that had been taken.
   C. The sharing (30:21-31): David distributes the plunder among two
      groups:
      1. *The soldiers of Israel* (30:21-25)
         a. Their objection (30:21-22): The 400 soldiers object to shar-
            ing the plunder with the 200 who stayed behind.
         b. His ordinance (30:23-25): David insists that the plunder be
            shared with those who guard the equipment as well as with
            those who fight.
      2. *The leaders of Judah* (30:26-31): The leaders of several towns
         of Judah also receive a portion of the plunder.
II. THE PHILISTINES' VICTORY (31:1-13): When the Philistines attack the
    Israelites, Saul and his sons are killed on the battlefield, just as
    Samuel foretold.
   A. The method (31:1-6): On Mount Gilboa, Saul's sons are killed,
      and Saul is critically wounded by the Philistines. He falls on his
      own sword to avoid capture and abuse by the enemy.

B. The mutilation (31:7-10): The Philistines cut off Saul's head and fasten his body to the wall of the city of Beth-shan.

C. The mission (31:11-13): Some men of Jabesh-gilead recover the bodies of Saul and his sons and give them a decent burial.

2 Samuel

SECTION OUTLINE ONE (2 SAMUEL 1–2)
David kills the young Amalekite who says he put Saul out of his
misery. David composes a song in honor of Saul and Jonathan. David
is crowned king over Judah, and Saul's son Ishbosheth is proclaimed
king over the other tribes. War breaks out between David and
Ishbosheth.

I. THE TEARS OF DAVID (1:1-27)
   A. **The foreigner** (1:1-16): An Amalekite comes to David, claiming
      to have put Saul out of his misery at Saul's request. David has
      him killed, since he admitted that he killed Saul, the Lord's
      anointed.
   B. **The funeral song** (1:17-27): David composes a funeral song for
      Saul and Jonathan.
      1. *The grief of David and Israel* (1:17-21, 24-27): In David's
         song, he expresses his deep sorrow over the deaths of Saul
         and Jonathan, and he calls for all Israel to mourn.
      2. *The glory of Saul and Jonathan* (1:22-23): David extols Saul
         and Jonathan, describing them as "swifter than eagles" and
         "stronger than lions."

II. THE TRIUMPH OF DAVID (2:1-32): David is proclaimed king by the
    tribe of Judah.
   A. **The ceremony** (2:1-7)
      1. *His crowning* (2:1-4): David is crowned king in the city of
         Hebron.
      2. *His commendation* (2:5-7): David praises the men of
         Jabesh-gilead for recovering Saul's body.
   B. **The competition** (2:8-11): Abner, Saul's military commander,
      now crowns Ishbosheth, Saul's 40-year-old son, king over the
      other tribes.
   C. **The contest** (2:12-17): Joab leads David's forces against Abner's
      forces. As the two armies face each other on opposite sides of a
      pool, Abner challenges Joab to a sword fight between 12 men
      from each side. This results in a major battle between the two
      armies.

    D. The chase (2:18-23): Joab's brother Asahel pursues Abner, who warns him to abandon the chase. Asahel refuses, so Abner kills him.

    E. The compromise (2:24-32): An angry Joab continues the pursuit, seeking to avenge his dead brother. At sunset, however, both sides agree to call off hostilities for a time.

SECTION OUTLINE TWO (2 SAMUEL 3–4)

The war between David and Ishbosheth continues. Abner defects to David and is murdered by Joab. David turns Abner's funeral into a public humiliation for Joab. Ishbosheth is killed by fellow Benjamites who, in turn, are put to death by David.

  I. THE BETRAYAL OF ABNER (3:1-39): As David's power increases, Abner switches loyalties, but he is betrayed when Joab kills him to avenge the murder of Asahel.

    A. The details (3:1-27)

      1. *David's fortune* (3:1-5)

        a. The strength of his house (3:1): Over time, David's power grows stronger and stronger.

        b. The sons born to his house (3:2-5): David fathers six sons during this time.

      2. *Ishbosheth's fall* (3:6-27)

        a. The argument (3:6-11): Ishbosheth and Abner have a falling-out over a concubine named Rizpah.

        b. The agreement (3:12-21): Abner switches his loyalties to David and makes an agreement with him to turn the rest of the tribes over to his side.

        c. The assassination (3:22-27): Upon learning of Abner's proposed agreement, Joab tells David that Abner is simply acting as a spy. Then Joab kills Abner to avenge the murder of his brother Asahel.

    B. The denunciation (3:28-30): Angry and sorrowful, David condemns Joab's brutal act of treachery toward Abner.

    C. The dejection (3:31-39): David mourns for Abner and fasts on the day of his funeral. He publicly condemns Joab and Abishai again.

  II. THE BETRAYAL OF ISHBOSHETH (4:1-12)

    A. The accident (4:4): In the middle of the account about Ishbosheth's assassination, there is a short digression about Mephibosheth, Jonathan's son, who is crippled when he is accidentally dropped by his nurse as she flees from the Philistines.

    B. The assassination (4:1-3, 5-7): Ishbosheth is murdered by two brothers, Baanah and Recab, two of the king's military leaders.

    C. The avenging (4:8-12): The two brothers bring the severed head of Ishbosheth to David, hoping to be rewarded. Instead, David orders them to be killed for murdering their king!

SECTION OUTLINE THREE (2 SAMUEL 5–6)
David is anointed king over all Israel. He captures Jerusalem, defeats the Philistines, and brings the Ark to Jerusalem. Michal despises David for dancing in worship before the Lord as the Ark is brought into the city.

I. THE ANOINTED OF GOD (5:1-25)
  A. **David's crowning** (5:1-5): The 12 tribes now come to Hebron and crown David king over all Israel.
  B. **David's city** (5:6-12): David captures Jerusalem and establishes it as Israel's new capital.
    1. *The taunts* (5:6): The pagan defenders of Jerusalem boast that their city can never be taken.
    2. *The triumphs* (5:7-12): After capturing the city, David begins enlarging it, thus increasing the strength of his kingdom.
  C. **David's children** (5:13-16): Eleven of David's sons, including Solomon and Nathan, are born in Jerusalem.
  D. **David's conquests** (5:17-25): David completely routs the attacking Philistines twice.
    1. *First occasion* (5:17-21)
    2. *Second occasion* (5:22-25)

II. THE ARK OF GOD (6:1-23): David transfers the Ark of God to Jerusalem.
  A. **The mission** (6:1-2): David goes to Baalah of Judah with 30,000 special troops to bring the Ark of God to Jerusalem.
  B. **The method** (6:3-4): They place the Ark on a new wagon, led by Uzzah and Ahio.
  C. **The music** (6:5): This is accompanied by singing and the playing of musical instruments.
  D. **The mistake** (6:6-8): The Lord strikes Uzzah dead when he reaches out to steady the Ark!
  E. **The months** (6:9-11): For the next 90 days, the Ark resides in the home of Obed-edom, who receives great blessing for his willingness to house the Ark.
  F. **The mad wife** (6:12-23): Michal becomes angry with David for dancing before the Ark, wearing only a priestly tunic.
    1. *David's celebration* (6:12-19): As the Ark is brought from the house of Obed-edom to Jerusalem, David joins in the celebration by dancing before the Lord in a priestly tunic.
    2. *Michal's condemnation* (6:20-23): David's wife sharply rebukes her husband for his behavior. David tells her that he is willing to look foolish in order to show his joy in the Lord. Michal remains childless throughout her life.

SECTION OUTLINE FOUR (2 SAMUEL 7–8)
The Lord grants an unconditional covenant to David, promising to
establish his dynasty forever. In response, David praises God. David's
military accomplishments are listed.

 I. THE COVENANT (7:1-29)
   A. The promise (7:1-17)
      1. *David's request* (7:1-7): to build a house for God.
         a. The purpose (7:1-3): David desires to build a dwelling that
            is fitting for the Ark of God, especially since David lives in
            a beautiful cedar palace while the Ark of God is housed in
            a tent. Nathan encourages David in his plan.
         b. The prohibition (7:4-7): The Lord tells Nathan that David is
            not the one chosen to build a house for the Lord.
      2. *The Lord's response* (7:8-17): to build a house for David.
         a. The promise to David (7:8-11): The Lord declares that
            David's kingdom will prosper and his name will be known
            throughout the world!
         b. The promise to David's descendant (7:12-15): The Lord
            promises to bless Solomon even after David's death.
         c. The promise to David's descendants (7:16-17): The Lord
            promises that David's dynasty will never end.
   B. The prayer (7:18-29): With his heart filled with awe and grati-
      tude, David praises the Lord for his promise.

 II. THE CONQUESTS (8:1-18): David continues to expand his kingdom
   and lead the Israelites to victory.
   A. David's campaigns (8:1-14)
      1. *Against the Philistines* (8:1): David captures their largest city.
      2. *Against the Moabites* (8:2): David executes two-thirds of the
         Moabites, and the rest are forced to pay him tribute money.
      3. *Against Hadadezer and the Arameans* (8:3-12): David defeats
         them and forces them to pay tribute money. He also seizes
         much gold, silver, and bronze from them.
      4. *Against the Edomites* (8:13-14): David defeats the Edomites
         and places garrisons throughout Edom.
   B. David's court (8:15-18): David was a fair ruler. His military,
      political, and religious leaders are listed.

SECTION OUTLINE FIVE (2 SAMUEL 9–10)
David shows kindness toward Mephibosheth and defeats the
Ammonites and Arameans.

 I. DAVID'S COMPASSION (9:1-13): David shows kindness toward Saul's
   family.
   A. The man (9:1-4): Seeking to make good on his promise to watch

over Jonathan's family, David asks Ziba, a former servant of Saul's, if anyone from Saul's family is still alive. Ziba tells him that Mephibosheth, Jonathan's son, lives in Lo-debar.

B. The meeting (9:5-6): David summons Mephibosheth, who fearfully and humbly appears before him.

C. The mercy (9:7-13): David tells Mephibosheth not to fear and promises him several generous gifts. David offers this kindness to Mephibosheth because of his love for his father, Jonathan.

1. *David promises to restore all of Saul's lands to Mephibosheth* (9:7-8).
2. *David provides him with many servants* (9:9-10, 12).
3. *David assigns him a special place in the royal palace* (9:10-11, 13).

II. DAVID'S CLENCHED FIST (10:1-19)

A. The respect (10:1-2): David sends ambassadors to express his sympathy to Hanun, king of the Ammonites, whose father recently died. Hanun's father had been loyal to David.

B. The ridicule (10:3-5): Hanun's advisers falsely conclude that the ambassadors are actually spies, so Hanun publicly humiliates them by cutting off their robes at the buttocks and shaving half their beards.

C. The retaliation (10:6-19)

1. *Hanun's fear* (10:6-8): Realizing his stupid blunder, the panic-filled Ammonite king hires 33,000 foreign soldiers to help him repel the anticipated Israelite attack.
2. *David's fury* (10:9-19): In a fierce battle alongside the Euphrates River, David defeats his enemies, killing 700 of their charioteers and 40,000 horsemen.

SECTION OUTLINE SIX (2 SAMUEL 11–12)

David commits adultery with Bathsheba, attempts to deceive Uriah, and arranges for Uriah's murder. When David is rebuked by Nathan, he repents, but their illegitimate child dies. David marries Bathsheba, and she becomes pregnant with Solomon. David seizes control of all the Ammonite cities.

I. DAVID THE SINNER (11:1-27)

A. His sin of adultery (11:1-5): Two factors lead to this tragic sin:

1. *David's laziness* (11:1): David stays behind in the royal palace and sends Joab to lead the Israelites to fight the Ammonites.
2. *David's lust* (11:2-5): David watches a beautiful woman named Bathsheba as she bathes. After learning that she is the wife of one of his soldiers, he sends for her and sleeps with her. Soon he learns she is pregnant with his child.

B. His sin of deceit (11:6-13): David tries to cover up his sin of adultery.

1. *The unscrupulous plan* (11:6-8): David recalls Uriah (Bathsheba's husband) from the battlefield, encouraging him to spend time with Bathsheba. David hopes that Uriah will sleep with his wife and think that David's child is his.

2. *The unsuccessful plan* (11:9-13): Twice Uriah refuses to go home to his wife.

C. **His sin of murder** (11:14-27): Failing to deceive Uriah into sleeping with his wife, David arranges for Uriah to be killed in battle so David can make Bathsheba one of his wives.

1. *The details* (11:14-21)

a. The treachery (11:14-15): David sends a sealed letter to Joab by way of Uriah, ordering Joab to arrange for loyal Uriah's death.

b. The tragedy (11:16-21): Joab places Uriah in the fiercest part of the battle, and he is killed just as David planned.

2. *The disapproval* (11:22-27): News reaches David that Uriah has been killed, so he marries the widowed Bathsheba after her period of mourning. Soon after this, a son is born. But the Lord is highly displeased with what David has done.

II. DAVID THE SORROWFUL (12:1-13)

A. **The confrontation** (12:1-12): The Lord sends Nathan the prophet to confront David regarding his sin.

1. *The illustration* (12:1-4): Nathan relates the story of how a rich farmer with many lambs takes the sole lamb of a poor farmer.

2. *The indignation* (12:5-6): David is furious, vowing to kill such a person unless he pays back the poor farmer fourfold!

3. *The identification* (12:7-9): Nathan tells David that he is the rich farmer in the story!

4. *The imprecation* (12:10-12): As punishment for David's sin, the Lord condemns David's family to terrible turmoil.

B. **The confession** (12:13): When David confesses his sin, Nathan tells him that the Lord has forgiven him and will not let him die for this sin.

III. DAVID THE SUBMISSIVE (12:14-25)

A. **The bitter event: the death of Bathsheba's first son** (12:15-23)

1. *David's travail* (12:15-19): For seven days David fasts and prays, asking God to spare his son. But the baby dies.

2. *David's testimony* (12:20-23): After the baby's death, David breaks his fast, ceases his mourning, and worships God. He testifies that one day he will join the baby in death, but the baby can never return to him.

B. **The blessed event: the birth of Bathsheba's foremost son** (12:24-25): Later Bathsheba gives birth to Solomon, whose name means "peace." The Lord, however, tells David that his name should be Jedidiah, meaning "beloved of the LORD."

IV. DAVID THE SOLDIER (12:26-31): David captures the Ammonite city of Rabbah, making slaves of the people and taking great amounts of gold, including a special golden crown set with precious stones.

SECTION OUTLINE SEVEN (2 SAMUEL 13–14)
Amnon rapes Tamar. Absalom avenges Tamar and flees to his maternal grandfather's home. David permits Absalom to return to Jerusalem but bars him from the palace. David meets with Absalom and is reconciled to him for a time.

I. THE RAPE (13:1-19)
   A. **Amnon desires Tamar** (13:1-10): David's son Amnon falls desperately in love with his half sister Tamar.
      1. *The suggestion by Jonadab* (13:1-5): Amnon's cousin Jonadab tells him to pretend he is sick and request Tamar to attend to him.
      2. *The subtlety by Amnon* (13:6-10): Amnon heeds Jonadab's advice and arranges for Tamar to be alone with him in his bedroom.
   B. **Amnon defiles Tamar** (13:11-19)
      1. *The sinful act* (13:11-14): Ignoring Tamar's cries of protest, Amnon rapes his half sister.
      2. *The sinful attitude* (13:15-19): Suddenly Amnon's lust turns to loathing, and Amnon has Tamar thrown out of his bedroom.

II. THE REVENGE (13:20-39)
   A. **Absalom and Tamar** (13:20-22): Absalom, Amnon's half brother, attempts to comfort Tamar, his full sister. Because of this terrible deed, Absalom hates Amnon, although he never speaks of it.
   B. **Absalom and Amnon** (13:23-33): Absalom conspires to murder Amnon in revenge for raping Tamar. He does so two years later as he is celebrating the shearing of his sheep.
   C. **Absalom and David** (13:34-39): Absalom flees the land of Israel to escape his father David. Eventually David desires to see Absalom again.

III. THE RETURN (14:1-33): Joab devises a plan to bring Absalom back to Israel.
   A. **The strategy by Joab** (14:1-20)
      1. *The person* (14:1-3): Joab enlists the help of a wise woman from Tekoa in effecting the return of Absalom.
      2. *The particulars* (14:4-20)
         a. Setting the trap (14:4-11): This woman approaches David, pretending that one of her two sons killed the other. She asks for mercy upon the survivor. David guarantees that her son will be allowed to safely return.

      b. Springing the trap (14:12-20): The woman then urges David
      to do this same thing for his son Absalom.
  B. The summons by David (14:21-33)
    1. *David sends for Absalom* (14:21-32): David instructs Joab to
      bring Absalom back from exile.
      a. Absalom's arrival (14:21-27): Absalom returns to Jerusalem,
      but David refuses to see him. Absalom is a very handsome
      man with long hair.
      b. Absalom's anger (14:28-32): After waiting two full years to
      see his father, Absalom sets a barley field on fire to get his
      attention.
    2. *David meets with Absalom* (14:33): Finally, David agrees to
      see his son, and the two men are reconciled to each other.

SECTION OUTLINE EIGHT (2 SAMUEL 15–16)
Absalom steals the hearts of the people and revolts against his father.
David flees into exile, returns the Ark of the Covenant to Jerusalem,
and plants an infiltrator named Hushai in Absalom's court. David
refuses to retaliate against Shimei. Ahithophel gives Absalom ungodly
counsel.

  I. THE PLOT EXECUTED (15:1-12): David's own son Absalom organizes
  a rebellion against him.
    A. The politics of the plot (15:1-6): Absalom captures the people's
    hearts by assuring them that his kingship would bring about a far
    more just society than did his father's.
    B. The place of the plot (15:7-12): The rebellion begins in the city
    of Hebron. He also sends messengers to other parts of Israel to
    stir up trouble.

  II. THE PEOPLE ENJOINED (15:13-29): David learns of the rebellion. As
  he flees Jerusalem to escape Absalom, he gives commands to three
  men who flee with him.
    A. Ittai (15:17-22)
      1. *The leader* (15:17-20): Ittai is the captain of the 600 Gittite
      soldiers who have joined David. David urges him to return to
      Jerusalem, since he and his men have only just arrived in
      Israel.
      2. *The loyal* (15:21-22): Ittai vows to support David whatever the
      cost, so David welcomes him.
    B. Zadok and Abiathar (15:23-29): David instructs a priest named
    Zadok to return the Ark of the Covenant to Jerusalem and send
    word to him before he disappears into the wilderness.

  III. THE PEOPLE ENCOUNTERED (15:30–16:19): David also encounters
  some people as he flees from Absalom.
    A. Hushai (15:30-37; 16:15-19)

1. *Hushai and David* (15:30-37): A faithful friend named Hushai is waiting for David on the Mount of Olives. David instructs him to return to Jerusalem and offer himself as Absalom's adviser, pretending he has turned against David, so he can offer Absalom wrong advice on how to conduct the rebellion.
2. *Hushai and Absalom* (16:15-19): Hushai and Ahithophel, David's former adviser who has turned against him, eventually meet with Absalom. After Hushai explains that he has turned against David, it appears that Absalom accepts him as his adviser.

B. Ziba (16:1-4): David encounters Ziba, the servant of Mephibosheth, who reports that his master has turned against David as well. So David grants Ziba all that he had formerly granted Mephibosheth.

C. Shimei (16:5-14): David meets Shimei, a member of Saul's family.

1. *The reviling* (16:5-8): Shimei curses David and throws stones at him as he calls him a murderer and tells him that the Lord is repaying him for stealing Saul's throne.
2. *The restraint* (16:9-14): David forbids his soldiers to harm Shimei, saying that his actions are understandable since he is Saul's relative.

IV. THE PROFANITY EMBRACED (16:20-23): At the advice of Ahithophel, Absalom sets up a tent on top of the palace roof and sleeps with David's concubines, publicly insulting David.

SECTION OUTLINE NINE (2 SAMUEL 17–18)
Hushai gives Absalom bad military counsel and warns David to flee. Absalom pursues David east of the Jordan, but David's men defeat Absalom's men. Twenty thousand men die in the battle, including Absalom. David mourns Absalom's death.

I. THE RUSE (17:1-14, 23): Ahithophel and Hushai offer conflicting advice to Absalom.

A. The correct advice of Ahithophel (17:1-4): Ahithophel urges Absalom to attack David's troops immediately while David is still weary and weak.

B. The crafty advice of Hushai (17:5-14, 23). Hushai advises that the attack be delayed until a large number of soldiers throughout the land can be assembled. Then Absalom himself should lead them into battle. Hushai's plan is accepted, causing Ahithophel to go home and hang himself.

II. THE RELAY (17:15-23): Hushai sends news of Absalom's plan to David, who now has time to mobilize his army.

III. THE REPLACEMENT (17:24-26): Absalom appoints Amasa to command the Israelite army in place of Joab.

IV. THE RENDEZVOUS (17:27-29): Three friends of David—Shobi, Makir, and Barzillai—bring him and his soldiers food in the wilderness.

V. THE REFUSAL (18:1-4): David's troops urge him not to lead them in battle, arguing that his life is worth 10,000 of theirs.

VI. THE REQUEST (18:5): Just before the battle, David instructs Joab, Abishai, and Ittai to deal gently with Absalom.

VII. THE ROUTING (18:6-8): David's troops defeat Absalom's army in the forest of Ephraim.

VIII. THE REPRISAL (18:9-18)
  A. **The helpless Absalom** (18:9-10): As he flees the battle on his mule, Absalom's hair gets caught in the thick branches of a large oak, and he is left dangling helplessly in the air.
  B. **The heartless Joab** (18:11-18): Disregarding David's instructions, Joab plunges three daggers into Absalom's heart.

IX. THE REPORT (18:19-32): David anxiously awaits news of the battle and Absalom's fate. Finally, a messenger brings him word that his enemies are defeated and Absalom is dead.

X. THE REMORSE (18:33): Bursting into tears, David wishes that he had died instead of his son.

SECTION OUTLINE TEN (2 SAMUEL 19)
David's kingship is restored in Jerusalem. David refuses to take vengeance on Shimei, deals with Mephibosheth, and attempts to reward Barzillai for his kindess to him. The tribe of Judah escorts David back to Jerusalem, causing some jealousy among the other tribes.

I. THE TEARS OF DAVID (19:1-7)
  A. **David's anguish** (19:1-4): The king continues to sorrow over the death of Absalom.
  B. **Joab's anger** (19:5-7): Joab sternly rebukes David, claiming that he seems to love those who hate him and hate those who love him! He warns David that his troops will desert him unless he congratulates them for winning the battle.

II. THE TRAVELS OF DAVID (19:8-43): David begins his long trip back to Jerusalem.
  A. **The resolution** (19:8-15)
    1. *The argument* (19:8-10): The people of Israel argue over whether David should return.

2. *The appeal* (19:11-12): David personally appeals to the leaders of Judah, asking them to support his return.

3. *The appointment* (19:13): The king promises to appoint Amasa as Joab's replacement.

4. *The agreement* (19:14): All of Judah agrees to support David's return.

B. The return (19:15-43)

1. *David and Shimei* (19:16-23)

   a. Shimei's fear (19:16-20): Shimei, who previously cursed David, meets David at the Jordan River and pleads for mercy.

   b. David's forgiveness (19:21-23): The king grants him mercy and assures him that his life will be spared.

2. *David and Mephibosheth* (19:24-30): Mephibosheth also comes to meet David; David asks him why he stayed in Jerusalem during the revolt. Mephibosheth claims that Ziba refused to help him leave and lied about his loyalty. So David divides Saul's land equally between Ziba and Mephibosheth.

3. *David and Barzillai* (19:31-39): David invites 80-year-old Barzillai to accompany him back to Jerusalem and live in the palace, but he declines the offer.

4. *David and the men of Judah* (19:40-43): The army of Judah escorts David across the Jordan and into Jerusalem. The other tribes complain about the favor shown to Judah in this way.

SECTION OUTLINE ELEVEN (2 SAMUEL 20–21)
Sheba rebels against David. Joab kills Amasa and attacks the city of Abel, but he retreats once the people cut off Sheba's head and throw it out to him. David makes amends for Saul's attack on the Gibeonites. Some military exploits of David and his men are recorded.

I. THE TROUBLEMAKING OF SHEBA (20:1-22)

A. Sheba's uprising (20:1-13)

1. *Sheba's conspiracy* (20:1-2): Sheba, a Benjaminite, leads a rebellion against David, supported by all Israel's tribes except Judah.

2. *David's concern* (20:3-7): David perceives Sheba's threat to be more dangerous than even Absalom's rebellion, so he orders Amasa to mobilize the entire army of Judah to fight against Sheba.

3. *Joab's cruelty* (20:8-13): Joab assassinates Amasa to regain his former position as David's military commander.

B. Sheba's undoing (20:14-22)

1. *The war against Abel* (20:14-15): Sheba seeks refuge in the city of Abel, so Joab attacks the city.

2. *The wise woman of Abel* (20:16-22): A woman from Abel

strikes a bargain with Joab to spare the city. She offers to throw Sheba's severed head over the wall. The woman makes good on her promise, and Joab calls off the attack on the city.

II. THE TALLY OF LEADERS (20:23-26): David's leaders are listed, including his military commanders, the leader of his labor force, his royal historian, his secretary, and his priests.

III. THE TRANSGRESSION OF SAUL (21:1-14)
   A. **The problem** (21:1-2): David asks God why Israel is being punished by a famine; he is told it is because Saul tried to wipe out the Gibeonites.
   B. **The plan** (21:3-9)
      1. *David's meeting* (21:3-6): The king confers with the Gibeonites, who demand that seven of Saul's descendants be handed over to them to be executed.
      2. *David's mercy* (21:7-9): David grants their demand, but he does not allow Jonathan's son Mephibosheth to be taken. So the Gibeonites execute seven of Saul's descendants on a nearby mountain.
   C. **The protective mother** (21:10-14): Rizpah, whose two sons were among those executed, faithfully remains by their bodies for many weeks, protecting them from being eaten by wild animals and vultures.

IV. THE TRIUMPHS OF THE FOUR (21:15-22): The military accomplishments of four of David's soldiers are recorded.

SECTION OUTLINE TWELVE (2 SAMUEL 22)
David composes a song to praise God and commemorate his victories over Saul and all his enemies.

I. THANKSGIVING FOR BEING SAVED FROM HIS ENEMIES (22:1-32)
   A. **God's protection** (22:2-7)
   B. **God's power** (22:8-16)
   C. **God's provision** (22:17-25)
   D. **God's perfect justice** (22:26-28)
   E. **God's proven dependability** (22:29-32)

II. THANKSGIVING FOR BEING SET OVER HIS ENEMIES (22:33-51)
   A. **The warrior for God** (22:33-46): David praises God for giving him what he needs to defeat his enemies.
      1. *The skill to defeat his foes* (22:33-37)
      2. *The strength to defeat his foes* (22:38-46)
   B. **The worshiper of God** (22:47-51): David praises God for all the victories he has given him.

SECTION OUTLINE THIRTEEN (2 SAMUEL 23–24)
David's last words are recorded, along with the deeds of his mighty
men. Because David takes a census of the people, he must choose
the punishment. After a plague kills 70,000 Israelites, David builds
an altar and the plague is stopped.

I. THE SONG OF DAVID (23:1-7)
  A. **God and the godly** (23:1-5)
    1. *His anointing of David* (23:1-4)
    2. *His agreement with David* (23:5)
  B. **God and the godless** (23:6-7): The godless will be cast away and
  burned like worthless and harmful thorns.

II. THE SOLDIERS OF DAVID (23:8-39): This passage lists the exploits of
David's mightiest warriors.
  A. **First grouping** (23:8-17): The first group, called the Three, con-
  sists of the three greatest warriors among David's men.
    1. *Jashobeam, the commander of the Three, killed 800 men in
    one battle.*
    2. *Eleazar struck down Philistines until his hand was too tired to
    hold his sword.*
    3. *Shammah single-handedly beat back a large number of
    attacking Philistines.*
    4. *These men once broke through the Philistine lines simply to
    bring David water from Bethlehem.*
  B. **Second grouping** (23:18-23): The second group of David's
  famous warriors are two leaders of the Thirty.
    1. *Abishai, the leader of the Thirty, once killed 300 enemy
    soldiers in a single battle. He became as famous as the Three.*
    2. *Benaiah, the commander of David's bodyguard, killed two of
    Moab's mightiest warriors and a lion in a pit. He also killed an
    Egyptian with the Egyptian's own spear.*
  C. **Final grouping** (23:24-39): The rest of the warriors among the
  Thirty are listed.

III. THE SIN OF DAVID (24:1-25)
  A. **The project** (24:1-2): David commands that a census be taken of
  all the tribes of Israel.
  B. **The protest** (24:3-4): Joab unsuccessfully attempts to change
  David's mind about taking a census.
  C. **The particulars** (24:5-9)
    1. *The territory of the census* (24:5-7): The itinerary of the census
    takers is given.
    2. *The time of the census* (24:8): It takes nine months and 20
    days to complete the census.
    3. *The total of the census* (24:9): There are 500,000 men of
    military age in Judah and 800,000 throughout the rest of
    Israel.

D. The prayer (24:10): After the census is taken, David realizes he sinned and asks for the Lord's forgiveness.

E. The punishment (24:11-15)

1. *The nature* (24:11-13): God allows David to choose one of three punishments for taking the census:
   a. three years of famine
   b. three months of military defeat
   c. three days of plague

2. *The number* (24:14-15): David chooses the plague, which results in 70,000 deaths throughout Israel.

F. The pardon (24:16-17): God stays the hand of the death angel as he is about to destroy Jerusalem.

G. The purchase (24:18-25): David is instructed to buy a certain threshing floor, build an altar there, and make a sacrifice to the Lord. He obeys, and the plague ceases.

1 Kings

I. THE COLDNESS OF DAVID (1:1-4): As David grows old, he becomes unable to keep warm, so his advisers find a beautiful young woman to keep him warm.

II. THE CONSPIRACY BY ADONIJAH (1:5-10): Adonijah, a half brother of Solomon, attempts to crown himself king in his father's place. He is helped by Joab and Abiathar the priest, and he invites most of the royal officials and David's sons to attend a sacrifice at En-rogel.

III. THE COUNTERPLOT BY NATHAN (1:11-27): Nathan hears of Adonijah's plan and works to ensure that Solomon will become the next king.
   A. **Nathan meets with Bathsheba** (1:11-21): Nathan instructs Solomon's mother, Bathsheba, to report Adonijah's behavior to David, reminding the dying king that he has already promised his throne to Solomon.
   B. **Nathan meets with David** (11:22-27): As planned, Nathan comes in just as Bathsheba is finishing talking with David, and he tells David the same thing that she has told him.

IV. THE COMMAND BY DAVID (1:28-37)
   A. **His intentions** (1:28-31): David reassures Nathan and Bathsheba that Solomon will indeed be Israel's next king.
   B. **His instructions** (1:32-37): Zadok the priest and Nathan the prophet are to anoint Solomon, place him on David's mule, blow trumpets, and shout, "Long live King Solomon!"

V. THE CROWNING BY ZADOK (1:38-40): The high priest does exactly what David instructed, causing a great celebration among the people of Jerusalem.

VI. THE COMPASSION OF SOLOMON (1:41-53): When Adonijah learns that Solomon is the new king, he seeks refuge at the altar of the sacred tent. He asks for mercy from Solomon, who grants it as long as Adonijah remains loyal to him.

SECTION OUTLINE TWO (1 KINGS 2)
David delivers a charge to Solomon and dies. Solomon executes Adonijah after he makes a request. For supporting Adonijah as king, Abiathar is deposed as priest but not killed. Joab seeks asylum but is put to death. Shimei is killed for disobeying Solomon's orders to remain in Jerusalem.

I. SOLOMON AND HIS FATHER (2:1-11): David, whose death is near, speaks his final words to Solomon, the new king.
   A. **David's reminder** (2:1-4): David urges Solomon to obey the Lord's commands written in the law of Moses.
   B. **David's requests** (2:5-9): David leaves instructions for Solomon to carry out after David's death.
      1. *Execute Joab and Shimei for their past crimes.*
      2. *Show kindness to the sons of Barzillai for their past faithfulness.*
   C. **David's resting place** (2:10-12): David dies after ruling Israel for 40 years. He is buried in the City of David. Solomon becomes king.

II. SOLOMON AND HIS FOES (2:13-46)
   A. **Adonijah** (2:13-25)
      1. *The petition* (2:13-18): Adonijah desires to marry Abishag, David's former attendant, so he persuades Bathsheba to ask Solomon for this favor.
      2. *The provocation* (2:19-25): Solomon is incensed at such a request, so he orders Adonijah to be put to death!
   B. **Abiathar** (2:26-27): Solomon deposes Abiathar as priest because he supported Adonijah as king, but Solomon does not kill him.
   C. **Joab** (2:28-35): Solomon orders Joab to be executed for brutally murdering Abner and Amasa.
   D. **Shimei** (2:36-46)
      1. *His disobedience* (2:36-40): Solomon allows Shimei to live peacefully in Jerusalem but warns that he will be executed if he leaves the city. Shimei agrees, but three years later he leaves the city to retrieve two runaway slaves.
      2. *His death* (2:41-46): Upon Shimei's return, Solomon has him executed.

I. THE RISE OF SOLOMON (3:1): As Solomon's power increases and his
building projects take shape, he forms an alliance with Pharaoh and
marries one of his daughters.

II. THE REVELATION TO SOLOMON (3:2-28): After Solomon sacrifices
1,000 burnt offerings, the Lord appears to him in a dream that
night.
   A. The details (3:5-15)
      1. *The assurance* (3:5): The Lord promises to give Solomon
      anything he asks for.
      2. *The answer* (3:6-9): Solomon asks for wisdom that he might
      govern justly.
      3. *The approval* (3:10-15): God is pleased with Solomon's choice
      and promises to give him wisdom plus riches and honor!
   B. The demonstration (3:16-28): Soon after Solomon is granted wisdom, he displays his ability to judge wisely by settling a difficult
   dispute.
      1. *The problem* (3:16-22): Two prostitutes gave birth to sons, but
      one of the babies died. One mother claims that the other
      mother switched babies and gave her the dead child.
      2. *The proposal* (3:23-25): Solomon proposes to cut the baby in
      two, giving half to each mother!
      3. *The protest* (3:26): One mother agrees, but the other cries out
      in protest and is willing to give up the infant that he might
      live.
      4. *The pronouncement* (3:27-28): Solomon awards the baby to
      the woman who protested, concluding that she is the real
      mother. News of Solomon's wisdom spreads throughout Israel.

III. THE REIGN OF SOLOMON (4:1-34)
   A. His people (4:1-19)
      1. *Solomon's high officials* (4:1-6)
      2. *Solomon's district governors* (4:7-19)
   B. His prosperity (4:20): The kingdom of Israel increases and pros-
   pers greatly under Solomon's reign.
   C. His places (4:21, 24): Solomon rules over all the land from the
   Euphrates River to the land of the Philistines to the borders of
   Egypt.
   D. His provisions (4:22-23, 27-28): Each district governor is respon-
   sible for providing food for Solomon's palace for one month of
   every year.

E. His peace (4:25): Throughout Solomon's reign, the land of Israel enjoys peace and prosperity.

F. His power (4:26): Solomon has thousands of horses and chariots.

G. His perceptiveness (4:29-34)

1. *The comparison of Solomon's wisdom* (4:29-31): Solomon is wiser than all the wise men of the east, including those in Egypt and the surrounding nations.

2. *The contents of Solomon's wisdom* (4:32-34)

   a. He writes 3,000 proverbs.

   b. He composes 1,005 songs.

   c. He possesses vast knowledge concerning plant and animal life.

   d. His advice is sought by the kings of every nation.

SECTION OUTLINE FOUR (1 KINGS 5–7)

Solomon gathers supplies and constructs a magnificent Temple for the Lord. He also constructs a palace for himself and supplies furnishings for the Temple.

I. A HOUSE FOR THE KING OF KINGS (5:1-18; 6:1-38; 7:13-51)

A. The preparations (5:1-18)

1. *The supplier* (5:1-12)

   a. Solomon's request (5:1-6): He asks Hiram, king of Tyre, to furnish cedar logs for the Temple.

   b. Hiram's reassurance (5:7-12): Hiram agrees; in return, he receives wheat and olive oil from Israel.

2. *The skilled workers* (5:13-18): Solomon conscripts thousands of stonecutters and carpenters to travel to Lebanon and prepare materials for the Temple.

B. The particulars (6:1-38; 7:13-51)

1. *The time schedules for the Temple* (6:1, 37-38)

   a. Its commissioning (6:1): Construction begins during the fourth year of Solomon's reign, 480 years after Israel's exodus from Egypt.

   b. Its completion (6:37-38): The Temple is finished seven years later.

2. *The size of the Temple* (6:2): It is 90 feet long, 30 feet wide, and 45 feet high.

3. *The structure of the Temple* (6:3-10, 14-36)

   a. The exterior (6:3-10): A description is given of the Temple's various rooms and staircases.

   b. The interior (6:14-36): A description is given of the elaborate decorations and paneling of the Temple's interior.

4. *The promise from the Temple* (6:11-13): The Lord assures Solomon that he will continue to live among his people if they obey his commands.

5. *The fixtures in the Temple* (7:13-51): A skilled craftsman from the tribe of Naphtali fashions the gold and bronze furnishings.
   a. The two bronze pillars (7:15-22)
   b. The bronze Sea (7:23-26)
   c. Ten bronze water carts (7:27-37)
   d. The gold altar, the gold table for the Bread of the Presence, the gold lampstands, etc. (7:48-51)

II. A HOUSE FOR THE KING OF ISRAEL (7:1-12): Solomon also builds a palace for himself.
   A. **The time** (7:1): The palace took 13 years to construct.
   B. **The dimensions** (7:2-12): Solomon's magnificent palace has many great rooms. One of the buildings, the Palace of the Forest of Lebanon, measures 150 feet long, 75 feet wide, 45 feet high, and is constructed almost entirely of cedar! Another room, the Hall of Pillars, measures 75 feet long by 45 feet wide.

SECTION OUTLINE FIVE (1 KINGS 8)
After the Ark is transferred to the Temple, Solomon blesses the people and dedicates the Temple.

I. THE SUMMONS (8:1-11)
   A. **The Ark of the Covenant** (8:1-9): Solomon gathers all of Israel's leaders to witness the placing of the Ark in the Temple.
   B. **The glory of God** (8:10-11): When the priests withdraw from the inner sanctuary, the glorious presence of the Lord fills the Temple.

II. THE SERMON (8:12-21): Solomon blesses the people and delivers a message.
   A. **Concerning the people who built the Temple** (8:12-19): David wanted to build a temple for the Lord, but Solomon is chosen to build it.
   B. **Concerning the purpose for building the Temple** (8:20-21)
      1. *To honor the name of God* (8:20)
      2. *To house the Ark of God* (8:21)

III. THE SUPPLICATION (8:22-53): Solomon prays, asking God for several things:
   A. **Continual blessing upon David's dynasty** (8:25-26)
   B. **Attentiveness to his prayers** (8:27-30)
   C. **Justice for the innocent** (8:31-32)
   D. **Forgiveness for the repentant** (8:33-40)
   E. **Attentiveness to the prayers of foreigners who visit the Temple** (8:41-43)
   F. **Victory in time of war** (8:44-45)
   G. **Restoration after captivity** (8:46-53)

IV. THE SOUND OF PRAISE (8:54-61): With outstretched arms, Solomon praises the Lord and blesses the people, calling upon the Lord to help them obey his laws.

V. THE SACRIFICES (8:62-66): Solomon and the people complete the dedication of the Temple by sacrificing 22,000 oxen and 120,000 sheep! Then they celebrate the Festival of Shelters.

SECTION OUTLINE SIX (1 KINGS 9–10)
The Lord responds to Solomon's prayer. Hiram is displeased with the towns that Solomon gave him as payment for the Temple materials. Solomon's triumphs and treasures are described. The queen of Sheba admires Solomon's wealth, wisdom, and fame.

I. THE WARNING TO SOLOMON (9:1-9)
   A. **The glory of obedience** (9:1-5): If Solomon continues to obey the Lord, the Lord will make his dynasty secure, just as he promised David.
   B. **The grief of disobedience** (9:6-9): If the people disobey and forsake the Lord, he will send two punishments upon them:
      1. *The dispersion of the people*
      2. *The destruction of the Temple*

II. THE WORK PROJECTS OF SOLOMON (9:10-19)
   A. **The complaint** (9:10-14): King Hiram is displeased with the 20 cities of Galilee that Solomon gave him as payment for his cedar, cypress, and gold.
   B. **The construction** (9:15-19): Solomon's many building projects include the Temple, the royal palace, the Millo, the wall of Jerusalem, the cities of Hazor, Megiddo, and Gezer, and various cities for storing grain and military equipment.

III. THE WORKFORCE OF SOLOMON (9:20-24): Solomon conscripts labor forces from the survivors of the nations he conquers.

IV. THE WORSHIP OF SOLOMON (9:25): Three times a year Solomon sacrifices burnt offerings and peace offerings in the Temple.

V. THE WISDOM OF SOLOMON (10:1-9): The Lord's marvelous gift of wisdom to Solomon is witnessed by the queen of Sheba during her visit to Jerusalem.
   A. **Solomon answers the queen** (10:1-3): The queen is determined to test Solomon's famed wisdom by asking him many difficult questions. Solomon wisely answers all her questions.
   B. **Solomon amazes the queen** (10:4-9): The queen is overwhelmed by Solomon's incredible wisdom and the glory of his kingdom.

VI. THE WEALTH OF SOLOMON (9:26-28; 10:10-29)
  A. **The sources** (9:26-28; 10:10-12, 14-15, 22-25): Solomon's vast
    wealth came from several sources, including:
    1. *The queen of Sheba* (10:10)
    2. *Visiting foreigners* (10:23-25)
    3. *Taxes* (10:14-15)
    4. *Merchant ships* (9:26-28; 10:11-12, 22)
  B. **The splendor** (10:13, 16-21, 26-29): As treasures flow into the
    royal coffers, Solomon's kingdom reflects his great wealth.
    1. *The gifts to the queen of Sheba* (10:13)
    2. *The 500 gold shields* (10:16-17)
    3. *The ivory throne overlaid with pure gold* (10:18-20)
    4. *The gold cups and dining utensils* (10:21)
    5. *The thousands of chariots and horses* (10:26-29)

SECTION OUTLINE SEVEN (1 KINGS 11)
Solomon allows his many wives and concubines to lead him into
idolatry. The Lord raises up enemies against Solomon. A prophet tells
Jeroboam, one of Solomon's leaders, that 10 of the northern tribes will
be taken from Solomon and given to him. Solomon dies and is buried.

  I. SOLOMON'S DISOBEDIENCE (11:1-40)
    A. **The causes** (11:1-8)
      1. *Polygamy* (11:1-3): Contrary to God's commands (Deut.
        17:17), Solomon has 700 wives and 300 concubines!
      2. *Paganism* (11:3-8): Solomon's pagan wives lead his heart
        astray, and he worships their idols.
    B. **The consequences** (11:9-40)
      1. *Future civil war* (11:9-13, 26-40): The Lord is angry and
        promises to tear the kingdom away from Solomon and give it
        to one of his servants. But for David's sake, the Lord reserves
        this punishment until after Solomon dies, and even then his
        son still reigns over one tribe.
        a. Jeroboam and Solomon (11:26-28): Prior to his rebellion,
          Jeroboam is a capable Ephraimite serving as one of Solo-
          mon's workforce leaders.
        b. Jeroboam and Ahijah (11:29-40): A prophet named Ahijah
          tells Jeroboam that the kingdom will be torn away from
          Solomon and given to him.
          (1) Ahijah's illustration (11:29-30): One day as Jeroboam
            leaves Jerusalem, Ahijah takes a new cloak and tears it
            into 12 pieces, giving Jeroboam 10 pieces.
          (2) Ahijah's interpretation (11:31-40): The prophet tells
            Jeroboam that the Lord will soon make him ruler over
            10 of Israel's tribes because of Solomon's many sins!
            Jeroboam flees to Egypt to escape Solomon's anger.

2. *Foreign enemies* (11:14-25): The Lord also allows foreign
enemies to trouble King Solomon's reign.
   a. Hadad (11:14-22): This Edomite sought asylum in Egypt
   after David's men killed most of the men in Edom. During
   Solomon's reign, he returns from Egypt and becomes a
   threat to Solomon.
   b. Rezon (11:23-25): Like Hadad, Rezon fled from David and
   became a bitter enemy of Israel. During Solomon's reign,
   Rezon rules in Damascus and causes trouble for Solomon.
II. SOLOMON'S DEATH (11:41-43): After reigning 40 years, Solomon
dies and is succeeded by his son Rehoboam.

SECTION OUTLINE EIGHT (1 KINGS 12–13)
Rehoboam succeeds his father, Solomon, as king. After Rehoboam
makes a poor decision to rule harshly, Jeroboam rebels against Rehoboam and rules the 10 northern tribes. An immediate war between
the two kingdoms is avoided. Jeroboam institutes idol worship at
Dan and Bethel.

I. REHOBOAM (12:1-24): After Solomon's death, Rehoboam is the new
king over all Israel.
   A. **The arrogance** (12:1-20)
      1. *The request by Israel's leaders* (12:1-11)
         a. The conditions (12:1-5): Before his coronation, Rehoboam
         is urged by the leaders of 10 of Israel's tribes to lessen the
         hardships placed upon them by King Solomon.
         b. The counsel (12:6-11)
            (1) The wise words of the old men (12:6-7): Rehoboam's
            older counselors, who had advised Solomon,
            recommend that he assure the tribes that there will be
            change for the good.
            (2) The wicked words of the young men (12:8-11):
            Rehoboam's younger, inexperienced friends from
            childhood urge him to threaten the tribes with even
            harsher rule.
      2. *The rejection of Israel's leaders* (12:12-15): Rehoboam rejects
      the counsel of the older men and follows the advice of his
      friends.
      3. *The reaction of Israel's leaders* (12:16-20): The 10 tribes
      denounce Rehoboam and form their own nation, with
      Jeroboam as their king.
   B. **The aborted attack** (12:21-24): Rehoboam gathers an army of
   180,000 troops to crush the rebellion, but a prophet named
   Shemaiah warns him not to fight against the northern kingdom.

II. JEROBOAM (12:25–13:34): After the 10 northern tribes revolt, they make Jeroboam their leader.
   A. His apostasy (12:25-33; 13:33-34)
      1. *What he does* (12:28-33; 13:33-34)
         a. Jeroboam builds two gold calf idols and places them in Bethel and Dan, two cities of the northern kingdom.
         b. He appoints non-Levites to serve as priests.
         c. He institutes his own religious festival.
      2. *Why he does it* (12:25-27): He does it to keep his people from returning to Jerusalem and sacrificing in the Temple.
   B. His altar (13:1-32)
      1. *The prophecy* (13:1-2): As Jeroboam offers a sacrifice on his pagan altar at Bethel, a man of God foretells that one day a future king will defile this altar by burning on it the bones of the very priests who are sacrificing upon it!
      2. *The proof* (13:3-5)
         a. The crack in the altar (13:3, 5): As proof that the predicted event will happen, the man of God states that the false altar will split apart, and its ashes will be poured out on the ground. This happens, just as the man of God foretold.
         b. The crippling of the hand (13:4): When Jeroboam hears this, he reaches out his hand and orders that the man be seized, but Jeroboam's hand becomes paralyzed!
      3. *The pleas* (13:6-10)
         a. The restoration (13:6): At the king's urging, the man of God prays to the Lord, who restores the king's hand.
         b. The refusal (13:7-10): Jeroboam offers to reward the man of God and invites him to the palace; the man refuses, for God has forbidden him to eat or drink anything in Bethel.
      4. *The prophet* (13:11-32)
         a. The sin (13:11-19): En route back to his home, the man of God is met by an old prophet, who tells him that an angel wants him to come home with him and share a meal. The old prophet is lying, but the man of God goes home and eats with him.
         b. The sentence (13:20-22): As the man of God eats with the prophet, the Lord sends a message to him through the prophet. The Lord rebukes him for his disobedience and tells him that his body will not be buried in the grave of his ancestors.
         c. The slaying (13:23-25): The man of God eats and then leaves on a donkey, but along the way he is killed by a lion.
         d. The sorrow (13:26-32): When the older prophet hears that the man of God has been killed, he retrieves the body and mourns for him. He instructs his sons to bury him beside the man of God, for his message is certainly true.

SECTION OUTLINE NINE (1 KINGS 14–15)

Ahijah pronounces doom on Jeroboam's family. Jeroboam dies, and Nadab becomes king of Israel. After leading Judah into idolatry, King Rehoboam dies, and Abijam becomes king. Asa succeeds Abijam and begins many reforms. Baasha assassinates Nadab and becomes king of Israel. There is constant war between Israel and Judah.

I. JEROBOAM, ISRAEL'S FIRST RULER (14:1-20): The final days of Jeroboam's reign are recorded.
   A. His deception (14:1-18)
      1. *The plot* (14:1-3): Jeroboam instructs his wife to disguise herself and find out from Ahijah the prophet if their sick son will recover.
      2. *The perception* (14:4-5): Before the queen arrives, the Lord informs Ahijah, who is old and almost blind, who his coming visitor is.
      3. *The prophecy* (14:6-18): Ahijah tells Jeroboam's wife of coming judgment for Jeroboam's evil.
         a. Concerning the house of Jeroboam (14:7-14, 17-18): Because Jeroboam promotes idolatry in Israel, his sick son will die along with all his other sons.
         b. Concerning the house of Israel (14:15-16): The Lord will cause the northern kingdom of Israel to be taken into captivity.
   B. His death (14:19-20): Jeroboam dies after a reign of 22 years. His son Nadab becomes king.

II. REHOBOAM, JUDAH'S FIRST RULER (14:21-31): The final days of Rehoboam's reign are recorded.
   A. His detestable practices (14:21-24): Rehoboam allows idolatry to flourish throughout Judah.
   B. His defeat (14:25-31): King Shishak of Egypt captures Jerusalem and steals the treasures of the Temple and the royal palace.

III. ABIJAM, JUDAH'S SECOND RULER (15:1-8)
   A. His wickedness (15:1-5): Abijam commits the same sins his father, Rehoboam, committed.
   B. His warfare (15:6-8): During Abijam's reign there is constant war between Israel and Judah.

IV. ASA, JUDAH'S THIRD RULER (15:9-24)
   A. His spiritual warfare (15:9-15): Asa initiates great reforms throughout Judah, removing the idols and even deposing his own grandmother for her pagan practices!
   B. His military warfare (15:16-24): Asa wages constant war against Baasha of Israel and reestablishes a treaty with the king of Aram to defeat Israel.

V. NADAB, ISRAEL'S SECOND RULER (15:25-28): King Nadab commits the same idolatrous sins that Jeroboam committed. After two years Nadab is assassinated by Baasha, one of his military commanders.

VI. BAASHA, ISRAEL'S THIRD RULER (15:29-34): Baasha kills Nadab and all of Jeroboam's descendants, thus fulfilling the prophecy of Ahijah the prophet. He is constantly at war with King Asa of Judah.

SECTION OUTLINE TEN (1 KINGS 16–17)

The reigns of the northern kings Baasha, Elah, Zimri, Omri, and Ahab are recorded. Elijah tells Ahab of a coming drought. Elijah flees to the east and is sustained by ravens and then by a widow at Zarephath. He restores the widow's dead son to life.

I. FIVE GODLESS POTENTATES (16:1-34)
   A. **Baasha, Israel's third ruler** (16:1-7)
      1. *The faithful messenger* (16:1): The Lord delivers a message to Baasha through the prophet Jehu.
      2. *The fearful message* (16:2-7): Jehu tells Baasha that he and all his descendants will be destroyed because of Baasha's wickedness.
   B. **Elah, Israel's fourth ruler** (16:8-10): After Baasha dies, his son Elah reigns, but he is killed in the second year of his reign.
   C. **Zimri, Israel's fifth ruler** (16:10-20)
      1. *Zimri kills his king* (16:10-14): Zimri, one of Elah's chariot commanders, kills Elah and all of Baasha's descendants, thus fulfilling Jehu's prophecy.
      2. *Zimri kills himself* (16:15-20): After a reign of only seven days, Zimri is overthrown by another military leader and commits suicide.
   D. **Omri, Israel's sixth ruler** (16:21-28)
      1. *The struggle* (16:21-22): After Zimri's death, Tibni and Omri struggle for power. Omri wins and becomes king.
      2. *The structure* (16:23-24): Omri builds the city of Samaria, which becomes the capital for the northern kingdom.
      3. *The sins* (16:25-28): Omri is more wicked than any other king up to his time. He continues to promote idolatry in Israel.
   E. **Ahab, Israel's seventh ruler** (16:29-34)
      1. *The model of Jeroboam* (16:29-30): Ahab follows Jeroboam's example and becomes Israel's worst king up to this time.
      2. *The marriage of Jezebel* (16:31-32): Ahab marries Jezebel, the daughter of the king of the Sidonians. She leads Ahab to worship Baal; he constructs a temple to Baal in Samaria.
      3. *The message of Joshua* (16:34): Hiel rebuilds Jericho, but just as Joshua had foretold, Hiel's first son dies when the

foundations are laid, and he loses his youngest son when the gates are in place.

II. ONE GODLY PROPHET (17:1-24): The Lord raises up a prophet from Gilead named Elijah.
    A. The word of the Lord (17:1): Elijah warns Ahab that there will be no rain in Israel unless he gives the word.
    B. The waiting at Kerith Brook (17:2-7)
        1. *The place* (17:2-3): The Lord instructs Elijah to hide by Kerith Brook east of where it enters the Jordan River.
        2. *The provisions* (17:4-6): Elijah drinks from the brook and is fed by ravens sent by the Lord.
        3. *The problem* (17:7): After a while the brook dries up, since there is no rain.
    C. The widow at Zarephath (17:8-24): The Lord tells Elijah to go to the village of Zarephath to be fed by a widow there.
        1. *The replenishing of the food* (17:8-16)
            a. Elijah's request (17:8-12): Elijah finds the widow and asks her for bread and water. She says that she has no food left except a handful of flour and some cooking oil.
            b. Elijah's reassurance (17:13-16)
                (1) The prediction (17:13-14): Elijah tells her that there will always be plenty of flour and oil in her containers until the famine has ended.
                (2) The provision (17:15-16): The widow cooks Elijah his meal, and everything happens exactly as Elijah said.
        2. *The raising of the boy* (17:17-24)
            a. The tragedy (17:17-21)
                (1) The boy's sickness (17:17): The widow's son becomes sick and dies.
                (2) The mother's sorrow (17:18): In great anguish the widow asks Elijah if he has come to punish her for some past sin.
                (3) The prophet's supplication (17:19-21): Elijah stretches himself upon the boy's body and asks the Lord to bring him back from the dead.
            b. The triumph (17:22-23): The Lord grants Elijah's request, and the boy is raised from the dead!
            c. The testimony (17:24): The grateful widow testifies that Elijah is indeed a man of God.

SECTION OUTLINE ELEVEN (1 KINGS 18–19)
Elijah challenges Ahab to a contest on Mount Carmel. The Lord
honors Elijah's prayer, sending fire from heaven. Rain falls once again
in Israel, and Elijah flees to Mount Sinai. The Lord tells him to anoint
Elisha as his prophet and Jehu as king. So Elijah finds Elisha and
makes him his assistant.

I. ELIJAH ON A ROAD (18:1-16): Elijah meets and talks with a follower
   of the Lord named Obadiah.
   A. Obadiah the faithful manager (18:1-6): Obadiah is in charge of
      Ahab's palace.
      1. *His ministry* (18:1-4): Once Obadiah hid and fed 100 of the
         Lord's prophets to keep them from being killed by Jezebel.
      2. *His mission* (18:5-6): Ahab instructs Obadiah to search the
         parched land for grass to feed the king's horses and mules.
   B. Obadiah the fearful manager (18:7-16)
      1. *The order* (18:7-8): As Obadiah is carrying out his duties, he
         meets Elijah, who tells him to arrange a meeting for him with
         King Ahab.
      2. *The objection* (18:9-14): Obadiah fears that Elijah might not
         show up for the meeting, which would result in Obadiah's
         death!
      3. *The obedience* (18:15-16): After being reassured by Elijah,
         Obadiah sets up the meeting.

II. ELIJAH ATOP A MOUNTAIN (18:17-46)
   A. Elijah and Ahab (18:17-19): Elijah challenges Ahab and his 850
      pagan prophets to meet him on Mount Carmel.
   B. Elijah and the people (18:20-24)
      1. *The chastening* (18:20-21): Elijah rebukes Israel for wavering
         between worshiping the Lord and Baal.
      2. *The contest* (18:22-24): Elijah proposes a contest between
         himself and the prophets of Baal.
         a. The preparation: Each side is to prepare a young bull as a
            sacrifice and place it on an altar.
         b. The proof: Elijah tells the prophets to call upon their god to
            send fire down to consume the sacrifice, and Elijah will call
            upon his God to do the same.
   C. Elijah and the prophets (18:25-29)
      1. *The shouting* (18:25-26): All morning the false prophets call
         out to Baal with no response.
      2. *The sarcasm* (18:27): At noon Elijah taunts them, suggesting
         that their god might be on a trip or sleeping!
      3. *The suffering* (18:28): In desperation, the prophets cut
         themselves with knives and swords!
      4. *The silence* (18:29): In spite of their frantic attempts to reach
         Baal, the only response is silence!

D. Elijah and the Lord (18:30-46)

1. *The fire from heaven* (18:30-40)

   a. The prayer (18:30-39): Following Elijah's prayer, fire falls from heaven, consuming the sacrifice. The people cry out, "The LORD is God!"

   b. The purge (18:40): Elijah tells the people to kill all the prophets of Baal, which they do.

2. *The flood from heaven* (18:41-46): Elijah announces the end of the three-year drought, and a terrific rainstorm sweeps over the land.

III. ELIJAH UNDER A TREE (19:1-7)

A. The curses (19:1-4): Jezebel vows to kill Elijah to avenge the death of her prophets. Elijah quickly flees to the desert.

B. The comfort (19:4-7): In the desert Elijah collapses under a broom tree and prays that he might die. But an angel of the Lord comforts and feeds him.

IV. ELIJAH IN A CAVE (19:8-18): After being strengthened by the angel, Elijah travels 40 days and nights to Mount Sinai, where he spends the night.

A. The confrontation from the Lord (19:9-14): After Elijah complains about his situation, the Lord tells him to stand outside the cave. The Lord passes by, but he is not in the windstorm, earthquake, or fire. Instead the Lord comes to Elijah in a gentle whisper, asking him why he is there.

B. The commissioning by the Lord (19:15-17): The Lord instructs Elijah to do three things:

1. *Anoint Hazael king of Aram* (19:15).

2. *Anoint Jehu king of Israel* (19:16).

3. *Anoint Elisha to succeed him as prophet* (19:16-17).

C. The correction by the Lord (19:18): The Lord tells Elijah that he is not alone, for there are 7,000 others in Israel who have not bowed to Baal or kissed him.

V. ELIJAH ALONGSIDE A FIELD (19:19-21): Elijah returns and finds Elisha plowing a field.

A. The selection (19:19-20): Elijah throws his cloak over Elisha's shoulders, indicating that he is calling him to follow. Elijah grants Elisha permission to say good-bye to his parents.

B. The sacrifice (19:21): Elisha sacrifices his oxen and shares the meat with the other plowmen, thus ending his old occupation and beginning his life as Elijah's assistant.

SECTION OUTLINE TWELVE (1 KINGS 20–21)
Ben-hadad's forces besiege Samaria. King Ahab defeats them twice;
Ahab makes a treaty with them but is condemned for sparing
Ben-hadad. Jezebel arranges Naboth's death so Ahab can have his
vineyard. Elijah condemns Ahab and Jezebel, but the Lord shows
mercy when Ahab is repentant.

I. AHAB'S CONQUEST (20:1-43): The Lord allows Ahab to defeat the
   Arameans on two occasions so he will know that the Lord is God.
   A. First occasion (20:1-21): Ben-hadad and his Aramean forces
      besiege Samaria and send demands to King Ahab.
      1. *Ahab's response* (20:1-4)
         a. Ben-hadad to Ahab (20:2-3): "Your silver and gold are
            mine, and so are the best of your wives and children!"
         b. Ahab to Ben-hadad (20:4): "All that I have is yours!"
      2. *Ahab's rebellion* (20:5-12)
         a. The further demands (20:5-6): Ben-hadad then demands
            that his officials be allowed to search the palace and take
            anything valuable.
         b. The fury of Ahab (20:7-9): Ahab becomes incensed at this
            last demand and refuses to grant it.
         c. The final words (20:10-12): Both men exchange hostile
            messages, and Ben-hadad prepares to destroy the city.
      3. *Ahab's reassurance* (20:13-14): A prophet tells Ahab that he
         will be victorious.
      4. *Ahab's routing* (20:15-21): Ahab defeats Ben-hadad's forces,
         destroying their horses and chariots and inflicting heavy
         losses.
   B. Second occasion (20:22-43)
      1. *The counsel* (20:22-28)
         a. The preparation (20:22): The prophet tells Ahab to prepare
            for another attack by Ben-hadad in the spring.
         b. The presumption (20:23-27): Ben-hadad's officers falsely
            presume that the Israelites worship gods of the hills. They
            assure Ben-hadad of victory if he attacks the Israelites on
            the plains.
         c. The prophecy (20:28): The prophet reassures Ahab that the
            Lord will defeat Ben-hadad's forces since they have
            defamed his name.
      2. *The conflict* (20:29-30): Israel utterly routs the Arameans,
         killing 127,000 of them! Ben-hadad runs and hides.
      3. *The conclusion* (20:31-43): Ben-hadad's officers beg for mercy
         before King Ahab.
         a. The agreement (20:31-34): Disobeying God's command,
            Ahab makes a treaty with the Arameans and spares Ben-
            hadad.
         b. The accusation (20:35-43)

    (1) The example (20:35-40): In order to convey a message to King Ahab, a prophet disguises himself as a soldier who irresponsibly allowed a prisoner to escape.

    (2) The explanation (20:40-43): King Ahab condemns the prophet, but then the prophet explains that the same is true of Ahab, since he allowed Ben-hadad to live.

II. AHAB'S CONSPIRACY (21:1-16)
  A. Ahab's request (21:1-2): Ahab desires to acquire a vineyard that is near his palace in Jezreel. Ahab offers to buy it from the owner, Naboth, or to exchange a better one for it.
  B. Naboth's refusal (21:3-4): Naboth declines, since the vineyard has belonged to his family for generations. Ahab becomes angry and sullen.
  C. Jezebel's reprisal (21:5-16)
    1. *Naboth is maligned* (21:5-10): Jezebel writes letters in Ahab's name, instructing the leaders of Jezreel to arrange for Naboth to be falsely accused of blasphemy and stoned to death.
    2. *Naboth is murdered* (21:11-16): Jezebel's plan is carried out. After Naboth is stoned to death, Ahab claims his vineyard.

III. AHAB'S CONDEMNATION (21:17-24): Elijah confronts Ahab in Naboth's vineyard and tells him that he and all his family will eventually be destroyed for their wickedness.

IV. AHAB'S CONTRITION (21:25-29): Hearing Elijah's terrible words, the king repents; the Lord chooses to carry out his sentence only after Ahab's death.

SECTION OUTLINE THIRTEEN (1 KINGS 22)
King Jehoshaphat of Judah joins forces with King Ahab of Israel to fight the Arameans. They ignore the warning of Micaiah the prophet and go to war. Ahab is killed in battle by an arrow. The reigns of Jehoshaphat and Ahaziah are summarized.

I. THE END OF AHAB'S REIGN (22:1-40)
  A. Ahab and Jehoshaphat (22:1-4): King Jehoshaphat of Judah agrees to an alliance with Ahab to fight the Arameans.
  B. Ahab and the prophets (22:5-28): At Jehoshaphat's urging, Ahab asks many prophets if he should go to war against Ramoth-gilead.
    1. *The prophets of Ahab* (22:5-6, 10-12): Ahab's prophets, about 400 in all, assure him of victory.
    2. *The prophet of the Lord* (22:7-9, 13-28): A prophet of the Lord named Micaiah is brought before King Ahab and asked if Israel will be victorious.
      a. What he says (22:13-16): At first Micaiah agrees with the other prophets, but Ahab demands that he tell the truth.

     b. What he saw (22:17-23): In a vision Micaiah saw the Israel-
     ites scattered like sheep because their shepherd (Ahab) had
     been killed. He also had a vision of the Lord allowing a
     spirit to inspire Ahab's prophets to speak lies.
     c. What he suggests (22:24-28): After Ahab's prophets protest,
     Micaiah advises the king to wait and see if his prophecies
     are correct.
  C. Ahab and the Arameans (22:29-40): Both kings decide to lead
  their armies into battle.
    1. *The royal apparel* (22:29-33): King Ahab disguises himself so
    as not to look like the king, while Jehoshaphat wears the royal
    robes. The Arameans see Jehoshaphat and chase him, but they
    stop when they realize that he is not King Ahab.
    2. *The random arrow* (22:34-40): An enemy arrow, shot at
    random, strikes King Ahab and mortally wounds him. Later,
    the dogs lick his blood just as Elijah and Micaiah had
    prophesied.

II. THE EVENTS OF JEHOSPHAPHAT'S REIGN (22:41-50): Judah's fourth
ruler, Jehoshaphat, is ultimately declared good, despite his mixed
record, including allowing pagan shrines to remain, making peace
with Israel, removing all the shrine prositutes, and building a fleet of
trading ships that are wrecked before they ever set sail.

III. THE EVILNESS OF AHAZIAH'S REIGN (22:51-53): Israel's eighth ruler,
Ahaziah, is declared wicked because he continues Jeroboam's sin
of idolatry in Israel.

2 Kings

SECTION OUTLINE ONE (2 KINGS 1–2)

Ahaziah consults the priests of Baal-zebub to see if he will recover from a fall, but Elijah prophesies that he will die. Elisha succeeds Elijah as prophet. Elijah is taken to heaven in a fiery chariot. Elisha is confirmed as Elijah's successor by the miracles he performs.

I. THE FINAL DAYS OF ELIJAH'S MINISTRY (1:1–2:11)
   A. **Elijah and Ahaziah** (1:1-18)
      1. *The fall* (1:1-2): Ahaziah suffers a serious fall and sends messengers to the temple of Baal-zebub to ask if he will recover.
      2. *The foretelling* (1:3-4): Elijah prophesies that Ahaziah will die from his injuries because he consulted Baal.
      3. *The fury* (1:5-9, 11): An angry Ahaziah sends soldiers to arrest Elijah.
      4. *The fire* (1:10, 12): Elijah calls down fire from heaven, which consumes the first two companies of soldiers.
      5. *The favor* (1:13-15): The captain of the third company begs for mercy. After the angel of the Lord tells Elijah to go with the captain, he does so.
      6. *The fulfillment* (1:16-18): Elijah repeats his prophecy to King Ahaziah himself, and the prophecy is fulfilled.
   B. **Elijah and Elisha** (2:1-11): Elijah and Elisha make a final journey together just before Elijah is taken up into heaven.
      1. *The route* (2:1-6): Traveling from Gilgal to Bethel to Jericho to the Jordan River, Elisha is repeatedly reminded that his master is going to be taken away. Elisha repeatedly affirms his loyalty to Elijah.
      2. *The river* (2:7-8): At the Jordan River, Elijah performs his final miracle by parting its waters.
      3. *The request* (2:9): Elisha asks to become Elijah's "rightful successor."
      4. *The requirement* (2:10): Elijah tells Elisha that he will receive his request if he witnesses Elijah's departure.
      5. *The removal* (2:11): As Elisha watches, a chariot of fire appears, and Elijah is carried into heaven by a whirlwind!

II. THE FIRST DAYS OF ELISHA'S MINISTRY (2:12-25)
   A. **He parts the Jordan** (2:12-14): Elisha takes up Elijah's cloak and parts the Jordan by striking its waters with it.
   B. **He pacifies some prophets** (2:15-18): Reluctantly Elisha permits 50 prophets to search for Elijah. They are unsuccessful.
   C. **He purifies some water** (2:19-22): Elisha throws salt into a polluted spring at Jericho and makes it wholesome.
   D. **He punishes some mocking youths** (2:23-25)
      1. *The mocking* (2:23): As Elisha heads to Bethel, some young boys ridicule his bald head.
      2. *The mauling* (2:24-25): Elisha curses the young boys, and two bears come out of the woods and maul 42 of them!

SECTION OUTLINE TWO   (2 KINGS 3–4)

Joram succeeds Ahaziah and goes to war with Moab. The Lord provides water for Israel and Judah and uses it to lure the Moabites to their destruction. Elisha provides oil for a widow, raises a dead child, purifies a pot of stew, and feeds 100 men with only a small amount of food.

I. ELISHA AND KING JORAM (3:1-14)
   A. **The incompetent king** (3:1-9)
      1. *Joram's idolatry* (3:1-3): Ahab's son Joram (sometimes called Jehoram) becomes Israel's ninth ruler. He practices idolatry, although he removes a sacred pillar of Baal.
      2. *Joram's intent* (3:4-8): King Joram persuades King Jehoshaphat of Judah to help him fight the Moabites, who have rebelled against him.
      3. *Joram's ineptness* (3:9): After a seven-day roundabout march, Joram's army runs out of water in the wilderness of Edom.
   B. **The indignant prophet** (3:10-27)
      1. *The request* (3:10-12): King Jehoshaphat asks King Joram to seek instruction from a prophet of the Lord.
      2. *The rebuke* (3:13-14): The two kings ask Elisha what they should do, but he tells the king of Israel that he wants no part of him. After King Joram pleads with him, Elisha agrees to help them for the sake of King Jehoshaphat.
      3. *The reply* (3:15-19): While a harp is played, Elisha receives a message from the Lord that the dry valley before them will be filled with water and that they will defeat the Moabites.
      4. *The red water* (3:20-23): The water appears, just as the Lord promised. The morning sun causes it to look like blood to the Moabites, and they think the armies have killed each other.
      5. *The routing* (3:24-27)
         a. Moab's defeat (3:24-25): When the Moabite soldiers arrive

to collect the plunder, Israel's soldiers rush out and destroy them.

b. Moab's desperation (3:26-27): The king of Moab realizes that his forces are being overwhelmed; he offers his oldest son as a burnt sacrifice, and the Israelite army returns home.

II. ELISHA AND A POOR WIDOW (4:1-7)

A. **The widow's crisis** (4:1-2): A widow of one of Elisha's fellow prophets is threatened with the enslavement of her two sons because of unpaid debts. All she has is a flask of olive oil.

B. **Elisha's command** (4:3-7): Elisha instructs the widow to borrow as many containers as possible. The olive oil fills all the containers. Elisha then tells her to sell the oil, pay her debts, and support her family with the rest of the money.

III. ELISHA AND THE WOMAN FROM SHUNEM (4:8-37)

A. **Her hospitality** (4:8-17)

1. *The room* (4:8-10): A wealthy woman from Shunem provides a special room for Elisha whenever he comes through the area.

2. *The reward* (4:11-17): Elisha wishes to reward this woman for her hospitality, so he promises her that she will have a son in one year. This all takes place just as Elisha says.

B. **Her heartache** (4:18-28)

1. *The source of her tears* (4:18-21): Years later, the woman's son becomes ill and dies.

2. *The solution for her tears* (4:22-31): The woman finds Elisha and tells him about her son. Elisha sends Gehazi ahead to lay his staff on the child's face, but nothing happens.

C. **Her happiness** (4:32-37): Elisha restores the boy to life and presents him to his mother, who is overwhelmed with gratitude.

IV. ELISHA AND THE PROPHETS (4:38-44): Elisha returns to Gilgal, and a famine comes upon the land.

A. **The poisonous food** (4:38-41): One of Elisha's prophets makes stew for the others, but he unknowingly uses poisonous gourds. Elisha purifies it by throwing some flour in the stew.

B. **The plentiful food** (4:42-44): Elisha instructs a man to give a sack of grain and 20 loaves of barley bread to 100 prophets. The man does so, and there is more than enough food for everyone.

SECTION OUTLINE THREE (2 KINGS 5)

Naaman, the commander of the Aramean army, seeks out Elisha in order to be healed of leprosy. Naaman is healed when he obeys Elisha's instructions, but Elisha's servant Gehazi is struck with leprosy for his greed.

I. THE CLEANSING OF LEPROSY (5:1-19)

   A. **Naaman's disease** (5:1): Naaman is a highly successful commander of the Aramean army, but he suffers from leprosy.

   B. **Naaman's determination** (5:2-5)

      1. *The little girl* (5:2-3): Naaman's wife's maid, a young Israelite captive, tells her mistress about Elisha's ability to heal Naaman's leprosy.

      2. *The large gift* (5:4-5): Believing the young girl, Naaman travels to meet Elisha, carrying with him considerable amounts of gold and silver.

   C. **Naaman's detainment** (5:6-8)

      1. *The request by the king of Aram* (5:6): The king of Aram addresses a letter to Israel's king, requesting that Naaman be healed.

      2. *The response by the king of Israel* (5:7): The king of Israel tears his clothes in frustration, concluding that the request is an excuse for Aram to attack Israel when it is not granted.

      3. *The reassurance by the man of God* (5:8): Elisha tells the king of Israel to send Naaman to him; Naaman will learn that there is a true prophet in Israel.

   D. **Naaman's displeasure** (5:9-13)

      1. *The announcement* (5:9-10): Naaman arrives at Elisha's house, but Elisha simply sends him a message telling him to wash himself seven times in the Jordan River.

      2. *The anger* (5:11-12): Naaman is furious, for he expects Elisha to come out and heal him personally.

      3. *The advice* (5:13): Naaman's officers convince him to obey the prophet.

   E. **Naaman's deliverance** (5:14): Naaman washes in the Jordan. He is healed of his leprosy, just as Elisha had said.

   F. **Naaman's dedication** (5:15-19)

      1. *His presents* (5:15-16): Naaman attempts to give gifts to Elisha, but Elisha refuses them.

      2. *His promises* (5:17-19): Naaman vows that he will worship the Lord from now on.

II. THE CURSE OF LEPROSY (5:20-27)

   A. **Gehazi's lust** (5:20): Elisha's servant, Gehazi, determines to receive a gift from Naaman, even though Elisha refused them.

   B. **Gehazi's lie** (5:21-24): Gehazi tells Naaman that Elisha has changed his mind and would like some gifts. Gehazi returns and hides the gifts.

C. **Gehazi's leprosy** (5:25-27): Elisha tells Gehazi that he knows what happened, and he curses Gehazi and his family with leprosy.

SECTION OUTLINE FOUR (2 KINGS 6–7)
Elisha causes an ax head to float. Elisha blinds the Aramean army and leads them to Samaria. Later, Ben-hadad besieges Samaria and cuts off its food supply. The Lord causes the Aramean army to flee, and four lepers inform the rest of the people about the abandoned supplies.

I. THE BORROWED AX (6:1-7): Elisha's prophets begin building a new meeting place near the Jordan River.

A. **The ax head falls** (6:4-5): As one of the prophets is chopping with a borrowed ax, the ax head falls into the Jordan River.

B. **The ax head floats** (6:6-7): Elisha throws a stick into the river where the ax head fell, and the head floats to the surface for the prophet to retrieve.

II. THE BLINDED ARMY (6:8-23)

A. **The background** (6:8-17)

1. *The revelations to Elisha* (6:8-10): On several occasions Elisha can foresee the king of Aram's plans to attack Israel. The prophet warns the king of Israel about each threat.

2. *The retaliation against Elisha* (6:11-14): The king of Aram learns that it is Elisha who is forewarning the king of Israel, so he sends his army of soldiers to arrest Elisha.

3. *The reassurance by Elisha* (6:15-17)

a. The panic (6:15): When Elisha's servant sees the Aramean army surrounding them, he becomes afraid.

b. The promise (6:16): Elisha reassures his servant that their army is bigger than the Aramean army!

c. The prayer (6:17): Elisha asks the Lord to open his servant's eyes.

d. The protection (6:17): The servant sees a massive army of fiery horses and chariots surrounding them.

B. **The blinding** (6:18-23)

1. *The miracle* (6:18): As the Aramean soldiers advance, Elisha prays for the Lord to blind them, and he does!

2. *The march* (6:19-20): Elisha leads the Arameans to the city of Samaria.

3. *The mercy* (6:21-23): When the king of Israel asks if he should kill the Arameans, Elisha tells him no. He tells the king to feed them and send them home, and the king does so.

III. THE BESIEGED CITY (6:24–7:20): Sometime later, the Arameans besiege Samaria.
   A. **The plight of the people** (6:24-29): Conditions inside Samaria become so terrible that people resort to cannibalism!
   B. **The prejudice of the king** (6:30-33): The king of Israel blames Elisha and the Lord for this terrible situation.
   C. **The prophecy of Elisha** (7:1-2): Elisha makes a twofold prophecy:
      1. *There will be abundant food for the famine-stricken city within 24 hours* (7:1).
      2. *The king's officer who doubted Elisha's first prophecy will not be able to eat any of the food* (7:2).
   D. **The panic of the Arameans** (7:3-11): Four Israelite men with leprosy enter the abandoned camp of the Arameans.
      1. *The desperation* (7:3-4): Since they are starving anyway, four Israelite men with leprosy decide to throw themselves upon the mercy of the Arameans outside Samaria.
      2. *The discovery* (7:5-8): When the men go to the Arameans, they find an abandoned camp still stocked with food, for the Lord had caused the Arameans to flee at the sound of a great army approaching.
      3. *The duty* (7:9-11): The lepers conclude that it is their moral obligation to share the news with Samaria's starving citizens, so they return to the city and tell the gatekeepers.
   E. **The plunder by the people** (7:12-16): After the king of Israel sends out scouts and confirms the discovery, the people rush out and collect the abundant plunder of food and silver. This fulfills Elisha's first prophecy.
   F. **The passing of the officer** (7:17-20): The king assigns the officer who scoffed at Elisha's words to control the traffic at the gate, but he is trampled to death in the rush, fulfilling Elisha's second prophecy.

SECTION OUTLINE FIVE   (2 KINGS 8)

The woman from Shunem tells the king of Israel about Elisha's deeds. Elisha tells Hazael that he will become the next king of Aram, so Hazael kills Ben-hadad and becomes king. Jehoram succeeds Jehoshaphat as king of Judah, and then Ahaziah succeeds Jehoram.

I. THE REMINISCING ABOUT ELISHA (8:1-6): Gehazi and the woman from Shunem tell the king of Israel of Elisha's deeds.
   A. **The relocation** (8:1-2): Elisha had warned the woman from Shunem about a seven-year famine, so she and her family had lived in Philistia.
   B. **The return** (8:3): When the famine is over, the woman returns to Israel and approaches the king to get her house and land back.
   C. **The restoration** (8:4-6): As the woman enters the palace, Gehazi

is telling the king about the time Elisha raised the woman's son from the dead. When Gehazi points out the woman, the king directs his officials to restore everything she had lost.

II. THE REGICIDE OF BEN-HADAD (8:7-15): Ben-Hadad, king of Aram, is sick and sends his officer Hazael to ask Elisha if he will recover.
   A. **The fatal sickness of Ben-hadad** (8:7-10): Elisha tells Hazael that his master will die.
   B. **The fearful reign of Hazael** (8:11-15): Elisha also tells Hazael that he will become king and commit many terrible acts against the people of Israel. The next day Hazael kills Ben-hadad and becomes king of Aram.

III. THE RULERS OF JUDAH (8:16-29)
   A. **Jehoram, Judah's fifth ruler** (8:16-24)
      1. *The elevation to power* (8:16-17): Jehoram succeeds Jehoshaphat as king of Judah.
      2. *The evil wife* (8:18): Jehoram is as evil as King Ahab, because he marries Athaliah, one of Ahab's daughters.
      3. *The everlasting covenant* (8:19): Despite Jehoram's wickedness, the Lord continues to honor his covenant regarding David's dynasty.
      4. *The Edomite war* (8:20-22): Jehoram is unable to put down the Edomite revolt against his kingdom.
      5. *The end of Jehoram* (8:23-24): Jehoram's death is recorded.
   B. **Ahaziah, Judah's sixth ruler** (8:25-29): Ahaziah succeeds his father Jehoram as king of Judah.
      1. *The wicked mother* (8:26-27): Ahaziah's mother is the cruel and corrupt Athaliah, a granddaughter of King Omri.
      2. *The wounded monarch* (8:28-29): King Ahaziah joins King Joram in a war against King Hazael of Aram. When Joram is wounded in battle, Ahaziah visits him.

SECTION OUTLINE SIX (2 KINGS 9-10)
Jehu is anointed king of Israel and kills King Joram and King Ahaziah. Jezebel is thrown to her death and eaten by dogs. Jehu kills all of Ahab's relatives and many from Ahaziah's family as well. Jehu kills many priests of Baal. Jehu dies after reigning 28 years.

I. THE ANOINTING OF JEHU (9:1-13)
   A. **The prophet** (9:1-6): Elisha instructs one of his young prophets to go to Ramoth-gilead and anoint Jehu as Israel's tenth ruler.
   B. **The prophecies** (9:7-10): After the young prophet anoints Jehu, he foretells of the destruction of Ahab's family.
   C. **The proclamation** (9:11-13): When Jehu tells his fellow officers what happened, they blow a trumpet and acknowledge him as king.

II. THE ATTACKS BY JEHU (9:14–10:29): Jehu kills Joram, Ahaziah, and their families, making him one of the bloodiest men in the Bible.
  A. **He kills King Joram of Israel** (9:14-26)
    1. *Where Joram is killed* (9:14-20): King Joram is in Jezreel, recovering from a wound suffered in battle.
    2. *How Joram is killed* (9:21-26): Jehu shoots King Joram between the shoulders, and the arrow pierces his heart. King Joram dies in his chariot.
  B. **He kills King Ahaziah of Judah** (9:27-29): When King Ahaziah sees what happened to King Joram, he flees in his chariot. But he is fatally shot in his chariot too.
  C. **He kills Jezebel** (9:30-37)
    1. *Her sarcasm* (9:30-33): When Jehu enters the gate of the palace at Jezreel, Jezebel calls him a murderer. Jehu tells her eunuchs to throw her from the window, which they do.
    2. *Her skull* (9:34-37): Wild dogs eat Jezebel's body, leaving only her skull, feet, and hands!
  D. **He kills Ahab's family** (10:1-11, 15-17)
    1. *The dare made by Jehu* (10:1-3): Jehu forewarns the people of Samaria that he will attack whichever of Ahab's sons is declared king.
    2. *The decapitation performed by the people* (10:4-8): The frightened people ask what Jehu wants them to do. Jehu instructs them to bring him the heads of Ahab's 70 sons, which they do.
    3. *The destruction unleashed on the rest* (10:9-11, 15-17): Jehu destroys the rest of Ahab's family and associates.
  E. **He kills Ahaziah's family** (10:12-14): As Jehu travels to Samaria to finish killing Ahab's relatives, he meets King Ahaziah's relatives and kills them all.
  F. **He kills the priests of Baal** (10:18-28)
    1. *The deception* (10:18-24): Jehu pretends that he wants to worship Baal and assembles all the priests of Baal in their own temple.
    2. *The destruction* (10:25-28): Jehu orders all the priests to be killed, and he destroys the temple of Baal.

III. THE ASSURANCE TO JEHU (10:29-30): Despite his failure to remove the gold calves at Bethel and Dan, the Lord commends Jehu for destroying Ahab's family. The Lord promises that Jehu's descendants will be kings to the fourth generation.

IV. THE APOSTASY OF JEHU (10:31-36)
  A. **His paganism** (10:31): Jehu continues to practice idolatry and disobey the law of the Lord.
  B. **His punishment** (10:32-33): The Lord allows King Hazael to con-

quer land east of the Jordan River that belonged to Israel's 2¹/₂ tribes.

C. His passing (10:34-36): Jehu dies after reigning for 28 years.

SECTION OUTLINE SEVEN (2 KINGS 11–12)
Athaliah becomes queen of Judah and destroys all the royal family except Joash, who is hidden in the Temple. A priest arranges for Athaliah's death and declares Joash king. Joash repairs the Temple but uses its treasures to pay off King Hazael so he wouldn't attack Jerusalem. His own officers assassinate him.

I. ATHALIAH, JUDAH'S SEVENTH RULER (11:1-18)
   A. The evil queen (11:1-3)
      1. *The ones she murders* (11:1): Athaliah tries to kill the entire royal family to secure her reign over Judah.
      2. *The one she misses* (11:2-3): Joash, infant grandson of Athaliah, is hidden in the Temple and raised there.
   B. The executed queen (11:4-18)
      1. *The priest* (11:4): After six years, Jehoiada the priest prepares to remove Athaliah as queen.
      2. *The plan* (11:5-16)
         a. Regarding Joash (11:5-12): Jehoiada presents him to the people and proclaims him Judah's king.
         b. Regarding Athaliah (11:13-16): She is taken out of the Temple and killed.
      3. *The pact* (11:17-18): Following the queen's death, Jehoiada makes covenants between the Lord, the king, and the people, and they destroy the idols of Baal.

II. JOASH, JUDAH'S EIGHTH RULER (11:19–12:21)
   A. The ascension of Joash (11:19-21): Seven-year-old Joash is led into the palace and takes his place as the new king of Judah.
   B. The activities of Joash (12:1-18)
      1. *Joash and the Temple money* (12:1-16)
         a. The command (12:1-5): Joash instructs the priests to begin much-needed repairs on the Temple.
         b. The concern (12:6-8): Years later, the king is upset when he learns that the priests still have not repaired the Temple.
         c. The chest (12:9-16): To finance the Temple repairs, Jehoiada bores a hole in the lid of a large chest and sets it beside the Temple entrance to receive money for repairs.
      2. *Joash and the tribute money* (12:17-18): When King Hazael of Aram attacks Jerusalem, King Joash pays him off with money and valuables taken from the Temple and the palace.
   C. The assassination of Joash (12:19-21): King Joash is assassinated by his own officers.

SECTION OUTLINE EIGHT (2 KINGS 13–14)
The reigns of Jehoahaz and Jehoash are recorded. Elisha makes a final
prophecy of victory over Aram. Elisha dies, and a man is revived from
the dead when his body touches Elisha's bones. Jehoash defeats Aram
three times. The reigns of Amaziah and Jeroboam II are recorded.

I. THE REIGNS OF FOUR MONARCHS (13:1-19, 22-25; 14:1-29)
   A. **Jehoahaz, Israel's eleventh ruler** (13:1-9)
      1. *The rebellion* (13:1-2, 6): Jehoahaz follows the wicked
         example of Jeroboam, Israel's first king.
      2. *The retribution* (13:3-9): Because of the Israelites' sin, the Lord
         allows the Arameans to defeat them. Jehoahaz prays for the
         Lord's help, so the Lord sends a deliverer. But the people
         continue to sin, and the Arameans reduce Jehoahaz's forces to
         a fraction of their original size.
   B. **Jehoash, Israel's twelfth ruler** (13:10-19, 22-25)
      1. *The iniquities against the Lord* (13:10-13): Like many before
         him, Jehoash worships idols. After he dies, Jeroboam II
         becomes king.
      2. *The instructions from the prophet* (13:14-25)
         a. The occasion for the event (13:14-15): The king visits Elisha
            when the prophet is very ill.
         b. The order to the king (13:16-18): Elisha prophesies victory
            for Israel as the king shoots an arrow out the window.
            Elisha orders the king to strike the floor repeatedly with the
            other arrows.
         c. The objection by Elisha (13:19): Elisha is angry that Jehoash
            struck the floor only three times instead of five or six times.
            Now the king will have only three victories over Aram
            instead of total victory.
         d. The ownership of the towns (13:22-25): Because of his
            mercy and his covenant with Abraham, the Lord keeps the
            people of Israel from being completely destroyed, and he
            enables Jehoash to recover some towns from Aram.
   C. **Amaziah, Judah's ninth ruler** (14:1-22)
      1. *His activities* (14:1-14)
         a. On the home front (14:1-6)
            (1) He pleases the Lord (14:1-4).
            (2) He punishes the guilty (14:5): Amaziah executes those
               who assassinated his father, Joash.
            (3) He protects the innocent (14:6): Obeying the law of
               Moses, the king did not kill the children of his father's
               assassins.
         b. On the battle front (14:7-14)
            (1) The war he wins (14:7): Amaziah completely defeats
               the Edomites.
            (2) The war he loses (14:8-14): Amaziah foolishly provokes

a war with Israel. He is captured and forced to pay
heavy tribute to his victors.

    2. *His assassination* (14:15-22): Like his father, Joash, Amaziah is
assassinated by his own people. He is succeeded by his son
Uzziah (also known as Azariah).

  D. Jeroboam II, Israel's thirteenth ruler (14:23-29)

    1. *Jeroboam's sinfulness* (14:23-24): Jeroboam II follows the
wicked example of his predecessor, Jeroboam I.

    2. *The Lord's sovereignty* (14:25-29): The Lord is moved with
compassion for his suffering people and uses this wicked ruler
to accomplish his purposes. Jeroboam II recovers much of
Israel's land that had been occupied by its enemies, just as
Jonah the prophet predicted.

II. THE REVIVAL OF ONE MAN (13:20-21): Sometime after Elisha's death,
a corpse comes back to life when his body is thrown on top of
Elisha's bones!

SECTION OUTLINE NINE   (2 KINGS 15–16)
The reigns of Uzziah, Zechariah, Shallum, Menahem, Pekahiah,
Pekah, Jotham, and Ahaz are recorded.

  I. THE GODLY KINGS (15:1-7, 32-38)

  A. Uzziah, Judah's tenth ruler (15:1-7)

    1. *His longevity* (15:1-3): For the most part, Uzziah does what is
pleasing to the Lord and rules Judah for 52 years.

    2. *His leprosy* (15:4-7): Uzziah allows idolatry to continue in
Judah, and the Lord strikes him with leprosy. Uzziah's son
governs Judah until his father's death.

  B. Jotham, Judah's eleventh ruler (15:32-38)

    1. *His behavior* (15:32-35): Jotham follows the example of his
father by pleasing the Lord while still allowing idolatry in
Judah.

    2. *His building project* (15:35-38): Jotham rebuilds the upper
gate of the Temple.

  II. THE GODLESS KINGS (15:8-31; 16:1-20)

  A. Zechariah, Israel's fourteenth ruler (15:8-12)

    1. *The abomination of Zechariah* (15:8-9): Like his father,
Zechariah worships idols.

    2. *The assassination of Zechariah* (15:10-12): After a reign of
only six months, Zechariah is assassinated.

      a. Who (15:10-11): Shallum murders him and becomes the
next king.

      b. Why (15:12): The Lord allows this to happen in order
to fulfill the words of Jehu the prophet (see 2 Kings
10:30).

B. Shallum, Israel's fifteenth ruler (15:13-15): After a reign of only one month, he is murdered by Menahem.

C. Menahem, Israel's sixteenth ruler (15:16-22)

1. *His brutality* (15:16): When the citizens of a town refuse to surrender to him, Menahem kills all the people and rips open the pregnant women.

2. *His blasphemy* (15:17-18): Menahem does what is evil in the Lord's sight, practicing idolatry like Jeroboam.

3. *His bribery* (15:19-22): When the Assyrians invade Israel, Menahem pays them a massive bribe to secure his reign over Israel.

D. Pekahiah, Israel's seventeenth ruler (15:23-26)

1. *The idolatry* (15:23-24): Pekahiah does what is evil in the Lord's sight, practicing idolatry like those before him.

2. *The insurrection* (15:25-26): After a reign of two years, Pekahiah is assassinated by his military general, Pekah.

E. Pekah, Israel's eighteenth ruler (15:27-31)

1. *The corruption* (15:27-28): Pekah worships idols, just as Jeroboam did.

2. *The captivity* (15:29): The Assyrians conquer several regions of Israel and take the people back to Assyria as captives.

3. *The conspiracy* (15:30-31): Hoshea plots against the king and kills him.

F. Ahaz, Judah's twelfth ruler (16:1-20)

1. *His wickedness* (16:1-4, 10-20): Ahaz sacrifices upon various pagan altars and even offers his own son as a sacrifice. He replaces the old bronze altar, built by Solomon, with one modeled after a pagan altar in Damascus. Ahaz rearranges some of the Temple furnishings.

2. *His war* (16:5-9): Ahaz enters into an alliance with the king of Assyria to stave off an attack by Israel and Aram.

SECTION OUTLINE TEN (2 KINGS 17)

The reign of Hoshea and the fall of Samaria are recorded. The reasons for the Assyrian invasion are given. Foreigners resettle in Israel and combine pagan worship with the worship of the Lord.

I. THE REVOLT BY HOSHEA (17:1-6): Hoshea becomes Israel's nineteenth ruler.

A. The abomination by Hoshea (17:1-2): Hoshea does what is evil in the Lord's sight.

B. The annual tribute to Assyria (17:3): King Shalmaneser of Assyria defeats Hoshea and forces Israel to pay a heavy annual tribute.

C. The attempt at freedom (17:4): Hoshea conspires with the king of Egypt to break free of Assyria's power.

D. The annihilation of Samaria (17:4-6): The king of Assyria hears of Hoshea's plan, so he arrests Hoshea, destroys Samaria, and exiles the people to Assyria.

II. THE REASON FOR THE ASSYRIAN CAPTIVITY (17:7-23): Despite the Lord's many warnings through his prophets, Israel chose to follow the example of Jeroboam, the first king, and practice idolatry.

III. THE RESETTLING FOLLOWING THE ASSYRIAN CAPTIVITY (17:24-41)
   A. **The people** (17:24): People from other conquered nations resettle in Samaria and the surrounding towns.
   B. **The problem** (17:25-26): Because these foreigners do not know how to worship the Lord properly, lions come and kill some of them.
   C. **The priests** (17:27-28): One of the deported Jewish priests is sent back to Israel to teach the people how to worship the Lord.
   D. **The paganism** (17:29-41): The people combine the worship of the Lord with the worship of their false gods. [This is probably the religion of the Samaritan woman at the well with whom Jesus spoke (see John 4:1-42).]

SECTION OUTLINE ELEVEN   (2 KINGS 18–19)
Hezekiah becomes king. Assyria invades Judah, and Sennacherib calls for the people of Jerusalem to surrender. Hezekiah seeks the Lord's help, and the prophet Isaiah sends a message to him from the Lord. The angel of the Lord kills 185,000 Assyrian soldiers, and Sennacherib is killed by his own men.

I. THE PLEASING DEEDS OF HEZEKIAH (18:1-8): Hezekiah becomes Judah's thirteenth ruler.
   A. **His destruction of idolatry** (18:1-4): Hezekiah launches a campaign against idolatry in Israel, destroying the pagan shrines and idols.
   B. **His dependence on the Lord** (18:5-8): Hezekiah trusts in the Lord and obeys him. As a result, the Lord gives him military success. Hezekiah revolts against the king of Assyria by refusing to pay him tribute.

II. THE PROVOCATION BY THE ASSYRIANS (18:9-18)
   A. **The review** (18:9-12): The capture of Samaria by the Assyrians is reviewed.
   B. **The retaliation** (18:13): The Assyrians invade Judah to punish Hezekiah for his revolt.
   C. **The regret** (18:14-18): Hezekiah asks the Assyrian king to forgive him concerning the revolt. Hezekiah strips the Temple of silver and gold to pay off the Assyrians.

III. THE PROPAGANDA OF SENNACHERIB (18:19–19:4, 8-13)
   A. **The forewarning** (18:19-35): The Assyrians surround Jerusalem

and taunt its citizens, promising them swift and severe punishment unless they surrender.

B. The fear (18:36–19:4): Hezekiah's officials report this to the king, and he becomes afraid. He dresses in sackcloth and prays in the Temple. He also asks Isaiah to pray for Judah.

C. The final warning (19:8-13): Sennacherib receives word that he must put down a rebellion in Ethiopa. Before he goes, he warns Hezekiah of the fate of all the nations that have opposed him and says that the same will happen to Judah.

IV. THE PRAYER OF THE KING (19:14-19): In desperation, Hezekiah lays Sennacherib's letter before the Lord and pleads with him to save Jerusalem.

V. THE PROMISES OF THE LORD (19:5-7, 20-34)
   A. First reassurance (19:5-7): The Lord informs Hezekiah through the prophet Isaiah that Jerusalem will be saved and that the Assyrian king will return home and be killed.
   B. Second reassurance (19:20-34): Isaiah sends Hezekiah a message from the Lord regarding Assyria's judgment.
      1. *Sennacherib's pride* (19:20-27): The Lord rebukes Sennacherib for his arrogance and for refusing to acknowledge that it was the Lord who granted him his accomplishments.
      2. *Sennacherib's punishment* (19:28): The Lord promises to bind Sennacherib and send him away from Israel.
      3. *Israel's protection* (19:29-34): The Lord promises to protect Israel, so that in three years they will be able to plant crops and harvest them.

VI. THE PASSING OF EVENTS (19:35-37)
   A. The army (19:35): One night the angel of the Lord kills 185,000 Assyrian troops.
   B. The assassination (19:36-37): Upon his return to Nineveh, Sennacherib is murdered by his own sons.

SECTION OUTLINE TWELVE (2 KINGS 20–21)
The Lord extends Hezekiah's life by 15 years. Hezekiah shows the treasures of the Temple to the Babylonian envoys. The reigns of Manasseh and Amon are recorded.

I. THE END OF HEZEKIAH'S REIGN (20:1-21): This chapter describes the final years of Hezekiah's life.
   A. The sickness (20:1): Hezekiah becomes very ill; Isaiah tells him that the Lord has said he will die.
   B. The supplication (20:2-3): Hezekiah cries out for the Lord to help him.
   C. The salvation (20:4-7)

1. *The Lord's message* (20:4-6): Isaiah tells Hezekiah that the Lord will heal him and he will live 15 more years.
2. *The Lord's medicine* (20:7): Isaiah instructs Hezekiah's servants to make an ointment from figs and spread it over Hezekiah's boil. They do, and Hezekiah recovers.

D. **The sign** (20:8-11): As a sign that Hezekiah will recover, Isaiah tells the king that the shadow on the sundial will move forward or backward, whichever way Hezekiah requests. The king asks that it move backward, which it does.

E. **The stupidity** (20:12-21)
   1. *The flaunting by Hezekiah* (20:12-13): When the king of Babylon sends envoys to visit Hezekiah while he is recovering, Hezekiah welcomes them and shows them all the kingdom's wealth.
   2. *The faulting of Hezekiah* (20:14-21): Isaiah rebukes Hezekiah for doing this and says that someday the Babylonian army will attack Jerusalem to steal Judah's great treasures.

II. THE EVIL OF MANASSEH'S AND AMON'S REIGNS (21:1-26)
   A. **Manasseh, Judah's fourteenth ruler** (21:1-17)
      1. *His perversions against God* (21:1-9, 16)
         a. Manasseh the blasphemer (21:1-5, 7-9): Manasseh practices idolatry and imitates the evil ways of the people whom the Lord drove out of the Promised Land. He sets up pagan altars and idols in the Temple.
         b. Manasseh the butcher (21:6, 16): Manasseh even sacrifices his own son and slaughters his innocent subjects.
      2. *His punishment from God* (21:10-15, 17): The Lord promises to bring disaster on Jerusalem, just as he did to Samaria.
   B. **Amon, Judah's fifteenth ruler** (21:18-26)
      1. *The apostasy by Amon* (21:18-22): Amon practices the same idolatry that his father, Manasseh, practiced.
      2. *The assassination of Amon* (21:23-26): Amon is killed by his own servants, who, in turn, are killed by the people.

SECTION OUTLINE THIRTEEN   (2 KINGS 22–24)
Josiah becomes king and orders repairs made to the Temple. The Book of the Law is discovered. Josiah institutes religious reforms, tearing down pagan shrines and reinstating the Passover celebration. Josiah is killed in battle. The reigns of Jehoahaz, Jehoiakim, Jehoiachin, and Zedekiah are recorded.

I. THE GODLY KING (22:1–23:30): Josiah becomes Judah's sixteenth ruler.
   A. **Doing God's work** (22:1-7): Josiah begins his reign by ordering repairs made to the Temple.

B. Discovering God's Word (22:8-20; 23:1-30): The Book of the
Law (or Book of the Covenant) is found, and it launches a religious revival throughout Judah.
1. *The priest* (22:8-13): Hilkiah the high priest finds the Book of
the Law in the Temple during the repair work. Josiah tells the
priests to find out what will happen because of the people's
disobedience to the law.
2. *The prophecy* (22:14-20): The priests consult the prophet
Huldah, and she tells them about the punishment that the Lord
will bring.
a. Regarding Judah (22:15-17): The city and its people will be
destroyed because of their many sins.
b. Regarding Josiah (22:18-20): Because of Josiah's repentance, the Lord promises to hold off the destruction until
after Josiah's death.
3. *The pledge* (23:1-3): Josiah assembles all the leaders of Judah
at the Temple and reads the Book of the Covenant. The king
renews the covenant. He and the people pledge to obey the
terms of the covenant.
4. *The purge* (23:4-20, 24-25): Josiah launches a campaign to
eradicate idolatry from Judah.
a. He removes all the pagan objects from the Temple (23:4,
6-7).
b. He removes the pagan priests and reinstalls the Lord's
priests (23:5, 8-9).
c. He destroys the pagan shrines and altars (23:10-15, 19-20,
24).
d. He burns the bones of some dead pagan prophets, fulfilling
a prophecy made during Jeroboam's reign (23:16-18; see
1 Kings 13:1-2).
5. *The Passover* (23:21-23): Josiah calls for all the people to
celebrate the Passover once again.
6. *The punishment* (23:25-30): Despite Josiah's reforms, the Lord
carries out his sentence of destruction on the people of Judah,
though it happens many years after Josiah's death (see 2 Kings
25:1-21). Josiah is killed in battle by Pharaoh Neco of Egypt.
II. THE GODLESS KINGS (23:31–24:20)
A. Jehoahaz, Judah's seventeenth ruler (23:31-34)
1. *His perversion* (23:31-32): Jehoahaz does what is evil in the
Lord's sight.
2. *His prison sentence* (23:33-34): Pharaoh Neco imprisons
Jehoahaz, forces Judah to pay a large tribute, and installs
Eliakim (whose name is changed to Jehoiakim) to reign in his
place.
B. Jehoiakim, Judah's eighteenth ruler (23:35–24:7)
1. *The raising of Neco's tribute* (23:35-37): Jehoiakim collects an

income tax to pay the tribute that Pharaoh Neco imposes on
him.

2. *The reign of Nebuchadnezzar* (24:1, 7): King Nebuchadnezzar
of Babylon attacks Judah and imposes another tribute on the
people for three years.

3. *The raiders from nearby lands* (24:2-4): The Lord continues to
punish Judah by allowing Babylonian, Aramean, Moabite, and
Ammonite raiders to harass the people.

4. *The rest of Jehoiakim's reign* (24:5-6): Jehoiakim dies and his
son Jehoiachin becomes the next king.

C. **Jehoiachin, Judah's nineteenth ruler** (24:8-17): During Jehoiachin's reign, Nebuchadnezzar besieges Jerusalem and takes
captive all those with any skill or status—about 10,000 people in
all. Jehoiachin is also taken captive, and his uncle is installed as
king.

D. **Zedekiah, Judah's twentieth ruler** (24:18-20): Zedekiah does evil
in the Lord's sight, so the Lord exiles the people of Jerusalem and
Judah. Zedekiah rebels against Nebuchadnezzar.

SECTION OUTLINE FOURTEEN   (2 KINGS 25)
Nebuchadnezzar overtakes Jerusalem a final time, and the Temple
is destroyed. Gedaliah is appointed governor of Judah but is assassinated. A new king ascends to the Babylonian throne, and he shows
favor to Jehoiachin, releasing him from prison and granting him
living expenses.

I. THE FALL OF JERUSALEM (25:1-21): When Zedekiah rebels against
Nebuchadnezzar, the Babylonians besiege Jerusalem again.

A. **The defeat** (25:1-7): After two years of siege, Jerusalem suffers
severe famine. So Zedekiah and his men flee the city by night,
but they are captured by the Babylonians. Zedekiah is forced to
watch as his sons are killed. Then his eyes are gouged out, and
he is taken to Babylon.

B. **The destruction** (25:8-10, 13-17): The city's walls are pulled
down, and the Temple and all the important buildings are
destroyed. The Temple's valuable furnishings are taken to Babylon.

C. **The deportation** (25:11-12, 18-21): The leading citizens are
exiled to Babylon, and those found hiding in the city are
killed.

II. THE FATE OF GEDALIAH (25:22-26)

A. **The appointment of Gedaliah** (25:22-24): Nebuchadnezzar
appoints Gedaliah as governor over Judah; he promises peace if
the inhabitants submit to the king of Babylon.

B. **The assassination of Gedaliah** (25:25-26): Gedaliah is murdered by a member of the royal family. Many people flee to Egypt, fearing how the king of Babylon will retaliate.

III. THE FAVOR TOWARD JEHOIACHIN (25:27-30): After many years, Evil-Merodach ascends to the Babylonian throne and shows favor toward Jehoiachin. He releases him from prison, supplies him with clothing and food, and provides him with living expenses.

1 Chronicles

III. THE RETURNING EXILES (9:1-34)
   A. **Returnees from assorted tribes** (9:1-9)
   B. **The priests** (9:10-13)
   C. **Other Levites and their duties** (9:14-34)

SECTION OUTLINE TWO (1 CHRONICLES 10–13)
Saul is killed, and David becomes king over all Israel. David captures Jerusalem and makes it his capital. The deeds of David's mighty men are recorded, and Saul's warriors transfer their loyalty to David. David attempts to bring the Ark of God to Jerusalem.

I. THE TRAGEDY OF SAUL (10:1-14): Israel's first king is killed in a battle with the Philistines.
   A. **The record of Saul's death** (10:1-12)
      1. *The actions of the battle* (10:1-6)
         a. The slaughter (10:1-3): The Philistines attack Israel; three of Saul's sons are killed on Mount Gilboa.
         b. The suicide (10:4-6): After being severely wounded by enemy archers, Saul falls upon his own sword to avoid capture and abuse.
      2. *The aftermath of the battle* (10:7-12)
         a. The routing (10:7): When the Israelites see that Saul is dead, they flee their towns. Philistines then occupy these towns.
         b. The ridicule (10:8-10): The Philistines cut off Saul's head and fasten it to the wall of the temple of Dagon.
         c. The recovery (10:11-12): Some warriors from Jabesh-gilead recover the bodies of Saul and his sons and give them a proper burial.
   B. **The reasons for Saul's death** (10:13-14): Saul was killed because he disobeyed the Lord and even consulted a medium.

II. THE TRIUMPHS OF DAVID (11:1–13:14)
   A. **His coronation** (11:1-3; 12:38-40): All Israel's leaders come to Hebron and anoint David king. The celebration lasts three days.
   B. **His city** (11:4-9): David captures Jerusalem and makes it his capital.
   C. **His champions** (11:10-47; 12:1-37): David's warriors are listed:
      1. *The mightiest* (11:10-19): These are the leaders of David's men.
      2. *The mighty* (11:20-47): Thirty of David's best warriors are listed.
      3. *The masses* (12:1-22): Those who defect to David from Saul's forces are listed.
      4. *The muster* (12:23-37): Over 300,000 warriors come to David's coronation at Hebron.

D. His challenge (13:1-14): David calls for the Israelites to bring the Ark of God to Jerusalem.
   1. *The consent* (13:1-6): Israel's leaders agree to join David in bringing the Ark to Jerusalem.
   2. *The celebration* (13:7-8): There is great joy among those who see the Ark.
   3. *The crisis* (13:9-11): When Uzzah reaches out to steady the Ark, the Lord strikes him dead.
   4. *The concern* (13:12-14): This incident makes David afraid to bring the Ark into Jerusalem, so he leaves it with Obed-edom for three months.

SECTION OUTLINE THREE (1 CHRONICLES 14–15)
David's power increases, and he defeats the Philistines. He brings the Ark to Jerusalem in proper fashion. There is great joy and rejoicing as the Ark enters Jerusalem, but David's wife Michal despises David for dancing joyfully before the Ark.

I. THE ANOINTED OF GOD (14:1-17)
   A. David's fame (14:1-2, 17): The Lord continues to exalt David for the sake of his people Israel.
   B. David's family (14:3-7): Thirteen of David's sons are listed, including Nathan and Solomon.
   C. David's foes (14:8-16): Twice David defeats the Philistines near the valley of Rephaim.
      1. *First occasion* (14:8-12)
         a. The assurance (14:8-10): The Lord promises David victory.
         b. The action (14:11-12): David's men burst through the enemies' line like a raging flood, so David names the place Baal-perazim (meaning "the Lord who bursts through").
      2. *Second occasion* (14:13-16)
         a. The assurance (14:13-15): Once again the Lord promises David victory. He tells him to circle around behind the Philistines and wait for the sound of marching feet in the trees.
         b. The action (14:16): This time David's victory is even greater and more extensive than the first.
II. THE ARK OF GOD (15:1-29): David prepares to bring the Ark of God from the house of Obed-edom to Jerusalem.
   A. The qualification (15:1-10): Only the Levites would be allowed the carry the Ark.
   B. The sanctification (15:11-14): David instructs the Levites to purify themselves in preparation for carrying the Ark.
   C. The transportation (15:15): The Levites carry the Ark on their shoulders with its carrying poles.

D. **The celebration** (15:16-28): The Ark arrives in Jerusalem accompanied by music, singing, dancing, and sacrificing!

E. **The condemnation** (15:29): David's wife Michal is filled with contempt when David dances and leaps for joy before the Ark.

SECTION OUTLINE FOUR (1 CHRONICLES 16–17)
David appoints several Levites to lead the people in worship and gives them a song of thanksgiving. David gives other assignments regarding worship. The Lord makes a covenant with David, promising to establish David's dynasty forever. David offers a prayer of thanks for the covenant.

I. THE PREFACE (16:1-6, 37-43)

A. **David blesses the people** (16:1-3): After the Ark is brought into its special tent, David blesses the people and gives them a gift of food.

B. **David bestows responsibilities** (16:4-6, 37-43): David assigns the Levites various responsibilities for leading worship.

II. THE PSALM OF PRAISE (16:7-36): David gives Asaph and the other Levites a song of thanksgiving.

A. **The explanation** (16:7-22): The Lord has been faithful to the promise he made to Abraham to give him and his descendants the land of Canaan forever.

B. **The exhortation** (16:23-36): David calls for the whole earth to recognize the glory of the Lord.

III. THE PROPHECY OF NATHAN (17:1-15): When David settles into his new palace, he speaks with the prophet Nathan.

A. **David plans to build a house for God** (17:1-6)
   1. *The reason* (17:1-2): David tells Nathan that he does not feel right living in a palace while the Ark is in a tent.
   2. *The rejection* (17:3-6): The Lord tells Nathan to inform David that David is not the one to build a temple for him.

B. **The Lord promises to build a house for David** (17:7-15)
   1. *David's past blessings* (17:7-8): The Lord selected David to lead Israel and protected him in battle.
   2. *David's present blessings* (17:9): The Lord has placed his people in a secure land.
   3. *David's future blessings* (17:10-15): The Lord promises to establish the throne of David's son Solomon. He also promises that David's dynasty will never end. This promise is fulfilled by Jesus Christ (see Luke 1:30-33).

IV. THE PRAYER OF DAVID (17:16-27): David offers a prayer of thanksgiving for the Lord's gracious covenant with him. He humbly acknowledges his total unworthiness and worships the Lord for all his blessings.

SECTION OUTLINE FIVE (1 CHRONICLES 18–21)
David's many military victories are recorded, including his defeat of
the Ammonites and the Philistines. He takes a census of the Israelites,
displeasing God; David chooses three days of plague throughout the
land as his punishment. When the Lord ends the plague, David builds
an altar on the threshing floor of Araunah.

I. THE CAMPAIGNS OF DAVID (18:1–20:8)
  A. **Against the Moabites** (18:2): David conquers the Moabites and
     forces them to pay tribute money.
  B. **Against the king of Zobah** (18:3-4): David conquers King
     Hadadezer of Zobah and cripples many of the chariot horses.
  C. **Against the Arameans** (18:5-11): David conquers the Arameans
     as they attempt to help King Hadadezer. He forces them to pay
     tribute money and receives vast amounts of gold, silver, and
     bronze.
  D. **Against the Edomites** (18:12-13): David destroys 18,000 Edomite
     forces in the Valley of Salt and stations garrisons throughout
     Edom.
  E. **Against the Ammonites** (19:1–20:3)
     1. *David the diplomat* (19:1-5)
        a. The sympathy (19:1-2): David sends a delegation to express
           his sympathy regarding the death of King Hanun's father,
           who had been loyal to David.
        b. The shame (19:3-5): Hanun foolishly thinks the ambassa-
           dors are spies and publicly humiliates them.
     2. *David the destroyer* (19:6–20:3)
        a. David's anger (19:6-17): An angry David quickly mobilizes
           his army.
        b. David's attacks (19:17–20:3): David's forces attack and
           completely rout the armies of Hanun and his ally, the
           Arameans. The following spring, David captures the key
           Ammonite city of Rabbah.
  F. **Against the Philistines** (18:1; 20:4-8)
     1. *First battle* (18:1): David captures Gath, one of the key
        Philistine cities.
     2. *Other battles* (20:4-8): During these confrontations, David and
        his warriors kill several of the notorious Philistine giants.

II. THE COURT OF DAVID (18:14-17): David's officials are listed.

III. THE CENSUS OF DAVID (21:1-30)
  A. **The prompting** (21:1-2): Satan leads David to take a census of
     the Israelites.
  B. **The protest** (21:3-6): Joab objects, but David insists, so Joab
     completes the census and reports the numbers to David.
  C. **The problem** (21:7): The Lord is displeased with David's actions.
  D. **The pleading** (21:8-13): Realizing his sin, David begs the Lord to

forgive him. The Lord offers David a choice between three pun-
ishments.
  E. **The punishment** (21:14): The Lord sends a plague, killing 70,000
     people throughout Israel.
  F. **The pardon** (21:15-17): The Lord forgives David, and at the
     threshing floor of Araunah, he stops the death angel from
     destroying Jerusalem.
  G. **The purchase** (21:18-30): At the Lord's command, David buys
     the threshing floor of Araunah and builds an altar there. After
     this, the plague is stopped.

SECTION OUTLINE SIX (1 CHRONICLES 22–27)
David gathers materials to build the Temple and charges Solomon
to complete the task since David is not the one chosen to build it.
David effectively organizes the religious, military, and political life
of the nation, assigning various duties to individuals and families.

  I. DAVID'S PREPARATIONS (22:1-19): David makes preparations for the
     Temple to be built.
     A. **The collection** (22:1-5): David begins to stockpile materials so
        that his son Solomon can build a magnificent temple for the
        Lord.
     B. **The charge** (22:6-19): David gives a charge to all who will take
        part in building the Temple, encouraging them to be diligent.
        1. *To Solomon* (22:6-16)
           a. The explanation (22:6-10): David explains why he cannot
              build the Temple himself. He has shed much blood, so the
              task will fall to his son, a man of peace.
           b. The exhortation (22:11-16): David encourages Solomon to
              obey the Lord and build a magnificent temple for him.
        2. *To Israel's leaders* (22:17-19): David orders them to seek the
           Lord with all their heart!
  II. DAVID'S PERSONNEL (23:1–27:34): David assigns the many tasks of
      the kingdom to various individuals and families.
      A. **The Levites** (23:1-32; 24:20-31; 25:1–26:32)
         1. *The counting* (23:1-3): A census reveals 38,000 Levites who
            are 30 years old or older.
         2. *The categorizing* (23:6-23; 24:20-31): David divides the
            Levites into three groups, separating them according to their
            ancestry and placing leaders over them.
            a. The Gershonites (23:7-11)
            b. The Kohathites (23:12-20)
            c. The Merarites (23:21-23)
         3. *The commissioning* (23:4-5, 24-32; 25:1–26:32): David
            assigns the Levites their various tasks.

  a. The musicians (25:1-31): Asaph, Heman, and Jeduthun are appointed as the leaders of the musicians, who are their descendants.

  b. The gatekeepers (26:1-19): The sons of Korah, Obed-edom, Hosah, and Shuppim are appointed as the gatekeepers of the house of the Lord.

  c. The treasurers and other officials (26:20-32): David assigns several of the Levites and their families to serve as treasurers and public administrators.

B. The priests (24:1-19): The descendants of Aaron, who are also Levites, are appointed various responsibilities by sacred lots. They are in charge of the rest of the Levites who serve at the Temple.

C. The military (27:1-15): David divides his army into 12 divisions, each with 24,000 troops, and assigns commanders over them. Each division is called up for active duty one month per year.

D. The officials (27:16-34): Other leaders are listed, including the leaders of each tribe, the overseers of David's property, and David's advisers.

SECTION OUTLINE SEVEN (1 CHRONICLES 28–29)

David delivers his farewell address, instructing both the people and Solomon. David gives Solomon the plans for the Temple, including a list of all the materials he has collected for it. David praises the Lord before all the people. The people crown Solomon as king, and David dies.

I. THE FINAL DAYS OF DAVID (28:1–29:20, 26-30): David makes one final speech regarding the building of the Temple.

 A. The clarification (28:1-7): David explains why he is not the one chosen to build the Temple and why his son Solomon is.

 B. The challenge (28:8-10): David challenges Solomon and the people to obey the Lord, and he urges Solomon to begin building the Temple.

 C. The contributions (28:11–29:9): David gives Solomon the plans for the Temple, including a catalog of the materials he has collected for it.

  1. *The details* (28:11-21): David gives Solomon specific details he has received from the Lord regarding the Temple.

  2. *The donations* (29:1-9)

   a. From David (29:1-5): David collects hundreds of tons of gold, silver, bronze, iron, wood, onyx, jewels, and marble for the Temple.

   b. From the people (29:6-9): The people of Israel give thousands of tons of gold, silver, bronze, iron, and jewelry for the Temple.

    D. The consecration (29:10-20): David stands before the people
and offers a dedicatory prayer for the materials.
      1. *David praises the Lord* (29:10-18).
        a. He testifies to God's glory (29:10-13).
        b. He testifies to God's grace (29:14-18).
      2. *David petitions the Lord* (29:19-20): David asks the Lord to
give Solomon a heart that is completely dedicated to him.
    E. The conclusion (29:26-30): After a fruitful reign of 40 years
(7 in Hebron and 33 in Jerusalem), David dies.

II. THE FIRST DAYS OF SOLOMON (29:21-25): Shortly after David's
dedicatory prayer, Solomon is anointed as Israel's next king, and
Zadok is anointed as Israel's priest.

2 Chronicles

SECTION OUTLINE ONE (2 CHRONICLES 1–5)
When Solomon requests wisdom, God grants it, along with riches
and honor. He acquires builders and materials for the Temple and
then builds it. The Ark is brought into the completed Temple, and
the presence of the Lord fills the Temple.

I. SOLOMON'S GREAT WISDOM FROM GOD (1:1-17)
   A. **The background** (1:1-5): Solomon summons Israel's leaders to
      Gibeon, where the Tabernacle is located.
   B. **The burnt offerings** (1:6): Solomon sacrifices 1,000 burnt offer-
      ings on the bronze altar.
   C. **The blessing** (1:7-17)
      1. *The announcement* (1:7): In a dream God promises to give
         Solomon anything he desires.
      2. *The answer* (1:8-10): Solomon asks for wisdom so that he
         might properly lead and govern Israel.
      3. *The approval* (1:11-12): God is pleased with Solomon's
         request and grants it, along with riches and honor.
      4. *The acquisition* (1:13-17): Just as God promised, Solomon
         acquires great prestige and wealth (see also 8:1-10, 17-18;
         9:10-11, 13-28).

II. SOLOMON'S GREAT WORK FOR GOD (2:1–5:14): Solomon builds the
    Temple and brings the Ark into it.
    A. **Arranging for the work** (2:1-18)
       1. *The resources* (2:1-2, 17-18): Solomon enlists a workforce of
          70,000 common laborers, 80,000 stonecutters, and 3,600
          foremen.
       2. *The request* (2:3-10): Solomon asks King Hiram of Tyre to
          provide the materials necessary to build the Temple.
          a. What he needs (2:3, 7-10): Solomon asks King Hiram for a
             master craftsman, a dyeing expert, and a skilled engraver.
             Solomon also wants cedar, cypress, and almug logs from
             Lebanon. Solomon offers payment of grain, wine, and olive
             oil.
          b. Why he needs it (2:4-6): The Temple will serve as a

worship center, allowing Israel to honor the Lord by burning incense and sacrificing animals.

3. *The reply* (2:11-16): King Hiram praises Solomon and agrees
to fulfill his request.

   a. The praise (2:11-12): Hiram commends Solomon for his
wisdom and skill.

   b. The promise (2:13-16): Hiram promises to send Huram-abi,
a master craftsman, dyer, and skilled engraver, to work
with Solomon's craftsmen. Hiram also promises to send the
timber that Solomon requested.

B. Assembling the Temple (3:1–4:22)

1. *The facts* (3:1-2): The Temple is built on Mount Moriah, where
Araunah's threshing floor is. Solomon begins construction in
the spring of the fourth year of his reign.

2. *The furnishings* (3:3–4:22)

   a. Foundation and foyer (3:3-4)

   b. Main room (3:5-7)

   c. Most Holy Place (3:8-13)

   d. Curtain (3:14)

   e. Two pillars (3:15-17)

   f. Bronze altar (4:1)

   g. Bronze Sea (4:2-5, 10)

   h. Ten basins (4:6)

   i. Ten lampstands (4:7)

   j. Ten tables and 100 gold basins (4:8)

   k. Courtyard for the priests (4:9)

   l. Articles made of bronze (4:11-18)

   m. Articles made of gold (4:19-22)

C. Acquiring the Ark (5:1-14)

1. *The accessories* (5:1): After the Temple is completed, Solomon
brings in the gifts dedicated by his father, David, and stores
them in the Temple treasuries.

2. *The Ark* (5:2-14): Finally, the Ark of God is brought into the
Temple.

   a. The carriers (5:2-10): The Levites and priests carry the Ark
into the Most Holy Place.

   b. The celebration (5:11-13): The Levites play music and sing
praises to the Lord.

   c. The cloud (5:13-14): The presence of the Lord fills the
Temple.

SECTION OUTLINE TWO   (2 CHRONICLES 6–7)
Solomon addresses the assembled people. Then he stands on a
specially built platform and prays to the Lord. Fire comes down from
heaven and burns up the offerings. The Israelites celebrate the Festival
of Shelters for seven days. The Lord responds to Solomon's prayer.

I. THE DEDICATION BY SOLOMON (6:1–7:10): Solomon addresses the
people who have assembled to see the Ark placed in the Temple.
  A. **Solomon's sermon** (6:1-11): Solomon mentions three points, all
  relating to the Temple.
    1. *Where the Temple is built* (6:1-6): The Lord had told David
    that the Temple would be constructed in Jerusalem.
    2. *Who was selected to build it* (6:7-10): David wanted to
    construct the Temple, but the Lord had chosen Solomon to do
    it.
    3. *Why the Temple was built* (6:11): The Temple was built to
    honor the Lord and house the Ark of God.
  B. **Solomon's supplication** (6:12-42)
    1. *His position* (6:12): Solomon spreads out his hands toward
    heaven.
    2. *His platform* (6:13): Solomon is on a bronze platform 7½ feet
    square and 4½ feet high.
    3. *His praise* (6:14-15): Solomon worships the Lord, Israel's
    unique and faithful God.
    4. *His petitions* (6:16-39)
      a. He prays for himself (6:16-21): Solomon calls on the Lord
      to hear his prayers in the Temple.
      b. He prays for his subjects concerning (6:22-39):
        (1) The innocent (6:22-23)
        (2) Defeat due to sin (6:24-25)
        (3) Famine due to sin (6:26-31)
        (4) Foreigners (6:32-33)
        (5) Israel's battles (6:34-35)
        (6) Israel's captivity (6:36-39)
    5. *His plea* (6:40-42): Solomon asks the Lord to dwell in the
    Temple, where the Ark resides, to clothe the priests with
    salvation, to cause the people to rejoice in his goodness, and
    to be faithful to the king.
  C. **Solomon's sign** (7:1-3): When Solomon finishes praying, fire
  comes down from heaven and burns up the sacrifices, and the
  Lord's glory fills the Temple.
  D. **Solomon's sacrifices** (7:4-10): Solomon and his people offer
  22,000 oxen and 120,000 sheep; then they celebrate the Festival
  of Shelters for seven days.

II. THE REVELATION TO SOLOMON (7:11-22): The Lord appears to
Solomon, reassuring him that his prayer has been heard. He tells

Solomon that he will punish his people for sin but also that he will forgive them if they repent and turn to him.
A. **Sin plus repentance equals restoration** (7:11-18).
B. **Sin minus repentance equals rejection** (7:19-22).

SECTION OUTLINE THREE (2 CHRONICLES 8–9)
Solomon's achievements are reviewed. The queen of Sheba visits Solomon and commends him for his wisdom. Solomon's wealth and splendor are summarized. Solomon reigned 40 years before he died.

I. SOLOMON'S RESOURCEFULNESS (8:1-18): Solomon accomplishes many great feats during his reign.
A. **Solomon the builder** (8:1-10): Solomon builds and fortifies dozens of cities and supply centers throughout his kingdom.
B. **Solomon the husband** (8:11): Solomon moves his wife, Pharaoh's daughter, from the City of David to a new palace he built for her.
C. **Solomon the religious leader** (8:12-16): Solomon carefully observes the religious festivals and assigns the priests their duties.
D. **Solomon the merchant** (8:17-18): Solomon has a fleet of ships on the Red Sea. These ships bring back almost 17 tons of gold from the land of Ophir!

II. SOLOMON'S REPUTATION (9:1-9, 12, 23-24): Solomon's reputation as a wise and capable ruler spreads throughout the nations.
A. **The queen of Sheba** (9:1-9, 12): The queen of Sheba hears of Solomon's wisdom and travels to Jerusalem to meet him.
1. *The purpose* (9:1-8): The queen tests Solomon to see if he is truly as wise as she has heard.
a. Solomon answers her (9:1-2): Solomon wisely answers all of the queen's questions.
b. Solomon amazes her (9:3-8): The queen is completely amazed by Solomon's wisdom and orderly reign.
2. *The presents* (9:9, 12): Solomon and the queen exchange gifts.
a. Her gifts to him (9:9): The queen gives Solomon great quantities of gold, spices, and jewels.
b. His gifts to her (9:12): Solomon gives the queen gifts that are even more valuable than those she gave him.
B. **The kings of the earth** (9:23-24): Kings from many nations visit Solomon and bring him valuable gifts.

III. SOLOMON'S RICHES (9:10-11, 13-22, 25, 27-28)
A. **His gold** (9:13-20): Solomon receives over 25 tons of gold each year! He makes 500 shields of hammered gold and overlays his ivory throne with gold. All his household articles are made of gold.
B. **His horses** (9:25, 28): Solomon owns 4,000 stalls for his many horses.

C. **His other riches** (9:10-11, 21-22, 27): Solomon also imports silver, ivory, apes, peacocks, and cedarwood.

IV. SOLOMON'S REIGN (9:26): Solomon's kingdom extends from the Euphrates River to the land of the Philistines and the border of Egypt!

V. SOLOMON'S REST (9:29-31): Solomon dies after ruling for 40 years.

SECTION OUTLINE FOUR   (2 CHRONICLES 10–12)
Rehoboam becomes king and threatens to rule harshly. After the northern tribes revolt, a prophet warns Rehoboam not to fight against them. Many Levites from the northern kingdom flee to Judah. When Judah is invaded by Egypt, the leaders repent. Rehoboam dies after an evil reign.

I. THE DIVISION OF THE KINGDOM (10:1-19)
   A. **The request to Rehoboam, Judah's first ruler** (10:1-11): Rehoboam succeeds his father, Solomon, as king of all Israel.
      1. *Jeroboam's complaint* (10:1-5): Jeroboam, who had fled to Egypt to escape Solomon after a prophet had predicted that he would reign over the 10 northern tribes, returns to act as a spokesman for the tribes. He and the leaders demand that Rehoboam treat them better than Solomon did.
      2. *Rehoboam's conference* (10:6-11): Rehoboam asks two groups of advisers what he should do.
         a. The wise advice of the older men (10:6-7): The older men who had been Solomon's advisers tell Rehoboam to treat his people with kindness.
         b. The wicked advice of the younger men (10:8-11): Rehoboam's boyhood friends tell him to deal with the people even more harshly than his father did!
   B. **The refusal by Rehoboam** (10:12-15): Rehoboam listens to the younger men and warns the people that he will be even harsher than Solomon was.
   C. **The revolt against Rehoboam** (10:16-19): Upon hearing this, the 10 northern tribes revolt and establish their own kingdom (Israel) with Jeroboam as their new ruler.

II. THE DETAILS OF REHOBOAM'S REIGN (11:1-23)
   A. **The restraint** (11:1-4): Heeding the Lord's message to him through the prophet Shemaiah, Rehoboam calls off his planned attack against the northern tribes.
   B. **The reinforcement** (11:5-12): Rehoboam rebuilds and strengthens key cities throughout Judah, including Bethlehem and Hebron.
   C. **The refugees** (11:13-17): Because of Jeroboam's idolatry and wickedness, many Levites flee the northern kingdom and settle in Jerusalem.

    D. The relationships (11:18-23): Rehoboam marries 18 wives and has 60 concubines, from whom come 28 sons and 60 daughters.

III. THE DESPOILING BY EGYPT (12:1-12)
    A. The rebellion (12:1): Once Rehoboam becomes strong, he abandons the law of the Lord, and all the people follow him.
    B. The retribution (12:2-5): Because of the people's rebellion, the Lord allows King Shishak of Egypt to conquer Judah's fortified cities and attack Jerusalem.
    C. The repentance (12:6): Rehoboam and the people humble themselves and confess their sin.
    D. The result (12:7-12): The Lord spares Jerusalem, but he allows Shishak to take all the treasures of the palace.

IV. THE DEEDS OF REHOBOAM (12:13-16): Rehoboam's reign is reviewed and declared evil. Rehoboam dies.

SECTION OUTLINE FIVE   (2 CHRONICLES 13–16)
Abijah succeeds Rehoboam and defeats Jeroboam's forces. Asa succeeds Abijah and removes pagan shrines from Judah. He defeats the Ethiopians and leads the people to recommit themselves to the Lord. Asa bribes the king of Aram to act as his ally, but a prophet rebukes Asa for this. Asa dies.

I. ABIJAH, JUDAH'S SECOND RULER (13:1-22)
    A. The fighter (13:1-20): Abijah becomes involved in a war with Jeroboam of Israel.
      1. *The armies* (13:1-3): Abijah's army is outnumbered two to one (800,000 troops to 400,000).
      2. *The address* (13:4-12): Before the battle, Abijah makes an impassioned speech.
        a. He condemns Jeroboam (13:4-9): Abijah recounts how Jeroboam led the northern tribes to rebel against the house of David.
        b. He cautions Jeroboam's troops (13:10-12): Abijah notes that his people have not abandoned the Lord and warns the northern tribes not to fight against the Lord by fighting the people of Judah.
      3. *The ambush* (13:13): During Abijah's the speech, Jeroboam's army secretly surrounds Abijah's army.
      4. *The alarm* (13:14): Judah's soldiers cry out to the Lord for help.
      5. *The attack* (13:15-20): The Lord answers and enables the forces of Judah to completely rout the forces of Israel.
    B. The father (13:21-22): Abijah marries 14 wives and fathers 22 sons and 16 daughters.

II. ASA, JUDAH'S THIRD RULER (14:1–16:14)
   A. **Asa's service** (14:1-8; 15:1-19)
      1. *The reforms* (14:1-5; 15:1-19): Asa destroys the pagan altars and shrines. Following a message from the Lord through the prophet Azariah, Asa continues his reforms, even deposing his own grandmother for her idolatrous practices. He leads the people to recommit themselves to follow the Lord.
      2. *The rebuilding* (14:6-8): Asa rebuilds and fortifies some of Judah's towns, and he amasses an army of 580,000 men!
   B. **Asa's salvation** (14:9-15): The Lord rescues Asa and his army from total destruction.
      1. *The danger* (14:9-10): The Ethiopians attack Judah with an enormous army.
      2. *The dependence* (14:11): Asa cries out to the Lord for help.
      3. *The deliverance* (14:12-15): The Lord enables the army of Judah to triumph over its enemies.
   C. **Asa's sins** (16:1-14)
      1. *The treachery* (16:1-10)
         a. The partnership (16:1-6): When King Baasha of Israel invades Judah, Asa bribes the king of Aram to break his ties with Baasha and attack him.
         b. The prophet (16:7-10): A prophet named Hanani rebukes Asa for depending on the king of Aram instead of the Lord. Asa becomes angry with Hanani and imprisons him.
      2. *The tragedy* (16:11-14): Asa develops a serious foot disease but still refuses to turn to the Lord for help, so he dies.

SECTION OUTLINE SIX (2 CHRONICLES 17–18)
Jehoshaphat succeeds Asa and strengthens Judah. He sends out officials to teach the Book of the Law. Later Jehoshaphat makes an alliance with King Ahab of Israel and attacks Ramoth-gilead despite the warnings of the prophet Micaiah. Ahab disguises himself in battle, but he is still killed.

I. THE GOOD DEEDS OF JEHOSHAPHAT, JUDAH'S FOURTH RULER (17:1-19)
   A. **His reinforcements** (17:1-2): Jehoshaphat stations troops in the lands that he controls.
   B. **His reforms** (17:3-4, 6-9): Jehoshaphat follows the Lord and sends out Levites to teach the Book of the Law to the people.
   C. **His rewards** (17:5, 10-19): The Lord honors Jehoshaphat for all his deeds and strengthens Judah.

II. THE GRIEVOUS DEEDS OF JEHOSHAPHAT (18:1-34)
   A. **His marital compromise** (18:1): Jehoshaphat arranges for his son to marry the daughter of wicked King Ahab of Israel.

B. His military compromise (18:2-34): Jehoshaphat unwisely joins with King Ahab to fight against Ramoth-gilead.

1. *The fateful decision* (18:2-27)

   a. The conference (18:2-3): At a great banquet Ahab entices Jehoshaphat to join him in attacking Ramoth-gilead.

   b. The concern (18:4): Before the battle, Jehoshaphat wants to seek God's will.

   c. The consultation (18:5-22): Ahab reluctantly agrees and seeks counsel from two sources:

      (1) From his 400 prophets (18:5, 9-11): When King Ahab asks his 400 prophets if he should attack Ramoth-gilead, they tell him what he wants to hear—that he will be victorious.

      (2) From a faithful prophet (18:6-8, 12-22): Jehoshaphat requests that advice be sought from a prophet of the Lord. The prophet Micaiah initially tells the kings the same thing that the other prophets did, but when Ahab orders him to tell the truth, Micaiah relates two visions:

         (a) The lost sheep (18:16): Micaiah sees the people of Israel scattered on the mountains, like sheep whose shepherd has been killed.

         (b) The lying spirit (18:18-22): Micaiah also sees an interaction in heaven where the Lord allows a spirit to cause Ahab's 400 prophets to lie to him so that Ahab will go to battle and be killed.

   d. The condemnation (18:23-27): After the truth of Micaiah's message is challenged and he is arrested, Micaiah tells Ahab that his message will be proven false if Ahab returns safely from battle.

2. *The futile disguise* (18:28-34): Ahab attempts to avoid the fate that Micaiah has predicted for him.

   a. The royal apparel (18:28-32)

      (1) Ahab's strategy (18:28-29): Ahab suggests that Jehoshaphat wear his kingly garments into battle while he disguises himself as a normal soldier.

      (2) Jehoshaphat's stupidity (18:30-32): The king of Judah foolishly agrees to Ahab's plan and is nearly killed by the Arameans, who mistake him for Ahab.

   b. The random arrow (18:33-34): Ahab is mortally wounded by a stray arrow.

I. JEHOSHAPHAT THE FAULTED KING (19:1-3; 20:35-37): Jehoshaphat
   displeases the Lord by some of his actions.
   A. **The military alliance** (19:1-3): Upon Jehoshaphat's return from
      Ramoth-gilead, the prophet Jehu rebukes him for helping "those
      who hate the Lord" (i.e., King Ahab of Israel).
   B. **The merchant ships** (20:35-37): Near the end of his life, Jehosh-
      aphat makes an alliance with wicked King Ahaziah of Israel.
      They build a fleet of merchant ships, but the ships are destroyed
      before they ever set sail.

II. JEHOSHAPHAT THE FRUITFUL KING (19:4-11; 20:31-34): Jehoshaphat
    pleases the Lord by most of his actions.
    A. **His appointments** (19:4-11): Jehoshaphat appoints godly judges
       throughout the land, admonishing them to deal justly with all
       people.
    B. **His actions** (20:31-34): Jehoshaphat does what is right in the
       Lord's eyes.

III. JEHOSHAPHAT THE FRIGHTENED KING (20:1-12)
     A. **The source of his fear** (20:1-2): Jehoshaphat learns that a vast
        enemy army is approaching from beyond the Dead Sea.
     B. **The solution to his fear** (20:3-12)
        1. *The king proclaims a public fast* (20:3).
        2. *The king prays a public prayer* (20:4-12).
           a. The location of the prayer (20:4-5): Jehoshaphat assembles
              the people in front of the new courtyard at the Temple in
              Jerusalem.
           b. The language of the prayer (20:6-12)
              (1) The review (20:6-9): Jehoshaphat reviews how the Lord
                  has faithfully protected his people in the past.
              (2) The request (20:10-12): Jehoshaphat asks the Lord to
                  protect his people again.

IV. JEHOSHAPHAT THE FAVORED KING (20:13-30): The Lord hears
    Jehoshaphat's prayer and prepares his people for victory.
    A. **The prophecy** (20:13-17): The Spirit of the Lord comes upon a
       Levite named Jahaziel, and he prophesies that the Lord will win
       a great victory for Judah.
    B. **The praise** (20:18-19): Jehoshaphat leads the people in
       worship.
    C. **The power of the Lord** (20:20-30)

1. *The choir* (20:20-22): Jehoshaphat appoints singers to lead the attack by singing praises to God!
2. *The conquest* (20:23-25): The enemy is defeated, providing much plunder for the people of Judah.
3. *The conclusion* (20:26-30): After three days of collecting plunder, the people assemble in the Valley of Blessing and give thanks to the Lord. Then they march into Jerusalem to singing and music.

SECTION OUTLINE EIGHT (2 CHRONICLES 21–23)
Jehoshaphat is succeeded by Jehoram, the Edomites revolt, and the Philistines and Arabs attack Jerusalem. Jehoram dies, and Ahaziah succeeds him, but he is soon killed. Ahaziah's mother, Athaliah kills all the royal family except for Joash and assumes the throne. After several years, Joash is brought before the people and crowned king, and Athaliah is killed.

I. JEHORAM, JUDAH'S FIFTH RULER (21:1-20): Jehoram does what is evil in the Lord's sight.
  A. **Jehoram's perversions** (21:1-7, 11)
    1. *His slaughter* (21:1-4): Jehoram becomes king and murders all his brothers.
    2. *His spouse* (21:5-7): Jehoram is influenced to do evil by his wife, who is one of Ahab's daughters.
    3. *His shrines* (21:11): Jehoram also leads the people of Judah to worship idols.
  B. **Jehoram's punishment** (21:8-10, 12-20)
    1. *Wars with other people* (21:8-10, 16-17)
      a. The insurrections (21:8-10): The Edomites and the town of Libnah revolt against Jehoram.
      b. The invasions (21:16-17): The Philistines and the Arabs attack Judah and plunder the royal palace.
    2. *Words from one prophet* (21:12-15, 18-20): Elijah writes Jehoram a letter prophesying the king's destruction.
      a. As foretold (21:12-15): Elijah sends a message from the Lord to Jehoram, denouncing him for his wickedness and foretelling his death.
      b. As fulfilled (21:18-20): Just as Elijah prophesied, Jehoram is struck with a severe intestinal disease and dies in agony.

II. AHAZIAH, JUDAH'S SIXTH RULER (22:1-9): Ahaziah succeeds Jehoram as king of Judah.
  A. **Ahaziah's apostasy** (22:1-6)
    1. *The evil advice* (22:1-3): Ahaziah's mother, Athaliah, a daughter of Ahab, encourages him to do evil.
    2. *The evil alliance* (22:4-6): Ahaziah's advisers, who are

members of Ahab's family, lead him into an alliance with
Joram, Israel's ninth ruler.
  B. **Ahaziah's assassination** (22:7-9): Ahaziah is captured and exe-
     cuted in Samaria by Jehu, who becomes Israel's tenth ruler.

III. ATHALIAH, JUDAH'S SEVENTH RULER (22:10–23:21)
  A. **The elimination of rivals** (22:10): When Athaliah learns that her
     son is dead, she sets out to destroy all rivals to the throne so that
     she can become queen.
  B. **The escape of Joash** (22:11-12): Ahaziah's infant son, Joash,
     escapes being killed by Athaliah because he is hidden in the
     Temple by Ahaziah's sister.
  C. **The execution of Athaliah** (23:1-21): After Athaliah rules for
     seven years, she is deposed and killed.
     1. *The persons* (23:1): Jehoiada the high priest and five military
        leaders prepare to depose Athaliah.
     2. *The plan* (23:2-10): Jehoiada secretly assembles Levites and
        leaders from throughout Judah and assigns them various posts
        around the Temple.
     3. *The proclamation* (23:11): When all is ready, seven-year-old
        Joash is brought out and loudly proclaimed as Judah's new
        king!
     4. *The purging* (23:12-15): Athaliah is taken out to one of the
        palace gates and killed.
     5. *The pact* (23:16): Jehoiada makes a covenant with the king
        and the people that they will serve the Lord.
     6. *The purification* (23:17-21): The people tear down the temple
        of Baal. Jehoiada places Levitical priests in charge of the
        Temple. The king is escorted to his throne, and the people
        rejoice.

SECTION OUTLINE NINE   (2 CHRONICLES 24–25)
Joash calls for Temple repairs but allows Judah to return to idolatry.
Joash orders Jehoiada's son to be killed. When the Arameans attack
Judah, Joash's servants kill him. Amaziah succeeds Joash and defeats
the Edomites, but he is defeated by King Jehoash of Israel. Later
Amaziah is assassinated for worshiping the gods of the Edomites.

I. JOASH, JUDAH'S EIGHTH RULER (24:1-27)
  A. **The better years of Joash's reign** (24:1-14): Early in his reign
     Joash pleases the Lord.
     1. *The command* (24:1-5): Joash orders the priests and Levites to
        collect money to repair the Temple.
     2. *The concern* (24:6-7): After a long delay, Joash demands to
        know why his order has not been carried out.
     3. *The chest* (24:8-14): Joash orders a chest to be made and set
        outside the Temple gate to receive money from the people.

Sufficient funds are collected, and the Temple repairs are completed.

B. The bitter years of Joash's reign (24:15-27): In his final years, Joash disobeys the Lord.

    1. *The reason* (24:15-17): Jehoiada the priest, who guided young Joash, dies.

    2. *The results* (24:18-27): Joash is influenced by some wicked leaders of Judah.

        a. The paganism (24:18-19): The people begin worshiping idols again.

        b. The prophet (24:20-22): Jehoiada's son Zechariah preaches against the people of Judah for abandoning the Lord. Joash orders Zechariah to be stoned to death.

        c. The plot (24:23-27): Because the people of Judah abandoned the Lord, he allows the Arameans to attack them, and Joash is wounded. Two of Joash's officials assassinate him in his bed.

II. AMAZIAH, JUDAH'S NINTH RULER (25:1-28): Amaziah succeeds Joash as king of Judah.

    A. The evaluation of Amaziah's behavior (25:1-2): Amaziah does what is right, but not wholeheartedly.

    B. The execution of Joash's assassins (25:3-4): Amaziah executes the officials who killed his father, but he obeys the law of Moses and does not kill their children.

    C. The encounter with the Edomite army (25:5-13): Amaziah goes to war against Edom.

        1. *The warriors* (25:5-6): Amaziah organizes and counts his troops.

            a. From the two tribes (25:5): Amaziah musters an army of 300,000 men from Judah and Benjamin.

            b. From the 10 tribes (25:6): Amaziah hires 100,000 mercenaries from Israel.

        2. *The warning* (25:7-10): A man of God rebukes Amaziah for hiring mercenaries instead of trusting God, so Amaziah dismisses them.

        3. *The war* (25:11-12): Amaziah is victorious, killing 20,000 enemy troops!

        4. *The wrath* (25:13): On their way home, the angry mercenaries from Israel plunder some towns of Judah.

    D. The errors of Amaziah's reign (25:14-24)

        1. *His paganism* (25:14-16): Amaziah angers the Lord by worshiping the gods of Edom, even though he has just defeated that nation in battle.

        2. *His pride* (25:17-20): Amaziah challenges King Jehoash of Israel to war. Despite Jehoash's warnings, Amaziah prepares to attack.

        3. *His punishment* (25:21-24): The Judean king is captured, and Jerusalem is plundered by Jehoash.

E. The end of Amaziah's life (25:25-28): Amaziah is assassinated for abandoning the Lord.

SECTION OUTLINE TEN (2 CHRONICLES 26–28)
The reigns of Uzziah, Jotham, and Ahaz are recorded. Uzziah pleases the Lord for most of his reign, but he disobeys near the end. Jotham is a good king of a corrupt nation. Ahaz is evil and is attacked by Aram, Israel, and Assyria. He also closes the Temple and offers sacrifices to foreign gods.

I. UZZIAH, JUDAH'S TENTH RULER (26:1-23): Amaziah's son Uzziah succeeds him as king of Judah.
  A. His accomplishments (26:1-15)
    1. *Uzziah the faithful* (26:1, 3-5): Uzziah begins his reign as a faithful follower of the Lord.
    2. *Uzziah the fortifier* (26:2, 9): He rebuilds the town of Elath and constructs towers in Jerusalem.
    3. *Uzziah the farmer* (26:10): Uzziah owns many livestock, farms, and vineyards.
    4. *Uzziah the fighter* (26:6-8, 11-15)
      a. His wars (26:6-8): Uzziah is successful in battle against the Philistines, the Arabs, and the Meunites.
      b. His warriors (26:11-13): Uzziah's army numbers 307,500 elite troops.
      c. His weapons (26:14-15): Uzziah provides his men with armor and produces machines that shoot arrows and huge stones.
  B. His arrogance (26:16-23): After Uzziah becomes powerful, he becomes proud.
    1. *Uzziah's lawlessness* (26:16-18)
      a. Uzziah's foolish action (26:16): Uzziah burns incense in the Temple, which only priests can do.
      b. Azariah's fearless reaction (26:17-18): Azariah the high priest confronts and condemns the king for his sinful act.
    2. *Uzziah's leprosy* (26:19-20): A furious and unrepentant Uzziah is struck with leprosy by the Lord.
    3. *Uzziah's loneliness* (26:21-23): Uzziah is forced to live in isolation until his death.

II. JOTHAM, JUDAH'S ELEVENTH RULER (27:1-9): Uzziah's son Jotham succeeds him as king of Judah.
  A. His worship (27:1-2): Jotham walks in the ways of the Lord.
  B. His works (27:3-4)
    1. *In Jerusalem* (27:3): Jotham rebuilds the Upper Gate and the wall at the hill of Ophel.
    2. *In Judah* (27:4): Jotham builds towns and fortresses throughout Judah.

C. His war (27:5-9)
1. *The record of his victory* (27:5): Jotham defeats the Ammonites and receives a huge annual tribute from them.
2. *The reason for his victory* (27:6-9): Jotham becomes powerful because the Lord blesses him for his obedience.

III. AHAZ, JUDAH'S TWELFTH RULER (28:1-27): Jotham's son Ahaz succeeds him as king of Judah.
  A. The adamant apostasy (28:1-4): Ahaz becomes a fanatical worshiper of Baal, even sacrificing his own sons to him.
  B. The attacking armies (28:5-15): Judah is punished for Ahaz's idolatry.
1. *The defeat by Aram* (28:5): Aram defeats Ahaz and deports large numbers of his people to Damascus.
2. *The defeat by Israel* (28:5-15): Israel also defeats Ahaz, killing 120,000 of his soldiers and capturing 200,000 Judean women and children! The prophet Oded warns Israel to return the captives from Judah, lest divine wrath fall upon them. Israel's leaders feed and clothe the captives and send them back to Judah.
  C. The attempted alliance (28:16-21): Ahaz asks the king of Assyria for help against his enemies. The Assyrian king takes Ahaz's money but oppresses him instead of helping him.
  D. The aggravated actions (28:22-27): In desperation, Ahaz sacrifices to the gods of Aram and closes the Temple, which leads to the ruin of both the king and all Israel.

SECTION OUTLINE ELEVEN (2 CHRONICLES 29–31)
Hezekiah succeeds Ahaz and reopens the Temple. The priests and Levites purify themselves and the Temple, and Passover is celebrated. Hezekiah reorganizes the priesthood and requires the people to obey the law of the Lord by supporting the priesthood.

I. REPAIRING THE TEMPLE (29:1-36): Hezekiah, Judah's thirteenth ruler, succeeds Ahaz as king; he reopens the Temple in the first month of his reign.
  A. The Temple overseers (29:4-19)
1. *The challenge to the Levites* (29:4-11): The king exhorts the priests and Levites to purify themselves and the Temple, making it ready for public worship.
2. *The cleansing by the Levites* (29:12-19): The priests and Levites complete the purification process in 16 days.
  B. The Temple offerings (29:20-36): Hezekiah rededicates the Temple by making offerings.
1. *The sacrifices* (29:20-24): Hezekiah commands the priests to sacrifice seven bulls, seven rams, seven lambs, and seven male goats as a sin offering.

  2. *The singing* (29:25-30): At Hezekiah's instruction, the
     sacrificing is accompanied by worshipful singing and musical
     instruments.
  3. *The sum total* (29:31-36): The assembled people offer 670
     bulls, 100 rams, and over 3,000 lambs and sheep.

II. REINSTITUTING PASSOVER (30:1-27)
  A. The request (30:1-5)
    1. *What* (30:1): Hezekiah invites the people to celebrate the
       Passover in Jerusalem.
    2. *When* (30:2): The Passover celebration will be in midspring, a
       month later than normal.
    3. *Why* (30:3-4): This delay is caused by the lack of purified
       priests on the earlier date.
    4. *Who* (30:5): An invitation is made to all Israel, from Dan to
       Beersheba!
  B. The reminder (30:6-9): Hezekiah promises that if Israel returns to
     the Lord, the Lord will return to Israel.
  C. The response (30:10-12)
    1. *Many mockingly reject the invitation* (30:10).
    2. *Some humbly accept the invitation* (30:11-12).
  D. The revival (30:13-14): The people assemble in Jerusalem for the
     Passover and destroy the pagan altars.
  E. The regulation (30:15-20): Many of the people are ceremonially
     unclean and ineligible to eat the Passover. Hezekiah prays for
     their forgiveness, so they can eat the Passover meal.
  F. The rejoicing (30:21-27): The people joyfully celebrate the
     Passover for another seven days, making the celebration the
     greatest since the days of Solomon!

III. REORGANIZING THE PRIESTS AND LEVITES (31:1-3): Hezekiah organizes
     the priests to offer daily sacrifices once again.

IV. REQUIRING THE PEOPLE TO TITHE (31:4-21): Hezekiah requires the
    people to fulfill the obligations set forth in the law of the Lord
    regarding tithes to the priesthood.
  A. The reason (31:4): Hezekiah requires the tithe to the priesthood
     so the priests and Levites can devote themselves fully to the Lord.
  B. The response (31:5-10): The people generously respond by
     bringing a portion of their crops and livestock.
  C. The reassignments (31:11-21): Hezekiah appoints officials to
     oversee the fair distribution of the tithes to the priests and
     Levites.

SECTION OUTLINE TWELVE (2 CHRONICLES 32)

King Sennacherib of Assyria invades Judah, and Hezekiah strengthens Jerusalem's defenses. Sennacherib warns the people of Jerusalem to surrender to him. Hezekiah prays, and the Lord sends an angel to destroy the Assyrian army. Hezekiah recovers from a serious illness, and his wealth increases.

I. THE HELPLESSNESS OF HEZEKIAH (32:1-22): King Sennacherib of Assyria invades Judah.
   A. The situation (32:1-8)
      1. *The plan* (32:1-2): Hezekiah realizes that Sennacherib intends to attack Jerusalem.
      2. *The preparations* (32:3-8)
         a. The reinforcements (32:3-5): Hezekiah fortifies Jerusalem and stops up the springs outside the city.
         b. The reassurance (32:6-8): Hezekiah encourages the people by reminding them that the Lord is on their side.
   B. The scorn (32:9-19): Sennacherib's ambassadors ridicule Hezekiah's attempts to defend Jerusalem. They note that the gods of the other nations were powerless to protect their cities and assume the God of the Hebrews will be powerless to protect Jerusalem.
   C. The supplication (32:20): Hezekiah and the prophet Isaiah cry out to God for deliverance.
   D. The salvation (32:21-22): The Lord sends an angel to destroy the Assyrian army. Sennacherib is killed by his own sons.

II. THE HEALING OF HEZEKIAH (32:24-26): Hezekiah becomes deathly ill and cries out to the Lord. When the Lord heals him, Hezekiah becomes very proud, but then he repents of his pride.

III. THE HONOR OF HEZEKIAH (32:23, 27-33): Hezekiah receives great respect and riches during his reign. The people honor him when he dies.

SECTION OUTLINE THIRTEEN (2 CHRONICLES 33)

Manasseh becomes king and practices many evils, including setting up idols in the Temple. After Manasseh is led away a captive, he repents and is released. He opposes idolatry and promotes worship of the Lord. Amon succeeds Manasseh as king and does much evil. He is assassinated by his own officials.

I. MANASSEH, JUDAH'S FOURTEENTH RULER (33:1-20): Hezekiah's son Manasseh succeeds him as king of Judah.
   A. The rebellious king (33:1-11)
      1. *Manasseh's perversions* (33:1-9): Manasseh commits idolatry and all sorts of evil. He even sacrifices his own sons to other gods and places an idol in the Temple of the Lord.

2. *Manasseh's punishment* (33:10-11): The Lord allows the Assyrians to capture Manasseh and lead him away in chains.

B. **The repentant king** (33:12-20)

1. *Manasseh's confession* (33:12-13): Manasseh repents of his wickedness and calls out to the Lord. The Lord hears Manasseh's prayer and allows him to return to his kingdom.

2. *Manasseh's changed conduct* (33:14-20): Manasseh returns to Judah, removes the idols, tears down the pagan altars he built, and promotes the worship of the Lord for the rest of his reign.

II. AMON, JUDAH'S FIFTEENTH RULER (33:21-25): Manasseh's son Amon succeeds him as king of Judah.

A. **His apostasy** (33:21-23): Amon does evil in the Lord's sight and worships idols.

B. **His assassination** (33:24-25): Amon's officials kill him in his palace.

SECTION OUTLINE FOURTEEN (2 CHRONICLES 34–35)

Josiah becomes king and removes idolatry from Judah. He orders repairs made to the Temple, and the Book of the Law is discovered. Josiah reads the scroll to all the leaders, and they recommit themselves to the Lord. Passover is celebrated. Josiah is killed in battle against King Neco.

I. JOSIAH, JUDAH'S SIXTEENTH RULER (34:1–35:27): Josiah succeeds his father, Amon, as king of Judah. He is Judah's last good king.

A. **The campaign launched** (34:1-7): Josiah begins a massive campaign against idol worship. He destroys pagan altars in Jerusalem, Judah, Manasseh, Ephraim, Simeon, and Naphtali.

B. **The construction undertaken** (34:8-13): Josiah orders repairs to be made to the Temple and appoints men to carry out the task.

C. **The covenant renewed** (34:14-33): While the Temple is being repaired, the high priest, Hilkiah, discovers the Book of the Law (Book of the Covenant).

1. *The pronouncement* (34:14-18): After Hilkiah finds the Book of the Covenant, he gives it to Shaphan, the court secretary. Shaphan takes it to the king and reads the book to him.

2. *The perplexity* (34:19-21): After listening to what is written in the book, Josiah despairs and instructs his leaders to ask the Lord what to do about the situation.

3. *The prophet* (34:22): The leaders consult the prophet Huldah.

4. *The prophecy* (34:23-28): Huldah issues a twofold prophecy:

   a. Concerning Judah (34:23-25): The Lord will soon punish the people because of their sins.

   b. Concerning Josiah (34:26-28): Because Josiah humbled himself before God, the Lord will not send his punishment until after Josiah dies.

      5. *The proclamation* (34:29-33): Josiah reads to the leaders and the people from the Book of the Covenant and renews the covenant between the Lord and his people.

D. The call sent out (35:1-6): Josiah calls for the people to celebrate the Passover in Jerusalem.

E. The contributions made (35:7-9): Josiah and his officials provide thousands of animals to be sacrificed. Josiah gives 30,000 lambs and goats and 3,000 bulls. Josiah's officials donate 7,600 lambs and goats and 800 bulls.

F. The ceremony conducted (35:10-15): The priests make the sacrifices, which are eaten by the people.

G. The celebration completed (35:16-19): The Passover is completed. Never since the time of Samuel has there been such a Passover celebration!

H. The casualty experienced (35:20-27)

    1. *Josiah's foolish war* (35:20-22): Josiah needlessly engages King Neco in battle.

    2. *Josiah's fatal wound* (35:22-27): Josiah is fatally wounded by enemy archers.

       a. The location of his death (35:22-23): The battle occurs on the plain of Megiddo.

       b. The lamentation over his death (35:24-27): All Judah mourns for Josiah, and the prophet Jeremiah composes funeral songs for him.

SECTION OUTLINE FIFTEEN (2 CHRONICLES 36)

The reigns of Jehoahaz, Jehoiakim, Jehoiachin, and Zedekiah are recorded. Jerusalem falls to the Babylonians, who exile the people to Babylon. Later Cyrus allows the exiles to return.

I. JEHOAHAZ, JUDAH'S SEVENTEENTH RULER (36:1-4): Josiah's son Jehoahaz succeeds him as king of Judah.

  A. The duration (36:1-2): Jehoahaz rules for only three months.

  B. The dethroning (36:3-4): Jehoahaz is dethroned and imprisoned in Egypt by King Neco, who appoints Jehoahaz's brother king of Judah.

II. JEHOIAKIM, JUDAH'S EIGHTEENTH RULER (36:5-8)

  A. The evil of his reign (36:5): Jehoiakim does what is evil in the Lord's sight.

  B. The events of his reign (36:6-8): Jerusalem is captured by Nebuchadnezzar, the Temple is plundered, and Jehoiakim is led away in chains.

III. JEHOIACHIN, JUDAH'S NINETEENTH RULER (36:9-10): Jehoiakim's son Jehoiachin succeeds him as king of Judah.

  A. His reign (36:9): Jehoiachin reigns for three months and ten days.

B. **His removal** (36:10): Nebuchadnezzar summons him to Babylon, and many of the Temple treasures are taken as well. Zedekiah is appointed the next king.

IV. ZEDEKIAH, JUDAH'S TWENTIETH RULER (36:11-23)
   A. **The disobedience** (36:11-14): Zedekiah rebels against the Lord and against Nebuchadnezzar. The priests and the people practice idolatry.
   B. **The destruction** (36:15-20): Because the people refuse to heed the prophets and repent, the Lord allows the king of Babylon to attack Jerusalem. The walls are broken down, the Temple is destroyed, and many people are killed or taken into exile.
   C. **The decree** (36:21-23): After 70 years, King Cyrus of Persia decrees that the Lord's people may return and rebuild their Temple.

Ezra

SECTION OUTLINE ONE (EZRA 1–3)

King Cyrus of Persia decrees that the Jews may return and rebuild the Temple. The return of the first group of the exiles is recorded. The offering of sacrifices is resumed, and the rebuilding of the Temple is begun.

I. THE DECREE (1:1-4)
   A. **The prophecy** (1:1): King Cyrus of Persia issues a decree that fulfills a prophecy made by Jeremiah many years earlier.
   B. **The proclamation** (1:2-4): Cyrus's decree allows all the Jews in the Persian Empire to return to Jerusalem and rebuild their Temple.

II. THE DONATIONS (1:6-11; 2:68-70)
   A. **Gifts from neighbors** (1:6): Many people, probably Jews choosing to stay in Babylon, give the returning Jews gold, silver, and supplies for the journey.
   B. **Gifts from King Cyrus** (1:7-11): King Cyrus donates the valuable items that Nebuchadnezzar took from the Temple.
   C. **Gifts from family leaders** (2:68-70): When the Jews arrive in Jerusalem, some family leaders already living there donate gold, silver, and robes for the Temple and the priests.

III. THE DEDICATED (1:5; 2:1-67): Nearly 50,000 devoted pilgrims return, including priests, Levites, descendants of Solomon's officials, and other Israelites. They bring along 736 horses, 245 mules, 435 camels, and 6,720 donkeys.

IV. THE DETERMINATION (3:1-9): Upon their return the Jews soon accomplish three of their goals:
   A. **The altar is rebuilt** (3:1-3): Daily sacrifices are immediately resumed.
   B. **The Festival of Shelters is observed** (3:4-6).
   C. **The Temple construction is begun** (3:7-9): In the second year after the Jews return, they begin rebuilding the Temple, with the Levites in charge.

V. THE DEDICATION (3:10-13): When the Temple foundation is
complete, there is a great celebration.
   A. **The singing** (3:10-11): The priests and Levites blow trumpets,
   clash cymbals, and sing praises to the Lord.
   B. **The sorrow** (3:12-13): Some older Jews remember Solomon's
   glorious Temple and weep over how much this one pales in
   comparison to it.

SECTION OUTLINE TWO (EZRA 4–6)
Enemies resist the rebuilding of the Temple. Artaxerxes halts the
work. Haggai and Zechariah encourage the people to continue
building the Temple. Permission is granted for the building of the
Temple to continue. The Temple is completed and dedicated, and
Passover is celebrated.

I. HINDRANCES TO THE PROJECT (4:1-24): As the Jews rebuild the
temple, their enemies try to hinder them in several ways.
   A. **Compromise** (4:1-3): Some enemies of the Jews try to make them
   compromise their standards.
      1. *The request* (4:1-2): Some pagans in the land offer to aid in the
      Temple construction.
      2. *The refusal* (4:3): The Jewish leaders decline their offer.
   B. **Coercion** (4:4-5): Local residents try to discourage and frighten
   the Jews as they rebuild. They even bribe agents to work against
   the Jews.
   C. **Condemnation** (4:6-24): The enemies write letters to King Xerxes
   and King Artaxerxes, accusing the Jews of being rebellious.
      1. *The message to the king* (4:6-16)
         a. The slander (4:6-13): The enemies warn King Artaxerxes
         that the Jews will revolt when the rebuilding is complete.
         b. The suggestion (4:14-16): The enemies suggest that King
         Artaxerxes check the ancient records himself to learn of the
         rebellious history of Jerusalem.
      2. *The message from the king* (4:17-24)
         a. What he discovers (4:17-20): Artaxerxes' search confirms
         the rebellious history of Jerusalem.
         b. What he demands (4:21-24): He orders all work on the
         Temple and the city to be halted immediately.

II. HEADWAY ON THE PROJECT (5:1–6:22): Eventually the Temple is
rebuilt, despite the many obstacles along the way.
   A. **The prophets in Judah** (5:1-2): The prophets Haggai and
   Zechariah spur the Jews on to restart the rebuilding of the Tem-
   ple.
   B. **The potentate in Persia** (5:3–6:22)
      1. *The rebuke* (5:3-5): Again the Jews' enemies create difficulties

for them. The governor of the province demands to know who
gave them permission to rebuild the Temple.
2. *The report* (5:6-16): The governor sends a letter to Darius, the
new king of Persia, reporting the Jews' activities.
3. *The request* (5:17): In his letter the governor mentions the
Jews' claim that Cyrus granted them permission to rebuild,
and he asks Darius to see if this is true.
4. *The reply* (6:1-12): Persian records reveal that Cyrus had
indeed granted the Jews permission to rebuild the Temple.
So Darius gives the following instructions:
   a. Allow the Jews to rebuild their Temple (6:6-7).
   b. Assist the Jews in rebuilding their Temple (6:8-12): Darius
   instructs the governor to use tax revenues to fund the
   project.
5. *The results* (6:13-22)
   a. The completion of the Temple (6:13-18)
      (1) The job ends (6:13-15): The Temple is finished during
      the sixth year of Darius's reign.
      (2) The joy begins (6:16-18): The Temple is dedicated with
      a joyous occasion of praise and thanksgiving!
   b. The celebration of Passover (6:19-22): All the returned
   exiles celebrate the Passover one month and nine days after
   the Temple is completed.

SECTION OUTLINE THREE (EZRA 7–8)

Artaxerxes authorizes Ezra to return to Jerusalem with more exiles.
The leaders of the returning families are recorded. After gathering at
the Ahava Canal, the people depart for Jerusalem and arrive safely.
They deposit many valuables at the Temple and sacrifice burnt
offerings to God.

I. THE PREPARATION (7:1-10): Many years after the first group of exiles
returns to Jerusalem, a man named Ezra comes on the scene.
   A. **Ezra and the line of Aaron** (7:1-5): Ezra belongs to the seventeenth generation of the priestly line of Aaron.
   B. **Ezra and the law of the Lord** (7:6-10): Ezra is a scribe, well
   versed in the law of Moses. Because of his commitment to study
   and obey the law, the Lord blesses him.

II. THE COOPERATION (7:11-28)
   A. **The king's edict concerning Ezra** (7:11-24)
      1. *What the ruler will do* (7:11-20): King Artaxerxes of Persia
      allows Ezra to return to Jerusalem and promises him the
      following:
         a. Any Jews who wish may go with him (7:13).
         b. Any finances he needs will be provided (7:14-20).
      2. *What the rest will do* (7:21-24): The king commands his

officials west of the Euphrates to supply Ezra with whatever he
requests.
B. The king's exhortation to Ezra (7:25-28)
1. *Ezra's task* (7:25-26): Artaxerxes directs Ezra to govern and
guide the people, no matter who they are, in the law of God.
2. *Ezra's thanksgiving* (7:27-28): Grateful, Ezra praises God for
granting him the king's favor.

III. THE PARTICIPATION (8:1-20): Ezra and those going with him to
Jerusalem camp at the Ahava Canal before leaving.
A. The exiles who come (8:1-14): Ezra lists the families returning
to Jerusalem.
B. The extras who are called (8:15-20)
1. *The absence of Levites* (8:15-17): Ezra notices that not one
Levite has volunteered to accompany him. So he sends 11
trusted men back to urge the Levites to join them.
2. *The arrival of Levites* (8:18-20): Over 40 Levites and 220
Temple servants respond and arrive at the camp.

IV. THE SUPPLICATION (8:21-23): Ezra calls for a time of prayer and
fasting before beginning the journey.

V. THE AUTHORIZATION (8:24-30): Ezra appoints 24 of the leading
priests to transport the silver, gold, and bronze items for the
Temple.

VI. THE DESTINATION (8:31-32): After a journey of some four months
(see Ezra 7:8-9), Ezra and the people arrive safely in Jerusalem.

VII. THE PRESENTATION (8:33-36): When Ezra's group of returnees arrives
in Jerusalem, they present several things:
A. Gold and silver to the Temple (8:33-34): All the valuables are
deposited at the Temple and carefully recorded.
B. Sacrifices to the Lord (8:35)
C. Decrees to the officials (8:36): The king's decrees are given to
his officials, who fully cooperate.

SECTION OUTLINE FOUR EZRA 9-10)
Ezra hears that many Jews are imitating the local pagans and have
intermarried with them. As Ezra confesses this sin to the Lord, many
people become sorrowful. Ezra calls the people to Jerusalem and
confronts them with their sin. The people agree to divorce their
pagan wives. Those who are guilty are listed.

I. THE TRANSGRESSION BY THE PEOPLE (9:1-15)
A. Ezra's pain (9:1-4)
1. *The report* (9:1-2): Ezra is told that many Jews—including
some priests and Levites—are imitating the local pagans.
Israelite men have even married pagan women.

    2. *The response* (9:3-4): Ezra tears his clothes, pulls hair from his head and beard, and sits down in sad shock.

  B. Ezra's prayer (9:5-15): Ezra prays to the Lord, confessing the faithlessness of Judah and the faithfulness of the Lord.

    1. *The faithlessness of the people of Judah* (9:6-7, 10-15)

      a. Their past sins (9:6-7)

      b. Their present sins (9:10-15)

    2. *The faithfulness of the Lord* (9:8-9)

II. THE CONFESSION BY THE PEOPLE (10:1-44)

  A. The repentance (10:1-2): Convicted of their sins after hearing Ezra's prayer, the people cry out to God for forgiveness.

  B. The resolve (10:3-12): The people promise to separate from the pagans in the land, and the men will divorce their pagan wives.

  C. The record (10:13-44): A process is decided upon to deal with all the intermarriages. The names of all the guilty leaders are recorded.

Nehemiah

SECTION OUTLINE ONE (NEHEMIAH 1–3)
After hearing about Jerusalem's situation, Nehemiah confesses his people's sins to God. He receives permission from King Artaxerxes to go to Jerusalem to repair the wall. After Nehemiah arrives and inspects the wall, he begins the repairs. Those who worked on various portions of the gates and wall are recorded.

I. THE REPORT (1:1-11)
   A. **Learning about the wall** (1:1-3): Nehemiah is told about the sad situation in Jerusalem. The wall of the city has been torn down, and the gates have been burned.
   B. **Lamenting over the wall** (1:4-11): Nehemiah is deeply saddened, and he mourns and fasts. He prays to the Lord about the following:
      1. *Israel's plight* (1:4-7): God's people have disobeyed his laws and are suffering the penalty.
      2. *God's promise* (1:8-10): If the people repent, the Lord has promised to restore them.
      3. *Nehemiah's petition* (1:11): Nehemiah prays that the Lord will cause the king to grant his request to return to Jerusalem.

II. THE REQUEST (2:1-10)
   A. **The petition to the king** (2:1-5): Nehemiah asks King Artaxerxes for a leave of absence so that he might return and rebuild Jerusalem.
   B. **The permission from the king** (2:6-10): Artaxerxes not only permits Nehemiah to go, he also agrees to help finance the project! Nehemiah travels to Jerusalem, despite the protests of a couple of non-Jews named Sanballat and Tobiah.

III. THE REVIEW (2:11-20): Nehemiah inspects the wall and makes a recommendation to the leaders.
   A. **Nehemiah's examination** (2:11-16): Nehemiah conducts a nighttime survey to inspect Jerusalem's wall.
   B. **Nehemiah's exhortation** (2:17-20)
      1. *The report* (2:17): Nehemiah calls a meeting of the Jewish

leaders and informs them of the terrible condition of the city's wall.

2. *The recommendation* (2:17-18): Nehemiah urges the leaders to begin the task of rebuilding the wall.
3. *The response* (2:18): The leaders cry out, "Good! Let's rebuild the wall!"
4. *The ridicule* (2:19): Sanballat, Tobiah, and an Arab named Geshem scoff at Nehemiah's plan, seeing it as rebellion against the king.
5. *The rebuke* (2:20): Nehemiah assures the three men that the wall will indeed be rebuilt without their help.

IV. THE REPAIRS (3:1-32): The work is divided up by the 10 various gates, each assigned to certain leaders.
   A. **The Sheep Gate** (3:1-2)
   B. **The Fish Gate** (3:3-5)
   C. **The Old City Gate** (3:6-12)
   D. **The Valley Gate** (3:13)
   E. **The Dung Gate** (3:14)
   F. **The Fountain Gate** (3:15-25)
   G. **The Water Gate** (3:25-27)
   H. **The Horse Gate** (3:28)
   I. **The East Gate** (3:29-30)
   J. **The Inspection Gate** (3:31-32)

SECTION OUTLINE TWO (NEHEMIAH 4–6)
The enemies ridicule and threaten the wall builders, but Nehemiah posts guards to protect them. He also eases the financial burdens of the people by convincing the lenders not to repossess their property. The enemies resume their opposition, but the wall is completed.

I. THE TROUBLES (4:1–6:14): As the Jews rebuild the wall of Jerusalem, they encounter various struggles along the way.
   A. **Ridicule** (4:1-6)
      1. *The pagans' scorn* (4:1-3): Sanballat and Tobiah, enemies of the Jews, mocked at the Jews' efforts to rebuild their wall.
      2. *The prophet's supplication* (4:4-5): Nehemiah prays to the Lord, asking him to punish the enemies for opposing the work.
      3. *The people's straining* (4:6): After intense effort, the workers rebuild the wall to half its original height.
   B. **Conspiracy** (4:7-9)
      1. *The plot* (4:7-8): Sanballat and Tobiah try to stop the work by making plans to lead an army against Jerusalem.
      2. *The prayers* (4:9): The Jews pray and post a 24-hour guard.
   C. **Discouragement** (4:10): Some of the Jews become discouraged about the amount of rubble that must be cleared away.

D. Intimidation (4:11-23)

1. *The craftiness of the enemy* (4:11-12): The enemies of the Jews make plans to swoop down upon them and kill them.
2. *The challenge of the prophet* (4:13-14): Nehemiah places armed guards in exposed areas and encourages the Jews to trust in the Lord.
3. *The commitment of the workers* (4:15-23): Nehemiah divides the workers in half. One half stands guard while the other half works. They labor from sunrise to sunset, being ever vigilant.

E. Internal strife (5:1-19)

1. *The ruthlessness* (5:1-5): During difficult times some of the wealthier Jews loan money to the poorer Jews and charge interest. When they cannot repay the loan, their property is repossessed, and they become slaves to the wealthy Jews.
2. *The reprimand* (5:6-11): At a public hearing Nehemiah demands that the wealthier Jews restore what they have taken from the poor.
3. *The repentance* (5:12-13): The wealthy Jews agree and do what Nehemiah demands.
4. *The role model* (5:14-19): Nehemiah is an excellent example for those in positions of authority or influence.
   a. What he does not do (5:14-16): Nehemiah refuses to accept any salary during his 12 years as governor of Judah.
   b. What he does do (5:17-19): Nehemiah regularly feeds 150 Jewish officials at his own expense.

F. Ruse (6:1-4): Four times Sanballat and Geshem attempt to meet with Nehemiah so they could harm him. Realizing their evil plot, Nehemiah refuses each time, saying his work is too important to stop.

G. Slander (6:5-9): Sanballat and Geshem show Nehemiah a letter to King Artaxerxes that claims Nehemiah and the Jews plan to rebel.

H. Treachery (6:10-14): The enemy uses a prophet named Shemaiah to try to persuade Nehemiah to seek refuge inside the Temple. Nehemiah sees through the scheme to intimidate and discredit him, and he refuses.

II. THE TRIUMPH (6:15-19): Despite the many obstacles, the Jews complete the wall in 52 days! The Jews' enemies are fearful, realizing that this project had indeed been done with God's help.

SECTION OUTLINE THREE (NEHEMIAH 7–10)
Nehemiah takes a census of the exiles who returned. Ezra reads the Book of the Law to the people, who then celebrate the Festival of Shelters. The Book of the Law is read aloud again, and some Levites lead the people in a prayer of confession, reviewing God's dealings with his people. The people make a written oath to obey the Lord.

I. THE CITY OF GOD (7:1-3): Nehemiah assigns his brother Hanani to govern Jerusalem, and he assigns a faithful man named Hananiah to command the fortress.

II. THE PEOPLE OF GOD (7:4-73): Nehemiah takes a census of all the exiles who have returned to Jerusalem and Judah.
   A. The names (7:4-65)
   1. *The 12 key leaders* (7:5-7)
   2. *The clan leaders* (7:8-38)
   3. *The priests* (7:39-42, 63-65)
      a. Those with genealogical records (7:39-42)
      b. Those without genealogical records (7:63-65)
   4. *The Levites* (7:43)
   5. *The singers* (7:44)
   6. *The gatekeepers* (7:45)
   7. *The Temple servants* (7:46-56)
   8. *The descendants of Solomon's officials* (7:57-60)
   9. *Families without genealogical records* (7:61-62)
   B. The numbers (7:66-73)
   1. *The count* (7:66-69): A total of 49,942 individuals return. They brought 8,136 animals with them.
   2. *The contributions* (7:70-73): Some of the leaders give expensive gifts to help finance the work.

III. THE WORD OF GOD (8:1-12)
   A. The communication (8:1-6): Ezra stands on a wooden platform in front of the Water Gate and reads the Book of the Law to the people.
   B. The clarification (8:7-8): As Ezra reads, the Levites explain the meaning of the passage being read.
   C. The celebration (8:9-12): The people weep as they listen to the law, but Ezra, Nehemiah, and the Levites tell them to rejoice since it is a sacred day. They instruct the people to celebrate and feast together.

IV. THE FESTIVAL OF GOD (8:13-18): Ezra, the priests, and the Levites study the law and realize the Lord has called the people to observe the Festival of Shelters. So the people build temporary shelters with cut branches and live there during the Festival.

V. THE CONFESSION TO GOD (9:1-38): The Book of the Law is read before the people again; the people confess their sins and worship God.

   A. The laity (9:1-3): The people dress in sackcloth and put dust on their heads as they confess their sins to God.

   B. The Levites (9:4-38): The leaders of the Levites lead the people in prayer and recount God's faithfulness and Israel's unfaithfulness throughout history.

    1. *From Abraham to Moses* (9:7-8): The Lord called Abram out of Ur of the Chaldeans and made a covenant with him, promising to give him and his descendants the land of Canaan.

    2. *From Moses to Joshua* (9:9-23)

      a. God's faithfulness (9:9-15, 19-23)

        (1) He delivered them from Egypt (9:9-11).

        (2) He led them day and night in the wilderness (9:12, 19).

        (3) He taught them his laws at Mount Sinai (9:13-14).

        (4) He provided food and water for them (9:15, 20).

        (5) He provided for all their needs (9:21).

        (6) He gave them victory over their enemies (9:22-23).

      b. Israel's unfaithfulness (9:16-18)

        (1) They refused to obey God; therefore he wouldn't let them enter the Promised Land (9:16-17).

        (2) They worshiped a calf idol (9:18).

    3. *From Joshua to the Judges* (9:24-26)

      a. God's faithfulness (9:24-25): God subdued the enemies of the Israelites.

      b. Israel's unfaithfulness (9:26): The Israelites disobeyed God, killing his prophets and committing terrible blasphemies.

    4. *From the Judges to Ezra and Nehemiah* (9:27-31): God allowed the Israelites' enemies to conquer them because of their repeated sin.

    5. *At the time of Ezra and Nehemiah* (9:32-38)

      a. The Levites' plea (9:32-37): The Levites implore God to extend mercy upon his sinful people.

      b. The Levites' promise (9:38): The Levites attest that the leaders of God's people are making a solemn written promise to obey God.

VI. THE VOW TO GOD (10:1-39): A special document is written up and signed by the leaders of the people.

   A. The parties (10:1-28): The document is signed by Nehemiah, the priests, the Levites, the political leaders, the gatekeepers, the singers, the Temple servants, and others.

   B. The promises (10:29-39): The document records six promises the people made to God.

    1. *They will not intermarry with non-Jews* (10:30).

2. *They will obey all the Sabbath laws* (10:31).
3. *They will take care of the Temple* (10:32, 34, 39).
4. *They will observe all the sacred festivals* (10:33).
5. *They will dedicate to the Lord the firstborn of their sons and animals* (10:36).
6. *They will pay their tithes* (10:35, 37-38).

SECTION OUTLINE FOUR (NEHEMIAH 11–13)
One tenth of the people from Judah and Benjamin resettle in Jerusalem. Many of the residents of Jerusalem are listed. The priests and Levites who returned with Zerubbabel are listed. The wall of Jerusalem is dedicated with a great ceremony. Nehemiah's various reforms are given.

I. THE RESETTLING OF THE CITIES (11:1-36)
   A. **Those living in Jerusalem** (11:1-24): Many people are relocated to Jerusalem to repopulate the city with others besides the leaders.
      1. *How they are selected* (11:1-2)
         a. Some are selected by the casting of lots (11:1).
         b. Some volunteer to relocate (11:2).
      2. *Who is selected* (11:3-24): A list of the leaders who relocate to Jerusalem is given.
         a. The provincial officials (11:3-9)
         b. The priests and others (11:10-24)
   B. **Those living in Judah and Benjamin** (11:25-36): Various cities that the people of Judah and Benjamin inhabit are listed.

II. THE RETURNING OF THE PRIESTS AND LEVITES (12:1-26): Priests and Levites who returned from exile with Zerubbabel and Jeshua the high priest are listed.

III. THE REJOICING OF THE PEOPLE (12:27-47): Jerusalem's newly completed wall is dedicated with a glorious celebration!
   A. **The music** (12:27-30): All the Levitical musicians throughout the land assemble by the wall in Jerusalem.
   B. **The marching** (12:31-43): Nehemiah divides the musicians and other leaders into two choirs; they are to march on the wall in opposite directions, praising God as they walk.
   C. **The ministers** (12:44-47): Nehemiah selects certain men to be in charge of the storerooms.

IV. THE REFORMS OF NEHEMIAH (13:1-31): Nehemiah records several reforms he instituted as he encountered various problems.
   A. **The separation** (13:1-3): When the people discover that the law of Moses forbids Ammonites and Moabites from entering the assembly of God, all people of mixed ancestry are immediately expelled.

B. The confrontations (13:4-31): On at least five occasions, Nehemiah sternly rebukes certain individuals.

1. *Eliashib* (13:4-9): Eliashib the priest is in charge of the Temple
   storerooms; he is also a relative of Tobiah, one of Nehemiah's
   opponents. Eliashib had provided Tobiah with a room in the
   Temple courtyards. When Nehemiah discovers this, he throws
   out Tobiah's belongings and orders the room to be purified.
2. *The Levites* (13:10-14): Because the Levites are not receiving
   the tithes due them, they neglect their Temple duties and work
   for pay. Nehemiah recalls them to their duties, and the people
   of Judah support them once again.
3. *Those who profane the Sabbath* (13:15-22)
   a. The sin (13:15-18): Merchants are entering and exiting
      through the gates of Jerusalem to conduct business on the
      Sabbath, just like on any other day.
   b. The solution (13:19-22): Nehemiah orders the gates closed
      during the Sabbath.
4. *Those who married pagan women* (13:23-27): Nehemiah
   encounters men who had married pagan women. After
   Nehemiah curses and beats them, the men agree to never
   allow their children to marry pagan spouses.
5. *Sanballat's son-in-law* (13:28-31): When Nehemiah discovers
   that one of the priests married the daughter of Sanballat, he
   drives him out of the Temple.

Esther

SECTION OUTLINE ONE (ESTHER 1–2)
King Xerxes deposes Queen Vashti for refusing to appear before him at a banquet. A search is made for a new queen, and Esther is selected. Her adoptive father Mordecai becomes a palace official. He overhears a plot to assassinate the king, and he reports it to Esther and saves the king's life.

I. THE REJECTION OF VASHTI (1:1-22): King Xerxes of Persia is rebuffed by his queen during one of his banquets, so he deposes her.

   A. **A banquet for his provincial officials** (1:1-4): King Xerxes gives a banquet for all his princes and officials from his 127 provinces, stretching from India to Ethiopia. The celebration lasts six months!

   B. **A banquet for his palace officials** (1:5-22): Apparently as a thank-you for helping with the previous banquet, King Xerxes gives another banquet for his palace officials.

      1. *The details* (1:5-9): The palace is richly decorated; all are allowed to completely gorge themselves for seven days!

      2. *The drunkenness* (1:10): On the final day of the banquet, the king becomes very intoxicated.

      3. *The demand* (1:11): King Xerxes orders Queen Vashti to parade her beauty before his drunken officials.

      4. *The defiance* (1:12): The queen refuses to obey Xerxes' order!

      5. *The dilemma* (1:13-18): The king consults his advisers concerning Vashti's defiance, and they convince him that all other women might rebel against their husbands as well.

      6. *The decision* (1:19-20): The advisers recommend that the king banish his queen.

      7. *The decree* (1:21-22): King Xerxes follows his advisers' counsel and decrees that each man should be the ruler of his own home.

II. THE SELECTION OF ESTHER (2:1-20): A young Jewish girl named Esther is eventually chosen to replace Vashti as queen.

   A. **The search** (2:1-4): In essence a "Miss Persia" beauty contest is now conducted; the winner will become Xerxes' new queen.

B. **The sending away** (2:5-8): A young Jewish girl named Esther is among those who are sent to appear before the king. She has been raised by her cousin Mordecai, who adopted her when her parents died.

C. **The special favor** (2:9): Hegai, the eunuch in charge of the royal harem, is very pleased with Esther and shows her special favor.

D. **The summons** (2:12-19)
   1. *The process* (2:12-14): Each young woman in the harem undergoes one year of beauty treatments before seeing the king. After spending the night with the king, the woman lives in a second harem and never sees the king again unless he requests her specifically.
   2. *The pleasing* (2:15-19): With help from Hegai, Esther delights the king and becomes his new queen. He gives a banquet in Esther's honor.

E. **The secret** (2:10-11, 20): Heeding Mordecai's advice, Esther does not reveal her Jewish nationality to anyone.

III. THE DETECTION BY MORDECAI (2:21-23): Mordecai becomes a palace official and saves the king's life.

A. **A plot revealed** (2:21-22): Mordecai overhears a plot by some palace guards to assassinate the king. He reports the information to Esther, and she tells the king.

B. **A plot recorded** (2:23): Because of Mordecai's report, the guards are hanged, and the entire episode is duly recorded in the king's archives.

SECTION OUTLINE TWO (ESTHER 3–5)

Because Mordecai refuses to bow before Haman, Haman requests permission to exterminate all the Jews. When this permission is granted, Mordecai urges Esther to intervene on behalf of her people. Esther makes plans to ask King Xerxes to spare the Jews. Haman constructs a gallows to kill Mordecai.

I. THE PROBLEM (3:1-15): Soon after Esther becomes queen, a wicked man named Haman plots to eliminate all Jews throughout the Persian empire.

A. **Haman the haughty** (3:1-2): King Xerxes promotes Haman to prime minister; all the royal officials bow down whenever Haman passes by.

B. **Haman the hateful** (3:3-5): Haman becomes furious when Mordecai refuses to bow down before him.

C. **Haman the heartless** (3:6-15)
   1. *The plot* (3:6-9): In his rage Haman seeks the king's permission to destroy all the Jews in the empire. He promises the king 375 tons of silver if he agrees to the plan.

2. *The permission* (3:10-11): King Xerxes agrees to the cruel purge even without payment.
3. *The proclamation* (3:12-15): Haman orders letters sent throughout the empire, announcing that all Jews will be killed on a certain day.

II. THE PLAN (4:1–5:14): Esther and Mordecai carry out a plan to thwart Haman's wicked intentions.
   A. **Mordecai's request** (4:1-14)
      1. *Mordecai's anguish* (4:1-4): Upon learning of Haman's cruel decree, Mordecai mourns deeply and refuses to be comforted.
      2. *Mordecai's advice* (4:5-14): Mordecai informs Esther of the plot and urges her to use her royal office to help deliver the Jews.
   B. **Esther's response** (4:15–5:14)
      1. *The faith* (4:15-17): Esther plans to visit the king after a three-day fast, even though it is against the law.
      2. *The fearlessness* (5:1): Risking her life, Esther enters the inner court and stands before the king.
      3. *The favor* (5:2-3): To Esther's great relief, King Xerxes welcomes her and offers to grant almost any request she might ask!
      4. *The feasts* (5:4-8)
         a. Esther's first request (5:4-5): Esther asks that the king and Haman attend a banquet she has prepared, and they do so.
         b. Esther's second request (5:6-8): At the banquet Esther asks that the king and Haman attend another banquet the next day.
      5. *The fury* (5:9-13): Returning home, Haman sees Mordecai and becomes furious that he still refuses to bow before him. He boasts to his wife and friends about his honors from the king, but he also tells of his anger toward Mordecai.
      6. *The fatal advice* (5:14): Haman's wife and friends advise him to build a gallows and hang Mordecai on it in the morning.

SECTION OUTLINE THREE (ESTHER 6–10)
Mordecai is honored for his loyalty, and Haman is hanged. The Jews are allowed to defend themselves against their enemies, and Mordecai is promoted. The Jews successfully defend themselves, and the Festival of Purim is established to commemorate the event. Mordecai becomes prime minister.

I. HONORING MORDECAI (6:1-14)
   A. **The discovery** (6:1-3): One night King Xerxes listens to an attendant read the historical records to help him fall asleep. He discovers Mordecai's role in saving his life and that Mordecai has never been rewarded for his deed.

B. The discussion (6:4-9): The king notices Haman arriving to visit him.

   1. *Haman's aspirations* (6:4-5): Haman is seeking permission to hang Mordecai.

   2. *Haman's arrogance* (6:6): The king asks Haman what should be done for someone who pleases him. Haman wrongly assumes that he is the one the king is talking about.

   3. *Haman's answer* (6:7-9): Haman tells the king to dress the person in royal robes and publicly honor him.

C. The decision (6:10-14)

   1. *Haman's assignment* (6:10-11): The king commands Haman to organize such an event for Mordecai!

   2. *Haman's apprehension* (6:12-14): The humiliated Haman is warned by his wife and friends that it would be fatal to continue his plot against Mordecai.

II. HANGING HAMAN (7:1-10)

   A. The treachery learned (7:1-6): During the second banquet, Esther tells the king about Haman's plot to kill her and her people.

   B. The tables turned (7:7-10): The furious king orders Haman to be hanged on the very gallows he built for Mordecai!

III. HELPING THE JEWS (8:1–9:16): Esther still must work to save her people from being annihilated on the appointed day.

   A. The anguish of Esther (8:1-6): Esther begs the king to reverse Haman's order to kill all the Jews.

   B. The actions of the king (8:7-17)

      1. *The proclamation* (8:7-14): The king issues a new decree allowing the Jews to defend themselves against those who try to kill them.

      2. *The celebration* (8:15-17): Because of this decree, Jews throughout the empire rejoice.

   C. The avenging of the Jews (9:1-16): The Jews kill several hundred people on the appointed day, and the king grants Esther's request to let the Jews defend themselves for another day. Over 75,000 attackers are killed, along with Haman's 10 sons.

IV. HALLOWING THE DAY (9:17–10:3)

   A. The announcing of Purim (9:17-32): A special two-day festival is declared, to be celebrated each year as a reminder of the Jews' deliverance from their enemies.

   B. The advancement of Mordecai (10:1-3): Mordecai is made prime minister over all of Persia, second in power only to the king himself!

PART THREE

Poetry

Job

SECTION OUTLINE ONE (JOB 1–2)

Job is introduced. God allows Satan to test Job's faithfulness by taking all that he has. Job responds with great sorrow, but he worships God. Satan accuses Job again and strikes him with boils. Job's wife tells him to curse God and die, but Job remains faithful. Three of Job's friends come and mourn with him.

I. JOB'S PRESTIGE (1:1-5)
   A. **His faith** (1:1): "There was a man named Job who lived in the land of Uz. He was blameless, a man of complete integrity. He feared God and stayed away from evil."
   B. **His fortune** (1:3): "He owned 7,000 sheep, and 3,000 camels, 500 teams of oxen, and 500 female donkeys, and he employed many servants. He was, in fact, the richest person in that entire area."
   C. **His family** (1:2, 4-5): "He had seven sons and three daughters."

II. JOB'S PAIN (1:6-22; 2:1-10): For reasons unknown to Job, he suffers two waves of tragedy.
   A. **The record of his trials** (1:13-19; 2:7-8)
      1. *First wave* (1:13-19): In one day Job experiences four terrible tragedies: The Sabeans steal all his oxen and donkeys and kill his farmhands. Fire falls from heaven and burns up his sheep and his shepherds. Chaldeans carry off all his camels and kill his servants. Finally, a mighty wind blows down the house where his sons and daughters are, killing all of them.
      2. *Second wave* (2:7-8): Job is afflicted with painful boils from head to foot.
   B. **The reason for his trials** (1:6-12; 2:1-6): All of Job's trials result from two confrontations between God and Satan.
      1. *The first confrontation* (1:6-12): This first confrontation gives rise to the first wave of Job's tragedies.
         a. The assembling (1:6-7): "One day the angels came to present themselves before the LORD, and Satan the Accuser came with them."
         b. The appraisal (1:8): "Then the LORD asked Satan, 'Have

you noticed my servant Job? He is the finest man in all the earth—a man of complete integrity. He fears God and will have nothing to do with evil.'"

   c. The accusation (1:9-11): Satan scoffs that Job only serves God because God blesses him. Satan says that if all Job's blessings were taken away, he would curse God.
   d. The agreement (1:12): God gives Satan permission to do anything to all that Job has, but he is not to touch him physically.
2. *The second confrontation* (2:1-6): This second confrontation gives rise to the second wave of Job's tragedies.
   a. The review (2:1-3): God reminds Satan that Job has remained faithful despite his trials.
   b. The reproach (2:4-5): Satan responds, "But take away his health, and he will surely curse you to your face!"
   c. The restriction (2:6): God allows Satan to take Job's health but not his life.

C. The reaction to his trials (1:20-22; 2:9-10)
1. *Following the first wave of tragedy* (1:20-22): Job is deeply grieved, but he recognizes that he has come into the world with nothing and will leave with nothing. Mindful of this, he chooses to praise God and not blame him.
2. *Following the second wave of tragedy* (2:9-10): Despite the urgings of Job's wife to "curse God and die," Job does not sin by anything he says.

III. JOB'S PITY (2:11-13): Three of Job's friends come to comfort him in his grief.
   A. Who they are (2:11): Their names are Eliphaz, Bildad, and Zophar.
   B. What they do (2:12-13): Seeing Job, they grieve by wailing loudly and throwing dust into the air. Then they sit with him on the ground for a week without saying a word.

SECTION OUTLINE TWO (JOB 3–7)
Job breaks his silence and wishes that he had never been born. Eliphaz responds and questions Job's innocence. He urges Job to accept God's discipline. Job maintains his innocence and asserts his right to complain. Job then asks God why he has bothered to make him his target.

I. JOB'S DESPAIR (3:1-26)
   A. I wish I had never been born (3:1-10): Job curses the day of his birth, wishing it could be blotted off the calendar.
   B. I wish I had been stillborn (3:11-19): For Job the next best thing to never having been born would have been dying at birth. He laments that his mother let him live.

C. **Why is life given to those in despair** (3:20-26): Job wonders why life is given to the miserable. He has no peace or rest—only trouble.

II. ELIPHAZ'S DENUNCIATIONS (4:1–5:27): Eliphaz responds to Job's groaning.
   A. **Practice what you preach** (4:1-6): Job has encouraged the weak in the past, and Eliphaz rebukes him for not heeding his own advice now.
   B. **Does the innocent person perish?** (4:7-11): Eliphaz makes the case that the Lord does not allow trouble to befall the innocent, implying that Job must be sinning.
   C. **It came in a vision at night** (4:12-17): Eliphaz claims to have received his knowledge from a spirit in the middle of the night!
   D. **Alive in the morning, dead by evening** (4:18-21): Eliphaz claims that humans cannot be trusted; they are frail and die in ignorance.
   E. **The godless are born to grief** (5:1-7): Again Job is said to be suffering for his sin.
   F. **Present your case to God** (5:8-16): Eliphaz urges Job to bring his case before God, who is able to do anything.
   G. **Don't despise God's discipline** (5:17-27): Eliphaz exhorts Job to trust that God will heal and protect him once he has punished him.

III. JOB'S DEFENSE (6:1–7:21): Job responds to Eliphaz's ill-informed rebuke.
   A. **Don't I have a right to complain?** (6:1-7): Job argues that the greatness of his sorrow gives him a right to complain.
   B. **I wish that God would kill me** (6:8-13): Though Job takes comfort in having never denied God's word, he still wishes to die.
   C. **You are unreliable** (6:14-21): Job accuses his friend of being as unreliable as a brook that overflows in the spring and dries up in the heat.
   D. **Show me where I am wrong** (6:22-24): Job challenges his critic Eliphaz to show him where he is guilty.
   E. **Stop assuming my guilt** (6:25-30): Job maintains his innocence and rebukes his friends for assuming that he is guilty.
   F. **Life is long and hard** (7:1-5): Job is enduring his miserable life like a worker longing for the day to end.
   G. **Life is but a breath** (7:6-10): Job describes life as being like a fleeting breath, for all people die and never return.
   H. **Why have you made me your target?** (7:11-21): Job complains that God has terrified him with nightmares and has made him his target. He asks why God should go to all this trouble for no apparent reason and for such an insignificant person.

SECTION OUTLINE THREE (JOB 8–14)

Bildad rebukes Job and asserts that sin brings punishment. Job longs for a mediator to approach God with his complaints. Zophar rebukes Job and reminds him that God is beyond understanding. He urges Job to confess his sins, but Job reasserts his innocence. Job wants to argue his case with God himself.

I. BILDAD'S DENUNCIATIONS (8:1-22)
   A. **Your words are a blustering wind** (8:1-7): Bildad tells Job that he is being senseless—if he confesses his sins, he will be restored.
   B. **The godless will die** (8:8-19): Bildad tells Job to ask the former generation and learn that those without God wither and die like a plant without water.
   C. **God rewards the righteous** (8:20-22): Bildad advises Job to repent and be restored.

II. JOB'S DEFENSE (9:1–10:22): Job defends himself against Bildad.
   A. **How can a mortal argue with God?** (9:1-14): Job is frustrated because, though he feels he is innocent, he cannot challenge such a mighty God.
   B. **God destroys both the blameless and the wicked** (9:15-31): Job argues that it doesn't matter if he is innocent, because God attacks him without reason.
   C. **If only there were a mediator** (9:32-35): Job longs for a mediator to bring him and God together to resolve the issue.
   D. **Why are you treating me so terribly?** (10:1-7): Job begins to formulate his complaint to God.
   E. **Did you create me to condemn me?** (10:8-17): Job asks if God's plan was to destroy him even as his body was being formed in his mother's womb.
   F. **Better to never have been born** (10:18-22): If Job was created only to be condemned, it would be better to have died at birth.

III. ZOPHAR'S DENUNCIATIONS (11:1-20): Zophar begins his rebuke.
   A. **God is punishing you less than you deserve** (11:1-6): Zophar wishes Job could see himself as God does.
   B. **You cannot comprehend God's ways** (11:7-12): God's ways are beyond human understanding.
   C. **Confess your sins and find hope** (11:13-20): Zophar, like the other friends, assumes that Job is suffering because of his sin.

IV. JOB'S DEFENSE (12:1–14:22): Now Job must defend himself before Zophar.
   A. **What a know-it-all!** (12:1-2): Job sarcastically says that Zophar knows everything.
   B. **Even the animals know** (12:3-12): Job asserts that even the animals know that God sometimes allows the evil to scoff at the good.

C. **God is omniscient and omnipotent** (12:13-25): Job knows that God knows all and that he is in control of everything that happens.

D. **Listen rather than accuse** (13:1-6): Job challenges Zophar to hear his defense.

E. **Don't put words in God's mouth!** (13:7-12): Job accuses Zophar of using lies to defend God's actions.

F. **I will risk death to declare my innocence** (13:13-19): Job is willing to risk death to speak his mind to God and prove his innocence.

G. **Two things I beg of you** (13:20-25): Job asks God to stop afflicting him and to cease terrifying him with his awesome presence.

H. **God's bitter accusations** (13:26-28): Job feels that God has been storing up accusations against him.

I. **Life is short and full of trouble** (14:1-6): Job asks for a little mercy from God since humans are so frail.

J. **Death is eternal** (14:7-12): Job declares that people, unlike trees that sprout again after they are cut down, never rise again after death.

K. **Oh, to live again after death** (14:13-22): Job wishes that God would think of him after he dies; that would give him hope. But he does not seem to believe that God will do so.

SECTION OUTLINE FOUR (JOB 15–19)

Eliphaz asserts that wise men have always believed that sin brings suffering. Job is frustrated with his friends and God; he longs for a mediator between him and God. Bildad says that terrors await the wicked. Job accuses his friends and God of unfairness. He feels forsaken, yet he expresses hope that his Redeemer lives.

I. ELIPHAZ'S DENUNCIATIONS (15:1-35): Eliphaz begins a second round of rebukes from Job's friends.

A. **Nothing but a windbag** (15:1-16): Eliphaz tells Job that he is acting like a wise man, but really he is foolish.

B. **Sinful people suffer** (15:17-35): Eliphaz again assumes that Job is suffering because of sin in his life, so he tells how the wicked suffer many troubles.

II. JOB'S DEFENSE (16:1–17:16): Job responds to Eliphaz with increased frustration.

A. **What miserable comforters!** (16:1-4): Job accuses his friends of an endless flow of foolish and critical words.

B. **I would help you** (16:5): Job says that he would help his friends if they were suffering.

C. **Betrayed by God and people** (16:6-18): Job says that both God and others have turned against him.

D. **An advocate in heaven** (16:19-22): Job trusts that someone is presenting his case before God.

E. **Defend my innocence** (17:1-9): Job calls upon God to defend him because Job has become a mockery to those around him.

F. **My hopes have disappeared** (17:10-16): Job despairs and resigns himself to death as he looks upon his seemingly hopeless situation.

III. BILDAD'S DENUNCIATIONS (18:1-21): Bildad begins his second round of rebukes.

A. **Be reasonable** (18:1-4): Bildad rebukes Job for merely reacting in his grief and not speaking reasonably to his friends.

B. **Terrors surround the wicked** (18:5-21): Assuming that Job is suffering because of his sin, Bildad describes the terrible woes of the wicked.

IV. JOB'S DEFENSE (19:1-29): Job continues to feel persecuted.

A. **Insulted 10 times** (19:1-5): Job complains that his three "friends" have reproached him 10 times.

B. **God must hate me** (19:6-12): Because of his suffering, Job concludes that God must have something against him.

C. **Forsaken by family and friends** (19:13-22): Job says that all his family and friends have turned against him.

D. **Chisel my words in stone** (19:23-24): Job wishes that his words could be eternally chiseled into a rock.

E. **My Redeemer lives** (19:25-29): Though Job is distressed that no one believes him now, he trusts that one day he will be vindicated and see God for himself.

SECTION OUTLINE FIVE (JOB 20–24)

Zophar tells Job that the wicked will be destroyed. Job insists that evil people prosper. Eliphaz lists sins Job may have committed and suggests that he repent. Job desires to find God and plead his case before him. Job asks why the ungodly continue to prosper.

I. ZOPHAR'S DENUNCIATIONS (20:1-29)

A. **I resent your rebuke** (20:1-3): Zophar feels insulted by Job's rebuke.

B. **The ways of the wicked** (20:4-29): Zophar returns to his theme of describing the sad fate of the wicked.

II. JOB'S DEFENSE (21:1-34): Job attacks Zophar's false assumption that the wicked are always punished for their sins in this life.

A. **The wicked prosper** (21:1-18): It seems to Job that the more wicked people are, the more they prosper!

B. **Don't punish their children** (21:19-21): Job rejects the theory that justice is served when the children of the ungodly are punished.

   C. **Death comes to good and bad alike** (21:22-26): The same fate
      eventually awaits all people—good or bad, rich or poor.
   D. **No guarantee of justice in this life** (21:27-34): Often the wicked
      flourish until death and then are buried with great honor.

III. ELIPHAZ'S DENUNCIATIONS (22:1-30): Eliphaz begins the third round
     of rebukes toward Job.
   A. **Your guilt has no limit** (22:1-5): Eliphaz accuses Job of endless
      sin.
   B. **A list of possible sins** (22:6-11): Eliphaz lists examples of sins
      that Job must have committed to incite God to punish him.
   C. **You think God doesn't see you** (22:12-20): Eliphaz says that Job
      must think that God does not see or care about what he does.
   D. **Repent and be restored** (22:21-30): Eliphaz advises Job to repent
      so that God can bless him once again.

IV. JOB'S DEFENSE (23:1–24:25): Job begins to respond less to Eliphaz
    and more directly to God himself.
   A. **Where can I find God?** (23:1-9): Job longs to find God and plead
      his case before him.
   B. **Tested like gold** (23:10-12): Job is certain that he will be found
      innocent after he endures his trials like gold in a refining fire.
   C. **God will do as he pleases** (23:13-17): Job acknowledges that
      God's decree concerning his life will be carried out regardless.
   D. **Why aren't the ungodly judged?** (24:1-17): Job cannot under-
      stand why God allows the unrighteous to go unpunished.
   E. **Fallen in a flash and forgotten** (24:18-25): Job admits that the
      wicked do not last long.

SECTION OUTLINE SIX (JOB 25–31)
Bildad argues that no one can stand before God. Job maintains his
innocence and tells how God possesses wisdom. Job longs to return
to his former days of blessing and contrasts them with his current
bitter situation. Job names many sins and challenges his friends to
find him guilty of any of them.

 I. BILDAD'S DENUNCIATIONS (25:1-6): Bildad gives the final rebuke of
    Job's three friends.
   A. **God is powerful** (25:1-3): Bildad begins by asserting that God is
      powerful.
   B. **No one is righteous** (25:4-6): Bildad tells Job that no one can
      stand before God and claim to be righteous.

II. JOB'S DEFENSE (26:1–31:40): Job begins his final defense before his
    friends.
   A. **How have you helped anyone?** (26:1-4): Job rebukes his critics
      by asking whom they have helped by their comments.
   B. **Creation is but a minor work of God** (26:5-14): Job reminds his

friends that the entire universe is only a feeble example of God's mighty power!

C. A twofold vow (27:1-6): Job vows to speak no evil and to maintain his innocence until he dies.

D. The godless have no hope (27:7-23): Job notes that the godless are ultimately headed for destruction.

E. Finding valuable things (28:1-11): Job notes how humans have amazing ways to find and extract valuables from the earth.

F. Wisdom cannot be found or bought (28:12-21): Wisdom is far more valuable than precious metals and stones. It cannot simply be discovered by people or bought for a price.

G. God knows where wisdom is hidden (28:22-28): God knows where to find wisdom: "The fear of the Lord is true wisdom; to forsake evil is real understanding."

H. Once respected for who I was (29:1-11): Job longs for the days when he was held in great honor by all who knew him.

I. Once respected for what I did (29:12-25): Before his sufferings began, Job championed the helpless and punished the wicked.

J. Now despised by the despicable (30:1-14): Now Job is mocked even by the lowly.

K. Unending pain and unanswered prayers (30:15-31): Job lives in terror and constant misery.

L. Have I lusted? (31:1-12): If evil sexual thoughts are the reason for Job's suffering, he is willing that his wife be given to another man.

M. Have I mistreated others? (31:13-23): Job is willing to be punished if he has wronged someone.

N. Have I worshiped money or idols? (31:24-28): Job recognizes that idolatry is justification for punishment as well.

O. Have I concealed any other sin? (31:29-40): Job would proudly face any accusation against him, if he only knew what he'd done. With these anguish-filled words Job concludes his defense.

SECTION OUTLINE SEVEN (JOB 32–37)

Elihu denounces Job for claiming to be innocent and his friends for failing to answer him well. Elihu argues that God does not condemn unfairly, and he calls Job arrogant for thinking he is righteous. Elihu says that God responds to us in his wisdom, and he condemns Job for questioning the Creator of the universe.

I. ELIHU'S MONOLOGUE: WHY ELIHU SPEAKS (32:1–33:7): Another man named Elihu rebukes Job and his three other friends.

A. An angry young man (32:1-15): Elihu, who is younger than Job and his friends, becomes angry with Job for refusing to acknowledge his sin. He rebukes the others for not giving adequate rebuttals to Job's answers.

B. **Listen to me** (32:16-22): Now that he has listened to Job and his friends, Elihu demands that they listen to his pent-up words.

C. **You can trust me** (33:1-7): Elihu assures Job that he will speak the truth sincerely and that he is not to be feared.

II. ELIHU'S MONOLOGUE: WHERE JOB IS WRONG (33:8–34:37): Elihu corrects what he believes are Job's wrong assumptions.

A. **God speaks to us in many ways** (33:8-22): Job accused God of not responding to people's complaints. Elihu argues that God speaks to people through dreams, visions, and even through pain and sickness, but people do not recognize it.

B. **God listens to us** (33:23-30): Elihu asserts that God listens and answers the prayers of those who have a mediator who shows that they are righteous.

C. **Be quiet and listen** (33:31-33): Elihu tells Job to speak if he has something to say. Otherwise he should remain silent and ponder the wisdom that Elihu will teach him.

D. **Listen to me, you wise men** (34:1-4): Elihu calls for all who are wise to discern whether Job is right.

E. **Job is bitter and arrogant** (34:5-9): Elihu accuses Job of being arrogant in his claim to be innocent. He believes that Job seeks the companionship of evil people.

F. **God repays people according to their deeds** (34:10-32): This is why Elihu believes Job is arrogant. He argues that Job cannot be righteous, because he is suffering, and God does not unjustly punish the righteous and allow the wicked to go unpunished.

G. **God does not answer to you** (34:33-37): Elihu accuses Job of blasphemy and rebellion because he has accused God of allowing him to suffer unjustly.

III. ELIHU'S MONOLOGUE: WHAT JOB MUST REALIZE (35:1–36:21): Elihu continues to correct Job's thinking.

A. **You cannot force God's hand** (35:1-8): Elihu tells Job that he should not expect God to respond to him simply because Job is righteous. Our actions cannot force God to do anything.

B. **In God's good timing** (35:9-16): The Almighty does indeed provide comfort for the oppressed, but all in his timing.

C. **God uses suffering for good** (36:1-15): Elihu asserts that God uses suffering to correct and instruct people.

D. **Change your attitude** (36:16-21): Elihu tells Job to be patient in his troubles and to view his suffering as God's way of helping him.

IV. ELIHU'S MONOLOGUE: WHAT GOD HAS DONE (36:22–37:24)

A. **Who understands God's ways?** (36:22–37:13): Elihu catalogs many wonders in nature that show God's greatness. In view of such greatness, how can Job tell God what to do?

B. **You know nothing** (37:14-24): Elihu tells Job to stand in awe of God and show him reverence.

SECTION OUTLINE EIGHT (JOB 38–42)
The Lord humbles Job by asking him a series of questions about nature. Job acknowledges his insignificance, but the Lord continues with questions about two imposing creatures, the behemoth and the leviathan. Job humbly repents of his complaints against God. The Lord rebukes the three friends and restores Job's fortunes.

I. THE LORD'S RESPONSE (38:1–39:30): The Lord finally speaks and humbles Job with a series of questions about nature.
   A. **First series of questions, concerning God's creation** (38:1-38):
      1. *The earth* (38:1-7, 17-18)
      2. *The oceans* (38:8-11, 16)
      3. *Light* (38:12-15, 19-21)
      4. *Snow and rain* (38:22-30, 34-38)
      5. *The stars* (38:31-33)
   B. **Second series of questions, concerning God's creatures** (38:39–39:30):
      1. *Lions* (38:39-40)
      2. *Ravens* (38:41)
      3. *Mountain goats* (39:1-4)
      4. *Wild donkeys* (39:5-8)
      5. *The wild ox* (39:9-12)
      6. *The ostrich* (39:13-18)
      7. *The horse* (39:19-25)
      8. *The hawk* (39:26-30)

II. JOB'S REACTION (40:1–42:17)
   A. **His repentance** (40:1–42:6)
      1. *First occasion* (40:1-5): Job is humbled regarding his wisdom.
         a. The confrontation (40:1-2): The Lord asks Job for his answers to all these questions.
         b. The confession (40:3-5): "I am nothing—how could I ever find the answers? I will put my hand over my mouth in silence."
      2. *Second occasion* (40:6–42:6): Job is humbled regarding his power.
         a. The confrontation (40:6–41:34): The Lord asks Job if he is able to capture two fearful creatures.
            (1) The behemoth (40:15-24): It is difficult to be certain what this creature was. Some scholars believe it may have been a land dinosaur; others believe it was a hippopotamus. Whatever it was, it was very imposing.
            (2) The leviathan (41:1-34): Some scholars believe this mysterious creature may have been an aquatic dinosaur; others believe it might have been a crocodile.
         b. The confession (42:1-6): Job admits his insignificance in comparison to the Lord's power.

B. His rewards (42:7-17): After Job recognizes his proper position before the Lord, the Lord restores his fortunes.

1. *The rebuke* (42:7-9): The Lord rebukes the three friends for their false accusations of Job. He instructs them to make a sacrifice and says that Job will pray for them.

2. *The restoration* (42:10-17): After Job prays for his friends, the Lord restores his fortunes to him, giving him twice as much as he had before. He blesses Job with seven more sons and three more daughters. Job lives 140 more years!

Psalms

SECTION OUTLINE ONE (PSALM 1)

The psalmist compares and contrasts the godly and the wicked and notes the eventual end of each.

I. THE GODLY (1:1-3)
   A. **The contrast** (1:1-2)
      1. *What they do not do* (1:1)
         a. Follow the advice of the wicked.
         b. Stand around with sinners.
         c. Join in with scoffers.
      2. *What they do* (1:2): They delight in the law of the Lord.
   B. **The comparison** (1:3): They are like fruitful, well-watered trees.

II. THE GODLESS (1:4-6): The Lord protects the godly, but the wicked are worthless chaff who will one day be condemned and destroyed.

SECTION OUTLINE TWO (PSALM 2)

This messianic psalm describes the nations' rebellion against God's chosen kings and warns against such foolish thinking.

I. THE APOSTATES (2:1-3): The earth's rulers plan to rebel against the Lord's anointed one.

II. THE ALMIGHTY (2:4-6)
   A. **The Lord's response** (2:4): He laughs at this pitiful attempt to rebel against his anointed king.
   B. **The Lord's rebuke** (2:5-6): "I have placed my chosen king on the throne in Jerusalem."

III. THE ANOINTED (2:7-9): The chosen king repeats the Lord's promises to him, asserting that the Lord will help him subdue all his enemies.

IV. THE ADVICE (2:10-12): "Serve the LORD with reverent fear."

SECTION OUTLINE THREE (PSALM 3)

David asks the Lord to protect him against his enemies and finds rest and security in the Lord's care.

I. THE SCORN (3:1-2): David is beset by many enemies; many say that God will not rescue him.

II. THE SUPPLICATION (3:4, 7): David prays to God and is heard.

III. THE SLEEP (3:3, 5-6, 8): Even when surrounded by 10,000 enemies, David can sleep in peace, for the Lord sustains him!

SECTION OUTLINE FOUR (PSALM 4)

David asks God to vindicate him from his accusers and finds rest in knowing that God will keep him safe.

I. THE SUPPLICATION (4:1, 6): David cries out to God for relief from his distress.

II. THE SHAME (4:2): David's enemies are attempting to ruin his reputation with groundless accusations.

III. THE SANCTIFICATION (4:3): God has set apart the godly for himself.

IV. THE SCRUTINY (4:4-5): David calls people to search their heart in silence and trust God.

V. THE SECURITY (4:7-8): Knowing that God will keep him safe, David can sleep in peace.

SECTION OUTLINE FIVE (PSALM 5)

David asks God to lead and protect him. He also calls upon God to destroy his wicked enemies.

I. THE DELIVERANCE OF THE GODLY (5:1-3, 7-8, 10-12)
   A. The petition (5:1-3, 7-8, 10)
   1. *Whom he prays to* (5:1-2): David calls upon the Lord alone to help him.
   2. *When he prays* (5:3): David prays to the Lord each morning.
   3. *Where he prays* (5:7): David prays and worships in the Temple.
   4. *What he prays* (5:8, 10)
      a. David asks the Lord to lead him in the right path (5:8).
      b. David asks the Lord to declare his enemies guilty (5:10).
   B. The praises (5:11-12): David calls all who find refuge in the Lord to rejoice and praise him.

II. THE DESTRUCTION OF THE GODLESS (5:4-6, 9): David professes that the Lord detests the wicked and will not let them stand in his presence.
   A. Why (5:4-5): The Lord detests the wicked and will not let them stand in his presence.
   B. Who (5:6, 9): This includes liars, murderers, and deceivers.

SECTION OUTLINE SIX (PSALM 6)
In this penitential psalm David says he is worn out from weeping and prays for the Lord to be merciful to him. David is confident that the Lord has heard his prayer.

I. DAVID'S REQUEST (6:1-7):
   A. What he desires (6:1-2, 4-5): David cries out for the Lord to be merciful to him.
      1. *Do not rebuke me* (6:1-2).
      2. *Do rescue me* (6:4-5).
   B. Why he desires it (6:3, 6-7)
      1. *He is sick at heart* (6:3).
      2. *He is worn out from sobbing (6:6-7).*

II. DAVID'S REASSURANCE (6:8-10): David is reassured that the Lord has heard his prayer and that his enemies will be disgraced.

SECTION OUTLINE SEVEN (PSALM 7)
David asks God to search his heart to see if he has sinned, for he knows that God protects the innocent and thwarts the plans of the wicked. David believes he is innocent, so he calls upon God to rescue him.

I. DAVID'S SUPPLICATION (7:1-9)
   A. Save me! (7:1-2, 6-9): David asks the Lord to rescue him from his enemies.
   B. Search me! (7:3-5): David calls upon the Lord to punish him if he is guilty of injustice.

II. DAVID'S SHIELD (7:10-16)
   A. God protects the righteous (7:10).
   B. God punishes the wicked (7:11-16).

III. DAVID'S SONG (7:17): David praises the Lord because the Lord is just.

SECTION OUTLINE EIGHT (PSALM 8)

David reflects on the Lord's majesty and his creation and is amazed that the Lord cares about human beings and crowns them with honor.

I. THE LORD'S GREATNESS (8:1-3, 9): David marvels at the glory of the Lord.
   A. **As seen in creation** (8:1, 3, 9): The majesty of the Lord fills the heavens and the earth.
   B. **As sung by children** (8:2): Little children praise the Lord.

II. THE LORD'S GOODNESS (8:3-8)
   A. **The amazement** (8:3-5): Considering the Lord's greatness, David is amazed that the Lord has shown such concern for humans and has crowned them with honor.
   B. **The assignment** (8:6-8): The Lord placed humans in charge of everything he has made.

SECTION OUTLINE NINE (PSALM 9)

David thanks the Lord for rescuing him and boasts that the Lord helps the helpless and punishes the wicked.

I. GOD'S RIGHTEOUS REDEMPTION OF THE ELECT (9:1-3, 9-14, 18)
   A. **What the Lord had done** (9:1-3, 9-10, 18)
      1. *He protected them* (9:1-3, 9-10).
      2. *He provided for them* (9:18).
   B. **What the psalmist would do** (9:11-14): He would sing God's praises at the gates of Jerusalem.

II. GOD'S RIGHTEOUS RESISTANCE OF EVIL (9:5-6, 15-17, 19-20)
   A. **The foolishness of the godless** (9:15-16): They eventually fall into their own pits and are caught by their own nets!
   B. **The fury upon the godless** (9:5-6, 17, 19-20)
      1. *God will fill them with terror* (9:19-20).
      2. *God will blot out their very names from memory* (9:5-6).
      3. *God will cast them into hell* (9:17).

III. GOD'S RIGHTEOUS RULE OVER THE EARTH (9:4, 7-8)
   A. **He will rule justly.**
   B. **He will rule eternally.**

IV. THE LORD'S RULE (9:7-10, 12, 17-18): The Lord reigns over the whole world with fairness and helps the oppressed.

V. THE LORD'S RESCUE (9:1-6, 9-16, 18-20)
   A. **What the Lord does** (9:3-6, 15-16): He lets the wicked fall into their own pits and get caught by their own nets!
   B. **What David does** (9:1-2, 11-14): David sings praises to the Lord and calls others to do the same.

C. What David wants the Lord to do (9:13-14, 19-20): David asks the Lord for mercy and for rescue from his enemies.

SECTION OUTLINE TEN (PSALM 10)

The psalmist asks the Lord why he allows the wicked to continue oppressing the poor and helpless. He calls upon the Lord to punish the wicked.

I. THE ARROGANCE AND CONTEMPT OF THE GODLESS (10:2-11)
   A. **Their vertical actions** (10:3-4, 11): The psalmist describes how the wicked regard the Lord.
      1. *They curse the Lord* (10:3).
      2. *They ignore the Lord* (10:4, 11).
   B. **Their horizontal actions** (10:2, 5-10): The psalmist describes how the wicked regard others.
      1. *They oppress the poor* (10:2).
      2. *They scorn their enemies* (10:5).
      3. *They boast that they cannot be stopped* (10:6).
      4. *They curse, threaten, and lie* (10:7).
      5. *They ambush and murder the innocent* (10:8-10).

II. THE ANGUISH AND CRY OF THE GODLY (10:1, 12-18)
   A. **Their response** (10:1, 13): The psalmist asks why the wicked are allowed to get away with their deeds.
   B. **Their request** (10:12, 15-18)
      1. *Punish the wicked* (10:12).
      2. *Break their arms* (10:15-16): The psalmist wants the Lord to render the wicked incapable of committing their deeds.
      3. *Bring justice to the oppressed* (10:17-18).

SECTION OUTLINE ELEVEN (PSALM 11)

David answers those who tell him to flee for fear of the wicked, assuring them that the Lord is in control.

I. THE SECURITY OF THE BELIEVER (11:1-3): The faithless wrongly advise David to flee to the mountains, for the wicked are attacking the righteous.

II. THE SOVEREIGNTY OF THE LORD (11:4-7): David finds security in three attributes of the Lord.
   A. **His sovereignty** (11:4): The Lord rules from heaven and controls everything.
   B. **His omniscience** (11:5): The Lord examines everyone's deeds.
   C. **His justice/righteousness** (11:6-7): The Lord punishes the wicked and shows himself to the righteous.

SECTION OUTLINE TWELVE (PSALM 12)

David cries out to the Lord because the wicked seem to overwhelm the godly, but he recognizes that the Lord knows their plight and will watch over them.

I. THE PROBLEM (12:1-4): David cries out to God with his concern.
   A. **The godly seem to be disappearing** (12:1).
   B. **Everyone is lying to each other** (12:2-4).

II. THE PURITY (12:6): David recognizes that the Lord's promises are pure and trustworthy.

III. THE PROTECTION (12:5, 7-8): David trusts that the Lord is aware of the situation and will defend the godly.

SECTION OUTLINE THIRTEEN (PSALM 13)

David feels isolated from the Lord and calls out to him to be vindicated. He again finds rest in the Lord's unfailing love.

I. DAVID'S PERPLEXITY (13:1-2): Four times David asks the Lord, "How long?":
   A. **"How long will you forget me?"** (13:1)
   B. **"How long will you look the other way?"** (13:1)
   C. **"How long must I struggle with anguish in my soul?"** (13:2)
   D. **"How long will my enemy have the upper hand?"** (13:2)

II. DAVID'S PETITION (13:3-4): David makes two requests of the Lord:
   A. **Restore me** (13:3).
   B. **Do not let my enemies gloat over me** (13:4).

III. DAVID'S PRAISE (13:5-6): David trusts in the Lord's unfailing love and rejoices because he is good to him.

SECTION OUTLINE FOURTEEN (PSALM 14)

David bemoans how everyone has turned away from God. He asserts that God opposes the wicked, and he calls for God to rescue his people.

I. GOD AND THE FOOLISH (14:1-5)
   A. **The arrogance of fools** (14:1): They say, "There is no God."
   B. **The actions of fools** (14:1, 4)
      1. *They are corrupt and evil* (14:1).
      2. *They devour the righteous* (14:4).
      3. *They do not pray to the Lord* (14:4).
   C. **The abundance of fools** (14:2-3): No one seeks God.
   D. **The anguish of fools** (14:5): God's judgment will someday overwhelm them.

II. GOD AND THE FAVORED (14:6-7)
- **A. The Lord watches** (14:6): The Lord watches over his people.
- **B. David wishes** (14:7): David calls upon the Lord to rescue his people.

SECTION OUTLINE FIFTEEN (PSALM 15)
David describes the behavior of those who truly worship the Lord.

I. THE QUESTION (15:1): David asks, "Who may worship in your sanctuary, LORD?"

II. THE QUALIFICATIONS (15:2-5): David describes the behavior of those who worship the Lord.
- **A. Positive aspects** (15:2, 4): Those who worship the Lord:
  1. *lead blameless lives* (15:2);
  2. *do what is right* (15:2);
  3. *speak the truth* (15:2);
  4. *despise persistent sinners* (15:4);
  5. *honor the Lord's faithful followers* (15:4); and
  6. *keep their promises even when it hurts* (15:4).
- **B. Negative aspects** (15:3, 5): Those who worship the Lord refuse to:
  1. *slander others* (15:3);
  2. *harm their neighbors* (15:3);
  3. *speak evil of their friends* (15:3);
  4. *charge interest on loans* (15:5); and
  5. *accept bribes to testify against the innocent* (15:5).

SECTION OUTLINE SIXTEEN (PSALM 16)
David rejoices in the Lord and recounts the blessings of following him. This psalm also prophesies of the relationship between the Messiah and God the Father.

I. DAVID'S SECURITY (16:1-7)
- **A. David's confidence** (16:1-2, 5-7): David finds security in the Lord.
  1. *The Lord protects him* (16:1).
  2. *The Lord provides for him* (16:2, 5-7).
- **B. David's companions** (16:3): David looks up to the godly of the land.
- **C. David's commitment** (16:4): David vows never to offer sacrifices to idols.

II. DAVID'S SON (16:8-11): These verses, although written by David, predict the future work of Christ.
- **A. Jesus' reliance upon his father** (16:8)

B. Jesus' resurrection by his father (16:9-10)
C. Jesus' reign with his father (16:11)

SECTION OUTLINE SEVENTEEN (PSALM 17)
David speaks of his sincere attempt to live a godly life and asks God to hear his prayer and protect him from his enemies.

I. HEAR ME! (17:1-2, 6): He asks the Lord to hear his righteous plea.

II. VINDICATE ME! (17:3-5): David is confident that he has not disobeyed God.

III. SHOW ME! (17:7): David longs for God's unfailing love.

IV. GUARD ME! (17:8-13)
   A. Where he wants to be hidden (17:8): "In the shadow of your wings."
   B. Why he wants to be hidden (17:9-12): David is assailed by many cruel enemies.

V. RESCUE ME! (17:13-14): David calls for God to overthrow his enemies.

VI. SATISFY ME! (17:15): David longs to see God face-to-face.

SECTION OUTLINE EIGHTEEN (PSALM 18)
In this psalm for public worship the psalmist praises God for delivering him from all his enemies, including Saul. He regards his deliverance as God's reward for living righteously.

I. DAVID'S DELIGHT (18:1-3): David expresses his deep love for the Lord.

II. DAVID'S DISTRESS (18:4-6): David is threatened with death and cries out to the Lord for help.

III. DAVID'S DELIVERANCE (18:7-49)
   A. The Lord arrives (18:7-15): Through poetic and majestic metaphors, David depicts the coming of the Lord to rescue him.
      1. *His appearance* (18:8-11)
         a. Smoke and fire pour from his mouth (18:8).
         b. Dark clouds shroud him (18:9, 11).
         c. Angelic beings accompany him (18:10).
      2. *His actions (18:7, 12-15)*
         a. He rocks the earth and shakes the mountains (18:7).
         b. He advances with hailstones and bolts of lightning (18:12, 14).
         c. He thunders from heaven (18:13).

       d. He shoots his arrows and scatters his enemies (18:14).
       e. He lays bare the earth and the sea (18:15).
    B. The Lord assists (18:16-49): The Lord acts to save David.
      1. *He rescues him* (18:16-19, 43-49).
       a. The Lord draws him out of deep waters (18:16).
       b. He leads him to a place of safety (18:17-19).
       c. He makes him ruler over nations (18:43-49).
      2. *He rewards him* (18:20-28): David considers these good things as a reward for his faithfulness to the Lord.
      3. *He revives him* (18:29-42): David is able, by God's strength, to defeat all his enemies.

IV. DAVID'S DESCENDANTS (18:50): God shows his unfailing love to David and his descendants.

SECTION OUTLINE NINETEEN (PSALM 19)
David shows that the Creator of the universe is the giver of the law and is worthy of praise, worship, and obedience.

I. NATURAL REVELATION (19:1-6)
    A. Where is this revelation? (19:1-2, 4-6): The heavens, including the sun, tell of God's glory.
    B. Who sees this revelation? (19:3-4): People all over the world can see this "soundless sermon."

II. SUPERNATURAL REVELATION (19:7-14)
    A. David describes God's Word (19:7-9).
      1. *What it is* (19:7-9): It is perfect, trustworthy, right, clear, true.
      2. *What it does* (19:7-9): It revives the soul, makes the simple wise, brings joy to the heart, and gives insight to life.
    B. David desires God's Word (19:10-14).
      1. *How he views it* (19:10): David considers God's word more precious than gold and sweeter than honey.
      2. *Why he values it* (19:11-14): David knows that God's word can keep him from sin.

SECTION OUTLINE TWENTY (PSALM 20)
David expresses the hope that God will lead the king and answer his requests.

I. THE REQUESTS (20:1-5, 9): David wishes several things for the king:
    A. May the Lord respond to your cry (20:1, 9).
    B. May the Lord keep you safe (20:1).
    C. May the Lord send you help and strengthen you (20:2).
    D. May the Lord look favorably on your offerings (20:3).
    E. May the Lord grant your heart's desire (20:4).

F. May we shout for joy over your victory (20:5).
G. May the Lord answer all your prayers (20:5).

II. THE REASSURANCE (20:6-8): The psalmist is confident in the Lord.

SECTION OUTLINE TWENTY-ONE (PSALM 21)
David thanks the Lord for answering his prayer for victory over his enemies.

I. THE LORD GIVES DAVID THE DESIRES OF HIS HEART (21:2-12).
   A. Regarding David (21:2-6)
      1. *Prosperity, success, and a crown of gold* (21:3)
      2. *Long life* (21:4)
      3. *Honor, splendor, and majesty* (21:5)
      4. *Joy in the Lord's presence* (21:6)
   B. Regarding David's enemies (21:7-12): David's enemies will be captured and destroyed.

II. DAVID GIVES THE LORD THE DEVOTION OF HIS HEART (21:1, 13): David praises the Lord for his strength and for his mighty acts.

SECTION OUTLINE TWENTY-TWO (PSALM 22)
The psalm simultaneously tells of both David's and Jesus' experiences. They feel abandoned by God. Their enemies have viciously attacked them, and they call out for deliverance. They then rejoice, knowing that the Lord defends the oppressed.

I. JESUS' GRIEVOUS CRUCIFIXION (22:1-21): As David speaks of his suffering, he also foretells Jesus' sufferings on the cross.
   A. The testimony (22:9-11, 19-21): Both Jesus and David share two things in common:
      1. *They have been raised to love God* (22:9-10).
      2. *They call upon God for deliverance* (22:11, 19-21).
   B. The travail (22:1-8, 12-18): David's experiences foretell of Jesus' experience of being alone on the cross.
      1. *Abandoned by God* (22:1-5): "My God, my God! Why have you forsaken me?"
      2. *Abused by his enemies* (22:6-8, 12-18): His enemies have done several things to him.
         a. He is scorned and despised (22:6).
         b. He is mocked and insulted (22:7-8).
         c. He is viciously attacked by his enemies (22:12-13, 16).
         d. His life is poured out like water (22:14).
         e. His bones are out of joint (22:14, 17).
         f. His heart is melted like wax (22:14).
         g. His strength is totally dried up (22:15).

      h. His hands and feet are pierced (22:16).

      i. His clothes are divided up and gambled for (22:18).

II. JESUS' GLORIOUS CORONATION (22:22-31)

    A. He praises the Lord for defending the oppressed (22:22-25): Some see this as an implied reference to Christ's resurrection (see Hebrews 2:12).

    B. All nations will worship the Lord (22:26-31): Some see this as a reference to Christ's future reign.

SECTION OUTLINE TWENTY-THREE (PSALM 23)

David uses the metaphors of a shepherd and his sheep and a host and his guests to describe the Lord's care for his people.

I. THE SHEPHERD AND HIS SHEEP (23:1-4): The Lord takes care of his people like a shepherd cares for his sheep.

    A. He provides for them (23:1).

    B. He renews their strength (23:3).

II. THE GUIDE AND THE TRAVELER (23:3-4): The Lord guides his people.

    A. He guides them along right paths (23:3).

    B. He protects and comforts them (23:4).

III. THE HOST AND HIS GUESTS (23:5): The Lord takes care of his people like a host cares for his guests.

IV. THE PHYSICIAN AND THE PATIENT (23:5): He anoints his head with oil.

V. THE PROPHET AND THE PROMISED (23:6): He shows them goodness and unfailing love (23:6).

SECTION OUTLINE TWENTY-FOUR (PSALM 24)

David describes the Lord as the glorious King who dwells in his Temple. Many think this psalm refers to Jesus the Messiah.

I. THE GLORIOUS KINGDOM (24:1-6)

    A. What it embraces (24:1-2): This kingdom includes the entire earth and everything in it.

    B. Whom it embraces (24:3-6): The Lord allows those with pure hands and hearts into his presence.

II. THE GLORIOUS KING (24:7-10): David calls for the gates to open so the Lord, the invincible King of glory, can enter.

SECTION OUTLINE TWENTY-FIVE (PSALM 25)

David wrote this psalm as an acrostic; each verse begins with a successive letter of the Hebrew alphabet. Believing that God rewards the righteous, David blends a prayer for deliverance from his enemies with a prayer for forgiveness and guidance.

I. PROTECT ME! (25:1-3, 15-22): David asks that his enemies would not be allowed to defeat him.

II. PILOT ME! (25:4-5, 8-10): David asks God to guide him in the right path.

III. PARDON ME! (25:6-7, 11)
  A. **What** (25:6-7): David asks God to forgive the sins of his youth.
  B. **Why** (25:11): David begs forgiveness for the honor of God's name.

IV. PROSPER ME! (25:12-14): David asserts that God blesses those who fear God.

SECTION OUTLINE TWENTY-SIX (PSALM 26)

David declares his innocence and asks God to examine and vindicate him.

I. DAVID'S SEPARATION FROM SIN (26:1-5, 9-11)
  A. **His request** (26:1): "Declare me innocent, O LORD."
  B. **His reasons** (26:1-5, 9-11)
    1. *He has trusted the Lord* (26:1).
    2. *He has lived according to God's truth* (26:2-3, 11).
    3. *He has refused to fellowship with the godless* (26:4-5, 9-10).

II. DAVID'S SEPARATION TO GOD (26:6-8, 12): David comes to the Lord's altar and gives thanks to him.

SECTION OUTLINE TWENTY-SEVEN (PSALM 27)

David expresses confidence in God's protection, even though he is surrounded by his enemies.

I. DAVID'S PRAISE (27:1-3): David trusts in the Lord to save him, strengthen him, and sustain him.

II. DAVID'S PETITIONS (27:4-14): David asks God to grant him three requests:
  A. **The Lord's house** (27:4-6): David desires to be in the Temple, where he can worship the Lord in safety.
  B. **The Lord's haven** (27:7-10): David begs the Lord to hold him close.

C. The Lord's help (27:11-14): David asks the Lord to show him how to live so he will not fall into his enemies' hands.

SECTION OUTLINE TWENTY-EIGHT (PSALM 28)
David asks the Lord to rescue him from his enemies and praises the Lord for hearing his prayer.

I. DAVID'S DEPENDENCE (28:1-5): David asks the Lord to do two things:
   A. Protect me! (28:1-2): David calls out for the Lord to have mercy on him and help him.
   B. Punish them! (28:4-5): David asks the Lord to punish the wicked, for they care nothing for what the Lord has done.

II. DAVID'S DELIGHT (28:6-9): David praises the Lord for hearing his prayer and calls upon the Lord to bless his people.

SECTION OUTLINE TWENTY-NINE (PSALM 29)
David calls the angels to worship the Lord in response to the wonders of creation and the power of storms. David attests to the great power of the Lord's voice.

I. THE VENERATION OF THE LORD (29:1-2): David calls the angels to worship and praise the Lord for his greatness.

II. THE VOICE OF THE LORD (29:3-9): David tells of the power of the Lord's voice.
   A. The sound of his voice (29:3): It thunders over the sea.
   B. The strength of his voice (29:4-9)
      1. *It splits the cedars of Lebanon* (29:4-5).
      2. *It shakes the mountains and the desert* (29:6-8).
      3. *It strips the forests bare* (29:9).

III. THE VICTORY OF THE LORD (29:10-11)
   A. The Lord reigns over the floodwaters (29:10).
   B. The Lord gives his people strength and peace (29:11).

SECTION OUTLINE THIRTY (PSALM 30)
David composed this psalm for the dedication of the Temple; he praises the Lord for answering his prayer and rescuing him.

I. DAVID'S TRIUMPHS (30:1-3): David praises God for victory over three things:
   A. Danger (30:1): David's enemies did not triumph over him.
   B. Disease (30:2): God restored David's health.
   C. Death (30:3): The Lord kept David from being killed.

II. DAVID'S TROUBLES (30:6-10): David recounts when he was overwhelmed and cried out to God.

III. DAVID'S TESTIMONY (30:4-5, 11-12): David praises God for rescuing him once again, turning his mourning into joy.

SECTION OUTLINE THIRTY-ONE (PSALM 31)
David expresses confidence in God in the midst of deep distress.

I. THE DELIVERANCE SOUGHT BY DAVID (31:1-5): David asks the Lord to listen to his cry and rescue him from his enemies.

II. THE DESPAIR SUFFERED BY DAVID (31:9-13)
   A. **His anguish** (31:9-10): David is physically weakened by his distress.
   B. **His alienation** (31:11-13)
      1. *He is scorned* (31:11-12).
      2. *He is slandered* (31:13).

III. THE DEDICATION SHOWN BY DAVID (31:6-8, 14-24): Despite his troubles, David expresses great confidence in the Lord.
   A. **He trusts God** (31:6-8, 14-18): He knows the Lord will save him from his enemies.
   B. **He thanks God** (31:19-24)
      1. *For his great goodness* (31:19-20)
      2. *For his unfailing love* (31:21-24)

SECTION OUTLINE THIRTY-TWO (PSALM 32)
David testifies to the blessings that come from confessing sin and receiving God's forgiveness.

I. THE CONFESSION (32:1-5): David recalls when he needed to confess his sins.
   A. **The bitterness** (32:3-4): David describes his agony before he confessed his sins.
      1. *He was weak and miserable* (32:3).
      2. *His strength evaporated* (32:4).
   B. **The blessedness** (32:1-2, 5): David describes his joy after he confessed his sins and received forgiveness.

II. THE COUNSEL (6-7): David advises the godly to repent of their sins.

III. THE COMMISSION (32:8-11)
   A. **What the Lord would do** (32:8, 10)
      1. *He promised to lead the King!*
      2. *He promised to love the King!*
   B. **What the King should do** (32:9-10): He should obediently follow God, having no need of a bit or bridle.

SECTION OUTLINE THIRTY-THREE (PSALM 33)
The psalmist praises the Lord for his attributes and his works.

I. THE METHODS OF PRAISE (33:1-3)
   A. **With joy from our hearts** (33:1)
   B. **With songs from our harps** (33:2-3)

II. THE MESSAGES OF PRAISE (33:4-22)
   A. **Praise God for his goodness** (33:4-5).
   B. **Praise God for his power over creation** (33:6-9): He simply spoke everything into existence.
   C. **Praise God for his sovereignty** (33:10-12): He is ultimately in charge of what happens on earth.
   D. **Praise God for his omniscience** (33:13-15): He knows everyone's heart.
   E. **Praise God for his omnipotence** (33:16-17): Security is found in God, not in kings and armies.
   F. **Praise God for his protection** (33:18-22): God watches over those who fear him.

SECTION OUTLINE THIRTY-FOUR (PSALM 34)
This psalm is an acrostic. David begins each verse with a successive letter of the Hebrew alphabet. David praises the Lord for freeing him from his fears and asserts that the Lord always watches over the righteous.

I. DAVID THE STUDENT (34:1-7): David proclaims what God has done for him.
   A. **He saved David** (34:4-6)
      1. *From his fears* (34:4)
      2. *From his foes* (34:5-6)
   B. **He surrounded David** (34:7): God's very presence had encamped around him.

II. DAVID THE TEACHER (34:8-22): David proclaims what God will do for others.
   A. **What he says to the righteous** (34:8-15, 17-20, 22)
      1. *He will give them their needs* (34:8-10).
      2. *He will grant them long, good lives* (34:11-15).
      3. *He will guard them from their enemies* (34;17-20, 22).
   B. **What he says to the unrighteous** (34:16, 21)
      1. *The face of God is against them!*
      2. *The fury of God is upon them!*

SECTION OUTLINE THIRTY-FIVE (PSALM 35)
David calls upon God to rescue him from his enemies.

   I. DAVID'S PERSECUTION (35:11-16): David's enemies persecute him in
      several ways:
      A. They falsely accuse him (35:11, 15).
      B. They repay his good with evil (35:12-13).
      C. They rejoice over his misfortunes (35:14-15).
      D. They mock and curse him (35:16).

  II. DAVID'S PETITION (35:1-8, 17-26): David asks God to do several
      things to his enemies:
      A. Declare war on them (35:1-3).
      B. Deny them (35:17-25).
      C. Dishonor them (35:4, 26).
      D. Darken their path (35:6-7).
      E. Destroy them (35:5, 8).

 III. DAVID'S PRAISE (35:9-10, 27-28): David promises to praise God if he
      rescues him from his enemies.

SECTION OUTLINE THIRTY-SIX (PSALM 36)
David contrasts the sinfulness of the wicked with the goodness of the
Lord and calls upon the Lord to bless the godly and humble the
wicked.

   I. THE CRUELTY OF THE GODLESS (36:1-4)
      A. They have no fear of God (36:1).
      B. They are conceited (36:2): They do not see how wicked they are.
      C. They are crooked and deceitful (36:3).
      D. They hatch sinful plots (36:4).

  II. CHARACTERISTICS OF GOD (36:5-12): In contrast to the wicked, the
      Lord possesses the following attributes:
      A. Unfailing love (36:5, 7)
      B. Faithfulness (36:5)
      C. Righteousness (36:6)
      D. Justice (36:6)
      E. Providence and protection (36:6-8, 10-12)
      F. Goodness: God provides life and light to the godly. (36:9)

SECTION OUTLINE THIRTY-SEVEN (PSALM 37)
David encourages the godly to trust in the Lord to rescue them from
evil. Though the wicked seem to prosper, they will ultimately be
destroyed.

I. THE GODLY (37:3-9, 11, 16-19, 21-31, 34, 37, 39-40)
   A. **What they sow** (37:3-5, 7-8, 16, 21, 30-31, 37)
      1. *They trust in God* (37:3).
      2. *They do good* (37:3).
      3. *They delight in the Lord* (37:4).
      4. *They commit their way to God* (37:5).
      5. *They rest in God* (37:7): The godly wait patiently for the Lord
         to act.
      6. *They refrain from anger* (37:8).
      7. *They are satisfied with little* (37:16).
      8. *They give generously* (37:21).
      9. *They speak wisely* (37:30): They know right from wrong.
      10. *They fill their hearts with God's law* (37:31).
      11. *They are honest and love peace* (37:37).
   B. **What they reap** (37:3-5, 6, 9, 11, 17-19, 22-29, 34, 37, 39-40)
      1. *They live safely in the land* (37:3, 11, 27).
      2. *They prosper* (37:3, 11).
      3. *They receive the desires of their hearts* (37:4).
      4. *They will be seen as innocent and just* (37:6).
      5. *They will inherit the land* (37:9, 11, 22, 29).
      6. *They are upheld by the Lord* (37:17, 24).
      7. *They are cared for* (37:17-19).
      8. *They will receive an eternal reward* (37:18).
      9. *They are directed by the Lord* (37:23).
      10. *They will never be forsaken* (37:25-28).
      11. *Their children are a blessing* (37:26).
      12. *They are protected* (37:28, 39-40).
      13. *They will be honored* (37:34).
      14. *They have a wonderful future* (37:37).

II. THE GODLESS (37:1-2, 9-10, 12-15, 17, 20-22, 28, 32-33, 35-36, 38)
   A. **What they sow** (37:12, 14, 21, 32)
      1. *They plot against the godly* (37:12, 14, 32).
      2. *They borrow and do not repay* (37:21).
   B. **What they reap** (37:1-2, 9-10, 13, 15, 17, 20, 22, 28, 33, 35-36, 38)
      1. *They will disappear* (37:1-2, 10, 35-36).
      2. *They will be destroyed* (37:9, 20, 22, 28).
      3. *They are laughed at by the Lord* (37:13): The Lord laughs
         because he knows their judgment is coming.
      4. *They will destroy themselves* (37:15).
      5. *Their strength will be shattered* (37:17).
      6. *They will not succeed* (37:33).
      7. *They have no future* (37:38).

David confesses his sins, which have caused him suffering, and calls upon the Lord to remember him and rescue him.

I. THE PENALTY (38:1-14): David is suffering because of his sins.
   A. **He is chastened by God** (38:1-10).
      1. *He is sick and his health is broken* (38:1-3).
      2. *His guilt overwhelms him* (38:4).
      3. *His wounds are festering* (38:5).
      4. *He is bent over and racked with pain* (38:6).
      5. *He burns with fever* (38:7).
      6. *He is going blind* (38:10).
   B. **He is cut off from his friends** (38:11).
   C. **He is conspired against by his enemies** (38:12-14).

II. THE PARDON (38:15-22)
   A. **His sin is confessed** (38:15-22)
      1. *"Lord, hear me!"* (38:15-16)
      2. *"Lord, heal me!"* (38:17)
      3. *"Lord, help me!" (38:18-22)*
   B. **His sin is cleansed. This is assumed.**

SECTION OUTLINE THIRTY-NINE (PSALM 39)
David confesses that he has failed to keep a resolution he had made and prays for God's compassion.

I. DAVID'S PLEDGE (39:1-3): David makes a vow to himself.
   A. **What he decides** (39:1): He vows not to sin in his speech and actions when the ungodly are in his presence.
   B. **What he does** (39:2-3): He does not keep silent about their sinful ways.

II. DAVID'S PETITION (39:4-13): David makes a fourfold request to the Lord.
   A. **Show me!** (39:4-6)
      1. *The frailty of life* (39:4-5): David knows his time on earth is brief and asks to be reminded of it.
      2. *The futility of life* (39:6): David asks God to show him the futility of rushing around for things that do not last.
   B. **Save me!** (39:7-9): He knows that his only hope is in God. He keeps silent before God because he knows that his punishment comes from him.
   C. **Spare me!** (39:10-11): He requests that God stop punishing him for his sin and hear his cry for help.
   D. **Satisfy me!** (39:12-13): He wants to experience the joy of the Lord.

SECTION OUTLINE FORTY (PSALM 40)
David recognizes the Lord's goodness to him in the past and calls for
the Lord to rescue him once again from his troubles.

I. DAVID'S PRAISE (40:1-10)
   A. **What God has done** (40:1-5)
      1. *Lifted him out of despair* (40:1-2)
      2. *Set his feet on solid ground* (40:2)
      3. *Given him a new song* (40:3-5)
   B. **What God desires** (40:6-10)
      1. *Negative* (40:6): The Lord does not delight in sacrifices and
         offerings.
      2. *Positive* (40:7-10): The Lord wants David to obey his law and
         tell others about his goodness.

II. DAVID'S PETITION (40:11-17): David asks the Lord to save him from
    two things:
   A. **From his troubles** (40:11-12): David confesses that they are more
      than the hairs on his head!
   B. **From his enemies** (40:13-17): David asks the Lord to rescue him
      quickly.

SECTION OUTLINE FORTY-ONE (PSALM 41)
David tells how the Lord blesses those who help the poor. He calls
upon the Lord to heal him and thwart the plans of those who are
waiting for him to die.

I. GOD'S FAVOR (41:1-3): Special blessings are bestowed on those who
   honor the poor.
   A. **Protection** (41:1-2)
   B. **Prosperity** (41:2)
   C. **Help in sickness** (41:3)

II. GOD'S FORGIVENESS (41:4): David asks the Lord for forgiveness and
    healing.

III. GOD'S FAITHFULNESS (41:5-13): David calls upon the Lord to rescue
     him from his enemies, who anxiously await David's death.

SECTION OUTLINE FORTY-TWO (PSALM 42)

The psalmist longs to be in God's presence. He feels abandoned by God but hopes that God will come to him once again.

I. DAVID'S DESIRE (42:1-2): He thirsts for God like a thirsty deer pants for water.

II. DAVID'S DESPAIR (42:3, 9-10)
   A. **He feels abandoned by God** (42:9).
   B. **He feels attacked by his enemies** (42:3, 9-10).

III. DAVID'S DETERMINATION (42:4-8, 11)
   A. **He remembers God's goodness** (42:4-8).
   B. **He rests in God's goodness** (42:11): Because of God's goodness in the past, David puts his hope in God to rescue him yet again.

SECTION OUTLINE FORTY-THREE (PSALM 43)

In this psalm, which complements Psalm 42, the psalmist calls upon God for deliverance from his enemies. He wants God's light and truth to lead him to worship him.

I. DEFEND ME! (43:1-2): The psalmist calls for God to defend him against ungodly people.

II. DIRECT ME! (43:3-5): The psalmist asks God to send his light and truth to guide him into God's presence.

SECTION OUTLINE FORTY-FOUR (PSALM 44)

The psalmist recounts the great deeds God did for his people in the past and asks God why he is allowing his people to be humiliated now.

I. ISRAEL'S PAST GLORY (44:1-8)
   A. **The power of God** (44:1-3)
      1. *The Lord led his people* (44:1-3).
         a. He drove the Canaanites from the land (44:1-2).
         b. He directed the Israelites into the land (44:2-3).
      2. *The Lord loved his people* (44:3): God used to smile on his people and favor them.
   B. **The praise to God** (44:4-8): The psalmist acknowledges that Israel's past victories came directly from the Lord, and he praises the Lord.

II. ISRAEL'S PRESENT GRIEF (44:9-26)
   A. **Their pain** (44:9-22)
      1. *Israel's physical suffering* (44:10-12, 22)
         a. They are defeated and plundered by their enemies (44:10).

b. They are slaughtered like sheep (44:11, 22).

c. They are sold and scattered among the nations (44:11-12): They feel they are of no value to God.

2. *Israel's psychological suffering* (44:9, 13-16)

a. They feel rejected by God (44:9): They feel God no longer leads them to battle.

b. They are mocked by their neighbors (44:13-16).

B. **Their perplexity** (44:17-22): The psalmist feels that they are innocent despite their suffering.

C. **Their petition** (44:23-26): The psalmist calls upon God to redeem his people.

SECTION OUTLINE FORTY-FIVE (PSALM 45)
This psalm praises a king on his wedding day.

I. THE KING (45:1-8): The psalmist composes a song to extol the king on his wedding day.

A. **His charm** (45:2): The king is handsome and gracious.

B. **His conquests** (45:3-5): The king should wield his mighty sword and defend truth, humility, and justice.

C. **His crown** (45:6-7): God gave the king the throne because he loves what is right and just.

D. **His clothing** (45:8): The king's robes are perfumed with myrrh, aloes, and cassia.

E. **His courts** (45:8): His palace is adorned with ivory and filled with beautiful music.

II. THE BRIDE (45:9-17): The psalmist speaks to the bride, who comes from far away.

A. **Her clothing** (45:9, 13-15)

1. *She wears jewelry made from the finest gold* (45:9).

2. *She wears a gown woven with gold* (45:13-15): In her beautiful robes she is led to the king.

B. **Her commitment** (45:10-11): The psalmist instructs the bride to accept two things:

1. *Her separation* (45:10): She has left her parents to marry the king of Israel.

2. *Her submission* (45:11): She must now honor her husband as her lord.

C. **Her coming glory** (45:16-17)

1. *Her sons will be kings* (45:16): They will rule many lands.

2. *She will receive honor* (45:17): Every generation will honor her name.

SECTION OUTLINE FORTY-SIX (PSALM 46)

The psalmist rests assured that God's people are safe and secure under God's mighty protection.

I. THE PROTECTION FROM GOD (46:1-3): The psalmist finds security and peace in knowing that God watches over his people.
   A. **Its availability** (46:1): God is always ready to be our refuge.
   B. **Its dependability** (46:2-3): We should not fear, since God is with us through all circumstances.
      1. *Though the world is destroyed* (46:2)
      2. *Though the oceans roar* (46:2-3)

II. THE PARADISE OF GOD (46:4-5): The psalmist describes the perfect tranquility of the city of God.
   A. **Its river brings joy** (46:4).
   B. **It is God's home** (46:4-5).
   C. **It is eternal** (46:5): The city cannot be destroyed.

III. THE POWER OF GOD (46:6-8): God brings destruction on the world.

IV. THE PEACE OF GOD (46:9): He will someday end wars throughout the earth.

V. THE PRAISE TO GOD (46:10-11): We are to be silent and honor the Lord Almighty.

SECTION OUTLINE FORTY-SEVEN (PSALM 47)

The psalmist describes a glorious kingdom!

I. THE RULER OVER THIS KINGDOM (47:2-3, 7-8)
   A. **What God reigns over** (47:2, 7): The entire earth!
   B. **Whom God reigns over** (47:3, 8): The nations of the earth!

II. THE REDEEMED IN THIS KINGDOM (47:1, 4-6, 9)
   A. **Their identity** (47:4, 9)
      1. *Saved Jewish believers* (47:4)
      2. *Saved Gentile believers* (47:9)
   B. **Their instruction** (47:1, 5-6): They are to shout and sing praises to their great king!

SECTION OUTLINE FORTY-EIGHT (PSALM 48)

The psalmist praises the Lord, who watches over the city of Jerusalem.

I. THE GOD OF JERUSALEM (48:1, 3-8, 10-11, 14)
   A. **He is great** (48:1): The Lord is to be praised in the city.
   B. **He defends the city** (48:3-7): Attacking kings run from the city in terror.

C. **He makes the city secure** (48:8).
D. **He executes justice** (48:10-11): God is praised because his judgments are just.
E. **He guides the people** (48:14).

II. THE JERUSALEM OF GOD (48:1-2, 9, 12-13): The city reflects the glory of its God.
  A. **It has magnificent elevation** (48:1-2): The earth rejoices to see the city, perched atop Mount Zion.
  B. **It has the Temple** (48:9): They meditate on God's unfailing love in his Temple.
  C. **It has towers** (48:12).
  D. **It has fortified walls and citadels** (48:13).

SECTION OUTLINE FORTY-NINE (PSALM 49)
The psalmist encourages the righteous not to fear or envy the prosperous wicked, for eventually they will die.

I. THE PSALMIST'S SUMMONS (49:1-4)
  A. **The crowd** (49:1-2): The psalmist tells the entire world to listen.
  B. **The competence** (49:3-4): The psalmist assures listeners that he will speak wisely, since he has pondered many proverbs and riddles.

II. THE PSALMIST'S SERMON (49:6-14, 17-20): He reminds hearers of the ultimate futility of wealth; it cannot help a person avoid death. The grave claims the wise and the foolish, the rich and the poor!

III. THE PSALMIST'S SAVIOR (49:5, 15-16): The psalmist has no fear when he is surrounded by wealthy enemies, knowing that God will rescue him from the power of death!

SECTION OUTLINE FIFTY (PSALM 50)
The psalmist delivers a blistering indictment against those who make offerings and recite God's laws but do not follow them with heartfelt obedience.

I. THE JUDGE (50:1-3, 6): The psalmist declares that God will make an indictment against his people.
  A. **His summons** (50:1, 6): God summons all humanity to the trial.
  B. **His splendor** (50:2-3): God shines with glorious radiance and approaches with thunder.

II. THE JUDGED (50:4-5, 7): The people of Israel are summoned to appear before him.

III. THE JUDGMENT (50:8-23)
   A. **What God desires** (50:8-15, 23)
      1. *No more bulls and goats* (50:8-13): God is not interested in receiving these offerings because he owns everything on earth!
      2. *Genuine commitment to him* (50:14-15, 23): God wants his people to be thankful, to fulfill their vows, and to trust in him.
   B. **What God despises** (50:16-21)
      1. *Empty religiosity* (50:16-17)
      2. *Participation in sin* (50:18): They help thieves and spend time with adulterers.
      3. *Wicked speech* (50:19-21): They lie and slander others.
   C. **What God declares** (50:22): "Repent . . . or I will tear you apart."

SECTION OUTLINE FIFTY-ONE (PSALM 51)
David confesses his sin to God and asks for forgiveness and mercy.

I. DAVID'S CONFESSION (51:1-6)
   A. **David appeals to God** (51:1-2): "Wash me clean from my guilt."
   B. **David acknowledges his sin** (51:3-6): "I recognize my shameful deeds."

II. DAVID'S CLEANSING (51:7-10): David asks God to do three things:
   A. **Remove his sin** (51:7).
   B. **Restore his joy** (51:8-9).
   C. **Renew his spirit** (51:10): David wants a clean heart and a right spirit.

III. DAVID'S CONCERN (51:11-12): He pleads that the Holy Spirit not be taken from him and that he be made willing to obey God.

IV. DAVID'S COMMITMENTS (51:13-15): If God responds to him, David promises to do three things:
   A. **Teach God's ways to sinners** (51:13).
   B. **Sing of God's forgiveness** (51:14).
   C. **Praise God** (51:15).

V. DAVID'S CONFIDENCE (51:16-19)
   A. **He knows God can forgive sins** (51:16-17): David recognizes that God wants broken spirits and repentant hearts.
   B. **He knows God can fortify the city** (51:18-19): David calls upon God to rebuild the walls of the city so that pleasing sacrifices can be offered.

SECTION OUTLINE FIFTY-TWO (PSALM 52)

David rebukes his enemy and foretells his downfall. He is confident that he will prosper as he trusts God.

I. THE BOAST OF THE GODLESS (52:1-5)
  A. Their perversion (52:1-4)
    1. *Their thoughts are evil!*
    2. *Their tongues are evil!*
  B. Their punishment (52:5)
    1. *God will strike them down!*
    2. *God will tear them up!*

II. THE BOAST OF THE GODLY (52:6-9)
  A. The contrast (52:6-8)
    1. *The unrighteous man will fail* (52:7): The godly will witness this and laugh.
    2. *The righteous man will flourish* (52:6, 8): He will be as an olive tree.
  B. The consecration (52:9)
    1. *David will offer thanksgiving to God.*
    2. *David will offer testimony for God.*

SECTION OUTLINE FIFTY-THREE (PSALM 53)

David observes the universal corruption of humanity and anticipates its judgment. David also longs for the salvation of Israel.

I. GOD AND HIS FOOLISH FOES (53:1-5): David bemoans the sinful state of humanity.
  A. Their atheism (53:1): Fools deny the existence of God.
  B. Their apostasy (53:1-3): They are completely corrupt and have turned away from God.
  C. Their attacks (53:4): They eat up God's people like bread.
  D. Their annihilation (53:5): God will destroy them.

II. GOD AND HIS FAITHFUL FRIENDS (53:6)
  A. The desire (53:6): David longs for God to rescue his people.
  B. The delight (53:6): When God restores his people, they will rejoice.

SECTION OUTLINE FIFTY-FOUR (PSALM 54)
David calls upon God to rescue him and offers a sacrifice.

I. DAVID'S TRAVAIL (54:1-3): David cries out to God that violent enemies are attacking him.

II. DAVID'S TRUST (54:4-5)
   A. **The Lord protects him** (54:4): David knows the Lord is keeping him alive.
   B. **The Lord punishes them** (54:5): David asks God to turn his enemies' plans against them.

III. DAVID'S TRIUMPH (54:6-7): David will make a voluntary offering to God for rescuing him.

SECTION OUTLINE FIFTY-FIVE (PSALM 55)
David complains about his enemies in general and about a specific enemy who he thought was his friend, expresses confidence of being delivered from his enemies and their destruction, and resolves to put his trust in the Lord.

I. DAVID'S TRIALS (55:2-15, 20-21)
   A. **Besieged by his foes** (55:2-8, 10-11)
      1. *The injustice David suffers* (55:2-8, 10-11)
         a. His enemies threaten him (55:2-8): David is terrified because his enemies are hunting him down.
         b. The city is filled with wickedness (55:10-11): Murder, robbery, threats, and cheating are everywhere.
      2. *The justice David seeks* (55:9, 15)
         a. Confuse my foes! (55:9)
         b. Consume my foes! (55:15): David wants death to come to his enemies by surprise.
   B. **Betrayed by his friend** (55:12-14, 20-21)
      1. *The friend's closeness* (55:12-14): He was one of David's most trusted companions.
      2. *The friend's corruptness* (55:20-21): He openly spoke kindly to David but secretly plotted against him.

II. DAVID'S TESTIMONY (55:1, 16-19, 22-23): During his trials, David constantly calls upon the Lord and trusts that he will save him.

SECTION OUTLINE FIFTY-SIX (PSALM 56)

David calls out to God to rescue him from his enemies. David is comforted knowing that God is aware of all his troubles, and he promises to offer sacrifices to him.

I. DAVID'S GRIEVOUS FOES (56:1-2, 5-6)
   A. **They dog his steps** (56:1-2): His enemies attack him all day long.
   B. **They twist his words** (56:5).
   C. **They plot his death** (56:6).

II. DAVID'S GLORIOUS FRIEND (56:3-4, 7-13): David calls out to God to rescue him.
   A. **God relieves his fears** (56:3-4, 9): "What can mere mortals do to me?"
   B. **God records his sorrows** (56:7-8): "You have collected all my tears in your bottle."
   C. **God receives his praise** (56:10-12): "I . . . offer a sacrifice of thanks for your help."
   D. **God redeems his life** (56:13): "You have rescued me from death."

SECTION OUTLINE FIFTY-SEVEN (PSALM 57)

David calls upon God to rescue him from his enemies. Confident that God will do so, David praises and thanks God.

I. DAVID'S PERSECUTORS (57:4, 6): Vicious enemies have set a trap for David.

II. DAVID'S PETITION (57:1-2): He cries out for God's mercy.

III. DAVID'S PROTECTION (57:1, 3): He takes refuge beneath the shadow of God's wings.

IV. DAVID'S PRAISE (57:5, 7-11)
   A. **His exaltation** (57:5, 11): "Be exalted, O God, above the highest heavens!"
   B. **His exuberance** (57:7-8): David sings God's praises upon his harp and lyre.
   C. **His expression** (57:9-10): David promises to tell everyone of God's love and faithfulness.

SECTION OUTLINE FIFTY-EIGHT (PSALM 58)

David rebukes wicked rulers and calls upon God to destroy them and avenge the godly.

I. GOD AND THE GODLESS (58:1-9): David cries out against wicked rulers.
   A. **Their perversions** (58:1-5)

1. *They pervert justice* (58:1-2): All their dealings are crooked.
2. *They lie* (58:3).
3. *They refuse to listen* (58:4-5).
B. Their punishment (58:6-9): David asks God to do two things to these rulers:
1. *Break off their fangs* (58:6).
2. *Make them disappear* (58:7-9).

II. GOD AND THE GODLY (58:10-11): The godly will rejoice when they see justice, and they will be assured that God rewards those who follow him.

SECTION OUTLINE FIFTY-NINE (PSALM 59)
David seeks God's protection from his enemies and is confident that God will defeat them. He asks that his enemies live on in defeat as an object lesson to his people.

I. DAVID'S WICKED FOES (59:1-7, 11-15): David is stalked by many enemies looking to ambush him.
A. Protect me! (59:1-2): David calls upon God to rescue him.
B. Punish them! (59:3-7, 11-15)
1. *The reasons* (59:3-4, 6-7, 14-15)
   a. They are bloodthirsty (59:3-4, 6, 14-15): They want to kill him.
   b. They are boastful (59:7): They speak filth and think no one can hurt them.
2. *The requests* (59:5, 11-12)
   a. Show them no mercy (59:5): He wants God to punish them.
   b. Bring them to their knees (59:11): God can stagger them with his power.
   c. Let them be captured by their evil words (59:12).
   d. Destroy them (59:13).
3. *The results* (59:13): When this is done, the world will know that God reigns in Israel.

II. DAVID'S WONDERFUL FRIEND (59:8-10, 16-17)
A. God laughs at David's enemies (59:8).
B. God is his strength (59:9-10, 17): God will help him triumph over his enemies.

III. DAVID'S TESTIMONY (59:16): David promises to sing about God's power.

SECTION OUTLINE SIXTY (PSALM 60)
David asks God why he has rejected his people. He calls upon God to help him overcome the nations they are fighting.

I. THE REJECTION (60:1-5, 10-12): David asks God why he has rejected his people.
   A. **The pain** (60:1-3): David expresses his people's pain.
      1. *You have split open our land* (60:1-2, 10-12).
      2. *You have been very hard on us* (60:3).
      3. *You have rejected us* (60:11-12).
   B. **The prospect** (60:4): David notes that God has still provided a rallying point in the face of attack.

II. THE REQUEST (60:5-12)
   A. **The plea** (60:5, 11-12): David asks God to help his people fight their enemies.
   B. **The promise** (60:6-8): David recalls God's promise to give Israel the Promised Land and to conquer their enemies.
   C. **The perplexity** (60:9-10): David asks God to bring them victory.

SECTION OUTLINE SIXTY-ONE (PSALM 61)
David prays for protection and long life and praises God for hearing his prayer.

I. LEAD (61:1-5): David asks God to lead him.
   A. **The rock of God** (61:1-2): God is his towering rock of safety.
   B. **The fortress of God** (61:3): God is his refuge and fortress.
   C. **The wings of God** (61:4-5): David wants to dwell in the shelter of God's wings.

II. LENGTHEN (61:6-8): David asks God to watch over him and add many years to his life.

III. LISTEN (61:8): David promises to praise God and fulfill his vows if God answers his prayer.

SECTION OUTLINE SIXTY-TWO (PSALM 62)
David trusts in God's protection despite the many enemies surrounding him.

I. THE TREACHERY (62:3-4)
   A. **The praising** (62:4): David's enemies are friendly when he is around.
   B. **The plotting** (62:3-4): David's enemies make plans to destroy him.

II. THE TRUST (62:1-2, 5-10)
   A. **David's advice to himself** (62:1-2, 5-7): David will not be
      shaken, for God is his fortress and hope.
   B. **David's advice to his people** (62:8-10)
      1. *What to do* (62:8)
         a. Place your trust in God (62:8).
         b. Pour out your hearts to God (62:8).
      2. *What not to do* (62:9-10)
         a. Do not become proud (62:9): All are lowly in God's sight.
         b. Do not practice extortion (62:10): Do not value riches so
            much that you extort or rob people.

III. THE TRUTHS (62:11-12): David testifies concerning two truths about
    God:
   A. **God reaches out to us** (62:11-12): God has spoken plainly of his
      unfailing love toward us.
   B. **God rewards us** (62:12): God judges all people according to
      what they have done.

SECTION OUTLINE SIXTY-THREE (PSALM 63)

David expresses his longing for God and his trust in God's provision.

I. DAVID'S THIRST FOR GOD (63:1-2): He longs for God in a parched
   and weary land.

II. DAVID'S THANKSGIVING TO GOD (63:3-5): He vows to honor and
    praise God.

III. DAVID'S THOUGHTS CONCERNING GOD (63:6-7)
   A. **The remembrance** (63:6): David declares, "I lie awake thinking
      of you."
   B. **The rejoicing** (63:7): David worships God in song.

IV. DAVID'S TRIUMPH IN GOD (63:8-11)
   A. **The deliverance** (63:8, 11): God's right hand holds David securely.
   B. **The destruction** (63:9-10): Those plotting against David will be
      ruined.

SECTION OUTLINE SIXTY-FOUR (PSALM 64)

David asks God to deliver him from the slanderous words of his
enemies and expresses confidence that God will do so.

I. PROTECT ME! (64:1-6): David calls out for God to protect him from
   his enemies.
   A. **The slander** (64:1-4): David's enemies attack him with words.
   B. **The snares** (64:5-6): David's enemies set traps for him.

II. PUNISH THEM! (64:7-8): David calls upon God to punish his
enemies.
A. **Strike them down** (64:7).
B. **Turn their words against them** (64:8).

III. PRAISE GOD! (64:9-10): David says that everyone will stand in awe
and praise God for what he has done.

SECTION OUTLINE SIXTY-FIVE (PSALM 65)
David tells of the joys of following God and praises him for sustaining
his creation and producing a bountiful harvest.

I. DAVID THANKS GOD FOR HIS REDEMPTIVE WORKS (65:1-5)
A. **For answering prayer** (65:1-2, 5): God answers prayers with
awesome deeds.
B. **For forgiving sin** (65:3)
C. **For imparting joy** (65:4): Joy is found in God's holy Temple.

II. DAVID THANKS GOD FOR HIS CREATIVE WORKS (65:6-13)
A. **For forming the mountains** (65:6): This demonstrates God's
power.
B. **For silencing the oceans** (65:7)
C. **For watering the earth** (65:8-10): God makes the ground rich
and fertile.
D. **For causing plants to grow** (65:11-13): God brings forth bounti-
ful harvests and lush pastures.

SECTION OUTLINE SIXTY-SIX (PSALM 66)
The psalmist reflects upon a time of deliverance for himself and for
God's people and summons people to worship and thank God.

I. THE DEEDS OF THE LORD (66:1-12): The psalmist speaks of all that the
Lord has done.
A. **God's preeminence** (66:1-2): The Lord's name is glorious.
B. **God's power** (66:3-7)
1. *He causes good and bad alike to worship him* (66:3-5, 7).
2. *He made a path through the Red Sea* (66:6).
C. **God's protection** (66:8-9): The psalmist praises God because our
lives are in his hands.
D. **God's purging** (66:10-12)
1. *The grief* (66:10-12): God has tested his people and refined
them like silver melted in a crucible.
2. *The glory* (66:12): In the end, God led his people to great
abundance.

II. THE DEDICATION TO THE LORD (66:13-20): The psalmist promises to fulfill his vows and make sacrifices, and he calls others to praise God.
   A. **The psalmist's ritual sacrifices** (66:13-15): He brings rams, bulls, and goats to the altar.
   B. **The psalmist's personal sacrifices** (66:16-20): The psalmist tells of God's deeds and calls others to praise God.

SECTION OUTLINE SIXTY-SEVEN (PSALM 67)
The psalmist desires that all the nations praise God for his power.

I. THE FEATURES OF THE PSALMIST'S PRAYER (67:1-5)
   A. **May God's glory be seen among his people** (67:1).
   B. **May God's grace be seen among the Gentiles** (67:2-5).

II. THE FRUITS OF THE PSALMIST'S PRAYER (67:6-7): The psalmist anticipates two occurrences if his prayer is answered:
   A. **Material blessing** (67:6): "The earth will yield its harvests."
   B. **Spiritual blessing** (67:7): God will bless his people, and all the world will fear him.

SECTION OUTLINE SIXTY-EIGHT (PSALM 68)
In this messianic psalm David praises God as a mighty victor over his enemies and calls others to praise him.

I. THE WORKS OF THE LORD (68:1-2, 4-17, 21-23): David recounts the Lord's mighty acts.
   A. **The Lord's punishment** (68:1-2, 21-23)
      1. *He scatters his enemies* (68:1-2): Those who hate God run for their lives.
      2. *He slays his enemies* (68:21-23): God smashes the heads of his enemies.
   B. **The Lord's power** (68:4-14)
      1. *Over the world* (68:4, 7-9)
         a. He rides the clouds (68:4).
         b. He shakes the land (68:7-8): The earth trembles and the heavens pour rain.
         c. He waters the land (68:9).
      2. *Over his enemies* (68:11-14): Enemy warriors flee in panic when he speaks!
      3. *Over his people* (68:5-6, 10)
         a. He defends orphans and widows (68:5).
         b. He places the lonely in families and frees prisoners (68:6).
         c. He provides for his people (68:10): The people have a bountiful harvest in the Promised Land.

    C. The Lord's place (68:15-17): God reigns from Mount Zion.

II. THE WORSHIP OF THE LORD (68:3, 18-20, 24-35)
    A. The praise to God (68:3, 19-20, 32-35): The psalmist calls people to praise God for his power and his salvation.
    B. The procession of God (68:24-28): This passage describes a procession marching toward the sanctuary.
    C. The presentations to God (68:18, 29-31): Many people give gifts to God.

SECTION OUTLINE SIXTY-NINE (PSALM 69)
A messianic psalm in which David asks God to rescue him from his enemies, who constantly insult him. David calls for God to severely punish these enemies and vindicate him.

I. DAVID'S SUFFERING (69:1-12, 19-28): David's pain comes from four sources.
    A. From his foes (69:1-4, 10-12, 19-21)
      1. *Many hate him for no reason* (69:1-4).
      2. *They ridicule and mock him* (69:10-12, 19-20): He endures his enemies' insults.
      3. *They give him poison for food and sour wine for drink* (69:21).
    B. From his flesh (69:5-6): Some of David's pain comes from his own sin.
    C. From his family (69:8): His own brothers have turned against him!
    D. From his faith (69:7, 9): David is mocked for his faith, and he feels insulted when people insult God.

II. DAVID'S SUPPLICATION (69:13-18, 22-29, 19): David makes requests of God.
    A. Regarding his enemies (69:22-28):
      1. *Take their security from them* (69:22).
      2. *Blind them and make them weak* (69:23).
      3. *Pour out your fury on them* (69:24).
      4. *Make their homes desolate* (69:25).
      5. *Do not let them go free* (69:26-27).
      6. *Erase their names from the Book of Life* (69:28).
    B. Regarding himself (69:13-18, 29): David prays for God to rescue him.

III. DAVID'S SONG (69:30-36): David praises God for hearing his prayer and helping his people.

SECTION OUTLINE SEVENTY (PSALM 70)

David calls upon God to vindicate him and humiliate his enemies.

I. DAVID'S CONCERN (70:1-3): "Punish your foes, O God!"
   A. **They have slandered him!**
   B. **God should scatter them!**

II. DAVID'S CONFIDENCE (70:4-5): "Protect Your Friends, Oh God!"
   A. **He will be rescued by the Lord!**
   B. **He then will rejoice in the Lord!**

SECTION OUTLINE SEVENTY-ONE (PSALM 71)

The psalmist, apparently aged and in trouble, cries out to God for deliverance and is confident that God will answer him.

I. THE PSALMIST'S TROUBLE (71:10-11): The psalmist cries out for God to rescue him from his enemies, who are plotting to destroy him.

II. THE PSALMIST'S TRIUMPH (71:1-7, 9, 12-14, 17-18): The psalmist's confidence is bolstered by two truths:
   A. **God is his help** (71:1-4, 7,12-13): Knowing that God will help him, the psalmist makes two requests:
      1. *Be a defense for me* (71:1-4, 7).
      2. *Bring disgrace on my foes* (71:12-13).
   B. **God is his hope** (71:5-6, 9, 14, 17-18): God has been the psalmist's hope throughout his life.
      1. *Since he was an infant* (71:6)
      2. *Since his childhood* (71:5, 17)
      3. *Now that he is old* (71:9, 14, 18)

III. THE PSALMIST'S TESTIMONY (71:8, 15-16, 19-24): The psalmist praises God.
   A. **What the psalmist praises God for** (71:8, 16, 19, 22-24)
      1. *For his righteous acts* (71:16, 19, 24)
      2. *For his faithfulness* (71:22)
   B. **When the psalmist praises God** (71:8, 15): He praises God all day long.
   C. **How the psalmist praises God** (71:22-23): He praises him with his voice and his harp and lyre.

SECTION OUTLINE SEVENTY-TWO (PSALM 72)
The psalmist prays for blessings and prosperity for the king. Many feel this psalm describes the world under the reign of Jesus Christ.

I. THE CONCERN FOR THE KING (72:1). Here David asks God:
   A. **To endow Solomon with divine justice.**
   B. **To endow Solomon with divine righteousness.**

II. THE CHARACTERISTICS OF THE KING (72:2-17): As has been previously noted, these royal characteristics had their partial fulfillment in Solomon, but their ultimate fulfillment awaits the reign of Christ.
   A. **The moral equity of the King's reign** (72:2)
   B. **The prosperity of the King's reign** (72:3, 6-7, 16): The entire earth will blossom, producing vast harvests of grain and fruit.
   C. **The security of the King's reign** (72:4): The poor, the needy, and the orphans will be delivered from their oppressors.
   D. **The duration of the King's reign** (72:5, 15, 17): It will outlast the sun and the moon.
   E. **The extent of the King's reign** (72:8)
      1. *"From sea to sea."*
      2. *"To the ends of the earth."*
   F. **The glory of the King's reign** (72:9-11, 15)
      1. *Desert nomads and kings will pay tribute to him.*
      2. *All nations will bow down to him and serve him.*
   G. **The compassion of the King's reign** (72:12-14): In great pity, he will rescue the weak and needy, viewing their lives as precious!

III. THE CONFIDENCE IN THE KING (72:18-19): The psalmist offers up praise to Israel's glorious God and coming ruler Jesus Christ.

SECTION OUTLINE SEVENTY-THREE (PSALM 73)
Asaph, a chief musician appointed by David and author of several psalms, deals with the question, Why do the wicked prosper and the righteous go unrewarded?

I. ASAPH AND THE EVIL ONES (73:1-20)
   A. **The consternation** (73:1-20): Psalmist Asaph is deeply troubled by two matters:
      1. *The prosperity of the godless* (73:3-12)
         a. They enjoy health and wealth (73:3-4).
         b. They have no worries or problems (73:5).
         c. They are proud and cruel (73:6).
         d. They have everything (73:7).
         e. They are arrogant toward God and people (73:8-12).

  2. *The pain of the godly* (73:1-2, 13-16)
    a. He feels like he is about to fall off a cliff (73:1-2).
    b. His life of purity seems unrewarded (73:13).
    c. He is constantly plagued with problems (73:14-16).
B. The clarification (73:17-20): Asaph realizes the destiny of the wicked.
  1. *The place of this revelation* (73:17): Asaph realizes this while he is in the sanctuary.
  2. *The particulars of this revelation* (73:18-20)
    a. The wicked are on a slippery path to destruction (73:18-19).
    b. The present life of the wicked is but a dream (73:20): They will vanish from the earth when the Lord arises.

II. ASAPH AND THE EXALTED ONE (73:21-28): Asaph acknowledges two great truths about God:
A. God is guiding him (73:21-24).
B. God is watching over him (73:25-28).

SECTION OUTLINE SEVENTY-FOUR (PSALM 74)
Asaph feels forsaken and laments the sad state of Jerusalem and the Temple. He recounts God's great deeds in the past and calls upon him to rescue his people from their enemies.

I. ASAPH'S FRUSTRATION (74:1-11): The psalmist is troubled by several things:
A. God seems to have angrily rejected his own people (74:1-2).
B. God has allowed Jerusalem and the Temple to be destroyed (74:3-8).
C. God has sent them no more prophets (74:9).
D. God has not destroyed their foes (74:10-11).

II. ASAPH'S FAITH (74:12-23): Asaph reflects on God's protection in the past and calls upon him to rescue his people.
A. What he acknowledges (74:12-17)
  1. *God is his eternal king* (74:12).
  2. *God rules over nature* (74:13-17).
B. What he asks for (74:18-23): Asaph asks two things of God:
  1. *Rescue your people* (74:18-19, 21-23): He prays that God will not let his people be destroyed.
  2. *Remember your promise* (74:20): Asaph asks God to remember his covenant promises in these dark, violent times.

SECTION OUTLINE SEVENTY-FIVE (PSALM 75)
Asaph is confident in God's sovereignty and trusts that God will one day overthrow the wicked.

I. ASAPH'S PRAISE (75:1, 9): Asaph praises God for his mighty deeds.
   A. **Asaph's thanksgiving** (75:1): He praises God for his mighty deeds!
   B. **Asaph's testimony** (75:9): He determines to proclaim this forever!

II. ASAPH'S PROMISE (75:2-8, 10)
   A. **God punishes the wicked** (75:2-5, 8, 10).
   B. **God will protect and promote the godly** (75:6-7): God decides who will rise and fall.

SECTION OUTLINE SEVENTY-SIX (PSALM 76)
Asaph celebrates God's greatness and sovereignty over his enemies.

I. GOD'S EXCELLENCE (76:1-10, 12)
   A. **His seat** (76:1-2): God lives in Jerusalem.
   B. **His splendor** (76:4): God is more glorious and majestic than the mountains.
   C. **His strength** (76:3, 5-10, 12)
     1. *God's power* (76:3, 5-9, 12)
       a. The enemy scatters (76:3, 5-6, 12): God breaks the power of the enemy.
       b. The earth shakes (76:7-8): God's sentence on his enemies causes the earth to tremble and stand silent.
     2. *God's purpose* (76:9-10): God uses human opposition to enhance his glory and judge others.

II. ASAPH'S EXHORTATION (76:11): The psalmist exhorts everyone to make vows to the Lord and fulfill them.

SECTION OUTLINE SEVENTY-SEVEN (PSALM 77)
Asaph feels deserted by God and begins to despair, but then he remembers the mighty acts of God in the past.

I. ASAPH'S SORROW (77:1-10)
   A. **Present grief** (77:1-4, 7-10)
     1. *He cries out to God* (77:1-3): Asaph is in deep trouble and searches for the Lord.
     2. *He is too distressed even to pray* (77:4): Asaph cannot pray or sleep.
     3. *He wonders if God has abandoned him* (77:7-10).
   B. **Past glory** (77:5-6): Asaph painfully remembers the good old days.

II. ASAPH'S SONG (77:11-20): He's encouraged as he remembers how God helped his people in the past.
   A. **God performed miracles** (77:11-18): He redeemed his people by his strength.
   B. **God led his people** (77:20): God used Moses and Aaron as their shepherds.

SECTION OUTLINE SEVENTY-EIGHT (PSALM 78)

Asaph recounts the mighty acts that God performed for his people and the rebellion they displayed throughout history. Asaph does this so that succeeding generations can learn from them and find hope in God.

I. THE COMMAND (78:1-7): Asaph calls his people to hear lessons from the past so they will learn to obey God and find hope in him.
   A. **I will teach** (78:1-3): Asaph tells people to listen to the lessons from God's people in the past.
   B. **You will teach** (78:4-7): The people should tell their children of God's truth and wonders.

II. THE CONSEQUENCES (78:8-72): Asaph relates the history of God's people.
   A. **Their rebellion against God** (78:8-12, 17-20, 22, 34-37, 40-41, 43, 56-58): The Israelites rebelled against God in several ways:
      1. *They disregarded his miracles* (78:11-12, 32, 43).
      2. *They refused to obey God* (78:8, 10, 17).
      3. *They complained against God* (78:18-20): They doubted that God could provide for their needs.
      4. *They lied to God* (78:34-36): They were insincere in their commitment to God.
      5. *They were faithless* (78:9, 22, 37, 40-41, 56-57).
      6. *They worshiped other gods* (78:58).
   B. **Their retribution from God** (78:21, 30-31, 33-35, 59-64, 67)
      1. *God became angry with them* (78:21).
      2. *God caused them to suffer failure and terror* (78:33).
      3. *God killed many of them* (78:30-31).
      4. *God allowed many of them to be killed* (78:62-64).
      5. *God abandoned his people* (78:59-60): God did not dwell among the people.
      6. *God allowed the Ark to be captured* (78:61).
      7. *God rejected the northern tribe of Ephraim* (78:67).
   C. **Their redemption from God** (78:13-16, 23-29, 38-55, 65-66, 68-72): Despite Israel's constant rebellion, God continued to help his people.
      1. *He miraculously delivered his people from Egypt* (78:42-51).
      2. *He divided the Red Sea for them* (78:13).

3. *He guided them by a cloud and pillar of fire* (78:14, 52-54).
4. *He provided water from a rock* (78:15-16).
5. *He fed them with manna and quail* (78:23-29).
6. *He forgave their sins* (78:38-39).
7. *He settled them in the Promised Land* (78:55): The nations in the land were driven out as God promised.
8. *He rescued them from their enemies* (78:65-66).
9. *He chose Jerusalem as the place for his Temple* (78:68-69).
10. *He chose David to rule over them* (78:70-72).

SECTION OUTLINE SEVENTY-NINE (PSALM 79)

Asaph cries out to God because pagans have overrun Jerusalem and the Temple and slaughtered the people. He calls upon God to vindicate his people and exact vengeance on their oppressors.

I. THE PAIN OF ISRAEL (79:1-4): Asaph cries out to God regarding the following troubles:
  A. **The land, the city of Jerusalem, and the Temple have been overrun by pagans** (79:1).
  B. **The people have been slaughtered** (79:2-3): The bodies of God's servants lie unburied.
  C. **The people are mocked by their neighbors** (79:4).

II. THE PRAYER FOR ISRAEL (79:5-13): Asaph asks several requests of God.
  A. **Concerning God's enemies** (79:6-7, 12): "Pour out your wrath on the nations that refuse to recognize you."
  B. **Concerning God's people** (79:5, 8-10)
    1. *Forgive us!* (79:5, 8): Asaph asks God to be merciful and not hold his people guilty for their sins.
    2. *Help us!* (79:9): Asaph asks God to save his people.
    3. *Avenge us!* (79:10-12): Asaph asks God to demonstrate his great power and avenge them.
    4. *The praise from Israel* (79:13): God's people will thank and praise him forever.

SECTION OUTLINE EIGHTY (PSALM 80)

Asaph cries out to God because his people are scorned by their enemies. He recalls God's past goodness to them and asks for favor once again. Asaph uses three images to describe God's people and their relationship to him.

I. THE SHEEP AND THE SHEPHERD (80:1-7): Asaph calls God the Shepherd of Israel.
  A. **Listen to us** (80:1-2): Asaph wants God, who is "enthroned above the cherubim," to respond to his people's cries and rescue them.

    B. Do not be angry with us (80:4-6): God has rejected them and made them the scorn of nations.

    C. Redeem your people (80:3, 7): Asaph asks God to cause his people to turn to him again so they can be saved.

II. THE VINE AND THE VINEYARD OWNER (80:8-16)

    A. The past vine (80:8-11)

      1. *It is brought out of Egypt as a tender vine* (80:8).

      2. *It is brought into Canaan, where it flourishes* (80:8-11).

    B. The present vine (80:12-13, 16): It is punished for its fruitlessness.

    C. The future vine (80:14-15): The psalmist begs God to return and care once again for his vine.

III. THE SINNERS AND THE SAVIOR (80:17-19)

    A. The person (80:17): "Strengthen the man you love, the son of your choice" is most likely a reference to the Messiah.

    B. The plea (80:18-19): "Make your face shine down upon us" is a plea for God to turn toward them and save them.

SECTION OUTLINE EIGHTY-ONE (PSALM 81)

Asaph exhorts Israel to praise God for delivering them from Egypt, complains about Israel's ingratitude, and portrays Israel's forfeited blessings.

I. THE PSALMIST EXHORTS ISRAEL TO REJOICE (81:1-4)

    A. How? (81:1-2): Everyone should praise God for his strength through singing, accompanied by tambourine, lyre, and the harp.

    B. When? (81:3-4): The law of God requires praise during Israel's scheduled feasts.

II. THE PSALMIST EXHORTS ISRAEL TO REMEMBER (81:5-16)

    A. What God has already done (81:5-7)

      1. *He brought them out of Egypt* (81:5-6): He set them free from slavery and relieved their burden.

      2. *He brought them through the desert* (81:7): He answered them from a thundercloud when they complained of no water.

    B. What God desires to do (81:8-16)

      1. *If they will listen and obey* (81:8-10, 16)

        a. Fill their lives with blessing (81:10, 16): He will fill their mouth with good things.

        b. Subdue their enemies (81:13-15): Their foes would cringe before God.

      2. *If they do not listen* (81:11-12): Because of Israel's rebellion, God will give them over to their own evil devices.

Asaph denounces Israel's corrupt judges who oppress the people. He reminds them of their God-intended role and that God will judge them.

I. GOD'S JUDGMENT UPON EARTHLY JUDGES (82:1-7)
   A. **His indictment** (82:1-2, 5-7)
      1. *They hand down unjust decisions and favor the wicked* (82:2).
      2. *They are ignorant and in darkness* (82:5).
      3. *They are responsible for shaking the whole world to the core* (82:5).
      4. *When it comes to death, they are mere mortals* (82:6-7).
   B. **His instruction** (82:3-4)
      1. *"Give fair judgment to the poor and the orphan; uphold the rights of the oppressed and the destitute"* (82:3).
      2. *"Rescue the poor and helpless; deliver them from the grasp of evil people"* (82:4).

II. GOD'S JUDGMENT UPON THE NATIONS (82:8): The plea for God to rise up and judge, for all nations belong to him.

Asaph petitions for divine help, describes the violence of Israel's enemies, and prays for deliverance as in ancient days, that God may be shown supreme.

I. THE PLOT AGAINST ISRAEL (83:1-8)
   A. **The iniquity** (83:1-4)
      1. *The grief inflicted by Israel's enemies* (83:1-3): These cruel and crafty foes are always conspiring against God's nation.
      2. *The goal intended of Israel's enemies* (83:4): They plan to wipe out Israel as a nation!
   B. **The identity** (83:5-8): Ten nations are allied against Israel, including Edom, Moab, Philistia, Tyre, and Assyria.

II. THE PETITION BY ISRAEL (83:9-18)
   A. **Concerning those nations** (83:13-17)
      1. *Blow them away like dust* (83:13): Make them like chaff in the wind.
      2. *Consume them by fire* (83:14): Make them as mountains set ablaze.
      3. *Terrify them* (83:15): Chase them with storms.
      4. *Shame and disgrace them* (83:16-18): Make them fail in all they do till they learn God alone is the Most High.
   B. **Concerning his name** (83:18): Vindicate your glorious name!

SECTION OUTLINE EIGHTY-FOUR (PSALM 84)
The psalmist expresses the joy of intimate communion with God.

I. WHAT THE TEMPLE OF THE LORD MEANS TO THE PSALMIST (84:1-10)
   A. **The desire** (84:1-3): He yearns to dwell near the altar, along with the sparrows and swallows that build their nests there.
   B. **The delights** (84:4-10)
      1. *The benefits* (84:4-9)
         a. Happiness (84:4-5): People who live in God's house constantly sing his praises.
         b. Strength (84:5, 7): The godly will make a pilgrimage to Jerusalem.
         c. Comfort (84:6): The Valley of Weeping becomes a refreshing spring.
         d. Protection (84:9): God has mercy on his anointed.
      2. *The bottom line* (84:10)
         a. One day there "is better than a thousand anywhere else!" (84:10).
         b. Living in a humble position in God's house is better than living a good life with the wicked (84:10)

II. WHAT THE LORD OF THE TEMPLE MEANS TO THE PSALMIST (84:11-12)
   A. **God is his light and protector** (84:11): He gives grace and glory.
   B. **God is the giver of all good things** (84:11-12): "Happy are those who trust in you."

SECTION OUTLINE EIGHTY-FIVE (PSALM 85)
The psalmist seeks God in his need on the basis of God's past faithfulness to him. He expresses confidence that God will pour out blessings.

I. ACKNOWLEDGING THE PAST (85:1-3)
   A. **God restores his people** (85:1): He blesses them.
   B. **God forgives his people** (85:2-3): He covers their sins and ends his anger.

II. QUESTIONING THE PRESENT (85:4-7)
   A. **"Will you be angry with us always?"** (85:4-6): They ask God to put aside his wrath against them and future generations.
   B. **"Show us your unfailing love, O LORD"** (85:7): They ask God to grant them salvation.

III. ANTICIPATING THE FUTURE (85:8-13)
   A. **The glorious message** (85:8-9): God promises peace and salvation to people who honor him.
   B. **The glorious meetings** (85:10-13)
      1. *Unfailing love and truth meet* (85:10).
      2. *Righteousness and peace kiss* (85:10-13).

SECTION OUTLINE EIGHTY-SIX (PSALM 86)

David acknowledges God's mercy, goodness, and uniqueness. He asks for God's guidance, supernatural strength, and a sign to reassure him amid all his enemies.

I. DAVID'S TROUBLES: What He Seeks from God (86:1-4, 6, 11, 14, 16-17)
   A. **His persecutors** (86:14): Insolent, violent, God-rejecting people are trying to kill him.
   B. **His petitions** (86:1-4, 6, 11, 16-17)
      1. *Hear me!* (86:1, 6): He needs God to hear his prayer for help.
      2. *Protect me!* (86:2): Because he serves and trusts God.
      3. *Be merciful to me!* (86:3, 6, 16): Because he calls on God constantly.
      4. *Give me happiness!* (86:4): Because his life depends on God.
      5. *Teach me!* (86:11): Because he wants to live according to God's truth.
      6. *Give me a sign!* (86:17): Because if he has God's favor, those who hate him will be put to shame.

II. DAVID'S TESTIMONY: What He Says about God (86:5, 7-10, 12-13, 15)
   A. **You are good and forgiving** (86:5): God is full of unfailing love to those who call on his name.
   B. **You answer prayer** (86:7): When trouble strikes, God is available.
   C. **You deserve to be worshiped by all nations** (86:9): They will bow before him and praise his name.
   D. **You deserve to be worshiped by me** (86:12): The author gives God glory forever.
   E. **You are unique** (86:8): There is no god like him or no other miracles like his.
   F. **You are a worker of miracles** (86:10): He alone is God.
   G. **You love me greatly** (86:13): God rescues him from death.
   H. **You are merciful and gracious** (86:15): God is slow to get angry and full of unfailing love and truth.

SECTION OUTLINE EIGHTY-SEVEN (PSALM 87)

This psalm is not only a religious lyric but a song of praise or triumph. The writer celebrates deliverance, tells of the glories of Jerusalem, and praises the universality of the Messiah's kingdom.

I. THE GREAT HONOR BESTOWED UPON JERUSALEM (87:1-3)
   A. **Because of its glorious present** (87:1-2)
      1. *God founded it* (87:1).
      2. *God loves it more than any other city* (87:2).
   B. **Because of its glorious past** (87:3): Wonderful things are said of it!

    II. THE GREAT HONOR OF BEING A CITIZEN OF JERUSALEM (87:4-7)
        A. To be known by many places, including Egypt, Babylon, Philistia, Tyre, and Ethiopia (87:4-5)
        B. To be registered by God himself (87:6-7)

SECTION OUTLINE EIGHTY-EIGHT (PSALM 88)
In this psalm of lamentation (deep despair) the psalmist's complaints are not relieved by joyful anticipation or expressions of strong confidence. Only darkness remains.

    I. SUFFERING FROM UNANSWERED PRAYER (88:1-2, 13)
        A. He cries out to God day and night (88:1-2).
        B. He pleads day by day (88:13).

    II. SUFFERING FROM UNENDING PAIN (88:3-5, 9, 15)
        A. The details (88:3-5, 9)
            1. *His life is full of trouble* (88:3).
            2. *He is at the point of death* (88:3-5).
            3. *His eyes are blinded by tears* (88:9): He begs the Lord for mercy and help.
        B. The duration (88:15): He has suffered these things from his youth.

    III. SUFFERING FROM UNDESERVED PERSECUTION (88:6-8, 10-12, 14, 16-18)
        A. Persecution from his Creator (88:6-7, 10-12, 14, 16-17): The psalmist feels God is unjustly punishing him.
            1. *He is in the darkest depths* (88:6-7, 16): God's anger overwhelms him, and God's terror cuts him off.
            2. *He feels utterly rejected* (88:14): God turns his face from him.
            3. *He is close to drowning* (88:17).
            4. *He asks God how he can glorify the Lord in death* (88:10-12).
        B. Persecution from his companions (88:8, 18)
            1. *His friends loathe him* (88:8).
            2. *His companions and loved ones are taken away* (88:18).

SECTION OUTLINE EIGHTY-NINE (PSALM 89)
In the midst of trouble, the psalmist celebrates God's everlasting and unconditional covenant with David and his descendants, including the special covenant with David (see 2 Samuel 7) in regard to his royal throne.

    I. THE PRAISE (89:1-37): The author offers thanks for four things.
        A. God's person (89:1-2, 5-8, 14)
            1. *For his mercy, love, faithfulness, and miracles* (89:1-2, 5)
            2. *For his uniqueness* (89:6-8): No one compares to him.

3. *For his righteousness and justice* (89:14): His throne is founded on these.

B. God's power (89:9-13)

1. *He creates all things* (89:11-13): He is strong and powerful.
2. *He rules over the sea* (89:9): He subdues the waves and storms.
3. *He crushes his enemies* (89:10): He also scatters them.

C. God's provisions (89:15-18): He gives to his people strength and joy!

D. God's promise (89:3-4, 19-37): This promise has to do with the Davidic covenant.

1. *The person* (89:3, 19-20): God himself made this covenant with King David.
2. *The duration* (89:4, 28-29, 35-37): The covenant is unconditional and unending.
3. *The method* (89:19-20): It is given in a vision from a prophet, probably Nathan, who then communicates it to David.
4. *The features* (89:21-27, 30-34)
   a. God will personally steady David (89:21): God will make him strong.
   b. David will be victorious over his foes (89:22-23): God will destroy those who hate him.
   c. He will have God's faithfulness and unfailing love (89:24): He will rise to power.
   d. He will rule from the Tigris and Euphrates rivers to the Mediterranean Sea (89:25).
   e. He will enjoy a relationship with God (89:26): God will be his Father, his God, and the Rock of his salvation.
   f. He will become God's firstborn son (89:27): He will become the mightiest king on earth.
   g. The covenant will prevail in spite of any sins committed by David's royal descendants (89:30-34): The covenant is everlasting, but sins committed by David's descendants will be punished.

II. THE PROBLEM (89:38-45): How can God's present rejection of Israel be reconciled to the Davidic covenant?

A. The time (89:38-39): The psalmist seems to be describing the Babylonian Captivity.

B. The tragedy (89:40-45)

1. *The Temple has been defiled* (89:40): Its protection is gone.
2. *The city of God has been destroyed* (89:40-45): David's enemies mock him because of his loss of power.

III. THE PLEA (89:46-52): The psalmist calls upon God to remember two things and show himself strong.

A. Our lives are short, empty, and futile (89:46-48): Everyone will die.

B. God's love is unfailing (89:49-52).

SECTION OUTLINE NINETY (PSALM 90)
This oldest psalm, written by Moses, addresses the frailty and brevity of human life as a consequence of sin and as a motive for repentance and obedience.

I. THE ETERNALITY OF THE CREATOR (90:1-4)
   A. **His identity** (90:1-3): From beginning to end God will always be God!
   B. **His immortality** (90:4) To God 1000 years are as:
      1. *Yesterday* (90:4)
      2. *A few hours* (90:4)

II. THE MORTALITY OF THE CREATURE (90:5-17)
   A. **The problems** (90:5-11)
      1. *The shortness* (90:5-6, 10)
         a. The comparison (90:5-6): Our lives are as grass, fresh at sunrise, withered and dry at sunset.
         b. The count (90:10): We are given an average of 70 years.
      2. *The sinfulness* (90:7-8): God sees all our iniquities, both secret and open.
      3. *The sorrow* (90:9-11): Our days are filled with pain and trouble.
   B. **The fourfold petition** (90:12-17)
      1. *Teach us* (90:12): That we might make the most of our time and grow in wisdom.
      2. *Satisfy us* (90:13-16): That we might experience God's love, sing for joy, and see God's miracles again.
      3. *Sanctify our children* (90:16): That they might see God's glory at work.
      4. *Make us successful* (90:17): That God might approve of us.

SECTION OUTLINE NINETY-ONE (PSALM 91)
This psalm is about faith and describes the perfect security of one who trusts in the Lord.

I. THE FOUNDATION OF FAITH (91:1-2)
   A. **Believing in the person of God** (91:1-2): The psalmist employs four names for God:
      1. *Elyon* (91:1): "The Most High"
      2. *Shaddai* (91:1): "The Almighty"
      3. *Yahweh* (91:2): "The LORD"
      4. *Elohim* (91:2): "My God"
   B. **Believing in the promises of God** (91:2): The psalmist trusts God as his refuge and place of safety.

II. THE FOES OF FAITH (91:3)
   A. **The trap** (91:3): God rescues us.
   B. **The fatal plague** (91:3): God protects us.

III. THE FRUITS OF FAITH (91:4-10, 13)
   A. **To find refuge under God's wings** (91:4)
   B. **To be protected by the armor of God's faithfulness** (91:4)
   C. **To be reassured in times of terror, danger, and evil** (91:5-7, 10)
   D. **To see the punishment of the wicked** (91:8-9)
   E. **To tread upon the lion and snake** (91:13)

IV. THE FRIENDS OF FAITH (91:11-12)
   A. **Who they are** (91:11): They are angels who do his bidding.
   B. **What they do** (91:11-12)
      1. *They guard believers* (91:11-12): They protect us wherever we go.
      2. *They guide believers* (91:12): They hold us with their hands.

V. THE FELLOWSHIP OF FAITH (91:14-16): Faith creates intimacy between the believer and the Lord.
   A. **A mutual love** (91:14): He rescues and protects those who love him.
   B. **Communication through prayer** (91:15): God answers those who call on him.
   C. **A long life of honor** (91:15-16): He is with them in trouble and satisfies them with a long life and salvation.

SECTION OUTLINE NINETY-TWO (PSALM 92)
This psalm was composed as a Sabbath song of praise to God for his power and wisdom in his providential dealings with the wicked and the righteous.

I. GOD AND THE REDEEMED (92:1-5, 8, 10-15)
   A. **What they are to do** (92:1, 8): Thank and praise the Lord God Most High!
   B. **When they are to do it** (92:2): In the morning (his unfailing love) and in the evening (his faithfulness)
   C. **How they are to do it** (92:3): With singing, accompanied by the harp, lute, and lyre.
   D. **Why they are to do it** (92:4-5, 10-15)
      1. *Because of God's person* (92:4-5)
         a. His actions (92:4)
         b. His thoughts (92:5)
      2. *Because of God's provision* (92:10-15)
         a. For strength (92:10): God's power refreshes.

     b. For victory (92:11): He sees the downfall of his enemies and hears the defeat of his opponents.

     c. For growth (92:12-15): The godly flourish in God's courts.

II. GOD AND THE REBELLIOUS (92:6-7, 9)

A. They do not comprehend God (92:6-7): Fools do not understand the destruction ahead of them.

B. They will be scattered by God (92:9): God's enemies will perish.

SECTION OUTLINE NINETY-THREE (PSALM 93)

In danger, the psalmist extols God's supremacy over all things and the resulting security of those who are his people.

I. THE LORD'S ROBES (93:1)

A. He is robed in majesty (93:1).

B. He is armed with strength (93:1).

II. THE LORD'S REIGN (93:2-4)

A. His throne has always existed (93:2-3): God himself is from the everlasting past.

B. His throne will always exist (93:4): The Lord is mightier than all.

III. THE LORD'S RIGHTEOUSNES (93:5)

A. His precepts (93:5): "Your royal decrees cannot be changed."

B. His purity (93:5): His reign is "holiness forever."

SECTION OUTLINE NINETY-FOUR (PSALM 94)

The psalmist complains about the Lord's apparent desertion yet expresses confidence in the Lord's return and his enemies' destruction.

I. THE LORD GOD AND HIS FOES (94:1-10, 20-21, 23)

A. The psalmist requests their punishment (94:1-3).

  1. *His impatience* (94:1, 3): "How long will the wicked be allowed to gloat?"

  2. *His insistence* (94:2): "Arise, O judge of the earth. Sentence the proud to the penalties they deserve."

B. The psalmist reviews their perversions (94:4-10, 20-21, 23).

  1. *Their godless actions* (94:4-6, 20-21)

    a. They spew out arrogant and boastful words (94:4).

    b. They oppress and hurt those God loves (94:5).

    c. They murder widows, foreigners, and orphans (94:6).

    d. They permit injustice (94:20-21): "They attack the righteous and condemn the innocent to death."

  2. *Their godless attitudes* (94:7-10, 23): They foolishly think God won't see, hear, or punish their evil. But he does, and he will.

II. The Lord God and His Friends (94:11-19, 22)
  A. **He disciplines them in love** (94:11-13): He gives them relief in troubled times and knows all their thoughts.
  B. **He never forsakes them** (94:14-15): The Lord does not reject his people, and the upright have a reward.
  C. **He keeps them from falling** (94:16-18, 22): The Lord supports them and provides a fortress where they can hide.
  D. **He causes them to rejoice** (94:19): God's comfort gives them hope and cheer.

SECTION OUTLINE NINETY-FIVE (PSALM 95)

This psalm, containing both positive and negative elements, invites the Jews not only to praise the Lord but also to respond to him.

I. The Positive: The Believer Should Always Praise God (95:1-7).
  A. **For his creative works** (95:4-5): He created and controls:
    1. *The dry land* (95:5): His hands formed it.
    2. *The sea* (95:5): It belongs to him.
    3. *The mountains and the depths* (95:4): Everything belongs to him.
  B. **For his redemptive works** (95:1-3, 6-7)
    1. *He is the rock of salvation* (95:1-3): Sing for joy to God for what he has done for us.
    2. *He is the shepherd of the sheep* (95:6-7): Kneel before God and worship him for his care.

II. The Negative: The Believer Should Never Provoke God. (95:8-11): The psalmist uses Israel's march to the Promised Land as an example.
  A. **The terrible rebellion** (95:8-9): In spite of God's mighty miracles, Israel refused to obey him.
  B. **The tragic results** (95:10-11)
    1. *During the 40-year march* (95:10): The older generation endured God's wrath.
    2. *Following the 40-year march* (95:11): The older generation could not enjoy God's rest.

SECTION OUTLINE NINETY-SIX (PSALM 96)

This psalm invites the Gentiles to praise and worship the Lord.

I. The Twofold Invitation (96:1-10)
  A. **The call to witness** (96:1-6, 10): Believers are to publish God's name worldwide!
    1. *Proclaiming his salvation* (96:1-2): Bless the Lord's name and sing to him.

2. *Proclaiming his splendor* (96:3, 6): Tell everyone about his deeds and his honor and glory.
3. *Proclaiming his sovereignty* (96:4-5, 10): God is most worthy of praise and judges all people fairly.
4. *Proclaiming his strength* (96:3, 6): He does amazing things.
   B. **The call to worship** (96:7-9)
   1. *Give glory to God* (96:7-8): All nations should recognize God and give him the glory he deserves.
   2. *Give gifts to God* (96:8-9): All nations should worship God in his splendor and tremble before him.

II. THE CELEBRATION (96:11-13)
   A. **The parties** (96:11-12): Both heaven and earth will rejoice!
   B. **The purpose** (96:13): The Lord will return to judge the earth with righteousness.

SECTION OUTLINE NINETY-SEVEN (PSALM 97)

The psalmist prophesies Messiah's righteous reign as king of all the earth.

I. OVER CREATION (97:1-2, 4-5): All God's creative works worship him.
   A. **The earth trembles and rejoices** (97:1-2, 4).
   B. **The farthest islands sing his praises** (97:1).
   C. **The mountains melt like wax** (97:5).

II. OVER THE CORRUPT (97:3): Fire burns up all his foes.

III. OVER THE COUNTRIES (97:6-9)
   A. **All the nations see his glory** (97:6-7): "Those who worship idols are disgraced . . . for every god must bow to him."
   B. **The Hebrew nation worships him** (97:8-9): They rejoice because God is Most High over the earth.

IV. OVER THE CONSECRATED ONES (97:10-12)
   A. **What he desires from them** (97:10)
   1. *That they love him* (97:10)
   2. *That they hate evil* (97:10)
   B. **What he does for them** (97:10-12)
   1. *He protects their lives* (97:10).
   2. *He rescues them from the wicked* (97:10).
   3. *He gives them light* (97:11).
   4. *He gives them joy and happiness* (97:11-12).

SECTION OUTLINE NINETY-EIGHT (PSALM 98)
This messianic psalm looks forward to the earthly millennial reign of David's greater Son, Jesus Christ. It urges believers to sing!

I. WHAT TO SING (98:1): A new song

II. HOW TO SING (98:4-6): Sing with joyful voices, accompanied by harp, trumpets, and the sound of the ram's horn.

III. WHY TO SING (98:2-3, 7-8)
   A. **Because of God's great redemptive work** (98:2-3): He shows his salvation to Jews and Gentiles alike.
   B. **Because of God's great creative work** (98:7-8): All nature joins in singing.

IV. WHEN TO SING (98:9)
   A. **At the present, anticipating his return** (98:9): The Lord is coming to judge the earth.
   B. **In the future, celebrating his return** (98:9): He will judge with justice and fairness.

SECTION OUTLINE NINETY-NINE (PSALM 99)
This psalm anticipates when Jesus Christ will establish his earthly kingdom and extols the kingship of the Lord.

I. THE PSALMIST CALLS PEOPLE TO EXALT THE LORD (99:1-5, 9):
   A. **Because of his splendor** (99:1): "He sits on his throne between the cherubim."
   B. **Because of his sovereignty** (99:2-3): He is "supreme above all the nations."
   C. **Because of his sinlessness** (99:4-5, 9): He is both just and holy.

II. THOSE WHO HAVE EXALTED THE LORD ARE DESCRIBED (99:6-8):
   A. **Who they are** (99:6): Moses, Aaron, and Samuel
   B. **What they did** (99:6-8)
      1. *They called upon God* (99:6): "They cried to the LORD for help, and he answered them."
      2. *They heard from God* (99:7-8): He spoke to them, and they followed his decrees.
      3. *God forgave their sins* (99:8): He "punished them when they went wrong."

SECTION OUTLINE ONE HUNDRED (PSALM 100)

This psalm looks forward to the glorious earthly reign of the Messiah and exhorts the entire world to receive the Lord as its Sovereign.

I. GOD IS THE SONG (100:1-2): We are his singers.

II. GOD IS THE CREATOR (100:3): We are his creation.

III. GOD IS THE SHEPHERD (100:3): We are his sheep.

IV. GOD IS THE BLESSED ONE (100:4): We are his blessed ones.

V. GOD IS LOVE (100:5): We are his loved ones.

SECTION OUTLINE ONE HUNDRED ONE (PSALM 101)

David determines to praise the Lord, to be blameless in his own walk, and to rule in a godly way and drive out evil.

I. DAVID'S WITNESS ABOUT GOD (101:1)
   A. **He sings of God's love** (101:1).
   B. **He testifies to God's justice** (101:1).
   C. **He praises God** (101:1).

II. DAVID'S WALK WITH GOD (101:2-7)
   A. **In his private life** (101:2-3): He attempts to conduct himself blamelessly in his own home.
   B. **In his public life** (101:3-7)
      1. *David vows to forsake the godless* (101:3-5, 7).
         a. He will have no part in their wicked works (101:3-4): He hates their vile doings and stays away from all evil.
         b. He will take no part in their wicked words (101:5, 7): He will not tolerate slanderers or liars.
      2. *David vows to fellowship with the godly* (101:6): Only those above reproach are allowed to serve him.

III. DAVID'S WARFARE FOR GOD (101:8): He vows to capture and destroy the criminals.

SECTION OUTLINE ONE HUNDRED TWO (PSALM 102)

While enemies attack, the psalmist—with broken health and heart—begs God to intervene. He also contemplates the Messiah's coming, when the present heaven and earth will be destroyed and all things will be new.

I. THE PSALMIST'S TRAVAIL (102:1-11, 23-24)
   A. **His plea** (102:1-2, 24)
      1. *"Hear my prayer! . . . Don't turn away from me."* (102:1-2)
      2. *"Don't take my life while I am still so young!"* (102:24)

B. His plight (102:3-11, 23)
    1. *His flesh* (102:3-7)
       a. His bones burn like red-hot coals (102:3).
       b. His heart withers away like grass (102:4).
       c. He is reduced to skin and bones (102:5).
       d. He is like a lonely owl in a far-off wilderness or a solitary
          bird on a roof (102:6-7).
    2. *His foes* (102:8-9): They taunt, mock, and curse him daily.
    3. *His friend* (102:10-11, 23): He feels even God is persecuting
       him.

II. THE PSALMIST'S TESTIMONY (102:12-22, 25-28): The sound of faith is
   now heard over the sighs of pain as he praises and worships God.
   A. For his eternality (102:12, 25-27)
   B. For his faithfulness (102:17): He hears the prayers of the desti-
      tute.
   C. For his millennial reign (102:15): All tremble before him.
   D. For his compassion (102:13-14, 16, 18-22)
      1. *Upon Jerusalem* (102:13-14, 16, 18, 21-22)
      2. *Upon prisoners* (102:19-20)
   E. For his omnipotence (102:25): He formed the earth and heavens.
   F. For his immutability (102:26-28): He never changes, and his
      children thrive in his presence.

SECTION OUTLINE ONE HUNDRED THREE (PSALM 103)
David praises the Lord, contemplates his blessing, and exhorts all of
God's creation to praise the Lord.

I. DAVID'S SUMMONS TO THE ADOPTED ON EARTH: "Praise the LORD!"
   (103:1-19): As members of God's adopted family, we must never
   forget two all-important facts:
   A. Who and what God is (103:1-13, 17-19)
      1. *His attributes* (qualities) (103:6-8, 17-19)
        a. He is righteous and just (103:6-7): "He revealed his charac-
          ter to Moses and his deeds to the people of Israel."
        b. He is merciful and gracious (103:8): "He is slow to get
          angry and full of unfailing love."
        c. He is loving, eternal, and faithful (103:17-18): "His salva-
          tion extends to the children's children of those who are
          faithful to his covenant."
        d. He is sovereign (103:19): He rules over everything from his
          throne in heaven.
      2. *His actions* (103:1-5, 8-13)
        a. He forgives sin (103:1-3, 8-12): Sin is removed from us as
          far as the east is from the west.
        b. He heals diseases (103:3).
        c. He protects from death (103:4).

       d. He satisfies (103:4-5): He surrounds us with love, tender mercies, and good things.
       e. He gives strength (103:5): Our youth is renewed like the eagle's.
       f. He functions as a loving father (103:13): The Lord is tender and compassionate.
    B. Who and what we are (103:14-16)
      1. *We are dust, soon to return to dust* (103:14-15): He knows how weak we are.
      2. *We are like wildflowers, soon to wither and die* (103:15-16)

II. DAVID'S SUMMONS TO THE ANGELS IN HEAVEN (103:20-22): "Praise the Lord!"

SECTION OUTLINE ONE HUNDRED FOUR (PSALM 104)
The psalmist recognizes that the universe is created by and is totally dependent upon a single Creator.

I. THE PRAISE TO GOD (104:1, 24, 31, 33-35): The psalmist worships the Lord for several reasons:
    A. For his greatness: "You are robed with honor and with majesty" (104:1).
    B. For his variety of creation: "The earth is full of your creatures" (104:24).
    C. For his glory: "May the glory of the LORD last forever!" (104:31).
    D. For his pleasure: "I will sing to the LORD as long as I live. I will praise my God to my last breath!" (104:33). The psalmist wants the Lord to be pleased with his praise.

II. THE POWER OF GOD (104:2-9, 32)
    A. He stretches out the heavens (104:2): He makes them a starry curtain.
    B. He rides the clouds as his chariots (104:3): He lays out the rafters of his home in the rain clouds.
    C. He sends forth fire and the winds (104:4): They are his messengers and servants.
    D. He placed the world on its foundation (104:5): It can never be moved.
    E. He controls the waters (104:6-9): He sent the great flood.
    F. He controls the earth and mountains (104:8, 32): They rise and sink, as God decrees. The earth trembles, and the mountains burst into flame at his glance.

III. THE PROVISIONS FROM GOD (104:10-23, 25-30): He cares and provides for all his creation.
    A. Water (104:10-13): He quenches the animals' thirst.
    B. Food (104:13, 15, 23, 27-28): He provides a crop from human

labor including wine, olive oil, and bread. Everyone and every-
thing depend on God for food.
- **C. Grass and plants** (104:13-14): He provides grass for cattle and plants for people.
- **D. Trees** (104:16): God plants trees and cares for them.
- **E. Home** (104:17-18, 22): God provides a place for rest for humans and animals, such as wild goats, rock badgers, and lions.
- **F. Night and day** (104:19-20): God also marks the seasons.

SECTION OUTLINE ONE HUNDRED FIVE (PSALM 105)
This psalm looks at God's dealings in history and encourages the people to hope for a deliverance similar to that of Moses' day.

I. GOD'S MAJESTY (105:1-4): The psalmist exhorts God's people to:
- **A. Sing his fame** (105:1-3): Proclaim his greatness and rejoice in him.
- **B. Seek his face** (105:4): Keep searching for the Lord and his strength.

II. GOD'S MIRACLES (105:5-45)
- **A. The invitation** (105:5): Israel is called upon to remember these supernatural acts.
- **B. The illustrations** (105:6-45)
  1. *As seen in Abraham's time* (105:6-15)
     a. The gift (105:6-10): Abraham receives the special promise known as the Abrahamic covenant.
     b. The geography (105:11): Abraham and his seed possess Canaan.
     c. The grace (105:12-15): From the very beginning God protected and cared for this tiny nation.
  2. *As seen in Joseph's time* (105:16-23)
     a. The crisis (105:16): God sends a famine upon the land.
     b. The champion (105:17-23)
        (1) Joseph the prisoner (105:17-19): He is falsely accused and cast into prison. There God tests his character.
        (2) Joseph the prophet (105:19-20): According to an earlier biblical account (see Genesis 41), Joseph predicts seven years of plenty and seven years of famine and is released from prison.
        (3) Joseph the prime minister (105:21-23): The king makes him second in command.
  3. *As seen in Moses' time* (105:24-43)
     a. The crisis (105:24-25): The Israelites become too mighty for Egypt, so Egypt makes the Israelites slaves.
     b. The champion (105:26-43)
        (1) God uses Moses to liberate his people (105:26-38): The miracles God allows Moses to perform make the Egyptians free the Israelites.

        (2) God uses Moses to lead and feed his people
           (105:39-43): God brings his people out with singing
           and rejoicing and takes care of them on the way to the
           Promised Land.
     4. *As seen in Joshua's time* (105:44-45): God brings Israel into
       the Promised Land.

SECTION OUTLINE ONE HUNDRED SIX (PSALM 106)

This psalm focuses on history and encourages God's people to look for deliverance.

  I. A REQUEST FOR THE PRESENT (106:1-5, 47-48): The psalmist asks for
    three things:
    A. Regard us (106:1-5, 48).
      1. *Israel wants to bless God* (106:1-3, 48): God can never be
        praised enough.
      2. *Israel wants to be blessed by God* (106:4-5): They want to be
        remembered by the Lord.
    B. Redeem us (106:47): They want to be saved.
    C. Regather us (106:47): They want to be gathered back from the
    nations.

 II. A REMEMBRANCE OF THE PAST (106:6-46): The psalmist reviews
    Israel's corruption and God's compassion in the wilderness.
    A. Israel's corruption (106:6-7, 13-43)
      1. *They forget God's miracles* (106:7, 13, 21-23).
      2. *They rebel against him* (106:6-7, 33): They act wickedly,
        rebelling against Moses.
      3. *They ignore his counsel* (106:13): They will not wait for him.
      4. *They test his patience* (106:14-15, 32): They anger God and
        Moses.
      5. *They envy Moses and Aaron* (106:16-18): As punishment,
        people are destroyed—swallowed up by the earth and fire.
      6. *They worship idols* (106:19-20, 28-31): They bow before gold
        images and eat sacrifices offered to the dead. The result is a
        plague.
      7. *They refuse to enter the Promised Land* (106:24).
      8. *They disbelieve his promises* (106:24): They think God will
        not care for them.
      9. *They grumble constantly* (106:25-27): They refuse to obey the
        Lord.
     10. *They adopt the sins of surrounding nations* (106:34-43): They
        mingle with the other nations instead of destroying them as
        the Lord commands.
    B. God's compassion (106:8-12, 43-46)
      1. *He saves his people for his name's sake* (106:8): He
        demonstrates his mighty power with their salvation.

2. *He divides the Red Sea for them* (106:9-12): They pass through on dry land; their pursuing enemies are drowned.
3. *He delivers them many times* (106:43): They continue to rebel and are finally destroyed by their sin.
4. *He takes note of their distress* (106:44): He listens to their cries.
5. *He remembers his covenant with them* (106:45): He relents because of his unfailing love.
6. *He even causes their enemies to treat them kindly* (106:46).

SECTION OUTLINE ONE HUNDRED SEVEN (PSALM 107)
The psalmist celebrates God's providential deliverances.

I. WHAT THE REDEEMED ARE TO DO (107:1, 8, 15, 21-22, 31-32, 42-43)
   A. **They are to give thanks to the Lord, praising him for his love** (107:1, 8, 15, 21, 31-32, 42-43): God's deeds are wonderful, and his love is faithful, enduring forever.
   B. **They are to sacrifice to the Lord** (107:22): They are to sing about God's glorious acts.

II. WHY THE REDEEMED ARE TO DO IT (107:2-7, 9-14, 16-20, 23-30, 33-41): The psalmist reviews Israel's sin and God's grace:
   A. **Israel's sin in spite of God's grace** (107:10-12, 17, 34)
      1. *They sit in darkness and gloom* (107:10): They are miserable prisoners in chains.
      2. *They rebel against his words* (107:11, 17, 34): They suffer for their rebellion.
      3. *They despise his counsel* (107:11-12): He breaks them with hard labor.
   B. **God's grace in spite of Israel's sin** (107:2-7, 9, 13-14, 16, 18-20, 23-30, 33-41)
      1. *He gathers them* (107:3-4): He brings them from many lands.
      2. *He feeds and leads them* (107:5-7, 9, 13-14, 33, 35): He provides food and water, and answers their calls for help.
      3. *He heals them with his voice* (107:20).
      4. *He saves them from imprisonment, death, and trouble* (107:2, 16, 18-20, 23-30): When they cry for help, he answers them.
      5. *He gives them abundant flocks and crops* (107:36-41): He helps them settle, build their cities, and increase their families.

SECTION OUTLINE ONE HUNDRED EIGHT (PSALM 108)

To provide this national psalm praising the Lord, David most likely combines material from Psalms 57:7-11 and 60:5-12.

I. DAVID PRAISES THE LORD (108:1-5, 7-10)
   A. **How?** (108:1-2): He sings, accompanied by the harp and lyre.
   B. **When?** (108:2): All day long, beginning at dawn
   C. **Where?** (108:3, 5): "Among the nations"
   D. **Why?** (108:4, 7-10)
      1. *Because of God's love* (108:4): His love is higher than the heavens.
      2. *Because of God's faithfulness* (108:4): His faithfulness reaches to the clouds.
      3. *Because of God's promises* (108:7-10): God has made us the holy promise that everything belongs to him.

II. DAVID PETITIONS THE LORD (108:6, 11-13)
   A. **To rescue them** (108:6): David wants God to use his strong right arm to save them.
   B. **To help them and give them success over their enemies** (108:11-13): David knows human help is useless.

SECTION OUTLINE ONE HUNDRED NINE (PSALM 109)

David examines the treachery suffered by him and the Israelite nation. He urges God to deal with his enemies to unmistakably demonstrate his great power.

I. THE PERSECUTION (109:1-5, 22-25)
   A. **The ruthless attacks** (109:1-5)
      1. *They slander him with horrible lies* (109:1-3): They use hateful words and fight against him for no reason.
      2. *They repay kindness with treachery* (109:4-5): They return evil for good, hatred for love.
   B. **The devastating results** (109:22-25)
      1. *They leave him poor, needy, and near death* (109:22-23, 25): He is full of pain, an object of mockery, and is fading like a shadow.
      2. *He is reduced to skin and bones* (109:24): His knees are weak.

II. THE PETITION (109:6-7, 9-20): David asks the following concerning his foes:
   A. **Give them a taste of their own medicine** (109:6-7, 16-20): Find them guilty and may their curses become their own punishment.
   B. **Do not heed their prayers** (109:7): Count them as sin.
   C. **Do not bless their families** (109:9-10, 12): Let no one pity their fatherless children and their widows.

    D. Do not bless them financially (109:11): May they lose their estates and all they have earned.

    E. May their family name be blotted out (109:13-15): Cut their family names off from memory.

III. THE PROPHECY (109:8): "Let his years be few; let his position be given to someone else." Centuries later, Simon Peter would refer to this prophecy about Judas Iscariot (see Acts 1:20).

IV. THE PROTECTION (109:21-22, 26-31)

    A. God's unfailing love (109:21, 26, 30-31): "Deal well with me, O Sovereign LORD, for the sake of your own reputation! Rescue me because you are so faithful and good."

    B. God's power (109:27-29): "Let them see that this is your doing, that you yourself have done it, LORD." Because David believes in God's plan, he rejoices in spite of the attacks against him.

SECTION OUTLINE ONE HUNDRED TEN (PSALM 110)

In this psalm, which depicts Christ in a fivefold light, David shows how the kingship of the Messiah connects with his priesthood.

I. HE IS GOD (110:1).

    A. The persons (110:1): The Father refers to his Son as "LORD."

    B. The promise (110:1): The Father assures the Son that his enemies will be humbled.

II. HE IS A KING (110:2-3).

    A. The place of his reign (110:2): It will extend from Jerusalem.

    B. The power of his reign (110:3): People will serve God willingly.

III. HE IS A PRIEST (110:4).

    A. The oath (110:4): The Father vows to establish his Son's priesthood.

    B. The order (110:4): It is after the order of Melchizedek.

IV. HE IS A JUDGE (110:6): He will punish the nations.

V. HE IS A VICTORIOUS WARRIOR (110:5, 6-7): God is nearby and will protect his people.

SECTION OUTLINE ONE HUNDRED ELEVEN (PSALM 111)

This psalm of praise celebrates the mighty deeds of the Lord, who is to be feared.

I. THE WORSHIP OF GOD (111:1-2): The psalmist testifies to the Lord's greatness before the people.

II. THE WONDERS OF GOD (111:2-9)
   A. **Who the Lord is** (111:2-4, 7): He is glorious, majestic, righteous, gracious, merciful, just, good, and trustworthy.
   B. **What the Lord does** (111:5-6, 8-9)
      1. *He provides food* (111:5): Those who trust him do not go hungry.
      2. *He remembers his covenant* (111:5, 9): He always keeps his promises.
      3. *He gives his people their inheritance* (111:6): He shows his power by giving them the lands of other nations.
      4. *His commandments are true* (111:8): He is to be obeyed faithfully and with integrity.
      5. *He redeems his people* (111:9): He pays a full ransom for his people.

III. THE WISDOM OF GOD (111:10)
   A. **The road** (111:10): "Reverence for the LORD is the foundation of true wisdom."
   B. **The results** (111:10): Those who obey him are rewarded with wisdom.

SECTION OUTLINE ONE HUNDRED TWELVE (PSALM 112)

This psalm of praise emphasizes the righteousness and uprightness of one who fears the Lord.

I. THE GODLY PERSON'S CONSECRATION (112:1, 4-5, 9)
   A. **He fears God and loves his word** (112:1): Happy is the one who does what God commands.
   B. **He is compassionate and righteous** (112:4): Light bursts in when he's overtaken by darkness.
   C. **He gives freely and generously** (112:4-5, 9): He conducts his business fairly.

II. THE GODLY PERSON'S COMPENSATION (112:2-3, 6-8, 9, 10)
   A. **His children will be successful** (112:2): An entire generation will be blessed.
   B. **He will have influence and honor** (112:9).
   C. **His financial needs are met** (112:3).
   D. **He is secure and never shaken by evil circumstances** (112:6).
   E. **He and his good deeds are not forgotten** (112:3, 6, 9): The righteous are long remembered.

F. He does not fear bad news (112:7-8): He confidently trusts the Lord.

G. He triumphs over his foes (112:8, 10): He is confident and fearless. As a result, the hopes of the wicked are thwarted.

SECTION OUTLINE ONE HUNDRED THIRTEEN (PSALM 113)
This hallelujah psalm praises the Lord for who and what he is.

I. THE MAJESTY OF THE LORD (113:1-6)
   A. **His horizontal glory** (113:1-3): It shines from east to west—so that all might praise the name of the Lord.
   B. **His vertical glory** (113:4-6): It ascends high above the nations and is greater than the heavens.

II. THE MERCY OF THE LORD (113:7-9)
   A. **It lifts up the poor and needy, setting them among princes** (113:7-8).
   B. **It gives a home and children to the barren** (113:9).

SECTION OUTLINE ONE HUNDRED FOURTEEN (PSALM 114)
To show that God is doing and will continue to do wondrous deeds for Israel, the psalmist uses two specific times in Israel's history—the crossings of the Red Sea and the Jordan River—when God led his people.

I. OUT OF THE LAND OF BONDAGE (114:1-3, 5)
   A. **Judah becomes God's sanctuary** (114:1-2): Israel becomes God's kingdom.
   B. **The Red Sea parts** (114:3, 5): In fact, it hurries out of their way!

II. INTO THE LAND OF BLESSING (114:3-4, 5-8)
   A. **The Lord's power parts the Jordan River** (114:3, 5).
   B. **The Lord's presence does two things** (114:4, 6-8):
      1. *It causes mountains to skip like rams and little hills like lambs* (114:4, 6).
      2. *It causes the earth to tremble* (114:7-8): Even rocks yield water.

SECTION OUTLINE ONE HUNDRED FIFTEEN (PSALM 115)
The psalmist delivers a strong polemic against idolatry by comparing the one true God with heathen idols.

I. THE TRUE GOD (115:1-3, 9-18)
   A. **The psalmist's description** (115:1-3)
      1. *The Lord is loving and faithful* (115:1): God gets all the glory for who he is.

2. *The Lord is sovereign* (115:2-3): God does as he wishes.
B. **The psalmist's desire** (115:9-18)
 1. *What he wanted Israel to do* (115:9-11): In essence, to trust and fear the Lord!
 2. *Why he wanted Israel to do it* (115:12-18): Because God will then remember and richly bless his people.

II. THE FALSE GODS (115:4-8)
 A. **They are merely silver and gold things** (115:4, 8): They are shaped by human hands.
 B. **They have mouths, eyes, ears, noses, hands, and feet, but cannot speak, see, hear, smell, feel, or walk** (115:5-7): These gods are powerless.

SECTION OUTLINE ONE HUNDRED SIXTEEN (PSALM 116)
The psalmist describes his attitudes toward the Lord, the deliverances he experiences, and determines to praise God.

I. WHAT GOD DOES FOR THE PSALMIST (116:1-11)
 A. **He hears his prayers** (116:1-2, 4-7).
 B. **He saves him from death** (116:3, 8-11).

II. WHAT THE PSALMIST DOES FOR GOD (116:12-19)
 A. **He praises the Lord for saving him** (116:13).
 B. **He fulfills his vows** (116:14-15, 18-19).
 C. **He serves him faithfully** (116:12-16).
 D. **He offers sacrifices of thanksgiving and calls upon the name of the Lord** (116:17).

SECTION OUTLINE ONE HUNDRED SEVENTEEN (PSALM 117)
This psalm issues an invitation for, justifies, and expresses universal praise to the Lord.

I. WHAT? (117:1-2): "Praise the LORD!"

II. WHY? (117:2): For his "unfailing love"

III. WHO? (117:1): "All you people of the earth"

SECTION OUTLINE ONE HUNDRED EIGHTEEN (PSALM 118)
This psalm invites praise to the Lord for his goodness, demonstrates his worthiness, testifies of his deliverance, and offers prayers of praise.

I. THE PSALMIST'S PROMPTING (118:1-4, 24)
 A. **To the people** (118:1-2, 4, 24): He urges the congregation to praise God by repeating "His faithful love endures forever."

B. To the priests (118:3): He urges Aaron's descendants to also praise God for his faithful love.

II. THE PSALMIST'S PAIN (118:5, 25): In great distress, he cries to the Lord to save him and give him success.

III. THE PSALMIST'S PEACE (118:6-9): Knowing God is with him, he is not afraid.

IV. THE PSALMIST'S POWER (118:10-13): In God's strength he defeats his enemies.

V. THE PSALMIST'S PRAISE (118:14-17)
   A. The method (118:14): He composes a song of worship.
   B. The message (118:15-17): He sings about his Savior's strong right arm, which does glorious things.

VI. THE PSALMIST'S PURGING (118:18): For his own good, he has been severely punished by God.

VII. THE PSALMIST'S PLEDGE (118:19-21, 27-29): He vows to offer sacrifices of thanksgiving to God and live in a godly manner.

VIII. THE PSALMIST'S PROPHECY (118:22-23, 26): The psalmist foretells two events in Jesus' life.
   A. His triumphal entry (118:26): See Matthew 21:9.
   B. His rejection by Israel (118:22-23): See Matthew 21:42.

SECTION OUTLINE ONE HUNDRED NINETEEN (PSALM 119)

This elaborate alphabetical psalm has 22 eight-verse stanzas that extol the Word of God. It is the longest chapter in the Bible (176 verses).

I. THE NAMES FOR GOD'S WORD: What It Is Called (119: 1, 3-37, 39-40, 42-69, 71-116, 119-120, 123-131, 133-148, 150-164, 166-176)
   A. His law or laws (119:1, 7, 13, 18, 20, 29-30, 34, 39, 43-44, 51-53, 55, 61-62, 70, 72, 77, 85, 91-92, 97, 102, 106, 108-109, 113, 126, 136, 142, 150, 153, 160, 163-165, 174-175): We must keep, not break, his laws—for our own good.
   B. His decrees (119:2, 14, 22, 24, 31, 36, 46, 79, 88, 95, 99, 111, 119, 125, 129, 138, 144, 146, 152, 157, 167-168): They provide us with discernment.
   C. His light (119:3, 105): God's word provides light for our way.
   D. His commands/commandments (119:4, 6, 10, 15, 19, 21, 27, 32, 35, 40, 45, 47-48, 56, 60, 63, 66, 69, 73, 78, 86-87, 93-94, 96, 98, 100, 104, 110, 115, 127-128, 131, 134, 141, 143, 151, 159, 166, 168, 172-173, 176): We must love them, not forget them, and study them.
   E. His principles (119:5, 8, 12, 16, 23, 26, 33, 48, 54, 64, 68, 71,

80, 83, 112, 117-118, 124, 135, 145, 155, 171): We must let
God teach us and then obey him.
  F. His rules (119:9): Following them will keep us pure.
  G. His ways (119:15): We should reflect on them.
  H. His statutes (119:59): If we follow them, they will give us direc-
  tion.
  I. His judgments or decisions (119:120, 137): God's decisions are
  fair, and we are to live by them.

II. THE NATURE OF GOD'S WORD: What It Accomplishes (119: 1-2, 9,
11, 24, 28-29, 37-38, 41-42, 45-46, 49-50, 62, 67, 70, 98-100,
103, 105, 111, 114, 116, 120-122, 132, 139, 141, 149, 165, 170)
  A. It brings blessing and happiness (119:1-2, 122).
  B. It keeps us pure (119:9).
  C. It keeps us from sin (119:11, 29, 121).
  D. It gives wise advice (119:24).
  E. It encourages the grieving (119:28).
  F. It reassures us of his promises for those who honor him (119:38).
  G. It provides answers, even for those who taunt us (119:42).
  H. It gives freedom (119:45).
  I. It offers hope (119:49).
  J. It comforts and revives (119:50).
  K. It provides a thankful heart (119:62).
  L. It brings us back to God (119:37, 67): God will discipline us if
  we turn from him.
  M. It instructs and gives wisdom (119:98-100).
  N. It nourishes (119:103): God's word is sweeter than honey.
  O. It enlightens (119:105): God's word provides a light for our path.
  P. It protects (119:114): God's word is a refuge.
  Q. It sustains our hope (119:116).
  R. It brings delight (119:70, 111).
  S. It brings peace (119:165): We do not have to fear stumbling.
  T. It delivers (119:170): God promises to rescue us.
  U. It brings love and salvation (119:41, 149).
  V. It shows mercy to all who love his name (119:132).
  W. It deserves respect (119:46, 120).
  X. It is important to remember (119:141).

SECTION OUTLINE ONE HUNDRED TWENTY (PSALM 120)
The psalmist petitions God for deliverance from those with deceitful
tongues and warring hearts.

I. SAVE ME FROM WICKED TONGUES (120:1-4).
  A. The psalmist's petition (120:1-2): Rescue me from liars and
  deceitful people.
  B. The psalmist's prediction (120:3-4): Divine punishment will fall
  upon his enemies.

II. SAVE ME FROM WARRING HEARTS (120:5-7).
   A. **His persecutors' identity** (120:5): They are of Meshech and Kedar.
   B. **His persecutors' iniquity** (120:6-7): They demand war when the psalmist pleads for peace.

SECTION OUTLINE ONE HUNDRED TWENTY-ONE (PSALM 121)
The psalmist describes the Lord as the guardian, protector of his people, or the keeper of Israel.

I. THE PSALMIST LOOKS UP TO THE LORD (121:1-2): When in need of help, he depends upon the Creator himself.
II. THE LORD LOOKS OUT FOR THE PSALMIST (121:3-8).
   A. **He will not allow him to fall or stumble** (121:3-4).
   B. **He will protect and preserve him day and night** (121:5-8).

SECTION OUTLINE ONE HUNDRED TWENTY-TWO (PSALM 122)
David utters blessings upon the holy city, Jerusalem, and prays for its prosperity.

I. PRAISE FOR JERUSALEM (122:1-5)
   A. **For its blessedness** (122:1-3): It is a joy to be within its gates.
   B. **For its busyness** (122:4-5): It is always crowded with worshipers and judges, holding court.
II. PRAYER FOR JERUSALEM (122:6-9)
   A. **For peace** (122:6-8)
   B. **For protection** (122:9)
   C. **For prosperity** (122:6-7): All who love Jerusalem and the walls of the city itself will prosper.

SECTION OUTLINE ONE HUNDRED TWENTY-THREE (PSALM 123)
The psalmist, in deep distress, expresses his need for mercy by describing two relationships between God and Israel.

I. THE SERVANT/MASTER RELATIONSHIP (123:1-2)
   A. **Israel's focused service to God** (123:2): As slaves and servants watch their masters, so Israel is to watch God.
   B. **Israel's total service to God** (123:1-2): Israel is to look to God for mercy.

II. THE PERSECUTED/PROTECTOR RELATIONSHIP (123:3-4)
   A. **Israel's prayer** (123:3): "Have mercy on us, LORD."
   B. **Israel's problem** (123:3-4): They are ridiculed and held in contempt by their foes.

SECTION OUTLINE ONE HUNDRED TWENTY-FOUR (PSALM 124)

David thanks God, who has been Israel's help and deliverer from all its woes, and encourages a right relationship with him.

I. THE WORST OF ALL POSSIBLE WORLDS (124:1-5): "If the LORD had not been on our side—"
   A. **The wicked would have swallowed Israel up** (124:1-3).
   B. **The waters would have engulfed Israel** (124:4-5).

II. THE BEST OF ALL POSSIBLE WORLDS (124:6-8): "Our help is from the LORD."
   A. **They are not torn apart by their foes!** (124:6).
   B. **They are delivered from their foes, as a bird escapes a hunter's trap** (124:7-8).

SECTION OUTLINE ONE HUNDRED TWENTY-FIVE (PSALM 125)

This psalm expresses confidence in the Lord's deliverance.

I. GOD'S DELIVERANCE (125:1-3)
   A. **The comparison** (125:1): Those who trust in God are as secure as Mount Zion.
   B. **The conclusion** (125:2-3): As the mountains surround the city, so God surrounds the redeemed, keeping them from doing wrong.

II. THE PSALMIST'S REQUEST (125:4-5)
   A. **"O LORD, do good to those who are good"** (125:4): God rewards those whose hearts are in tune with him.
   B. **"Banish those who turn to crooked ways, O LORD"** (125:5): The evil are taken away.

SECTION OUTLINE ONE HUNDRED TWENTY-SIX (PSALM 126)

The psalmist remembers God's great deliverance and prays it will continue until completion. He describes the nation Judah's emotion upon being released from a terrible captivity.

I. THE REALITY (126:1): At first the freed captives have difficulty comprehending the truth of this wonderful event.

II. THE REACTION (126:2-3)
   A. **Among the people** (126:2-3): They are filled with laughter and testify to God's faithfulness.

B. Among the pagans (126:2): They acknowledge God's care and amazing things he does for his people.

III. THE REQUEST (126:4-6)
   A. The petition (126:4): "Restore our fortunes, LORD."
   B. The promise (126:5-6): Those who plant in tears will harvest in joy.

SECTION OUTLINE ONE HUNDRED TWENTY-SEVEN (PSALM 127)
The psalmist reminds us that human care and toil in any area of life are of no value without God's blessings.

I. THE FOUNDATION FOR A SUCCESSFUL FAMILY (127:1-2)
   A. What is necessary (127:1)
      1. *The home must be built by the Lord* (127:1).
      2. *The home must be protected by the Lord* (127:1).
   B. What is needless (127:2): The breadwinner need not burn the candle at both ends and be overly anxious, for God will supply rest and what we need.

II. THE FRUITS FROM A SUCCESSFUL FAMILY (127:3-5): Children
   A. The parents will be honored (127:3-4): Children are a reward and like sharp arrows.
   B. The parents will be helped (127:5): They will not be ashamed in front of their accusers.

SECTION OUTLINE ONE HUNDRED TWENTY-EIGHT (PSALM 128)
The psalmist proclaims that a truly happy person fears the Lord, not merely with speech, but in the way he lives.

I. THE REQUIREMENTS (128:1): Those who follow the Lord will be happy.

II. THE REWARDS (128:2-6)
   A. The parents (128:2, 6)
      1. *Prosperity* (128:2): They enjoy the fruits of their labor and their lives are rich.
      2. *Longevity* (128:6): They live to enjoy their grandchildren and have quietness and peace.
   B. The children (128:3-5): They are as vigorous and healthy as young olive trees.

SECTION OUTLINE ONE HUNDRED TWENTY-NINE (PSALM 129)

The psalmist reminds Israel of how God delivered them from bondage, judged their enemies, and encourages them to hope for future deliverance.

I. THE PERSECUTION (129:1-4)

    A. Israel's enemies often attack (129:1-2).

    B. Israel's enemies can never annihilate her (129:2, 4).

II. THE PETITION (129:5-8)

    A. May Israel's enemies be defeated and disgraced, not receiving God's blessing (129:5, 8).

    B. May they dry up like grass, which is ignored by the harvester and despised by the binder (129:6-7).

SECTION OUTLINE ONE HUNDRED THIRTY (PSALM 130)

The psalmist admits his sins and seeks the Lord's forgiveness. He confidently encourages the nation to do as he has done—confess.

I. THE PSALMIST SPEAKS TO GOD (130:1-6).

    A. Save us in spite of our corruption (130:1-3).

    B. Save us because of your compassion (130:4-6).

        1. *The psalmist looks with hope toward God* (130:5).

        2. *The psalmist longs anxiously for God* (130:6).

II. THE PSALMIST SPEAKS TO ISRAEL (130:7-8).

    A. The plea (130:7): "O Israel, hope in the LORD."

    B. The promise (130:7-8): "He himself will free Israel from every kind of sin."

SECTION OUTLINE ONE HUNDRED THIRTY-ONE (PSALM 131)

David quietly expresses his dependence upon the Lord for accomplishing all his purposes.

I. THE PSALMIST (131:1-2)

    A. He is not haughty (131:1).

    B. He is still and quiet (131:2).

II. THE PEOPLE (131:3): "O Israel, put your hope in the LORD."

SECTION OUTLINE ONE HUNDRED THIRTY-TWO (PSALM 132)

This is a prayer for God's blessing upon Israel and the fulfillment of all his promises made to David.

I. DAVID DESIRES TO BUILD A HOUSE FOR GOD (132:1-10).

    A. The nature of this house (132:1-5): It will be a "sanctuary for the Mighty One of Israel."

B. The need for this house (132:6-10): It will be a permanent dwelling place for the Ark of the Covenant.
1. *It has been moved about by the people* (132:6): They found the Ark in Jaar.
2. *It will now be ministered to by the priests, who will be agents of salvation* (132:7-10).

II. GOD DECREES TO BUILD A HOUSE FOR DAVID (132:11-18).
   A. The promise (132:11-12, 17-18): This "house" involves a continual dynasty, known as the House of David.
   1. *It will be a permanent dynasty* (132:11-12): If David's descendants are obedient, his kingdom will never end.
   2. *It will be a powerful dynasty* (132:17-18): David's enemies will be shamed before him.
   B. The place (132:13-14): The center of this dynasty will be Jerusalem, God's own chosen city.
   C. The provisions (132:15-16): God will provide prosperity, salvation, and joy.

SECTION OUTLINE ONE HUNDRED THIRTY-THREE (PSALM 133)
David expresses the sweet joys of worshiping God in fellowship with other believers.

I. EXHORTATION TO UNITY AND FELLOWSHIP (133:1): It is good and pleasant.

II. EXAMPLES OF UNITY AND FELLOWSHIP (133:2-3)
   A. It is as precious as the anointing oil used on Aaron (133:2).
   B. It is as refreshing as the dew falling on Mount Zion (133:3).

SECTION OUTLINE ONE HUNDRED THIRTY-FOUR (PSALM 134)
The psalmist pronounces a benediction upon the worshipers as the service ends.

I. RENDER A BLESSING TO THE LORD (134:1-2).
   A. Who? (134:1): The watchmen of Israel
   B. When? (134:1): During the night
   C. Where? (134:1): In the Temple
   D. How? (134:2): Lifting up hands

II. RECEIVE A BLESSING FROM THE LORD (134:3): The Lord blesses from Jerusalem.

SECTION OUTLINE ONE HUNDRED THIRTY-FIVE (PSALM 135)

The psalmist calls upon his people to praise the Lord for his mighty works in creation and history. He contrasts the true God, who made his people, with the false gods, who were made by their people.

I. THE ONLY TRUE GOD (135:1-14, 19-21)
   A. **Who should worship him?** (135:1-2, 19-21): Everyone, but especially those who minister in the Temple!
   B. **Why should we worship him?** (135:3-14)
      1. *Because of who he is* (135:3, 5-7)
         a. He is great (135:3, 5): His name should be celebrated.
         b. He is sovereign (135:6): He does whatever pleases him.
         c. He is creative (135:7): He controls clouds, lightning, winds, and rain.
      2. *Because of what he does* (135:4, 8-14)
         a. He chose Israel as his special treasure (135:4).
         b. He delivered Israel from Egypt (135:8-9).
         c. He gave Israel its inheritance (135:10-12): He destroyed the kings in Canaan to give the Israelites their land.
         d. He loves Israel (135:13-14): He vindicates and has compassion on his people.

II. THE MANY FALSE GODS (135:15-18)
   A. **They are made by mortals out of silver and gold** (135:15).
   B. **They are made like mortals** (135:18).
   C. **They have mouths, eyes, ears, and noses, but cannot speak, see, hear, or smell** (135:16-17).

SECTION OUTLINE ONE HUNDRED THIRTY-SIX (PSALM 136)

The psalmist thanks God for his works in creation and redemption.

I. THE REASONS TO GIVE THANKS (136:1-26)
   A. **Because of God's goodness** (136:1, 26)
   B. **Because of his uniqueness** (136:2-3): He is God of gods and Lord of lords.
   C. **Because of his miracles** (136:4)
   D. **Because of his creative works** (136:5-9, 25)
      1. *He made all nonliving things* (136:5-9): The earth, the heavenly lights, the sun, and the moon.
      2. *He cares for all living things* (136:25): He gives them food.
   E. **Because of his relationship to Israel** (136:10-24)
      1. *He performed miracles to get his people out of Egypt* (136:10-16).
      2. *He brought his people into Canaan* (136:17-24): He struck down the foreign kings and gave the land to Israel.

II. The Refrain for Giving Thanks (136:1-26): Each of this psalm's 26 verses ends with "His faithful love endures forever."

SECTION OUTLINE ONE HUNDRED THIRTY-SEVEN (PSALM 137)
The psalmist recalls the sad saga of Israel's Babylonian captivity and prays that God would severely punish their captors.

I. Judah and Its Captors (137:1-6)
   A. **Their despair** (137:1-2): The Jewish captives weep beside the rivers of Babylon, thinking about Jerusalem.
   B. **Their derision** (137:3-4): The Babylonian soldiers taunt them, demanding that they "sing us one of those songs of Jerusalem!"
   C. **Their determination** (137:5-6): The captives will never forget Jerusalem, regardless of what happens!

II. Judah and Its Creator (137:7-9): The captives pray that God will punish:
   A. **The Babylonians, who burned Jerusalem** (137:7-9)
   B. **The Edomites, who encouraged the Babylonians to level Jerusalem** (137:7)

SECTION OUTLINE ONE HUNDRED THIRTY-EIGHT (PSALM 138)
David comments on the promises God made to him in the Davidic covenant (2 Samuel 7:1-16).

I. The Personal Worship of God (138:1-3, 7-8): The psalmist praises God and acknowledges:
   A. **His love and faithfulness** (138:1-2): He praises God and worships him.
   B. **His very person and promises** (138:2): God's promises are backed by the honor of his name.
   C. **His answering of prayer** (138:3)
   D. **His manifold provisions** (138:3, 7-8)
      1. *Encouragement and strength* (138:3)
      2. *Preservation* (138:7): God's power saves him from his enemies.
      3. *Guidance* (138:8): God works out the plan for his life.

II. The Universal Worship of God (138:4-6): The psalmist predicts that all of earth's rulers will praise God and acknowledge:
   A. **His glory** (138:4-5)
   B. **His ways** (138:5-6)
      1. *In caring for the humble* (138:6)
      2. *In resisting the proud* (138:6)

SECTION OUTLINE ONE HUNDRED THIRTY-NINE (PSALM 139)

David comments upon the greatness of God in the three "omnis"—omniscience, omnipresence, and omnipotence.

I. His OMNISCIENCE (139:1-6): God knows all about us.
   A. **What we do** (139:1-3)
   B. **What we think** (139:2)
   C. **What we say** (139:4-6)

II. His OMNIPRESENCE (139:7-12): God is always with us.
   A. **He is in heaven** (139:7-8).
   B. **He is in the place of the dead** (139:8).
   C. **He can be found by the farthest oceans** (139:9-10): God's hand will guide and support us wherever we go.
   D. **He shines forth in the darkness** (139:11-12): Darkness and light are the same to God.

III. His OMNIPOTENCE (139:13-24): God can do all things for us.
   A. **David's review** (139:13-18)
      1. *God creates and arranges our bodies within the womb* (139:13-15): He knows us before we are born.
      2. *He schedules each day of our lives before we are born* (139:16).
      3. *He records our every day in his book* (139:16).
      4. *He thinks wonderful and innumerable thoughts about us constantly* (139:17-18).
   B. **David's request** (139:19-24)
      1. *"O God, if only you would destroy the wicked!"* (139:19-22)
      2. *"Search me, O God, and know my heart"* (139:23-24): He wants God to test him and point out anything that offends him.

SECTION OUTLINE ONE HUNDRED FORTY (PSALM 140)

David reflects upon the perils that befall him because of his enemies' persecution and trusts in the protection of God's word until the promise can be realized.

I. DAVID'S PETITION REGARDING THE GODLESS (140:1-11)
   A. **What they do** (140:1-5)
      1. *They plot evil and stir up trouble* (140:1-2).
      2. *Their tongues sting like a snake's poison* (140:3).
      3. *They often attempt to snare David* (140:4-5).
   B. **What they deserve** (140:6-10)
      1. *To suffer from failure and poverty* (140:6-8, 11)
      2. *To have their evil deeds destroy them* (140:9)
      3. *To be burned by coals, consumed by fire, or thrown into deep pits* (140:10)

II. DAVID'S PETITION REGARDING THE GODLY (140:12-13)
   A. **The requests** (140:12)
      1. *Secure justice for them* (140:12): The Lord will help those who are persecuted.
      2. *Uphold them* (140:12): God will maintain the rights of the poor.
   B. **The results** (140:13)
      1. *The godly praise his name* (140:13).
      2. *The godly live in his presence* (140:13).

SECTION OUTLINE ONE HUNDRED FORTY-ONE (PSALM 141)
A young David fellowships with God and expresses the concerns closest to his heart.

I. HEAR MY PRAYER, O GOD (141:1-2): David asks that his request ascend to heaven like incense.

II. HONOR MY PRAYER, O GOD (141:3-10)
   A. **Regarding his conversation** (141:3): David wants the Lord to guide his speech.
   B. **Regarding his conduct** (141:4): "Don't let me lust for evil things."
   C. **Regarding his companionship** (141:4-10)
      1. *With godless people* (141:4, 6-10)
         a. That he not be part of them (141:4): He does not want to share in the acts of the wicked.
         b. That he not be punished with them (141:6-10): He wants the wicked to fall into their own traps. He also wants to be spared.
      2. *With godly people* (141:5): When he needs it, David requests that:
         a. The godly reprove him in the Lord (141:5): The reproach of the godly is a kindness.
         b. He receive it from the Lord (141:5): He will not refuse their reproof.

SECTION OUTLINE ONE HUNDRED FORTY-TWO (PSALM 142)
A personal psalm in which David, overwhelmed and alone, expresses confidence that God hears his cry for refuge, rescue, and release.

I. DAVID'S DESPERATION (142:1-4)
   A. **The abundance of foes** (142:1-3): He is surrounded by enemies who constantly threaten his life.
   B. **The absence of friends** (142:4): He feels no one on earth cares what happens to him.

II. DAVID'S REALIZATION (142:5-7)
   A. God alone is his refuge (142:5).
   B. God alone is his strength (142:6).
   C. God alone is all he wants in life (142:6).
   D. God alone is his rescuer (142:6-7): God brings him out of prison.

SECTION OUTLINE ONE HUNDRED FORTY-THREE (PSALM 143)
Crushed by his enemies, David longs for time alone with God. He
prays for victory (as in times of old), deliverance, spiritual guidance,
and revival. David petitions God for three things.

I. SAVE ME! (143:1-7, 9, 11-12)
   A. The facts (143:3-4, 7)
       1. *The enemy is crushing David* (143:3): His enemy chases him
          and knocks him to the ground.
       2. *The hopeless situation paralyzes him with fear* (143:4).
       3. *His depression deepens* (143:7): He feels he will die.
   B. The foundation (143:1-2, 5-6, 9, 11-12)
       1. *Negative* (143:2): David does not plead his own righteousness
          as the basis for the salvation he seeks.
       2. *Positive* (143:1, 5-6, 9, 11-12)
           a. Save me because of your faithfulness and righteousness
              (143:1): He wants God to listen to his plea.
           b. Save me because you previously saved others (143:5): He
              remembers all God has done.
           c. Save me because I reach out to you (143:6): He thirsts for
              God as parched land thirsts for rain.
           d. Save me because I run to hide in you (143:9).
           e. Save me for your name's sake (143:11-12): He wants God
              to act for his glory and because of his unfailing love.

II. SHOW ME! (143:8): "Show me where to walk."

III. SANCTIFY ME! (143:10)
   A. Teach me to do your will (143:10): He belongs to God and
      wants to please him.
   B. Touch me with your Spirit (143:10): He wants God to lead him
      onto firm footing.

SECTION OUTLINE ONE HUNDRED FORTY-FOUR (PSALM 144)

David notes the greatness of God and the insignificance of human beings. He asks for divine help against human enemies and envisions a time of peace and personal prosperity that can only come from God.

I. DAVID'S SOURCE OF VICTORY (144:1-8): Victory comes from God, not people.
   A. **God is powerful** (144:1-2, 5-8).
      1. *He protects David* (144:2): "He is my loving ally and . . . my deliverer."
      2. *He prepares David* (144:1, 5-8): "He gives me strength for war."
   B. **Mortals are puny** (144:3-4).
      1. *Our meagerness* (144:3): "O LORD, what are mortals that you should notice us?"
      2. *Our mortality* (144:4): "We are like a breath . . . a passing shadow."

II. DAVID'S SONG OF VICTORY (144:9-15)
   A. **The rejoicing of the redeemed** (144:9-11): "I will sing a new song to you, O God!"
   B. **The rewarding of the redeemed** (144:12-15)
      1. *In the homes* (144:12): There are flourishing sons and graceful daughters.
      2. *In the fields* (144:13-14): There are abundant crops and flocks.
      3. *In the streets* (144:14-15): There is no crime in the cities.

SECTION OUTLINE ONE HUNDRED FORTY-FIVE (PSALM 145)

David extols the righteousness and goodness of the Lord to people in general and to his own people in particular.

I. GOD'S GREATNESS (145:1-6)
   A. **Its depth** (145:1-3): No one can fathom it.
   B. **Its breadth** (145:4-6): God's greatness is extolled universally by each generation.

II. GOD'S GOODNESS (145:7-10)
   A. **He is slow to anger** (145:8): He is kind, merciful, and full of love.
   B. **He is good to all** (145:7, 9-10): He showers compassion on all creation.

III. GOD'S GLORY (145:11-13): God's divine kingdom is glorious.
   A. **Its dynamics** (145:11-12): It will be filled with majesty and splendor.
   B. **Its duration** (145:13): It will be an everlasting kingdom.

IV. GOD'S GUARANTEE (145:13): "The LORD is faithful in all he says; he is gracious in all he does."

V. GOD'S GRACE (145:14-21)
 A. **He lifts up the fallen** (145:14): He lifts those bent beneath their loads.
 B. **He feeds the hungry** (145:15-18): He satisfies the thirst of every living thing.
 C. **He rescues the persecuted** (145:19-21): The Lord protects all who fear him but destroys the wicked.

SECTION OUTLINE ONE HUNDRED FORTY-SIX (PSALM 146)
The psalmist exhorts the people to praise and trust the Lord.

I. THE BASIS FOR TRUSTING GOD (146:1-4, 10)
 A. **God's reliability** (146:1-2, 10): God is eternal.
 B. **Our fallibility** (146:3-4): The psalmist warns against depending upon mortals.

II. THE BLESSINGS OF TRUSTING GOD (146:5-9)
 A. **Who God is** (146:5-6)
  1. *He is Israel's helper and hope* (146:5).
  2. *He is the creator of everything* (146:6).
 B. **What God does** (146:6-9)
  1. *He keeps his promises* (146:6).
  2. *He upholds the oppressed and feeds the hungry* (146:7).
  3. *He frees the prisoners* (146:7).
  4. *He gives sight to the blind* (146:8).
  5. *He protects the foreigners and cares for orphans and widows* (146:9).

SECTION OUTLINE ONE HUNDRED FORTY-SEVEN (PSALM 147)
The psalmist exhorts the people to praise the Lord because of his goodness to his creatures and his people.

I. WHAT ISRAEL SHOULD DO (147:1, 7, 12)
 A. **Praise God with your mouth** (147:1, 12).
 B. **Praise God with your music** (147:7): Sing to God, accompanied by harps.

II. WHY ISRAEL SHOULD DO IT (147:2-6, 8-11, 13-20): The psalmist gives four reasons God should be praised.
 A. **For his work with Israel** (147:2, 13-14, 19-20)
  1. *He rebuilds Jerusalem* (147:2).
  2. *He brings back the exiles* (147:2).
  3. *He fortifies the gates and sends peace across the nation* (147:13-14).
  4. *He supplies the finest wheat for food* (147:14).
  5. *He gives his law to Israel alone* (147:19-20).

B. For his work with nature (147:8-10, 15-18)
   1. *He sends rain for the grass* (147:8).
   2. *He feeds the wild animals* (147:9-10).
   3. *He creates and controls the weather* (147:15-18).
      a. The cold snows, frosts, and hail of winter (147:15-17)
      b. The warm winds of spring (147:18): The ice melts at his command.
C. For his work with the heavens (147:4-5)
   1. *He counts and names the stars* (147:4).
   2. *He has absolute power over the heavens* (147:5).
D. For his work with the redeemed (147:3, 6, 11)
   1. *He heals the brokenhearted and binds their wounds* (147:3).
   2. *He supports the humble* (147:6).
   3. *He brings down the wicked* (147:6).
   4. *He delights in those who honor him and hope in his unfailing love* (147:11).

SECTION OUTLINE ONE HUNDRED FORTY-EIGHT (PSALM 148)

The psalmist poetically calls upon the universe to praise God as its maker because he is infinitely worthy of adoration.

I. PRAISE FROM CREATION (148:3-6, 8-9): All nonliving creation praises him.

II. PRAISE FROM LIVING CREATURES (148:1-2, 7, 10-14): All God's created beings praise him.

SECTION OUTLINE ONE HUNDRED FORTY-NINE (PSALM 149)

The psalmist praises the Lord for his mercies and for the hope of future triumphs over hostile, heathen powers.

I. WHAT ISRAEL SHOULD DO (149:2): They are to rejoice in their Maker and exult in their King.

II. HOW ISRAEL SHOULD DO IT (149:1, 3, 6)
   A. Praise him with your mouth (149:1, 6): They are to sing to the Lord.
   B. Praise him with your music (149:3): They are to praise him with dancing, tambourine, and harp.

III. WHERE ISRAEL SHOULD DO IT (149:5): "Let them sing for joy as they lie on their beds."

IV. WHY ISRAEL SHOULD DO IT (149:4, 6-9)
   A. Because the Lord delights in his people (149:4)
   B. Because he crowns the humble with salvation (149:4)

C. Because he punishes the enemies of his people (149:6-9)
D. Because he is the glory of his people (149:9)

SECTION OUTLINE ONE HUNDRED FIFTY (PSALM 150)
The psalmist calls upon God's people, along with every other living thing, to praise the Lord for his greatness.

I. WHERE (150:1): God is praised in his heavenly dwelling.

II. WHAT (150:2): God is praised for his works and unequaled greatness.

III. HOW (150:3-5)
   A. Praise him with trumpet, lyre, harp, tambourine, stringed instruments, flutes, and cymbals (150:3-5).
   B. Praise him with dancing (150:4).

IV. WHO (150:6): "Let everything that lives sing praises to the LORD!"

Proverbs

SECTION OUTLINE ONE (PROVERBS 1)
Wisdom warns about being enticed by sinners.

I. THE REASONS FOR THE PROVERBS (1:1-7)
   A. **To grasp wisdom and discipline** (1:1-2): They help with the understanding of wise sayings.
   B. **To receive guidance and understand deep thoughts** (1:3, 5-7): People who listen to the proverbs learn the fear of the Lord.
   C. **To give insight to the immature and mature alike** (1:4): The Proverbs give knowledge and purpose.

II. THE RECIPIENTS OF THE PROVERBS (1:8-33): Solomon's son in particular
   A. **Advice regarding wicked companions** (1:8-19): Stay away from them! Why?
      1. *They terrorize others* (1:8-17).
      2. *They trap themselves and rob themselves of life* (1:18-19).
   B. **Advice regarding wisdom's counsel** (1:20-33): Stay close to her!
      1. *Her call* (1:20-21): She shouts out in the streets.
      2. *Her condemnation* (1:22-32): She calls; fools do not listen or come to her.
      3. *Her consolation* (1:33): All who listen to her live in peace and safety.

SECTION OUTLINE TWO (PROVERBS 2)
Wisdom saves from evil and pays benefits.

I. IT WILL SANCTIFY YOU (2:1-6): We are to treasure wisdom's instructions and learn to fear the Lord.

II. IT WILL SECURE YOU (2:7-9): It serves as a shield and guard.

III. IT WILL SATISFY YOU (2:10-11): "Knowledge will fill you with joy."

IV. IT WILL SAVE YOU (2:12-22)
   A. **From godless men** (2:12-15, 20-22): "Follow the steps of good men . . . and stay on the paths of the righteous."

B. From godless women (2:16-19): Wisdom saves you from immoral women.

SECTION OUTLINE THREE (PROVERBS 3)
Wisdom results in right relationships and gives life and honor.

I. THE ROUTE (3:1, 3)
   A. Keep its precepts in your heart (3:1): Never forget what the Lord teaches you.
   B. Fasten them around your neck (3:3): God's teachings should be like a necklace you wear always.
   C. Write them deep within your heart (3:3).

II. THE RULES (3:5-12, 19-21, 25-35)
   A. What to do (3:5-10)
      1. *Trust in the Lord* (3:5-8): We should seek God's will in all we do. If we fear him and turn from evil, we will gain renewed health and vitality.
      2. *Tithe to the Lord* (3:9-10): If we honor the Lord with the best from our wages, he will reward us.
   B. What not to do (3:11-12, 21, 25-35)
      1. *Do not despise his discipline* (3:11-12): The Lord corrects those he loves.
      2. *Do not lose sight of good planning and insight* (3:21).
      3. *Do not be overtaken by fear* (3:25-26): "The LORD is your security."
      4. *Do not wrong your neighbor* (3:27-30): Do not plot against your neighbor or make accusations against someone who has not wronged you. Help your neighbor if you are able.
      5. *Do not envy a violent man* (3:31-35): Wicked people are an abomination to the Lord and are put to shame.

III. THE RELEASE (3:19-20)
   A. By wisdom God lays the foundation of the earth, clouds, and rain (3:19-20).
   B. By wisdom he established the heavens (3:19).

IV. THE REWARDS (3:2, 4, 13-18, 22-24)
   A. A long and satisfying life (3:2)
   B. Favor with both God and people (3:4): "You will gain a good reputation."
   C. A possession more precious than silver, gold, and jewels (3:13-15): Nothing can compare with wisdom.
   D. Riches and honor (3:16-17): "All her ways are satisfying."
   E. A tree of life (3:18): Happy are those who embrace wisdom.
   F. Confidence and security (3:22-24): "You can lie down without fear and enjoy pleasant dreams."

SECTION OUTLINE FOUR (PROVERBS 4)
Wisdom results in self-discipline.

I. DAVID'S COUNSEL TO SOLOMON (4:1-9)
   A. **Acquire wisdom** (4:1-2, 5, 7): Learn to be wise, for that is the most important thing.
   B. **Embrace wisdom** (4:4, 8): If you take wisdom to heart, you will live.
   C. **Love and cherish wisdom** (4:3, 6, 8-9): Wisdom will protect and exalt you.

II. SOLOMON'S COUNSEL TO REHOBOAM (4:10-27).
   A. **Let wisdom guard your feet** (4:10-19, 26-27).
      1. *To keep you from limping or stumbling* (4:10-12): If you do this, you will have a long, good life.
      2. *To keep you from straying* (4:13-19, 26-27): Avoid evildoers. "Mark out a straight path for your feet; then stick to the path and stay safe."
   B. **Let wisdom guard your heart** (4:20-23).
      1. *It is the wellspring of one's body* (4:20, 22): Let wisdom's words bring life and health.
      2. *It is the wellspring of one's soul* (4:21, 23): Let wisdom guard your heart.
   C. **Let wisdom guard your tongue** (4:24): Stay away from corrupt speech.
   D. **Let wisdom guard your eyes** (4:25): "Fix your eyes on what lies before you."

SECTION OUTLINE FIVE (PROVERBS 5)
Wisdom instructs about sexuality.

I. THE WOMAN IN THE STREET: DEPART FROM HER (5:1-14, 21-23).
   A. **The pleasure she offers** (5:3)
      1. *Her lips are as sweet as honey* (5:3).
      2. *Her mouth is smoother than oil* (5:3).
   B. **The price you pay** (5:4-14, 21-23)
      1. *"The result is as bitter as poison"* (5:4): It is "sharp as a double-edged sword."
      2. *"Her feet go down to death"* (5:5): "Her steps lead straight to the grave."
      3. *"She does not care about the path to life"* (5:6): "She staggers down a crooked trail and doesn't even realize where it leads."
      4. *The loss of one's reputation* (5:7-9): She will take your honor.
      5. *The loss of one's self-respect* (5:12-14): You come to the brink of utter ruin.
      6. *The loss of one's wealth* (5:10): Others will enjoy the fruit of your labor.

    7. *The loss of one's health* (5:11): Disease consumes your body.
    8. *The loss of one's very soul* (5:21-23)

II. THE WIFE IN THE HOME: DELIGHT IN HER (5:15-20).
    A. The rule: Remain faithful to her (5:15-18).
    B. The reward: Her love will satisfy you (5:19-20).

SECTION OUTLINE SIX (PROVERBS 6)
Wisdom warns of pitfalls to avoid.

I. GOD'S ADMONITIONS (6:1-15, 24-35): Four people are warned:
    A. The thoughtless (6:1-5): God advises to think carefully before guaranteeing a loan to anyone.
    B. The shiftless (6:6-11)
        1. *The example* (6:6-8): God counsels the lazy to learn from the industrious ant.
        2. *The results* (6:9-11): Extreme poverty in the future.
    C. The ruthless (6:12-15)
        1. *Their debauchery* (6:12-14)
            a. They are filled with hypocrisy (6:12-13): They lie constantly.
            b. They continuously devise evil (6:14): They are perverted.
            c. They spread conflict (6:14): They stir up trouble constantly.
        2. *Their destruction* (6:15): It will be swift and total.
    D. The virtueless (6:24-35): Illicit sex has tragic consequences.
        1. *An immoral woman's beauty seduces* (6:24-25): Keep away from her smooth tongue.
        2. *She reduces the person to poverty* (6:26): She can cost him his life.
        3. *She burns both character and reputation* (6:27-29, 33): His shame can never be erased.
        4. *She makes a fool out of a man* (6:32): "He destroys his own soul."

II. GOD'S ASSURANCES (6:20-23)
    A. His word will guard us (6:20-22): It protects us.
    B. His word will guide us (6:23): His word is a lamp to lead the way.

III. SEVEN ABOMINATIONS IN GOD'S SIGHT (6:16-19): "Haughty eyes, a lying tongue, hands that kill the innocent, a heart that plots evil, feet that race to do wrong, a false witness who pours out lies, a person who sows discord among brothers."

SECTION OUTLINE SEVEN (PROVERBS 7)
Wisdom warns against fornication.

I. RECEIVE MY WORDS AND LIVE! (7:1-5)
   A. **"Guard my teachings as your most precious possession"** (7:1-2).
   B. **"Tie them on your fingers as a reminder"** (7:3).
   C. **"Write them deep within your heart"** (7:3).
   D. **"Love wisdom like a sister"** (7:4-5): "Make insight a beloved member of your family."

II. REJECT MY WORDS AND DIE! (7:6-27)
   A. **Solomon's observation** (7:6-23): He views a harlot approaching a simpleminded youth.
      1. *The seduction* (7:6-21)
         a. Where he is (7:6-12): The simpleminded youth is passing her house at twilight.
         b. What she does (7:13): She grabs him and kisses him.
         c. What she says (7:14-21)
            (1) My bed is ready! (7:14-18): She wants to enjoy his caresses through the night.
            (2) My husband is gone on a long trip! (7:19-21).
      2. *The destruction* (7:22-23): Immediately he follows her:
         a. Like an animal about to be slaughtered (7:22-23).
         b. Like a bird about to be snared (7:23): He doesn't realize it will cost him his life.
   B. **Solomon's twofold conclusion** (7:24-27):
      1. *Listen and live!* (7:24-25): Do not let your heart stray toward her.
      2. *Disobey and die!* (7:26-27): "Her house is the road to the grave."

SECTION OUTLINE EIGHT (PROVERBS 8)
Wisdom proclaims her worth, availability, and accomplishments.

I. WISDOM'S ENTREATY (8:1-21, 32-36): Wisdom calls from the hilltops and crossroads, telling all who will listen about the importance of accepting her words. Her words are:
   A. **Valid** (8:1-9)
      1. *"Let me give you common sense"* (8:1-5).
      2. *"Everything I say is right"* (8:6).
      3. *"I speak the truth and hate every kind of deception"* (8:7).
      4. *"My advice is wholesome and good"* (8:8).
      5. *"My words are plain to anyone with understanding"* (8:9).
   B. **Valuable** (8:10-11, 18-21): Wisdom is more precious than silver, gold, or rubies.
   C. **Vital** (8:12-17): All earth's rulers need wisdom to lead and judge wisely.

D. Vibrant (8:32-36)
1. *They bring abundant life* (8:32-35).
2. *They bring about God's approval* (8:35-36): But those who miss wisdom injure themselves and love death.

II. WISDOM'S ETERNALITY (8:22-31): Many believe that Jesus himself is referred to in these verses.
A. Wisdom creates with God in eternity past (8:22-29): Wisdom is with God during Creation.
B. Wisdom is God's companion from eternity past (8:30-31): Wisdom is God's constant delight.

SECTION OUTLINE NINE (PROVERBS 9)
Wisdom spreads a banquet and gives instructions.

I. WISDOM'S FRUITS (9:1-12)
A. Its palace (9:1): "Wisdom has built her spacious house with seven pillars."
B. Its provisions (9:2, 5-6): Wisdom "has prepared a great banquet, mixed the wines, and set the table."
C. Its plea (9:3-4): "She has sent her servants to invite everyone to come."
D. Its platform (9:10): "Fear of the LORD is the beginning of wisdom."
E. Its promises (9:7-9, 11-12)
1. *The effects of rebuking the wise* (9:7-8): Rebuking a wicked man will cause hurt; the wise will love you all the more.
2. *The effects of teaching the wise* (9:9): The righteous will learn more, and the wise will be wiser.
3. *The benefits of gained wisdom* (9:11-12): It will add abundant years to one's life.

II. WHOREDOM'S FOLLY (9:13-18): Folly is likened to a loud and brash harlot.
A. What sexual immorality promises (9:13-17): "Stolen water is refreshing; food eaten in secret tastes the best!"
B. What sexual immorality produces (9:18): "Her former guests are now in the grave."

SECTION OUTLINE TEN (PROVERBS 10)
Wisdom instructs on right and wrong.

I. THE TWO CHILDREN (10:1-7)
A. The wise child brings joy to his father (10:1-7).
B. The foolish child brings grief to his mother (10:1-7).

II. THE TWO LIFESTYLES AND THEIR RESULTS (10:8-32)
  A. **The wise vs. the foolish** (10:8-9, 13-14, 19-21, 23, 26): The wise are careful with their words and actions; the foolish care only about what they want.
  B. **The obedient vs. the disobedient** (10:10, 17): The obedient accept correction; the disobedient "wink at wrong."
  C. **The rich vs. the poor** (10:15-16, 22): Godly people use their money wisely; fools squander it.
  D. **The godly vs. the godless** (10:11-12, 18, 24-25, 27-32): The words of the godly lead to life; evil people hide their intentions and cut their lives short.

SECTION OUTLINE ELEVEN (PROVERBS 11)
Wisdom avoids all kinds of wickedness.

  I. GOD HATES DISHONESTY (11:1-3): "He delights in honesty."

  II. RICHES WON'T HELP (11:4-9): Only right living safeguards against death.

  III. THE UPRIGHT UPHOLD THE CITY (11:10-11):The godly succeed and bless others.

  IV. THE GODLY LIVE RIGHT (11:12-21): A person with good sense does not gossip; your soul is nourished when you are kind.

  V. THE GODLY USE DISCRETION (11:22-23): Discretion is more important than beauty. "The godly can look forward to happiness, while the wicked can expect only wrath."

  VI. THE GODLY ARE GENEROUS (11:24-26): "The generous prosper and are satisfied"; the greedy are cursed.

  VII. THE RIGHTEOUS ARE REWARDED (11:27-31): They find favor and flourish.

SECTION OUTLINE TWELVE (PROVERBS 12)
Wisdom contrasts righteousness and wickedness.

  I. CHARACTER COUNTS (12:1-14): The Lord is happy with those who are good but condemns the wicked.

  II. THE WISE WEIGH THEIR WORDS (12:15-16): "Fools think they need no advice."

  III. WORDS CAN WOUND (12:17-23): "Some people make cutting remarks, but the words of the wise bring healing."

  IV. THE WORKER WINS (12:24-28): But a hard worker becomes a leader.

SECTION OUTLINE THIRTEEN (PROVERBS 13)
Wisdom instructs on right living.

I. CORRECTION (13:1): He accepts his parents' discipline.

II. CONTROL (13:2-4): Work hard and prosper; control your tongue and have a long life.

III. CONSEQUENCES (13:5-25): The godly hate lies, work hard for their money, and are rewarded with respect. The wicked ruin their lives with their tongues, get wealth quickly and lose it, and their lives are snuffed out quickly.

SECTION OUTLINE FOURTEEN (PROVERBS 14)
Wisdom instructs about the fear of the Lord.

I. THE WISE AND THE FOOLISH (14:1-9): The wise build up their houses; the wicked tear them down.

II. TRUE JOY (14:10-13): Laughter conceals a heavy heart.

III. PERSONALITY PATTERNS (14:14-21): The prudent carefully consider what they do while fools rush in without a thought.

IV. GENERAL DOS AND DON'TS (14:22-28): Plan for good, work hard, be truthful, and fear the Lord.

V. ANGER AND ENVY (14:29-33): If you control your anger, you have great understanding. If you are jealous, your life rots away.

VI. LIFTING UP KINGDOM AND KING (14:34-35): Godliness exalts a nation, and a king rejoices in it.

SECTION OUTLINE FIFTEEN (PROVERBS 15)
Wisdom instructs on right emotions and the right way to live.

I. USE WORDS WISELY (15:1-7): "Gentle words bring life and health; a deceitful tongue crushes the spirit."

II. REMEMBER WHAT THE LORD LOVES (15:8-9): The prayers of the upright and those who pursue godliness.

III. CONSIDER THE CONSEQUENCES (15:10-19): Abandoning the right path brings serious consequences.

IV. USE GOOD SENSE (15:20-29): The Lord is far from the wicked but close to the righteous.

V. LOOK AND LISTEN WELL (15:30-33): A cheerful look brings joy to the heart.

SECTION OUTLINE SIXTEEN (PROVERBS 16)
Wisdom instructs on God's providential care.

I. A PURPOSE FOR EVERYTHING (16:1-9): "Commit your work to the
LORD, and then your plans will succeed."

II. KINGLY ADVICE (16:10-15): Kings must never judge unfairly.

III. MORE GLORIOUS THAN GOLD (16:16-17): Wisdom and understanding
are better than riches.

IV. PRIDE AND PROSPERITY (16:18-24): It is better to be humble and poor
than proud and rich.

V. A GODLESS GROUPING (16:25-30): The way that seems right actually
leads to death.

VI. TEMPER YOUR TEMPER! (16:31-33): "It is better to be patient than
powerful."

SECTION OUTLINE SEVENTEEN (PROVERBS 17)
Wisdom instructs on fools.

I. A REFINING FIRE (17:1-5): God tests the heart; fools are punished.

II. FAMILY PRIDE (17:6): "Grandchildren are the crowning glory of the
aged; parents are the pride of their children."

III. A CATALOG OF FOOLS (17:7-28): "The crooked heart will not
prosper; the twisted tongue tumbles into trouble."

SECTION OUTLINE EIGHTEEN (PROVERBS 18)
Wisdom instructs on moral virtues and their contrary vices.

I. THE MOUTH OF A FOOL (18:1-9): Fools only want to air their own
opinions, they get into constant quarrels, and their mouths are their
ruin.

II. THE SAFETY OF THE LORD (18:10-11): The godly run to the Lord when
in trouble.

III. THE POWER OF THE TONGUE (18:12-21): It "can kill or nourish life."

IV. THE WONDERS OF A WIFE (18:22): "The man who finds a wife finds a
treasure and receives favor from the LORD."

V. THE BEST OF ALL BROTHERS (18:23-24): "A real friend sticks closer
than a brother."

SECTION OUTLINE NINETEEN (PROVERBS 19)
Wisdom instructs on character.

 I. WEALTH AND WISDOM (19:1-4): "Wealth makes many 'friends';
    poverty drives them away."

 II. DECEIVERS AND LIARS (19:5-9): A false witness will be punished, and
     a liar will be destroyed.

 III. FOOLS, KINGS, AND CHILDREN (19:10-14): Fools should not live in
      luxury and should restrain their anger.

 IV. LAZINESS AND LIFE (19:15-16): "A lazy person sleeps soundly—and
     goes hungry." If you keep the commandments, you keep your life.

 V. DISCIPLINE AND DEDICATION (19:17-25): If you discipline your
    children, you will save their lives. "Loyalty makes a person
    attractive."

 VI. PARENTAL ABUSE (19:26-29): Children who abuse their parents are a
     disgrace.

SECTION OUTLINE TWENTY (PROVERBS 20)
Wisdom instructs on avoiding drunkenness, sloth, and a contentious
spirit.

 I. DO NOT BE LED ASTRAY BY DRINK (20:1).

 II. DO NOT ROUSE THE KING'S ANGER (20:2-8): His judgment is always
     just.

 III. DO NOT HAVE DOUBLE STANDARDS (20:9-13): The Lord despises
      them. You need to work and not be lazy. Be pure in all your conduct.

 IV. WATCH OUT FOR BAD BARGAINS (20:14-18): Do not accept a
     guarantee for the debt of a stranger without collateral.

 V. DO NOT GOSSIP OR HOLD GRUDGES (20:19-25): "It is the LORD who
    directs our steps."

 VI. DO NOT TOLERATE WICKEDNESS (20:26-30): A wise king knows how
     to handle the wicked. "The LORD's searchlight penetrates the human
     spirit, exposing every hidden motive."

SECTION OUTLINE TWENTY-ONE (PROVERBS 21)
Wisdom instructs on integrity, patience, and God's sovereignty.

I. GOD WATCHES THE HEART (21:1-8): The Lord examines our heart more than our actions.

II. IT'S SIMPLER BEING ALONE (21:9-19): It is better than having a contentious wife or simple, wicked companions.

III. THE WAY OF THE WISE (21:20-29): "Whoever pursues godliness and unfailing love will find life, godliness, and honor."

IV. "VICTORY BELONGS TO THE LORD" (21:30-31): "Human plans, no matter how wise or well advised, cannot stand against the LORD."

SECTION OUTLINE TWENTY-TWO (PROVERBS 22)
Wisdom instructs on how to secure and keep a good name. It emphasizes wise words and justice toward others, especially the poor.

I. A GOOD NAME (22:1): A good reputation is better than silver or gold.

II. SOME GENERAL GUIDANCE (22:2-16): The Lord made all of us, and we all have the choice to do right.

III. SOME GOOD ADVICE (22:17-29): The wise will heed these sayings as they trust in the Lord.

SECTION OUTLINE TWENTY-THREE (PROVERBS 23)
Wisdom instructs on greediness, intemperance, and impurity.

I. DINING WITH A KING (23:1-5): Pay attention to what is before you since deception may be involved.

II. DINING WITH THE STINGY (23:6-8): Do not go, because he doesn't mean to be hospitable.

III. FELLOWSHIPING WITH FOOLS (23:9): "They will despise the wisest advice," so do not waste your time with them.

IV. DISCIPLINING YOUR CHILDREN (23:10-18): Do everything you can to gain wisdom for yourself and for your children.

V. AVOIDING PITFALLS (23:19-28): Too much of anything sends a person to poverty or a deep pit.

VI. AVOIDING DRUNKENNESS (23:29-35): A drunk does not care how bad it gets. He is always looking for another drink.

SECTION OUTLINE TWENTY-FOUR (PROVERBS 24)
Wisdom tells how to relate to the wicked and foolish and conduct oneself with neighbors, and warns against sloth.

I. THE HOUSE WISDOM BUILT (24:1-9): It "becomes strong through good sense" and "through knowledge its rooms are filled with all sorts of precious riches and valuables."

II. RESCUE THE PERISHING (24:10-12): If you do not help those unjustly sentenced, God will punish you.

III. LIKE HONEY TO THE SOUL (24:13-14): If you eat wisdom, you will have a bright future and your hopes will be fulfilled.

IV. DOWN SEVEN TIMES (24:15-16): The godly are able to overcome misfortune.

V. WHEN ENEMIES FALL (24:17-22): If you rejoice over the misfortune of the wicked, God will be displeased with you.

VI. PARTIALITY AND PREPARATION (24:23-27): Do not declare the guilty innocent or you will be denounced by the nations. Develop your business before building your house.

VII. RETURN GOOD FOR EVIL (24:28-29): Do not lie or testify spitefully against others.

VIII. LEARN FROM THE LAZY (24:30-34): Laziness will bring poverty.

SECTION OUTLINE TWENTY-FIVE (PROVERBS 25)
Wisdom instructs kings and their subjects on the fear of God and righteousness.

I. THE SOURCE OF PROVERBS (25:1): They were collected by Hezekiah's advisers.

II. THE RIGHTS OF RULERS (25:2-7): Kings have the right to exalt people or to bring them down.

III. BE SLOW TO SUE (25:8-10): Try to settle a dispute with your neighbor privately.

IV. THE RIGHT USE OF WORDS (25:11-15): Words should be used to give good advice and build up, not to make promises that won't be kept.

V. MODERATION IN ALL THINGS (25:16-17): Do not eat too much or you will be sick; do not visit too often or you will wear out your welcome.

VI. DEALING WITH OTHERS (25:18-20): Do not do things that common sense tells you are not good for you or others, such as lying or shooting someone.

VII. KILL HIM WITH KINDNESS (25:21-22): The Lord will reward you for giving your enemy food and drink.

VIII. BETTER OFF ON A ROOF (25:23-24): It is better to live alone in an attic than with a contentious person or a gossip.

IX. GOOD NEWS AND SELF-CONTROL (25:25-28): Good news is like cold water to the thirsty. A person without self-control is like a city with broken-down walls.

SECTION OUTLINE TWENTY-SIX (PROVERBS 26)
Wisdom instructs against dishonorable conduct.

I. FACTS ON THE FOOL (26:1-12): A fool should not be trusted or honored.

II. SEVEN TIMES SMARTER (26:13-16): A lazy person thinks he's smart, but he's only full of excuses.

III. MIND YOUR OWN BUSINESS (26:17-19): You should not interfere in other people's arguments.

IV. GOSSIP GENERATES GRIEF (26:20-28): The hurt you intend for others by gossiping about them will come back on you.

SECTION OUTLINE TWENTY-SEVEN (PROVERBS 27)
Wisdom instructs on human relations.

I. NEITHER BOAST NOR BRAG (27:1-3): You do not know what the future will bring. Let others praise you.

II. MORE DANGEROUS THAN ANGER (27:4): Jealousy is more destructive than wrath.

III. SWEETER THAN KISSES (27:5-9): A friend's criticism is better than kisses from the enemy.

IV. NEVER FORGET A FRIEND (27:10-14): If you remember your friends, they will help you when you need it.

V. A RAINY DAY AND A CRANKY WOMAN (27:15-18): They are equally annoying.

VI. MORE REFLECTIVE THAN A MIRROR (27:19-22): "As a face is reflected in water, so the heart reflects the person."

VII. CARING FOR THE LAMBS (27:23-27): Put your heart into caring for your flock, because it will provide food and clothing for you.

SECTION OUTLINE TWENTY-EIGHT (PROVERBS 28)

Wisdom instructs on the unscrupulous and unlawful dealings of the rich against the poor.

I. A STABLE GOVERNMENT (28:1-2): Wise and knowledgeable leaders make a stable nation.

II. A POURING RAIN (28:3): "A poor person who oppresses the poor is like a pounding rain that destroys the crops."

III. INTEGRITY (28:4-9): People of integrity follow the Lord and understand justice. God does not answer the prayers of the evil, who are unjust and ignore the law.

IV. THE BLESSINGS OF THE GODLY, THE PLIGHT OF THE GODLESS (28:10-15): Honest people inherit good things; everyone is glad when they succeed. If people confess their sins and stubbornness and adopt a tender conscience, they will receive mercy.

V. THE RISE OF THE JUST, THE FALL OF THE UNJUST (28:16-20): An honest king will have a long reign, but a stupid king will oppress the people. The honest will be rescued, while the crooked are destroyed.

VI. PARTIALITY AND PUNISHMENT (28:21): It is never good to show favoritism, but some may do so for almost nothing.

VII. BEING CRITICAL (28:22-24): "People appreciate frankness more than flattery."

VIII. GREED AND GENEROSITY (28:25-28): "Greed causes fighting. . . . Whoever gives to the poor will lack nothing."

SECTION OUTLINE TWENTY-NINE (PROVERBS 29)

Wisdom instructs against stubbornness and insubordination.

I. ACCEPTING CRITICISM (29:1): If you refuse to accept criticism, you will be broken.

II. WISDOM AND WICKEDNESS (29:2-8): "The man who loves wisdom brings joy to his father. . . . Evil people are trapped by sin."

III. FACTS ABOUT A FOOL (29:9-11): A fool has no restraint on his emotions.

IV. POTENTATES AND THE POOR (29:12-14): If a king honors liars, all his advisers will be wicked. He will have a long reign if he is fair to the poor.

V. SPANKING, NOT SPOILING (29:15-17): Discipline produces wisdom, but spoiling a child brings a mother disgrace.

VI. NO REVELATION, NO RESTRAINT (29:18-19): If people are not wise and accept guidance, they run wild.

VII. THOUGHTLESS SPEECH (29:20-26): There is more hope for a fool than for one who speaks without thinking.

VIII. THE GODLY AND THE UNGODLY (29:27): They detest each other.

SECTION OUTLINE THIRTY (PROVERBS 30)
Wisdom instructs on God's Word and other subjects.

I. THE WRITER (30:1-3, 7-9)
   A. **His identity** (30:1): He is Agur, son of Jakeh.
   B. **His ignorance** (30:2-3)
      1. *He lacks common sense* (30:2).
      2. *He has not mastered human wisdom* (30:3).
      3. *He does not understand God* (30:3).
   C. **His inquiry** (30:7-9): Agur asks God for two favors:
      1. *"Help me never to tell a lie"* (30:8).
      2. *"Give me neither poverty nor riches!"* (30:8-9): If he becomes rich, he may become too proud, and if he becomes poor, he may dishonor God's name. He wants just enough to satisfy his needs.

II. GOD'S WONDERS (30:4): God has complete control over himself and everything he made.

III. GOD'S WORD (30:5-6)
   A. **"Every word of God proves true"** (30:5).
   B. **We dare not add to it!** (30:6): If we do, he will rebuke us, and we will be found a liar.

IV. GOD'S WORLD (30:10-33)
   A. **Seven kinds of people** (30:10-14, 17, 20, 32)
      1. *Those who slander someone to their employer* (30:10): They will receive a curse and pay for their folly.
      2. *Those who curse and dishonor their parents* (30:11, 17): They will be eaten by vultures.
      3. *Those who are pure in their own eyes* (30:12): They are actually filthy and unwashed.
      4. *Those with proud, disdainful attitudes* (30:13)
      5. *Those who devour the poor* (30:14): They destroy the needy with teeth as sharp as swords or knives.
      6. *The brash and defiant harlot* (30:20): She thinks she's done nothing wrong.
      7. *The arrogant fools, plotting evil* (30:32): They should not brag about it; they should be ashamed.

    B. Two suckers belonging to the leech (30:15): They cry out, "More, more!"

    C. Four things that are never satisfied (30:15-16): "The grave, the barren womb, the thirsty desert, the blazing fire."

    D. Four wonderful and mysterious things (30:18-19): "How an eagle glides through the sky, how a snake slithers on a rock, how a ship navigates the ocean, how a man loves a woman."

    E. Four things the earth finds unbearable (30:21-23): "A slave who becomes a king, an overbearing fool who prospers, a bitter woman who finally gets a husband, a servant girl who supplants her mistress."

    F. Four small but wise things (30:24-28)

        1. *Ants* (30:25): "They store up food for the winter."

        2. *Rock badgers* (30:26): "They make their homes among the rocky cliffs."

        3. *Locusts* (30:27): "They march like an army in ranks."

        4. *Lizards* (30:28): They manage to exist everywhere.

    G. Four stately monarchs (30:29-31): "The lion . . . the strutting rooster, the male goat, a king as he leads his army."

    H. Three by-products of life (30:33): Churning milk yields butter; twisting the nose produces blood, just as anger produces quarrels.

SECTION OUTLINE THIRTY-ONE (PROVERBS 31)

Wisdom instructs kings and praises the virtuous, wise, and industrious woman.

  I. A GODLY MOTHER'S COUNSEL (31:1-9)

    A. Whom she taught (31:1-2): She taught her son, King Lemuel

    B. What she taught (31:3-9)

        1. *The Negative* (31:3-7)

          a. "Do not spend your strength on women, on those who ruin kings" (31:3).

          b. Do not guzzle wine or crave liquor (31:4-7).

        2. *The Positive* (31:8-9): Stand up for the poor and needy.

  II. A GODLY WIFE'S CHARACTER (31:10-31)

    A. Her worth (31:10, 25, 29)

        1. *She is more precious than rubies* (31:10).

        2. *"She is clothed with strength and dignity"* (31:25): "She laughs with no fear of the future."

        3. *She surpasses all other women* (31:29).

    B. Her works (31:13-22, 24, 27)

        1. *With her family* (31:13-15, 17-19, 21-22, 27)

          a. She provides them with proper clothing (31:13, 21): She finds wool and flax and spins it.

      b. She plans meals and her day (31:14-15): She brings food from afar and gets up before dawn to prepare breakfast.

      c. She is tireless in her work (31:17-19): She is a hard worker, looking for bargains and working late into the night.

      d. She cares for and watches over the entire household (31:22, 27): She makes her own clothes and bedspreads.

  2. *With her finances* (31:16, 24)

      a. She buys and sells property (31:16).

      b. She plants vineyards with her earnings (31:16).

      c. She makes and sells belted linen garments and sashes (31:24).

  3. *With the less fortunate* (31:20): She extends her arms to the poor and needy.

C. Her wisdom (31:26): Her words of instruction are wise and kind.

D. Her witnesses (31:11-12, 23, 28, 31)

  1. *Her husband* (31:11-12, 23)

      a. Trusts her (31:11): "She will greatly enrich his life."

      b. Knows she helps him (31:12): "She will not hinder him."

      c. Is respected among the city elders (31:23).

  2. *Her children* (31:28): They "stand and bless her."

  3. *Her fellow citizens* (31:31): She should be publicly praised.

E. Her worship (31:30): She fears and reverences God.

Ecclesiastes

SECTION OUTLINE ONE (ECCLESIASTES 1)

The Teacher declares that everything is meaningless. He begins reviewing his search for meaning, and his first conclusion is that wisdom is futile.

I. THE MAN (1:1, 12): The author introduces himself as King David's son—presumably Solomon—and notes that he once ruled over Israel.

II. THE MISSION (1:13, 16)
   A. **His quest** (1:13): Solomon devotes himself to searching out the purpose of life.
   B. **His qualifications** (1:16): Because of his great wisdom and power, Solomon feels he possesses the necessary credentials to conduct this search.

III. THE MADNESS (1:2-11, 14-15, 17-18): A preliminary investigation quickly reveals some bitter truths about life.
   A. **No real purpose** (1:2-7, 14, 17): Life is futile and meaningless.
   B. **No new thing** (1:9-10): History merely repeats itself.
   C. **No cure** (1:15): What is wrong cannot be righted.
   D. **No lasting honor** (1:11): The dead are quickly forgotten.

SECTION OUTLINE TWO (ECCLESIASTES 2)

Solomon tries to find meaning through various things.

I. THE KING'S DELUSIONS (2:1-10): Solomon travels down many roads in his search for peace and purpose. This includes:
   A. **Pleasure** (2:1-2)
   B. **Alcohol** (2:3)
   C. **Great building projects** (2:4a)
   D. **The planting of vineyards** (2:4b)
   E. **The creation of beautiful parks with exotic trees** (2:5-6)
   F. **The accumulation of possessions, including:**
      1. *Human slaves* (2:7a)

      2. *Herds and flocks* (2:7b)
      3. *Silver and gold* (2:8a)
      4. *Gifted musicians* (2:8b)
      5. *Beautiful concubines* (2:8c)
   G. A universal reputation (2:9)
   H. Total indulgence (2:10)

II. THE KING'S CONCLUSIONS (2:11-26)
   A. The bitter truth (2:11-23)
      1. *What Solomon finds* (2:11-16)
         a. Everything is useless and empty (2:11).
         b. Everyone must eventually die (2:12-16).
      2. *What Solomon fears* (2:17-23): He realizes that in most instances the achievements of good men are left to fools.
   B. The better truth (2:24-26): Be content with what you have, and enjoy your work!

SECTION OUTLINE THREE (ECCLESIASTES 3)
Solomon views life from a human perspective and from God's perspective.

I. EARTHLY EVENTS FROM A HUMAN PERSPECTIVE (3:1-14, 22)
   A. The categories (3:1-8): There is a proper time for all events.
      1. *To be born and to die* (3:2a)
      2. *To plant and to harvest* (3:2b)
      3. *To kill and to heal* (3:3a)
      4. *To tear down and to rebuild* (3:3b)
      5. *To cry and to laugh* (3:4a)
      6. *To grieve and to dance* (3:4b)
      7. *To scatter and to gather* (3:5a)
      8. *To embrace and to turn away* (3:5b)
      9. *To search and to lose* (3:6a)
      10. *To keep and to throw away* (3:6b)
      11. *To tear and to mend* (3:7a)
      12. *To be quiet and to speak* (3:7b)
      13. *To love and to hate* (3:8a)
      14. *To wage war and to pursue peace* (3:8b)
   B. The conclusions (3:9-14, 22)
      1. *The ultimate truth* (3:9-11, 14): God—and God alone—can separate time from eternity.
      2. *The "until-then" truth* (3:12-13, 22): Enjoy both your work and the fruits proceeding from it.

II. EARTHLY EVENTS FROM GOD'S PERSPECTIVE (3:15-21)
   A. **What God has done** (3:15): He has supervised all past actions.
   B. **What God now does** (3:18-21): He tests people so that they can see they are no better than animals.
   C. **What God will do** (3:16-17): He will bring to judgment both the righteous and the wicked.

SECTION OUTLINE FOUR (ECCLESIASTES 4)
Solomon continues his observations about life.

I. THE WRETCHED THINGS IN THIS LIFE (4:1-8, 13-16)
   A. **The people Solomon finds** (4:1, 4-8)
      1. *The oppressed poor* (4:1)
      2. *The selfish rich* (4:4, 7-8)
      3. *The lazy fool* (4:5-6)
   B. **The pessimism Solomon feels** (4:2-3, 13-16)
      1. *Concerning life and death* (4:2-3)
         a. It is better to be dead than living (4:2)!
         b. It is best never to have been born (4:3)!
      2. *Concerning prisoners and potentates* (4:13-16)
         a. It is better to be a poor but wise youth with a prison record than to be a rich but foolish king (4:13-16a)!
         b. However, in the final analysis, it matters little who and what one is (4:16b).

II. THE WORKABLE THINGS IN THIS LIFE (4:9-12)
   A. **Two are better than one** (4:9-12a).
      1. *If one falls, the other can help* (4:10).
      2. *If one is cold, the other can provide warmth* (4:11).
      3. *If one is attacked, the other can defend* (4:12a).
   B. **Three are better than two** (4:12b): A triple-braided cord is not easily broken.

SECTION OUTLINE FIVE (ECCLESIASTES 5)
Solomon observes humanity.

I. HUMAN WORDS (5:1-7)
   A. **Be cautious in making a vow** (5:1-3).
   B. **Be committed in keeping a vow** (5:4-7).

II. HUMAN WICKEDNESS (5:8-12)
   A. **Our injustice** (5:8-9): This can be seen from the poor person to the king on the throne.
   B. **Our greed** (5:10-12): The more people receive, the more they desire.

III. HUMAN WRETCHEDNESS (5:13-17)
  A. Our birth (5:15): We enter this world with nothing.
  B. Our life (5:13-14): We may be financially reduced to nothing in this life.
  C. Our death (5:16): We leave the world with nothing.

IV. HUMAN WISDOM (5:18-20): Once again Solomon advises us to enjoy our work and to be content with our life.

SECTION OUTLINE SIX (ECCLESIASTES 6)
Solomon considers the source of joy.

I. FORTUNE DOES NOT BRING JOY (6:1-2).
  A. Most wealthy people are unhappy with their possessions in life (6:2a).
  B. All wealthy people leave their possessions to others in death (6:2b).

II. FAMILY DOES NOT BRING JOY (6:3-5): A stillborn child is better off than the unhappy father of 100 children.

III. FULLNESS OF YEARS DOES NOT BRING JOY (6:6-12): This is true even if a person could live to observe his or her 2000th birthday!

SECTION OUTLINE SEVEN (ECCLESIASTES 7)
Solomon considers the better things in life.

I. THE "BETTERS" (7:1-12, 19)
  A. A good reputation is better than fine perfume (7:1a).
  B. The day of death is better than the day of birth (7:1b).
  C. Funerals are better than festivals (7:2).
  D. Sorrow is better than laughter (7:3-4).
  E. Criticism from a wise man is better than praise from a fool (7:5-6).
  F. Finishing is better than starting (7:8a).
  G. Patience is better than pride (7:8b).
  H. Wisdom is better than wealth (7:11-12).
  I. Wisdom is better than power (7:19).

II. THE BITTER (7:26): The snares of a prostitute are more bitter than death!

III. THE BOTTOM LINE (7:13-18, 20-25, 27-29): Solomon concludes the following:
  A. What is crooked cannot be made straight (7:13).
  B. Enjoy today, for tomorrow is uncertain (7:14).
  C. Don't be too good or too wise (7:15-18).

    D. There is no one who has not sinned (7:20).
    E. Don't eavesdrop (7:21-22).
    F. Wisdom without God is impossible (7:23-25, 27-29).

SECTION OUTLINE EIGHT (ECCLESIASTES 8)
Solomon makes further observations about life.

  I. CONCERNING UNDERSTANDING (8:1, 16-17)
    A. Wisdom brightens a person's appearance (8:1).
    B. Wisdom comes only from God (8:16-17).

  II. CONCERNING UNQUESTIONED OBEDIENCE (8:2-5): Obey the king, for his word is supreme.

  III. CONCERNING UNCERTAINTY (8:6-8): No one can escape death.

  IV. CONCERNING UNFAIRNESS (8:9-14)
    A. Solomon's frustration (8:9-11, 14)
      1. *Why do the wicked often receive that which the righteous deserve (8:9-11)?*
      2. *Why do the righteous often receive that which the wicked deserve (8:14)?*
    B. Solomon's realization (8:12-13): God will eventually punish the wicked!

  V. CONCERNING THE ULTIMATE (8:15): Be content, and enjoy life!

SECTION OUTLINE NINE (ECCLESIASTES 9)
Solomon reflects on the things that control human destiny.

  I. THE INFINITE ONE (9:1): The affairs of all people are in the hands of God.

  II. THE INSANITY (9:2-6, 11-12)
    A. Death ends every person's life (9:2-6).
      1. *The living know they will die* (9:5a).
      2. *The dead know nothing at all* (9:5b).
    B. Chance controls every person's life (9:11).
      1. *The swift do not always win the race* (9:11a).
      2. *The strong do not always win the battle* (9:11b).
      3. *The smart do not always acquire the wealth* (9:11c).
    C. Calamity stalks every person's path (9:12).

  III. THE INSTRUCTIONS (9:7-10)
    A. Enjoy life with your wife (9:9).
    B. Whatever you do, do well (9:10).

IV. The Illustration (9:13-18)
  A. **The contents** (9:13-15)
    1. *The saving* (9:13-15a): By his wisdom a poor but wise man once saved his town from a powerful king whose armies had surrounded it.
    2. *The sorrow* (9:15b): His noble achievements were soon forgotten because he was poor.
  B. **The conclusion** (9:16-18): Wisdom is still better than strength!

SECTION OUTLINE TEN (ECCLESIASTES 10)
Solomon reflects on different kinds of people.

I. The Individuals Described by Solomon (10:1-7, 12-18, 20)
  A. **The wise** (10:2a, 12a)
    1. *Their hearts direct them to do right* (10:2a).
    2. *Their mouths give forth gracious words* (10:12a).
  B. **The foolish** (10:2b-3, 6-7, 12b-15)
    1. *Their hearts direct them to do evil* (10:2b).
    2. *The way they walk betrays them as fools* (10:3).
    3. *They are often* (tragically) given great authority (10:6-7).
    4. *They are consumed by their own words* (10:12b-14).
    5. *They are exhausted by even the simplest tasks* (10:15).
  C. **Those in authority** (10:4-5, 16-17, 20)
    1. *Stay calm, and don't quit if your boss is angry with you* (10:4).
    2. *Woe to the land whose king is a child* (10:16).
    3. *Happy is the land whose king is a nobleman* (10:17).
    4. *Don't make light of a king, even in your thoughts* (10:20).
  D. **The lazy man** (10:18): He lets the roof leak and the rafters rot.

II. The Injuries Warned about by Solomon (10:8-11): He cautions concerning:
  A. **Digging a well, lest you fall into it** (10:8a)
  B. **Demolishing an old wall, lest a snake bite you** (10:8b)
  C. **Working a quarry, lest the stones crush you** (10:9a)
  D. **Chopping wood, lest the axe strike you** (10:9b-10)

III. The Insights Observed by Solomon (10:19)
  A. **A party gives laughter** (10:19a).
  B. **Wine gives happiness** (10:19b).
  C. **Money gives everything** (10:19c).

SECTION OUTLINE ELEVEN (ECCLESIASTES 11)
Solomon considers various rules for life.

I. GENERAL RULES FOR ALL PEOPLE (11:1-6)
   A. **Be generous** (11:1-2).
   B. **Don't delay in matters of sowing and reaping** (11:3-4).
   C. **Don't try to understand the work of God** (11:5).
   D. **Keep on sowing your seed** (11:6).

II. SPECIAL RULES FOR YOUNG PEOPLE (11:7-10)
   A. **Rejoice** (11:7-9a): Enjoy your youth. Live life to the hilt.
   B. **Remember** (11:9b-10): Keep in mind that someday you must account to God for everything you do.

SECTION OUTLINE TWELVE (ECCLESIASTES 12)
Solomon gives some concluding thoughts.

I. THE COMMAND (12:1-8)
   A. **What his readers are to do** (12:1-2): They are to honor their Creator early in life.
   B. **Why they are to do it** (12:3-8): God desires the strength of his people when they are young, before old age reduces the body to a pitiful shell of its former days.

II. THE COLLECTION (12:9-12)
   A. **The information** (12:9): The Teacher collected and classified many proverbs.
   B. **The instruction** (12:10): The gifted Teacher then taught the proverbs to his people.

III. THE CONCLUSION (12:13-14)
   A. **What his readers are to do** (12:13): "Fear God and obey his commandments."
   B. **Why his readers are to do it** (12:14): "God will judge us for everything we do."

Song of Songs

SECTION OUTLINE ONE (SONG OF SOLOMON 1–8)
A description is given of the events preceding the wedding, the events accompanying the wedding, and the events following the wedding.

I. THE EVENTS PRECEDING THE WEDDING (1:1–3:5)
  A. **"You light up my life"** (1:1-4a, 5-7, 12-14, 16-17, 2:1, 3-13, 16-17, 3:1-5): The bride speaks to the groom, Solomon.
    1. *Your love is sweeter than wine* (1:2).
    2. *How pleasing is your name* (1:3).
    3. *I am darkened by the sun but beautiful* (1:5-6).
    4. *Where do you graze your flocks, O my love* (1:7)?
    5. *I desire to hold you in my bosom* (1:12-14; 2:4-7).
    6. *I will be to you as a rose of Sharon, the lily of the valley* (2:1).
    7. *You will be to me as an apple tree* (2:3).
    8. *I hear you coming for me* (2:8-13, 16-17).
    9. *I dreamed that I searched for you in the streets of the city* (3:1-5).
  B. **"You light up my life"** (1:8-11, 15): The groom speaks to the bride.
    1. *You are like a lovely filly* (1:9).
    2. *How lovely are your cheeks and neck* (1:10).
    3. *Your eyes are soft like doves* (1:15).
  C. **"They light up each other's life"** (1:4b, 2:15): The young women of Jerusalem speak to the couple.
    1. *We rejoice and delight in you* (1:4b).
    2. *Guard the vineyard of your love* (2:15).

II. THE EVENTS ACCOMPANYING THE WEDDING (3:6–5:1)
  A. **The wedding day** (3:6-11)
    1. *The coming of King Solomon* (3:6): Solomon is seen sweeping in from the deserts like a cloud of smoke, coming for his bride.
    2. *The carriage of King Solomon* (3:7-10)
      a. The soldiers (3:7-8): Solomon's carriage is guarded by 60 of Israel's strongest and most experienced warriors.
      b. The splendor (3:9-10)
        (1) Made from wood imported from Lebanon (3:9)

        (2) Has silver posts and a golden canopy (3:10a)

        (3) Is upholstered with purple (3:10b)

    3. *The crown of King Solomon* (3:11): The bride invites the daughters of Jerusalem to see and admire his crown, given him by his mother on the very day of his wedding.

  B. The wedding night (4:1–5:1)

    1. *As spoken by the husband to his wife* (4:1-15; 5:1a): He praises her as follows:

      a. Her eyes are like doves (4:1a).

      b. Her hair is like a flock of goats (4:1b).

      c. Her teeth are like shorn sheep (4:2).

      d. Her lips are like a scarlet ribbon (4:3a).

      e. Her cheeks are like the halves of a pomegranate (4:3b).

      f. Her neck is like the tower of David (4:4).

      g. Her breasts are like twin fawns of a gazelle (4:5).

      h. Her love is much better than wine (4:10a).

      i. Her perfume is more fragrant than the richest spices. Her virginity is his own private garden, an enclosed spring, a sealed fountain, a lovely orchard holding precious fruit (4:10b-15; 5:1a).

    2. *As spoken by the wife to her husband* (4:16): She urges him to take his fill of love.

    3. *As spoken by the young women of Jerusalem to both* (5:1b): "Eat and drink deeply of this love!"

III. THE EVENTS FOLLOWING THE WEDDING (5:2–8:14)

  A. In regard to the wife (5:2-8, 10-16; 7:10–8:4, 6-7, 10-14)

    1. *Her dream* (5:2-8)

      a. The sin (5:2-4): In her dream she rebuffs her husband, causing him to walk away sadly.

      b. The search (5:5-8): Regretting this, she searches for him in the city streets and is mistreated by the watchmen.

    2. *Her desire* (7:10–8:4)

      a. To visit the countryside and spend the night in one of the fields (7:10-13)

      b. To publicly demonstrate her love for him (8:1-4)

      c. To offer herself totally to him (8:10-12, 14)

    3. *Her description* (5:10-16; 8:6-7)

      a. She describes her lover (5:10-16).

      b. She describes her love (8:6-7).

  B. In regard to the husband (6:4-12-13; 7:1-9; 8:5b, 13)

    1. *He characterizes the beauty of his wife* (6:4-7): Solomon speaks in glowing terms concerning his wife's hair, teeth, cheeks, etc.

    2. *He contrasts the beauty of his wife* (6:8-10): Her beauty far surpasses that of his 60 other wives, 80 concubines, and unnumbered virgins!

C. In regard to the young women of Jerusalem (5:9; 6:1, 13a; 8:5a): They ask the wife several questions.
D. In regard to the wife's brothers (8:8-9)
    1. *The question* (8:8): "What will happen to our little sister?"
    2. *The answer* (8:9): "We will help her to remain pure until she marries."

PART FOUR

Prophets

Isaiah

PART ONE (Isaiah 1–12)
Isaiah tells of the Lord's indictment of Israel and Judah, then foretells their deliverance.

SECTION OUTLINE ONE (ISAIAH 1–2)
Isaiah describes the Lord's complaint against Judah, the future glory of Zion, and the coming day of the Lord.

I. GOD'S DEALINGS WITH ONE NATION (1:1-31): Israel
   A. **The iniquities** (1:1-19, 21-25, 28-31)
      1. *Judah's actions* (1:1-8, 16-24)
         a. They have rebelled (1:2).
         b. They have spurned and abandoned God and his laws (1:1, 3-4, 21-24).
         c. They have rejected God's correction (1:5-8): Their country lies in ruins, and their cities are barren.
      2. *God's response* (1:9-15, 25, 28-31): Israel was once faithful to God, but she turned from him, so he will pour out his fury on her.
         a. He will reject her sacrifices and refuse her prayers (1:9-15).
         b. He will pour out his anger upon her (1:25, 28-31): All the sinners will be completely destroyed.
   B. **The invitation** (1:16-19, 26-27): God urges his people to repent and to return to him, promising to cleanse and restore them.

II. GOD'S DEALINGS WITH ALL NATIONS (2:1-22)
   A. **Promised horror** (2:6-22): Isaiah foretells what will happen to those who have rebelled.
      1. *They will cower in fear* (2:6-10, 19-22).
      2. *They will be cast down* (2:11-13): The proud will be humbled.
      3. *They will be crushed* (2:14-18).
   B. **Promised hope** (2:1-5): Isaiah describes what the Lord will do in the future.
      1. *We will learn God's ways* (2:1-3): All nations will come to the Temple in Jerusalem for worship and instruction in the Scriptures.

2. *We will live God's ways* (2:4-5): The Lord himself will settle disputes and bring peace. Nations will beat their swords into plowshares and their spears into pruning hooks.

SECTION OUTLINE TWO (ISAIAH 3–4)
Isaiah describes God's judgment upon the rulers and daughters of Zion and Zion's future cleansing and glory.

I. THE CONDEMNATION (3:1–4:1)
   A. **God's judgment on the leaders** (3:1-15)
      1. *He will cut off their food and water supplies* (3:1).
      2. *Their armies will be destroyed* (3:2-3).
      3. *Anarchy will prevail* (3:4-12).
      4. *God himself will serve as the great prosecuting attorney* (3:13-15): The leaders and princes are the first to feel his wrath.
   B. **God's judgment on the women** (3:16–4:1)
      1. *Their perversions* (3:16, 18-23)
         a. They are haughty and self-centered (3:16): They walk around with their noses in the air, flirting with the men.
         b. They attire themselves in an extravagant way (3:18-23): They wear ornaments, headbands, and gaudy clothes and accessories.
      2. *Their punishment* (3:17-18, 24-26; 4:1)
         a. God will make their scalps bald from sores and scabs (3:17).
         b. He will strip them of their finery and their beauty (3:18, 24-26).
         c. Seven women will be forced to fight over one man (4:1).

II. THE CONVERSION (4:2-6)
   A. **God the Son will minister to the people** (4:2-3): The title "the branch of the LORD" refers to the Messiah.
   B. **God the Spirit will minister to the people** (4:4-6): Israel will be washed and cleansed of all its moral filth and will be protected by God's glory cloud!

SECTION OUTLINE THREE (ISAIAH 5)
This chapter describes God's judgment upon his vineyard.

I. THE PARABLE OF THE VINEYARD (5:1-7)
   A. **The identity of this vineyard—Israel** (5:1-2): God himself laid out this vineyard on a very fertile hill, planting in it the choicest vines.
   B. **The indictment of this vineyard** (5:3-7): At harvesttime, instead of the expected sweet grapes, it produced only bad fruit.

II. THE PAGANISM OF ISRAEL (5:8-24): Six judgments are pronounced against Israel for her sins.
  A. **First judgment** (5:8-10): The rich have bought up all the desirable property, leaving the rest of the people with nowhere to live.
  B. **Second judgment** (5:11-17): They have become a nation of God-rejecting drunks, living only for carnal pleasure.
  C. **Third judgment** (5:18-19): They are filled with deceit and have mocked God, daring him to punish them.
  D. **Fourth judgment** (5:20): They twist the truth, saying that right is wrong and wrong is right.
  E. **Fifth judgment** (5:21): They are wise and shrewd in their own eyes.
  F. **Sixth judgment** (5:22-24): They release the guilty for a bribe but deny justice to the innocent.

III. THE PUNISHMENT OF ISRAEL (5:25-30): The Lord's people will suffer punishment for their sinful ways.
  A. **Their dead bodies will rot in the streets** (5:25).
  B. **The Lord will bring foreign nations into Jerusalem, resulting in the captivity of the people** (5:26-30).

SECTION OUTLINE FOUR (ISAIAH 6–8)
Isaiah records his vision and new commission, his ministry of comfort to King Ahaz, and his message of destruction to the northern kingdom.

I. THE CALL OF THE PROPHET (6:1-13)
  A. **Isaiah and the heaven of God** (6:1-7)
    1. *Isaiah's vision* (6:1-4)
      a. What he sees (6:1): The Lord seated upon his exalted throne in glory
      b. What he hears (6:2-4): The mighty seraphim (angelic beings) praising God for his holiness
    2. *Isaiah's vexation* (6:5): This awesome sight causes Isaiah to cry out, acknowledging his own sin and that of his people.
    3. *Isaiah's visitation* (6:6-7): One of the angelic seraphim touches Isaiah's tongue with a burning coal from heaven's altar, purifying the prophet.
  B. **Isaiah and the God of heaven** (6:8-13)
    1. *Isaiah hears God's voice* (6:8a): God wants to know whom he should send as his messenger to his people.
    2. *Isaiah heeds God's voice* (6:8b-13): Isaiah volunteers.

II. THE CHRIST OF THE PROPHET (7:1-25)
  A. **Isaiah's first prophecy** (7:1-12): God sends the prophet to reassure young Ahaz, the terrified king of Judah.

1. *The need for this reassurance* (7:1-2): The southern tribe of Judah is threatened with invasion by the northern ten tribes and Aram.
2. *The nature of this reassurance* (7:3-9): God instructs Isaiah to assure Ahaz that this simply will not happen, for the enemy armies will soon be crushed and broken.
3. *The negative response to this reassurance* (7:10-12)
   a. The Lord's sign (7:10-11): God invites Ahaz to ask for any sign he might desire to validate Isaiah's promise.
   b. The king's scorn (7:12): Wicked Ahaz refuses, not allowing God to show his mighty power.
B. **Isaiah's second prophecy** (7:13-16): Many believe these verses predict the births of two babies, one to be born supernaturally in the distant future, the other to be born naturally in the immediate future.
   1. *The first baby* (7:13-14): This will be the Messiah, born centuries later to the Virgin Mary.
   2. *The second baby* (7:15-16): This will be Maher-shalal-hash-baz, born less than a year later to Isaiah and his wife. Ahaz is told that even before this baby is weaned, the enemy kings of both the northern kingdom and Aram will be dead.
C. **Isaiah's third prophecy** (7:17-25): He warns of a terrible Assyrian attack on Judah.

III. THE CHILDREN OF THE PROPHET (8:1-22): In this chapter Isaiah's own name and the names of his two sons are given prophetic significance by God himself (see 8:18). *Isaiah,* meaning "The LORD will save," refers to Israel's eventual restoration. *Shear-jashub,* meaning "A remnant will return," refers to Israel's return to the land after various deportations. *Maher-shalal-hash-baz,* meaning "Swift to the plunder," refers to the destruction of Judah's enemies.
A. **Isaiah's first message from God** (8:1-4): "Father a second son through your wife."
B. **Isaiah's second message from God** (8:5-16): "Tell Judah to neither fear nor compromise with her enemies."
C. **Isaiah's third message from God** (8:17-18): "Judah's enemies will soon be destroyed."
D. **Isaiah's fourth message from God** (8:19-22): "Tell Judah she will be punished if she turns to the occult instead of to me."

SECTION OUTLINE FIVE (ISAIAH 9–10)

Isaiah gives a message of hope concerning Israel's future and foretells the Assyrians' invasion of Immanuel's land.

I. GOD'S SON (9:1-7)
   A. **The twofold ministry of the Messiah** (9:1-5, 7)
      1. *Christ's first coming* (9:1-2): He displays his glory to both Jews and Gentiles living in Israel at that time.
      2. *Christ's second coming* (9:3-5, 7): He ushers in universal peace and rules the world in righteousness.
   B. **The twofold nature of the Messiah** (9:6): "For a child is born to us, a son is given to us."
      1. *The Messiah will be born as a human baby* (9:6a).
      2. *The Messiah will be sent as a gift from heaven* (9:6b).

II. GOD'S SOVEREIGNTY (9:8–10:34)
   A. **Regarding his friends** (9:8–10:11, 20-25)
      1. *The Lord will punish Israel* (9:8–10:11).
         a. At the hands of the Arameans and Philistines (9:8-21): Even though Israel is destroyed, the people will not repent and turn to the Lord.
         b. At the hands of the Assyrians (10:1-11): Assyria will destroy Israel but will not realize that it is the Lord allowing it to happen.
      2. *The Lord will protect and purify Israel* (10:20-25): Someday God's chosen remnant will turn to him and be forever restored to their land.
   B. **Regarding his foes** (10:12-19, 26-34)
      1. *He will destroy the Assyrians because of their pride* (10:12-15).
      2. *The results of this destruction* (10:16-19, 26-34)
         a. An angel will send a terrible plague among the troops (10:16-18, 26-32): They will be destroyed in a single night.
         b. Only a handful of soldiers will survive (10:19): A child will be able to count their number.
         c. God will cut them down as a woodsman fells trees (10:33-34).

SECTION OUTLINE SIX (ISAIAH 11–12)

Isaiah tells of the coming King and his Kingdom and recites Israel's salvation hymn.

I. THE PERSON OF THE MESSIAH (11:1-16)
   A. **His ancestry** (11:1): The Messiah will come from David's family.
   B. **His anointing** (11:2): God's Holy Spirit will rest on the Messiah, giving him unlimited power and wisdom.

C. His administration (11:3-5): His reign will be just and righteous as he defends the helpless and defeats the wicked.
D. His accomplishments (11:6-16)
  1. *The Messiah will usher in universal peace among mankind and perfect harmony among the animals* (11:6-9): Everyone will live together in peace.
  2. *All nations will rally to him* (11:10, 12a).
  3. *He will gather the outcasts of Israel from all over the world and will restore them to the land* (11:11, 12b-14): The jealousy between Israel and Judah will end, and they will join together to fight against their enemies.
  4. *He will build a highway of peace from the Red Sea to the Euphrates River* (11:15-16).

II. THE PRAISE TO THE MESSIAH (12:1-6): Isaiah recites a song of praise that will be sung by God's people when the Messiah accomplishes his mission.
  A. Their thanksgiving to the Lord (12:1-3)
    1. *For forgiving them* (12:1): God was angry with them, but now he has forgiven them.
    2. *For strength and deliverance* (12:2-3): God is their salvation; they trust in him and are not afraid.
  B. Their testimony to the world (12:4-6): The people of Israel will praise God for what he has done and will become a testimony to the nations of God's presence among them.

PART TWO (Isaiah 13–23)
Isaiah tells of the Lord's judgment of the nations.

SECTION OUTLINE SEVEN (ISAIAH 13–14)
Isaiah prophesies judgment for Babylon, Assyria, and Philistia.

I. GOD'S CONDEMNATION OF HIS FOES (13:1-22; 14:12-32)
  A. Babylon (13:1-22; 14:12-27)
    1. *The destruction foretold* (13:1-22)
      a. The severity of the destruction (13:6-16)
        (1) All the people will be paralyzed with fear as God destroys Babylon (13:6-8).
        (2) The land will be devastated, and the people will be destroyed (13:9).
        (3) The very heavens will be blackened (13:10): No light will shine from the sun, the stars, or the moon.
        (4) Survivors will be as scarce as gold (13:11-13).
        (5) Babylon's armies will flee to their own lands like hunted deer (13:14).
        (6) The children will be killed and the wives raped

(13:15-16): Everyone who is caught will be run through by a sword, and all their homes will be sacked.

  b. The source of the destruction (13:1-5, 17-22): God will raise up the Medes and Persians against Babylon.

2. *The destruction fulfilled (14:12-27)*

  a. The symbol (14:12-14): Some believe these verses refer to the fall of Satan, history's first rebel, who was cut down because of his terrible pride and self-will. If this is the case, Isaiah here uses the Devil as an object lesson in regard to Babylon's destruction, due to its arrogance and cruelty.

  b. The slaughter (14:15-27): Babylon's cities will be destroyed, its people will be killed, and the land will become a desolate and deserted swampland.

B. Philistia (14:28-32)

1. *The warning* (14:28-30): God tells Philistia not to rejoice over the death of its terrible oppressor (Shalmaneser V), for his son will prove to be an even greater scourge!

2. *The weeping* (14:31-32): The Philistines will soon begin wailing, for their nation is doomed.

II. GOD'S COMPASSION ON HIS FRIENDS (14:1-11)

  A. The salvation (14:1-3): God promises to forgive, restore, and resettle his people in their land forever.

  B. The sarcasm (14:4-11): Israel is invited to taunt its enemies, especially Babylon.

SECTION OUTLINE EIGHT (ISAIAH 15–18)
Isaiah prophesies judgment for Moab, Damascus, and Ethiopia.

I. PROPHECIES AGAINST MOAB (15:1–16:14)

  A. The suffering of Moab (15:1, 9; 16:1-5, 13-14)

  1. *Its two key cities, Ar and Kir, will be destroyed in one night* (15:1).

  2. *Its women will be abandoned like homeless birds* (16:1-5): They will cry out for help and for defense against their enemies.

  3. *Within three years, few of the people will be left alive* (16:13-14): The glory of Moab will be ended.

  4. *Lions will hunt down the survivors* (15:9): The streams will run red with blood.

  B. The sin of Moab (16:6): The land is filled with arrogance and insolence.

  C. The sorrow over Moab (15:2-8; 16:7-12)

  1. *The tears of the people* (15:2-4, 8; 16:7-8, 12): The Moabites will show their grief.

  a. They will shave their heads and cut off their beards (15:2).

      b. They will put on sackcloth (15:3-4): They will wander the
         streets, and weeping will be heard from every home.

      c. Their cries will be heard throughout the land (15:8; 16:7-8).

      d. They will pray to their idols for help (16:12): They will
         cry to the gods in their temples, but no one will save
         them.

    2. *The tears of the prophet* (15:5-7; 16:9-11): Isaiah himself
       weeps over the Moabite judgment!

II. PROPHECIES AGAINST ARAM AND THE NORTHERN KINGDOM (17:1-14)
    A. The severity (17:1-6, 9-11): First, both nations will be punished
       for their terrible idolatry.
    B. The salvation (17:7-8, 12-14): Finally, one nation (Israel) will
       turn to God and be delivered!

III. PROPHECIES AGAINST ETHIOPIA (18:1-7): Destruction will come to
    Ethiopia.
    A. Ethiopia, the strong nation (18:1-4): It is feared far and wide for
       its mighty power to destroy other nations.
    B. Ethiopia, the stricken nation (18:5-6): God himself will cut down
       the Ethiopian armies as a man prunes his vineyard, even as they
       plan to destroy Jerusalem.
    C. Ethiopia, the saved nation (18:7): During the glorious Millen-
       nium, the people will bring their gifts to the Lord in Jerusalem!

SECTION OUTLINE NINE (ISAIAH 19:1–21:16)
Isaiah prophesies judgment for Egypt, Ethiopia, Babylon, Edom, and
Arabia.

I. GOD'S DEALINGS WITH EGYPT (19:1–20:6)
    A. The sentence on Egypt (19:1-3, 5-17): That nation receives a
       fourfold punishment from God because of its sin.
      1. *Dread* (19:1, 16-17): The hearts of the people are filled with
         fear, especially upon hearing the mention of Israel.
      2. *Discord* (19:2): God sets them fighting, one against another.
      3. *Dumbness* (19:3, 11-15): God turns the wisdom of their sages
         into foolishness and stupidity.
      4. *Drought* (19:5-10): The Nile River fails to flood, causing the
         fish and crops to die.
    B. The slave master over Egypt (19:4; 20:1): This refers to the Assyr-
       ian king Sargon, who captures the land and deports its citizens.
    C. The sign against Egypt (20:2-6)
      1. *The motion* (20:2): For a space of three years, Isaiah is
         commanded to walk around naked and barefooted!
      2. *The meaning* (20:3-6): God will later allow Assyria to strip and
         humble the land of Egypt.

    D. The salvation of Egypt (19:18-25)

        1. *Egypt's speech* (19:18): Five of its cities will begin to speak the Hebrew language!

        2. *Egypt's sacrifices* (19:19, 21): An altar, on which sacrifices will be offered to God, will be built in one of these five cities.

        3. *Egypt's supplication* (19:20, 22): God will hear the prayers of the Egyptians and will deliver them.

        4. *Egypt's safety* (19:23-25): A highway will connect Egypt with Israel and Assyria, thus guaranteeing the unity and safety of all three nations!

  II. GOD'S DEALINGS WITH BABYLON (21:1-10)

    A. Babylon's destruction foretold (21:1-4)

        1. *The revelation to the prophet* (21:1-2): Isaiah sees this terrible event occurring in a vision from God.

        2. *The response by the prophet* (21:3-4): Isaiah is physically sickened at the slaughter that will soon occur.

    B. Babylon's destruction fulfilled (21:5-10)

        1. *The attack* (21:5-7): Isaiah refers to a banquet, likely referring to Belshazzar's banquet in process when the Medes and Persians attack Babylon (see Daniel 5).

        2. *The announcement* (21:8-10): It consists of the frightful words *"Babylon is fallen!"*

  III. GOD'S DEALINGS WITH EDOM (21:11-12): The divine message to Edom is: "Your judgment day is at hand! Your only hope is to repent!"

  IV. GOD'S DEALINGS WITH ARABIA (21:13-17): Within a year this mighty nation will be reduced to a few survivors!

SECTION OUTLINE TEN (ISAIAH 22–23)

Isaiah prophesies judgment for Edom, Arabia, Jerusalem, Tyre, and Sidon.

  I. GOD'S JUDGMENT ON JERUSALEM (22:1-14)

    A. The revelation (22:1-7): In a vision Isaiah sees the city of Jerusalem being attacked by a powerful and cruel enemy (probably either Assyria or Babylon).

    B. The reason (22:8-14): Judah in the past has turned against God, so God will turn against Judah.

  II. GOD'S JUDGMENT ON SHEBNA (22:15-25)

    A. His removal (22:15-19, 25): God will discard this greedy and pompous palace administrator, who disgraces his office, and will allow him to be carried off into captivity.

    B. His replacement (22:20-24): Eliakim, the godly son of Hilkiah, will be chosen to assume the duties of the disgraced Shebna.

III. GOD'S JUDGMENT ON TYRE (23:1-18)
  A. **The destruction of Tyre by the Lord** (23:1-14)
    1. *The travail* (23:1-14)
      a. The sorrow (23:1-7): Isaiah tells the merchants to weep over the coming destruction of Tyre's harbors. No more will they receive cargo from the various far-flung ports of the world.
      b. The source (23:8-14): God himself will bring the Babylonian armies against Tyre to accomplish what the Assyrians can't do, namely, to totally destroy its palaces and make its very location a heap of ruins!
    2. *The time* (23:15-17): For seventy years Tyre will be forgotten. After this, God will revive it, but to no avail, for soon Tyre will return to its sinful ways!
  B. **The devotion of Tyre to the Lord** (23:18): Tyre will eventually give a portion of her vast riches to help support the priests of God!

P A R T   T H R E E   (Isaiah 24–27)
Isaiah tells of the future judgment of all peoples and the future blessing of God's people.

SECTION OUTLINE ELEVEN (ISAIAH 24–25)
Isaiah prophesies universal judgment and God's ultimate triumph over evil.

I. THE COMING GREAT TRIBULATION (24:1-13, 16b-22): While the immediate context here may refer to the devastation of Judah following the Babylonian captivity, it would seem to have its ultimate fulfillment during the Great Tribulation.
  A. **The Great Tribulation—what it is** (24:1-4, 6-13, 16b-22)
    1. *God himself will lay waste to the entire earth* (24:1): The earth will become a great wasteland, and the people will be scattered.
    2. *All people and fallen angels will be judged* (24:2-4, 21-22): No one will be spared from God's wrath, and the fallen angels will be put in prison.
    3. *Very few will survive* (24:6): A curse will consume the earth and its people, who will be destroyed by fire.
    4. *Happiness will no longer exist* (24:7-13): All joy in life will be gone.
    5. *Evil and treachery will be everywhere* (24:16b-18): People possessed by sheer terror will flee from one danger only to be confronted with something even more horrifying.
    6. *The earth will stagger like a drunkard* (24:19-20): It will fall and collapse like a tent, unable to rise again because of the weight of its sins.

B. The Great Tribulation—why it occurs (24:5): Humanity has twisted the laws of God and has broken his holy commands.

II. THE COMING GLORIOUS MILLENNIUM (24:14-16a, 23; 25:1-12)
   A. The promise (24:14-16a, 23)
      1. *Joy and singing will fill the earth* (24:14-16a): The people will shout and sing for joy, declaring God's majesty.
      2. *God's glory will outshine the sun* (24:23): He will rule gloriously from Jerusalem.
   B. The praises (25:1-12): Isaiah now worships and exalts God for the following:
      1. *His faithfulness* (25:1): God promises wonderful things, and he accomplishes them.
      2. *His salvation of the Gentiles* (25:2-3): Strong nations will declare his glory, and ruthless nations will adore him.
      3. *His mercy* (25:4-5): He is kind to the poor and needy.
      4. *His provision* (25:6-7): He will spread a feast for everyone and will remove the cloud of gloom hanging over the earth.
      5. *His victory over death* (25:8): He will swallow up death forever.
      6. *His restoration of Israel* (25:9): Israel will rejoice in his salvation.
      7. *His judgment of his enemies* (25:10-12): God will destroy the Moabites and will end their evil works.

SECTION OUTLINE TWELVE (ISAIAH 26–27)
These chapters, recorded in the lyrics of two songs, contain Isaiah's messages of God's ultimate exaltation of Israel.

I. STANZA ONE—ISRAEL'S SAVIOR (26:1-15): This part of the song will be sung as Israel's testimony to God during the Millennium. It will do three things:
   A. Thank God for his strength and peace (26:1-6)
   B. Thank God for his righteous judgment (26:7-11)
   C. Thank God for his uniqueness (26:12-15): He alone, unlike the dead idols Israel once worshiped, is the true and only God.

II. STANZA TWO—ISRAEL'S SUFFERING (26:16-18; 27:7-11): It will speak of two things:
   A. The sin (26:16; 27:7-11): God himself allows Israel's suffering as punishment for sin.
   B. The symbol (26:17-18): Israel suffers as a woman giving birth.

III. STANZA THREE—ISRAEL'S SALVATION (26:19; 27:12-13): Israel will experience two things:
  A. Resurrection from the dead (26:19)
  B. Restoration to the land (27:12-13)

IV. STANZA FOUR—ISRAEL'S SECURITY (Isaiah 26:20-21; 27:1-6): Israel will enjoy two things:
  A. Protection during the Great Tribulation (Isaiah 26:20-21; 27:1)
  B. Productivity during the glorious Millennium (Isaiah 27:2-6)

P A R T   F O U R   (Isaiah 28–35)
Isaiah conveys six woes, or messages of judgment, against Israel, Jerusalem, and the surrounding nations (28–33), and a message of blessing for Israel (34–35).

SECTION OUTLINE THIRTEEN (ISAIAH 28–29)
Isaiah prophesies his first three messages of woe—against Ephraim, Jerusalem, and Lebanon.

I. ISRAEL'S REJECTION (28:1-4, 7-29; 29:1-4, 9-16)
  A. The northern ten tribes (28:1-4)
    1. *The sin* (28:1): The northern kingdom has become a nation of arrogant drunkards.
    2. *The suffering* (28:2-4): God will bring the Assyrians against his people, resulting in their deportation.
  B. The southern two tribes (28:7-29; 29:1-4, 9-13, 15-16)
    1. *The perversions* (28:7-10, 14-15; 29:9, 15-16)
      a. Drunkenness (28:7-8): The priests and prophets are unable to carry out their responsibilities.
      b. Disdain (28:9-10): The religious leaders ridicule Isaiah's warning.
      c. Disbelief (28:14-15; 29:9)
        (1) In God's power (28:14-15): In time of danger, they turn to Egypt for help.
        (2) In God's promise (29:9)
      d. Deceit (29:15-16): They attempt to hide both their sin and themselves from God.
    2. *The punishment* (28:11-13, 16-22; 29:1-4, 10-13): God's terrible wrath upon his people will be twofold:
      a. For Judah, the horrors of the Babylonian Captivity (28:11-13, 17-22; 29:1-4): The people refuse to listen to God, so he will send the enemy like a flood to destroy them.
      b. For all Israel, a spiritual sleep, causing the people in their blindness to later reject their own Messiah (28:16;

29:10-13): The events of the future have been made like a sealed book.

3. *The parable* (28:23-29): Isaiah compares God's workings among the nations to those of a farmer working his soil.

II. ISRAEL'S RESTORATION (28:5-6, 16; 29:5-8, 17-24)
   A. **The Redeemer** (28:16): Jesus Christ himself is Israel's chief cornerstone.
   B. **The redemption** (28:5-6; 29:5-8, 17-24)
      1. *He will provide justice and strength for his people* (28:5-6): He will be the pride and joy of the remnant.
      2. *He will provide victory and protection for his people* (29:5-8, 20, 22): Israel's enemies will disappear, and the people will no longer be afraid.
      3. *He will provide healing and joy for his people* (29:17-19, 21, 23-24): The fields will become fertile and lush, the deaf will hear, the blind will see, and justice will prevail.

SECTION OUTLINE FOURTEEN (ISAIAH 30–31)
Isaiah prophesies his fourth and fifth messages of woe, both of which warn against making an alliance with Egypt.

I. THE DEVASTATION UPON ISRAEL (30:1-14, 16-17; 31:1-3)
   A. **What Israel has done to God** (30:1-11): They make plans without consulting God, they demand that their prophets cease from preaching on sin, and they listen only to soothing sermons.
   B. **What God will do to Israel** (30:12-14, 16-17)
      1. *His judgment will fall on them like a bulging wall* (30:12-14): They will be smashed like pieces of pottery.
      2. *A thousand of them will flee from one enemy soldier* (30:16-17): They have put their trust in Egypt instead of in God and will be punished for it.

II. THE INVITATION TO ISRAEL (30:15, 18; 31:6-7): God issues invitations urging his people to repent and to return to him.

III. THE SALVATION OF ISRAEL (30:19-33; 31:4-5): The Lord will do several things for Israel:
   A. **Comfort his people and hear their prayers** (30:19): God will be gracious and respond to their cries.
   B. **Teach and guide them** (30:20-22)
   C. **Give them abundant crops** (30:23-26): The animals will be well fed, and the sun and moon will be bright.
   D. **Defeat their enemies** (30:27-28, 30-33; 31:4-5, 8-9): The Lord will come and sift out the proud nations and will lead them to destruction.
   E. **Fill their hearts with joy** (30:29): They will sing songs like those sung at holy festivals.

I. ISRAEL'S FUTURE: The Wonders (32:1-8, 15-20; 33:16-24): Here the prophet speaks concerning the Millennium.
  A. **The ministry of the Son of God** (32:1-8; 33:16-24): The Messiah himself will appear in all his glory and beauty to accomplish a fivefold ministry:
    1. *To reign as earth's righteous king* (32:1): Honest princes will rule under him.
    2. *To restore and regenerate Israel* (32:2-4): Everyone will look to God and will listen to him.
    3. *To right all wrongs* (32:5-8): The ungodly will be exposed, but generous people will be blessed for all they do.
    4. *To meet the needs of all people* (33:16): They will have a fortress, food, and water.
    5. *To usher in universal peace* (33:18-24): The Lord will reign and be the judge and king. He will care for his people and save them.
  B. **The ministry of the Spirit of God** (32:15-20)
    1. *To anoint the people of God* (32:15): The Spirit will be poured down from heaven.
    2. *To bring about worldwide justice* (32:16-17): The righteousness of God will bring peace.
    3. *To guarantee abundant crops* (32:18-20): Wherever the people plant seed, they will have bountiful crops.
II. ISRAEL'S PRESENT: The Warnings (32:9-14; 33:1-15): Here the prophet speaks concerning his own day.
  A. **He warns the women of Israel** (32:9-14).
    1. *Hear God's word* (32:9-10): The harvest will not take place, because they have been lazy.
    2. *Heed God's word* (32:11-14): Their land will be overgrown, and their homes will be gone.
  B. **He warns the warriors of Assyria** (33:1-15): Judah will be threatened and terrified by the advancing Assyrian troops.
    1. *The prayer for deliverance* (33:2-4): Judah wants to be rescued from Assyrian domination.
    2. *The promise of deliverance* (33:1, 5-15)
      a. The Assyrian destroyers will be destroyed themselves (33:1): They have never felt destruction, but they will be betrayed and destroyed.
      b. The Assyrian armies will be cut down like thorns and burned (33:5-15): God will show his power and might against the Assyrians.

I. GOD'S GRIEVOUS PUNISHMENT (34:1-17)
   A. **Judgment upon all nations** (34:1-4): These verses refer to the
      coming Great Tribulation.
      1. *The world's armies will be destroyed* (34:1-2): The Lord's
         anger will be brought down upon them.
      2. *The mountains will flow with the blood of unburied corpses*
         (34:3): The bodies of the dead will be left unburied.
      3. *The heavens will dissolve, and the stars will fall* (34:4): They
         will be like withered leaves and fruit falling from a tree.
   B. **Judgment upon one nation** (34:5-17): This doomed nation is
      Edom.
      1. *The severity of God's judgment* (34:5-15)
         a. Edom's people will be cut down like animals (34:5-8): The
            Lord's sword will be covered in blood and fat as if used for
            sacrifices.
         b. The ground will be covered with fire (34:9): Even the
            streams will be filled with burning pitch.
         c. The land will become desolate and uninhabited (34:10-15).
      2. *The surety of God's judgment* (34:16-17): He guarantees all
         this by putting it in writing!

II. GOD'S GLORIOUS PROVISION (35:1-10): This chapter refers to the
    Millennium.
    A. **Life in the perfect age—the characteristics** (35:1-2, 5-10)
       1. *The deserts will bloom* (35:1-2, 6-7): The lame will walk, and
          the mute will shout and sing.
       2. *The blind will see, and the deaf will hear* (35:5).
       3. *A Highway of Holiness will be built* (35:8-10).
    B. **Life in the present age—the challenge** (35:3-4): The glorious fact
       of the coming Millennium should serve as strength and comfort
       to all believers living in difficult times.

PART FIVE (Isaiah 36–39)
A historical section is included, telling of an Assyrian attack and of
Hezekiah's sickness and recovery.

SECTION OUTLINE SEVENTEEN (ISAIAH 36–37)
These chapters contain historical information, drawing the curtain
on the Assyrian crisis. Isaiah describes the siege of Jerusalem under
Sennacherib and the glorious deliverance by the Lord.

I. HEZEKIAH AND THE ASSYRIAN DANGER (36:1-22; 37:1-20): Just prior to
attacking Jerusalem, King Sennacherib of Assyria sends his military
commander to threaten, ridicule, and intimidate King Hezekiah and
his people.
   A. **Sennacherib and Hezekiah—Round One** (36:1-22; 37:1-7)
      1. *The men from the king* (36:1-3): Three of Hezekiah's top
      officials—Eliakim, Shebna, and Joah—meet with
      Sennacherib's military commander.
      2. *The message to the king* (36:4-21): In essence the commander's
      warning is twofold:
         a. What Judah cannot do (36:4-12, 18-21)
            (1) They cannot depend on Egypt (36:4-6): Pharaoh is
            unreliable.
            (2) They cannot depend on God (36:7-12, 18-21):
            Hezekiah has insulted God.
         b. What Judah should do (36:13-17): In a word, *surrender!*
      3. *The misery of the king* (36:22; 37:1): Hezekiah tears his
      clothes and dresses in sackcloth.
      4. *The man of God and the king* (37:2-7)
         a. Hezekiah's request to Isaiah (37:2-4): The king informs
         Isaiah of the terrible danger and begs him to pray for God's
         help.
         b. Hezekiah's reassurance from Isaiah (37:5-7): Isaiah tells the
         king that his foe Sennacherib will soon experience defeat
         and death.
   B. **Sennacherib and Hezekiah—Round Two** (37:8-20)
      1. *The Assyrian king to the Judean king* (37:8-13): "I'll destroy
      you!"
      2. *The Judean king to the King of kings* (37:14-20): "Please
      deliver us!"

II. HEZEKIAH AND THE ANGELIC DELIVERANCE (37:21-38)
   A. **God condemns Sennacherib** (37:21-29).
      1. *His pride* (37:21-28): The wicked king arrogantly ridicules the
      Holy One of Israel.
      2. *His punishment* (37:29): Sennacherib will be led back to
      Assyria with a hook in his nose and a bit in his mouth.
   B. **God consoles Hezekiah** (37:30-38).
      1. *The promises* (37:30-35): God assures the king of two things:

a. The land will soon enjoy abundant crops (37:30-32): In the third year, the people will be able to plant crops and vineyards.
b. The Assyrians will never enter Jerusalem (37:33-35): God will defend the city.
2. *The power* (37:36-38): That very night God's angel destroys 185,000 Assyrian troops! Sennacherib flees back to Nineveh, where he is killed by his own sons.

SECTION OUTLINE EIGHTEEN (ISAIAH 38–39)
These chapters contain historical information, raising the curtain on the Babylonian crisis. Isaiah describes King Hezekiah's sickness, healing, and self-exaltation.

I. THE HEALING OF HEZEKIAH (38:1-22)
   A. **The sickness of the king** (38:1): He is afflicted by a fatal illness.
   B. **The supplication by the king** (38:2-3): In desperation he cries out to the Lord.
   C. **The salvation of the king** (38:4-6): Isaiah tells Hezekiah that God will add fifteen more years to his life.
   D. **The sign for the king** (38:7-8): God says the shadow on Hezekiah's sundial will go backward ten degrees as a sign to assure him that he will be healed.
   E. **The summary by the king** (38:9-22)
      1. *Regarding his depression* (38:9-16)
         a. He feels betrayed (38:9-12): It seems unfair to be cut down while in the prime of life.
         b. He feels broken (38:13-16): It is like being torn apart by lions.
      2. *Regarding his deliverance (38:17-22)*
         a. What God has done (38:17-18): God has healed Hezekiah's body and has forgiven his sins.
         b. What Hezekiah will do (38:19-20): He will write songs of God's faithfulness and will sing them daily.
         c. What Isaiah tells Hezekiah's servants (38:21): Make an ointment of figs to spread over the king's boils so that he will recover.
         d. What Hezekiah asks (38:22): He asks for a sign assuring him that he will go to the Temple in three days.

II. THE HOSPITALITY OF HEZEKIAH (39:1-8)
   A. **The foolishness of the king** (39:1-2): He unwisely shows some visiting Babylonian officials all of Judah's treasures.
   B. **The faulting of the king** (39:3-8)
      1. *The rebuke* (39:3-7): Isaiah warns the king that someday the entire Babylonian army will be back, this time to plunder and enslave the people of Judah.

2. *The response* (39:8): The selfish king responds, "At least there will be peace and security during my lifetime!"

P A R T   S I X (Isaiah 40–48)
Isaiah conveys words of comfort and deliverance to God's people.

SECTION OUTLINE NINETEEN (ISAIAH 40)
This chapter is the key to the remainder of the prophecy and contains the prophet's message that after judging his people, God will comfort them.

I. AN INTRODUCTION TO THE GOD OF ISRAEL (40:1-26): This chapter describes eight attributes of God.
   A. **His mercy** (40:1-2)
      1. *He comforts* (40:1): He wants his people to be comforted.
      2. *He forgives* (40:2): Jerusalem has been pardoned and punished in full for her sins.
   B. **His glory** (40:3-5)
      1. *The messenger* (40:3): Isaiah predicts the ministry of John the Baptist.
      2. *The message* (40:4-5): John calls Israel to repentance in preparation for the glorious appearance of the Messiah.
   C. **His eternality** (40:6-9): God's word stands forever, unlike people, and his people are called to proclaim the Lord's coming.
   D. **His gentleness** (40:11): God will treat his own with the same tenderness a shepherd displays for his flock.
   E. **His omnipotence** (40:10, 12, 26): He is master over all nature.
   F. **His omniscience** (40:13-14): He knows and understands all things and needs no one to counsel or advise him.
   G. **His sovereignty** (40:15-17, 21-24)
      1. *All nations are as a drop in the bucket, as dust on the scales to him* (40:15-17).
      2. *He is enthroned above the circle of the earth* (40:21-22): He spreads out the heavens like a curtain and makes his tent from them.
      3. *He rules over all people* (40:23-24).
   H. **His uniqueness** (40:18-20, 25): He cannot be compared to anyone or anything.

II. AN INVITATION BY THE GOD OF ISRAEL (40:27-31)
   A. **Israel's problem** (40:27-28): Having apparently forgotten God's wondrous attributes, the Israelites conclude he does not know or care about them.
   B. **Israel's promise** (40:29-31): If they ask, God will renew their strength, allowing them to mount up with wings like eagles!

SECTION OUTLINE TWENTY (ISAIAH 41–42)
Isaiah assures his people that God will deliver them and introduces
the true servant of the Lord.

I. THE CONQUESTS OF CYRUS (41:1-7, 25-29): Some two centuries
before this Persian king is born, Isaiah predicts his victories, even
calling him by name (see also 44:28; 45:1).
  A. **The source of Cyrus's power** (41:1-4, 25-29): God himself
  directs and permits the victories of Cyrus.
  B. **The strength of Cyrus's power** (41:5-7): No nation is able to
  withstand his assaults.

II. THE CHOSEN OF GOD (41:8-24; 42:18-25): In these passages God
both consoles and corrects Israel, his chosen nation.
  A. **The consolation of Israel** (41:8-24): God has chosen Israel as his
  people.
    1. *The reason for God's choice* (41:8-9): Israel was selected
    because Abraham, its founder, was a special friend of God.
    2. *The results of God's choice* (41:10-24)
      a. Divine protection (41:10-16): He will strengthen, help, and
      uphold his people. Anyone who opposes them will be cut
      off by the Lord.
      b. Divine provision (41:17-24): He plants trees and provides
      water.
  B. **The correction of Israel (42:18-25)**
    1. *Their sin* (42:18-21): They will not listen or see what God
    does.
    2. *Their suffering* (42:22-25): They are robbed, enslaved, and
    imprisoned.

III. THE COMING OF CHRIST (42:1-9)
  A. **The Messiah's anointing** (42:1): He is filled by the Holy Spirit.
  B. **The Messiah's achievements** (42:2-4)
    1. *What he does not do* (42:2b, 3a, 4a)
      a. Shout or quarrel in public (42:2b)
      b. Crush the weak (42:3a)
      c. Stop until truth and righteousness prevail (42:4a)
    2. *What he does do* (42:2a, 3b, 4b)
      a. Acts with gentleness (42:2a)
      b. Brings justice to all (42:3b)
      c. Ushers in a reign of righteousness (42:4b): Even distant
      lands will wait for his instruction.
  C. **The Messiah's assurance** (42:5-9): God the Father himself guar-
  antees all of the above.

IV. THE CHORUS OF CREATION (42:10-17)
  A. **The singers** (42:10-12): All creatures on earth are urged to praise
  God.

B. The song (42:13-17): God is to be praised for two things:
1. *Defeating his enemies* (42:13-15)
2. *Delivering his people* (42:16-17)

SECTION OUTLINE TWENTY-ONE (ISAIAH 43–44)
Isaiah proclaims God's love for his servant Israel and God's superiority over idols.

I. ISAIAH REVEALS THE ONE TRUE GOD (43:1-28; 44:1-8, 21-28).
   A. Because of his grace (43:1-21; 44:1-8, 21-28): The Lord does many things for the people of Israel:
   1. *He protects them* (43:1-2, 14-17)
      a. From the fire and water (43:1-2)
      b. From their enemies (43:14-17)
   2. *He prefers them* (43:3-4): They are chosen above all other nations.
   3. *He gathers them* (43:5-9): He brings them back to Israel.
   4. *He appoints them as his special witnesses* (43:10-13; 44:6-8): They know that he alone is God.
   5. *He ushers in the Millennium for them with his Spirit* (43:18-21): He prepares all things for his people to come home.
   6. *He fills them with his Spirit* (44:1-5).
   7. *He forgives them* (44:21-24).
   8. *He rebuilds their Temple* (44:25-28): He causes Cyrus to command that Jerusalem be rebuilt and the Temple be restored.
   B. In spite of their sin (43:22-28): God does all the above even though Israel has often grieved him.

II. ISAIAH RIDICULES THE MANY FALSE GODS (44:9-20).
   A. The worthlessness of false idols (44:9-10): Those who make and worship them are fools.
   B. The wrath upon false idols (44:11): Someday God will judge all paganism.
   C. The workmanship of false idols (44:12-17): Isaiah describes the backbreaking labor required to shape these expensive idols.
   D. The wickedness prompting false idols (44:18-20): Those who carve out idols willfully blind themselves to the truth.

SECTION OUTLINE TWENTY-TWO (ISAIAH 45–48)
Isaiah proclaims God's message to Cyrus concerning the fall of Babylon, God's sovereignty, and God's deliverance of his people.

I. THE ANOINTED OF GOD (45:1-21): Isaiah predicts that Cyrus the Great, founder of the mighty Persian Empire, will function as God's chosen servant.

A. **Cyrus and the Gentile nations** (45:1-3, 14-21): He is divinely empowered to crush the Babylonians, Egyptians, Ethiopians, and other armies.

B. **Cyrus and the Jewish nation** (45:4-13): God allows Cyrus to be successful for the sake of Israel.

II. THE ANGER OF GOD (46:1-2; 47:1-15): Isaiah describes the judgment of Babylon by God.

  A. **The sins of Babylon** (47:6-8, 10)

    1. *Cruelty* (47:6-7): Babylon shows the Israelites no mercy.

    2. *Materialism and pride* (47:8, 10): The people feel self-sufficient and are pleasure-crazy.

  B. **The shame of Babylon** (47:1-4): Babylon is stripped and exposed to public viewing.

  C. **The suffering of Babylon** (46:1-2; 47:5, 9, 11-15)

    1. *Its idols are crushed* (46:1-2): The idols cannot protect the people, and the people cannot protect their idols.

    2. *Babylon is crushed, never to rise again* (47:5).

    3. *This destruction strikes suddenly, in a single day* (47:9, 11-15).

III. THE ATTRIBUTES OF GOD (45:22-25; 46:3-13; 48:1-22): In these passages Isaiah lists at least seven characteristics or attributes of God.

  A. **His salvation** (45:22-25; 48:20-22)

    1. *Offered universally, to all nations* (45:22-25): Every knee bows, and every tongue confesses allegiance to God's name.

    2. *Offered nationally, to Israel* (48:20-22): The Lord redeems the people of Israel.

  B. **His faithfulness** (46:3-4; 48:16-17)

    1. *In caring for his own* (46:3-4): He created them and has cared for them throughout their lives.

    2. *In correcting his own* (48:16-17): He teaches them what is good and which paths to follow.

  C. **His uniqueness** (46:5-9): No idol, regardless of its craftsmanship or costliness, can even remotely depict him!

  D. **His omnipotence** (46:10-13; 48:13-15)

    1. *He created all things* (48:13): He spoke, and everything came into being.

    2. *He has chosen a pagan Persian named Cyrus to accomplish the rebuilding of the Temple* (46:11-13; 48:14-15): Cyrus will destroy Babylon and allow the Temple to be rebuilt.

    3. *He does whatever he desires to do* (46:10): He is the only one who can tell what is going to happen, for he has it all in his control.

  E. **His eternality** (48:12): He is both the first and last.

  F. **His grace** (48:1-11): In spite of the Israelites' rebellion, he refines them in the furnace of affliction and redeems them for his name's sake.

G. His grief (48:18-19): His heart aches when he contemplates the blessings Israel would have enjoyed if that nation had obeyed him.

PART SEVEN   (Isaiah 49–57)
Isaiah foretells the Suffering Servant's work of restoring God's people to their land.

SECTION OUTLINE TWENTY-THREE (ISAIAH 49–50)
Isaiah prophesies of the Servant of the Lord (the Messiah), his mission, and his obedience. These chapters record for us the communication between the Father, his Son, and Israel.

  I. THE FATHER AND IMMANUEL (49:1-13; 50:4-9)
     A. The words of God to Christ (49:3, 5-13)
        1. *"I will display my glory through you"* (49:3).
        2. *"You will redeem and restore Israel"* (49:5): God commissions the Son to bring Israel back to him.
        3. *"You will be a light to the Gentiles"* (49:6): The Son will bring salvation to the ends of the earth.
        4. *"After suffering rejection, you will be honored by all nations"* (49:7): Kings will stand at attention, and princes will bow low when the Lord walks by.
        5. *"You will usher in the Millennium"* (49:8-13): Everything will be made perfect for Israel.
     B. The words of Christ to God (49:4): "My labor seems in vain, but I'll leave everything in your hands!"
     C. The words of Christ to himself (49:1-2; 50:4-9)
        1. *"He commissioned me before my physical birth"* (49:1).
        2. *"I am a mighty weapon in his hands"* (49:2): His words of judgment are as sharp as a sword.
        3. *"He gives me perfect wisdom, that I might comfort those in need"* (50:4).
        4. *"I obediently follow him, even when I suffer for it"* (50:5-7): He does not rebel or turn away from his Father's plan.
        5. *"He totally vindicates me"* (50:8-9): All his enemies are destroyed.

 II. THE FATHER AND ISRAEL (49:14-26; 50:1-3, 10-11)
     A. The complaint (49:14): Jerusalem feels that God has forsaken and forgotten her.
     B. The correction (50:1-3): God quickly points out that in reality it is Israel that has forsaken and forgotten him.
     C. The comfort (49:15-26): In spite of Israel's sin, God reassures his people that he still loves them.
        1. *The power of God's love* (49:15): It is stronger than that of a nursing mother for her infant.

2. *The picture of God's love* (49:16): He has engraved them on the palms of his hands.
3. *The promises of God's love* (49:17-26)
   a. Their enemies will be destroyed (49:17-18).
   b. They will be regathered to Jerusalem (49:19-21): The land will be filled with the people who come back.
   c. They will be honored by all nations (49:22-26): All of their needs will be cared for.
   D. **The challenge** (50:10-11): Fear and obey God! Look to him and not to yourselves.

SECTION OUTLINE TWENTY-FOUR (ISAIAH 51–52)
Isaiah conveys the Lord's encouragement to his faithful people and calls Israel to be ready for the coming of the Lord.

I. THE CHOSEN SEED (51:1-23; 52:1-12): Isaiah continues his discussion of God's dealings with the nation of Israel.
   A. **The patriarch** (51:1-2): God reminds the Israelites that they are descendants of Abraham and Sarah.
   B. **The promise** (51:3-8): These verses refer to the coming Millennium, at which time God promises to destroy Israel's enemies and to rule over the nations.
   C. **The prayer** (51:9-11): By faith Israel calls upon God to do all he promised to do.
   D. **The protection** (51:12-16): The Lord personally assures the Israelites that he will protect them.
   E. **The proclamations** (51:17-23; 52:1-6, 11-12): Jerusalem receives two divine "wake-up" calls!
      1. *First call—regarding God's punishment* (51:17-23): This punishment has to do with transferring the cup of God's wrath.
         a. It will be taken from the city of Jerusalem (51:17-22): They have suffered long enough! Their pain will be taken away.
         b. It will be given to the enemies of Jerusalem (51:23): They will drink of that terrible cup.
      2. *Second call—regarding God's power* (52:1-6, 11-12)
         a. Be clothed with God's strength (52:1-2).
         b. Be delivered by God's strength (52:3-6, 11-12): God's people will be delivered from Babylon, and they will recognize his voice.
   F. **The preaching** (52:7-10): Israel is to shout the glorious news of God's salvation from the mountaintops.

II. THE CHOSEN SERVANT (52:13-15): Here, it would seem, Isaiah presents the entire work of Christ in capsule form.
   A. **His earthly ministry** (52:13a): My servant prospers.
   B. **His crucifixion** (52:14): He is beaten, bloody, and disfigured.

C. His resurrection (52:13b): He is highly exalted.
D. His redemption (52:15): He startles many nations.

SECTION OUTLINE TWENTY-FIVE (ISAIAH 53)
This chapter contains the prophet's message describing the suffering of Messiah. In this supremely important chapter, Isaiah describes in graphic detail the crucifixion of Christ nearly 800 years before it actually occurs!

I. THE OVERVIEW (53:1-2)
   A. Facts about Isaiah's message (53:1): Isaiah realizes his Calvary predictions are so amazing that few will believe him.
   B. Facts about Isaiah's Messiah (53:2)
      1. *His background* (53:2a): Jesus grows up like a tender green shoot from a root in dry and sterile ground.
      2. *His beauty* (53:2b): There is nothing striking about his appearance—nothing to attract us to him.

II. THE ORIGIN (53:4, 10a): Who is responsible for the death of Christ?
   A. The Messiah's foes (53:4): He dies for the sins of those who hate him, namely, all of us!
   B. The Messiah's Father (53:10a): Amazingly, it is God's plan to bruise his own Son!

III. THE ORDEAL (53:3, 5-6, 8-9)
   A. He is belittled in life (53:3): Christ is despised and rejected by Israel's leaders.
   B. He is brutalized in death (53:5-6, 8-9).
      1. *He endures imprisonment and various unfair trials* (53:8): They lead him from prison to trial to death.
      2. *He is wounded, beaten, and bruised* (53:5-6): This happens for our sins.
      3. *He is buried like a common criminal* (53:9): He is put in a rich man's grave.

IV. THE OBEDIENCE (53:7): As a sheep awaiting shearing, the Messiah silently endures all his sufferings. He is led like a lamb to the slaughter.

V. THE OUTCOME (53:10b-12)
   A. His death assures spiritual life for countless multitudes (53:10b): They will enjoy a long life and will prosper.
   B. He is raised again and enjoys the fruits of his sacrifice (53:11).
   C. He is honored for his greatness (53:12).

SECTION OUTLINE TWENTY-SIX (ISAIAH 54–55)
Isaiah describes Messiah's mission and issues a call to accept
Messiah.

I. A NATIONAL PROCLAMATION—IN REGARD TO THE CITY OF GOD
(54:1-17): Isaiah describes the relationship between a special wife
and her husband.
  A. The grieving wife (54:1-4)
    1. *Who she is* (54:1): She represents Jerusalem, pictured both as
    a barren woman and as a sorrowing widow because of the
    sins of her youth.
    2. *What she is to do* (54:2-4): She is to enlarge her house,
    preparing for the multitude of children that will soon be hers.
  B. The glorious husband (54:5-17)
    1. *Who he is* (54:5): He is none other than her Creator and
    Redeemer, the Holy One of Israel and God of all the earth!
    2. *What he does* (54:6-17)
      a. God had once briefly punished Jerusalem (54:6-10): He
      now forever blesses her.
      b. The city is restored to a state of unparalleled beauty
      (54:11-12): The city is made of precious jewels.
      c. He instructs, protects, and prospers Jerusalem's citizens
      (54:13-17): They have a just government, and their enemies
      stay far away.

II. A UNIVERSAL INVITATION—IN REGARD TO THE GRACE OF GOD (55:1-9):
This is one of Scripture's greatest invitations.
  A. The participants (55:1a): It is only for the thirsty.
  B. The product (55:1b): Free wine or milk.
  C. The price (55:1c-2): It is absolutely free!
  D. The promise (55:3-5): This free drink saves one's soul!
  E. The plea (55:6-9): Sinners are urged to seek the Lord now, before
  it is too late.

III. A NATURAL ILLUSTRATION—IN REGARD TO THE WORD OF GOD
(55:10-11): Isaiah compares the weather to God's word.
  A. God's weather (55:10): The rain comes down from heaven to
  produce food for people's bodies.
  B. God's word (55:11): God's word comes down from heaven to
  produce food for people's souls.

IV. A PERSONAL APPLICATION—IN REGARD TO THE PEOPLE OF GOD
(55:12-13): Someday during the Millennium all believers will dwell
peacefully and joyfully in a perfect world!

SECTION OUTLINE TWENTY-SEVEN (ISAIAH 56–57)
Isaiah proclaims salvation for the Gentiles and grace for Israel's wicked leaders. He describes God's dealings with seven kinds of individuals.

I. GODLY INDIVIDUALS (56:1-8; 57:1-2, 14-21)
   A. **Those who do right** (56:1-2): God blesses those who are fair and those who honor his special day.
   B. **Saved Gentiles** (56:3a, 6-8)
      1. *They are not looked upon as second-class citizens* (56:3a): When they turn to the Lord, they are accepted as Jews are.
      2. *Their sacrifices are accepted* (56:6-7).
      3. *They experience God's joy in the Temple* (56:7-8): His Temple is a house of prayer for all nations.
   C. **Dedicated eunuchs** (56:3b-5): God gives them more honor than sons or daughters could ever offer!
   D. **The good who die young** (57:1-2): Sometimes God allows this to happen that they might be spared future evil.
   E. **The contrite** (57:14-21): Isaiah describes God's relationship with repentant and humble individuals.
      1. *Concerning the person of God* (57:15a): He is the holy, high, and lofty one who inhabits eternity.
      2. *Concerning the promises of God (57:14, 15b-21)*
         a. To safely regather the contrite (57:14): God clears the way for his people to return from captivity.
         b. To revive their spirits (57:15b): He refreshes them and gives them courage.
         c. To never again accuse them of sin (57:16-17): He does not fight against them forever.
         d. To heal, lead, and comfort them (57:18)
         e. To impart to them his peace (57:19): He heals them, and they praise him.

II. GODLESS INDIVIDUALS (56:9-12; 57:3-13)
   A. **Israel's religious leaders (56:9-12)**
      1. *The transgression* (56:10-12)
         a. They suffer from self-induced blindness (56:10): They give no warning when danger comes.
         b. They are greedy and totally self-centered (56:11): They follow their own paths, intent on personal gain.
         c. They are materialistic drunkards (56:12): They buy wine to get drunk.
      2. *The tragedy* (56:9): Because of their sin, God's flock is torn apart by the wild beasts of the field.
   B. **Israel's idolators** (57:3-13)
      1. *Their wickedness* (57:3-4): They are the offspring of adulterers and prostitutes, children of sinners and liars.

2. *Their worship* (57:5-11): They worship and love gods of stone.
3. *Their hope* (57:12-13): Nothing can save them but trust in God.

P A R T   E I G H T   (Isaiah 58–66)
Isaiah foretells of the coming of the Lord and the completion of the restoration of God's people.

SECTION OUTLINE TWENTY-EIGHT (ISAIAH 58–59)
Isaiah details the nation's hypocrisy and need for repentance.

I. ISRAEL'S SINS (58:1-14; 59:3-8)
   A. **Hypocrisy** (58:1-12): This sin surfaces during their last days of fasting.
      1. *The wrong way to fast* (58:1-5): They boast of their fasting and think God will be happy.
      2. *The right way to fast* (58:6-12)
         a. The facts (58:6-10): They should share their food and clothes with the poor and with relatives who need it.
         b. The fruits (58:11-12): They will be guided by the Lord.
   B. **Neglect** (58:13-14): Apparently the nation has not been properly observing the Sabbath.
   C. **Bloodshed** (59:3a): Their hands are those of murderers, and their fingers are filthy with sin.
   D. **Lying** (59:3b-4): No one cares about honesty.
   E. **Dishonesty** (59:5-8): They rush to do what is wrong.

II. ISRAEL'S SUFFERING (59:1-2, 9-11): Their sin brings about the following:
   A. **Unanswered prayer** (59:1-2): God does not hear their prayers because of their sins.
   B. **Despair** (59:9): They are in darkness and gloom because of their disobedience.
   C. **Spiritual blindness** (59:10): They wander about as though they are blind.
   D. **Utter frustration** (59:11): They look for justice, but none can be found.

III. ISRAEL'S SUPPLICATION (59:12-15a): The nation responds to Isaiah's rebuke and confesses its sin.

IV. ISRAEL'S SAVIOR (59:15b-21)
   A. **The plight of Israel** (59:15b-16): God sees there is no justice on earth, nor is there anyone who sides with Israel, so he personally intervenes.
   B. **The plans of God** (59:17-21): They are twofold: first, to punish sin, and second, to usher in righteousness.
      1. *The Great Tribulation* (59:17-18): At this time the entire world feels his wrath.

2. *The glorious Millennium* (59:19-21): During this period his name is glorified, and his people are wonderfully blessed!

SECTION OUTLINE TWENTY-NINE (ISAIAH 60–62)
Isaiah prophesies of Zion's glory and restoration.

I. THE SPLENDOR OF GOD'S PEOPLE (60:1-22; 61:4–62:12)
  A. Facts concerning their city (60:1-3, 5-7, 10-22; 62:1-4, 12)
    1. *Jerusalem will illuminate the entire earth* (60:1-3): All the nations will see its light.
    2. *It will be visited and honored by the Gentiles* (60:5-7, 10-16): The nations will come to see Jerusalem and bring its people goods.
    3. *It will be protected by God himself* (60:17-18): Violence will disappear from the land.
    4. *It will shine forever in its splendor* (60:19-21): The people will have no need for sun or moon, for the Lord will be their everlasting light.
    5. *Its population will vastly increase* (60:22): The smallest family will become a large clan.
    6. *It will be known by various new names* (62:1-4, 12): Isaiah prays for God to take away Israel's shame and to give them a new name.
      a. Hephzibah, meaning "City of God's Delight," and Beulah, meaning "Bride of God" (62:4): Jerusalem will lose its shameful names.
      b. "The City No Longer Forsaken" (62:12): They will be called "the Holy People" and "the People Redeemed by the LORD."
  B. Facts concerning their country (60:4, 8-9; 61:4-11; 62:5-11)
    1. *The promise to the nation of Israel* (60:4, 8-9; 61:4-9; 62:5, 8-11)
      a. Their children will care for them (62:5): God will rejoice over them.
      b. They will be regathered from among all other nations (60:8-9; 62:10-11): They will come home, bringing their wealth with them.
      c. They will rebuild long-destroyed cities (61:4).
      d. The Gentiles will serve Israel (61:5): They will feed the Israelites' flocks, plow their fields, and tend their vineyards.
      e. They will be a priestly nation (61:6): They will be called priests of the Lord.
      f. All reproach will be replaced with great honor among the Gentile nations (61:7-9): They will be a people the Lord has blessed.
      g. They will never suffer defeat again (62:8-9): They will be safe from their enemies forever.

2. *The praise of the nation of Israel* (61:10-11): In the future Israel will testify throughout the earth concerning God's faithfulness.
3. *The prayers for the nation of Israel* (62:6-7)
   a. The people are to give themselves no rest until Jerusalem is established (62:6): They will pray to the Lord night and day for fulfillment of his promises.
   b. The people are to give God no rest until Jerusalem is established (62:7): Jerusalem will be the object of praise throughout the earth.

II. THE SAVIOR OF GOD'S PEOPLE (61:1-3)
   A. **His anointing** (61:1a): The Messiah is appointed by the Father and anointed by the Spirit.
   B. **His assignments** (61:1b-3)
      1. *He preaches good news to the poor* (61:1b)
      2. *He comforts the brokenhearted* (61:1c)
      3. *He releases captives and frees prisoners* (61:1d)
      4. *He transforms ashes into beauty, sorrow into joy, and despair into praise* (61:2-3): The Lord is with them for his own glory.

SECTION OUTLINE THIRTY (ISAIAH 63–64)
Isaiah prophesies judgment and salvation.

I. THE GOD OF ISRAEL (63:1-9)
   A. **As a soldier** (63:1-6)
      1. *Question* (63:1a, 2): Who is the warrior dressed as a king, with his royal apparel stained with the blood of his enemies?
      2. *Answer* (63:1b, 3-6)
         a. The victor (63:1b): It is the Lord God himself.
         b. The victory (63:3-6): In righteous indignation God utterly crushes his enemies (probably at Armageddon) as a man would tread on grapes in a winepress!
   B. **As a Savior** (63:7-9): With love and mercy, God redeems and tenderly cares for Israel throughout the ages.

II. THE ISRAEL OF GOD (63:10–64:12)
   A. **Their rebellion** (63:10): Israel turned against God in the wilderness.
   B. **Their reflection** (63:11-14): The nation later remembered God's faithfulness during the Red Sea crossing.
   C. **Their realization** (63:15-16; 64:5-8): Israel freely acknowledges just who they are and who God is.
      1. *He is their eternal Father and Redeemer* (63:16): He has been with them from ages past.
      2. *In his sight even their righteous acts are as filthy rags* (64:5-7): Like autumn leaves they wither and fall and are swept away.

3. *He is the Potter; they are the clay* (64:8): They are formed by God's hand.
  D. **Their requests** (63:17-19: 64:1-4, 9-12)
    1. *To return and save them from all their enemies* (63:17-19; 64:1-4): They want God to treat them like they are still his people.
    2. *To forgive and forget all their sins* (64:9-12): They think they have suffered enough.

SECTION OUTLINE THIRTY-ONE (ISAIAH 65–66)
Isaiah gives glimpses of God's Kingdom established on earth.

I. THE PAGANS AND GOD (65:1, 17, 20-25; 66:6, 15-17, 22-24)
  A. **His current dealings with the Gentile nations** (65:1): God is revealing himself to non-Jewish people, and for a while he is choosing saved Gentiles instead of Israel to perform his will.
  B. **His future dealings with the Gentile nations** (65:17, 20-25; 66:6, 15-17, 22-24): The entire world will be subjected to universal punishment and then to perfection.
    1. *The punishment* (66:6, 15-17): A reference to the great tribulation
      a. God takes fiery vengeance on his enemies (66:6): There is a great commotion in the city, and a terrible noise comes from the Temple.
      b. Multiplied millions of sinners are slain at that time (66:15-17): The Lord comes with fire to mete out his punishment.
    2. *The perfection* (65:17, 20-25; 66:22-24): A reference to the glorious Millennium. Here are some features of this perfect age:
      a. There are no infant deaths (65:20a).
      b. All but the rebellious live to celebrate their 100th birthdays (65:20b): Only sinners die young.
      c. A time of great prosperity (65:21-23): They live in their own houses, eat from their own vineyards, and are blessed by the Lord.
      d. A time when prayers are instantly answered (65:24): Before the prayers are spoken, God answers them.
      e. The wolf, lamb, lion, and ox dwell in perfect harmony (65:25).
      f. The permanent creation of new heavens and earth (65:17; 66:22): No one thinks of the old ones anymore, for the new ones are so beautiful and will last forever.
      g. Universal worship of God (66:23): Everyone worships God regularly.
      h. A sober reminder of the holiness of God (66:24): The rebellious are devoured by worms and are destroyed by fire.

II. THE PEOPLE OF GOD (65:2-16, 18-19; 66:1-5, 7-14, 18-21)
   A. The old Israel (65:2-15; 66:1-5)
      1. *The rebellious ones* (65:2-7, 11-15; 66:3-4)
         a. Their perversions (65:2-5; 66:3)
            (1) Idolatry (65:2-3): The people have rebelled against God
               and have insulted him.
            (2) Witchcraft (65:4): They worship evil spirits and eat
               forbidden food.
            (3) Hypocrisy (65:5; 66:3): They are a stench in God's
               nostrils because they choose their own ways.
         b. Their punishment (65:6-7, 11-15; 66:4)
            (1) To be paid in full for their sins (65:6-7): They pay for
               their sins and for the sins of their ancestors.
            (2) To be cut down by the sword (65:11-12): They are
               destroyed because they did not listen to the Lord.
            (3) To suffer from hunger and thirst (65:13)
            (4) To cry out in sorrow (65:14)
            (5) To become a curse among the people (65:15): The Lord
               destroys them.
            (6) To bring upon them all these things (66:4): They do not
               listen to the Lord.
      2. *The righteous ones* (65:8-10; 66:1-2, 5): These verses refer to
         God's faithful remnant throughout the ages.
         a. They will be preserved and made prosperous in the land
            (65:8-10).
         b. They will be esteemed by God for their humility (66:1-2).
         c. They will hear his reassuring voice (66:5): They will hear
            God telling them not to be discouraged if they are scorned.
   B. The new Israel (65:16, 18-19; 66:7-14, 18-21)
      1. *The duration* (66:7-9): The nation will be reborn in a single
         day!
      2. *The description* (65:16, 18-19; 66:10-14, 18-21)
         a. The people will be totally forgiven (65:16): God will put
            aside his anger and forgive their evil.
         b. Jerusalem will be rebuilt and filled with rejoicing
            (65:18-19): There will be no more crying in the city.
         c. The city will enjoy financial prosperity (66:10-12): The
            wealth of nations will flow to the city, and it will be blessed
            with peace.
         d. The people will be comforted by God himself (66:13): He
            will comfort them as a mother comforts her child.
         e. The people will rejoice (66:14): When they see their city,
            they will be filled with joy.
         f. The people will see God's glory (66:18-21): They will come
            from every nation to his holy mountain.

Jeremiah

The book of Jeremiah is outlined in the following manner:

I. JEREMIAH AND JUDAH (1–45; 52)
   A. **Events preceding Jerusalem's fall** (1–38)
      1. *During King Josiah's reign* (1–20)
      2. *During the reigns of kings Jehoahaz, Jehoiakim, Jehoiachin, and Zedekiah* (21–38)
   B. **Events during Jerusalem's fall** (39; 52)
   C. **Events following Jerusalem's fall** (40–45)
      1. *The prophet and survivors* (40–44)
         a. In Judah (40–42)
         b. In Egypt (43–44)
      2. *The prophet and the scribe* (45:1-5)

II. JEREMIAH AND THE GENTILES (46–51): Jeremiah delivers prophecies against nine nations:
   A. **Egypt** (46)
   B. **Philistia** (47)
   C. **Moab** (48)
   D. **Ammon, Edom, Damascus, Elam, and the two Arab tribes of Kedar and Hazor** (49)
   E. **Babylon** (50–51)

SECTION OUTLINE ONE (JEREMIAH 1–2)
Jeremiah is called by the Lord, is consecrated for service in spite of his doubts, and preaches his first sermon.

I. JEREMIAH'S CONSECRATION (1:1-19)
   A. **His call** (1:1-5)
      1. *The official call* (1:1-3): It happens during the thirteenth year of King Josiah's reign.
      2. *The original call* (1:4-5): Jeremiah is chosen by God before his birth.
   B. **His concern** (1:6): Am I too young to be a spokesman to the world?
   C. **His consolation** (1:7-10): God's hand touches Jeremiah's mouth, assuring him that he will be given the very words to say.

D. His confirmation (1:11-19): God confirms Jeremiah's call by showing him two visions.
  1. *The almond-tree branch* (1:11-12): "It means that I am watching, and I will surely carry out my threats of punishment."
  2. *The pot of boiling water* (1:13-19): It means that "terror from the north will boil out on the people of this land."

II. JEREMIAH'S FIRST PROCLAMATION (2:1-37): It begins in 2:1 and ends in 3:5.
  A. The parable (2:1-3): God depicts Israel as a new bride in her younger days, anxious to please her husband.
  B. The perversions (2:4-13, 18-30, 33-37): This young bride later becomes an unfaithful wife, guilty of many sins.
    1. *The description of Israel's sin* (2:4-13, 18-20, 23-30, 36-37)
      a. Of idolatry (2:4-11, 20, 23-30): They worship foolish idols and defile the land.
      b. Of forsaking God (2:12-13): Instead of choosing the fountain of living water, they dig for themselves cracked cisterns that can hold no water.
      c. Of godless alliances (2:18-19, 36-37): They are led into exile as a result.
    2. *The depths of Israel's sin* (2:21-22, 33-35): They are so stained with guilt that no amount of soap or lye can make them clean.
  C. The punishment (2:14-17): Massive and fierce armies invade Israel from all directions, leaving her cities in ruins and her people as slaves.
  D. The pleading (2:31-32): God appeals to his people to hear and heed his word.

SECTION OUTLINE TWO (JEREMIAH 3–6)
In his second sermon, Jeremiah talks about divorce, disobedience, and destruction.

I. DIVORCE (3:1-25)
  A. The illustration (3:1-11): Jeremiah likens God's relationship with Israel to that of an innocent husband who divorces his adulterous wife and then, due to his great love for her, desires to rebuild the fractured marriage.
  B. The invitation (3:12-25)
    1. *The Lord's appeal* (3:12-22a)
      a. The basis (3:12-15): Israel must confess and renounce its terrible sins of idolatry in order to be restored.
      b. The blessings (3:16-22a): "'My wayward children,' says the LORD, 'come back to me, and I will heal your wayward hearts.'" God dwells among his people as a loving and faithful Father.

     2. *Jeremiah's prediction* (3:22b-25): Someday Israel will repent and return to God.

II. DISOBEDIENCE (5:1-31)
  A. Israel's terrible sins (5:1-5, 7-13, 20-31)
    1. *Dishonesty* (5:1-5)
      a. Among the poor and ignorant (5:1-4)
      b. Among the leaders (5:5)
    2. *Idolatry and immorality* (5:7-10): No matter what God does for the people, they worship idols and visit brothels.
    3. *Treachery* (5:11-13, 20-31): They lie about the Lord.
  B. Israel's terrible punishment (5:6, 14-19)
    1. *To be set upon by wild animals* (5:6): A lion, a wolf, and a leopard will tear them apart.
    2. *To be attacked and defeated by hostile armies* (5:14-19): God will bring disaster on his people and will make them serve foreigners because they refuse to listen to him.

III. DESTRUCTION (4:1-31; 6:1-30): Jeremiah predicts Jerusalem's destruction.
  A. The warnings (4:1-4, 14; 6:1-3, 8-10)
    1. *First* (4:1-4, 14): Plow up your hard heart.
    2. *Second* (6:1-3): If you are righteous, flee from Jerusalem.
    3. *Third* (6:8-10): The last warning before judgment.
  B. The wrath (4:5-9, 11-13, 15-18; 6:4-7, 11-26)
    1. *It comes from the north* (4:5-6): This refers to the Babylonian invasion in 606 B.C.
    2. *It destroys Judah's cities* (4:7-9, 11-13, 15-18): The Lord's tools are a burning wind and enemies.
    3. *It breaches Jerusalem's walls* (6:4-7): Why? Because the city is "wicked through and through."
    4. *It punishes everyone for their wickedness* (6:11-17): This includes the least to the greatest.
    5. *It refuses the people's Temple offerings* (6:18-26): Their sacrifices mean nothing to God because of their sins.
  C. The witness—Jeremiah (4:10, 19-31; 6:27-30)
    1. *His agitation over Israel's punishment* (4:10)
    2. *His agony over sinful Israel's future* (4:19-31)
    3. *His assignment as a tester of metals* (6:27-30): Jeremiah is to determine Israel's spiritual condition.

SECTION OUTLINE THREE (JEREMIAH 7–10)

Jeremiah condemns God's people who deceive themselves, he grieves over the sin and suffering of Israel, and he contrasts the one true God with false idols.

I. JEREMIAH'S CONDEMNATION OF THE PEOPLE (7:1–8:17)
   A. **They deceive themselves** (7:1-15).
      1. *The fallacies* (7:1-7): "Do not be fooled by those who repeatedly promise your safety because the Temple of the LORD is here."
      2. *The facts* (7:8-15): Jeremiah reminds them of the destroyed Tabernacle at Shiloh: "See what I did there because of all the wickedness of my people."
   B. **They destroy themselves** (7:16–8:17).
      1. *The command* (7:16): God instructs Jeremiah to cease praying for the people.
      2. *The corruption* (7:17-31; 8:4-15)
         a. They worship idols (7:17-18): They make cakes to offer to the Queen of Heaven and give drink offerings to other gods.
         b. They hurt themselves (7:19).
         c. They feel God's fury and are consumed (7:20).
         d. They are like the people God led out of Egypt (7:21-26): God continues to send prophets, but no one listens.
         e. They do not respond to truth (7:27-29): "It is no longer heard on their lips."
         f. They sin right before God's eyes (7:30): They set up idols in God's own Temple.
         g. They sacrifice their own children (7:31).
         h. They refuse to heed God's law (8:4-7): "They do not know what the LORD requires of them."
         i. They allow themselves to be governed by lying leaders (8:8-15): Their "wise" teachers twist the law.
      3. *The condemnation involved* (7:32–8:3, 16-17)
         a. The place where they worship idols will become the Valley of Slaughter (7:32-34): God will kill so many people that there won't be room for the graves.
         b. Enemy troops will desecrate their graves, digging up the bones (8:1-3): The people still alive will wish to be dead.
         c. Soldiers will bite them like poisonous serpents (8:16-17): They will die.

II. JEREMIAH'S RESPONSE (8:18–9:26)
   A. **Jeremiah's sorrow** (8:18–9:1, 10-12)
      1. *The extent* (8:18-19, 21-22; 9:1, 10-12)
         a. His heart is broken and beyond healing (8:18-19).
         b. His weeping continues day and night (8:21-22; 9:1, 10-12).
      2. *The explanation* (8:20): "'The harvest is finished, and the summer gone,' the people cry, 'yet we are not saved!'"

B. Judah's sins and sufferings (9:2-9, 13-26)
  1. *The sins* (9:2-9, 13-14)
    a. Adultery (9:2)
    b. Dishonesty (9:3): They only tell lies.
    c. Treachery (9:2, 4-9): They take advantage of one another.
    d. Idolatry (9:13-14): They worship images of Baal.
  2. *The sufferings (9:15-26)*
    a. To be given bitter food and poisoned water (9:15)
    b. To be scattered among distant lands (9:16)
    c. To be afflicted with anguish, death, and mourning (9:17-26)

III. JEREMIAH'S CONTRAST (10:1-25)
  A. Judah's false gods: (10:1-5, 8-16): Jeremiah preaches that idolatry—the worship of man-made gods—is foolish and destructive.
  B. Judah's true God (10:6-7, 17-25): Jeremiah tells of God's greatness, power, and coming judgment. He then pleads for God's gentle correction upon him but a pouring out of wrath upon the nations that refuse to recognize God as Lord.

SECTION OUTLINE FOUR   (JEREMIAH 11–15)
Jeremiah gives his fourth, fifth, and sixth sermons, concerning God's covenant with his people, a linen belt, and Judah's sin and suffering.

I. FOURTH SERMON (11:1–12:17)
  A. The covenant (11:1-13)
    1. *Past covenant* (11:1-8)
      a. The reminder (11:1-7): God promises to bless his people when he brings them out of Egypt if they obey him.
      b. The rejection (11:8a): Israel refuses to obey.
      c. The results (11:8b): "I brought upon them all the curses described in our covenant."
    2. *Present covenant* (11:9-13): Jeremiah's generation also disobeys the Lord and is judged.
  B. The command (11:14-17): Once again Jeremiah is instructed not to weep or pray for Judah.
  C. The conspiracy (11:18-23)
    1. *The plot against Jeremiah* (11:18-19): God tells him that his hometown people are planning to kill him.
    2. *The prayer by Jeremiah* (11:20): He prays for divine help—God's vengeance against his enemies.
    3. *The promise to Jeremiah* (11:21-23): God reassures his prophet that not one of the plotters will live.
  D. The complaint (12:1-4): Jeremiah is upset with God at the apparent prosperity of the wicked.
  E. The chastening (12:5-14)

      1. *Of Jeremiah* (12:5-6): God rebukes the prophet for
complaining and warns him not to trust anyone.

      2. *Of Judah* (12:7-14): The entire land falls victim to invading
hostile armies.

  F. The compassion (12:15-17): In spite of their terrible transgressions, God's love prompts him to someday regather and regenerate his people.

II. FIFTH SERMON (13:1-27)

  A. The instructions (13:1-7)

      1. *The order* (13:1-6): Jeremiah is to buy and bury a linen belt
and then later dig it up again.

      2. *The outcome* (3:7): It is mildewed, falling apart, and useless.

  B. The illustration (13:8-14): God rots and ruins the pride of Judah
as the ground does to the belt.

  C. The invitation (13:15-27)

      1. *Jeremiah's plea* (13:15-22): In vain he urges the nation to
repent of its pride and to return to God.

      2. *Judah's problem* (13:23-27): Their sin disease is terminal, and
their destruction is sure.

III. SIXTH SERMON (14:1–15:21)

  A. Jehovah and Judah (14:1-10)

      1. *The suffering* (14:1-6): A terrible drought plagues the land.

      2. *The supplication* (14:7-9): The people cry out to God for
mercy, wanting to know the reason for their suffering.

      3. *The sinfulness* (14:10): God explains that their sin has brought
about the suffering.

  B. Jehovah and Jeremiah (14:11–15:21): These verses record a
ninefold dialogue between the Lord and his prophet.

      1. *God* (14:11-12): "Do not pray for these people anymore."

      2. *Jeremiah* (14:13): "O Sovereign LORD, their prophets are
telling them, 'All is well—no war or famine will come.'"

      3. *God* (14:14-16): "I will punish these lying prophets, for they
have spoken in my name even though I never sent them."

      4. *Jeremiah* (14:17-22): "Night and day my eyes overflow with
tears. . . . LORD, have you completely rejected Judah?"

      5. *God* (15:1-9): "Even if Moses and Samuel stood before me
pleading for these people, I wouldn't help them. . . . I will
make my people an object of horror to all the kingdoms of the
earth."

      6. *Jeremiah* (15:10): "Oh, that I had died at birth! I am hated
everywhere I go."

      7. *God* (15:11-14): "All will be well with you, Jeremiah."

      8. *Jeremiah* (15:15-18): "Your words are what sustain me. . . .
[But] your help seems as uncertain as a seasonal brook."

      9. *God* (15:19-21): "If you return to me, I will restore you so you

can continue to serve me. . . . You are to influence them; do
not let them influence you!"

SECTION OUTLINE FIVE (JEREMIAH 16–20)
Jeremiah gives his seventh and eighth sermons, concerning what he
is to do and not do and a parable about a potter.

I. SEVENTH SERMON (16:1–17:27)
  A. **The prohibitions—what Jeremiah is not to do** (16:1-9)
     1. *Marry or have children* (16:1-4): They will die.
     2. *Mourn* (16:5-7): He is forbidden to sorrow over sinful Israel's
        punishment.
     3. *Mingle* (16:8-9): He cannot eat or fellowship with Judah's
        people.
  B. **The proclamations—what Jeremiah is to do** (16:10-18; 17:1-4,
     9-11, 19-27)
     1. *Explain* (16:10-13, 16-18; 17:1-4, 9-11)
        a. The reason for God's coming judgment (16:10-13, 18;
           17:1-4, 9-11): The people have sinned.
           (1) The description of their sin (16:10-13, 18): They
               worship idols and do evil deeds.
           (2) The depths of their sin (17:1-4, 9-11): Even their
               children worship idols, and their wealth comes from
               unjust means.
        b. The certainty of God's coming judgment (16:16-17): The
           people cannot hide from him.
     2. *Encourage* (16:14-15): Someday God will regather Israel and
        will resettle her in the land.
     3. *Exhort* (17:19-27): Jeremiah urges the people to observe a
        proper Sabbath.
  C. **The pair of personalities** (17:5-8)
     1. *The godless and fruitless man* (17:5-6): He is like a stunted
        shrub in the desert.
     2. *The godly and fruitful man* (17:7-8): He is like a deeply rooted
        tree planted by the riverbank.
  D. **The prayers** (16:19-21; 17:12-18)
     1. *First* (16:19-21): Jeremiah is confident that God is with him.
     2. *Second* (17:12-18): Jeremiah prays that God will not desert
        him.
II. EIGHTH SERMON (18:1–20:18)
  A. **The prophet and the potter** (18:1–19:15)
     1. *Jeremiah's first visit to the potter's house* (18:1-23)
        a. The parable (18:1-17)
           (1) What he sees (18:1-4): He views a potter remolding a
               previously marred clay pot.
           (2) What he hears (18:5-10): God tells Jeremiah that he is

the divine Potter and will soon remold his sinfully
marred vessel, Israel.

   (3) What he says (18:11-17): Jeremiah is to warn the
people that God will soon destroy them and their land
for idolatry.

  b. The plot (18:18): The Jewish leaders decide to attack Jeremiah for his fearless preaching.

  c. The prayers (18:19-23): Jeremiah cries out for God to
deliver him and to execute his enemies.

2. *Jeremiah's second visit to the potter's house* (19:1-15)

  a. The jar (19:1-2): "The LORD said to me, 'Go and buy a clay
jar.'"

  b. The judgment (19:3-15)

    (1) It is severe (19:3-9): Jeremiah warns that God will soon
pour out punishment upon Judah for its sin.

    (2) It is symbolic (19:10-15): The prophet is to smash the
jar beyond repair to illustrate what God will do to
Judah.

B. The prophet and the priest (20:1-18)

1. *The confrontation* (20:1-6)

  a. Jeremiah's imprisonment (20:1-2): Pashhur, Judah's wicked
high priest, arrests Jeremiah and has him whipped and put
in stocks overnight.

  b. Jeremiah's indictment (20:3-6): Upon being released, the
prophet predicts the evil priest's doom.

    (1) All his friends are killed or taken to Babylon (20:3-5).

    (2) He and his family are carried into captivity, never to
return (20:6).

2. *The complaints* (20:7-8, 10, 14-18).

  a. You have deceived me (20:7).

  b. "These messages from the LORD have made me a household joke" (20:8).

  c. "Even my old friends are watching me, waiting for a fatal
slip" (20:10).

  d. "I curse the day I was born!" (20:14-18).

3. *The constraint* (20:9): Jeremiah wants to quit, but he cannot,
for God's word burns in his heart like a fire.

4. *The consolation* (20:11-13): "But the LORD stands beside me
like a great warrior. Before him they will stumble. They cannot
defeat me."

I. ZEDEKIAH, JUDAH'S 20TH AND FINAL KING (21:1-14)
  A. **Zedekiah's request** (21:1-2): The king begs Jeremiah to plead
     with God for delivery from Nebuchadnezzar and the Babylo-
     nians.
  B. **Jeremiah's refusal** (21:3-14)
     1. *His warnings to the king* (21:3-7, 11-14)
        a. That God will help their enemies by making Judah's weap-
           ons useless (21:3-5, 11-14)
        b. That a plague will sweep Jerusalem, killing people and
           animals (21:6-7)
     2. *His warning to the people* (21:8-10): Choose between life and
        death!
        a. To stay in Jerusalem means to die (21:8-10).
        b. To surrender to Nebuchadnezzar means to live (21:9).

II. SHALLUM OR JEHOAHAZ, JUDAH'S 17TH KING (22:10-12): God
    commands Jeremiah to:
  A. **Stop weeping over the death of godly King Josiah** (22:10a).
  B. **Start weeping over the deportation of godless King Jehoahaz**
     (22:10b-12): He will never see his land again and will die in a
     distant country.

III. JEHOIAKIM, JUDAH'S 18TH KING (22:1-9, 13-23)
  A. **The choice** (22:1-9): The wicked king must choose between:
     1. *Repentance* (22:1-4): If the king repents, there will always be a
        descendant of David on the throne.
     2. *Ruin* (22:5-9): If he violates the Lord's covenant, everything he
        has will be destroyed.
  B. **The corruption** (22:13-14): The greedy and cruel Jehoiakim has
     built his lavish palace with forced labor.
  C. **The contrast** (22:15-17): The reigns of the godless Jehoiakim and
     Josiah, his godly father.
     1. *Josiah's blessed reign* (22:15-16): "Why did your father, Josiah,
        reign so long? Because he was just and right in all his
        dealings."
     2. *Jehoiakim's bloody reign* (22:17): "But you! You are full of
        selfish greed and dishonesty! You murder the innocent,
        oppress the poor, and reign ruthlessly."
  D. **The condemnation** (22:18-23)
     1. *Jehoiakim will die unlamented* (22:18): His family and
        subjects will not even care that he is dead.
     2. *He will be buried on a garbage dump like a dead donkey*
        (22:19): He will be dragged out of the city and dumped
        outside the gate.

3. *He is abandoned by his allies and friends* (22:20-23):
Everything is taken away, and he is in anguish.

IV. JEHOIACHIN OR CONIAH, JUDAH'S 19TH KING (22:24-30): Jeremiah
issues a twofold prophecy against the evil ruler:
   A. **About him and his mother** (22:24-28)
      1. *He is utterly removed from God's favor, discarded like a
      broken dish* (22:24-25, 28): He is abandoned and turned over
      to be killed.
      2. *Both he and his mother will die as captives in Babylon*
      (22:26-27): They never again will return to their own land.
   B. **About his sons** (22:29-30): None of them will ever sit on the
   throne of David.

SECTION OUTLINE SEVEN (JEREMIAH 23–25)
Jeremiah's 10th, 11th, and 12th sermons are about Judah's spiritual
leaders, a basket of figs, and the prophetic cup of anger.

I. TENTH SERMON (23:1-40)
   A. **Regarding Judah's politicians** (23:1-8)
      1. *The ruthless* (23:1-2): Jeremiah condemns Judah's godless
      shepherds, who destroy and scatter their flocks.
      2. *The responsible* (23:3-4): God appoints faithful leaders to
      govern his people.
      3. *The righteous* (23:5-8): "He will be a King who rules with
      wisdom." This is a reference to the coming Messiah.
         a. What he is called (23:5a, 6a)
            (1) King David's righteous branch (23:5a)
            (2) "The LORD Is Our Righteousness" (23:6a)
         b. What he does (23:5b, 6b-8)
            (1) Rules over the world (23:5b, 6b): The people are safe.
            (2) Regathers Israel (23:7-8): They live again in their own
            land.
   B. **Regarding Judah's prophets and priests** (23:9-40)
      1. *Their perversions* (23:9-11, 13-14, 16-38)
         a. Adultery (23:9-10): The land lies under a curse.
         b. Blasphemy (23:11): They do wicked things—even in the
         Temple.
         c. Idolatry (23:13-14): The prophets of Jerusalem are worse
         than the evil prophets of Samaria.
         d. Falsely representing God (23:16-32)
            (1) During the day (23:16-24): They claim he speaks
            through them, but they make up the words.
            (2) During the night (23:25-32): They tell false dreams,
            telling lies in God's name.
         e. Ridiculing Jeremiah, making light of God's warnings about

judgment (23:33-38): People use the Lord's name to give authority to their own ideas.
2. *Their punishment* (23:12, 15, 39-40)
   a. Their paths are made dark and slippery (23:12): They are chased till they fall.
   b. They are fed with bitterness and are given poison to drink (23:15): It is their fault that wickedness fills the land.
   c. They are forever cast out of God's sight (23:39-40): They are an object of ridicule throughout the ages.

II. ELEVENTH SERMON (24:1-10): Received in a vision, Jeremiah undoubtedly preached its contents later.
   A. When (24:1): After King Jehoiachin (Jeconiah) is carried off to Babylon.
   B. What (24:2-10)
      1. *The information* (24:2-3): Jeremiah sees two baskets, one filled with fresh figs, the other with rotten ones.
      2. *The explanation* (24:4-10)
         a. The good figs—the Jewish exiles already in Babylon (24:4-7)
            (1) God will bless them while they are in captivity (24:4-6): He has brought them there for their own good.
            (2) God later restores them to Jerusalem as his people (24:6-7): They follow him wholeheartedly.
         b. The bad figs—King Zedekiah and his corrupt leaders, who are destroyed by war, famine, and disease (24:8-10)

III. TWELFTH SERMON (25:1-38)
   A. The chronology (25:1-3)
      1. *During the fourth year of Jehoiakim's reign* (25:1): This is the first year of Nebuchadnezzar's reign in Babylon.
      2. *During the 23rd year of Jeremiah's ministry* (25:2-3): The Lord has been giving Jeremiah messages all this time, but the people have not listened.
   B. The contents (25:4-7)
      1. *Jeremiah's declaration* (25:4-6): For over two decades, the prophet has warned the people to repent.
      2. *Judah's deafness* (25:7): Jeremiah's messages fall on deaf ears and defiant hearts.
   C. The cup (25:8-38): Sinners are forced to drink the terrible cup of God's anger.
      1. *The historical cup* (25:8-14): It includes two nations:
         a. Judah (25:8-11): The Babylonian monarch Nebuchadnezzar is allowed to destroy their land and enslave the people for 70 years.
         b. Babylon (25:12-14): After these 70 years, Babylon is destroyed and enslaved.

2. *The prophetic cup* (25:15-38): Probably a reference to all nations during the great tribulation
   a. The victims (25:15-26): Jeremiah goes to all the kingdoms of the world and gives them the cup of God's anger.
   b. The victor (25:27-38): The Lord God Almighty is victorious over all nations.

SECTION OUTLINE EIGHT (JEREMIAH 26–28)
These chapters detail Jeremiah's sufferings for preaching the truth, and they use a yoke as an object lesson.

I. JEREMIAH'S SUFFERINGS (26:1-24)
   A. **His twofold warnings** (26:1-6)
      1. *God will deliver us if we repent of our evil* (26:1-3).
      2. *God will destroy us and the Temple if we refuse* (26:4-6).
   B. **His enemies' wrath** (26:7-11): They mob the prophet and threaten him.
      1. *Who they are* (26:7-10): Judah's wicked priests, prophets, and other people
      2. *What they want* (26:11): His death
   C. **His witnesses** (26:12-24)
      1. *The prophet himself* (26:12-15): Jeremiah reminds the crowd that his words are from God. If they kill him, they are killing an innocent man.
      2. *Certain political officials and other people* (26:16): They say that Jeremiah speaks in the name of the Lord and does not deserve death.
      3. *A number of wise old men* (26:17-23): They point to two historical events that support Jeremiah's ministry.
         a. Micah's example (26:17-19): When Micah prophesied, the people turned from their sins and worshiped the Lord. "Then the LORD held back the terrible disaster he had pronounced against them."
         b. Uriah's example (26:20-23): Uriah predicts the same destruction as Jeremiah.
      4. *The royal secretary, Ahikam, son of Shaphan* (26:24): He stands with Jeremiah to persuade the court not to turn him over to the mob to be killed.
II. JEREMIAH'S SYMBOL (27:1–28:17)
   A. **His object lesson** (27:1-22)
      1. *What it is* (27:1-2): Jeremiah is to make a yoke and to fasten it on his neck with leather thongs.
      2. *What it means* (27:3-22)
         a. To certain nations it symbolizes destruction (27:3-11): Five pagan countries (Edom, Moab, Ammon, Tyre, and Sidon)

will fall victim to Nebuchadnezzar and his Babylonian
armies.
    b. To the chosen nation (Judah), it symbolizes either life or
    destruction (27:12-22): Jeremiah says, "Surrender to the
    king of Babylon, and you will live."
  B. **His opposition** (28:1-17): A prophet from Gibeon now confronts
  Jeremiah.
    1. *Hananiah's deceit* (28:1-9)
      a. Hananiah (28:1-4): God has told me there will be peace in
      two years! Therefore, Jeremiah is wrong!
      b. Jeremiah (28:5-9): "A prophet who predicts peace must
      carry the burden of proof. Only when his predictions come
      true can it be known that he is really from the LORD."
    2. *Hananiah's defiance* (28:10-11): He takes the yoke off
    Jeremiah's neck and breaks it.
    3. *Hananiah's doom* (28:12-17): God tells Jeremiah to say to
    Hananiah that he will die for his sins that very year. Two
    months later Hananiah dies.

SECTION OUTLINE NINE (JEREMIAH 29)

In this chapter Jeremiah records the contents of three letters.

I. FIRST LETTER (29:1-23)
  A. **The person and place** (29:1a): Jeremiah writes this letter from
  Jerusalem.
  B. **The parties and purpose** (29:1b-23): He writes to the Jewish
  exiles living in Babylon, for a twofold purpose:
    1. *To comfort and instruct* (29:1b-14)
      a. Build, plant, marry, and raise children, for you'll be in
      Babylon for 70 years (29:1b-7, 10).
      b. Realize that after 70 years, God will bring you back to the
      land and will greatly prosper you (29:11-14): His plans are
      for good and not for evil.
      c. Don't believe the lying prophets in Babylon who tell you
      differently (29:8-9): They do not prophesy in God's name.
    2. *To condemn* (29:15-23): Jeremiah warns the exiles that soon
    two groups of people will be severely punished by God.
      a. First group (29:15-19): The countrymen of the exiles
      (including King Zedekiah), still living their sinful lives in
      Jerusalem
      b. Second group (29:20-23): The lying and immoral prophets
      like Ahab and Zedekiah who conduct their godless minis-
      tries in Babylon
II. SECOND LETTER (29:24-29)
  A. **The person and place** (29:24): Shemaiah, another false prophet
  in Babylon, writes this letter.

B. **The parties and purpose** (29:25-29): Shemaiah tells Zephaniah, a priest living in Jerusalem, that God has appointed him (Zephaniah) to:
   1. *Replace the current high priest, Jehoiada* (29:25-26): He is also to put anyone claiming to be a prophet in the stocks and neck irons.
   2. *Silence Jeremiah the prophet* (29:27-29).

III. THIRD LETTER (29:30-32)
   A. **The person and place** (29:30): Jeremiah writes from Jerusalem.
   B. **The parties and purpose** (29:31-32): He informs the exiles that God will soon judge Shemaiah and his family for his lying and wickedness.

SECTION OUTLINE TEN (JEREMIAH 30–31)
Jeremiah predicts Israel's future restoration.

I. THE CLEANSING PRECEDING THIS RESTORATION (30:4-8, 11-16, 23-24; 31:15): Jeremiah predicts a time of terror and trouble—probably a reference to the coming great tribulation.
   A. **For the Gentile nations** (30:16, 23-24)
      1. *Their armies will be utterly destroyed* (30:16).
      2. *God's wrath will descend on them like a driving wind* (30:23-24).
   B. **For the Jewish nation** (30:4-8, 11-15; 31:15)
      1. *The need for suffering* (30:11-15): It is necessary to punish and purify the nation because of its sin.
      2. *The nature of suffering* (30:4-8; 31:15): It proves to be the most severe ever endured by the nation.

II. THE CONDITIONS DURING THIS RESTORATION (30:1-3, 9-10, 17-22; 31:1-14, 16-30)
   A. **Israel will be regathered and resettled in its land from throughout the world** (30:1-3, 10; 31:8-10): The people's fortunes will be restored.
   B. **They will serve the Lord their God and David their king** (30:9).
   C. **The capital (Jerusalem) and other cities will be rebuilt** (30:17-18): The palace will be restored.
   D. **Their population will be greatly increased** (30:19-21; 31:27-30).
   E. **They once again will become God's special people** (30:22; 31:1-3): God loves them with an everlasting love.
   F. **They will experience unprecedented joy** (31:4-7, 11-14, 16-26).

III. THE COVENANT GUARANTEEING THIS RESTORATION (31:31-40)
   A. **Its superiority** (31:31-34): It is unconditional, unlike the covenant God made with Moses, which was dissolved because of Israel's continual sin.

B. Its security (31:35-40): It lasts as long as the sun and stars give forth their light.

I. JEREMIAH IS PERSECUTED (32:1-5).
  A. **How** (32:1-2): He is imprisoned in the courtyard of the guard in the royal palace.
  B. **Why** (32:3-5): He is punished for preaching that the Babylonians will destroy Jerusalem and carry off its people, including King Zedekiah himself.

II. JEREMIAH MAKES A PURCHASE (32:6-25): God commands him to buy a field.
  A. **The person** (32:6-8): Jeremiah is to purchase the land from Hanamel, son of Shallum.
  B. **The price** (32:9-13): He pays 17 pieces of silver.
  C. **The purpose** (32:14-15): Jeremiah is commanded to preserve the title deeds to the land in a pottery jar, thus signifying that someday all the land of Judah, now worthless because of the invading Babylonians, will once again become valuable ground, occupied by Jewish people.
  D. **The prayer** (32:16-25): The prophet acknowledges God's sovereignty over Israel in the past and in the present.

III. JEREMIAH RECEIVES PROMISES (32:26–33:26)
  A. **About God's omnipotence** (32:26): "I am the LORD, the God of all the peoples of the world. Is anything too hard for me?"
  B. **About God's objectives** (32:27–33:26): He must punish his people to purify them.
    1. *The punishment (32:27-36; 33:1-5)*
      a. What Israel has done against God (32:30-35)
        (1) Rebelled and disobeyed (32:30-33)
        (2) Sacrificed to idols (32:34-35)
      b. What God does against Israel (32:27-29, 36; 33:1-5)
        (1) Allows Jerusalem to be destroyed by the Babylonians (32:27-29; 33:1-5)
        (2) Allows war, famine, and disease (32:36)
    2. *The purification (32:36-44; 33:6-26)*: Israel will:
      a. Be regathered and restored (32:36-37)
      b. Receive a new heart and mind to worship God (32:38-39)
      c. Be given an everlasting covenant (32:40-42; 33:19-26)
      d. Experience great joy and singing (33:10-11)
      e. Enjoy great prosperity (32:43-44; 33:6-9, 12-14)
      f. Be ruled over by the Messiah, the son of David (33:15-18)

SECTION OUTLINE TWELVE (JEREMIAH 34–36)
Jeremiah warns wicked King Zedekiah again about God's coming
judgment. When the monarch does not listen, Jerusalem is captured,
and Zedekiah is taken into captivity. God then sends Jeremiah to
search for godly role models for Judah.

I. JUDAH'S RULERS (34:1-22; 36:1-32)
   A. **King Zedekiah** (34:1-22)
      1. *The prophecy* (34:1-7)
         a. Jerusalem will be destroyed and burned by the Babylonians
            (34:1-2).
         b. Zedekiah will be exiled to Babylon, where he will die a
            peaceful death (34:3-7): The people will mourn him and
            will burn incense for him.
      2. *The pact* (34:8-10): Zedekiah makes a covenant with the
         people in Jerusalem to free all the Judean slaves.
      3. *The profaning* (34:11-16): The people change their minds and
         refuse to free the slaves.
      4. *The punishment* (34:17-22): God punishes his people by war,
         famine, and disease.
   B. **King Jehoiakim** (36:1-32)
      1. *Jeremiah's first scroll* (36:1-26)
         a. As read by Baruch (36:1-20)
            (1) The reading (36:1-15): Following Jeremiah's orders,
                Baruch reads the scroll first to the people and then to
                the administrative officials.
            (2) The reaction (36:16-20): Upon hearing Jeremiah's
                terrible words of coming judgment, the frightened
                administrative officials feel the king also needs to hear
                the scroll.
         b. As read by Jehudi (36:21-26)
            (1) The reading (36:21-22): Jehudi reads the scroll to
                Zedekiah as the king sits beside his fireplace.
            (2) The reaction (36:23-26): The wicked monarch cuts up
                the scroll and burns the pieces.
      2. *Jeremiah's second scroll* (36:27-32)
         a. It includes all the old material (36:27-28, 32).
         b. It introduces much new material, including a twofold
            prophecy against King Jehoiakim (36:29-31):
            (1) His dynasty will not continue (36:29-30a): None of
                Jehoiakim's heirs will sit on the throne.
            (2) "His dead body will be thrown out to lie unburied"
                (36:30b-31).

II. JUDAH'S ROLE MODELS (35:1-19): God commands Jeremiah to visit a
    settlement in Judah where the Recabites live.
    A. **Jeremiah's offer** (35:1-5): He tests the Recabites by offering them
       some wine.

B. The Recabites' objection (35:6-11): They correctly refuse, on the grounds that it would ruin their testimony and would cause them to disobey the command of their ancestor Jehonadab, son of Recab, who had forbidden such wine drinking (along with other commands).

C. God's object lesson (35:12-19): God commends this action and instructs Jeremiah to present the Recabites as role models to Judah.

SECTION OUTLINE THIRTEEN (JEREMIAH 37–38)
Jeremiah is falsely accused of desertion and dissension.

I. THE CHARGE—DESERTION (37:1-21)
  A. Zedekiah's request (37:1-10)
    1. *What the king asks* (37:1-5): That Jeremiah ask God to save Jerusalem from the Babylonians
    2. *Jeremiah's twofold reply* (37:6-10)
      a. That Pharaoh, who came to help Zedekiah, will return to Egypt (37:6-7)
      b. That the Babylonians will then destroy Jerusalem (37:8-10)
  B. Irijah's persecution (37:11-16): This Jewish captain of the guard falsely accuses Jeremiah of treason and orders him arrested, beaten, and imprisoned.
  C. Jeremiah's prophecy (37:17-21): The prophet warns Zedekiah that he will soon be handed over to the king of Babylon.

II. THE CHARGE—DISSENSION (38:1-28)
  A. Jeremiah's foes (38:1-6): They demand and receive from King Zedekiah permission to throw Jeremiah into an empty cistern covered with a thick layer of mud at the bottom, planning to leave him there.
  B. Jeremiah's friend (38:7-13): A palace official named Ebed-melech persuades Zedekiah to remove Jeremiah from this death pit.
  C. Jeremiah's final meeting with Zedekiah (38:14-28): The prophet once again summarizes God's message:
    1. *Surrender to the Babylonians, and Jerusalem will be spared* (38:14-17, 20): The city will not be burned.
    2. *Fight against the Babylonians, and Jerusalem will be destroyed* (38:18-19, 21-28): The city will be burned to the ground.

SECTION OUTLINE FOURTEEN (JEREMIAH 39; 52)

Jeremiah describes Jerusalem's destruction by the Babylonian armies and the events that take place preceding, during, and following this devastation.

I. EVENTS PRECEDING (39:15-18; 52:1-7)
   A. **Jeremiah's reassurance** (39:15-18): That Ebed-melech will be protected in the hour of Jerusalem's agony because of his faithfulness.
   B. **Zedekiah's rebellion** (52:1-3): Zedekiah instigates a revolt against the Babylonian king.
   C. **Nebuchadnezzar's retaliation** (52:4-7): Nebuchadnezzar lays siege to Jerusalem for two years, resulting in severe famine within the city.

II. EVENTS DURING (39:1-8; 52:8-14)
   A. **The walls are breached** (39:1-3): The wall falls, and the Babylonians march in and sit in triumph at the Middle Gate.
   B. **The king is blinded** (39:4-7; 52:8-11): Zedekiah is captured at Jericho, bound in chains, and sent away to exile in Babylon.
   C. **The Temple and city are burned** (39:8; 52:12-14): The walls are torn down.

III. EVENTS FOLLOWING (39:9-14; 52:15-34)
   A. **Judah's officials are executed** (52:24-27).
   B. **Judah's people are enslaved** (39:9-10; 52:15-16, 28-30).
   C. **Judah's wealth is exported** (52:17-23): The Temple fixtures are dismantled and sent to Babylon.
   D. **Judah's prophet is encouraged** (39:11-14): At Nebuchadnezzar's order, Jeremiah is treated very kindly.
   E. **Judah's former king, Jehoiachin, is elevated** (52:31-34): Previously imprisoned in Babylon, he is released and given a seat of honor by the new Babylonian ruler.

SECTION OUTLINE FIFTEEN (JEREMIAH 40–42)

The Babylonians free Jeremiah from prison and appoint Gedaliah governor over Judah. When Gedaliah is killed by Ishmael, Johanan asks Jeremiah whether the people should stay in Judah or go to Egypt.

I. THE RELEASE (40:1-6): Following the destruction of Jerusalem, Jeremiah is freed from prison by the Babylonian army commander Nebuzaradan.

II. THE REASSURANCE (40:7-10)
   A. **The concern** (40:7-8): Some Jewish military men meet with

Gedaliah, the newly appointed Jewish governor over Judah, to determine what his policies will be.

B. The confidence (40:9-10): Gedaliah promises a safe and prosperous reign.

III. THE RETURN (40:11-12): Upon hearing this, many exiled Jews return to Judah.

IV. THE REPORT (40:13-16): Johanan, a leading Jewish soldier, gives Gedaliah a special warning.

A. The details (40:13-15): Ishmael, another soldier, is planning to kill him.

B. The dismissal (40:16): Gedaliah refuses to believe the report.

V. THE REBELLION (41:1-10): Johanan's warning is soon tragically fulfilled.

A. Ishmael assassinates Gedaliah (41:1-3): He also kills the Judean officials and Babylonian guards who are with him.

B. Ishmael kills 70 worshipers (41:4-9): He throws their bodies into a cistern.

C. Ishmael then enslaves many of Judah's leading women (41:10): He starts back to the land of Ammon.

VI. THE RESCUE (41:11-18): Johanan's soldiers defeat Ishmael's band and free the captives.

VII. THE REQUEST (42:1-6): Johanan asks Jeremiah to pray concerning God's will as to where the people should go.

VIII. THE REPLY (42:7-22): After 10 days, Jeremiah announces God's twofold will in this matter:

A. Remain in Judah, and live (42:7-12): They are not to fear the king of Babylon any longer.

B. Retire to Egypt, and die (42:13-22). If they go to Egypt, all the bad things that have happened to them in Judah will follow them.

SECTION OUTLINE SIXTEEN (JEREMIAH 43–45)
Jeremiah ministers to the survivors in Egypt and comforts Baruch the scribe.

I. JEREMIAH'S MINISTRY TO THE SURVIVORS IN EGYPT (43:1–44:30)

A. The people's sin (43:1-7): In spite of the prophet's previous warning not to go to Egypt, the people journey there, forcing Jeremiah to accompany them.

B. The prophet's sign (43:8-13): God tells Jeremiah to bury some large rocks at the entrance of Pharaoh's palace to signify that someday Nebuchadnezzar, king of Babylon, will occupy Egypt and place his throne on the very spot of those buried rocks.

C. **The prophet's sermons** (44:1-30)
  1. *First sermon* (44:1-19)
      a. The prophet's rebuke (44:1-14)
          (1) He reminds the people how God punishes Judah for sin (44:1-6).
          (2) He warns them that God will judge them for worshiping the Egyptians' gods (44:7-14).
      b. The people's twofold rejection (44:15-19)
          (1) "We will not listen to your messages from the LORD!" (44:15-16).
          (2) "We will burn incense to the Queen of Heaven and sacrifice to her just as much as we like" (44:17-19).
  2. *Second sermon* (44:20-30)
      a. Remain in Egypt, and die (44:20-27): "You will suffer war and famine until all of you are dead."
      b. Return to Judah, and live (44:28-30): "Only a small number will escape death and return to Judah from Egypt."

II. JEREMIAH'S MINISTRY TO BARUCH (45:1-5): These events transpire sometime before the destruction of Jerusalem.
  A. **Baruch's complaint** (45:1-3): Jeremiah's scribe suffers from deep depression, no doubt caused by seeing King Jehoiakim burn the scroll he had written (see Jeremiah 36).
  B. **Baruch's comfort** (45:4-5): Jeremiah reassures him, promising divine protection during Jerusalem's future destruction.

SECTION OUTLINE SEVENTEEN (JEREMIAH 46; 48)
Jeremiah prophesies about the future of two foreign nations: Egypt and Moab.

I. EGYPT (46:1-28): Jeremiah prophesies the world-famous battle of Carchemish.
  A. **The parties** (46:1-2): Egyptian pharaoh Neco is soundly defeated by Babylonian king Nebuchadnezzar beside the Euphrates River.
  B. **The pride** (46:3-4, 7-9): Egypt is defeated because of its arrogance and boasting that it would destroy every foe.
  C. **The panic** (46:5-6, 13-18)
      1. *Terror fills the hearts of the strongest Egyptian warriors* (46:5-6): They flee without a backward glance.
      2. *They lose total confidence in their pharaoh to deliver them* (46:13-18): "Pharaoh, the king of Egypt, is a loudmouth who missed his opportunity!"
  D. **The punishment** (46:10-12, 19-26)
      1. *Babylonian swords are covered with Egyptian blood* (46:10-11).
      2. *Egypt becomes the shame of nations* (46:12): The earth is filled with their cries of despair.

      3. *Their capital cities are destroyed* (46:19-24): Not a single person in those cities lives.

      4. *Their gods are punished* (46:25).

      5. *Pharaoh and the people are enslaved by Babylon* (46:26): However, the Lord says, "Afterward the land will recover from the ravages of war."

  E. The promise (46:27-28): Israel is reassured of a future restoration to its land.

II. MOAB (48:1-47)

  A. The apostasy (48:7, 35): The people worship the idol Chemosh and other false gods instead of Jehovah.

  B. The arrogance (48:11-14, 25-30): Everyone knows of Moab's pride and insolence.

  C. The divine anger (48:8-10, 15-16; 40-46): Its cities will be destroyed and burned.

  D. The anguish (48:1-6, 17-24, 31-34, 36-39)

      1. *Of the Moabites* (48:1-6, 37-39)

        a. They will climb the hills and will hide in the wilderness, weeping bitterly (48:1-6): They trust in themselves and in their god, and neither can save them.

        b. They will shave their heads, slash their hands, and put on sackcloth (48:37-39): Moab will be smashed like an old, unwanted bottle.

      2. *Of its neighbors* (48:17-24): Even surrounding nations will sorrow over Moab's pain.

      3. *Of Jeremiah* (48:31-34, 36): His heart is broken over God's judgment on Moab.

  E. The assurance (48:47): "'In the latter days I will restore the fortunes of Moab,' says the LORD."

SECTION OUTLINE EIGHTEEN (JEREMIAH 47; 49)

Jeremiah prophesies other foreign nations' futures: Philistia, Ammon, Edom, Kedar, and Hazor.

I. PHILISTIA (47:1-7): Jeremiah predicts this nation's destruction.

  A. The source (47:1, 6-7): God will empower the Egyptian army.

  B. The severity (47:2-5)

      1. *The enemy will overrun Philistia like a mighty flood* (47:2): It will destroy the land and the people.

      2. *Fathers will abandon their children, attempting to escape* (47:3-4).

      3. *The chief cities of Gaza and Ashkelon will be utterly destroyed* (47:5).

II. AMMON (49:1-6)
   A. The reason for punishment (49:1): The Ammonites have driven out the Israelite tribe of Gad and are occupying their homes.
   B. The results (49:2-5): God will burn the Ammonite cities, drive them from the occupied lands, and allow their neighbors to chase them from the land.
   C. The reassurance (49:6): "'But afterward I will restore the fortunes of the Ammonites,' says the LORD."

III. EDOM (49:7-22)
   A. The punishment (49:7-10, 12-15, 17-22)
      1. *The entire land will be stripped bare and its people killed* (49:7-10).
      2. *The chief Edomite city Bozrah will be cursed, mocked, and destroyed* (49:12-15, 17-21).
      3. *Its young people will be enslaved, its mighty warriors frightened* (49:20-22).
   B. The pride (49:16): Dwelling high in the mountains in a rock fortress, the people think themselves untouchable.
   C. The protection (49:11): God promises to protect the surviving widows and orphans.

IV. DAMASCUS (49:23-27)
   A. The towns are filled with fear (49:23-24): They hear the news of their destruction.
   B. The famous "city of joy" will be abandoned and forsaken (49:25-27): The warriors will all be killed.

V. KEDAR AND HAZOR (49:28-33)
   A. God's message to the victor (49:28-29, 31-33)
      1. *Who* (49:28, 31): God issues a direct command to the Babylonian king Nebuchadnezzar.
      2. *What* (49:29, 31-33): He is to attack these two rich Bedouin tribes and take all their wealth.
      3. *Why* (49:31): Because of their pride.
   B. God's message to the victims (49:30): He warns the people of these two tribes to flee.

VI. EDOM (49:34-39)
   A. It will be destroyed (49:34-38).
   B. Its fortunes will be restored in the latter days (49:39).

SECTION OUTLINE NINETEEN (JEREMIAH 50–51)
Jeremiah describes Babylon's destruction and Israel's deliverance.

I. BABYLON'S DESTRUCTION (50:1-3, 9-16, 21-27, 29-32, 35-46; 51:1-14, 20-33, 37-64)
   A. The source (50:1-3, 9, 41-46; 51:1-6, 9-12, 20-24, 45-46)

1. *The one who directs it* (50:9; 51:1-6, 9-12, 45-46): God himself has decreed Babylon's ruin.
2. *The one who delivers it* (50:1-3, 41-46; 51:20-24, 45-46): God will use Cyrus the Great, founder of the mighty Persian Empire.

B. The sins (50:11, 32, 38; 51:7-8, 44, 47-51)

1. *She has plundered Judah, God's chosen people* (50:11).
2. *She has defiled the Temple* (51:51).
3. *She is proud* (50:32).
4. *She is totally given over to idolatry* (50:38; 51:7-8, 44, 47-50).

C. The severity (50:10, 12-16, 21-27, 29-31, 35-37, 39-40; 51:13-14, 25-33, 37-43, 52-58)

1. *Her walls will be leveled, and her gates will be burned* (51:53-58).
2. *The city will be utterly sacked* (50:10).
3. *Her wise men will become fools* (50:35-36).
4. *Her young men and warriors will be killed* (50:30-31).
5. *The groans of her wounded will be heard throughout the land* (51:52): Her idols will be destroyed.
6. *Her horses will be slaughtered, and her chariots will be smashed* (50:37).
7. *Her homeland will become a deserted wasteland* (50:12-16, 21-27, 29; 51:27-33): All who pass by will be horrified.
8. *Her city will be inhabited by wild animals* (50:39; 51:37-43): "Never again will people live there; it will lie desolate forever."
9. *Her city will be destroyed like Sodom, Gomorrah, and their neighboring towns* (50:40): No one will live there anymore.
10. *Her debris will never again be used for building* (51:25-26): The nation will be completely wiped out.
11. *Her cities will be filled with enemies* (51:13-14): They will shout their triumph over them.

D. The symbolic scroll (51:59-64)

1. *The individual* (51:59): Jeremiah gives a special scroll to Seraiah, an exile and former officer under Zedekiah, who was en route to Babylon.
2. *The information* (51:60): It describes God's judgment upon Babylon.
3. *The instructions* (51:61-64): Upon arriving in Babylon, Seraiah is to read the scroll, then tie a rock to it and throw it into the Euphrates River, illustrating that Babylon will soon sink, never to rise again.

II. ISRAEL'S DELIVERANCE (50:4-8, 17-20, 28, 33-34; 51:15-19)

A. The sheep (50:4-8, 17-20, 28; 51:9-10, 35-36)

1. *They have been led astray by their own leaders* (50:6-8).
2. *They are devoured by both the Assyrians and Babylonians*

(50:17-20): The Assyrians eat them, and the Babylonians crack their bones.
3. *They will repent and be restored* (50:4-5, 28; 51:10): They will come back to Jerusalem and will tell what the Lord has done.
B. The shepherd (50:33-34; 51:15-19)
1. *"The one who redeems them is strong. His name is the LORD Almighty. He will defend them and give them rest again in Israel"* (50:33-34).
2. *"He made the earth by his power, and he preserves it by his wisdom"* (51:15-16).
3. *He alone, unlike the idols, is the true God* (51:17-19): All idols will be destroyed, but God is "the Creator of everything that exists."

Lamentations

SECTION OUTLINE ONE (LAMENTATIONS 1)

Jeremiah describes Jerusalem's great sins and resultant suffering.

I. HER SINS (1:8-9): "Jerusalem has sinned greatly. . . . She defiled herself with immorality."

II. HER SUFFERING (1:1-7, 10-11)
   A. **Jerusalem sits alone, like a grief-stricken widow** (1:1, 4).
   B. **She weeps throughout the night with no one to comfort her** (1:2).
   C. **Judah has been taken into exile** (1:3, 5).
   D. **Her former beauty and majesty are gone** (1:6).
   E. **The enemy laughs as she falls** (1:7).
   F. **The enemy has looted her treasure and violated her Temple** (1:10).
   G. **Her people are starving** (1:11).

III. HER SPEECH (1:12-22)
   A. **The punishment** (1:12-15): She is treated with contempt.
   B. **The pain** (1:16-21): She weeps uncontrollably over her people's plight.
   C. **The prayer** (1:22): She asks the Lord to punish the enemy as he has punished his own people.

SECTION OUTLINE TWO (LAMENTATIONS 2)

Jeremiah describes the Lord's wrath against Jerusalem—and his own anger over the city's desperate state.

I. JERUSALEM'S CRISIS (2:1-19): The city's troubles are recounted.
   A. **The agony** (2:1-17)
      1. *The nation* (2:2-5): The Lord's anger consumes the land like a raging fire.
      2. *The city* (2:1, 8-9a, 13, 15-17): The Lord humiliates Jerusalem.
         a. Her walls and ramparts are destroyed (2:8).
         b. Her gates sink into the ground (2:9a).

c. Her wound is as deep as the sea (2:13).
d. Her enemies scoff and jeer at her (2:15-17).
3. *The Temple* (2:6-7): It has been broken down as though it were a garden shelter, and the holy festivals are no longer observed.
4. *The people* (2:9b-12, 14)
a. The displacement (2:9b): The king and princes are in exile.
b. The darkness (2:9c, 14): The prophets no longer receive visions from the Lord.
c. The despair (2:10): The leaders sit on the ground in silence.
d. The deaths (2:11-12): Little children die in the streets.
B. The anguish (2:18-19): The city is to cry out in her grief and is to pray for deliverance.

II. JERUSALEM'S CRY (2:20-22): In utter anguish, Jerusalem calls out to the Lord, "O LORD, think about this! . . . Should mothers eat their little children . . . ? Should priests and prophets die within the Lord's Temple?"

SECTION OUTLINE THREE (LAMENTATIONS 3)
Jeremiah recalls his sufferings but expresses hope in the Lord. He tells the people to repent and asks the Lord to vindicate him by punishing his oppressors.

I. THE AFFLICTIONS (3:1-20, 43-46, 52-66)
A. Of Jeremiah (3:1-20, 52-66): The Lord and the people plague him.
1. *From the Lord* (3:1-20)
a. The Lord brings him into deep darkness (3:2-3).
b. The Lord makes him old and breaks his bones (3:4).
c. The Lord walls him in a dark place and chains him down (3:5-7).
d. The Lord ignores his prayers (3:8).
e. The Lord blocks his path (3:9).
f. The Lord attacks him like a bear (3:10-11).
g. The Lord pierces his heart with arrows (3:12-13).
h. The Lord makes him the object of ridicule (3:14).
i. The Lord fills him with bitterness (3:15).
j. The Lord takes away his peace and prosperity (3:16-20).
2. *From the people* (3:52-66): Mistreated and imprisoned by his own people for preaching against their sins, Jeremiah calls upon the Lord to pay them back.
B. Of Jerusalem (3:43-46)
1. *From the Lord* (3:43-45): Jeremiah laments that the Lord has treated them in the following ways:
a. He has chased them down and slaughtered them without mercy (3:43).

b. He refuses to hear their prayers (3:44).

c. He has discarded them as garbage (3:45).

2. *From their enemies* (3:46): They speak out against Jerusalem.

II. THE AGONY (3:47-51): Jeremiah cries out, "My tears flow down endlessly."

III. THE ASSURANCE (3:21-24, 31-33): Despite Jeremiah's groaning, he finds hope in the Lord. He rejoices that the Lord's unfailing love keeps his people from complete destruction.

IV. THE ADMONITION (3:25-30, 34-42): Jeremiah's threefold advice to the people:

A. Wait patiently for the Lord to respond (3:25-26).

B. Accept the Lord's discipline (3:27-30, 34-39).

C. Repent of your sin (3:40-42).

SECTION OUTLINE FOUR (LAMENTATIONS 4)

Jeremiah clarifies the desperate situation in Jerusalem, detailing the causes and events of the city's destruction. He warns Edom not to rejoice, for they, too, will be judged.

I. JERUSALEM'S CURRENT JUDGMENT (4:1-20)

A. The consequences (4:1-10): Various people endure terrible suffering when the Babylonians destroy the city.

1. *Children* (4:1-4)

2. *Rich people* (4:5-6)

3. *Princes* (4:7-9)

4. *Mothers* (4:10)

B. The causes (4:11-20)

1. *The priests' and prophets' sins* (4:11-16): Because they shed innocent blood, the Lord sends his people into exile.

2. *The enemy's strength* (4:17-20): The people can't withstand the Babylonians. They put their trust in man, not God.

II. EDOM'S COMING JUDGMENT (4:21-22): Jeremiah says not to laugh at suffering Jerusalem, for Edom, too, will be judged.

SECTION OUTLINE FIVE (LAMENTATIONS 5)

Jeremiah pleads with the Lord to remember his people's desperate situation—and to restore them.

I. REMEMBER US (5:1-18): Jeremiah reviews Jerusalem's pitiful condition after the Babylonian destruction and asks the Lord to remember his people.

A. The suffering (5:2-14): Jeremiah notes the suffering of

1. *The homeless* (5:2)

        2. *The fatherless* (5:3)

        3. *The hungry* (5:4, 6-7, 9-10)

        4. *The persecuted* (5:5, 8)

        5. *The women* (5:11)

        6. *The noble* (5:12)

        7. *The old and the young* (5:13-14)

    B. The sadness (5:15-18): Jeremiah summarizes the people's plight, declaring that "our dancing has turned to mourning."

II. RESTORE US (5:19-22): Jeremiah asserts that the Lord remains the same forever and calls upon him to restore his people once again.

Ezekiel

SECTION OUTLINE ONE (EZEKIEL 1–3)
Ezekiel describes a vision of God that he has received. He also
describes his call from God.

I. THE VISION (1:1-28): Ezekiel receives visions of God.
  A. **Ezekiel and the cherubim of God** (1:1-25)
    1. *He sees these heavenly creatures* (1:1-23).
      a. The appearance of the living beings (1:5-11): Ezekiel is
        visited by four of these special beings.
        (1) Each has four faces (1:5, 10).
          (a) The face in front is a man's face (1:10a).
          (b) The face on the right is a lion's face (1:10b).
          (c) The face on the left is an ox's face (1:10c).
          (d) The face in back is an eagle's face (1:5, 10d).
        (2) Each has two pairs of wings (1:6, 9, 11).
        (3) Each has human hands beneath its wings (1:8).
        (4) Each possesses legs like those of men but feet like
          calves' feet (1:7).
      b. The vision of God (1:1-4): Ezekiel feels the hand of the Lord
        on him.
      c. The activities of the living beings (1:12-23)
        (1) They go in whatever direction the spirit chooses (1:12,
          17, 20-23): They move straight forward in all
          directions, without turning.
        (2) They glow like bright coals of fire when they move
          (1:13): It looks as though lightning is flashing among
          them.
        (3) Their movement is swift as lightning (1:14).
        (4) Each is accompanied by a polished chrysolite wheel,
          with a second wheel crosswise inside (1:15-16, 19):
          When the beings move, the wheels move with them.
        (5) The wheels have rims and spokes (1:18a).
        (6) The rims are filled with eyes (1:18b).
    2. *He hears these heavenly creatures* (1:24-25).
      a. Their wings roar like waves against the shore (1:24a).

  b. Their wings sound like the voice of God (1:24b).
  c. Their wings sound like the shout of a mighty army
     (1:24c-25).
B. Ezekiel and the Christ of God (1:26-28)
  1. *Ezekiel sees a man seated upon a throne made of beautiful
     blue sapphire stones* (1:26).
  2. *His appearance is like glowing amber, surrounded by a
     rainbowlike halo* (1:27-28): Ezekiel falls down in the dust and
     hears someone speaking to him.

II. THE VOICE (2:1–3:27): Ezekiel is called by God to deliver a certain
    message.
  A. The recipients (2:1-5; 3:4-7)
    1. *Who they are* (2:1-3; 3:4): His message is directed to the
       nation of Israel.
    2. *What they are* (2:4-5; 3:5-7): They are hard, impudent,
       rebellious, and stubborn.
  B. The reassurance (2:6–3:3, 8-9)
    1. *God gives Ezekiel the sermon he needs* (2:6–3:3): God's words
       are on a scroll, which he gives Ezekiel to eat.
    2. *God gives Ezekiel the strength he needs* (3:8-9): Ezekiel is not
       to be afraid.
  C. The reflection (3:10-11): Before delivering his message, Ezekiel
     is to allow God's words to sink down deep in his own heart.
  D. The reaction (3:12-15): Ezekiel's initial response to all this is one
     of bitterness and turmoil! However, God's hand is strong upon
     him.
  E. The role (3:16-21): Ezekiel assumes the role of a spiritual watch-
     man by delivering a twofold warning:
    1. *To the godless* (3:16-19): Cease your wicked ways, or die!
    2. *To the godly* (3:20-21): Continue your good ways, or die!
  F. The restriction (3:22-27): Ezekiel is to imprison himself in his
     own house, where God will temporarily cause him to be unable
     to speak.

SECTION OUTLINE TWO (EZEKIEL 4–7)
Ezekiel employs both visual aids and sermons to describe the tragic
spiritual decline among the people of Israel.

I. THE FIRST SYMBOLS PRESENTED BY EZEKIEL (4–6)
  A. First illustration (4:1-3)
    1. *The symbol* (4:1-2): He draws a picture of Jerusalem upon a
       clay tablet and then places an iron plate next to it.
    2. *The significance* (4:3): The Babylonian army, like an iron wall,
       will soon surround Jerusalem.
  B. Second illustration (4:4-6)
    1. *The symbol* (4:5-6)

       a. He is to lie on his left side for 390 days (4:5): This is for the years of Israel's sin.

       b. He is then to lie on his right side for 40 days (4:6): This represents the years of Judah's sin.

    2. *The significance* (4:4): Each day represents one year of punishment for Israel and Judah.

C. Third illustration (4:7-8)

    1. *The symbol* (4:7): He is to lie on his back with his arms tied.

    2. *The significance* (4:8): This depicts the helplessness of Jerusalem against the Babylonian attack.

D. Fourth illustration (4:9-17)

    1. *The symbol* (4:9-15): He is to prepare a meager meal and cook it over some dried cow dung.

    2. *The significance* (4:16-17): This is a warning that the people of Israel will be forced to eat defiled food among the nations where God will drive them.

E. Fifth illustration (5:1-17)

    1. *The symbol* (5:1-4): He is to shave both his head and his beard and is to place the hair into three equal parts. One part is then to be burned, the second part is to be struck with his sword, and the third part is to be scattered to the wind.

    2. *The significance* (5:5-17): This is to predict that one third of Jerusalem's people will soon die by fire, another third will die by the sword, and the final third will go into captivity.

F. Sixth illustration (6:1-10)

    1. *The symbol* (6:1-2): He is to set his face against the mountains of Israel and is to prophesy against them.

    2. *The significance* (6:3-10): This means that those living in the valley below will soon be destroyed by their enemies.

G. Seventh illustration (6:11-14)

    1. *The symbol* (6:11): He is to clap his hands and stomp his feet.

    2. *The significance* (6:12-14): This is done in horror, predicting the disease and death that await Israel.

II. THE FIRST SERMON PREACHED BY EZEKIEL (7:1-27): The prophet warns Jerusalem that the terrible day of God's judgment is at hand.

A. The sin causing this judgment (7:1-4, 19-21, 23-24)

    1. *Idolatry* (7:1-4): Ezekiel calls the people to account for their disgusting behavior.

    2. *Greed* (7:19-21): The love of money makes them stumble into sin.

    3. *Bloodshed* (7:23): The land is bloodied by terrible crimes.

    4. *Pride* (7:24): God will break down their proud fortresses.

B. The severity of this judgment (7:5-18, 22, 25-27)

    1. *Continuous disaster and calamity* (7:5-6, 22, 25-27): They will have terror after terror and calamity after calamity. No one will be there to guide them.

2. *God's punishment without his pity* (7:7-14): He will neither spare nor pity them.
3. *Death by plagues inside the city, death by sword outside the city* (7:15-18): The few who survive will moan for their sins.

SECTION OUTLINE THREE (EZEKIEL 8–11)
Ezekiel has a vision of some of Jerusalem's sins and of the impending departure of God's glory from the Temple.

I. EZEKIEL SEES THE GOD OF GLORY DEFILED IN THE CITY OF JERUSALEM (8:1–10:3, 5-17; 11:1-22, 24-25).
   A. The man (8:1-4): Ezekiel is supernaturally transferred from Babylon to Jerusalem by a glowing figure from heaven who is probably the Messiah himself.
   B. The mockery (8:5-18; 11:1-13): Ezekiel witnesses God's holiness mocked and blasphemed on four occasions.
   1. *The perversions* (8:5-18)
      a. The people are worshiping a large idol north of the altar gate in the Temple entrance (8:5-6): The people have made God so angry that he is going to leave the Temple.
      b. Seventy Jewish elders are burning incense to devilish images inside the Temple (8:7-12): The people think the Lord doesn't see them.
      c. Some Jewish women are weeping for the false god Tammuz (8:13-15).
      d. Twenty-five men are worshiping the sun (8:16-18): The people of Judah are leading the whole nation into violence.
   2. *The promoters* (11:1-13): God holds 25 of Judah's most prominent leaders responsible for the people's sins. The most important of these men, Pelatiah, is suddenly struck dead before the horrified eyes of Ezekiel.
   C. The marking (9:1-11): God orders six men (possibly angels) to put a mark on the foreheads of the godly individuals in Jerusalem. Another group of men is then instructed to kill all those with unmarked foreheads, beginning with the 70 Jewish elders.
   D. The magnificent ones (10:1-3, 5-17): The four cherubim Ezekiel described in chapter 1 suddenly reappear and begin their ministry before God.
   E. The message (11:14-22, 24-25): God gives Ezekiel a note of encouragement to the Babylonian exiles, assuring them they will someday be regathered, returned, and regenerated.

II. EZEKIEL SEES THE GLORY OF GOD DEPART FROM THE CITY OF JERUSALEM (10:4, 18-22; 11:23).
   A. From the Holy of Holies to the entrance of the Temple (10:4): The Temple courtyard glows with the cloud of God's glory.

B. From the entrance of the Temple to the east gate (10:18-22): The glory of God hovers above the cherubim.

C. From the east gate to the Mount of Olives (11:23): The glory of God departs from Jerusalem.

SECTION OUTLINE FOUR (EZEKIEL 12–15)
Ezekiel continues his ministry as a "watchman on the wall."

I. HIS ILLUSTRATIONS TO THE NATION OF ISRAEL (12:1-28; 15:1-8)
   A. Through demonstrations (12:1-20)
      1. *First illustration* (12:1-16)
         a. The symbol (12:1-7): Ezekiel is commanded to pack his belongings on his shoulders and dig a tunnel through the city wall.
         b. The significance (12:8-16): This depicts how Jerusalem's frightened citizens will attempt to escape the Babylonian siege.
      2. *Second illustration* (12:17-20)
         a. The symbol (12:17-18): Ezekiel is to tremble and shudder with fear as he eats his food and drinks his water.
         b. The significance (12:19-20): This depicts how the people of Jerusalem will soon eat their food and drink their water.
   B. Through proverbs (12:21-28)
      1. *The old proverb of the people* (12:21-22): "Those who predict judgment are wrong! Each passing day proves it!"
      2. *The new proverb of the prophet* (12:23-28): "These predictions are true! The coming day of destruction will prove it!"
   C. Through analogy (15:1-8): Ezekiel compares the city of Jerusalem to a useless vine.

II. HIS INDICTMENT OF THE NATION OF ISRAEL (13:1–14:23)
   A. Ezekiel condemns the false prophets (13:1-23).
      1. *The male prophets* (13:1-16)
         a. Their perversions (13:1-7, 10, 16): They assure the people that God will not punish them but rather will send peace their way!
         b. Their punishment (13:8-9, 11-15): God's wrath will crash down upon them like great hailstones.
      2. *The female prophets* (13:17-23)
         a. Their perversions (13:17-20, 22): Prompted by greed, they deceive the people by their magic charms and veils.
         b. Their punishment (13:21, 23): God will rescue the people from their grasp.
   B. Ezekiel condemns the idol worshipers (14:1-23).
      1. *Three people* (14:1-20): God says the sins of the nation have become so great that his terrible wrath will fall even if

righteous men like Noah, Daniel, and Job are numbered among the citizens. If so, they alone will be saved!

 2. *Four punishments* (14:21-23): These four dreadful judgments are sword, famine, wild beasts, and plague.

SECTION OUTLINE FIVE (EZEKIEL 16)
Ezekiel employs an extended allegory, depicting Israel as God's unfaithful wife.

I. THE PLIGHT (16:1-5): As the story opens, Israel is seen as a helpless and unloved baby girl who has been dumped into a field and left to die.

II. THE PITY (16:6-14)

 A. God and the baby girl (16:6-7): He rescues, cleanses, clothes, and raises her.

 B. God and the young woman (16:8-14): When she is of age, God marries her, dresses her in the finest apparel, and bestows lavish gifts upon her.

III. THE PROSTITUTION (16:15-26, 28-34)

 A. The corruption of this young wife (16:15-25, 30-34): Israel soon betrays her divine husband by playing the role of a common harlot.

 B. The clients of this young wife (16:26, 28-29): She commits spiritual adultery with the gods of other nations.

  1. *Egypt* (16:26): She fans the flames of God's anger with her promiscuity.

  2. *Assyria* (16:28): She never seems to find enough new lovers.

  3. *Babylon* (16:29): Even after she adds Babylon, she isn't satisfied.

IV. THE PUNISHMENT (16:27, 35-58)

 A. She will be given over to her enemies (16:27): She will be handed over to the Philistines, who also will be shocked by her conduct.

 B. She will be stripped naked before them (16:37-41): The many nations that have been her lovers will destroy her.

 C. She will be repaid for her sins (16:35-36, 42-52): God will pour out all his jealous anger on her.

 D. She will be restored (16:53): When God's anger is spent, he will bring her back.

 E. She will be ashamed for her sins (16:54-58): Her wickedness will be exposed to the world.

V. THE PARDON (16:59-63): In spite of all her sin, a loving and faithful God will someday reaffirm his covenant of grace with Israel!

SECTION OUTLINE SIX (EZEKIEL 17–19)
Ezekiel continues his message of judgment to Israel by additional parables and proverbs.

I. THE PARABLES (17:1-24; 19:1-14)
   A. **First parable** (17:1-6, 11-14)
      1. *Information in the parable* (17:1-6): A great eagle plucks off the top of a tall cedar tree and replants it elsewhere, in fertile soil.
      2. *Interpretation of the parable* (17:11-14): The eagle is Nebuchadnezzar, who carries off many Jewish citizens (the top of the cedar tree) into the Babylonian captivity, where they fare well, for the most part, due to God's faithfulness.
   B. **Second parable** (17:7-10, 15-21)
      1. *Information in the parable* (17:7-10): A part of that cedar-tree replant, however, soon gives its allegiance to another eagle that arrives on the scene. Because of this, that section of the replanted tree is destroyed by God.
      2. *Interpretation of the parable* (17:15-21): The second eagle represents Egypt's pharaoh, with whom Judean king Zedekiah allies against Nebuchadnezzar, resulting in Jerusalem's destruction.
   C. **Third parable** (17:22-24)
      1. *Information in the parable* (17:22-23): God himself one day takes a tender sprout from a tall cedar and plants it atop Israel's highest mountains, where it becomes the ultimate and universal tree!
      2. *Interpretation of the parable* (17:24): The original tree seems to be a reference to the house of David, from which eventually comes the Messiah himself, the second tree.
   D. **Fourth parable** (19:1-9): A lioness has two cubs that become man-eaters. Both are eventually trapped. The first cub is taken to Egypt, and the second cub is taken to Babylon.
   E. **Fifth parable** (19:10-14): A strong and fruitful vine planted in fertile soil alongside a stream is suddenly uprooted and replanted in a barren desert, where it begins to wither away.

II. THE PROVERB (18:1-32): Ezekiel begins this chapter by referring to a popular proverb, widely quoted in Israel at the time.
   A. **The contents of this proverb** (18:1-4)
      1. *The information* (18:1-2): It says, "The parents have eaten sour grapes, but their children's mouths pucker at the taste."
      2. *The interpretation* (18:3-4): The proverb says Israel is simply being punished for the sins of her fathers.
   B. **The correction of the proverb** (18:5-28): Ezekiel refutes this false teaching by pointing out that God punishes only the individual for his or her sin. He cites five examples to illustrate his point.

1. *The case of the righteous versus the unrighteous* (18:20, 25): The one who sins is the one who dies.
2. *The case of a righteous man* (18:5-9): He will surely live.
3. *The case of a righteous man's unrighteous son* (18:10-13): The righteous man's son will surely die and take full blame.
4. *The case of an unrighteous man's righteous son* (18:14-19): The son will not die because of his father's sins.
5. *The case of a righteous man who becomes unrighteous* (18:24, 26): He will die.
6. *The case of unrighteous people who become righteous* (18:21-23, 27-28): They will live.
C. **The challenge from the proverb** (18:29-32): In light of all this, God urges the people of Israel to repent so that they will not be punished for their unrighteous ways.

SECTION OUTLINE SEVEN (EZEKIEL 20–21)
Ezekiel warns Israel of the consequences of her sins by physically acting out messages of judgment.

I. ISRAEL'S CONDEMNATION (20:1-32, 45-49; 21:1-32)
   A. **The indictments** (20:1-32, 45-49; 21:1-5, 24-32)
      1. *Upon the people* (20:1-32, 45-49; 21:1-5, 24): Israel is reminded of her constant sinning against God throughout her history.
         a. In Egypt (20:1-9): The people of Israel did not get rid of their idols as God instructed.
         b. In the wilderness (20:10-26): The people refused to obey God's laws.
         c. In Canaan (20:27-28): They continued to blaspheme and betray God.
         d. In Ezekiel's time (20:29-32, 45-49; 21:1-5, 24): They continue to sin and are not ashamed of it. God has become their enemy and will unleash his anger on them.
      2. *Upon the prince* (21:25-27): The "wicked prince of Israel" is Zedekiah, Judah's final ruler.
      3. *Upon the pagans* (21:28-32): Here judgment is handed down against the Ammonites for their many national sins.
   B. **The illustrations** (21:6-23): Once again Ezekiel acts out his message of judgment.
      1. *First illustration* (21:6-7)
         a. What he does (21:6): He groans.
         b. What it means (21:7): This will be Jerusalem's reaction as the Babylonian army marches against the city.
      2. *Second illustration* (21:8-12)
         a. What he does (21:12): He beats upon his thighs.

b. What it means (21:8-11): Soon enemy swords will pierce through the hearts of Judah's people.

3. *Third illustration* (21:13-17)
   a. What he does (21:13-16): He claps his hands and slashes a sword from left to right.
   b. What it means (21:17): The same message is conveyed as that of the second illustration.

4. *Fourth illustration* (21:18-23)
   a. What he does (21:18-21): He draws a map showing two roads with a fork in the middle.
   b. What it means (21:22-23): This signifies that the king of Babylon will decide to attack Jerusalem before the Ammonite capital city of Rabbah.

II. ISRAEL'S RESTORATION (20:33-44): In spite of their terrible sins, God will someday regenerate, regather, and restore his people!

SECTION OUTLINE EIGHT (EZEKIEL 22–24)
Ezekiel details the sins of Israel and compares Samaria and Jerusalem to two prostitutes.

I. THE SINS OF ISRAEL (22:1-31)
   A. The perversions (22:1-12, 23-29)
   1. *Bloodshed and idolatry* (22:1-6, 9, 27): Everyone in the city is murderous and idolatrous.
   2. *Contempt for parents, orphans, and widows* (22:7, 23-25): Fathers and mothers are ignored, the number of widows increases, and people are destroyed for profit.
   3. *Utter disregard for the Sabbath* (22:8, 26): They violate the Lord's holy days of rest.
   4. *Adultery and incest* (22:10-11): They defile themselves.
   5. *Bribe taking and extortion* (22:12, 29)
   6. *Lying prophets* (22:28): They say their message is from the Lord when the Lord hasn't spoken.

   B. The punishment (22:13-22, 30-31)
   1. *They are scattered among the nations* (22:13-16): God purges their wickedness.
   2. *They are thrown into the furnace of God's fiery wrath* (22:17-22, 30-31): God heaps on them the full penalty for their sins.

II. THE SISTERS DEPICTING ISRAEL (23:1-49): In this parable Ezekiel compares Israel to two sisters who become prostitutes.
   A. The identity of these sisters (23:1-4): The elder sister is named Oholah and represents Samaria. The younger sister is named Oholibah and represents Jerusalem. God "marries" both sisters and "fathers" sons and daughters through them.

B. The immorality of these sisters (23:5-49): Both sisters prove untrue to their divine husband.
  1. *The sins of Oholah, the older sister* (23:5-10)
     a. Her perversion (23:5-8): She commits spiritual adultery with the Assyrian gods.
     b. Her punishment (23:9-10): God allows the Assyrians to capture and enslave the city of Samaria.
  2. *The sins of Oholibah, the younger sister* (23:11-35, 43-49)
     a. Her perversions (23:11-21)
        (1) She, like her sister, commits spiritual adultery with the Assyrian gods (23:11-13).
        (2) She then does the same with the Babylonian gods (23:14-21).
     b. Her punishment (23:22-35, 43-49): She is captured and enslaved by the Babylonians.
  3. *The sins of both sisters* (23:36-42): Each sister city is guilty of the following:
     a. Murder (23:36-37a)
     b. Idolatry (23:37b)
     c. Child sacrifice (23:37c)
     d. Total hypocrisy (23:38-39): After doing these terrible things, they come to worship God at his Temple.
     e. Gaudy lifestyle (23:40-41): They paint themselves and put on their finest jewels.
     f. Drunkenness (23:42): The sound of carousing comes from their room.

III. THE SIGNS TO ISRAEL (24:1-27)
  A. The food sign (24:1-14)
     1. *What he does* (24:1-7): Ezekiel is commanded to boil some meat in a pot of water until the flesh falls off the bones; then he is to cast out everything upon the ground.
     2. *What it means* (24:8-14): God will consume Israel, corrupted by her sin, in his pot of judgment and then will cast her out!
  B. The funeral sign (24:15-27)
     1. *What he does* (24:15-18): God instructs Ezekiel to remain tearless at the funeral of his beloved wife, who dies suddenly.
     2. *Why he does it* (24:19-27): When asked why he shows no sorrow, Ezekiel responds by telling the people that they will likewise not be allowed to display any tears over the coming destruction of their nation.

SECTION OUTLINE NINE (EZEKIEL 25–28)
In these chapters Ezekiel pronounces judgment against six pagan nations.

I. THE PROPHECY AGAINST AMMON (25:1-7)
   A. **Their crimes** (25:1-3, 6): They rejoice over the destruction of Israel's Temple and mock the Jewish exiles on their way to the Babylonian captivity.
   B. **Their condemnation** (25:4-5, 7): Their land will be overrun by enemy forces, and their people will be enslaved.

II. THE PROPHECY AGAINST MOAB (25:8-11): They, too, are condemned for applauding the destruction of Jerusalem.

III. THE PROPHECY AGAINST EDOM (25:12-14): A similar judgment awaits the Edomites.

IV. THE PROPHECY AGAINST PHILISTIA (25:15-17): The same punishment will soon fall upon the Philistines.

V. THE PROPHECY AGAINST TYRE (26:1–28:19)
   A. **The splendor of Tyre** (27:1-9)
      1. *The shipbuilding* (27:1-7)
         a. Its harbor is the most beautiful in the world (27:1-4): It is the gateway to the sea.
         b. Its ships are the finest in the world (27:5-7): The ships are made of cypress, cedar, oak, pine, ivory, and linen.
      2. *The sailors* (27:8-9): They come from many nations to join the fleet.
   B. **The soldiers of Tyre** (27:10-11): The most experienced and best-equipped men serve in the army of Tyre.
   C. **The substance of Tyre** (27:12-25): The city is one of the richest of its day! Note the exotic items imported to Tyre:
      1. *Silver, iron, tin, and lead* (27:12)
      2. *Slaves* (27:13)
      3. *Chariot horses, steeds, and mules* (27:14)
      4. *Ebony and ivory* (27:15)
      5. *Emeralds, purple dyes, fine linen, and jewelry of coral and rubies* (27:16)
      6. *Wheat, honey, oil, balm, wine, and wool* (27:17-18)
      7. *Iron and saddle cloths* (27:19-20)
      8. *Rams, lambs, and goats* (27:21)
      9. *Spices and gold* (27:22)
      10. *Blue cloth, embroidery, and carpets* (27:23-25)
   D. **The sin of Tyre** (26:1-2; 28:1-5)
      1. *The city celebrates the fall of Jerusalem* (26:1-2): Tyre thinks it will benefit from Jerusalem's destruction.
      2. *The prince of Tyre is filled with pride, conducting himself as a*

little god (28:1-5): His wisdom and treasure have made him rich.

E. The sentence on Tyre (26:3-21; 27:26-36; 28:6-10)

1. *The city will be destroyed down to its bare foundation* (26:3-21; 28:6-10).

   a. The attack by the Babylonians (26:3-21): Babylon will destroy Tyre's villages and tear down her walls and her gates.

   b. The attack by the Greeks (28:6-10): They draw their swords against the king of Tyre, and he dies.

2. *An ocean storm destroys its ships* (27:26-36).

F. The satanic force behind Tyre (28:11-19): Many Bible students feel these verses describe the original sin and fall of Satan himself! If this be the case, observe:

1. *The perfection* (28:11-13): This magnificent angel is created by God as the ultimate in wisdom and beauty.

2. *The position* (28:14): He is then appointed to be the anointed guardian angel.

3. *The pride* (28:15-16a): All this causes Lucifer to be filled with pride, prompting him to attempt a violent overthrow of God himself!

4. *The punishment* (28:16b-19): He is removed from his lofty position, cast to the ground, and made an example of concerning God's wrath toward sin!

VI. THE PROPHECY AGAINST SIDON (28:20-26)

A. Sidon is destroyed (28:20-24): Invading armies and terrible plagues will devastate both the land and the people.

B. Israel is delivered (28:25-26): The people will be regathered, regenerated, and restored to the land.

SECTION OUTLINE TEN (EZEKIEL 29–32)

These chapters describe for us God's relationship with the nation of Egypt.

I. THE PARABLE DESCRIBING EGYPT (31:1-9): Egypt is pictured as a mighty and magnificent cedar tree in Lebanon, envied by all other trees.

II. THE PRIDE OF EGYPT (29:1-3; 31:10; 32:1-2)

A. She feels she owns the Nile River (29:1-3): God is her enemy.

B. She boasts of being the greatest (31:10).

C. She claims to be a lion among the nations (32:1-2): She is really just a sea monster, heaving around and stirring up mud.

III. THE PLUNDERING OF EGYPT (29:4-10, 17-21; 30:1-26; 31:11-18; 32:3-32): No less than seven times, Ezekiel predicts the enemies of Egypt invading and spoiling her land!

A. First occasion (29:4-10): God will put hooks in her jaws and drag her out on the land.

B. Second occasion (29:17-21): God will give Egypt to Nebuchadnezzar.

C. Third occasion (30:1-19): A sword will come against Egypt, and those who are slaughtered will cover the ground.

D. Fourth occasion (30:20-26): Pharaoh's arms will be broken and his people scattered.

E. Fifth occasion (31:11-18): They will be cut down and left on the ground.

F. Sixth occasion (32:3-16): They will be completely destroyed.

G. Seventh occasion (32:17-32): They will be dragged away to judgment.

IV. THE PITY ON EGYPT (29:11-16): Mercifully, God will partially restore Egypt.

    A. The decades (29:11-12): Egypt first will suffer God's wrath for a period of 40 years.

    B. The deliverance (29:13-16): Following this, God will partially regather and restore the Egyptians to their land.

SECTION OUTLINE ELEVEN (EZEKIEL 33–34)
Ezekiel uses various images to depict Israel's relationship with her leaders.

I. THE WATCHMAN AND THE WALL (33:1-33)

    A. God and the messengers to Israel (33:1-9): Here a distinction is made between a faithful watchman and an unfaithful watchman (or messenger).

        1. *The faithful watchman* (33:1-5, 7, 9): This kind of prophet (like Ezekiel) keeps on warning the people to repent even if they refuse to listen.

        2. *The faithless watchman* (33:6, 8): The blood of the guilty is on his hands for not warning the people.

    B. God and the messenger to Israel (33:10-33): Ezekiel is instructed to preach two sermons to Israel.

        1. *The message before the fall of Jerusalem* (33:10-20): The message is twofold:

            a. "Your past good deeds will not deliver you from the coming judgment unless you repent!" (33:10-12a)

            b. "Your present bad deeds will not deliver you to the coming judgment if you repent!" (33:12b-20)

        2. *The message after the fall of Jerusalem* (33:21-33)

            a. The report (33:21): A Jew who escaped the destruction of Jerusalem tells Ezekiel about it.

            b. The restoration (33:22): God now opens the mouth of the previously mute Ezekiel.

      c. The rebuke (33:23-29): Ezekiel predicts that severe punish-
ment will soon fall upon those Jews who have survived
Jerusalem's destruction but still continue in their evil
ways!

      d. The ridicule (33:30-33): Some of the Jewish exiles already
in Babylon are laughing at Ezekiel behind his back.

II. THE SHEPHERDS AND THE SHEEP (34:1-31)
  A. The false shepherds (34:1-8, 18-19)
    1. *They feed and water themselves and ignore their flocks*
(34:1-3, 18-19): What they don't use for themselves, they
trample or make muddy.
    2. *They refuse to care for the weak, sick, and injured sheep*
(34:4): They rule with force and cruelty.
    3. *They allow wild animals to devour the sheep* (34:5-8): The
sheep are easy prey for any wild animal.
  B. The faithful shepherd (34:9-17, 20-31): These verses doubtless
refer to the Messiah himself, Jesus Christ!
    1. *His relationship with the false shepherds* (34:9-10, 20-21)
      a. He removes them and holds them responsible (34:9-10):
He considers them his enemies.
      b. He judges them (34:20-21): He will separate the fat, unruly
sheep from the scrawny, downtrodden sheep.
    2. *His relationship with the sheep* (34:11-16, 22, 25-31)
      a. He rescues and regathers them (34:11-12, 22): The Lord is
their shepherd.
      b. He feeds them (34:13): He brings them back home.
      c. He gives them good pasture (34:14-15, 26-27): They lie in
pleasant places and feed in lush pastures.
      d. He binds up the injured and strengthens the weak (34:16):
He destroys those who have hurt his own.
      e. He protects them (34:25, 28): They live in safety and fear
no one.
      f. He adopts them as his own (34:29-31): They know God is
with them.
    3. *His relationship with the goats* (34:17): He separates them
from the sheep.
    4. *His relationship with the undershepherd* (34:23-24): He allows
King David to assist him in feeding and leading the sheep.

SECTION OUTLINE TWELVE (EZEKIEL 35–37)
Ezekiel foretells Edom's destruction and Israel's salvation.

I. THE CONDEMNATION OF EDOM (35:1-15; 36:1-7)
  A. The perversions of Edom (35:5, 10-13; 36:1-5)
    1. *They hate and betray Israel* (35:5): Edom butchered Israel after
Israel had already been punished by God.

2. *They plan to occupy Israel* (35:10): They don't care that the Lord is there.
3. *They slander Israel* (35:11-12): They say Israel has been given to them.
4. *They slander God* (35:13; 36:1-5): They boast against God, and he hears them.
  B. **The punishment of Edom** (35:1-4, 6-9, 14-15; 36:6-7)
1. *To be smashed by God's fist* (35:1-4): They will be completely destroyed.
2. *To suffer a bloodbath* (35:6-9): God will fill the mountains with their dead since they have no distaste for blood.
3. *To be wiped out* (35:14-15): Then they will know that he is the Lord.
4. *To be filled with shame* (36:6-7): They will have their turn at being wiped out.

II. THE SALVATION OF ISRAEL (36:8–37:28)
  A. **The sin** (36:16-17): Israel defiles her own land by shedding blood and worshiping idols.
  B. **The scattering** (36:18-19): For this the people are scattered among the nations.
  C. **The slander** (36:20-21): This, however, gives rise to a problem, for the pagans are defaming God's name, saying he cannot take care of his own people.
  D. **The solution** (36:8-15, 22-38): God determines to vindicate his great name through the following actions:
1. *He will give Israel crops* (36:8-12): The ground will be tilled and planted.
2. *He will keep other nations from devouring Israel* (36:13-15): Other nations will no longer sneer at her.
3. *He will regather his people from among the nations* (36:22-24): He will bring them back to honor his name.
4. *He will regenerate his people, giving them new hearts* (36:25-27): Their filth will be washed away.
5. *He will restore his people, allowing them to rebuild their cities and harvest their crops* (36:28-38): They will be his people, and he will be their God.
  E. **The symbols** (37:1-28): Ezekiel is given two symbols to illustrate all this:
1. *The symbol of the skeletons, illustrating Israel's resurrection* (37:1-14)
    a. The miracle of the dead bones (37:1-10): An amazed Ezekiel sees dry bones in a valley suddenly reassemble themselves and then become covered with muscles, flesh, and skin!
    b. The meaning of the dead bones (37:11-14): God explains that he will someday do a similar thing for the nation of Israel!

2. *The symbol of the two sticks, illustrating Israel's reunion* (37:15-28)
   a. The merging (37:15-17): Ezekiel takes two sticks, writing the name *Juda* on one stick and *Ephrai* on the other. These then are joined together in his hand.
   b. The meaning (37:18-23): God will someday reunite the northern and southern kingdoms of Israel and Judah.
   c. The monarchy (37:24-25): David will then be appointed to rule over both kingdoms.
   d. The mercy (37:26-28): God will make an everlasting covenant of peace with Israel.

SECTION OUTLINE THIRTEEN (EZEKIEL 38–39)
Ezekiel predicts that Israel will someday be attacked by an enemy confederation led by a warrior named Gog, from the land of Magog.

I. THE ABHORRENCE OF GOG (38:1-3): God states his anger concerning the evil plans of Gog.

II. THE ALLIES OF GOG (38:4-7): Ezekiel identifies these nations as Persia, Ethiopia, Libya, Gomer, and Beth-togarmah.

III. THE ATTACK BY GOG (38:8-16)
   A. **When Gog will attack** (38:8-11): The invasion will occur "in the latter days" when Israel is at peace in their own land.
   B. **Why Gog will attack** (38:12-16): This will be done to plunder and loot.

IV. THE ANNIHILATION OF GOG (38:17–39:24)
   A. **As foretold in the former days** (38:17-18): This destruction was predicted by the prophets long ago.
   B. **As fulfilled in the final days** (38:19–39:24)
      1. *The plan* (38:19-22): God will accomplish this annihilation by a threefold method:
         a. A mighty earthquake (38:19-20): All living things will quake in terror at God's presence.
         b. Mutiny among the enemy troops (38:21): Their men will turn against each other.
         c. The use of sword, disease, floods, hailstorms, fire, and brimstone (38:22)
      2. *The place* (39:1-6): This will occur on the mountains of Israel.
      3. *The purpose* (38:23; 39:7-8, 21-24)
         a. In regard to the Gentile nations (38:23; 39:21, 23-24): Upon witnessing this destruction, the pagan nations will acknowledge the person and power of the true God.
         b. In regard to the Jewish nation (39:7-8, 22): They also will know that Israel's God is indeed the only true God!
      4. *The purifying* (39:9-16)

a. Seven years of fuel (39:9-10): There will be sufficient war debris to serve as fuel for the people of Israel for seven years.

b. Seven months of funerals (39:11-16): It will take Israel seven months to bury the dead.

5. *The proclamation* (39:17-20): God will personally invite the wild birds and animals to consume the flesh of the fallen enemy warriors.

V. THE ASSEMBLING AFTER GOG (39:25-29): God will then regather, regenerate, and restore his people to their land.

SECTION OUTLINE FOURTEEN (EZEKIEL 40–48)

These chapters describe for us the glories of the Millennium, including facts about the new Temple—its size, its priests, its location, etc.

I. THE TEMPLE (40:1–43:27)

A. The man (40:1-4): Ezekiel is introduced to a man carrying a measuring stick, his face shining like bronze.

B. The measurement (40:5–42:20; 43:13-27): This man proceeds to measure the following:

1. *The outer court* (40:5-27)

2. *The inner court* (40:28-47): It is 175 feet square.

3. *The Temple vestibule* (40:48-49): It is 35 feet in depth and 19 {1/4} feet wide.

4. *The Temple itself* (41:1-26)

5. *The chamber in the outer court* (42:1-14): It is 175 feet long and 87 {1/2} feet wide.

6. *The place of separation* (42:15-20): It is 875 feet on each side.

7. *The altar of burnt offerings* (43:13-27)

C. The magnificence (43:1-12): Ezekiel, who previously saw the glory of God depart from the Temple, now witnesses its return.

1. *The sound of God's glory cloud* (43:1-5): It is like the roar of rushing waters.

2. *The speech from God's glory cloud* (43:6-12): God reassures Ezekiel that he will someday permanently dwell with Israel!

II. THE TRUSTEES (44:1–46:24)

A. The officials (44:1–45:17; 46:1-8, 16-18)

1. *The prince* (44:1-3; 45:13-17; 46:1-8, 16-18): Here Ezekiel describes an especially important Temple official known only as "the prince."

2. *The priests and Levites* (44:4–45:12): The Levites, except for the family of Zadok, will no longer be able to serve as priests, because they encouraged the people to worship foreign gods.

B. The offerings (45:18-25; 46:9-15, 19-24): On the first day of each new year, in the early spring, they are to sacrifice a bull to purify the Temple.

III. THE TERRITORY (47:1–48:35)
   A. **Facts concerning the millennial soil** (47:1–48:29)
      1. *The river* (47:1-12): Water flows from the Temple to the Dead Sea, bringing new life to Israel!
      2. *The dimensions* (47:13-23): Here the northern, southern, eastern, and western dimensions are given.
      3. *The tribal land divisions* (48:1-29): The specific land area for each tribe is now allotted.
   B. **Facts concerning the millennial city** (48:30-35)
      1. *The gates in the city* (48:30-34): It has 12 gates, each gate bearing the name of one of the Old Testament tribes.
      2. *The name of the city* (48:35): It is called "Yahweh-Shammah," meaning, "The LORD Is There."

Daniel

SECTION OUTLINE ONE (DANIEL 1–2)
As a captive in Babylonia, the brave Daniel refuses to eat the king's food—and prospers. He also is able, with God's help, to interpret the king's disturbing dream.

I. THE KING'S DIET REFUSED BY DANIEL (1:1-21)
   A. Daniel the selected (1:1-7)
      1. *The conquest* (1:1-2): The Babylonian monarch Nebuchadnezzar attacks and conquers Jerusalem.
      2. *The command* (1:3-5): Nebuchadnezzar orders Ashpenaz (the head palace official) to begin training some of the most promising Jewish captives for public service.
      3. *The candidates* (1:6-7): Daniel (Belteshazzar), Hananiah (Shadrach), Mishael (Meshach), and Azariah (Abednego) are among those chosen.
   B. Daniel the steadfast (1:8-20)
      1. *The request* (1:8-9): Determining not to defile himself by eating the king's food and wine, Daniel seeks permission to eat other, more wholesome food.
      2. *The reluctance* (1:10): His superintendent fears he will be executed if the Jewish captives do not fare well with this menu.
      3. *The recommendation* (1:11-14): Daniel suggests a 10-day test.
      4. *The results* (1:15-16): Daniel and his three friends are healthier than the rest!
      5. *The reward* (1:17-20): Three years later Nebuchadnezzar declares that the four young men are 10 times smarter than all the magicians and enchanters in his kingdom.
   C. Daniel the statesman (1:21): Daniel now begins his service in Babylonian politics.

II. THE KING'S DREAM REVEALED BY DANIEL (2:1-49)
   A. The king and his pagan advisors (2:1-13)
      1. *The fear* (2:1): The king has a disturbing dream.
      2. *The frustration* (2:2-13): The king is unable to remember his dream.

a. His demand (2:2-4): The king calls for his wise men and commands them to tell him what he has dreamed and what it means.

b. His decree (2:5-13): Because the wise men are unable to do this, they are sentenced to death.

B. The king and God's prophet (2:14-49)

1. *God reveals the dream to Daniel* (2:14-23).

a. The request (2:14-16): Daniel learns that he and his three friends are among those to be executed and asks the king for a little more time.

b. The revelation (2:17-19): After Daniel and his friends pray, God tells Daniel the dream and its meaning.

c. The rejoicing (2:20-23): Daniel praises God for his omnipotence and omniscience.

2. *Daniel reveals the dream to Nebuchadnezzar* (2:24-49).

a. The information (2:24-35)

(1) The statue (2:24-33): The king saw a huge statue with a gold head, silver chest and arms, bronze belly and thighs, iron legs, and feet that are a combination of iron and clay.

(2) The stone (2:34-35): A massive rock was cut out from a mountain by supernatural means. It struck the feet of iron and clay, smashing them to bits so that the whole statue collapsed.

b. The interpretation (2:36-45)

(1) Of the statue (2:36-43): It represents four successive Gentile powers—Babylon, Persia, Greece, and Rome.

(2) Of the stone (2:44-45): It represents God's kingdom, which will someday destroy pagan power.

c. The elevation (2:46-49): An amazed Nebuchadnezzar worships Daniel and appoints him to be ruler over the entire province of Babylon as well as chief over all his wise men!

SECTION OUTLINE TWO (DANIEL 3–4)

Shadrach, Meshach, and Abednego refuse to worship Nebuchadnezzar's gold statue and are thrown into a blazing furnace—but survive. Nebuchadnezzar has a second dream, which Daniel also interprets. When the king refuses to repent, he has to live like an animal for seven years. His kingdom and sanity are restored when he acknowledges God.

I. THREE MEN AND A TEST (3:1-30)

A. The flamboyant Babylonian monarch (3:1-7)

1. *The project* (3:1): Nebuchadnezzar builds a gold statue that is 90 feet tall and 9 feet wide.

2. *The politicians* (3:2-3): The king summons all his political leaders to attend the statue's dedication.
3. *The proclamation* (3:4-5): When the band plays, all those present are to bow down and worship the gold statue.
4. *The penalty* (3:6-7): All those who refuse to bow down will be cast into a blazing furnace.

B. The faithful men (3:8-23)

1. *The threat* (3:8-15)
   a. The astrologers' report (3:8-12): The king learns that Shadrach, Meshach, and Abednego have refused to bow.
   b. The king's reasoning (3:13-15): He offers the three men a second chance.
2. *The testimony* (3:16-23)
   a. The three men's answer (3:16-18): "We will burn, if need be, before we will serve anything other than God."
   b. The king's anger (3:19-23): He orders the young men thrown into the furnace, which has been heated seven times hotter than usual.

C. The fourth man (3:24-30)

1. *The discovery* (3:24-25): Looking into the fire, an amazed Nebuchadnezzar sees two incredible things:
   a. The three men are still alive (3:24-25a).
   b. Another man has joined them, and he looks like a divine being (3:25b).
2. *The deliverance* (3:26-28): At the king's urging, the three men walk out of the fire, not even smelling of smoke.
3. *The decree* (3:29-30): Nebuchadnezzar imposes the death sentence upon anyone who speaks against God, and the three men are promoted to higher positions.

II. TWO MEN AND A TREE (4:1-37): This chapter records the second of Nebuchadnezzar's three dreams. Daniel interprets this dream also.

A. The prologue (4:1-3)

1. *The proclamation* (4:1): Nebuchadnezzar issues a special announcement throughout his kingdom.
2. *The praise* (4:2-3): The king testifies of God's awesome power.

B. The particulars (4:4-37)

1. *The king is corrupted through vanity* (4:4-27).
   a. Nebuchadnezzar's dream (4:4-18)
      (1) He sees a large tree spreading out (4:4-12).
      (2) He sees the tree struck down (4:13-18): A messenger, a holy one, cuts down this tree and says it represents a man who will lose his mind and will live like a wild animal for seven years.
   b. Daniel's interpretation (4:19-27)
      (1) His explanation (4:19-26): Daniel identifies the tree as Nebuchadnezzar, who will suffer from a divinely caused insanity due to his pride. However, in seven

years, after he acknowledges God's power, his
kingdom will be restored.

(2) His exhortation (4:27): Daniel urges the king to repent
and thus avoid this terrible judgment.

2. *The king is corrected through insanity* (4:28-37).

a. The pride (4:28-30): Refusing to repent, the king remains
arrogant, boasting to all about his building of Babylon.

b. The punishment (4:31-33): As predicted, the king is given
an animal's mind for seven years.

c. The postscript (4:34-37): Upon receiving his right mind and
being restored to the kingdom, Nebuchadnezzar worships,
praises, honors, and glorifies Daniel's God.

SECTION OUTLINE THREE (DANIEL 5–6)

Belshazzar sees a hand writing on the wall and calls Daniel for
an interpretation. He dies that very night when Darius the Mede
captures the city. Daniel's enemies plot against him, and he is
thrown into the lions' den.

I. GOD'S HAND AT DINNER (5:1-31)

   A. **The ball** (5:1): Babylonian king Belshazzar invites a thousand of
   his officers to a great feast.

   B. **The gall** (5:2-4)

   1. *The order* (5:2): Belshazzar asks that the vessels
   Nebuchadnezzar took from the Jerusalem Temple be brought
   to his feast.

   2. *The outrage* (5:3-4): Both king and guests drink wine from
   these vessels and praise the Babylonian gods.

   C. **The wall** (5:5-6)

   1. *The hand* (5:5): Belshazzar sees a human hand (with no arm)
   writing a message on the wall.

   2. *The horror* (5:6): He's filled with fear.

   D. **The call** (5:7-29)

   1. *To the magicians* (5:7-9): Belshazzar promises great rewards to
   any who can interpret the mysterious writing. But no one is
   able to do so.

   2. *To the prophet* (5:10-29)

      a. The recommendation (5:10-12): The queen mother advises
      Belshazzar to call for Daniel.

      b. The reward (5:13-16): The king offers to promote Daniel to
      the third highest position in the kingdom if he can interpret
      the writing.

      c. The refusal (5:17): Daniel spurns the bribe but offers to
      interpret the message without cost.

      d. The rebuke (5:18-23): Daniel contrasts the reigns of Nebu-
      chadnezzar and Belshazzar.

>>> *(1)* Lessons Nebuchadnezzar learned (5:18-21): He testified to God's sovereignty after being humbled by insanity.
>>> *(2)* Lessons Belshazzar spurns (5:22-23): Although he knows history, he still chooses to defy and insult God!
>> e. The revelation (5:24-28): Daniel tells the king that his kingdom will be given to the Medes and Persians—and that he will soon die.
>> f. The robing (5:29): In a futile attempt to escape God's judgment, the king clothes Daniel in purple and proclaims him third ruler in the kingdom.
> **E. The fall** (5:30-31): That very night Darius the Mede enters Babylon, kills Belshazzar, and rules over the city.

II. GOD'S HAND IN A DREAM (6:1-28)
A. A hostile plan (6:1-9)
> 1. *The organization* (6:1-3): Darius appoints Daniel as one of the kingdom's three top administrators.
> 2. *The orchestration* (6:4-9)
>> a. The sinister search (6:4): Daniel's envious enemies unsuccessfully attempt to find something in his life that can be used against him.
>> b. The solution (6:5): They finally conclude that he can only be trapped by his religious life.
>> c. The subtlety (6:6-9): Darius is tricked into signing a decree that imposes the death penalty upon anyone who prays to any god except the king for 30 days.

B. A holy man (6:10-15)
> 1. *The fearless prophet* (6:10): Even though he knows about the decree, Daniel continues his usual three-times-a-day prayers to God.
> 2. *The heartless plotters* (6:11-13): Daniel's devilish foes gleefully report this to the king.
> 3. *The tireless potentate* (6:14-15): Realizing he has been tricked, Darius spends the rest of the day trying—unsuccessfully—to find a legal loophole whereby Daniel can be saved.

C. A heavenly ban (6:16-28)
> 1. *The king's concern* (6:16-18): With great sorrow, Darius gives orders for Daniel to be arrested and thrown into the lions' den. He returns home to spend a sleepless night.
> 2. *The king's cry* (6:19-22): Early the next morning, hoping against hope, Darius cries out to Daniel in the lions' den.
>> a. The question (6:19-20): Was God able to save you?
>> b. The answer (6:21-22): God shut the lions' mouths!
> 3. *The king's command* (6:23-28)
>> a. About Daniel (6:23): Overjoyed, Darius orders Daniel (who doesn't even have a scratch) removed from the lions' den.

b. About his foes (6:24): They are thrown into the same lions' den and are instantly torn apart.

c. About his God (6:25-28): Darius sends a message: All people in the kingdom are to fear and reverence Daniel's God.

SECTION OUTLINE FOUR (DANIEL 7–8)
During the first and third years of Belshazzar's reign in Babylon, Daniel has two visions of future Gentile world powers.

I. THE FIRST VISION (7:1-28): During the first year of Belshazzar's reign
   A. The information (7:1-14): Daniel sees:
   1. *A lionlike beast* (7:1-4): "As I watched, its wings were pulled off, and it was left standing with its two hind feet on the ground, like a human being. And a human mind was given to it."
   2. *A bearlike beast* (7:5): It holds three ribs between its teeth.
   3. *A leopardlike beast* (7:6): It has four birds' wings on its back and four heads and is given great authority.
   4. *A 10-horned beast* (7:7-8): It is by far the most dreadful and terrifying creature yet. An 11th horn grows, yanking out 3 of the 10 horns.
   5. *The Ancient One* (7:9-12)
      a. Who it is (7:9): God himself is seated in all his heavenly glory, preparing to judge the world.
      b. What happens (7:10-12)
         (1) A river of fire flows from God's presence (7:10a).
         (2) Millions of angels minister to him (7:10b).
         (3) Tens of millions of people await judgment (7:10c).
         (4) The fourth beast is thrown into hell (7:11-12).
   6. *The man* (7:13-14)
      a. Who it is (7:13): Some believe the "man" who approaches the Ancient One is a reference to God's Son, Jesus Christ.
      b. What happens (7:14): The Son is given a mighty, glorious, and eternal kingdom.
   B. The interpretation (7:15-28)
   1. *Of the four beasts in general* (7:15-18)
      a. Their rise (7:15-17): They represent the four ancient kingdoms of Babylon, Persia, Greece, and Rome.
      b. Their replacement (7:18): They will give way to God's glorious kingdom.
   2. *Of the fourth beast in particular* (7:19-28)
      a. The confusion (7:19-22): Daniel desires more information on the cruelty and conquests of this vicious beast.
      b. The clarification (7:23-27): He is given three facts concerning the fourth beast. It will:

(1) Devour the earth (7:23-24)

(2) Defy the Most High (7:25)

(3) Be destroyed by the Most High (7:26-27)

c. The consternation (7:28): The prophet is terrified by this vision.

II. THE SECOND VISION (8:1-27): During the third year of Belshazzar's reign

A. **The animals** (8:1-12)

1. *A two-horned ram* (8:1-4): It is able to defeat and utterly crush all its enemies.

2. *A one-horned male goat* (8:5-8)

a. Its destructiveness (8:5-7): The goat attacks and utterly destroys the ram.

b. Its death (8:8): At the height of its power, the goat's horn is broken and replaced by four smaller horns.

3. *Another creature that comes from the goat* (8:9-12)

a. The conquests (8:9-10): He invades and occupies much of the Holy Land.

b. The contempt (8:11-12): He even challenges God!

B. **The answers** (8:13-27)

1. *From a regular angel* (8:13-14)

a. The question (8:13): How long will it take for Daniel's vision to be fulfilled? How long until the defiled Jewish Temple will be purified, thus allowing the daily sacrifices to once again take place?

b. The answer (8:14): A period of 2,300 days!

2. *From a ruling angel* (8:15-27)

a. His identity (8:15-19): He is none other than Gabriel himself.

b. His information (8:20-27):

(1) About the two-horned ram (8:20): It represents the Medo-Persian Empire.

(2) About the one-horned goat (8:21-22): It represents Greece, which will break into four sections following the death of Alexander the Great.

(3) About the third creature (8:23-27): This probably refers to a brutal Syrian king, Antiochus Epiphanes IV, who defiled the Temple in December of 167 B.C. Later, it would be cleansed by Judas Maccabeus.

SECTION OUTLINE FIVE (DANIEL 9–10)
After being visited by the angel Gabriel, Daniel goes on an
extended fast in order to pray for Israel's repentance—and
future restoration.

I. THE CHRONOLOGY (9:1-27): This chapter records two time
periods—one historical, the other prophetic. Both periods involve
the number 70.
  A. The historical 70 (9:1-19): Daniel and God
    1. *The Scriptures as pondered by Daniel* (9:1-2): He understands
      that Israel's 70-year Babylonian captivity, prophesied by
      Jeremiah, is almost over.
    2. *The supplication as prayed by Daniel* (9:3-19)
      a. The review (9:3-14)
        (1) Israel's sin (9:3-11)
        (2) Israel's suffering (9:12-14)
      b. The request (9:15-19): Daniel asks God to forgive his
        people and to restore them to their land.
  B. The prophetic 70 (9:20-27): Daniel and Gabriel's visit
    1. *The nature of Gabriel's mission* (9:20-23): He has been sent to
      help Daniel understand God's future plan for Israel.
    2. *The nature of Gabriel's message* (9:24-27): God will
      successfully accomplish his total plan for Israel during a
      specified number of years.
      a. The number (9:24): It will involve "seventy sets of seven,"
        for a total of 490 years, beginning with the command to
        rebuild the walls of Jerusalem.
      b. The nature (9:25-27): These years will fall into three cate-
        gories:
        (1) First period, 49 years, during which Jerusalem will be
          rebuilt (9:25)
        (2) Second period, 434 years, at which time the Messiah
          will be crucified (9:26)
        (3) Third period, 7 years, a reference to the coming Great
          Tribulation (9:27)

II. THE CONFLICT (10:1-21)
  A. Daniel's vexation (10:1-4): He undergoes an extended fast as a
    result of the fearful visions.
    1. *The duration of his fast* (10:1-3): Three weeks
    2. *The location of his fast* (10:4): On the bank of the Tigris River
  B. Daniel's visitation (10:5-21): An angel from heaven appears!
    1. *The radiance* (10:5-6): Clothed in linen and a gold belt, the
      angel's body looks "like a dazzling gem." He sounds like an
      entire multitude as he speaks.
    2. *The reaction* (10:7-8): Daniel feels faint and weak with fear.
      Although his companions see nothing, all of a sudden they
      become terrified and flee.

3. *The reassurance* (10:9-12): A trembling Daniel is gently lifted and comforted by the angel.
4. *The revelation* (10:14): He has come to instruct Daniel concerning the future of Israel.
5. *The resistance against this angel* (10:13, 15-21): The heavenly messenger tells Daniel why it has taken him a full three weeks to arrive.
   a. The hostility (10:13a, 15-20)
      (1) He was hindered by the demonic leader of Persia en route (10:13a).
      (2) He will be hindered by the demonic leader of Greece upon his return (10:15-20).
   b. The helper (10:13b, 21): Michael the archangel helped Gabriel as he came and will help him again as he leaves.

SECTION OUTLINE SIX (DANIEL 11–12)
God's angel describes for Daniel the future reigns of various Persian, Greek, Egyptian, and Syrian kings. The angel concludes by predicting the eventual rule of the Antichrist himself!

I. A CHRONOLOGY OF CHRISTLESS CONQUERORS (11:1-45)
  A. Four Persian kings (11:1-2): Daniel learns that three Persian kings will succeed Darius the Mede, followed by a powerful fourth ruler who will use his great wealth to wage total war against Greece.
  B. A mighty king of Greece (11:3-4): Here is a reference to Alexander the Great, who will suddenly die soon after building his vast empire, resulting in the empire being fragmented into four divisions.
  C. The kings of Syria and Egypt (11:5-20)
   1. *The alliance between Syria and Egypt* (11:5-6): The daughter of the king of Egypt will be given in marriage to the king of Syria to secure an alliance.
   2. *The defeat of Syria by Egypt* (11:7-12): The king of Egypt will carry Syria's treasures back to his land.
   3. *The defeat of Egypt by Syria* (11:13-16): Even though Egypt is fortified, it will be destroyed.
   4. *The stalemate between Syria and Egypt* (11:17-20): The king of Syria will give his daughter to the king of Egypt in marriage to overthrow the kingdom from within.
  D. An evil Syrian king (11:21-35): This is a reference to Antiochus Epiphanes IV, who will come to power around 175 B.C.
   1. *His craftiness* (11:21-23): He will secure his kingdom by flattery and intrigue.
   2. *His conquests* (11:24): He will besiege and capture powerful strongholds.

    3. *His confrontations* (11:25-30)
       a. With Egypt (11:25-27): The king of Syria will defeat him.
       b. With Israel (11:28-30): He will set himself against the
          people of the covenant, doing great damage.
    4. *His cruelty* (11:31-35): Antiochus Epiphanes IV will possess a
      hellish hatred for Israel.
       a. He will desecrate the Temple and cause the daily sacrifices
          to cease (11:31-32): He will flatter those who violate the
          covenant.
       b. He will murder many Jews (11:33-35): Many who are wise
          will die, but those who survive will be made pure till the
          time of the end.
  E. The satanic, self-willed king (11:36-45): These verses describe
    the frightful reign of the coming Antichrist.
    1. *The wickedness of the Antichrist* (11:36-39)
       a. His impudence (11:36-37): He will blaspheme God in
          unthinkable and unheard-of ways!
       b. His idolatry (11:38-39): He will worship the god of
          fortresses.
    2. *The warfare of the Antichrist* (11:40-45)
       a. The ones he will defeat (11:40-44a): He will sweep through
          many countries like a flood, including Israel, Egypt, and
          Libya.
       b. The one who will defeat him (11:45): The context here
          suggests that God himself will utterly crush the Antichrist
          near the city of Jerusalem!
    3. *The wrath of the Antichrist* (11:44b): Hearing some alarming
      news from the east and the north, he will return in great anger,
      destroying as he goes.

II. A Chronology of Closing Conditions (12:1-13)
  A. The description of the end times (12:1-4)
    1. *The suffering* (12:1)
       a. The pain (12:1b): During the Great Tribulation, Israel will
          suffer as never before.
       b. The prince (12:1a): Israel will be helped at that time by
          Michael the archangel.
       c. The perseverance (12:1c): All those whose names are writ-
          ten in God's book will be delivered.
    2. *The separation* (12:2): In the last day, all will be resurrected,
      some to everlasting life, others to everlasting punishment.
    3. *The shining* (12:3): The righteous will shine like stars!
    4. *The sealing* (12:4): Daniel's prophecies are sealed until the
      end times.
  B. The duration of the end times (12:5-13): Three separate time
    periods are specified.

1. *A period of 1,260 days* (12:5-10): This probably refers to the last three and one-half years of the Great Tribulation.
2. *A period of 1,290 days* (12:11): The previous 1,260 days plus 30 additional days.
3. *A period of 1,335 days* (12:12-13): The previous 1,290 days plus 45 additional days.

Hosea

SECTION OUTLINE ONE (HOSEA 1–3)
God tells Hosea to marry a prostitute, so some of her children will
have been born from other men. Why? To illustrate the way God's
people have been untrue to him. Then, even when Hosea's wife goes
and sins again, Hosea is to take her back and love her—demonstrating
God's never-failing love for his people.

I. AN INNOCENT HUSBAND AND AN IMMORAL WIFE: Hosea and Gomer
   (1:1-9; 2:2-7; 3:1-3)
   A. **The command** (1:1-2): God orders Hosea to marry a prostitute.
   B. **The children** (1:3-9)
      1. *What their names are* (1:4a, 6a, 9a)
         a. Jezreel, a son (1:4a)
         b. Lo-ruhamah, a daughter (1:6a)
         c. Lo-ammi, another son (1:9a)
      2. *What their names mean* (1:4b-5, 6b, 9b)
         a. "Scattered" (Jezreel) (1:4b-5)
         b. "Not loved" (Lo-ruhamah) (1:6b)
         c. "Not my people" (Lo-ammi) (1:9b)
   C. **The corruption** (2:2): Gomer, who was a prostitute before marry-
      ing Hosea, now becomes an adulterous wife. Gomer represents
      Israel.
   D. **The chastisement** (2:3-5): God says he will severely punish
      Gomer/Israel if she does not repent.
   E. **The confinement** (2:6-7): Hosea tries to wall Gomer/Israel in,
      thus preventing her from returning to her immoral ways, but all
      to no avail!
   F. **The compassion** (3:1-3): Because of his great love for her, and in
      spite of her terrible sin, Hosea purchases Gomer/Israel from the
      slave market where she has sold herself sexually.

II. AN INNOCENT HUSBAND AND AN IMMORAL WIFE: The Lord and Israel
    (1:10–2:1, 8-23; 3:4-5)
    A. **Israel's sin** (2:8): She is guilty of both immorality and idolatry.
    B. **Israel's suffering** (2:9-13): She will suffer famine, shame, and
       destruction.

C. Israel's salvation (1:10–2:1, 14-23; 3:4-5)

    1. *The chronology* (3:4): Israel will be a long time without a king, prince, sacrifices, Temple, priests, or even idols.

    2. *The conditions* (1:10–2:1, 14-23; 3:5)

        a. She will be multiplied, received, and restored by God (1:10–2:1, 23).

        b. God will once again be her husband (2:16-17).

        c. She will know his love as never before (2:19-20).

        d. Her Valley of Trouble will become the gateway of hope (2:14-15).

        e. She will live in a perfect environment and will enjoy abundant crops (2:18, 21-22).

        f. The great King David will rule over her (3:5).

SECTION OUTLINE TWO (HOSEA 4–10)

Hosea describes Israel's rebellion, ruin, and repentance.

I. HER REBELLION (4:1–5:15; 6:4–8:14; 9:7-10; 10:1-4)

  A. Swearing, lying, killing, stealing, and adultery (4:1-3, 14-17)

  B. Godless religious leaders (4:4-5, 8-10; 5:1-4, 10-15)

  C. Godless political leaders (7:1-7)

  D. Willful ignorance (4:6)

  E. Idolatry (4:7, 12-13, 19; 7:8-16; 8:1-14; 10:1-3)

  F. Drunkenness (4:11, 18)

  G. Arrogance (5:5-9)

  H. Insincere sacrifices (6:4-6)

  I. Breaking the covenant (6:7-11; 10:4)

  J. Refusing to hear God's Word (9:7-10)

II. HER RUIN (9:1-6, 11-17; 10:5-15)

  A. The child mortality rate will soar (9:11-16).

  B. Her idols will be destroyed (10:5-9).

  C. Her people will be carried off into captivity by the Assyrians (9:1-6; 10:10-15).

  D. They will wander around, homeless (9:17).

III. HER REPENTANCE (6:1-3)

  A. The confession (6:1a, 3)

    1. *"Let us return to the LORD!"* (6:1a).

    2. *"Let us press on to know him!"* (6:3).

  B. The cleansing (6:1b-2)

    1. *"He will bandage our wounds"* (6:1b).

    2. *"He will restore us so we can live in his presence"* (6:2).

SECTION OUTLINE THREE (HOSEA 11–14)
Hosea explains God's case against Israel, then shares God's invitation
to and hope for Israel.

I. THE CASE (11:5-7, 12; 12:1-2, 7-14; 13:1-3, 6-16)
  A. **Their sin** (11:12; 12:1-2, 7-8; 13:1-2, 6)
    1. *Deceit* (11:12)
    2. *Ungodly alliances* (12:1-2)
    3. *Dishonesty* (12:7)
    4. *Boasting* (12:8)
    5. *Pride* (13:6)
    6. *Idolatry* (13:1-2)
  B. **Their suffering** (11:5-7; 12:9-14; 13:3, 7-16)
    1. *Poverty* (12:9-13)
    2. *Physical death for some* (12:14; 13:7-16)
    3. *Exile for the rest* (11:5-7; 13:3)

II. THE INVITATION (12:6; 14:1-3, 8-9)
  A. **Realize your helplessness** (14:3).
  B. **Confess and forsake your sin** (14:1-2, 8-9).
  C. **Return to God** (12:6).

III. THE LOVE (11:1-4, 8-11; 12:3-5; 13:4-5; 14:4-7)
  A. **In the past** (11:1-4; 12:3-5; 13:4-5)
  B. **At the present** (11:8-9)
  C. **In the future** (11:10-11; 14:4-7)

Joel

SECTION OUTLINE ONE (JOEL 1–3)
Joel writes about current and future conditions in Israel.

I. CURRENT CONDITIONS (1:1-20): The worst locust plague in Judah's history has settled upon the land.
  A. **The devastation** (1:1-12, 15-18)
    1. *The severity* (1:1-4, 6-7, 15): The crops are consumed by a fourfold attack:
      a. The cutting locusts (1:1-4a, 15)
      b. The swarming locusts (1:4b)
      c. The hopping locusts (1:4c)
      d. The stripping locusts (1:4d, 6-7)
    2. *The sorrow* (1:5, 8-12, 16-18): Hungry cries of anguish are heard everywhere.
  B. **The proclamation** (1:13-14)
    1. *Dress in sackcloth* (1:13a).
    2. *Declare a fast* (1:13b-14a).
    3. *Gather in the Temple* (1:14b).
  C. **The supplication** (1:19-20): Both people and animals cry out for divine intervention.

II. COMING CONDITIONS (2:1–3:21): There will be three future "days."
  A. **The day of Pentecost** (2:28-32; see also Acts 2:14-18; Rev. 6:12-14)
    1. *The contents* (2:28-32)
      a. God's Spirit will be poured out upon Israel (2:28-29).
      b. Great signs will occur in the heavens (2:30-31).
      c. Salvation will be offered to all (2:32).
    2. *The chronology* (see Acts 2:14-18; Rev. 6:12-14)
      a. Present fulfillment (see Acts 2:14-18)
      b. Future fulfillment (see Rev. 6:12-14)
  B. **The day of the Lord—a title for the coming Great Tribulation** (2:1-21; 3:1-16): Using the locust plague as an object lesson, Joel describes a future invasion where enemy soldiers (not insects) will ravage the land.
    1. *The alarm* (2:1, 15)

2. *The admonition* (2:12-14, 16-17): God calls for Israel's repentance.
3. *The assurance* (2:18-21): God promises deliverance following this repentance.
4. *The attack* (2:2-11): A fierce and seemingly unstoppable foreign army will invade Israel, marching in precise fashion, causing great fear.
5. *The anger* (3:3-8): God is furious concerning Israel's past and future mistreatment by the pagan Gentiles.
6. *The announcement* (3:9-11): These pagan Gentiles are warned to prepare for the worst, for God himself will soon battle against them.
7. *The assembling* (3:1-2, 12): God plans to drive his enemies into the valley of Jehoshaphat (called the Kidron Valley in the New Testament) so he can kill them.
8. *The annihilation* (3:13-16): The enemies will be crushed like overripe grapes.

C. The day of Christ—a title for the Millennium (2:22-27; 3:17-21)
1. *Body blessings—the provision of food* (2:22-26; 3:18-19)
2. *Soul blessings—the presence of God* (2:27; 3:17, 20-21)

Amos

SECTION OUTLINE ONE (AMOS 1–2)
These chapters describe Amos's vision of God's judgment on
Damascus, Philistia, Tyre, Ammon, Moab, Judah, and Israel.

I. THE REVELATION OF GOD'S JUDGMENT (1:1-2): In a vision Amos sees
divine wrath falling upon certain nations.

II. THE RECIPIENTS OF GOD'S JUDGMENT (1:3–2:16)
   A. **Damascus** (1:3-5)
      1. *Their sin* (1:3): They have ravished the Israelite city of Gilead.
      2. *Their sentence* (1:4-5): Damascus will be burned, and its
         people will be enslaved.
   B. **Philistia** (1:6-8)
      1. *Their sin* (1:6): They have sold God's people into slavery.
      2. *Their sentence* (1:7-8): The Philistine cities will be torched,
         and the people will be killed.
   C. **Tyre** (1:9-10)
      1. *Their sin* (1:9): They have broken their treaty with the people
         of Israel and have betrayed them.
      2. *Their sentence* (1:10): The city will be burned.
   D. **Edom** (1:11-12)
      1. *Their sin* (1:11): They have hounded Israel with the sword.
      2. *Their sentence* (1:12): Their cities will be burned.
   E. **Ammon** (1:13-15)
      1. *Their sin* (1:13): They ripped open the pregnant women of
         Gilead.
      2. *Their sentence* (1:14-15): Their cities will be burned, and their
         people will be enslaved.
   F. **Moab** (2:1-3)
      1. *Their sin* (2:1): They have desecrated tombs, showing no
         respect for the dead.
      2. *Their sentence* (2:2-3): Their cities will be burned, and their
         people will be killed.
   G. **Judah** (2:4-5)
      1. *Their sin* (2:4): They have rejected the law of God.
      2. *Their sentence* (2:5): Jerusalem will be destroyed.

H. Israel (2:6-16)
  1. *Their sins* (2:6-12)
    a. Bribery (2:6): They pervert justice with dishonest scales.
    b. Cruelty to the poor (2:7a): They trample helpless people in the dirt.
    c. Immorality (2:7b): Father and son sleep with the same woman.
    d. Hypocrisy (2:8): They go to religious festivals in stolen clothing.
    e. Tempting the godly to sin (2:9-12): They cause the Nazirites to sin by making them drink wine.
  2. *Their sentence* (2:13-16)
    a. They will groan as an overloaded wagon (2:13)
    b. Their enemies will defeat them (2:14-16): The runners, the warriors, and those on horses will be unable to get away.

SECTION OUTLINE TWO (AMOS 3–6)
These chapters record for us three sermons preached by Amos.

I. AMOS'S FIRST SERMON (3:1-15)
  A. The privileges of Israel (3:1-3): Amos reminds the nation that God treats them as a special nation.
  B. The perversions of Israel (3:10)
    1. *They do not know right from wrong* (3:10a).
    2. *Their homes are full of loot they have stolen from others* (3:10b).
  C. The prophecy against Israel (3:4-9, 11-15)
    1. *God will roar out his wrath as a hungry lion* (3:4-9): God warns the people, but they do not listen.
    2. *Their enemies will devour them* (3:11-14): They will be torn into pieces.
    3. *Their beautiful homes will be destroyed* (3:15).

II. AMOS'S SECOND SERMON (4:1-13)
  A. He denounces the Israel of God (4:1-5).
    1. *Their godless women* (4:1-3): They will be led away with hooks in their noses.
    2. *Their hypocrisy* (4:4-5): They offer sacrifices to idols.
  B. He defends the God of Israel (4:6-13).
    1. *The past patience of God* (4:6-11): He has given Israel repeated opportunities to repent, all to no avail.
    2. *The future punishment from God* (4:12-13): The nation will soon face him in judgment.

III. Amos's Third Sermon (5:1–6:14)
  A. **God's invitation to Israel** (5:4-9, 14-15): Amos makes one final plea, urging his people to repent.
    1. *Seek God and live* (5:4, 7-9): God is all-powerful.
    2. *Renounce your idolatry* (5:5-6): They are to worship idols no longer.
    3. *Do what is good* (5:14-15): The Lord will be their helper if they are obedient.
  B. **God's indictment of Israel** (5:1-3, 10-13, 16-27; 6:1-14)
    1. *The nation's perversions* (5:10-13, 25-26; 6:1-7, 12-13)
      a. They hate the truth (5:10): They hate honest judges and people who tell the truth.
      b. They oppose the good (5:11): They trample the poor and take what they have.
      c. They are guilty of extortion and bribery (5:12-13): They oppress good people by taking bribes.
      d. They are lazy and complacent (6:1-3): They lounge in luxury and think they are safe.
      e. They are materialistic and indulgent (6:4-5): They lie on comfortable beds eating choice meat and singing idle songs.
      f. They are a nation of drunkards (6:6-7): They drink wine by the bowlful.
      g. They have turned justice into poison (6:12): They make bitter the sweet fruit of righteousness.
      h. They are arrogant (6:13): They boast that they have made conquests on their own.
      i. They worship idols (5:25-26): Their real interest is in the gods they have made themselves.
    2. *The nation's punishment* (5:1-3, 16-24, 27; 6:8-11, 14)
      a. To be broken and deserted (5:1-2): She will fall, never to rise again.
      b. To lose 90 percent of her soldiers in battle (5:3)
      c. To grieve (5:16-18): Weeping will be heard throughout the land.
      d. To go from bad to worse (5:19-20): It will be a day without a ray of hope.
      e. To have hypocritical offerings rejected by God (5:21-22)
      f. To have her songs rejected (5:23-24): God wants to see a river of righteous living instead.
      g. To go into slavery in exile (5:27; 6:14)
      h. To lose their pride and glory (6:8-11): God will give everything to their enemies.

I. THE PLAGUES (7:1-9; 8:1–9:10): These verses describe five visions received by Amos, all dealing with God's judgment on Israel.
   A. **Vision of the locusts** (7:1-3)
      1. *God's intention* (7:1): He is preparing a vast locust plague to destroy Israel's crops.
      2. *Amos's intervention* (7:2-3): The prophet prays, and this judgment is set aside.
   B. **Vision of the fire** (7:4-6)
      1. *God's intention* (7:4): A great fire will soon devour the land.
      2. *Amos's intervention* (7:5-6): Again the prophet prays, and judgment is averted.
   C. **Vision of the plumb line** (7:7-9)
      1. *The revelation* (7:7): Amos sees God measuring the "spiritual straightness" of Israel with a plumb line.
      2. *The results* (7:8-9): The moral crookedness of the nation demands divine judgment.
   D. **Vision of the summer fruit** (8:1-14)
      1. *The symbol* (8:1-2): Israel is pictured as a basket of fruit, ripe for judgment because of sin.
      2. *The sin* (8:4-6)
         a. The rich are robbing and enslaving the poor, buying and selling them for a pair of sandals (8:4a, 6).
         b. The needy in the land are being trampled on (8:4b).
         c. Gross dishonesty can be witnessed everywhere (8:5).
      3. *The suffering* (8:3, 7-14): Sin always results in sorrow, pain, and disaster! Amos now describes a fourfold judgment:
         a. In regard to sinners (8:3, 10)
            (1) Dead bodies will be scattered everywhere (8:3): Singing will turn to wailing.
            (2) Sheer misery will replace mirth (8:10): Celebrations will become times of mourning, and songs of joy will become weeping.
         b. In regard to the soil (8:7-8): The entire land will rise and fall like the Nile River.
         c. In regard to the skies (8:9): The sun will go down at noon.
         d. In regard to the Scriptures (8:11-14)
            (1) The famine (8:11): God himself will send a famine of hearing the words of the Lord.
            (2) The fruitless search (8:12-14): Men will wander everywhere attempting to find it!
   E. **The vision of God at the altar** (9:1-10): Amos sees the Lord standing at the altar, and God tells Amos that he will destroy the people.

II. THE PRIEST (7:10-17)
   A. Amos's confrontation with Amaziah (7:10-13)
      1. *He slanders Amos* (7:10-11): Amaziah tells King Jeroboam II that Amos is a traitor and a rebel.
      2. *He scorns Amos* (7:12-13): Amaziah tells Amos to take his foolish preaching back to Judah.
   B. Amos's clarification to Amaziah (7:14-15): He acknowledges that he is neither a prophet nor the son of a prophet. But he then adds that:
      1. *He feels unworthy* (7:14): "I'm just a shepherd, and I take care of fig trees."
      2. *He knows God has called him to prophesy* (7:15).
   C. Amos's condemnation of Amaziah (7:16-17)
      1. *Amaziah's wife will become a prostitute* (7:16-17a).
      2. *Amaziah's sons and daughters will be killed* (7:17b).
      3. *Amaziah's land will be divided up* (7:17c).
      4. *Amaziah will die as a slave in a pagan land* (7:17d).

III. THE PROMISES (9:11-15)
   A. Jerusalem will be rebuilt to its former glory (9:11-12): The walls will be rebuilt.
   B. Israel will be restored to her former land (9:13-15): The people will rebuild the ruined cities and will live in them.

Obadiah

SECTION OUTLINE ONE (OBADIAH 1)

Obadiah receives two visions: the first, about Edom; the second, about Israel.

I. THE HOUSE OF EDOM REDUCED BY GOD (1:1-16)
   A. **Edom's contempt** (1:3, 10-14)
      1. *Their thankless hearts* (1:3): Dwelling in the high and inaccessible cliffs of their land has made the Edomites boastful.
      2. *Their treacherous hand* (1:10-14): The Edomites, relatives of the Israelites (the nations are descendants of the twin brothers Jacob and Esau), have sided with Jerusalem's enemies on a number of occasions.
   B. **Edom's condemnation** (1:1-2, 4-9, 15-16)
      1. *The source* (1:1-2, 7)
         a. Her foes (1:1-2)
         b. Her friends (1:7)
      2. *The severity* (1:4-6, 8-9, 15-16)
         a. Her wealth will be removed (1:4-6).
         b. Her wisdom will be reduced (1:8-9).
         c. Her wickedness will be returned (1:15-16): Edom will now reap what she has sown.

II. THE HOUSE OF JACOB RESTORED BY GOD (1:17-21)
   A. **They will repossess their land** (1:17-20).
   B. **They will rule over their land** (1:21).

Jonah

SECTION OUTLINE ONE (JONAH 1–2)
When God commands Jonah to go to Nineveh, Jonah protests—and
learns his lesson. After being swallowed by a huge fish, he prays for
deliverance.

I. JONAH'S REFUSAL SHOWS GOD'S PATIENCE (1:1-17).
   A. **The order** (1:1-2): God commands Jonah to go to Nineveh and
      preach against its wickedness.
   B. **The objection** (1:3): Jonah refuses and boards a ship going to
      Tarshish, in the opposite direction from Nineveh!
   C. **The ordeal** (1:4-17)
      1. *The furious storm* (1:4): God sends a violent wind that
         threatens to sink the ship.
      2. *The fear* (1:5-7)
         a. The sailors attempt to protect the boat in the storm (1:5-6):
            The sailors pray to their gods and throw the cargo over-
            board to lighten the ship.
         b. The sailors attempt to point the blame for the storm (1:7):
            They cast lots to determine who is responsible for their
            trouble, and the lot falls upon Jonah.
      3. *The fault* (1:8-16)
         a. The confrontation (1:8): The sailors confront Jonah,
            demanding to know who he is and what he has done.
         b. The confession (1:9-11): Jonah acknowledges that he is
            running from God.
         c. The counsel (1:12-14): Jonah advises them that if they
            throw him overboard, the storm will calm.
         d. The calm (1:15-16): The sailors throw Jonah overboard,
            and the storm stops at once.
      4. *The fish (1:17):* God arranges for a great fish to swallow Jonah.
II. JONAH'S PRAYER SHOWS GOD'S POWER (2:1-10).
   A. **Jonah's despair** (2:1-6)
      1. *The waters close around him* (2:1-5a).
      2. *Seaweed wraps itself around his head* (2:5b).
      3. *He sinks to the bottom of the sea* (2:6).

  B. Jonah's dedication (2:7-9): He remembers and renews his previous vow to serve and obey God.

  C. Jonah's deliverance (2:10): God commands the fish to spit Jonah up on the beach.

SECTION OUTLINE TWO (JONAH 3–4)

When Jonah preaches to the Ninevites, they repent and are saved. But Jonah resents God for saving his enemies, so God has to teach him about compassion.

I. NINEVEH'S REVIVAL SHOWS GOD'S PARDON (3:1-10).

 A. Jonah's commission (3:1-4)

  1. *The nature* (3:1-2): For the second time, the prophet is ordered to Nineveh.

  2. *The numbers* (3:3-4)

   a. Three days (3:3): Nineveh is so big, it takes three days to see it all.

   b. Forty days (3:4): Jonah says God will destroy the city after this time if the people do not repent.

 B. Nineveh's confession (3:5-9)

  1. *The ruler repents* (3:6-9).

  2. *The rest repent* (3:5).

 C. God's compassion (3:10): Nineveh's repentance saves the city from divine destruction.

II. JONAH'S RESENTMENT SHOWS GOD'S COMPASSION AND JONAH'S LACK OF PITY (4:1-11).

 A. Jonah's twofold complaint (4:1-9)

  1. *About God sparing Nineveh* (4:1-3)

  2. *About the sun's glare* (4:4-9)

   a. The watch (4:4-5): Jonah waits outside the city to see what will happen.

   b. The wonders (4:6-8): God now creates three things:

    (1) A welcome vine (4:6): It shades Jonah from the fierce heat.

    (2) A worm (4:7): It destroys the vine.

    (3) A wind (4:8): It almost scorches Jonah.

   c. The whining (4:9): Jonah continues to complain, this time about the death of the vine.

 B. God's manifold compassion (4:10-11)

  1. *The rebuke* (4:10): God chastens Jonah for his concern over the vine.

  2. *The revelation* (4:11): God says his concern is for the people and animals living in Nineveh.

Micah

SECTION OUTLINE ONE (MICAH 1–3)
Micah receives visions of God's grief over Judah's and Israel's evil
deeds, their coming destruction and later deliverance, the capture of
Jerusalem, and the future arrival of the Son of Man.

I. THE DEPRAVITY OF JUDAH AND ISRAEL (2:1-2, 6-11; 3:1-5, 8-11)
   A. **Among the laity** (2:1-2, 6-10)
      1. *They continually plot evil* (2:1).
      2. *They practice fraud and violence* (2:2).
      3. *They reject the Holy Spirit* (2:6-7).
      4. *They are insolent thieves* (2:8).
      5. *They mistreat widows and orphans* (2:9-10).
   B. **Among the leaders** (2:11; 3:1-5, 8-11)
      1. *They are drunken liars* (2:11).
      2. *They hate good and love evil* (3:1).
      3. *They devour the sheep* (3:2-5).
      4. *They despise justice* (3:8-9).
      5. *They shed innocent blood* (3:10).
      6. *They accept bribes* (3:11).

II. THE DESTRUCTION OF JUDAH AND ISRAEL (1:1-16; 2:3-5; 3:6-7, 12)
   A. **The Judge** (1:1-4): Using fearful, poetic language, Micah
      describes an angry God coming from his Temple in judgment.
   B. **The judged** (1:5-16)
      1. *Samaria* (1:5-8)
      2. *Judah* (1:9-16)
   C. **The judgment** (2:3-5; 3:6-7, 12)
      1. *Israel and Judah will be rewarded evil for evil* (2:3).
      2. *Their enemies will mock them* (2:4-5).
      3. *God will refuse to communicate with them* (3:6-7).
      4. *Both Jerusalem and the Temple will be destroyed* (3:12).

III. THE DELIVERANCE OF JUDAH AND ISRAEL (2:12-13)
   A. **They will be regathered** (2:12).
   B. **They will be restored** (2:13).

SECTION OUTLINE TWO (MICAH 4–5)
Micah discusses two key events: the capture of the City of David and the coming of the Son of David.

I. THE CAPTURE OF THE CITY OF DAVID (4:9-10a; 5:1)
   A. The defeat (5:1): Jerusalem will be taken and its king (Zedekiah) humbled.
   B. The deportation (4:9-10a): The people will suffer much and will be carried off as captives to Babylonia.

II. THE COMING OF THE SON OF DAVID (4:1-8, 10b-13; 5:2-15)
   A. Christ's first coming (5:2-3)
      1. *His birth in Bethlehem* (5:2)
      2. *His rejection by Israel* (5:3)
   B. Christ's second coming (4:1-8, 10b-13; 5:4-15)
      1. *The Temple will become the universal worship center* (4:1).
      2. *All nations will learn the Word of God* (4:2).
      3. *Wars will cease* (4:3-5).
      4. *The exiles will be strengthened* (4:6-7).
      5. *Israel will be reestablished in the land* (4:8, 10b).
      6. *Israel's enemies will be destroyed* (4:11-13; 5:5b-15).
      7. *King Jesus will meet all human needs* (5:4-5a).

SECTION OUTLINE THREE (MICAH 6–7)
As Micah addresses God's case against Israel—and his compassion for the people—his confidence in God grows.

I. THE LORD AND ISRAEL (6:1-16; 7:1-6, 11-20)
   A. God's case against Israel (6:1-2, 10-12; 7:1-6)
      1. *The witnesses* (6:1-2): God calls upon the mountains and hills as witnesses.
      2. *The wickedness* (6:10-12; 7:1-6)
         a. Ill-gotten gain (6:10-11)
         b. Violent lying (6:12)
         c. Nonexistent goodness (7:1)
         d. Shedding of innocent blood (7:2)
         e. Taking of bribes (7:3)
         f. As harmful as briars and thorns (7:4)
         g. Betrayal by family and friends (7:5-6)
   B. God's compassion for Israel (6:3-9)
      1. *In the past* (6:3-5)
      2. *At the present* (6:6-9): He desires for them to "do what is right, to love mercy, and to walk humbly."
   C. God's chastening of Israel (6:13-16; 7:13)
      1. *Their land will become empty and desolate* (7:13).
      2. *They will fail at whatever they do* (6:14-15).
      3. *Misery will become their close companion* (6:13).

       4. *Their enemies will treat them with contempt* (6:16).

  D. God's conversion of Israel (7:11-12, 14-20)

      1. *The Millennium of God* (7:11-12, 14-17)

         a. Their cities will be rebuilt (7:11).

         b. Honor will come to them from the nations (7:12).

         c. Peace and prosperity will be their lot (7:14).

         d. Their foes will tremble before them (7:15-17).

      2. *The God of the Millennium* (7:18-20): Micah ends his book with a fivefold description of the awesome God of Israel:

         a. He is unique (7:18a).

         b. He does away with sin (7:18b).

         c. He is merciful (7:18c).

         d. He is compassionate (7:19).

         e. He is faithful (7:20).

II. THE LORD AND MICAH (7:7-10)

  A. Micah's confession to God (7:9): "I will be patient as God punishes me."

  B. Micah's confidence in God (7:7-8, 10): "I wait confidently for God to save me."

Nahum

I. NAHUM'S PREDICTION OF NINEVEH'S FALL (1:1-7, 9-15; 2:12; 3:1, 4-10)
   A. The purpose (1:1-2, 7, 9-15; 2:12; 3:1, 4-10): God will accomplish this for two reasons:
      1. *To protect Judah* (1:1-2, 7, 13, 15)
         a. Jehovah's confirmation (1:1-2, 7): Nahum says God is jealous over those he loves and takes vengeance on all who would harm them.
         b. Judah's celebration (1:13, 15): The people will soon rejoice over the destruction of the cruel Assyrian Empire.
      2. *To punish Nineveh* (1:9-12, 14; 2:12; 3:1, 4-10): Her wickedness will bring down God's wrath. Nineveh will be destroyed for her:
         a. Defiance of God (1:9-12)
         b. Idolatry (1:14)
         c. Terrible bloodshed (2:12; 3:1)
         d. Involvement in the occult (3:4-10)
   B. The power (1:3-6): Nahum says when sinful men (in this case the Assyrians) exhaust God's patience, they face the terrible power of God's wrath, which is like:
      1. *A raging storm* (1:3-5)
      2. *A consuming fire* (1:6)

II. NAHUM'S DESCRIPTION OF NINEVEH'S FALL (1:8; 2:1-11, 13; 3:2-3, 11-19)
   A. The sources of her destruction (1:8; 2:3-4)
      1. *Waters will overflow her* (1:8): The Tigris River will rush through a breach in the walls and will help to destroy the city.
      2. *Babylonian warriors will invade her* (2:3-4).
   B. The severity of her destruction (2:1-2, 6-11, 13; 3:2-3, 11-19)
      1. *As foretold by God* (3:11-15)
         a. The city will stagger like a terrified drunkard (3:11).
         b. All its fortresses will fall (3:12).

    c. Its soldiers will be helpless (3:13a).
    d. Nineveh will be sacked and burned (3:13b-15).
  2. *As fulfilled by God* (2:1-2, 6-11, 13; 3:2-3, 16-19)
    a. The overview of the battle for Nineveh (2:1-2): The
       Ninevites struggle to defend themselves, but to no avail.
    b. The outcome following the battle for Nineveh (2:6-11, 13;
       3:2-3, 16-19): Ninevah is completely obliterated.

Habakkuk

SECTION OUTLINE ONE (HABAKKUK 1–3)
Habakkuk searches for answers to two questions and is reassured by God.

I. THE SEARCH (1:1–2:13, 15-20): Habakkuk asks God two questions.
  A. The first Q&A (1:1-11)
    1. *Q: Will Judah be punished?* (1:1-4): Habakkuk is troubled over:
       a. Jehovah's silence (1:1-2): Habakkuk's prayers about the terrible violence in the land have gone unanswered.
       b. Judah's sins (1:3-4): There is destruction, violence, arguing, fighting, and injustice everywhere.
    2. *A: Judah will be punished* (1:5-11).
       a. The soldiers (1:5-6): God will send the Babylonians to chasten his people.
       b. The severity (1:7): These warriors are notorious for their cruelty.
       c. The symbols (1:8-9): Their soldiers are like
          (1) Swift leopards (1:8a)
          (2) Fierce wolves (1:8b)
          (3) Devouring eagles (1:8c-9)
       d. The scorn (1:10-11): They laugh at their enemies, holding them in great contempt.
  B. The second Q&A (1:12-17; 2:1-13, 15-20)
    1. *Q: Will Babylon be punished?* (1:12-17): Babylon is even more wicked than Judah.
    2. *A: Babylon will be punished* (2:1-13, 15-20).
       a. The record (2:1-2): God tells Habakkuk to write the answer on a tablet in large, clear letters so that everyone can get the message.
       b. The reassurance (2:3): Even though it might appear that God is delaying judgment, Babylon will eventually be crushed.
       c. The righteous (2:4): Until then, those in exile should live by faith.

   d. The reasons (2:5-13, 15-19): God will judge Babylon for her many sins:
    (1) Drunkenness and greed (2:5)
    (2) Brutal treatment of the nations (2:6)
    (3) The shedding of blood (2:7-13)
    (4) Being merchants of terror (2:15-16)
    (5) Destroying other lands (2:17)
    (6) Gross idolatry (2:18-19)
   e. The respect (2:20): "The LORD is in his holy Temple. Let all the earth be silent before him."

II. THE SOLUTION (2:14; 3:1-19): Habakkuk is reassured.
  A. Because of what he has heard (2:14; 3:1-2)
   1. *About God's fame and deeds* (3:1-2)
   2. *About the entire earth someday being filled with God's glory* (2:14)
  B. Because of what he now sees (3:3-19): In essence, he views the majesty of the Almighty moving across the earth.
   1. *God's splendor* (3:3-4): His glory is as the sunrise. "Rays of brilliant light flash from his hands."
   2. *God's strength* (3:5-12, 14-15)
    a. He judges with pestilence and plague (3:5).
    b. He shakes the nations, shatters the mountains, and levels the hills (3:6).
    c. He utterly crushes his enemies (3:7-12, 14-15).
   3. *God's salvation* (3:13): He delivers his chosen people.
   4. *God's security* (3:16-19): Because of all he has seen, heard, and experienced, Habakkuk determines that he will:
    a. Trust God in time of fear (3:16)
    b. Trust God in time of famine (3:17-19)

Zephaniah

SECTION OUTLINE ONE (ZEPHANIAH 1–3)
Zephaniah describes three special "days," two of which are grievous, while the third is glorious.

I. THE GRIEVOUS DAYS (1:1–3:8): Zephaniah pronounces judgment.
   A. **The first grievous day** (1:1-13; 2:1-15; 3:1-5): Historical in scope, it includes Judah and her surrounding neighbors and is fulfilled by the king of Babylon.
      1. *Judah* (1:1-13; 2:1-3; 3:1-5)
         a. Zephaniah's condemnation (1:1-13; 3:1-5)
            (1) Her sins (1:4-6, 8-9, 11-12; 3:1-5)
               (a) Idolatry (1:4-6)
               (b) Greed (1:11)
               (c) Utter indifference to God (1:12; 3:2)
               (d) Rebellion, violence, and crime (3:1)
               (e) Leaders who follow pagan customs (1:8-9)
               (f) Judges who are like ravenous wolves that leave no trace of their prey (3:3)
               (g) Godless prophets and priests (3:4-5)
            (2) Her sentence (1:1-3, 7, 10, 13)
               (a) Cries of anguish will be heard throughout the land (1:10).
               (b) The land will be reduced to rubble (1:1-3, 7).
               (c) The people's wealth will be plundered and their homes demolished (1:13).
         b. Zephaniah's invitation (2:1-3): He tells Judah to repent and escape God's wrath.
      2. *The Gentiles* (2:4-15)
         a. The Philistine cities of Gaza, Ashkelon, Ashdod, and Ekron (2:4-7): Israel's western enemies
         b. Moab and Ammon (2:8-11): Israel's eastern enemies
         c. Ethiopia (2:12): Israel's southern enemy
         d. Assyria and its capital, Nineveh (2:13-15): Israel's northern enemy

B. The second grevious day (1:14-18; 3:6-8): Prophetic in scope, it will include all nations and is yet to be fulfilled by the King of heaven.
  1. *The designation* (1:14): Zephaniah calls it the "day of the LORD," a probable reference to the coming Great Tribulation.
  2. *The devastation* (1:15-18; 3:6-8)
      a. Earth's citizens will stumble as blind men (1:15-17a).
      b. Their blood will be poured out into the dust (1:17b).
      c. Wealth will become absolutely useless (1:18).
      d. Few survivors will be left (3:6-7).
      e. The entire earth will be devoured by the fire of divine wrath (3:8).

II. THE GLORIOUS DAY (3:9-20): Zephaniah proclaims justice.
  A. To the Gentiles (3:9): Their many languages will be unified and purified, thus allowing all people to worship God together.
  B. To the Jews (3:10-20)
    1. *Their regathering* (3:10, 19-20a)
    2. *Their restoring* (3:20b)
    3. *Their refining* (3:11-13)
    4. *Their rejoicing* (3:14-18): God himself will join in their happy song.

Haggai

SECTION OUTLINE ONE (HAGGAI 1–2)
Haggai preaches three messages to the returning Jewish remnant:
the first, to their hands; the second, to their hearts; and the third,
to their heads.

I. HIS AUGUST MESSAGE (1:1-15): Directed to the people's hands, it
   says, *Reform.*
   A. **God's exhortation** (1:2, 4-11): Build the Temple!
      1. *The people's complacency* (1:2): "The people are saying, 'The
         time has not yet come to rebuild the LORD's house—the
         Temple.'"
      2. *The Lord's chastisement* (1:4-11)
         a. His reminder (1:4-6, 9-11)
            (1) The people's materialism (1:4-5): They live in luxurious
                homes while the Temple lies in ruins.
            (2) The people's misery (1:6, 9-11): They plant much but
                harvest little. They attempt many things but fail in
                everything.
         b. His reassurance (1:7-8): If you build, I'll bless!
   B. **God's exhorters** (1:1, 3, 12-15): God now speaks through three
      of his choice servants: Zerubbabel (Judah's governor), Jeshua (or
      Joshua—the high priest), and Haggai (Judah's prophet).

II. HIS OCTOBER MESSAGE (2:1-9): Directed to the people's hearts, it
    says, *Patience:* There is weeping and rejoicing at the modest second
    Temple's dedication, for some old men remember the glories of the
    first one (Solomon's Temple). In light of this, Haggai attempts to
    encourage all as he speaks of the future magnificent millennial
    Temple.
    A. **The buildings** (2:1-5, 9)
       1. *The first and second Temples* (2:1-5): Haggai tells them to take
          courage, for God's presence among them is far more
          important than the size of any earthly Temple.
       2. *The future Temple* (2:9): The people are reassured that the
          millennial Temple will be the biggest and best of all.
    B. **The builder** (2:6-8): God himself will build the future Temple.

However, this glorious event will be preceded by two key events:
1. *The nations' chastening* (2:6-7a)
2. *The Messiah's coming* (2:7b-8)

III. HIS DECEMBER MESSAGE (2:10-23): Directed to the people's heads, it says, *Ponder:* Two facts Haggai wants the people to think about are
  A. **Judah's contamination** (2:10-19)
      1. *Past problems* (2:10-17)
          a. The examples (2:10-13)
              (1) God's first question (2:10-12)
                  (a) The question (2:10-11): If a person carrying a holy offering brushes against an object, does that object become holy?
                  (b) The answer (2:12): No, for holiness does not pass on to other things that way.
              (2) God's second question (2:13)
                  (a) The question (2:13a): If a person defiled by contact with a dead body touches an object, does that object become defiled?
                  (b) The answer (2:13b): Yes!
          b. The explanation (2:14-17): Haggai applies this principle to the people, saying that their sinful ways have contaminated their consecrated offerings to God, resulting in crop failures, famine, etc.
      2. *Future promises* (2:18-19): Because the people repent of all this and lay the Temple's foundation, God will now abundantly bless them.
  B. **Zerubbabel's elevation** (2:20-23): God promises to honor and elevate this faithful governor of Judah someday. This will occur
      1. *After the Great Tribulation* (2:20-22)
      2. *During the glorious Millennium* (2:23)

Zechariah

SECTION OUTLINE ONE (ZECHARIAH 1–6)
Zechariah encourages Judah's repentance, receives eight visions from God in one night, and is told how to reward Joshua (Judah's high priest).

I. JUDAH'S REPENTANCE (1:1-6)
   A. **In the past God's people have been chastened for their corruption** (1:1-2).
   B. **Now God's people will be cleansed by their confession** (1:3-6).

II. JEHOVAH'S REVELATIONS (1:7–6:8): The eight visions
   A. **First vision—the man among the myrtle trees** (1:7-17): He is seated upon a red horse, accompanied by other horses and riders. Two questions are now asked and answered.
      1. *By the prophet* (1:7-11)
         a. The question (1:7-9a): "What are all those horses for?"
         b. The answer (1:9b-11): They have been sent by the Lord to patrol the earth.
      2. *By the angel* (1:12-17)
         a. The question (1:12): "How long will it be until you again show mercy to them?"
         b. The answer (1:13-17): God will indeed someday bless his people abundantly.
   B. **Second vision—the four horns and the four blacksmiths** (1:18-21)
      1. *The four horns* (1:18-19): Israel and Judah are scattered by these four world powers.
      2. *The four blacksmiths* (1:20-21): God will use them to destroy the four horns.
   C. **Third vision—the man with the measuring line** (2:1-13)
      1. *The plan to measure Jerusalem* (2:1-3): How wide and long is it?
      2. *The promise to magnify Jerusalem* (2:4-13)
         a. Great crowds will live both within and outside its walls—in safety (2:4-7, 10-13).
         b. Judah's enemies will be totally defeated (2:8-9).

D. Fourth vision—the cleansing and clothing of Jeshua (Joshua), Judah's high priest (3:1-10)
   1. *The prejudice* (3:1): Satan is seen in heaven, accusing Jeshua of many things.
   2. *The person* (3:2): God himself now rebukes the Devil.
   3. *The purifying* (3:3-5): Jeshua is cleansed from his sins and clothed in divine righteousness.
   4. *The promises* (3:6-10)
      a. To be a steward in God's building (3:6-7): Jeshua will be put in charge of God's Temple.
      b. To be a symbol for the Branch of God (3:8-10): He will become a type of the Messiah himself, God's Branch and the Foundation Stone.
E. Fifth vision—the gold lampstand and the two olive trees (4:1-14)
   1. *The gold lampstand* (4:1-2, 10)
      a. The information (4:1-2): Zechariah sees a gold lampstand holding seven lamps, each supplied with olive oil from a reservoir at the top.
      b. The interpretation (4:10): The seven lamps represent God's eyes that search all around the earth.
   2. *The two olive trees* (4:3-9, 11-14)
      a. The information (4:3): Zechariah sees two olive trees carved upon the lampstand, one on each side.
      b. The interpretation (4:4-9, 11-14): The two olive trees represent God's two anointed servants who will, through divine power, complete the Temple building.
F. Sixth vision—the flying scroll (5:1-4)
   1. *The size* (5:1-2): Zechariah sees a flying scroll, 30 feet long and 15 feet wide.
   2. *The symbol* (5:3-4): This scroll represents God's curse upon every home in the land whose occupants use God's name in a false or blasphemous way.
G. Seventh vision—the woman in the basket (5:5-11)
   1. *The transgressions* (5:5-8)
      a. The scope (5:5-6): The basket contains the sins of all those living in Judah.
      b. The symbol (5:7-8): A woman who represents the wickedness of the people sits inside the basket.
   2. *The transporters* (5:9): He sees two women with wings like those of a stork.
   3. *The terminal point* (5:10-11): The destination is Babylon, where a temple will be built to house the basket.
H. Eighth vision—the four chariots (6:1-8)
   1. *What he sees* (6:1-3): Zechariah sees four chariots coming from between two bronze mountains, each pulled by a different team of colored horses.

2. *What it symbolizes* (6:4-8): The four heavenly spirits sent from God to do his work on earth.

III. JESHUA'S REWARD (6:9-15)
  A. **What Zechariah is to do** (6:9-11): Collect the gifts of gold brought to Jerusalem by four Jewish exiles who arrive from Babylon and make a crown of gold for Jeshua the high priest, setting it upon his head.
  B. **Why Zechariah is to do it** (6:12-15)
    1. *By this action the high priest represents the future reign of the Messiah over Israel* (6:12-13).
    2. *By this action the four exiles represent the future return of the Jews to Israel* (6:14-15).

SECTION OUTLINE TWO (ZECHARIAH 7–14)
Zechariah asks for clarification about God's law, predicts conquests in battle, and addresses the first and second comings of Christ.

I. THE CLARIFICATION (7:1-14; 8:9-19)
  A. **Judah's request** (7:1-3): The people want to know if they should continue their traditional custom of fasting and mourning during the fifth month as they have done in the past.
  B. **Jehovah's reply** (7:4-14; 8:9-19)
    1. *He chastens them for what they have done* (7:4-7, 11-14).
      a. Their hearts are insincere when they do observe the fifth-month fast (7:4-7).
      b. They are proud and rebellious (7:11-12).
      c. Their sin has led to their dispersion among the nations (7:13-14).
    2. *He challenges them to do what they must do now* (7:8-10; 8:9-19).
      a. Be honest, merciful, and kind (7:8-9).
      b. Don't oppress the helpless (7:10).
      c. Complete the Temple building, and you will be blessed (8:9-15).
      d. Always tell the truth (8:16-18).
      e. Turn the fifth-month fast into a godly celebration (8:19).

II. THE CONQUESTS (9:1-8, 11-13): These verses seem to predict the successful warfare of some Gentile pagans and Jewish patriots.
  A. **The Gentile pagans** (9:1-8): Here is the record of the conquests of Alexander the Great in 333 B.C.
    1. *The destruction of Phoenicia, Syria, and Philistia* (9:1-7)
    2. *The deliverance of Judah* (9:8): Alexander does not destroy Jerusalem.
  B. **The Jewish patriots** (9:11-13): This passage probably refers to the victory of the Maccabean Jews over the Syrians in 165 B.C.

III. THE COMINGS (8:1-8, 20-23; 9:9-10, 14-17; 10:1–14:21): Zechariah gives graphic details about the first and second comings of Christ.
   A. The first coming (9:9; 11:4-14; 12:10; 13:7)
      1. *His role as a shepherd* (11:4-7)
      2. *His triumphal entry* (9:9)
      3. *His twofold rejection* (11:8-14; 12:10; 13:7)
         a. Israel rejects the Messiah (11:8, 12-13; 12:10; 13:7).
            (1) He is hated (11:8).
            (2) He is betrayed (11:12-13).
            (3) He is abandoned (13:7).
            (4) He is crucified (12:10).
         b. The Messiah rejects Israel (11:9-11, 14).
   B. The second coming (8:1-8, 20-23; 9:10, 14-17; 10:1–11:3; 11:15–13:6, 8-9; 14:1-21)
      1. *Pre-appearance events* (11:15-17; 12:1-8; 13:8-9; 14:1-2, 12-15)
         a. The Antichrist's reign (11:15-17)
         b. The Jewish remnant's survival (13:8-9)
         c. The battle for Jerusalem (12:1-8; 14:1-2, 12-15)
      2. *Appearance events* (8:1-8, 20-23; 9:14-15; 10:4-5; 11:1-3; 12:9-14; 14:3-5)
         a. Christ's return (14:4-5)
         b. The Battle of Armageddon (9:14-15; 10:4-5; 11:1-3; 12:9; 14:3)
         c. Israel's recognition of Christ (12:10-14)
         d. Jerusalem's salvation (8:1-8, 20-23)
      3. *Post-appearance events* (9:10, 16-17; 10:1-3, 6-12; 13:1-6; 14:6-11, 16-21)
         a. Unfaithful Israel's judgment (10:2-3)
         b. Faithful Israel's regathering (10:8-12)
         c. Israel's cleansing (13:1-6)
         d. Jerusalem's elevation (14:10-11)
         e. The lifting of nature's curse (10:1)
         f. Wondrous changes in the heavens (14:6-7)
         g. Living waters proceeding from Jerusalem to purify the land (14:8)
         h. Christ's universal reign (9:10)
         i. Universal joy (9:16-17; 10:6-7)
         j. Universal worship (14:9, 16-19)
         k. Universal holiness (14:20-21)

Malachi

SECTION OUTLINE ONE (MALACHI 1–4)
Malachi talks about Israel's privileged status and transgressions and God's future promises. He also refers to two key prophets: John the Baptist and Elijah.

I. ISRAEL'S PRIVILEGE (1:1-5)
   A. God's devotion to Jacob's descendants (1:1-2, 5)
   B. God's destruction of Esau's descendants (1:3-4)

II. ISRAEL'S POLLUTIONS (1:6–2:17; 3:5-15)
   A. The priests' sins (1:6–2:9)
      1. *Their rebellion* (1:6-14; 2:7-9)
         a. They despise and dishonor God's holy name (1:6, 11, 14b).
         b. They offer polluted sacrifices (1:7-10; 12-14a).
         c. They pervert God's Word, causing many to stumble (2:7-9).
      2. *Their rebuke* (2:1-3): God warns that the priests and their descendants will be severely punished if they do not repent.
      3. *Their role model* (2:4-6): Levi, the tribe's founder
   B. The people's sins (2:10-17; 3:5-15)
      1. *Their iniquities* (2:10-17; 3:5, 8-15)
         a. They are untrue to each other (2:10).
         b. They divorce their wives (2:13-16).
         c. They marry pagan wives (2:11-12).
         d. They claim evil is good (2:17).
         e. They are sorcerers, adulterers, liars, cheaters, oppressors, and unjust people (3:5).
         f. They slander God (3:13-15).
         g. They rob God (3:8-12).
      2. *God's invitation* (3:6-7): Repent!

III. ISRAEL'S PROPHETS (3:1a; 4:5-6): Malachi refers to two key prophets:
   A. John the Baptist, who introduces Christ's first coming (3:1a)
   B. Elijah, who will introduce Christ's second coming (4:5-6)

IV. GOD'S PROMISES TO ISRAEL (3:1b-4, 16-18; 4:1-4)
   A. Christ's coming (3:1b, 16; 4:1-4)
      1. *The place* (3:1b): The millennial Temple

    2. *The particulars* (3:16; 4:1-4)
       a. The journal (3:16): Christ will bring with him a scroll of
          remembrance, in which he will record the names of those
          who love and fear him.
       b. The judgment (4:1): He will punish the wicked.
       c. The joy (4:2-4): The Sun of Righteousness will rise with
          healing in his wings!
B. Israel's cleansing (3:2-4, 17-18)
    1. *To be refined as silver and gold* (3:2-4)
    2. *To be regarded as treasure* (3:17-18)

PART FIVE

Gospels

Matthew

SECTION OUTLINE ONE (MATTHEW 1–2)
The genealogy of Christ is presented. The Virgin Mary miraculously conceives, and her fiancé, Joseph, receives a visit from an angel. Mary and Joseph are married, and the baby Jesus is born.

I. THE RECORD OF THE MESSIAH (1:1-17): Matthew traces the genealogy leading to Jesus Christ, beginning with Abraham and concluding with Joseph, husband of Mary, Jesus' mother.
   A. **The preview** (1:1): The account begins with a reference to two all-important individuals:
      1. *David, Israel's royal father* (1:1a)
      2. *Abraham, Israel's racial father* (1:1b)
   B. **The overview** (1:2-16)
      1. *From Abraham to David* (1:2-6)
      2. *From Solomon to Jehoiachin (Jeconiah)* (1:7-11)
      3. *From Shealtiel to Jesus* (1:12-16)
   C. **The review** (1:17): Each phase of the threefold genealogical account encompasses fourteen generations.

II. THE REVELATION CONCERNING THE MESSIAH (1:18-25)
   A. **Joseph's distress** (1:18): He is heartbroken, assuming his pregnant wife-to-be has been unfaithful.
   B. **Joseph's decision** (1:19): Not wanting to disgrace Mary, he determines to break their engagement secretly.
   C. **Joseph's dream** (1:20-25)
      1. *The message in the dream* (1:20-23)
         a. Concerning the purity of Mary (1:20): Joseph is reassured that Mary's pregnancy is caused by the Holy Spirit.
         b. Concerning the person within Mary (1:21): The Angel of the Lord tells Joseph that Mary will bare a son and that he shall be named Jesus.
         c. Concerning the prophecy about Mary (1:22-23): This son, conceived without the aid of a human father, is the fulfillment of Isaiah's prophecy (Isa. 7:14).
      2. *The marriage following the dream* (1:24-25): Joseph takes Mary to be his wife.

III. THE REQUEST TO SEE THE MESSIAH (2:1-12)
   A. The wise men's journey (2:1-8): They travel to Jerusalem.
      1. *Their public meeting with King Herod* (2:1-6)
         a. The magi's request (2:1-2): "Where is the newborn King of the Jews?"
         b. The monarch's reaction (2:3-4)
            (1) His concern (2:3): Herod is greatly troubled!
            (2) His command (2:4): Herod demands that the Jewish priests tell him where the Messiah will be born.
         c. The ministers' reply (2:5-6)
            (1) The place (2:5): In Bethlehem!
            (2) The prophecy (2:6): This was the prediction of Micah the prophet (Micah 5:2).
      2. *Their private meeting with King Herod* (2:7-8)
         a. Herod's demand (2:7): He asks them when they first saw the star.
         b. Herod's deception (2:8): He says, "When you find the child, tell me, so that I can worship him, too."
   B. The wise men's joy (2:9-12): They rejoice when they find the child.
      1. *The witness of the star* (2:9): It leads them to the very house where Jesus is living.
      2. *The worship by the wise men* (2:10-11): They present him with gifts of gold, frankincense, and myrrh.
      3. *The warning from the Lord* (2:12): They are told to bypass Herod en route to their home.

IV. THE ESCAPE ROUTE OF THE MESSIAH (2:13-23): Joseph takes Mary and the young Jesus to Egypt.
   A. The reasons for the trip (2:13-15)
      1. *To flee the wrath of Herod* (2:13-14): Joseph is warned by God in a dream that Herod will try to kill Jesus.
      2. *To fulfill the words of Hosea* (2:15): This Old Testament prophet foretold the trip to Egypt (Hos. 11:1).
   B. The retaliation during the trip (2:16-18)
      1. *The purge of Herod* (2:16): He kills all the male babies in Bethlehem in an attempt to eliminate Jesus.
      2. *The prophecy of Jeremiah* (2:17-18): This Old Testament prophet predicted the Bethlehem massacre (Jer. 31:15).
   C. The return from the trip (2:19-23): Joseph receives two more dreams.
      1. *First dream* (2:19-21): Joseph is told that Herod is now dead and that he should depart from Egypt with his family.
      2. *Second dream* (2:22-23): Joseph is told that he should dwell in Nazareth.

SECTION OUTLINE TWO (MATTHEW 3)

John the Baptist begins his ministry and baptizes Jesus. The Holy Spirit descends upon Jesus, and God declares that he is pleased with his Son.

I. JOHN MINISTERS TO THE MULTITUDES (3:1-12)
   A. **What John preaches** (3:1-4)
      1. *His message* (3:1-3)
         a. As proclaimed (3:1-2): "Repent, for the Kingdom of Heaven is at hand."
         b. As predicted (3:3): Isaiah the prophet foretold John's ministry and message some 700 years earlier (Isa. 40:3).
      2. *His mantle* (3:4): He wears a garment of camel's hair and a leather belt, and he eats locusts and wild honey.
   B. **To whom John preaches (3:5-10)**
      1. *To the people of Israel* (3:5-6): Many accept his message, repent of their sins, and are baptized.
      2. *To the religious leaders of Israel* (3:7-10)
         a. John's description of these wicked men (3:7): He refers to them as a brood of snakes!
         b. The leaders' demand of John (3:8-10): He warns them to truly repent and do good works or be destroyed.
   C. **For whom John preaches** (3:11-12): He is preparing the way for the coming of the Messiah.

II. JOHN MINISTERS TO THE MESSIAH (3:13-17)
   A. **The agreement by the Baptist** (3:13-15)
      1. *John's objection* (3:13-14): John at first refuses Christ's request to be baptized, feeling he is unworthy to do so.
      2. *John's obedience* (3:15): After the second request he baptizes the Savior.
   B. **The anointing by the Spirit** (3:16): The Holy Spirit descends like a dove upon Jesus.
   C. **The approval by the Father** (3:17): A voice from heaven says, "This is my beloved Son, and I am fully pleased with him."

SECTION OUTLINE THREE (MATTHEW 4)

The Holy Spirit leads Jesus into the wilderness to be tempted by the Devil. Jesus triumphs over Satan, then returns to Galilee to begin his ministry and calls his first four disciples.

I. JESUS AND THE DEVIL (4:1-11): Jesus is led by the Spirit into the wilderness to be tempted by Satan.
   A. **The attacks** (4:1-10)
      1. *First round* (4:1-4)
         a. The temptation (4:1-3): "Change these stones into loaves of bread!"

b. The triumph (4:4): "People need more than bread for their life; they must feed on every word of God."
   2. *Second round* (4:5-7)
       a. The temptation (4:5-6): "If you are the Son of God, jump off [the pinnacle of the Temple]!"
       b. The triumph (4:7): "Do not test the Lord your God!"
   3. *Third round* (4:8-10)
       a. The temptation (4:8-9): "I will give [all the glory of the world] to you if you will only kneel down and worship me."
       b. The triumph (4:10): "Get out of here, Satan. For the Scriptures say, 'You must worship the Lord your God; serve only him.'"
   B. The angels (4:11): Following the temptations, angels come and care for Jesus.

II. JESUS AND THE DESPERATE (4:12-17, 23-25): He officially begins his ministry to needy people everywhere!
   A. To the spiritually darkened (4:12-17): He preaches to the people, urging them to turn from sin.
   B. To the physically disabled (4:23-25): He heals the sick wherever he goes.

III. JESUS AND THE DISCIPLES (4:18-22): He now extends a call to four future apostles.
   A. Peter and Andrew (4:18-20)
       1. *The fishermen* (4:18): Jesus meets these brothers by the Galilean Sea.
       2. *The fishers of men* (4:19-20): Jesus promises to make them successful soul winners.
   B. James and John (4:21-22)
       1. *Repairing their nets* (4:21): Jesus calls them to leave their work and come with him.
       2. *Renouncing their nets* (4:22): Like Peter and Andrew, these brothers follow Jesus.

SECTION OUTLINE FOUR (MATTHEW 5)
The Sermon on the Mount, part 1: Jesus lays down the principles and rules of the Kingdom.

I. THE KINGDOM AND BELIEVERS (5:1-16)
   A. Kingdom attributes (5:1-12)
       1. *The poor in spirit* (5:3)
           a. The role (5:3a): God blesses those who realize their need for him.
           b. The reward (5:3b): The Kingdom of Heaven is given to them.

2. *Those who mourn* (5:4)
   a. The role (5:4a): God blesses those who mourn.
   b. The reward (5:4b): They will be comforted.
3. *The meek* (5:5)
   a. The role (5:5a): God blesses the gentle and lowly.
   b. The reward (5:5b): The whole earth will belong to them.
4. *Those who hunger and thirst for righteousness* (5:6)
   a. The role (5:6a): God blesses those who seek after justice.
   b. The reward (5:6b): They will receive it in full.
5. *The merciful* (5:7)
   a. The role (5:7a): God blesses those who are merciful.
   b. The reward (5:7b): They will be shown mercy.
6. *The pure in heart* (5:8)
   a. The role (5:8a): God blesses those whose hearts are pure.
   b. The reward (5:8b): They will see God.
7. *The peacemakers* (5:9)
   a. The role (5:9a): God blesses those who work for peace.
   b. The reward (5:9b): They will be called the children of God.
8. *Those who are persecuted for the sake of righteousness* (5:10-12)
   a. The role (5:10a, 11): God blesses those who are persecuted because they live for God.
   b. The reward (5:10b, 12): The Kingdom of Heaven is theirs.
B. **Kingdom actions (5:13-16)**
1. *To function as the salt of the earth* (5:13)
2. *To function as the light of the world* (5:14-16): Their light and good deeds shine for all.

II. THE KINGDOM AND THE LAW (5:17-20)
A. **The Redeemer and the law** (5:17-18): Christ did not come to abolish the law but to fulfill it.
B. **The redeemed and the law** (5:19): Those who obey and teach God's laws will be great in the Kingdom of Heaven.
C. **The religious leaders and the law** (5:20): People like the godless Pharisees, who do not obey the law, will not enter into the Kingdom.

III. THE KINGDOM AND THE OLD TESTAMENT (5:21-48)
A. **In regard to murder** (5:21-26)
1. *The basic concept* (5:21): The law says, "Do not murder."
2. *The broadened concept* (5:22-26): Jesus says that hating someone is the same as murder. Our relationship with God is dependent on our relationship with others.
B. **In regard to adultery** (5:27-30)
1. *The basic concept* (5:27): The law says, "Do not commit adultery."
2. *The broadened concept* (5:28-30): Jesus says that looking lustfully at someone is the same as adultery.

   C. In regard to divorce (5:31-32)
     1. *The basic concept* (5:31): The law says, "A man can divorce his wife by merely giving her a letter of divorce."
     2. *The broadened concept* (5:32): Jesus says that unlawful divorce and remarriage is the same as adultery.
   D. In regard to oaths (5:33-37)
     1. *The basic concept* (5:33): The law says, "You must carry out the vows you have made to the Lord."
     2. *The broadened concept* (5:34-37): Jesus says, "Don't make any vows!" A simple yes or no should suffice.
   E. In regard to retaliation (5:38-42)
     1. *The basic concept* (5:38): The law says, "An eye for an eye and a tooth for a tooth."
     2. *The broadened concept* (5:39-42): Jesus says to turn the other cheek and to do more than is demanded.
   F. In regard to love (5:43-48)
     1. *The basic concept* (5:43): The law says, "'Love your neighbor' and hate your enemy."
     2. *The broadened concept* (5:44-48): Jesus says, "Love your enemies! Pray for those who persecute you!"

SECTION OUTLINE FIVE (MATTHEW 6)
The Sermon on the Mount, part 2: Jesus presents models for giving, prayer, fasting, money, and trust.

I. Jesus Talks about Giving (6:1-4)
   A. The rules (6:1-3)
     1. *Give sincerely* (6:1): You will receive reward from your Father in heaven.
     2. *Give secretly* (6:2-3): Calling attention to your giving will cause that to be your only reward.
   B. The reward (6:4): Give your gifts in secret, and God will reward you openly.

II. Jesus Talks about Praying (6:5-15)
   A. Essentials in prayer (6:5-8)
     1. *Prayers God rejects* (6:5, 7-8)
       a. Boasting prayers (6:5): Praying publicly brings reward from men only.
       b. Babbling prayers (6:7-8): God knows what you need before you ask.
     2. *Prayers God receives* (6:6): We should pray from the heart, in private.
   B. Elements in prayer (6:9-15): Jesus lists nine aspects of prayer.
     1. *Faith* (6:9a): "Our Father in heaven."
     2. *Worship* (6:9b): "May your name be honored."
     3. *Expectation* (6:10a): "May your kingdom come soon."

4. *Submission* (6:10b): "May your will be done here on earth, just as it is in heaven."
5. *Petition* (6:11): "Give us our food for today."
6. *Confession* (6:12a): "And forgive us our sins."
7. *Compassion* (6:12b, see also 14-15): "Just as we have forgiven those who have sinned against us."
8. *Dependence* (6:13a): "And don't let us yield to temptation."
9. *Acknowledgment* (6:13b): "For yours is the kingdom and the power and the glory forever. Amen."

III. JESUS TALKS ABOUT FASTING (6:16-18)
   A. **By hypocrites** (6:16): They disfigure their faces to show people they are fasting.
   B. **By the humble** (6:17-18): They comb their hair and wash their faces so only God knows what they are doing. Then the Father rewards them.

IV. JESUS TALKS ABOUT TREASURES (6:19-24)
   A. **Earthly treasures are insecure and corruptible** (6:19, 22-24): No one can serve two masters, but all must choose between God and gold!
   B. **Heavenly treasures are secure and incorruptible** (6:20-21): Where your treasure is, there your heart will be.

V. JESUS TALKS ABOUT TRUSTING (6:25-34)
   A. **The information** (6:25): We are told not to worry about food or clothes, for life consists of more than these things.
   B. **The illustrations** (6:26-30)
      1. *Consider the birds* (6:26-27): They do not sow, reap, or store up food, yet God feeds them!
      2. *Consider the lilies* (6:28-30): They don't worry about clothes, yet Solomon in all his glory was not dressed as beautifully as they are!
   C. **The invitation** (6:31-34): Put God in first place, and he will meet all your needs!

SECTION OUTLINE SIX (MATTHEW 7)

The Sermon on the Mount, part 3: Jesus teaches us to ask God for what we need, how to treat others, and how to live as a true child of the heavenly Father.

I. JESUS' EXHORTATIONS (7:1-12)
   A. **Our responsibilities to the saved** (7:1-2): We are not to harshly judge other believers.
   B. **Our responsibilities to ourselves** (7:3-5): We are to harshly judge ourselves!
   C. **Our responsibilities to the ungodly** (7:6): We are not to give holy things to depraved men.

D. Our responsibilities to the Lord (7:7-11)
   1. *The command* (7:7): We are to diligently seek God's will.
   2. *The confidence* (7:8): He promises to reveal his will if we ask!
   3. *The comparison* (7:9-11): If we, being sinful, can give good gifts to our children, how much more will the sinless Father impart to his children!
E. Our responsibilities to the world (7:12): We are to treat others as we would want them to treat us.

II. JESUS' ILLUSTRATION (7:13-27)
   A. The two roads (7:13-14)
      1. *The broad highway to hell* (7:13): The gate is wide, and many choose this way to destruction.
      2. *The narrow road to heaven* (7:14): The gate is narrow, and only a few ever find it.
   B. The two animals (a condemnation of false prophets) (7:1)
      1. *They pretend to be sheep* (7:15a): They seem harmless.
      2. *They prove to be wolves* (7:15b): They tear you apart.
   C. The two kinds of disciples (7:21-23)
      1. *True disciples* (7:21a): On judgment day, the true disciples will be separated from the false ones.
      2. *False disciples* (7:21b-23): On judgment day, the false disciples will be condemned.
         a. The wondrous deeds they will say they did (7:22): They will say they prophesied, cast out demons, and performed miracles in his name.
         b. The wicked deeds Christ will say they did (7:21b, 23): They disobeyed the Father, and God will say he never knew them.
   D. The two trees (7:16-20)
      1. *A good tree cannot produce bad fruit* (7:16, 18).
      2. *A bad tree cannot produce good fruit* (7:17, 19-20).
   E. The two builders (7:24-27)
      1. *The structures* (7:24, 26)
         a. One man built his house on solid rock (7:24).
         b. One man built his house on shifting sand (7:26).
      2. *The storm* (7:25, 27)
         a. The house on the rock stood firm (7:25).
         b. The house on the sand fell flat (7:27).

III. JESUS' DEMONSTRATIONS (7:28-29): Jesus continues to teach, amazing his listeners with his authority.

SECTION OUTLINE SEVEN (MATTHEW 8)
Jesus heals many, including a leper, a Roman officer's slave, Peter's mother-in-law, and a number of demon-possessed people. He amazes his disciples by calming a storm and talks about the costs of being his follower.

I. THE MIRACLES OF JESUS (8:1-17, 23-34)
  A. Curing the sick (8:1-17, 28-34)
    1. *A leper* (8:1-4)
      a. The cry (8:1-2): He begs the Savior to heal him.
      b. The compassion (8:3): Jesus restores the man by the touch of his hand.
      c. The command (8:4): The cleansed leper is instructed to tell no one about his miracle.
    2. *A centurion's servant* (8:5-13)
      a. The favor desired by the centurion (8:5-7): He wants Jesus to visit his home and heal his servant, which the Lord agrees to do.
      b. The faith demonstrated by the centurion (8:8-13)
        (1) The confidence (8:8-9): He feels the Lord can heal the servant without even coming to his home!
        (2) The commendation (8:10): Jesus commends him for so much faith!
        (3) The conclusion (8:11-12): Jesus says his kind of faith will result in the eventual salvation of a number of Gentiles, while many faithless Jews will suffer eternal loss.
        (4) The cure (8:13): The servant is healed at that very hour.
    3. *Peter's mother-in-law* (8:14-15)
      a. The suffering hostess (8:14): Jesus finds her in bed with a high fever.
      b. The serving hostess (8:15): After Jesus touches her hand, she gets up and begins to wait on him.
    4. *A number of demon-possessed people* (8:16-17, 28-34)
      a. On the western side of the Galilean Sea (8:16-17)
        (1) The possessed (8:16): Many of these people are brought to Jesus for deliverance.
        (2) The prophecy (8:17): He heals them all, that Isaiah's prophecy might be fulfilled (Isa. 53:4).
      b. On the eastern side of the Galilean Sea (8:28-34)
        (1) The Gadarene maniacs, controlled by demons (8:28): Demons have made these two men violent, causing them to live among the tombs!
        (2) The panic of these demons (8:29): They are filled with fear as the Savior approaches.
        (3) The plea from these demons (8:30-31): They beg Jesus to send them into a herd of nearby pigs!

(4) The Galilean Messiah, controller of demons (8:32-34)
- (a) The release (8:32): He delivers the two men by ordering the demons into the herd of pigs!
- (b) The rejection (8:33-34): The foolish people living in that area plead with Christ to depart and leave them alone.

B. Calming the sea (8:23-27)
1. *The furious storm* (8:23-24): A terrible storm threatens to sink the disciples' boat.
2. *The fearful sailors* (8:25): In desperation they awaken the sleeping Jesus, crying out for him to save them.
3. *The faithful Savior* (8:26-27): He quickly stills the waters, to the amazement of the disciples!

II. THE MANDATE OF JESUS (8:18-22): He describes the cost of true discipleship to several would-be followers.
A. Concerning one's finances (8:18-20): They will have no place to lay their heads.
B. Concerning one's family (8:21-22): They must forsake their families in order to follow Jesus.

SECTION OUTLINE EIGHT (MATTHEW 9)

Jesus continues his ministry of healing people's bodies while ministering to their souls.

I. JESUS MINISTERS TO INDIVIDUALS (9:1-8, 18-38)
A. A paralytic (9:1-8)
1. *The helpful companions* (9:1-2)
   a. The place (9:1): The miracle occurs in Capernaum.
   b. The paralytic (9:2a): His friends carry him to Jesus.
   c. The pardon (9:2b): Jesus first forgives the man of his sins.
2. *The hostile critics* (9:3-7)
   a. The disdain of the Pharisees (9:3): They accuse Jesus of blasphemy.
   b. The defense of the Savior (9:4-6): He says he will prove his authority to forgive sin by his ability to heal the man.
   c. The deliverance of the paralytic (9:7): At Jesus' command, the man rises up and walks away!
3. *The happy crowd* (9:8): The people rejoice over this great miracle!
B. A dead girl (9:18-19, 23-26)
1. *The request to Jesus* (9:18-19): A heartbroken ruler begs Jesus to come to his home to raise his dead daughter.
2. *The ridicule of Jesus* (9:23-24)
   a. The confusion (9:23): Upon entering the ruler's home, Jesus is met by a noisy crowd and loud funeral music.

      b. The command (9:24a): He orders the crowd to leave,
        saying the little girl is only sleeping.
      c. The contempt (9:24b): The crowd laughs at him.
    3. *The restoration by Jesus* (9:25-26): He takes the girl by the
      hand, and she rises!
  C. A sick woman (9:20-22)
    1. *Her disease* (9:20a): For twelve years she has suffered from
      internal bleeding.
    2. *Her determination* (9:20b-21):She touches the hem of Jesus'
      robe, believing this will heal her.
    3. *Her deliverance* (9:22): Immediately the Savior restores her!
  D. Two blind men (9:27-31)
    1. *The request* (9:27): They cry out for Jesus to heal them.
    2. *The response* (9:28-31)
      a. The test (9:28)
        (1) "Do you believe?" he says (9:28a).
        (2) "Yes, we believe!" they say (9:28b).
      b. The touch (9:29-30a): He touches their eyes and heals
        them.
      c. The task (9:30b): He then instructs them to tell no one.
      d. The telling (9:31): They, however, go out and tell many.
  E. A demon-possessed mute (9:32-34)
    1. *The helpless one* (9:32): This desperate man is brought to
      Jesus.
    2. *The Holy One* (9:33)
      a. The miracle (9:33a): Jesus frees him.
      b. The marvel (9:33b): The watching crowd is amazed!
    3. *The hostile ones* (9:34): He is blasphemed by the Pharisees!
  F. Many sick people throughout Galilee (9:35-38)
    1. *The Savior's compassion* (9:35-36): He travels through all the
      cities of that area, preaching and healing the multitudes.
    2. *The Savior's command* (9:37-38)
      a. The situation (9:37): The harvest is plentiful, but the work-
        ers are few.
      b. The solution (9:38): Pray that God will send forth laborers!

II. JESUS MEETS WITH INDIVIDUALS (9:9-17)
  A. A tax collector (9:9-13)
    1. *The call* (9:9): Jesus summons Matthew to become his
      disciple.
    2. *The celebration* (9:10): Matthew gives a banquet to celebrate
      this occasion.
    3. *The criticism* (9:11): The Pharisees are upset because there are
      sinners at the banquet.
    4. *The chastening* (9:12-13): Jesus rebukes them, saying he has
      come to call sinners, not those who think they are good
      enough.

B. Some disciples of John the Baptist (9:14-17)
  1. *Their inquiry* (9:14): They want to know why his disciples do not fast.
  2. *His illustrations* (9:15-17)
     a. The bridegroom (9:15): The wedding guests don't mourn while the groom is with them.
     b. The old garment (9:16): An old garment is not patched with unshrunk cloth.
     c. The old wineskin (9:17): New wine is not put in old wineskins.

SECTION OUTLINE NINE (MATTHEW 10)
Jesus seems to give instructions to three kinds of disciples, each group living at a different time.

I. TO FORMER DISCIPLES, LIVING IN THE TIME OF CHRIST (10:1-15): Jesus speaks to the disciples of his day.
  A. The individuals (10:2-4): Here Matthew lists the names of the twelve apostles.
  B. The instructions (10:1, 5-15)
    1. *Their mission field* (10:5-6): They are to go only to the lost sheep of Israel.
    2. *Their mission* (10:1, 7-15)
       a. To preach that God's Kingdom is near (10:7)
       b. To heal the sick, raise the dead, and cast out demons (10:1, 8a): They are given authority to do these things.
       c. To give freely (10:8b): They are to give as freely as they have received.
       d. To remain unburdened (10:9-10): They are not to take money or extra clothes with them.
       e. To bless or curse each town upon leaving (10:11-15): They are to bless worthy towns and curse unbelieving towns.

II. TO FUTURE DISCIPLES, LIVING DURING THE TIME OF THE GREAT TRIBULATION (10:16-23): This is assumed, based on Jesus' statement in 10:23.
  A. The enemies of God will hate them (10:16-18, 23).
    1. *Religious persecution* (10:16-17): They will be handed over to courts and beaten in synagogues.
    2. *Political persecution* (10:18): They will be called before governors and kings; this will give them a chance to witness.
    3. *Family persecution* (10:21): Family members will betray each other.
    4. *General persecution* (10:22-23): Everyone will hate them because of their allegiance to Christ.
  B. The Spirit of God will help them (10:19-20): He will give them the right words to say!

III. To Faithful Disciples, Living throughout Church History
(10:24-42): Jesus speaks of discipleship and persecution.
   A. **The certainty** (10:24-25): Just as he is persecuted, his disciples
      also will be.
   B. **The confidence** (10:26-31)
      1. *What people may do* (10:26-28): They may kill the body, but
         they cannot touch the soul.
      2. *What God will do* (10:29-31): He cares for both body and
         soul.
   C. **The conflict** (10:34-36): Faith in Christ may well turn a person's
      family against him or her!
   D. **The conditions** (10:37-38)
      1. *The priority of our love for Christ* (10:37): We are to place him
         even above our families!
      2. *The proof of our love for Christ* (10:38): We are to take up our
         cross and follow him.
   E. **The compensation** (10:32-33, 39-42): These are the benefits of
      true discipleship:
      1. *To be honored by the Son in the presence of the Father*
         (10:32-33)
      2. *To fully gain one's life* (10:39)
      3. *To be given great rewards* (10:40-42)

SECTION OUTLINE TEN (MATTHEW 11)

Jesus reassures the disciples of John the Baptist, rebukes several cities,
rejoices in his Father's wisdom, and reveals that he is the only way
to the Father.

I. The Reassuring by the Savior (11:1-19)
   A. **John's request to Jesus** (11:1-3): In a moment of doubt, the
      imprisoned Baptist sends a group of men to Jesus.
      1. *Who they are* (11:1-2): They are John's disciples.
      2. *What they ask* (11:3): John wants to know if Christ is really the
         Messiah.
   B. **John's reassurance by Jesus** (11:4-19)
      1. *The proof for John* (11:4-6): They are to return and tell John
         concerning all the miracles they see Christ do.
      2. *The praise of John* (11:7-11): Jesus says John is one of history's
         greatest men!
      3. *The prophet like John* (11:12-15): Jesus compares John's
         ministry with that of Elijah.
      4. *The prejudice against John* (11:16-19): Jesus condemns his
         generation, who accuses John of being demon-possessed!
II. The Rebuking by the Savior (11:20-24): Jesus denounces three
    Galilean cities.

A. **Korazin and Bethsaida** (11:20-22)
   1. *Their privilege* (11:20-21a): He did many miracles among them.
   2. *Their pride* (11:21b): They rejected him.
   3. *Their punishment* (11:22): Wicked Tyre and Sidon will be better off on judgment day than they!
B. **Capernaum** (11:23-24)
   1. *Its privilege* (11:23b): Identical to that of the above cities.
   2. *Its pride* (11:23a): Identical to that of the above cities.
   3. *Its punishment* (11:24): Wicked Sodom will be better off on the judgment day than Capernaum!

III. THE REJOICING BY THE SAVIOR (11:25-26): Jesus thanks his heavenly Father for revealing spiritual truth to the childlike and for hiding it from those who think themselves wise.

IV. THE REVEALING BY THE SAVIOR (11:27-30)
A. **The illumination** (11:27): The believer can only know the Father through the Son.
B. **The invitation** (11:28-30): Jesus invites the weary and burdened to find their rest in him.

SECTION OUTLINE ELEVEN (MATTHEW 12)

Jesus heals the sick, confronts the Pharisees, and fulfills ancient prophecies.

I. JESUS AND THE PHARISEES (12:1-14, 22-45) On three separate occasions, Jesus is confronted by these wicked men.
A. **The Sabbath conflict** (12:1-14): The Pharisees take issue with Jesus when he performs his miracles.
   1. *In regard to eating on the Sabbath* (12:1-8): Jesus is criticized by the Pharisees for allowing his disciples to pluck some heads of grain from a field on the Sabbath. The Savior reports by pointing out two facts:
      a. The purpose of the Sabbath (12:1-7): The Sabbath was made for man, and not the reverse!
         (1) As seen in the life of David (12:3-4): David and his men ate the bread reserved for the priests.
         (2) As seen in the law of Moses (12:5-6): The priests are allowed to serve in the Temple on the Sabbath.
         (3) As seen in the Book of Hosea (12:7): God wants them to be merciful; he doesn't care that much about their sacrifices.
      b. The person of the Sabbath (12:8): The Son of Man is Lord even of the Sabbath!
   2. *In regard to healing on the Sabbath* (12:9-14): Jesus notices a man with a deformed hand.

a. The accusation (12:9-10): The Pharisees ask Jesus whether it is legal to work by healing on the Sabbath day.

b. The answer (12:11-12): Jesus replies by asking them if they would rescue a sheep on the Sabbath. He says, "Of course you would! And how much more valuable is a person than a sheep!"

c. The action by the Savior (12:13-14): He heals the man's hand.

B. **The source conflict** (12:22-37): The Pharisees claim that Satan is the source of Jesus' miracles. On this occasion Jesus has just healed a demon-possessed, blind, mute man.

1. *The criticism by the Pharisees* (12:22-29)

a. Their accusation (12:22-24): "He gets his power from Satan, the prince of demons."

b. His argument (12:25-29)

(1) "A city or home divided against itself is doomed" (12:25).

(2) "If Satan is casting out Satan, he is fighting against himself" (12:26-29).

2. *The condemnation of the Pharisees* (12:30-37)

a. Jesus says their sin is terrible (12:30-34).

(1) They are corrupt fruit trees (12:30-33): A tree is known by its fruit.

(2) They are poisonous snakes (12:34): Whatever is in their hearts determines what they say.

b. Jesus says their sin is terminal (12:35-37): The words they say now will determine their fate on judgment day.

C. **The sign conflict** (12:38-45): The Pharisees insist that Jesus do something spectacular just for them.

1. *Jesus refers to Jonah and Nineveh* (12:38-41).

a. The illustration from the life of the prophet of God (12:38-40): Jonah's experience in the belly of the fish depicts Jesus' death and resurrection; this is the only sign he gives them!

b. The indictment from the lips of the people of Nineveh (12:41): The Ninevites will someday condemn Jesus' generation, for Nineveh repented at the preaching of Jonah, but Jesus is greater than Jonah.

2. *Jesus refers to Solomon and the Queen of Sheba* (12:42): She will condemn Jesus' generation because she had great respect for Solomon, and Jesus is greater than Solomon.

3. *Jesus refers to eight evil spirits* (12:43-45): Here Jesus likens his generation to a demon-possessed man.

a. The first state of the man (12:43): The original demon living within him departs.

b. The final state of the man (12:44-45): Unable to find

another person to indwell, the spirit returns to the man, this time bringing seven other spirits more wicked than himself.

II. JESUS AND THE PROPHECIES (12:15-21): Jesus fulfills the prophecies of Isaiah, who predicted the earthly ministry of the Messiah (Isa. 42:1-4).
  A. **Jesus' heavenly relationships** (12:18a-18b)
    1. *Concerning the Father* (12:18a): The Father would love him.
    2. *Concerning the Spirit* (12:18b): The Spirit would fill him.
  B. **Jesus' earthly actions** (12:15-17, 18c-21)
    1. *Concerning the nations* (12:18c, 21): He would proclaim justice to the nations.
    2. *Concerning himself* (12:19): He would not be quarrelsome or rebellious.
    3. *Concerning the weak and hopeless* (12:20): He would treat them with gentleness and understanding.
    4. *Concerning the sick* (12:15-17): He would heal the sick.

III. JESUS AND HIS FAMILY (12:46-50)
  A. **His earthly family** (12:46-47): Jesus is told his mother and brothers are waiting to meet with him.
  B. **His eternal family** (12:48-50): He says all who obey his heavenly Father are part of his family!

SECTION OUTLINE TWELVE (MATTHEW 13)
Jesus explains the Kingdom of Heaven using eight parables.

I. THE RELATING OF HIS PARABLES (13:1-8, 18-33, 36-50, 52)
  A. **The sower, the seed, and the soil** (13:1-8, 18-23)
    1. *Information in this parable* (13:1-8): A farmer sows grain, which falls upon four different kinds of soil, producing four different results.
      a. Roadside soil (13:1-4): This seed is soon devoured by the birds.
      b. Shallow, rocky soil (13:5-6): This seed springs up quickly but soon withers, being scorched by the sun.
      c. Thorn-infested soil (13:7): This seed is quickly choked by the thorns.
      d. Fertile soil (13:8): This seed produces a thirty, sixty, and even hundredfold crop!
    2. *Interpretation of this parable* (13:18-23)
      a. The seed (13:18-19a): The seed represents the Good News about the Kingdom.
      a. The roadside soil (13:19b): The hard soil represents those who hear the message but do not understand it, thus allowing Satan to steal it from them.
      b. The rocky soil (13:20-21): The shallow, rocky soil

represents those who have no depth and thus drop out upon encountering any trouble or persecution.

    c. The thorn-infested soil (13:22): The thorny ground represents those who allow the lure of wealth to snuff out the Good News.

    d. Fertile soil (13:23): The good soil represents those who truly accept God's message, producing an abundant harvest.

B. The wheat and the thistle (13:24-30, 36-43)

    1. *Information in the parable* (13:24-30)

      a. The diligence of a sower (13:24): A farmer sows good seed throughout his field.

      b. The discovery by the sower (13:25-28): He learns his enemy later secretly visited the field and sowed thistles among the wheat.

      c. The dilemma of the sower (13:29): He knows that if he attempts to pull out the thistles, he will also harm the wheat.

      d. The decision of the sower (13:30): He will wait until harvesttime, when he will sort out the thistles from the wheat and burn them.

    2. *Interpretation of the parable* (13:36-43)

      a. The sower is Christ (13:36-37).

      b. The enemy is the devil (13:39a).

      c. The field is the world (13:38a).

      d. The good seed is believers (13:38b).

      e. The thistles are unbelievers (13:38c).

      f. The harvest is the end of the age (13:39b).

      g. The reapers are angels (13:39c-41).

      h. The granary is heaven (13:43).

      i. The furnace is hell(13:42).

C. The mustard seed (13:31-32)

    1. *It goes into the ground the smallest of seeds* (13:31-32a).

    2. *It grows out of the ground the largest of plants* (13:32b).

D. The yeast (13:33)

    1. *It is placed in the flour* (13:33a): Only a small amount of yeast is used.

    2. *It permeates every part of the dough* (13:33b).

E. The treasure in the field (13:44)

    1. *The discovery* (13:44a): A man finds a precious treasure.

    2. *The delight* (13:44b): He is overjoyed at what he finds.

    3. *The decision* (13:44c): He sells all that he has to buy the field.

F. The merchant and the pearl (13:45-46)

    1. *He seeks this pearl* (13:45).

    2. *He buys this pearl* (13:46).

G. The sorting of fish (13:47-50)

    1. *The information in this parable* (13:47-48): Upon catching a net filled with fish, the fishermen sort out the good from the bad.

2. *The interpretation of this parable* (13:49-50): At the end of the world, the angels will likewise separate the righteous from the wicked.

H. **The homeowner and his treasure** (13:52): A wise teacher of God's Word can display both old and new precious truths (Old and New Testament) like a homeowner can show off both old and new treasures.

II. THE REASON FOR HIS PARABLES (13:9-17, 34-35, 51)

A. **The purpose** (13:9-13, 34-35, 51): Jesus uses his parables to accomplish a twofold goal.

1. *To reveal God's truth to the righteous* (13:9-12a, 34-35, 51)
2. *To conceal God's truth from the unrighteous* (13:12b-13)

B. **The prophecy** (13:14-17): Isaiah predicted that Israel would not be able to understand or accept the truths in Christ's parables (Isa. 6:9-10).

III. THE REACTION TO HIS PARABLES (13:53-58): The people in Jesus' hometown of Nazareth react to his parables in a twofold way.

A. **First they are amazed** (13:53-56).

B. **Then they are angered** (13:57-58): Jesus does only a few miracles there because of their unbelief.

SECTION OUTLINE THIRTEEN (MATTHEW 14)

Herod Antipas martyrs John the Baptist. Jesus feeds the 5,000 and walks on water.

I. THE MARTYRDOM OF JOHN (14:1-12)

A. **John is mistreated by Herod Antipas** (14:3-8).

1. *The persecution* (14:3-5): John is imprisoned by Herod for fearlessly condemning Herod's unlawful marriage to Herodias, the king's ex-sister-in-law.
2. *The performance* (14:6): The daughter of Herodias performs a dance for Herod during his birthday celebration.
3. *The promise* (14:7): A highly pleased Herod vows to give her anything she desires.
4. *The plot* (14:8): At her mother's urging, the girl demands the head of John the Baptist.

B. **John is murdered by Herod Antipas** (14:9-12): The reluctant king, forced to keep his promise, has John beheaded.

C. **Jesus is misunderstood by Herod Antipas** (14:1-2): When the king first hears of Jesus' ministry, he fears the Savior is John, come back to life.

II. THE MIRACLES OF JESUS (14:13-36)

A. **He feeds the 5,000** (14:13-21): Jesus meets a twofold need.

1. *He heals the hurting* (14:13-14): The sick in the crowd are restored.

2. *He feeds the hungry* (14:15-21)
   a. The scarcity of food (14:15-17): A quick check reveals only five small loaves of bread and two fish are available for the hungry crowd.
   b. The surplus of food (14:18-21): After all have eaten their fill, twelve basketfuls are left over!
B. **He walks on water** (14:22-36).
   1. *Events preceding his walk* (14:22-24)
      a. The command (14:22): Jesus instructs his disciples to cross to the other side of the lake.
      b. The communion (14:23): He then retires to a hill and prays.
      c. The crisis (14:24): A violent storm suddenly threatens the disciples' boat.
   2. *Events during his walk* (14:25-33)
      a. The approach (14:25): In the middle of the night, Jesus comes to the disciples, walking on the water.
      b. The alarm (14:26): The disciples are terrified, thinking Jesus is a ghost!
      c. The assurance (14:27): Jesus tells them who he is.
      d. The attempt (14:28-31): Peter tries to walk to Jesus but soon begins to sink and cries out for help.
      e. The awe (14:32-33): At Jesus' command, the wind stops, causing the disciples to worship him.
   3. *Events following his walk* (14:34-36): Jesus heals many sick people on the eastern side of the lake.

SECTION OUTLINE FOURTEEN (MATTHEW 15)
Jesus confronts the Pharisees, teaches the crowds, and explains his teachings to Peter and the other disciples. He heals a Canaanite woman's daughter and feeds the 4,000.

I. THE MEETINGS (15:1-20)
   A. **Jesus' meeting with the Pharisees** (15:1-9)
      1. *Their accusation* (15:1-2): They accuse Jesus of breaking the Mosaic law by permitting his disciples to ignore the ceremonial hand washing ritual before eating.
      2. *His condemnation* (15:3-9)
         a. Jesus speaks concerning their corruption (15:3-6): The Pharisees twist God's law in such a way that it allows them to ignore their responsibilities concerning their parents!
         b. Jesus speaks concerning their character (15:7-9): Jesus calls the Pharisees hypocrites and says they fulfill Isaiah's terrible prophecy concerning them (Isa. 29:13).
   B. **Jesus' meeting with the people** (15:10-11): Jesus tells the crowd that uncleanness is not caused by what goes into a person's mouth (nonkosher food) but rather by what comes out!

C. Jesus' meeting with Peter (15:12-20): He says the same thing to Peter and the disciples.

II. THE MIRACLES (15:21-39)

A. Healing a Canaanite woman's daughter (15:21-28)

1. *The brokenhearted mother* (15:21-23)
   a. The place (15:21): Jesus is in the region of Tyre and Sidon.
   b. The plea (15:22-23): A mother in this area begs him to heal her demon-possessed daughter.

2. *The kindhearted Messiah* (15:24-28)
   a. His reminder (15:24-26): He tells her that his key ministry is to the Jews, not the Gentiles.
   b. Her response (15:27-28)
      (1) The reasoning (15:27): She agrees but asks for some of the crumbs that might fall from Israel's spiritual table.
      (2) The reward (15:28): Jesus immediately grants her request.

B. Feeding the 4,000 (15:29-39): Jesus ministers to this group of 4,000 men as he did previously for the 5,000.

1. *Meeting the needs of the hurting* (15:29-31): Jesus heals the lame, blind, crippled, and the mute.

2. *Meeting the needs of the hungry* (15:32-39)
   a. The amount of food (15:32-34): He has only seven loaves of bread and a few small fishes.
   b. The abundance of food (15:35-39): Seven full baskets remain after all have eaten their fill!

SECTION OUTLINE FIFTEEN (MATTHEW 16)

Jesus again refuses to give the Pharisees a sign to prove his divine identity, and he warns his disciples to beware the false teachings of these evil men. Peter correctly identifies Jesus as the Messiah.

I. JESUS AND HIS FOES (16:1-4)

A. Their demand (16:1): The Pharisees insist that he prove himself through some great sign from heaven.

B. His denial (16:2-4)

1. *What they would not do* (16:2-3): Jesus reminds them of the many previous miracles he has already performed, which they would not accept!

2. *What he will not do* (16:4): He will give them no sign except that of Jonah, a reference to his death and resurrection.

II. JESUS AND HIS FOLLOWERS (16:5-28)

A. The reminder (16:5-12): Jesus reminds his disciples to beware of the yeast of the Pharisees, a reference to their false teaching.

B. The revelation (16:13-21)

1. *The probing by Christ* (16:13-17)

　　　a. The request (16:13): He asks the disciples what people are
　　　　saying about him.
　　　b. The rumors (16:14): Some believe he is John the Baptist,
　　　　Elijah, Jeremiah, or one of the other prophets.
　　　c. The recognition (16:15-17): He then asks the disciples what
　　　　they think about him.
　　　　　(1) What Peter says (16:15-16): He acknowledges the deity
　　　　　　of Jesus Christ!
　　　　　(2) Why Peter says it (16:17): God the Father has revealed
　　　　　　this to him!
　　2. *The promise by Christ* (16:18-19)
　　　a. The announcement (16:18): He will soon build his church.
　　　b. The authority (16:19): He will entrust them with the keys to
　　　　the Kingdom!
　　3. *The prohibition by Christ* (16:20): They are not to tell anyone
　　　that he is the Messiah.
　　4. *The passion of Christ* (16:21): Jesus predicts his future
　　　sufferings, death, and resurrection.
　C. The rebukes (16:22-23)
　　1. *Peter rebukes Jesus* (16:22): He is upset that the Savior would
　　　talk about his sufferings and death.
　　2. *Jesus rebukes Satan* (16:23): Jesus rebukes the Devil for
　　　influencing Peter to speak as he has.
　D. The requirements (16:24-26): Jesus lists the conditions for true
　discipleship.
　E. The rewards (16:27-28)
　　1. *General rewards to all of Jesus' disciples* (16:27): This will
　　　occur at his second coming.
　　2. *Specific reward to three of Jesus' disciples* (16:28): Peter,
　　　James, and John will soon be allowed to witness the
　　　transfiguration of Christ!

SECTION OUTLINE SIXTEEN (MATTHEW 17)

God confirms Peter's earlier acknowledgment of the deity of Christ
by transfiguring Jesus on the mountaintop. Jesus heals a
demon-possessed boy, predicts his own death, and instructs Peter
to pay the Temple tax with a coin found in the mouth of a fish.

I. THE SPLENDOR OF THE SAVIOR (17:1-13)
　A. The confirmation on top of the mountain (17:1-8): Jesus takes
　Peter, James, and John with him.
　　1. *What they see* (17:1-3)
　　　a. The appearance of God's Messiah (17:1-2): His face and
　　　　clothing shine like the noonday sun!
　　　b. The arrival of God's messengers (17:3): Moses and Elijah
　　　　appear and speak to Jesus.

2. *What they say* (17:4): Peter wants to build three shelters, one each for Jesus, Moses, and Elijah.
3. *What they hear* (17:5): The Father speaks from heaven, attesting to the love he has for his Son.
4. *What they do* (17:6-8): They fall to the ground, terrified, but are reassured by Jesus.

   B. The conversation coming down the mountain (17:9-13)
   1. *The command* (17:9): Jesus instructs the three to say nothing concerning what they saw until his resurrection.
   2. *The confusion* (17:10): They want to know if Elijah will come before the return of the Messiah.
   3. *The clarification* (17:11-13)
      a. His answer (17:11-12)
         (1) Elijah will indeed come (17:11).
         (2) Elijah has already come (17:12).
      b. Their assumption (17:13): By this they understand that he is referring to John the Baptist.

II. THE SOVEREIGNTY OF THE SAVIOR (17:14-21, 24-27): Jesus demonstrates his deity through two miracles.
   A. The boy with a demon (17:14-21)
   1. *The desperation of the father* (17:14-16): He begs Jesus to heal his son.
   2. *The exorcism by the Lord* (17:17-18): Jesus quickly drives the demon from the lad.
   3. *The frustration of the disciples* (17:19-21)
      a. They say, "Why couldn't we cast out that demon?" (17:19).
      b. He says, "You didn't have enough faith" (17:21).

   B. The fish with a coin (17:24-27)
   1. *The who* (17:24b): Some tax collectors approach Peter.
   2. *The what* (17:24c): They demand to know if Jesus will pay the Temple tax.
   3. *The where* (17:24a): This takes place upon Jesus' arrival in Capernaum.
   4. *The why* (17:25-26): Jesus informs Peter of two things.
      a. Why he should not have to pay this tax (17:25): Kings tax the conquered, not their own people.
      b. Why he should pay the tax anyway (17:26): Though he is free, he should try not to offend anyone.
   4. *The how* (17:27): Jesus tells Peter to throw a line in the lake, open the mouth of the first fish he catches, and use the coin he will find there to pay the tax!

III. THE SUFFERING OF THE SAVIOR (17:22-23)
   A. His revelation (17:22-23a): He tells the disciples of his coming betrayal, death, and resurrection.
   B. Their reaction (17:23b): The disciples are filled with grief.

SECTION OUTLINE SEVENTEEN (MATTHEW 18)
Jesus addresses the issues of how to determine greatness, how to
escape hell, how to exercise church discipline, and how to forgive
a sinning brother.

I. HOW TO DETERMINE GREATNESS (18:1-6, 10-14)
  A. **The illustration of a little child** (18:1-5)
    1. *The statement* (18:1-4): True greatness is to humble oneself as
    a little child.
    2. *The spiritual truth* (18:5): To honor a little child is to honor the
    Savior himself.
  B. **The ill treatment of a little child** (18:6, 10-14)
    1. *The penalty* (18:6): It is better for a person to have a large
    millstone hung around the neck and be cast into the sea than
    to mistreat a little child!
    2. *The protection* (18:10): Angels are assigned to protect
    children.
    3. *The priority* (18:11-14): In the parable of the lost sheep, Jesus
    says that it is the will of his Father to bring all little ones into
    the safety of the sheepfold.

II. HOW TO ESCAPE HELL (18:7-9): In highly metaphorical language,
Jesus says:
  A. **Control what you do** (18:7-8): If your hand or foot causes you to
  sin, cut it off!
  B. **Control what you see** (18:9): If your eye causes you to sin, pluck
  it out!

III. HOW TO EXERCISE CHURCH DISCIPLINE (18:15-20)
  A. **The procedure** (18:15-17)
    1. *If your brother sins against you, go to him in private, and
    attempt to reconcile the matter* (18:15).
    2. *If this fails, take someone with you* (18:16).
    3. *If this fails, bring the matter before the church* (18:17a).
    4. *If this fails, dismiss the unrepentant brother* (18:17b).
  B. **The promise** (18:18-20): The authority of heaven itself will sup-
  port this kind of church decision.

IV. HOW TO FORGIVE YOUR BROTHER (18:21-35)
  A. **The percentage** (18:21-22)
    1. *Peter to Jesus* (18:21): "How often should I forgive someone
    who sins against me? Seven times?"
    2. *Jesus to Peter* (18:22): "No! Seventy times seven!"
  B. **The parable** (18:23-35): Jesus relates the story of a king, his ser-
  vant, and another servant.
    1. *Scene one* (18:23-27): The servant and his master, the king.
      a. The debt (18:23-24): He owes his master a staggering sum
      of money!

b. The decree (18:25): Unable to pay, he and his entire family are to be sold into slavery by the king.

c. The desperation (18:26): He falls on his knees before the king, begging for mercy.

d. The deliverance (18:27): Moved with compassion, the king forgives his entire debt.

2. *Scene two* (18:28-30): The forgiven servant and another servant—the second servant owes the forgiven servant a very small amount of money.

a. The pitiful request (18:28-29): He begs for a little more time to pay the debt.

b. The pitiless response (18:30): Unmoved, the first servant orders the second servant thrown in prison!

3. *Scene three* (18:31-35): The forgiven servant and the king.

a. The outrage (18:31-33): The forgiven (but unforgiving) servant is summoned before the furious king.

(1) The reminder (18:31-32): "You evil servant! I forgave you that tremendous debt because you pleaded with me."

(2) The rebuke (18:33): "Shouldn't you have mercy on your fellow servant, just as I had mercy on you?"

b. The outcome (18:34): The king throws the servant into prison until he pays back his debt in full!

c. The overall lesson (18:35): God does not forgive the unforgiving!

SECTION OUTLINE EIGHTEEN (MATTHEW 19)

Jesus teaches about divorce and tells his disciples that one must be childlike in order to enter the Kingdom of Heaven. He also talks about the difficulty of having both worldly riches and spiritual riches.

I. PART ONE (19:1-15)

A. The confrontation—Jesus and the Pharisees (19:1-9): The wicked Pharisees ask Jesus two trick questions, and Jesus answers them.

1. *What they ask—first question* (19:3): "Should a man be allowed to divorce his wife for any reason?"

2. *How he answers—first reply* (19:4-6): "'A man . . . is joined to his wife, and the two are united into one.' . . . Let no one separate them, for God has joined them together."

3. *What they ask—second question* (19:7): "Then why did Moses say a man could merely write an official letter of divorce and send her away?"

4. *How he answers—second reply* (19:8-9)

a. The insolence (19:8a): Moses only allowed it due to the hardness of their hearts!

      b. The intention (19:8b): Divorce was not God's original intention!

      c. The immorality (19:9): The man who unlawfully divorces his wife and remarries commits adultery!

B. The clarification—Jesus and his disciples (19:10-12)

    1. *What they ask* (19:10): "Then it is better not to marry!"

    2. *How he answers* (19:11-12): This is true only for those whom God has called to remain single.

C. The consecration—Jesus and some little children (19:13-15)

    1. *The disciples rebuke the parents* (19:13): They scold the parents for "bothering" Jesus with their request that he bless their little ones.

    2. *The Savior receives the children* (19:14-15): Jesus rebukes the rebukers and blesses the children, saying that "the Kingdom of Heaven belongs to such as these."

II. PART TWO (19:16-30)

A. Jesus speaks concerning riches (19:16-26): Jesus meets with a rich young ruler and is asked a question by his disciples.

    1. *Jesus and the ruler* (19:16-22)

      a. The seeking ruler (19:16-21)

        (1) The ruler's confusion (19:16): "What good things must I do to have eternal life?"

        (2) The Savior's clarification (19:17): "Keep the commandments!"

        (3) The ruler's confirmation (19:18-20): "I've obeyed all these commandments."

        (4) The Savior's conclusion (19:21): "If you want to be perfect, go and sell all you have and give the money to the poor. . . . Then come, follow me."

      b. The sorrowing ruler (19:22): He turns away with sadness, not willing to give up his wealth.

    2. *Jesus and the disciples* (19:23-26)

      a. The allegory (19:23-24): Jesus says it is easier for a camel to go through the eye of a needle than for a rich man to enter heaven.

      b. The amazement (19:25): The disciples ask who can possibly be saved.

      c. The assurance (19:26): Jesus says with God all things are possible.

B. Jesus speaks concerning rewards (19:27-30)

    1. *What the disciples have renounced for Jesus* (19:27): They have given up everything to follow him.

    2. *What the disciples will receive from Jesus* (19:28-30): They will sit on thrones next to him and will judge the twelve tribes of Israel.

SECTION OUTLINE NINETEEN (MATTHEW 20)
Jesus tells the parable of the vineyard workers, again predicts his death, receives a peculiar request from the mother of James and John, and heals two blind men.

I. THE PARABLE (20:1-16)
   A. **The analogy** (20:1a): Here Jesus likens the kingdom of heaven to a landowner who hires men to work in his vineyard.
   B. **The agreement** (20:1b-7)
      1. *The work wages* (20:2): He agrees to pay each worker one denarius per day.
      2. *The work schedule* (20:1b, 3-7)
         a. Some work from 6:00 A.M. to 6:00 P.M. (20:1b).
         b. Some work from 9:00 A.M. to 6:00 P.M. (20:3-4).
         c. Some work from noon to 6:00 P.M. (20:5a).
         d. Some work from 3:00 P.M. to 6:00 P.M. (20:5b).
         e. Some work from 5:00 P.M. to 6:00 P.M. (20:6-7).
   C. **The argument** (20:8-15)
      1. *The payoff* (20:8): In the evening the owner instructs his foreman to pay them their wages, beginning with the last one hired and going on to the first.
      2. *The pay* (20:9-10): Each worker receives identical wages—one denarius!
      3. *The protest* (20:11-12): The workers who began at 6:00 A.M. protest that they should receive more than the late-afternoon workers.
      4. *The pronouncement* (20:13-15): The owner reminds the complainers of two things.
         a. He has paid them what he promised (20:13).
         b. He can pay anyone anything he wants (20:14-15).
   D. **The application** (20:16): Jesus says the last will be first, and the first, last!

II. THE PREDICTION (20:17-19): Jesus predicts two events in regard to himself.
   A. **The grievous event** (20:17-19a)
      1. *His betrayal by Judas* (20:17-18a): He will be betrayed to the priests.
      2. *His condemnation by the Jewish leaders* (20:18b): He will be sentenced to death.
      3. *His mockery, whipping, and crucifixion by the Romans* (20:19a)
   B. **The glorious event** (20:19b): He will rise again on the third day!

III. THE PETITION (20:20-28)
   A. **The request** (20:20-21): The mother of James and John asks Jesus to allow her two sons to sit on his right and left side in the Kingdom.

B. The response (20:22-23): Jesus denies this favor on two counts:
   1. *Their ignorance* (20:22) Neither the mother or the sons really understand what they are asking!
   2. *His inability* (20:23): Seating arrangements in the Kingdom will be assigned by the Father, not the Son!
C. The resentment (20:24): The other ten disciples are indignant when they hear what James and John asked.
D. The requirement (20:25-28): Jesus uses this tense situation to set forth the conditions for true greatness.
   1. *Greatness as viewed by the Gentiles* (20:25): Greatness to them is the powerful lording of their authority over others.
   2. *Greatness as viewed by God* (20:26-28): It consists of becoming a servant to others!

IV. THE PITY (20:29-34)
   A. The cries of the blind (20:29-30): Two blind men cry out to Jesus as he passes by.
   B. The criticism of the crowd (20:31): The people tell them to be quiet.
   C. The compassion of the Savior (20:32-34): Filled with pity, Jesus restores their sight!

SECTION OUTLINE TWENTY (MATTHEW 21)
Jesus rides triumphantly into Jerusalem on a donkey and drives the corrupt merchants out of the Temple. He curses a fig tree, answers a challenge to his authority, and tells two parables.

I. THE ACCLAMATION (21:1-11): The Triumphal Entry.
   A. The preparation (21:1-3)
      1. *The mountain* (21:1): From the Mount of Olives, Jesus sends two of his disciples into the next village.
      2. *The mission* (21:2-3): They are to bring back a donkey and its colt for the master to ride on.
   B. The prophecy (21:4-5): This is done to fulfill prophecy (Zech. 9:9).
   C. The parade (21:6-11): Jesus is welcomed by a huge crowd.
      1. *They prepare his path* (21:6-8): The people spread coats and branches on the road.
      2. *They proclaim his praises* (21:9-11): They shout, "Praise God for the Son of David! Bless the one who comes in the name of the Lord!"

II. THE PURIFICATION (21:12-13)
   A. Jesus removes the money tables from the Temple (21:12): He drives them out.
   B. Jesus rebukes the money changers in the Temple (21:13): They have made the Temple a den of thieves.

III. THE RESTORATION (21:14): Jesus heals the blind and lame who come to him in the Temple.

IV. THE PROTESTATION (21:15-17)
   A. The praise (21:15a): Some little children are singing praises to Jesus in the Temple.
   B. The protest (21:15b): The Pharisees object to this.
   C. The prophecy (21:16-17): Jesus reminds the critics that this was a fulfillment of prophecy (Ps. 8:2).

V. THE DETERIORATION (21:18-22)
   A. The authority (21:18-19): Jesus causes a fruitless fig tree to wither up and die.
   B. The amazement (21:20): The disciples are astonished by this supernatural action.
   C. The application (21:21-22): Jesus says that if one exercises true faith and genuine prayer, he or she can:
   1. *Do what he just did* (21:21a)
   2. *Cast the Mount of Olives into the ocean* (21:21b-22)

VI. THE CONFRONTATION (21:23-27)
   A. The demand by the Pharisees (21:23): They want to know who gives Jesus the right to do the things he does.
   B. The dilemma of the Pharisees (21:24-26): Jesus traps the trappers by asking them the source of John the Baptist's authority.
   C. The defeat of the Pharisees (21:27): When they are unable to answer his question, Jesus refuses to answer theirs!

VII. THE ILLUSTRATIONS (21:28-46): Jesus relates two parables.
   A. The parable of the two sons (21:28-32)
   1. *The contents* (21:28-30): A father asks his two sons to work in his vineyard.
      a. One son says he won't but later does (21:28-29).
      b. The other son says he will but later doesn't (21:30).
   2. *The conclusion* (21:31-32)
      a. Corrupt tax collectors and prostitutes can be compared to the first son (21:31).
      b. The scribes and Pharisees can be compared to the second son (21:32).
   B. The parable of the evil farmers (21:33-46)
   1. *The work* (21:33): A landowner spends considerable time and labor developing a vineyard and then leases it to some tenants.
   2. *The wickedness* (21:34-39)
      a. The mission of his servants and son (21:34, 36a, 37-38): Over a period of time, the landowner sends these men to gather his share of the crop.
      b. The mistreatment of his servants and son (21:35, 36b, 39): The godless tenants beat and stone the servants and kill the son!

3. *The wrath* (21:40-41): Filled with anger, the landowner destroys these wicked tenants and hires others, whom he can trust.
4. *The witness* (21:42): David predicted in Psalm 118:22-23 that this would occur when the Messiah came—he would be rejected and killed by the godless Jewish leaders!
5. *The withdrawal* (21:43-46): Jesus removes the privileges of the Kingdom of God from Israel.

SECTION OUTLINE TWENTY-ONE (MATTHEW 22)
Jesus continues to teach about the Kingdom of Heaven and avoids more verbal traps set for him by the Pharisees and Sadducees.

I. The Lord of Israel Overviews the Kingdom of Heaven (22:1-14)
 A. **The illustration of the wedding** (22:1-2): Jesus likens the Kingdom of Heaven to a wedding banquet given by a king for his son.
 B. **The invitations to the wedding** (22:3-10)
  1. *The exclusive guest list* (22:3-7)
   a. Their first invitation (22:3)
    (1) The request (22:3a): Many guests are invited.
    (2) The refusal (22:3b): All of the invited guests refuse to come.
   b. Their second invitation (22:4-7)
    (1) The request (22:4): The king prepares more exotic food and again sends servants out to bring the guests.
    (2) The ridicule (22:5): The invited guests ignore the invitations!
    (3) The ruthlessness (22:6): Other guests actually mistreat and kill the king's servants!
    (4) The rage (22:7): The furious king sends his army to destroy those evil guests and to burn their city!
  2. *The expanded guest list* (22:8-10)
   a. The command (22:8-9): The servants are now instructed to go out to the street corners and invite everybody they see to the wedding!
   b. The crowd (22:10): Soon the royal palace is filled with people.
 C. **The indignation at the wedding** (22:11-14)
  1. *The problem* (22:11-12)
   a. The guest who has no robe (22:11): He isn't wearing the proper wedding attire.
   b. The guest who has no reply (22:12): When asked why he has no wedding clothes, the man cannot respond.
  2. *The punishment* (22:13-14): The guest who insults the king by refusing to wear the robe required by all in attendance is imprisoned!

II. THE LEADERS OF ISRAEL OPPOSE THE KINGDOM OF HEAVEN (22:15-46): The wicked Pharisees and Sadducees attempt to trap Jesus on four occasions.

A. **First occasion** (22:15-22): Concerning paying taxes to Caesar

　　1. *Their deceit* (22:15-17): "Is it right to pay taxes to the Roman government or not?"

　　2. *Their denunciation* (22:18): Jesus calls them a group of hypocrites!

　　3. *Their defeat* (22:19-22): The Savior says, "Give to Caesar what is his and to God what is God's!"

B. **Second occasion** (22:23-29): Concerning marriage and the resurrection.

　　1. *The confrontation by the Sadducees* (22:23-33)

　　　　a. Their silly example (22:24-28): They want to know if a woman married seven times on the earth will have a husband in heaven.

　　　　b. Their serious errors (22:23, 29)

　　　　　　(1) Their intolerance concerning the resurrection (22:23): They don't believe in the resurrection.

　　　　　　(2) Their ignorance concerning the Scriptures (22:29): They don't understand the power of God.

　　2. *The clarification by the Savior (22:30-33)*

　　　　a. There will be no marriage in the resurrection (22:30): Why? Because people will be like the angels in heaven.

　　　　b. There will be a resurrection (22:31-33): Why? Because God is not the God of the dead but of the living.

C. **Third occasion: Concerning the greatest commandment** (22:34-40): Once again the Jewish leaders attempt to trick Jesus.

　　1. *Their request* (22:34-36): "Which is the greatest commandment in the law?"

　　2. *His response* (22:37-40): Jesus gives them both the greatest and second greatest of all the commandments.

　　　　a. The identifying of these two commandments (22:37-39)

　　　　　　(1) The first (22:37-38): "Love the Lord your God with all your heart, all your soul, and all your mind."

　　　　　　(2) The second (22:39): "Love your neighbor as yourself."

　　　　b. The importance of these two commandments (22:40): "All the other commandments and the demands of the prophets are based on these two commandments."

D. **Fourth occasion: Concerning the Son of David** (22:41-46)

　　1. *Christ points out the fact that the Messiah is David's son, thus affirming the Messiah's humanity (22:41-42).*

　　2. *Christ points out the fact that the Messiah is also David's Lord, thus affirming the Messiah's deity (22:43-46).*

SECTION OUTLINE TWENTY-TWO (MATTHEW 23)
Jesus warns the religious leaders that their evil ways will lead to judgment, and he grieves over the rebellion of Jerusalem.

I. THE ANGER OF JESUS (23:1-36): His anger is directed toward the wicked Pharisees, whom he condemns both publicly and personally.
   A. **Jesus publicly condemns the Pharisees** (23:1-12).
      1. *The wickedness of these men* (23:1-7)
         a. They do not practice what they preach (23:1-3).
         b. They place heavy burdens upon the people (23:4).
         c. They do everything for show (23:5, 7).
         d. They demand to occupy the place of prominence (23:6).
      2. *The warning against these men* (23:8-12): Jesus warns that whoever exalts himself will be humbled, and the one who humbles himself will be exalted!
   B. **Jesus personally condemns the Pharisees** (23:13-36): This he does through seven judgments.
      1. *First judgment* (23:13): "You won't let others enter the Kingdom of Heaven, and you won't go in yourselves."
      2. *Second judgment* (23:15): "You cross land and sea to make one convert, and then you turn him into twice the son of hell as you yourselves are."
      3. *Third judgment* (23:16-22)
         a. "Blind guides! . . . You say that it means nothing to swear 'by God's Temple'—you can break that oath. But then you say that it is binding to swear 'by the gold in the Temple'" (23:16-17).
         b. "Blind fools! . . . You say that to take an oath 'by the altar' can be broken, but to swear 'by the gifts on the altar' is binding!" (23:18-22).
      4. *Fourth judgment* (23:23-24)
         a. "You are careful to tithe even the tiniest part of your income, but you ignore the important things of the law—justice, mercy, and faith" (23:23).
         b. "You strain your water so you won't accidentally swallow a gnat; then you swallow a camel!" (23:24).
      5. *Fifth judgment* (23:25-26): "You are so careful to clean the outside of the cup and the dish, but inside you are filthy—full of greed and self-indulgence!"
      6. *Sixth judgment* (23:27-28): "You are like whitewashed tombs—beautiful on the outside but filled on the inside with dead people's bones and all sorts of impurity."
      7. *Seventh judgment* (23:29-36)
         a. "You will become guilty of murdering all the godly people from righteous Abel to Zechariah" (23:29-35).

(1) By their ancestors' hands (23:29-31): They admit that they are descendants of those who killed the prophets.
(2) By their own hands (23:32-35): They will kill those sent to warn them.
b. "All the accumulated judgment of the centuries will break upon the heads of this very generation" (23:36).

II. THE ANGUISH OF JESUS (23:37-39)
A. **The desire—what Jesus wants to do** (23:37a): He longs to gather and protect his people.
B. **The denial—what Jesus cannot do** (23:37b): Israel rejects and despises him.
C. **The desolation—what Jesus will do** (23:38-39): He will remove his presence from Israel until the Great Tribulation!

SECTION OUTLINE TWENTY-THREE (MATTHEW 24)
The Olivet Discourse, part 1: Jesus foretells the future while speaking to his disciples on the Mount of Olives.

I. THE CONTENT OF CHRIST'S SERMON (24:1-26, 29)
A. **His remarks concerning the Temple destruction** (24:1-3)
1. *The pride* (24:1): Israel takes great pride in the Temple.
2. *The prophecy* (24:2-3)
a. Jesus' revelation (24:2): The Temple will someday be completely demolished!
b. The disciples' request (24:3): The disciples want to know when!
B. **His remarks concerning the Tribulation destruction** (24:4-14): Events of the first three and a half years.
1. *A time of apostasy* (24:4-5, 11)
a. The rise of false prophets (24:11): False prophets will lead the people astray.
b. The rise of false Christs (24:4-5): False messiahs will lead the people astray.
2. *A time of anarchy* (24:6-8): Wars will break out!
3. *A time of apathy* (24:12-13): The love of many will grow cold.
4. *A time of affliction* (24:9-10): Believers will be hated, betrayed, and martyred.
5. *A time of accomplishment* (24:14): The gospel will be preached to all nations.
C. **His remarks concerning the Tribulation destruction** (24:15-26, 29): Events of the final three and a half years—the most severe part of the Great Tribulation.
1. *The wickedness against God* (24:15-26)
a. What the enemy will do (24:15, 23-26): Construct the sacrilegious object that causes desecration.
(1) The statue (24:15): Assumed from Revelation 13:14-18.

(2) The subtlety (24:23-26): Many claim to be Christ.
  b. What the elect are to do (24:16-22): Run for the mountains!
  2. *The wrath from God* (24:29)
    a. The sun will be darkened (24:29a).
    b. The moon will not give light (24:29b).
    c. The stars will fall from the sky (24:29c).
    d. The powers of heaven will be shaken (24:29d).

II. THE CLIMAX OF CHRIST'S SERMON (24:27-28, 30-31, 40-41): The Second Coming.
  A. **The signal** (24:30): The Son of Man will appear in the heavens.
  B. **The swiftness** (24:27): As the lightning flashes across the sky.
  C. **The summons** (24:31): Angels will be sent forth with a mighty trumpet blast to gather the people of Israel from the farthest ends of the earth and heaven.
  D. **The slaughter** (24:28, 40-41): Armageddon!
    1. *The assembling of the victims* (24:40-41): One will be taken, another left.
    2. *The appearing of the vultures* (24:28): To eat the bodies of the slain warriors!

III. THE CLUE TO CHRIST'S SERMON (24:32-35): The rebirth of Israel.
  A. **The parable** (24:32): A sprouting fig tree.
  B. **The prophecy** (24:33-34)
    1. *The when (24:33)*
    2. *The who (24:34)*
  C. **The permanence** (24:35): Heaven and earth will pass away, but his word is eternal.

IV. THE CHALLENGE FROM CHRIST'S SERMON (24:36-39, 42-51): Be watchful.
  A. **The reason for this watchfulness** (24:36, 42): No one knows when Christ will come!
  B. **The reminder of this watchfulness** (24:37-39)
  C. **The reaction to this watchfulness** (24:43-51)
    1. *The wise servant* (24:43-47): He watches and is rewarded.
    2. *The wicked servant* (24:48-51): He ignores the warning and is condemned.

SECTION OUTLINE TWENTY-FOUR (MATTHEW 25)
The Olivet Discourse, part 2: Jesus tells two stories to illustrate the Kingdom of Heaven, and he talks about the final judgment of unbelievers.

I. THE PARABLE OF THE TEN VIRGINS (25:1-13)
  A. **The purpose** (25:1): Jesus relates this parable to explain the Kingdom of Heaven, comparing it to ten bridesmaids who go out to meet the bridegroom.

    B. The people (25:2-4)

       1. *Five of the bridesmaids are foolish and don't fill their lamps with oil* (25:2a, 3).

       2. *Five of the bridesmaids are wise, for they have extra oil* (25:2b, 4).

    C. The particulars (25:5-13)

       1. *The cry* (25:5-6): At midnight, a shout is heard: "The bridegroom is coming!"

       2. *The crisis* (25:7-9)

         a. The request by the foolish (25:7-8): "Give us some of your oil!"

         b. The refusal by the wise (25:9): "We don't have enough for all of us. Go to a shop and buy some for yourselves."

       3. *The closed door* (25:10-12): Upon returning with fresh oil, the foolish bridesmaids find the door to the marriage feast closed.

       4. *The challenge* (25:13): Maintain a diligent watch, and be prepared for the bridegroom's return!

II. THE PARABLE OF THE TALENTS (25:14-30)

    A. The responsibility (25:14-15): Jesus likens the Kingdom of Heaven to a man entrusting his property to three servants before going to another country.

       1. *The first servant is given five bags of gold* (25:14-15a).

       2. *The second servant is given two bags of gold* (25:15b).

       3. *The third servant is given one bag of gold* (25:15c).

    B. The reliability (25:16-18)

       1. *The first servant doubles his money* (25:16).

       2. *The second servant also doubles his money* (25:17).

       3. *The third servant buries his one bag of gold* (25:18).

    C. The accountability (25:19-30): Upon his return, the man meets with his three servants.

       1. *The first servant is rewarded for his faithfulness* (25:19-21).

       2. *The second servant is also rewarded for his faithfulness* (25:22-23).

       3. *The third servant is severely rebuked for his unfaithfulness* (25:24-30).

III. THE PARABLE OF THE SHEEP AND GOATS (25:31-46): Jesus compares the final judgment to a shepherd's separating sheep from goats.

    A. The separator (25:31): The Savior himself will occupy this role.

    B. The separation (25:32-33): The goats (lost people) will be placed on his left hand, and the sheep (saved people) on his right hand.

    C. The separated (25:34-46)

       1. *The sheep* (25:34-40): They will be rewarded!

         a. The contents (25:34): They will receive the Father's Kingdom, prepared for them from the foundation of the world.

b. The cause (25:35-36): It is due to their loving ministry in feeding, clothing, caring for, and even assisting Jesus in prison!

c. The confusion (25:37-39): The saved ask when all this takes place.

d. The clarification (25:40): Jesus says that when they ministered to others, they ministered to him!

2. *The goats* (25:41-46): They will be punished!

a. The contents (25:41): Eternal hell!

b. The cause (25:42-43): They did not minister to Jesus!

c. The confusion (25:44): The unsaved ask when it was that they did not minister to Jesus.

d. The clarification (25:45-46): Jesus says because they did not minister to others, they did not minister to him!

SECTION OUTLINE TWENTY-FIVE (MATTHEW 26)

Jesus and disciples celebrate Passover in the upper room. Jesus predicts Judas's betrayal and Peter's denial, both of which come to pass. After supper Jesus prays in Gethsemane, then is arrested and taken before the high priest.

I. THE ACTION PRECEDING THE UPPER ROOM (26:1-16)

A. The prediction (26:1-2): Once again Jesus predicts his betrayal and crucifixion.

B. The plots (26:3-5, 14-16): On two occasions wicked plans are made to kill Jesus.

1. *The plot by Caiaphas* (26:3-5): Jewish leaders meet at the palace of this high priest to discuss ways to murder the Savior!

2. *The plot by Judas* (26:14-16): He agrees with Jesus' enemies to betray the Messiah for thirty pieces of silver.

C. The preparation (26:6-13): Jesus is anointed by a woman at Bethany.

1. *The dedication* (26:6-7): A woman pours a very expensive alabaster jar of perfume over his head.

2. *The denunciation* (26:8-9): The disciples criticize her for not selling the perfume and giving the proceeds to the poor.

3. *The defense* (26:10-13): Jesus defends the woman, referring to two aspects:

a. The preparation aspect (26:10-12): She did this to prepare his body for burial.

b. The prophetic aspect (26:13): Her act will be remembered wherever the gospel is preached!

II. THE ACTION IN THE UPPER ROOM (26:17-30)

A. The instructions (26:17-19): Jesus directs two of his disciples to prepare a room in Jerusalem for the Passover.

B. The indictment (26:20-25)

1. *Jesus' betrayal* (26:20-24): The Savior announces that one of the Twelve will betray him.
2. *Jesus' betrayer* (26:25): He then identifies Judas as the one.
C. **The institution** (26:26-30)
  1. *The supper* (26:26-29): The Lord's Supper is now instituted.
    a. He speaks concerning the bread (26:26): It is his body.
    b. He speaks concerning the cup (26:27-29): It is his blood, poured out to forgive sins.
  2. *The song* (26:30): They sing a hymn, then go out to the Mount of Olives.

III. THE ACTION FOLLOWING THE UPPER ROOM (26:31-75)
  A. **The prophecy of Jesus** (26:31-35, 56b, 69-75)
    1. *As foretold* (26:31-35): Jesus makes a twofold prediction concerning the disciples.
      a. All will desert him (26:31-32): He will meet them in Galilee after the Resurrection.
      b. One will deny him (26:33-35): He says Peter will deny him three times before the rooster crows!
    2. *As fulfilled* (26:56b, 69-75)
      a. The desertion (26:56b): All the disciples flee.
      b. The denial (26:69-75): Peter denies Jesus three times.
  B. **The prayers of Jesus** (26:36-46)
    1. *The assistance he seeks* (26:36-38): Jesus requests that Peter, James, and John keep watch with him.
    2. *The agony he suffers* (26:39-46)
      a. His first prayer (26:39-41)
        (1) The struggle (26:39): Jesus begs his Father to remove the suffering he is about to endure but emphasizes that he desires the Father's will, not his own.
        (2) The sleepers (26:40-41): Returning, he finds the three disciples asleep.
      b. His second prayer (26:42-43)
        (1) The struggle (26:42): Similar to the first prayer.
        (2) The sleepers (26:43): Again he finds them asleep.
      c. His third prayer (26:44-46)
        (1) The struggle (26:44): Similar to the first two prayers.
        (2) The sleepers (26:45-46): Upon awakening them, he warns of his imminent arrest.
  C. **The persecutions of Jesus** (26:47-56a, 57-68)
    1. *He is arrested* (26:47-56)
      a. Jesus and Judas (26:47-50a): Judas betrays him to the soldiers by a kiss.
      b. Jesus and Peter (26:50b-54): Peter is rebuked for cutting off the ear of the high priest's servant.
      c. Judas and the soldiers (26:55-56a): He reminds the arresting soldiers of his innocence.
    2. *He is accused* (26:57-66)

a. The attempts (26:57-61)
  (1) The frantic efforts to locate false witnesses against Jesus (26:57-59)
  (2) The futile efforts to locate false witnesses against Jesus (26:60-61): No two people can agree in their testimony.
b. The affirmation (26:62-64): Jesus acknowledges to the high priest that he is indeed the Messiah.
c. The agreement (26:65-66): The Sanhedrin votes to put him to death for blasphemy!
3. *He is assaulted* (26:67-68): The Jewish leaders spit upon him and strike him.

SECTION OUTLINE TWENTY-SIX (MATTHEW 27)
Judas, overcome with guilt for betraying Jesus, hangs himself. Jesus goes on trial before Pilate, the Roman governor. Pilate finds Jesus innocent but gives in to the demands of the crowd and sentences Jesus to death. Jesus dies on the cross, saving the entire world from sin once and for all time.

I. EVENTS PRECEDING THE CRUCIFIXION (27:1-31)
  A. **The tragedy of Judas** (27:3-10)
    1. *The bloody silver* (27:3-5)
      a. His despair (27:3-4): Filled with remorse, Judas returns the thirty coins to the Jewish leaders.
      b. His death (27:5): He then goes out and hangs himself!
    2. *The bloody soil* (27:6-10)
      a. The priests' deliberation (27:6): They ponder what to do with the returned blood money.
      b. The priests' decision (27:7-10)
        (1) The property they find (27:7-8): They use the money to buy a field for a burial place for foreigners.
        (2) The prophecy they fulfill (27:9-10): This event was predicted centuries before (see Jer. 32:6-9; Zech. 11:12-13).
  B. **The trial before Pilate** (27:1-2, 11-26)
    1. *The confabulation* (27:1-2): The religious leaders meet to discuss how to persuade the Roman authorities to sentence Jesus to death.
    2. *The confusion* (27:11-14): Pilate is somewhat confused in two areas in regard to his famous prisoner.
      a. The sovereignty of Jesus (27:11): Is he really a king? The Savior says he is.
      b. The silence of Jesus (27:12-14): Why does he offer no defense before his accusers?
    3. *The custom* (27:15): Each Passover feast Pilate releases any one Jewish prisoner the crowd might desire.

4. *The criminal* (27:16-18): This year there is a particularly notorious criminal in jail named Barabbas.

5. *The concern* (27:19): At this moment Pilate's wife warns her husband concerning Jesus: "Leave that innocent man alone, because I had a terrible nightmare about him last night!"

6. *The choice* (27:20-23): When offered a choice, the wicked Pharisees demand:
   a. The deliverance of Barabbas (27:20-22)
   b. The death of Jesus (27:23)

7. *The (attempted) cleansing* (27:24-25): Pilate washes his hands to signify his innocence in Jesus' execution.

8. *The cruel chastening* (27:26): Pilate now orders Jesus to be flogged.

C. **The travesty by the soldiers** (27:27-31)
   1. *Their contempt* (27:27-29): They strip, spit upon, and mock Jesus, giving him a crown of thorns, a wooden scepter, and a scarlet robe.
   2. *Their cruelty* (27:30-31): They repeatedly strike him on the head.

II. EVENTS DURING THE CRUCIFIXION (27:32-50)

A. **The carrier of the cross** (27:32-33): An African named Simon is forced by the Romans to carry Jesus' cross.

B. **The cup for the cross** (27:34): Jesus refuses to drink a cup of drugged wine offered him to ease the pain.

C. **The clothing below the cross** (27:35-36): The soldiers cast lots for the Savior's clothes.

D. **The citation of the cross** (27:37): A sign reads, "This is Jesus, the King of the Jews."

E. **The criminals alongside the cross** (27:38): Two robbers are crucified with Jesus on either side of his cross.

F. **The contempt at the cross** (27:39-44)
   1. *Where the contempt comes from* (27:39, 41, 44)
      a. The passing crowd (27:39)
      b. The Jewish leaders (27:41)
      c. The two criminals (27:44)
   2. *What the contempt consists of* (27:40, 42-43)
      a. "So! You can destroy the Temple and build it again in three days, can you?" (27:40a).
      b. "If you are the Son of God, save yourself and come down from the cross!" (27:40b).
      c. "He saved others, but he can't save himself!" (27:42).
      d. "He trusted God—let God show his approval by delivering him!" (27:43).

G. **The cloud covering the cross** (27:45): A strange darkness falls on that area from noon till 3 P.M.

H. The cry from the cross (27:46-49)

    1. *The call* (27:46): *"Eli, Eli, lema sabachthani?"* ("My God, my God, why have you forsaken me?").

    2. *The confusion* (27:47-49): Some mistakenly think he is calling for Elijah to save him.

I. The cessation on the cross (27:50): Jesus cries out once more and gives up his spirit.

III. EVENTS FOLLOWING THE CRUCIFIXION (27:51-66)

  A. The heavenly action (27:51-53): Three supernatural events now occur.

    1. *Regarding the Temple* (27:51a): The heavy curtain secluding the Holy of Holies is torn in two, from top to bottom!

    2. *Regarding the terrain* (27:51b): The earth shakes, and rocks break!

    3. *Regarding the tombs* (27:52-53): The bodies of some godly people rise from their graves and live again!

  B. The human reaction (27:54-66)

    1. *The soldiers* (27:54): Those at the cross are terrified, acknowledging that Jesus is indeed the Son of God!

    2. *The women* (27:55-56, 61): Mary Magdalene and other godly women witness these things with great awe.

    3. *A rich man* (27:57-60): Joseph of Arimathea obtains the dead body of Jesus, wraps it in a clean linen cloth, and places it in his own tomb.

    4. *The chief priests* (27:62-66)

      a. What they do (27:62, 64-66): They secure permission to station a guard at Jesus' tomb and seal it.

      b. Why they do it (27:63): They remember the words of Jesus that he will rise again from the dead!

SECTION OUTLINE TWENTY-SEVEN (MATTHEW 28)

In this final chapter, Matthew records two postresurrection appearances of Jesus.

I. JESUS' APPEARANCE TO TWO WOMEN (28:1-15)

  A. The action preceding this appearance (28:1-8)

    1. *The arrival at the tomb* (28:1): Mary Magdalene and the other Mary come to the tomb.

    2. *The angel beside the tomb* (28:2-8)

      a. His radiance (28:2-4): His face shines like lightning, and his clothing is a brilliant white, causing the guards to become as dead men in their fear!

      b. His reassurance (28:5-6): He announces the resurrection of Christ from the dead!

       c. His request (28:7-8): The women are to tell the disciples this glorious news, informing them the Savior will meet them in Galilee.

B. The action during this appearance (28:9-10)

    1. *The women meet Jesus* (28:9a).

    2. *The women hear Jesus* (28:9b).

    3. *The women worship Jesus* (28:9c).

    4. *The women obey Jesus* (28:10): Again they are to remind the disciples concerning the Galilean meeting.

C. The action following this appearance (28:11-15): The frightened guards tell the chief priests what happened at Jesus' tomb.

    1. *First they tell the truth* (28:11): The soldiers give a factual account concerning what happened at the tomb.

    2. *Then they sell the truth* (28:12-15): For a sum of money they agree to lie, claiming the disciples of Jesus stole his body!

II. JESUS' APPEARANCE TO THE ELEVEN DISCIPLES (28:16-20)

A. The mountain (28:16): They meet on a mountain in Galilee as he had instructed them.

B. The mixed reaction (28:17): Some worship him, while others still doubt.

C. The mandate (28:18-20)

    1. *Jesus' authority* (28:18): He has been given all authority in heaven and on earth.

    2. *Jesus' assignment* (28:19-20a): They are to reach and teach all nations.

    3. *Jesus' assurance* (28:20b): He will always be with them!

Mark

SECTION OUTLINE ONE (MARK 1)
John the Baptist preaches the coming of the Messiah. John baptizes
Jesus, and Jesus is tempted for 40 days by Satan in the wilderness.
Jesus calls his first four disciples and begins his ministry of teaching
and healing.

I. EVENTS PRIOR TO JESUS' MINISTRY (1:1-13)
   A. **The witnesses of the Old Testament** (1:1-3): Mark begins his
      account by quoting from two Old Testament prophets.
      1. *Malachi, who spoke of God's messenger* (Mal. 3:1) (1:1-2):
         The messenger is John the Baptist.
      2. *Isaiah, who spoke of God's message* (Isa. 40:3) (Mark 1:3): The
         message is, "Prepare a pathway for the Lord's coming!"
   B. **The work of the Baptist** (1:4-11)
      1. *John baptizes the Jewish multitudes* (1:4-8): People confess
         their sins and are baptized.
      2. *John baptizes the Jewish Messiah* (1:9-11): The Holy Spirit
         lights on Jesus, and there is a voice from heaven, announcing
         God's pleasure with him.
   C. **The wrath of the Devil** (1:12-13): Jesus is tempted by Satan for
      forty days.

II. EVENTS EARLY IN JESUS' MINISTRY (1:14-45)
   A. **The promise of the Savior** (1:16-20): Jesus calls Andrew, Peter,
      James, and John, promising to make them fishers of men!
   B. **The preaching of the Savior** (1:14-15, 38-39)
      1. *What he preaches* (1:14-15): He preaches the Good News that
         the Kingdom of God is near.
      2. *Where he preaches* (1:38-39): He travels throughout all
         Galilee.
   C. **The praying of the Savior** (1:35-37): Jesus goes out into the wil-
      derness early one morning to pray.
   D. **The power of the Savior** (1:21-34, 40-45): Jesus heals many sick
      and demon-possessed people.
      1. *Individual healings* (1:21-31, 40-45)
         a. A demon-possessed man (1:21-28)

(1) The torment of the man (1:21-23): He is possessed by an evil spirit.

(2) The acknowledgment by the demon (1:24): The evil spirit immediately recognizes Jesus as the Son of God!

(3) The commandment of the Lord (1:25-26): He orders the demon to leave the man, and it does.

(4) The amazement of the crowd (1:27-28): They are overcome by the power and message of Jesus!

b. Peter's mother-in-law (1:29-31)

(1) The suffering woman (1:29-30): She is in bed with a high fever.

(2) The serving woman (1:31): Jesus heals her, and immediately she begins to wait upon him and the disciples.

c. A man with leprosy (1:40-45)

(1) The tears (1:40): The leper falls to his knees, begging Jesus to heal him.

(2) The touch (1:41-42): Filled with compassion, Jesus reaches out and restores him.

(3) The testimony (1:43-45)

(a) What Jesus tells the man not to do (1:43-44): "Don't talk to anyone."

(b) What the man does (1:45): He tells everybody what has happened to him!

2. *Corporate healings* (1:32-34): Multitudes now flock to Jesus for healing and deliverance.

SECTION OUTLINE TWO (MARK 2)
Jesus' enemies criticize him on four separate occasions: two for doing what they think he should *not* do, and two for not doing what they think he *should* do!

I. THE FIRST TWO CRITICISMS (2:1-17): What the Pharisees think Jesus should not be doing.

A. Jesus and a man on a bed (2:1-12)

1. *Some helpful friends* (2:1-5, 11-17)

a. The helplessness of the paralytic (2:1-4): He is totally immobile, confined to a stretcher.

(1) The intervening by his friends (2:1-3): Four men carry him to Jesus.

(2) The ingenuity of his friends (2:4): Unable to get in the front door because of the crowd, they cut a hole in the roof and lower him into the room!

b. The healing of the paralytic (2:5, 11-12)

(1) His spiritual healing (2:5): Jesus says, "My son, your sins are forgiven."

(2) His physical healing (2:11-12): Jesus says, "Stand up, take your mat, and go on home, because you are healed!"

   2. *Some hostile foes* (2:6-10)

      a. The denunciation by the scribes (2:6-7): They accuse him of blasphemy for forgiving sin.

      b. The defense by the Savior (2:8-10): He says his authority to forgive sin is seen by his power to heal!

B. Jesus and a man in a booth (2:13-17)

   1. *The conversion of Levi* (2:13-14): Jesus finds Levi sitting at his tax-collection booth and invites him to become a disciple.

   2. *The celebration by Levi* (2:15-17): He invites many friends to dinner so that they might meet Jesus.

      a. The background of these guests (2:15): Many are notorious sinners in the community.

      b. The bitterness against these guests (2:16): The Pharisees are outraged at this, demanding to know why Jesus associates with such sinners!

      c. The basis for these guests (2:17): Jesus explains that he has not come to call the righteous to repentance but sinners!

II. THE FINAL TWO CRITICISMS (2:18-28) What the Pharisees think Jesus should be doing.

A. They say he is not observing fasting (2:18-22)

   1. *Their rebuke* (2:18): They want to know why Jesus' disciples don't fast when their disciples do.

   2. *His response* (2:19-22)

      a. Wedding guests do not fast while the bridegroom is with them (2:19-20).

      b. No one sews a patch of unshrunk cloth on an old garment (2:21).

      c. No one puts new wine into old wineskins (2:22).

B. They say he is not observing the Sabbath (2:23-28).

   1. *Their rebuke* (2:23-24): He is allowing his disciples to break off heads of wheat and eat the grain on the Sabbath.

   2. *His response* (2:25-28)

      a. David was given consecrated bread, which was lawful only for priests to eat (2:25-26).

      b. The Sabbath was made for man, not man for the Sabbath, and Jesus is master of the Sabbath (2:27-28).

SECTION OUTLINE THREE (MARK 3)

Jesus heals a man on the Sabbath, provoking the Pharisees' rage. Crowds continue to follow him, and he heals the sick and demon-possessed among them. He chooses his twelve disciples and talks about the source of his power and about his true family.

I. THE COURAGE OF JESUS (3:1-6)
   A. **The miracle** (3:1-5): Jesus heals a man of a withered hand on the Sabbath in the presence of the wicked Pharisees.
   B. **The malice** (3:6): Outraged by the act, the Pharisees plot with the Herodians how to kill Jesus.

II. THE COMPASSION OF JESUS (3:7-12)
   A. **What he does** (3:7-11)
      1. *He restores those who are sick* (3:7-10).
      2. *He releases those who are possessed* (3:11).
   B. **What he says** (3:12): He warns those possessed by demons not to say who he is.

III. THE CALL OF JESUS (3:13-19): He invites a group of men to become his disciples.
   A. **The number** (3:13-14): Twelve men are called.
   B. **The nature** (3:15): They are to preach and cast out demons.
   C. **The names** (3:16-19): Peter, James, John, Andrew, Philip, Bartholomew, Matthew, Thomas, James (son of Alphaeus), Thaddaeus, Simon, and Judas Iscariot.

IV. THE CRITICS OF JESUS (3:20-30)
   A. **Criticism from his family** (3:20-21): They fear that his zeal for God has affected his mind!
   B. **Criticism from his foes** (3:22-30)
      1. *The accusation by the Jewish leaders* (3:22): They say he is casting out demons by Satan, the prince of demons.
      2. *The answer by the Savior* (3:23-30)
         a. His words of wisdom (3:23-27): "How can Satan cast out Satan?"
         b. His words of warning (3:28-30): He warns his wicked enemies that blasphemy against the Holy Spirit—which they are committing—is the unpardonable sin!

V. THE CLARIFICATION OF JESUS (3:31-35)
   A. **The desire of his earthly kin** (3:31-32): Jesus' family members want to see him!
   B. **The description of his eternal kin** (3:33-35): Jesus explains all who do God's will are part of his family!

SECTION OUTLINE FOUR (MARK 4)
Jesus teaches about the Kingdom by telling the parables of a farmer
and his seed, a lamp on a stand, growing seeds, and a mustard
seed. He amazes his disciples by calming a fierce storm.

I. JESUS RELATES HIS PARABLES (4:1-34)
  A. **Parable of the sower and the seed** (4:1-20)
    1. *Information in the parable* (4:1-9): A farmer sows grain which
      falls on four kinds of soil, producing four different results.
      a. Roadside soil (4:1-4): This seed is soon devoured by the
        birds.
      b. Shallow, rocky soil (4:5-6): This seed springs up quickly,
        but soon withers, scorched by the sun.
      c. Thorn-infested soil (4:7): This seed is quickly choked by the
        thorns.
      d. Fertile soil (4:8-9): This seed produces a thirty, sixty, or
        even hundredfold crop.
    2. *Isaiah and the parables* (4:10-12): This Old Testament prophet
      predicted that the wise would understand God's parables, but
      not the foolish.
    3. *Interpretation of the parable* (4:13-20)
      a. Roadside soil (4:13-15): This soil represents those who hear
        the message but do not understand it, thus allowing Satan
        to steal it from them.
      b. Shallow, rocky soil (4:16-17): This soil represents those
        who have no depth and thus drop out when encountering
        persecution.
      c. Thorn-infested soil (4:18-19): This soil represents those who
        allow the deceitfulness of riches to snuff out the seed.
      d. Fertile soil (4:20): This soil represents those who both hear
        and understand, permitting the seed to produce abundantly.
  B. **Parable of the lamp on a stand** (4:21-25): Jesus says the more
    one allows his or her light to shine, the clearer the truths in the
    parable will become!
  C. **Parable of the growing seed** (4:26-29): God's word, once it takes
    root in the heart of a believer, will in and by itself bring forth
    much fruit!
  D. **Parable of the mustard seed** (4:30-34): God's kingdom is like a
    mustard seed, so small when it is planted, yet eventually it
    becomes one of the largest plants!

II. JESUS REVEALS HIS POWER (4:35-41)
  A. **The crisis** (4:35-38a)
    1. *The stormy sea* (4:35-37): Jesus and the disciples suddenly
      encounter a furious squall while crossing the Sea of Galilee in
      a boat.
    2. *The sleeping Savior* (4:38a): Jesus is asleep at the back of the
      boat.

B. The cry (4:38b): Filled with fear, they shout to him: "Don't you even care that we are going to drown?"
C. The calm (4:39-41)
1. *The rebuke* (4:39): He rebukes the wind and sea, saying, "Quiet down!"
2. *The reproof* (4:40): Jesus chides the disciples for their lack of faith.
3. *The reaction* (4:41): They are filled with awe at his power!

SECTION OUTLINE FIVE (MARK 5)

Jesus heals a man possessed by many evil spirits by sending the demons into a herd of pigs. When a woman touches Jesus' robe, Jesus rewards her faith and heals her. He also rewards the faith of a synagogue leader by bringing his dead daughter back to life.

I. JESUS RELEASES A DEMON-POSSESSED MAN (5:1-20)
A. The despair (5:1-5): This man is continuously tormented by a large number of demons.
1. *The man lives among the tombs* (5:1-3a).
2. *No one can keep him chained* (5:3b-4).
3. *He constantly screams out and hits himself with stones* (5:5).
B. The deliverance (5:6-13): Jesus speaks to the evil spirits within the man.
1. *The panic of these demons* (5:6-7): In great fear they beg Jesus not to torment them before their time.
2. *The plea of these demons* (5:8-13)
   a. The request (5:9-12): The demons ask for permission to enter a large herd of pigs nearby.
   b. The results (5:13): Jesus allows it, and the possessed pigs run into the lake and drown.
   c. The release (5:8): The man is set free!
C. The disbelief (5:14-17): The pig owners and townspeople come running out to see what has happened.
1. *What they see* (5:14-16): They see the former madman now sitting, clothed, and in his right mind!
2. *What they say* (5:17): They all urge Jesus to go away and leave them alone!
D. The desire (5:18-20)
1. *The request by the man* (5:18): He begs to be allowed to go with Jesus.
2. *The reply by the Messiah* (5:19-20): The Savior declines, asking the man to share his testimony with others.

II. JESUS RESTORES A SUFFERING WOMAN (5:25-34)
A. Her disease (5:25-26)
1. *The description* (5:25): For twelve years she has suffered from internal bleeding.

2. *The deterioration* (5:26): Her condition is worsening.
B. Her determination (5:27-28): She fights her way through a crowd and touches Jesus' cloak, believing this will heal her!
C. Her deliverance (5:29-34)
  1. *The cure* (5:29): Immediately her bleeding stops.
  2. *The concern* (5:30-32): Turning around, Jesus wants to know who has touched him.
  3. *The confession* (5:33): The woman acknowledges to Jesus that she touched him.
  4. *The commendation* (5:34): Jesus reassures the woman that her faith has brought about her healing!

III. JESUS RESURRECTS A DEAD GIRL (5:21-24, 35-43)
  A. The request (5:21-24)
    1. *The person* (5:21-22): A synagogue leader named Jairus approaches Jesus.
    2. *The problem* (5:23-24): He begs the Savior to come and heal his dying daughter.
  B. The report (5:35): Jairus receives word that his daughter has just died.
  C. The reassurance (5:36): Jesus says to Jairus: "Don't be afraid. Just trust me."
  D. The restriction (5:37): Jesus allows only Peter, James, and John to accompany him to Jairus's home.
  E. The ridicule (5:38-40a)
    1. *The confusion* (5:38): Jesus encounters uncontrolled weeping and wailing upon entering Jairus's home.
    2. *The contempt* (5:39-40a): The Savior is ridiculed when he says the child is simply asleep.
  F. The resurrection (5:40b-43)
    1. *His order* (5:40b-41): "Get up, little girl!"
    2. *Her obedience* (5:42): She does, to the amazement of her parents!
  G. The restraint (5:43): Jesus commands the girl's parents not to tell anyone what has happened and to give their daughter something to eat.

SECTION OUTLINE SIX (MARK 6)
The people of Jesus' hometown reject him. Jesus sends out his disciples on a mission of preaching and healing. Herod has John the Baptist beheaded. Jesus feeds the 5,000 and walks on water.

I. THE MALICE OF THE NAZARENES (6:1-6a): Jesus visits his hometown but is rejected by the people of Nazareth.
  A. Their hostility (6:1-3): They resent the fact that this hometown boy has somehow acquired so much wisdom and power.

B. His helplessness (6:4-6a): Because of their unbelief, he can do few miracles among them.

II. THE MISSIONS OF THE TWELVE (6:6b-13): Jesus sends his disciples out two by two.
    A. Their assignments (6:6b-11)
        1. *To cast out demons* (6:6b-7)
        2. *To take no food, money, or extra clothes* (6:8-10)
        3. *To condemn unbelieving cities* (6:11)
    B. Their accomplishments (6:12-13)
        1. *They cast out demons* (6:13a).
        2. *They preach the gospel* (6:12).
        3. *They heal the sick* (6:13b).

III. THE MARTYRDOM OF THE BAPTIST (6:14-29)
    A. John is mistreated by Herod Antipas (6:17-20).
        1. *What Herod does* (6:17): He orders John arrested, bound, and imprisoned!
        2. *Why Herod does it* (6:18-20): John condemned the adulterous marriage between the king and his wife, thus invoking the wrath of Queen Herodias.
    B. John is murdered by Herod Antipas (6:21-29).
        1. *The party* (6:21): Herod hosts a banquet to celebrate his birthday.
        2. *The performance* (6:22a): Herodias's daughter gives a dance that greatly pleases the king.
        3. *The promise* (6:22b-23): As a sign of his pleasure, Herod promises to grant any favor the girl desires!
        4. *The plot* (6:24-29): At the urging of wicked Queen Herodias, the daughter asks for John's head on a platter, and the favor is quickly granted!
    C. Jesus is misunderstood by Herod Antipas (6:14-16): At first Herod thinks Jesus is the reincarnation of John!

IV. THE MIRACLES OF JESUS (6:30-56): Jesus feeds the 5,000, walks on water, and heals many people.
    A. Feeding the Five Thousand (6:30-44)
        1. *Events preceding this miracle* (6:30-38)
            a. The consideration of Jesus (6:30-31): Realizing the exhaustion of his disciples, Jesus leads them to a quiet place where they can rest.
            b. The compassion of Jesus (6:32-34): A large crowd of people soon arrives upon the scene, however, and Jesus is filled with compassion for them because they are like sheep without a shepherd.
            c. The command of Jesus (6:35-38)
                (1) The disciples' despair (6:35-36): Realizing that there is no food, they advise Jesus to send the hungry crowd away.

          (2) The Savior's directive (6:37-38): At his order the
          disciples search the crowd for food and locate five
          loaves of bread and two fish among the people.
  2. *Events accompanying this miracle* (6:39-42)
    a. The arrangement (6:39-40): Jesus has the people sit down
    in groups of 50 or 100.
    b. The acknowledgment (6:41): He thanks his heavenly Father
    for the food about to be received.
    c. The abundance (6:42): All eat their fill!
  3. *Events following this miracle (6:43-44)*
    a. The meals (6:43): Twelve basketfuls of bread and fish are
    picked up by the disciples.
    b. The men (6:44): Five thousand men are fed!

B. Walking on the water (6:45-52)
  1. *The awareness* (6:45-48a): Standing on a hillside, Jesus sees
    his disciples struggling for their lives in a boat during a terrible
    storm on the Sea of Galilee.
  2. *The approach* (6:48b): He comes walking on the water to
    them in the middle of the night.
  3. *The alarm* (6:49-50a): The disciples are terrified, thinking he is
    a ghost!
  4. *The assurance* (6:50b-51a): He reassures them and climbs into
    their boat, and the storm immediately dies!
  5. *The amazement* (6:51b-52): They are astonished at his mighty
    power.

C. Healing the multitudes (6:53-56): Upon landing at Gennesaret,
the Savior heals many.

SECTION OUTLINE SEVEN (MARK 7)

Jesus teaches about inner purity and rewards the faith of a Gentile
woman by healing her demon-possessed daughter. He also heals
a deaf-mute, to the amazement of the onlookers.

I. THE HOLINESS MESSAGE PREACHED BY JESUS (7:1-23)
  A. The reason for the message (7:1-5): The godless Pharisees
    demand to know why Jesus does not always observe their laws
    and regulations for outer cleansing.
  B. The rebuke in the message (7:6-23)
    1. *The prophecy* (7:6-7): He reminds them of Isaiah's prediction
      that God's people would honor the Messiah with their lips but
      hate him in their hearts (Isa. 29:13)!
    2. *The parental example* (7:8-13): Jesus says the Pharisees twist
      God's laws to avoid the responsibility of financially supporting
      their own parents!
    3. *The preaching* (7:14-23)
      a. Proclaiming the message (7:14-16): Jesus says defilement

has nothing to do with what one eats but rather with what one says and does.

  b. Explaining the message (7:17-23)
    (1) The intake of supposedly unclean food does not cause defilement (7:17-19).
    (2) The output of an unclean thought-life—including lust, theft, murder, adultery, deceit, envy, slander, and pride—does cause defilement (7:20-23).

II. THE HEALING MIRACLES PERFORMED BY JESUS (7:24-37)
  A. The healing of a demon-possessed daughter (7:24-30)
    1. *The brokenhearted mother* (7:24-26)
      a. The place (7:24): The region of Tyre.
      b. The problem (7:25): A Gentile girl is possessed by an evil spirit.
      c. The plea (7:26): The girl's desperate mother begs Jesus to heal her daughter.
    2. *The kindhearted Messiah (7:27-30)*
      a. His reminder (7:27): He says he has come to help the Jewish people and that "it isn't right to take food from the children and throw it to the dogs."
      b. Her response (7:28-30)
        (1) The reasoning (7:28): She replies: "True, but even the dogs under the table are given some crumbs from the children's plates."
        (2) The reward (7:29-30): For this reply Jesus heals the woman's daughter!
  B. The healing of a deaf and dumb man (7:31-37)
    1. *The desperation of the man* (7:31-32): The people bring the man to Jesus and beg the Savior to heal him.
    2. *The declaration of the Messiah* (7:33-37)
      a. What he does: (7:33): Jesus touches both the man's ears and tongue.
      b. What he says (7:34-37)
        (1) To the deaf ears (7:34-35): Jesus says, "Be opened!" And the man can hear and speak perfectly!
        (2) To the crowd (7:36-37): Jesus tells the people not to tell anyone. But they do!

SECTION OUTLINE EIGHT (MARK 8)
Jesus feeds the 4,000. The Pharisees demand a miraculous sign from Jesus, but he refuses. He heals a blind man and predicts his own death. Jesus asks his disciples who they think he is, and Peter correctly identifies Jesus as the Messiah.

I. THE PROVISION BY THE SAVIOR (8:1-10)
   A. **His concern** (8:1-4, 9-10)
      1. *The problem he faces* (8:1, 9-10): A crowd of 4,000 men has assembled to hear him preach when the food runs out.
      2. *The pity he feels* (8:2-3): Jesus' heart is moved. He knows the people are hungry.
      3. *The pessimism he finds* (8:4): The disciples conclude that nothing can be done.
   B. **His command** (8:5-8)
      1. *The amount of food* (8:5-7): Only seven loaves and a few small fish can be found among the crowd.
      2. *The abundance of food* (8:8)
         a. All eat until full! (8:8a)
         b. Seven basketfuls remain! (8:8b)

II. THE PROVOKING OF THE SAVIOR (8:11-13)
   A. **The Pharisees' demand** (8:11): "Give us a miraculous sign."
   B. **The Messiah's denial** (8:12-13): "I will not give this generation any such sign."

III. THE PATIENCE OF THE SAVIOR (8:14-21)
   A. **The caution** (8:14-15): Jesus warns the disciples to "beware of the yeast of the Pharisees and of Herod."
   B. **The confusion** (8:16): They think he is referring to actual bread.
   C. **The clarification** (8:17-21): Jesus asks the disciples why they think he would be worried about bread when they have seen him feed 5,000 and then 4,000 people, starting with next to nothing.

IV. THE POWER OF THE SAVIOR (8:22-26) Jesus heals a blind man at Bethsaida.
   A. **Jesus' first touch** (8:22-24): This causes the blind man to see people as walking trees.
   B. **Jesus' second touch** (8:25-26): This causes the blind man to see everything clearly.

V. THE PROMPTING BY THE SAVIOR (8:27-30) Jesus asks his disciples two questions.
   A. **First question** (8:27-28)
      1. *Jesus' question* (8:27): "Who do people say I am?"
      2. *The disciples' answer* (8:28): "Some say John the Baptist, some say Elijah, and others say you are one of the other prophets."
   B. **Second question** (8:29-30)

1. *Jesus' question* (8:29a): "Who do you say I am?"
2. *Peter's answer* (8:29b): "You are the Messiah."
3. *Jesus' warning* (8:30): Jesus warns them not to tell anyone about him.

VI. THE PREDICTION BY THE SAVIOR (8:31-38)
   A. **The revelation** (8:31): Jesus predicts his rejection, death, and resurrection.
   B. **The rebukes** (8:32-33)
      1. *Peter rebukes Jesus* (8:32).
      2. *Jesus rebukes Peter* (8:33).
   C. **The requirements** (8:34): To be Jesus' disciple, a person must take up his or her cross and follow Christ!
   D. **The rewards** (8:35-38): To lose one's life for Christ is to gain it!

SECTION OUTLINE NINE (MARK 9)
Peter, James, and John witness Jesus' transfiguration on a mountaintop. Jesus heals a demon-possessed boy and again predicts his own death and resurrection.

I. TRANSFIGURATION (9:1-13)
   A. **Ascending the Mount of Transfiguration** (9:1-2a)
      1. *The prophecy* (9:1): Jesus tells his disciples that some of them will see God's Kingdom in its glory.
      2. *The people* (9:2a): Jesus chooses Peter, James, and John to accompany him.
   B. **On the Mount of Transfiguration** (9:2b-8)
      1. *The appearance by Moses and Elijah* (9:2b-4)
      2. *The assumption by Peter* (9:5-6): He wrongly places Jesus, Moses, and Elijah on the same level!
      3. *The approval by the Father* (9:7-8): "This is my beloved Son. Listen to him."
   C. **Descending the Mount of Transfiguration** (9:9-13)
      1. *The command* (9:9-10): Jesus warns them to keep silent concerning his transfiguration.
      2. *The confusion* (9:11): They ask him why the teachers of religious law insist that Elijah must return before the Messiah comes.
      3. *The clarification* (9:12-13): Jesus tells them that Elijah has already come, in the person of John the Baptist.

II. RESTORATION (9:14-32) Jesus heals a demon-possessed boy.
   A. **The preliminaries** (9:14-16): Jesus finds nine of his disciples arguing with some teachers of religious law.
   B. **The particulars** (9:17-29)
      1. *The victim* (9:17-22)

a. The helpless father (9:17a): A desperate father tells Jesus that the disciples were unable to cast out an evil spirit from his son.
b. The hopeless son (9:17b-18a, 20-22)
   (1) The source of his problem (9:17b): He is demon-possessed!
   (2) The symptoms of his problem (9:18a): The evil spirit throws the boy into violent fits.
   (3) The span of his problem (9:20-22): He has been possessed since childhood!
c. The hapless disciples (9:18b-19): They are powerless to help.
2. *The victor* (9:23-29)
   a. Jesus reassures the father (9:23-24)
      (1) The strength of faith (9:23): The Savior says, "Anything is possible if a person believes."
      (2) The struggle for faith (9:24): The father says, "I do believe, but help me not to doubt!"
   b. Jesus rebukes the demon (9:25-26).
   c. Jesus restores the son (9:27).
   d. Jesus reveals the secret (9:28-29).
      (1) The disciples (9:28): "Why couldn't we cast out that evil spirit?"
      (2) The Savior (9:29): "This kind can be cast out only by prayer."
C. The prophecy (9:30-32): Jesus again predicts his betrayal, death, and resurrection.

III. CLARIFICATION (9:33-50) Jesus now addresses three subjects.
   A. He speaks concerning humility (9:33-37): Humility is the secret of greatness!
   B. He speaks concerning harmony (9:38-41): We are to fellowship with all Christ's followers.
   C. He speaks concerning hell (9:42-50): Do what must be done to avoid hell!

SECTION OUTLINE TEN (MARK 10)
Jesus blesses some children and teaches about childlike faith. He talks about divorce and the difficulty of having both worldly and heavenly riches. He predicts his death. James and John ask for glory in the Kingdom. Jesus heals a blind man.

I. JESUS AND THE SUBJECT OF DIVORCE (10:1-12) He is confronted by two groups regarding the divorce issue.
   A. The insincere group (10:1-9)
   1. *What Moses said* (10:1-4): The Pharisees tell Jesus that Moses permitted divorce.
   2. *Why Moses said it* (10:5-9): Jesus tells the Pharisees that:

a. Divorce was only God's permissive plan (10:5): He allowed it only because of the hard-hearted wickedness of people!

b. Divorce is not God's perfect plan (10:6-9): He made man and woman to be joined together permanently in marriage.

B. The sincere group (10:10-12): In a private meeting, Jesus explains his comments to the confused disciples.

1. *To divorce one's wife and marry another is to commit adultery* (10:10-11).

2. *To divorce one's husband and marry another is to commit adultery* (10:12).

II. JESUS AND SOME LITTLE CHILDREN (10:13-16): Jesus rebukes his disciples and receives some children.

A. He rebukes his disciples for attempting to prevent some children from seeing him (10:13-14).

B. He receives the children and blesses them (10:15-16).

III. JESUS AND THE RICH YOUNG RULER (10:17-22)

A. The seeking ruler (10:17-21)

1. *What he longs for* (10:17): He desires eternal life.

2. *What he lacks* (10:18-21)

a. He says he has observed all God's precepts (10:18-20).

b. Jesus says he must abandon all his possessions (10:21).

B. The sorrowing ruler (10:22): He goes away sadly, for he is very rich!

IV. JESUS AND THE DISCIPLES (10:23-31): After the departure of the rich man, Jesus discusses the subject of riches.

A. The allegory (10:23-25): Jesus says it is easier for a camel to go through the eye of a needle than for a rich man to enter the Kingdom of God!

B. The amazement (10:26): The stunned disciples then ask who can possibly be saved!

C. The assurance (10:27-31)

1. *He assures them in regard to redemption* (10:27): With God all things are possible.

2. *He assures them in regard to rewards* (10:28-31): All who follow Jesus will be amply rewarded!

V. JESUS AND THE CROSS (10:32-34): Once again he predicts his betrayal, death, and resurrection.

VI. JESUS AND TWO BROTHERS (10:35-45): James and John ask a favor from Jesus.

A. The request (10:35-37): "In your glorious Kingdom, we want to sit in places of honor next to you."

B. The refusal (10:38-39): Jesus says they don't know what they are asking.

C. **The restriction** (10:40): He then says that the Father, not the Son, will determine future seating arrangements!

D. **The resentment** (10:41): Upon learning of all this, the other ten apostles become upset with James and John.

E. **The review** (10:42-45): Jesus uses this tense situation to set forth the conditions for true greatness.

VII. JESUS AND THE BLIND MAN (10:46-52)

A. **The request by the blind man** (10:46-47)
   1. *Who he is* (10:46): His name is Bartimaeus.
   2. *What he wants* (10:47): He cries out for Jesus to have mercy on him.

B. **The response by the crowd** (10:48-50)
   1. *First they rebuke him* (10:48): "Be quiet!" they say.
   2. *Then they reassure him* (10:49-50): "Cheer up," they say. "Come on, he's calling you!"

C. **The restoration by the Savior** (10:51-52): Jesus restores Bartimaeus's sight!

SECTION OUTLINE ELEVEN (MARK 11)

Jesus fulfills prophecy by riding triumphantly into Jerusalem on a donkey. He drives the corrupt merchants from the Temple and declines to answer a challenge to his authority by his enemies when they can't answer a question he asks them.

I. THE CELEBRATION (11:1-11) Mark describes Jesus' triumphal entry into Jerusalem.

A. **The preparation** (11:1-7)
   1. *The mountain* (11:1a): Jesus stands on the Mount of Olives.
   2. *The two men* (11:1b): He speaks to two of his disciples.
   3. *The mission* (11:2-7)
      a. Their orders (11:2-3): The two men are to bring back to the Savior an unridden colt, upon which he will ride into Jerusalem.
      b. Their obedience (11:4-7): They do as they are commanded.

B. **The parade** (11:8-11)
   1. *The crowd prepares his path* (11:8): They spread their coats and branches in the road in front of the colt on which Jesus is riding.
   2. *The crowd proclaims his praises* (11:9-11): "Bless the one who comes in the name of the Lord!"

II. THE CLEANSING (11:15-19)

A. **Jesus removes the money tables from the Temple** (11:15-16).

B. **Jesus rebukes the money takers in the Temple** (11:17-19).
   1. *The prophecy* (11:17): Jesus says that Jeremiah predicted this event (Jer. 7:11).

2. *The plot* (11:18-19): The Pharisees meet and plan to kill Jesus.

III. THE CURSING (11:12-14, 20-26): Jesus pronounces judgment on a fig tree.
   A. **The reason for this judgment** (11:12-14): The tree has no fruit!
   B. **The results of this judgment** (11:20-21): Overnight the fruitless fig tree withers.
   C. **The reflection on this judgment** (11:22-26): Jesus uses this event to stress the power of faith and prayer!

IV. THE CONFLICT (11:27-33): The wicked Jewish leaders now confront Jesus.
   A. **Their demand** (11:27-28): They ask Jesus what authority he has to drive the merchants out of the Temple and from where this authority has come.
   B. **His defense** (11:29-30): In return, Jesus asks them from where the authority of John the Baptist came—was it heavenly authority or human authority?
   C. **Their dilemma** (11:31-32): They realize whatever answer they give will trap them!
   D. **Their defeat** (11:33)
      1. *Their response* (11:33a): "We don't know."
      2. *He says* (11:33b): "Then I won't answer your question either."

SECTION OUTLINE TWELVE (MARK 12)
Jesus tells a parable and answers questions about paying taxes and about the resurrection. He identifies the two most important commandments, talks about the Messiah's divine identity, and commends a poor widow for her offering.

I. ILLUSTRATION (12:1-12): Jesus relates the parable of the vineyard tenants to illustrate his rejection by the nation of Israel.
   A. **The workman** (12:1)
      1. *The labor* (12:1a): A man plants a vineyard, builds a wall around it, digs a pit for the winepress, and constructs a watchtower.
      2. *The lease* (12:1b): He then rents it out and goes away on a journey.
   B. **The wickedness** (12:2-12): At harvesttime the man sends some servants back to his vineyard.
      1. *Their mission* (12:2, 4a, 5a, 6): They are to collect his share of the crop.
      2. *Their mistreatment* (12:3, 4b, 5b, 7-12)
         a. The wicked tenants ridicule, beat, and even kill some of the owner's servants (12:3, 4b, 5b).
         b. The wicked tenants finally murder the owner's son (12:7-8).

c. The wrath (12:9): The furious owner returns, kills the godless tenants, and leases the vineyard to others!

d. The witness (12:10-12): Jesus reminds his listeners that David predicted Israel's rejection and murder of God's Son (Ps. 118:22-23).

II. CONFRONTATION (12:13-37): The Jewish leaders confront Jesus in regard to four issues.

A. **Concerning the paying of tribute** (12:13-17)
1. *Their deceit* (12:13-15a): In derision they ask: "As a man of great integrity, we ask you: Is it right to pay taxes to Caesar?"
2. *Their defeat* (12:15b-17): He answers: "Give to Caesar what belongs to him. But everything that belongs to God must be given to God."

B. **Concerning marriage in the resurrection** (12:18-27)
1. *Their silly example* (12:18-23): They demand to know to which husband a wife will be married in heaven if she has been married seven times while on earth!
2. *The Savior's education* (12:24-27)
a. Concerning the resurrection (12:24-25): There will be a resurrection!
b. Concerning marriage (12:26-27): There will be no marriage in the resurrection!

C. **Concerning the greatest commandment** (12:28-34)
1. *Jesus and a Jewish teacher: Round one* (12:28-31)
a. The question asked of Jesus (12:28): "Of all the commandments, which is the most important?"
b. The question answered by Jesus (12:29-31)
(1) "The most important commandment is this: 'Hear, O Israel! . . . You must love the Lord your God with all your heart, all your soul, all your mind, and all your strength (12:29-30).
(2) "The second is equally important: 'Love your neighbor as yourself'" (12:31).
2. *Jesus and a Jewish teacher: Round two* (12:32-34)
a. The teacher (12:32-33): "You have spoken the truth."
b. The master (12:34): "You are not far from the Kingdom of God."

D. **Concerning the Son of David** (12:35-37): Jesus points out two facts about the Messiah.
1. *He is David's son, thus affirming his humanity* (12:35-36).
2. *He is David's Lord, thus affirming his deity* (12:37).

III. CONDEMNATION (12:38-40): Jesus warns against the teachers of religious law.

A. **Haughtiness** (12:38-39): They strut about in fine robes and expect the best places at banquets.

B. **Cheating** (12:40): They cheat widows out of their property.

IV. DONATION (12:41-44): Jesus compares the small offering of a poor widow to the large offerings of the rich.

    A. The ones who give much, amounting to little (12:41): Jesus watches some rich people putting great sums of money into the Temple treasury.

    B. The one who gives little, amounting to much (12:42-44): Jesus says a poor widow who drops in two small coins has given the most, for it is all she has!

SECTION OUTLINE THIRTEEN (MARK 13)
Jesus teaches about events of the end times.

I. THE TWO PROPHECIES OF JESUS (13:1-27)

    A. In regard to the Temple (13:1-2): He predicts the total destruction of the Jewish Temple!

    B. In regard to the Tribulation (13:3-27): Jesus describes the events that will transpire during the first and final halves of the future Great Tribulation.

        1. *Events during the first half of the Tribulation* (13:4-13)

            a. The appearance of false Messiahs (13:4-6)

            b. Worldwide wars (13:7-8a)

            c. Earthquakes and famines (13:8b)

            d. Persecution of the godly (13:9, 12-13)

                (1) Political and religious persecution (13:9)

                (2) Family persecution (13:12-13)

            e. Universal preaching of the Gospel (13:10)

            f. Ministry of the Holy Spirit (13:11)

        2. *Events during the final half of the Tribulation* (13:14-27)

            a. Desecration of the third Temple (13:14-16)

            b. Unprecedented horror (13:17-20)

            c. False rumors of Christ's return (13:21-23)

            d. Fearful happenings concerning the sun, moon, and stars (13:24-25)

            e. The second coming of Christ (13:26)

            f. The gathering of Israel (13:27)

II. THE TWO PARABLES OF JESUS (13:28-37)

    A. Parable of the fig tree (13:28-31): Jesus talks about observing signs.

        1. *The sign* (13:28): "When [the fig tree's] buds become tender and its leaves begin to sprout, you know without being told that summer is near."

        2. *The significance* (13:29-30): "Just so, when you see the events I've described beginning to happen, you can be sure that [my] return is very near, right at the door."

3. *The surety* (13:31): "Heaven and earth will disappear, but my words will remain forever."
B. Parable of the alert servants (13:32-37): Jesus urges his servants to be watchful, giving two reasons for this.
1. *Because of the task* (13:34-35): God has assigned each believer a specific task to accomplish.
2. *Because of the time* (13:32-33, 36-37): No servant knows when the Master will return, thus constant watchfulness is required!

SECTION OUTLINE FOURTEEN (MARK 14)
This chapter records events before, during, and after Jesus' agony in Gethsemane.

I. Events Preceding Gethsemane (14:1-31)
A. The plots (14:1-2, 10-11): Wicked plans are laid on two occasions to kill Jesus.
1. *The plot by the chief priests* (14:1-2)
2. *The plot by Judas Iscariot* (14:10-11): He agrees to betray Jesus.
B. The preparation (14:3-9): A woman pours expensive perfume over Jesus' head, to which Jesus responds by saying that she has prepared his body for burial.
1. *The place* (14:3a): It occurs in Bethany.
2. *The person* (14:3b): A woman anoints Jesus.
3. *The perfume* (14:3c): She pours out an alabaster jar of very costly perfume on Jesus.
4. *The protest* (14:4-9)
   a. The woman is denounced by some of the guests (14:4-5): "Why was this expensive perfume wasted? She could have sold it for a small fortune and given the money to the poor!"
   b. The woman is defended by the Savior (14:6-9).
      (1) Concerning the poor (14:6-7): "You will always have the poor among you, and you can help them whenever you want to. But I will not be here with you much longer."
      (2) Concerning the perfume (14:8-9): "Wherever the Good News is preached throughout the world, this woman's deed will be talked about in her memory."
C. The Passover meal (14:12-26)
1. *The instructions* (14:12-16): Jesus sends two of his disciples to Jerusalem to secure an upper room where the Passover supper can be observed, and they obey.
2. *The indictment* (14:17-20)
   a. The betrayal (14:17-18): In the upper room, Jesus announces that one of the disciples will betray him!

      b. The baffled (14:19): One by one they ask him, "I'm not the
         one, am I?"
      c. The betrayer (14:20-21): Jesus says of the one who will
         betray him, "Far better for him if he had never been born!"
   3. *The institution* (14:22-26)
      a. The supper (14:22-25): Jesus institutes the first Christian
         Communion service.
         (1) The bread (14:22): "This is my body."
         (2) The wine (14:23-25): "This is my blood."
      b. The song (14:26): They now sing a hymn and depart the
         upper room.
  D. The predictions (14:27-31): Jesus warns:
   1. *That he will be deserted by all* (14:27-28)
   2. *That he will be denied by one* (14:29-31)

II. Events Occurring in Gethsemane (14:32-52)
  A. The agony of Jesus (14:32-42)
   1. *His first prayer* (14:32-38)
      a. The struggle (14:32-35): Feeling his soul crushed with
         sorrow, he prays that, if possible, his terrible cup of suffer-
         ing might be removed.
      b. The submission (14:36): He emphasizes that he desires his
         Father's will above his own.
      c. The sleepers (14:37-38): Upon returning to where he left
         them, Jesus finds Peter, James, and John asleep!
         (1) He awakens them (14:37).
         (2) He admonishes them (14:38): "Keep alert and pray."
   2. *His second prayer* (14:39-40): Jesus again leaves his disciples
     and prays alone, and again he returns to find them sleeping.
   3. *His third prayer* (14:41-42): Yet a third time he finds the
     disciples asleep.
  B. The arrest of Jesus (14:43-49)
   1. *Jesus and Judas* (14:43-45): Judas betrays Jesus into the hands
     of a mob with a deceitful kiss.
   2. *Jesus and Peter* (14:46-49): Jesus rebukes Peter's act of cutting
     off the ear of the high priest's servant (see also John 18:10).
  C. The abandonment of Jesus (14:50-52)
   1. *He is forsaken by the eleven* (14:50).
   2. *He is forsaken by a young man* (14:51-52).

III. Events Following Gethsemane (14:53-72)
  A. Jesus is denounced by his foes (14:55-65).
   1. *He is arraigned before the Sanhedrin* (14:55-64).
      a. The attempts involved (14:55-59)
         (1) The frantic efforts to indict him (14:55-56): False
         witnesses are assembled to testify against him.
         (2) The futile efforts to indict him (14:57-59): None of the
         witnesses get their stories straight.

      b. The affirmation (14:60-62): When asked, Jesus affirms that he is indeed the Messiah!

      c. The agreement (14:63-64): The Sanhedrin now agrees that Jesus should be put to death as a blasphemer.

    2. *He is assaulted by the Sanhedrin* (14:65): Jesus is blindfolded, spit upon, struck, and ridiculed!

B. Jesus is denied by his follower (14:53-54, 66-72)

    1. *The person* (14:53-54a): Simon Peter denies Jesus on three occasions.

    2. *The place* (14:54b): It occurs beside a fire in the courtyard of the Sanhedrin.

    3. *The particulars* (14:66-72)

      a. First occasion (14:66-68): A servant girl accuses him of being a disciple of Jesus.

      b. Second occasion (14:69-70a): This charge is repeated by the same girl.

      c. Third occasion (14:70b-72)

        (1) Several others now accuse Peter, causing him to curse out his denials (14:70b-71).

        (2) The rooster crows (14:72a).

        (3) Peter breaks down and weeps bitterly (14:72b).

SECTION OUTLINE FIFTEEN (MARK 15)

Jesus is put on trial, sentenced to death, crucified, and buried, taking upon himself the sins of the entire world!

I. EVENTS PRECEDING THE CRUCIFIXION (15:1-21)

  A. The conspiracy (15:1): The Sanhedrin binds Jesus and brings him before Pilate to be crucified.

  B. The confusion (15:2)

    1. *Pilate* (15:2a): "Are you the King of the Jews?"

    2. *Jesus* (15:2b): "It is as you say."

  C. The charges (15:3-5)

    1. *The slander against Jesus* (15:3-4): The Pharisees accuse him of many crimes.

    2. *The silence of Jesus* (15:5): He makes no reply!

  D. The custom (15:6): It is Pilate's custom to release one Jewish prisoner each year at Passover.

  E. The choice (15:7-14)

    1. *The crowd demands the deliverance of Barabbas the murderer* (15:7-11).

    2. *The crowd demands the death of Jesus the Messiah* (15:12-14).

  F. The chastening (15:15): Pilate now orders Jesus flogged.

  G. The contempt (15:16-20): Jesus is handed over to the Roman soldiers.

1. *He is mocked* (15:16-18): "Hail, King of the Jews!"
2. *He is mistreated* (15:19-20): They spit on him and strike him!

H. **The crossbearer** (15:21): Simon of Cyrene is pressed into service by the Romans to carry Jesus' cross.

II. EVENTS DURING THE CRUCIFIXION (15:22-37)

A. **The cup for the cross** (15:22-23): Jesus refuses the cup of wine drugged with bitter herbs offered him.

B. **The clothing below the cross** (15:24-25)
1. *What is done* (15:24): The soldiers throw dice for his clothes.
2. *When it is done* (15:25): He is crucified at 9 A.M.

C. **The citation on the cross** (15:26): The sign reads, "The King of the Jews."

D. **The criminals alongside the cross** (15:27-28): Jesus is crucified between two robbers.

E. **The contempt toward the cross** (15:29-32)
1. *Where it comes from* (15:29a, 31, 32b)
   a. Those passing by (15:29a)
   b. The Jewish religious leaders (15:31)
   c. The two robbers (15:32b)
2. *What it consists of* (15:29b-30, 32a)
   a. "You can destroy the Temple and rebuild it in three days, can you? Well then, save yourself and come down from the cross!" (15:29b-30).
   b. "He saved others, but he can't save himself!" (15:32a).

F. **The cloud covering the cross** (15:33): Darkness covers the cross from noon till 3 P.M.

G. **The cry from the cross** (15:34): Jesus shouts, *"Eloi, Eloi, lema sabachthani?"* ("My God, my God, why have you forsaken me?")

H. **The confusion around the cross** (15:35-36): Some people who hear his cry think Jesus is calling for Elijah to help him.

I. **The consummation of the cross** (15:37): At 3 P.M. Jesus dies.

III. EVENTS FOLLOWING THE CRUCIFIXION (15:38-47)

A. **Regarding the tearing of the veil** (15:38): The Temple curtain is torn in two from top to bottom.

B. **Regarding the tribute by the centurion** (15:39): As he watches Jesus die, the Roman officer in charge cries out, "Truly, this was the Son of God!"

C. **Regarding the testimony of the women** (15:40-41): A number of faithful women are at the cross when Jesus dies.

D. **Regarding the tomb of Joseph of Arimathea** (15:42-47)
1. *The mission of Joseph* (15:42-45): He requests and receives from Pilate the lifeless body of Jesus.
2. *The ministry of Joseph* (15:46-47): He wraps the body of Jesus in a linen cloth and places it in his own personal tomb.

SECTION OUTLINE SIXTEEN (MARK 16)
Jesus rises from the grave, defeating death for all time, and ascends to heaven after giving his disciples the command to preach the Good News throughout the whole world.

I. HE ARISES (16:1-18)
  A. **The resurrection announcement** (16:1-8)
    1. *The grief* (16:1-3): Three heavyhearted women come to the tomb, wondering how they might roll aside the huge stone from the entrance.
    2. *The glory* (16:4-8): An angel announces Jesus' resurrection to the startled women.
  B. **The resurrection appearances** (16:9-18)
    1. *First appearance, to Mary Magdalene* (16:9-11)
    2. *Second appearance, to two believers* (16:12-13)
    3. *Third appearance, to the disciples as they are eating* (16:14-18)
      a. The command (16:14-15): They are to preach the gospel to all nations.
      b. The confirmation (16:16-18): Supernatural signs will accompany them!

II. HE ASCENDS (16:19-20): Jesus is taken up into heaven and sits down at God's right hand!

Luke

SECTION OUTLINE ONE (LUKE 1)
This first chapter of Luke includes a preface, two proclamations, and three songs of praise.

I. THE PREFACE (1:1-4)
   A. **The review** (1:1-2): Luke explains just why he is writing this Gospel.
   B. **The recipient** (1:3): He dedicates his book to someone named Theophilus.
   C. **The reason** (1:4): "To reassure you of the truth of all you were taught."

II. THE TWO PROCLAMATIONS (1:5-38)
   A. **To Zechariah, concerning the birth of John** (1:5-25)
      1. *Zechariah's spouse* (1:5-7)
         a. Elizabeth is blameless (1:5-6): "Righteous in God's eyes, careful to obey all of the Lord's commandments."
         b. Elizabeth is barren (1:7): She is a childless old woman.
      2. *Zechariah's service* (1:8-10) He prepares the burnt incense on the altar of incense as the people wait and pray outside.
      3. *Zechariah's shock* (1:11-25)
         a. The reason (1:11-12): He sees the angel Gabriel standing at the right side of the altar!
         b. The revelation (1:13-17): Gabriel tells Zechariah that Elizabeth will bear a son.
            (1) He will be called John (1:13-14).
            (2) He will become a Nazirite (1:15).
            (3) He will serve as the Messiah's forerunner (1:16-17).
         c. The reluctance (1:18): Zechariah finds all this hard to believe.
         d. The rebuke (1:19-20): Gabriel says that due to his unbelief, Zechariah will be unable to speak until the child is born!
         e. The restraint (1:21-22): Upon leaving the Temple, Zechariah is unable to pronounce the priestly blessing for the waiting crowd.

      f. The rejoicing (1:23-25): The barren Elizabeth soon becomes pregnant, causing great joy in the household.

B. To Mary, concerning the birth of Jesus (1:26-38)

    1. *The salutation to Mary* (1:26-37): She receives a heavenly visit.

      a. The messenger (1:26-28): The angel Gabriel appears to this virgin girl in Nazareth; Mary is engaged to Joseph the carpenter.

      b. The message (1:29-33)

        (1) Gabriel's assurance (1:29-30): He comforts Mary, saying she has found favor with God.

        (2) Gabriel's announcement (1:31-33): Mary will give birth to Jesus, the Messiah, whose Kingdom and reign over Israel will never end!

      c. The mystery (1:34): Being a virgin, Mary is perplexed, wondering how this can be accomplished.

      d. The method (1:35): Gabriel tells her that the Holy Spirit will father the baby!

      e. The miracle (1:36-37): Mary now learns that her aged relative Elizabeth is already six months into her pregnancy!

    2. *The submission by Mary* (1:38): "I am the Lord's servant, and I am willing to accept whatever he wants."

III. THE THREE SONGS OF PRAISE (1:39-80)

    A. The praise of Elizabeth to God (1:39-45)

      1. *The babe within Elizabeth* (1:39-41): Mary visits Elizabeth, and upon hearing Mary's voice, Elizabeth's child leaps within her womb, and she is filled with the Holy Spirit.

      2. *The blessing from Elizabeth* (1:42-45): She tells Mary what an honor it is to be visited by the mother of the Messiah!

    B. The praise of Mary to God (1:46-56)

      1. *The testimony* (1:46-55): Mary thanks God for six things.

        a. His condescension (1:46-48): God took notice of her.

        b. His holiness (1:49): He has done great things for her.

        c. His mercy (1:50): His mercy goes on from generation to generation.

        d. His power (1:51): He does tremendous things with his power.

        e. His sovereignty (1:52-53): He humbles the proud and exalts the lowly.

        f. His faithfulness (1:54-55): He has kept all his promises to Israel.

      2. *The time* (1:56): Mary stays with Elizabeth for three months, then returns home.

    C. The praise of Zechariah to God (1:57-80)

      1. *Zechariah the father* (1:57-66)

        a. He is seen writing (1:57-63).

        (1) The celebration (1:57-58): John's parents, neighbors, and relatives meet and rejoice at his birth.

(2) The circumcision (1:59): This is performed on the eighth day.

(3) The confusion (1:60-61): People are puzzled that the baby will be named John. Does the mute Zechariah agree with this?

(4) The confirmation (1:62-63): Calling for a tablet, Zechariah writes, "His name is John!"

    b. He is seen worshiping (1:64-66): Zechariah is suddenly able to speak again and begins praising God!

  2. *Zechariah, the foreteller* (1:67-80)

    a. His prophecy concerning his Savior (1:67-75)

(1) The birth of Jesus assures the fulfillment of the Davidic covenant (1:67-72).

(2) The birth of Jesus assures the fulfillment of the Abrahamic covenant (1:73-75).

    b. His prophecy concerning his son (1:76-80)

(1) He will prepare the way of the Lord (1:76).

(2) He will proclaim the words of the Lord (1:77-80).

SECTION OUTLINE TWO (LUKE 2)

Mary and Joseph travel to Bethlehem, and Jesus is born. Shepherds receive a visit from some angels and come to worship the baby, and Simeon and Anna bless the child in the Temple. When Jesus is 12, he amazes the religious teachers in the Temple with his wisdom. Jesus and his parents settle in Nazareth.

  I. BETHLEHEM (2:1-21)

    A. Jehovah's Son is born (2:1-7).

      1. *The decree by Caesar* (2:1-5)

        a. The law (2:1-3): All are required to return to their ancestral homes because of a census.

        b. The location (2:4-5): Joseph and Mary must travel to Bethlehem.

      2. *The delivery by Mary* (2:6-7): While in Bethlehem, Mary gives birth to Jesus.

    B. Judah's shepherds are briefed (2:8-21).

      1. *They watch* (2:8): They are in the fields guarding their sheep.

      2. *They wonder* (2:9-14): The shepherds are confused and terrified when the horizon is suddenly filled with God's glory!

        a. The reassurance by the angel of the Lord (2:9-10): "Don't be afraid! I bring you good news of great joy for everyone!"

        b. The revelation by the angel of the Lord (2:11-12)

(1) In regard to God's Son (2:11): The Messiah has just been born in Bethlehem!

(2) In regard to God's sign (2:12): They will find him wrapped in strips of cloth, lying in a manger.

c. The rejoicing by the angels of the Lord (2:13-14): "Glory to God in the highest heaven and peace on earth to all whom God favors!"

3. *They worship* (2:15-16): The shepherds kneel before the babe in the manger.

4. *They witness* (2:17-21)
   a. The confirming (2:17-18, 20): When they leave, they tell everyone what has happened.
   b. The contemplating (2:19): Mary treasures these things in her heart and thinks about them.
   c. The circumcising (2:21): On the eighth day, the babe is circumcised and named Jesus, in accordance with what the angel said before the baby was even conceived.

II. JERUSALEM (2:22-38, 41-50)
   A. **Jesus' first recorded Temple visit** (2:22-38): Mary and Joseph bring him to the Temple to dedicate him to the Lord. Two individuals are there to greet him.
      1. *The testimony of Simeon* (2:25-35)
         a. His reassurance (2:25-26): This devout man has been promised by the Holy Spirit that he would live to see the Messiah.
         b. His recognition (2:27-32): The Holy Spirit tells him that Mary's baby is the Messiah!
         c. His revelation (2:33-35)
            (1) Concerning the Messiah (2:33-34): He will cause the rising and falling of many in Israel.
            (2) Concerning the mother (2:35): He says a sword will someday pierce the soul of Mary!
      2. *The testimony of Anna* (2:36-38): This aged and godly widow joins Simeon in praising God for Israel's Messiah.
   B. **Jesus' second recorded Temple visit** (2:41-50)
      1. *The missing son* (2:41-47)
         a. The occasion (2:41-42): Jesus attends the Passover festival in Jerusalem with his parents at age 12.
         b. The oversight (2:43-45): He is accidentally left behind by his parents.
         c. The outcome (2:46-47): After looking for him everywhere, they finally locate him in the Temple, discussing theology with the Jewish teachers.
      2. *The messianic Son (2:48-49)*
         a. Mary's rebuke (2:48): "Why have you done this to us?"
         b. Jesus' reminder (2:49): "You should have known that I would be in my Father's house."
      3. *The misunderstood Son* (2:50): They cannot comprehend what he is saying!

III. NAZARETH (2:39-40, 51-52): While growing up in Nazareth, Jesus grows in the following areas:
   A. **In height** (physical maturity) (2:39-40a, 52a)
   B. **In wisdom** (mental maturity) (2:40b)
   C. **In favor with God** (spiritual maturity) (2:52b)
   D. **In favor with man** (social maturity) (2:52c)

SECTION OUTLINE THREE (LUKE 3)

John the Baptist prepares the way of the Messiah. Jesus is baptized, and God declares his pleasure with his Son. Luke records Jesus' ancestral records.

I. THE LABOR OF JOHN THE BAPTIST (3:1-22)
   A. **The message of John** (3:1-14, 19-20)
      1. *When he preaches* (3:1-2)
         a. Tiberius Caesar is ruler over the Roman Empire (3:1a).
         b. Pilate is governor over Judea (3:1b).
         c. Herod Antipas is governor over Galilee (3:1c).
         d. Annas and Caiaphas are the high priests (3:2).
      2. *What he preaches* (3:3-6): "Repent of your sins and be baptized! Prepare the way for the Lord!"
      3. *To whom he preaches* (3:7-11, 13-14, 19-20)
         a. The Jewish religious leaders and lay people (3:7-11)
         b. Tax collectors (3:13)
         c. Soldiers (3:14)
         d. King Herod Antipas and Queen Herodias (3:19-20): Herod will eventually become so frustrated by John's preaching that he will put John in prison.
   B. **The misunderstanding about John** (3:15-18)
      1. *The confusion* (3:15): Some people feel John is the Messiah!
      2. *The clarification* (3:16-18): John declares, "Someone is coming soon who is greater than I am—so much greater that I am not even worthy to be his slave."
   C. **The ministry of John** (3:3, 21-22)
      1. *He baptizes the converts of Israel* (3:3).
      2. *He baptizes the Christ of Israel* (3:21-22).

II. THE LINE OF JESUS THE MESSIAH (3:23-38)
   A. **From Jesus, the legal son of Joseph, to Nathan, the biological son of David** (3:23-31)
   B. **From Obed, the son of Boaz, to Adam, the son of God** (3:32-38)

SECTION OUTLINE FOUR (LUKE 4)

Jesus is tempted by Satan in the wilderness. The people of Nazareth, his hometown, reject him. He heals many sick and demon-possessed people, to the amazement of the people. Everywhere he goes, he preaches the Good News of the Kingdom of God.

I. THE MEASURING OF JESUS (4:1-13): The Holy Spirit allows Jesus to be tempted by the Devil.

  A. **The terrain** (4:1): The tempting occurs in the barren wastelands of Judea.

  B. **The time** (4:2): The ordeal lasts for forty days.

  C. **The test** (4:3-12)

   1. *First temptation* (4:3-4)

    a. The test (4:3): "Change this stone into a loaf of bread!"

    b. The triumph (4:4): "People need more than bread for their life."

   2. *Second temptation* (4:5-8)

    a. The test (4:5-7): "I will give you the glory of these kingdoms and authority over them . . . if you will bow down and worship me."

    b. The triumph (4:8): "You must worship the Lord your God; serve only him."

   3. *Third temptation* (4:9-12)

    a. The test (4:9-11): "If you are the Son of God, jump off [the highest point of the Temple]!"

    b. The triumph (4:12-13): "Do not test the Lord your God." At this point Satan leaves Jesus alone.

II. THE MESSAGES OF JESUS (4:14-15, 16-30, 31, 42-44)

  A. **In a Nazareth synagogue** (4:16-30): Jesus preaches a sermon in his hometown.

   1. *The contents of his sermon* (4:16-27)

    a. What he reads (4:16-19): He reads from Isaiah 61, where the prophet describes the supernatural ministry of the Messiah.

    b. What he says (4:20-27)

     (1) The identification (4:20-23): Jesus says he is the Messiah Isaiah wrote about!

     (2) The illustrations (4:24-27): Jesus gives two Old Testament examples to illustrate why he cannot perform the miracles in Nazareth that he has elsewhere—namely, because of the people's unbelief!

      (a) The example of Elijah and the Zarephath widow (4:24-26)

      (b) The example of Elisha and the leper Naaman (4:27)

   2. *The contempt for his sermon* (4:28-30): Jesus' remarks so infuriate the audience that they actually attempt to kill him!

  B. **In numerous synagogues** (4:14-15, 31-32, 42-44): He preaches in many places throughout Galilee.

III. THE MIRACLES OF JESUS (4:33-41)
   A. **He heals a demon-possessed man** (4:33-37)
      1. *The acknowledgment by the demon* (4:33-34): He recognizes and fears Jesus!
      2. *The commandment by the Lord* (4:35): Jesus orders the demon to leave the man, and it does.
      3. *The amazement of the crowd* (4:36-37): The people don't understand Jesus' authority.
   B. **He heals Simon's (Peter's) mother-in-law** (4:38-39): She is immediately cured.
   C. **He heals the multitudes** (4:40-41): He heals people with any disease.

SECTION OUTLINE FIVE (LUKE 5)
Jesus calls his first disciples. He heals a leper and a paralyzed man and teaches about fasting.

I. THE INVITATIONS (5:1-11, 27-32)
   A. **Jesus calls Peter, James, and John to become his disciples** (5:1-11).
      1. *Jesus' sermon from Peter's boat* (5:1-3): He uses the boat as a platform to preach to the crowd on the shore.
      2. *Jesus' summons from Peter's boat* (5:4-11)
         a. "Go out where it is deeper and let down your nets, and you will catch many fish" (5:4-10a): They do, and they catch so many fish that their boats nearly sink!
         b. "From now on, you'll be fishing for people!" (5:10b-11): They follow Jesus and become his disciples.
   B. **Jesus calls Levi to become his disciple** (5:27-32).
      1. *The conversion of Levi* (5:27-28): This tax collector leaves his business to follow Jesus.
      2. *The celebration by Levi* (5:29-32)
         a. The background (5:29): Levi invites some of his business associates to meet Jesus and to help him celebrate his new calling.
         b. The bitterness (5:30): The Pharisees fault Jesus for association with such sinners.
         c. The basis (5:31-32): Jesus explains these are the very people he has come to save!

II. THE RESTORATIONS (5:12-26): Jesus restores a leper and a paralytic.
   A. **The healing of a leper** (5:12-16)
      1. *His tears* (5:12): The leper begs Jesus to help him.
      2. *His touch* (5:13): The Savior touches the leper, causing the disease to disappear.

3. *His instruction* (5:14): The leper is not to tell anyone but to go straight to the priests.
4. *His testimony* (5:15-16): Word of his healing spreads everywhere.
B. **The healing of a paralytic** (5:17-26)
   1. *The companions of the sufferer* (5:17-20, 24b-26): Some friends help the paralytic.
      a. The helplessness (5:17-19): He is totally immobile, lying on a mat.
         (1) The intervening by his friends (5:17-18): They carry him to Jesus.
         (2) The ingenuity of his friends (5:19): Unable to approach Jesus because of the crowd in the house where he is teaching, they lower the paralytic through the roof.
      b. The healing (5:20, 24b-26)
         (1) Spiritual healing (5:20): "Your sins are forgiven."
         (2) Physical healing (5:24b-26): "Stand up, take your mat, and go on home, because you are healed!"
   2. *The critics of the Savior* (5:21-24a)
      a. Their denunciation (5:21): The Pharisees accuse Jesus of blasphemy for forgiving the man's sins, saying only God could do this!
      b. His defense (5:22-24a): Jesus says that his power to heal the man's body proves his authority to save the man's soul!

III. THE ILLUSTRATIONS (5:33-39): Jesus gives three illustrations to explain why he does not require the disciples to observe the Jewish traditions of fasting.
   A. **First illustration** (5:33-35): Wedding guests don't fast while the bridegroom is still with them.
   B. **Second illustration** (5:36): No one sews an old patch on a new garment.
   C. **Third illustration** (5:37-39): No one puts new wine into old wineskins.

SECTION OUTLINE SIX (LUKE 6)
Jesus declares himself Lord of the Sabbath and heals a deformed man on another Sabbath day. He chooses his twelve disciples and preaches the Sermon on the Mount.

I. THE PREEMINENCE OF JESUS (6:1-11): He declares himself to be Lord of the Sabbath!
   A. **In regard to harvesting on the Sabbath** (6:1-5)
      1. *The rebuke by the Pharisees* (6:1-2): They criticize Jesus for allowing his disciples to harvest grain on the Sabbath.
      2. *The reply by the Savior* (6:3-5): He defends his actions by referring to an event in the life of David.

   B. In regard to healing on the Sabbath (6:6-11)
   1. *The deed* (6:6-8, 10-11): To the amazement and anger of the
      Pharisees, Jesus heals a man with a deformed hand right
      before their eyes on the Sabbath!
   2. *The defense* (6:9): He asks the Pharisees a question with an
      obvious answer: "Is it right to do good and save lives on the
      Sabbath?"

II. THE PROTÉGÉS OF JESUS (6:12-16)
   A. The communion (6:12): Jesus retires to the mountains and prays
      all night.
   B. The call (6:13-16): In the morning he chooses his twelve disciples.

III. THE POWER OF JESUS (6:17-19): Jesus heals many people.
   A. Where these people are from (6:17): Jerusalem, all Judea, Tyre,
      and Sidon.
   B. What these people suffer from (6:18-19): Both physical and
      demon-related problems.

IV. THE PREACHING OF JESUS (6:20-49): He summarizes various subjects
   in a twofold manner:
   A. Two attitudes (6:20-26)
   1. *The attitudes of the godly* (6:20-23): Jesus gives the Beatitudes,
      showing their blessedness.
      a. Those who are poor (6:20): The Kingdom of God is given to
         them.
      b. Those who are hungry (6:21a): They will be satisfied.
      c. Those who weep (6:21b): They will laugh with joy.
      d. Those who are persecuted because of Christ (6:22-23): A
         great reward awaits them in heaven.
   2. *The attitudes of the godless* (6:24-26): They have mourning
      and sorrow.
      a. Those who are rich (6:24): They have their only happiness
         now.
      b. Those who are prosperous (6:25a): A time of awful hunger
         is before them.
      c. Those who laugh carelessly (6:25b): Their laughing will
         turn to mourning and sorrow.
      d. Those who are praised by the crowds (6:26): Their ances-
         tors praised false prophets.
   B. Two commands (6:27-38)
   1. *Love your foes* (6:27-36).
      a. The reason for this (6:27-35a, 36): Be different from the
         unsaved who only love those who love them!
      b. The rewards for this (6-35b): This will demonstrate to the
         world that you are indeed sons and daughters of the Most
         High!
   2. *Don't judge your friends* (6:37-38): Judging and criticizing will
      come back on you.

C. Two illustrations (6:39-42)
1. *The blind leading the blind* (6:39-40): They will both fall into a ditch.
2. *The "log" judging the "speck"* (6:41-42): Get rid of the log in your own eye, and then you can help with the speck in your neighbor's eye.

D. Two trees (6:43-45)
1. *Good trees do not produce bad fruit* (6:43a).
2. *Bad trees do not produce good fruit* (6:43b-44).
3. *A good person does good deeds, and an evil person does evil deeds* (6:45).

E. Two buildings (6:46-49)
1. *The structures* (6:46-48a, 49a)
   a. The wise man builds his house on solid rock (6:46-48a).
   b. The foolish man builds his house with no foundation (6:49a).
2. *The storm* (6:48b, 49b)
   a. The house on solid rock will stand firm (6:48b).
   b. The house with no foundation will fall flat (6:49b).

SECTION OUTLINE SEVEN (LUKE 7)

Jesus rewards the faith of a Roman officer by healing his slave and raises a widow's only son from the dead. He reassures John the Baptist that he is indeed the Messiah; an immoral woman anoints Jesus' head with perfume and washes his feet with tears.

I. JESUS REWARDS AN OFFICER (7:1-10)
 A. **What he requests of Jesus** (7:1-5): He sends some Jewish elders to Jesus, asking him to come and heal his slave.
 B. **What he reveals to Jesus** (7:6-9): He tells the Savior all he needs to do is to speak the word, and the servant will be healed.
 C. **What he receives from the Savior** (7:10): The officer's faith is rewarded by instant healing!

II. JESUS RESURRECTS A SON (7:11-17)
 A. **The brokenhearted mother** (7:11-12): A weeping widow is about to bury her only son.
 B. **The tenderhearted Messiah** (7:13-17)
    1. *His words to the hopeless mother* (7:13): "Don't cry!"
    2. *His words to the lifeless son* (7:14-17): "Young man, get up."

III. JESUS REASSURES A PROPHET (7:18-35)
 A. **John's request to Jesus** (7:18-20): The imprisoned prophet sends his disciples to Jesus, asking if he indeed is the Messiah.
 B. **Jesus' reply to John** (7:21-35)
    1. *The proof for John* (7:21-23): Yes, Jesus is indeed the Messiah!
       a. He heals the sick (7:21a, 22a).

b. He raises the dead (7:22b).

c. He delivers the demon-possessed (7:21b).

d. He preaches the gospel to the poor (7:22c-23).

2. *The praise of John* (7:24-26): Jesus gives honor to his rugged, faithful, and fearless forerunner!

3. *The prophecy about John* (7:27-28): Jesus says John is the one the Old Testament prophet Malachi wrote about (Mal. 3:1).

4. *The people and John* (7:29): Many Israelites have repented at John's preaching.

5. *The prejudice against John* (7:30-35): The Pharisees, however, have refused and ridiculed his baptism and preaching of repentance.

IV. JESUS REDEEMS A HARLOT (7:36-38, 50)
   A. **Her sin** (7:36-37a): She is a woman of the streets.
   B. **Her sacrifice** (7:37b): She brings an expensive alabaster jar of perfume to Jesus.
   C. **Her sorrow** (7:38a): She weeps over her sin.
   D. **Her service** (7:38b): She anoints Jesus' feet.
   E. **Her salvation** (7:50): Her sins are forgiven.

V. JESUS REBUKES A PHARISEE (7:39-49)
   A. **The resentment by the Pharisee** (7:39): In his heart this Jewish leader named Simon condemns Jesus for associating with the harlot who anointed his feet.
   B. **The response by the Savior** (7:40-49): Jesus relates a parable to defend his action.
      1. *The contents of the parable* (7:40-43): A creditor freely forgives two debtors of all they owe him.
         a. The first owes him 500 pieces of silver (7:40-41a).
         b. The second owes him 50 pieces of silver (7:41b).
         c. The one with the larger debt will be the most grateful (7:42-43).
      2. *The conclusions from the parable* (7:42-49): The Pharisee demonstrates little respect and affection for Jesus, thus he will receive little forgiveness.

SECTION OUTLINE EIGHT (LUKE 8)

Jesus teaches about the Kingdom of Heaven by telling several stories. He performs more miracles, including healing many people. He amazes his disciples by calming a life-threatening storm.

I. EVENTS PRECEDING THE CALMING OF THE STORM (8:1-21)
   A. **Illustrations related by Jesus** (8:4-18): The Savior gives two parables at this point.
      1. *The parable of the sower, seed, and soil* (8:4-15)

      a. Information in this parable (8:4-8): A farmer sows seed on four kinds of soil, producing four different results.

        (1) Roadside soil (8:4-5): This seed is devoured by the birds.

        (2) Shallow, rocky soil (8:6): This seed springs up, but soon withers for lack of moisture.

        (3) Thorn-infested soil (8:7): This seed is quickly choked by the thorns.

        (4) Fertile soil (8:8): This seed produces one hundred times as much as had been planted.

      b. Interpretation of this parable (8:11-15)

        (1) Roadside soil (8:11-12): This represents those who hear but do not heed, thus allowing Satan to steal it from them.

        (2) Shallow, rocky soil (8:13): This represents those who have no depth, causing them to fall away in the hour of testing.

        (3) Thorn-infested soil (8:14): This represents those who allow life's worries, riches, and pleasures to choke the seed.

        (4) Fertile soil (8:15): This represents those who both hear and heed, thus producing an abundant crop.

      c. The intention behind this parable (8:9-10)

        (1) To enlighten the hearts of the sincere (8:9-10a)

        (2) To darken the hearts of the insincere (8:10b)

    2. *The parable of the elevated lamp stand* (8:16-18)

      a. Its light reveals all things in the house (8:16).

      b. Someday God's light will reveal all things in our heart (8:17-18).

  B. Individuals related to Jesus (8:1-3, 19-21)

    1. *His physical, earthly kin* (8:19-20): This is a reference to Jesus' mother and brothers.

    2. *His spiritual, eternal kin* (8:1-3, 21): This is a reference to all who hear and obey God's Word.

II. EVENTS DURING THE CALMING OF THE STORM (8:22-25)

  A. The crisis (8:22-23): A severe squall threatens to sink the disciples' boat on the Sea of Galilee.

  B. The cry (8:24a): In desperation they cry out for Jesus to save them.

  C. The command (8:24b-25): Jesus orders the winds and water to subside.

    1. *His rebuke* (8:24b-25a): "Where is your faith?"

    2. *Their response* (8:25b): "Who is this man?"

III. EVENTS FOLLOWING THE CALMING OF THE STORM (8:26-56): This passage records three of Jesus' miracles.

  A. He releases a demon-possessed man (8:26-39).

1. *The Gadarene maniac, controlled by demons* (8:26-28, 29b-33)
   a. What they did to the maniac (8:27, 29b)
      (1) He is living naked among the tombs (8:27).
      (2) He is violent and cannot be chained (8:29b).
   b. What the demons now desire from the Messiah (8:28, 30-33)
      (1) Their perception (8:28): The demons recognize Jesus as God's Son!
      (2) Their panic (8:30-31): They beg him not to send them into the Bottomless Pit.
      (3) Their plea (8:32-33): The demons beg Jesus to send them into a nearby herd of pigs. Jesus does, resulting in the death of the pigs by drowning!
2. *The Galilean Messiah, controller of demons* (8:29a, 34-39)
   a. The cleansing of the maniac (8:29a): Jesus drives the demons from the possessed man.
   b. The clothing of the maniac (8:34-37): The restored man sits at Jesus' feet, dressed and in his right mind!
   c. The commissioning of the maniac (8:38-39): Jesus sends him on his way to "tell . . . all the wonderful things God has done for you."

B. He resurrects a dead girl (8:40-42, 49-56).
   1. *The request to Jesus* (8:40-42): Jairus begs the Savior to come and heal his dying daughter.
   2. *The reassurance from Jesus* (8:49-50): Jairus learns that his daughter has died, but Jesus promises that she will be all right.
   3. *The restriction of Jesus* (8:51): He allows only Peter, James, and John to enter the dead girl's room.
   4. *The ridicule toward Jesus* (8:52-53): The crowd laughs at him for saying the girl will be healed.
   5. *The resurrection by Jesus* (8:54-56): He raises the girl from the dead!

C. He restores a sick woman (8:43-48).
   1. *Her disease* (8:43): She has been slowly bleeding for twelve years.
   2. *Her determination* (8:44a): Fighting the crowd, she touches the edge of Jesus' cloak.
   3. *Her deliverance* (8:44b-48): She is healed and sent on her way by the Savior.

SECTION OUTLINE NINE (LUKE 9)
Jesus sends the disciples out on a mission of preaching and healing.
He feeds the 5,000. Peter correctly affirms that Jesus is the Messiah,
and Jesus predicts his own death. Peter, James, and John witness the
transfiguration of Christ.

I. EVENTS PRECEDING THE TRANSFIGURATION (9:1-27)
   A. **Jesus, the source of authority** (9:1-9)
      1. *The men he empowers* (9:1-6)
         a. The individuals (9:1a): The twelve apostles.
         b. The instructions (9:1b-6)
            (1) Heal all diseases, and cast out demons (9:1b).
            (2) Preach God's Kingdom (9:2).
            (3) Travel fast and light (9:3-6): Don't take a walking stick,
            a bag, food, or money.
      2. *The misunderstanding he encounters* (9:7-9): At first Herod
      Antipas thinks Jesus is a reincarnation of John the Baptist!
   B. **Jesus, the supplier of food** (9:10-17): He feeds 5,000.
      1. *The scarcity of food* (9:10-14): When he begins the miracle,
      there are only five loaves of bread and two small fish.
      2. *The surplus of food* (9:15-17): When he completes the miracle,
      all have been fed, and twelve basketfuls of food remain.
   C. **Jesus, the Son of God** (9:18-27)
      1. *The request* (9:18): Jesus asks the disciples who people say
      that he is.
      2. *The rumors* (9:19): They reply that some think he is John the
      Baptist, Elijah, etc.
      3. *The recognition* (9:20): Peter says, however, that the disciples
      know him as the Son of God!
      4. *The restriction* (9:21): He then warns them not to tell anyone
      of this.
      5. *The rejection and resurrection* (9:22-23): Jesus predicts
      Calvary and the empty tomb!
      6. *The requirements* (9:24-26): He speaks of the cost of true
      discipleship.
      7. *The return* (9:27): He predicts his second coming.

II. EVENTS DURING THE TRANSFIGURATION (9:28-36)
   A. **The disciples** (9:28): Jesus takes Peter, James, and John with him
   to the top of a mountain.
   B. **The details** (9:29-36)
      1. *What they see* (9:29-32)
         a. The splendor of the Messiah (9:29): His face shines, and his
         clothes become dazzling white and blaze with light.
         b. The splendor of two men (9:30-32): Moses and Elijah now
         appear, also in glorious splendor.

2. *What they say* (9:33): In his ignorance, Peter the spokesman suggests they build three shelters—one for Jesus, one for Moses, and one for Elijah.

3. *What they hear* (9:34-36): From a cloud, they hear the Father's voice, saying, "This is my Son, my Chosen One. Listen to him."

III. EVENTS FOLLOWING THE TRANSFIGURATION (9:37-62)

A. **Jesus and a desperate father** (9:37-42)

1. *The victims* (9:37-40)

a. The heartbroken father (9:37-38): He begs Jesus to help his son.

b. The helpless son (9:39): He is possessed by a vicious demon.

c. The hopeless disciples (9:40): They cannot drive the demon out.

2. *The victor* (9:41-42): Jesus rebukes the demon and heals the boy.

B. **Jesus and the twelve disciples** (9:43-50)

1. *He talks to them about suffering* (9:43-45): The Savior predicts his betrayal by Judas.

2. *He talks about spiritual greatness* (9:46-48)

a. The illustration (9:46-47): He stands a little child before him.

b. The application (9:48): He says the one who welcomes a child on his behalf welcomes both the Father and Son and is therefore the greatest among men!

3. *He talks about sectarianism* (9:49-50).

a. John to Jesus (9:49): John says that the disciples tried to keep a man who wasn't in their group from casting out demons.

b. Jesus to John (9:50): "Don't stop him! Anyone who is not against you is for you."

C. **Jesus and the Samaritans** (9:51-56)

1. *The rejection of Jesus* (9:51-53): He is refused entrance into a Samaritan village because he is going to Jerusalem.

2. *The request to Jesus* (9:54): James and John want to call down fire from heaven and destroy the city.

3. *The rebuke by Jesus* (9:55-56): He faults them for their vindictive spirit.

D. **Jesus and three would-be disciples** (9:57-62): All three promise to follow him but then draw back.

1. *Hardship keeps the first from becoming Jesus' disciple* (9:57-58).

2. *Kinship keeps the second and third from becoming Jesus' disciples* (9:59-62): One wants to bury his father; the other wants to say good-bye to his family.

I. SEVENTY-TWO SPOKESMEN (10:1-24): Jesus selects 72 other disciples and sends them out in pairs to canvas the entire Galilean area.
   A. **The job given to the 72 by the Savior** (10:1-16)
      1. *Their assignment* (10:1-15)
         a. Pray before going (10:1-2): Ask the Lord to send more workers to the fields.
         b. Travel fast and light (10:3-7): Don't take money or even sandals.
         c. Heal the sick, and preach the gospel (10:8-9): Do this in towns that accept you.
         d. Reject those cities that reject me (10:10-15).
            (1) Wipe the dust of the city from your feet as a sign of its doom (10:10-12).
            (2) Korazin, Bethsaida, and Capernaum have all rejected Jesus (10:13-15).
      2. *Their authority* (10:16): Those who accept or reject them also accept or reject Christ!
   B. **The joy felt by the 72 and the Savior** (10:17-24)
      1. *The joy of the 72* (10:17-20, 23-24)
         a. The passing joy (10:17): They are excited because even the demons submit to them in Jesus' name.
         b. The permanent joy (10:18-20, 23-24): Jesus says there are things even more glorious to rejoice over.
            (1) Satan's fall from heaven (10:18-19)
            (2) Their heavenly position (10:20): Their names are written in heaven.
            (3) Their earthly privilege (10:23-24): He says Old Testament prophets and kings wanted to see and hear what they have seen and heard.
      2. *The joy of the Savior (10:21-22)*
         a. Because of the Father's revelation to the elect (10:21)
         b. Because of the Father's revelation through the Son (10:22): The Father gives the Son authority over everything.

II. ONE SAMARITAN (10:25-37): Jesus relates the parable of the Good Samaritan.
   A. **The occasion for the parable** (10:25-29): Jesus is challenged by a Jewish lawyer.
      1. *Question* (10:25-26): "What must I do to receive eternal life?"
      2. *Answer* (10:27-28): "'Love the Lord your God with all your heart, all your soul, all your strength, and all your mind.' And, 'Love your neighbor as yourself.'"

3. *Question* (10:29): "Who is my neighbor?"
B. The overview of the parable (10:30-35)
  1. *The trip* (10:30a): A man is going from Jerusalem to Jericho.
  2. *The trouble* (10:30b): He is attacked by some robbers who take his money, beat him, and leave him for dead.
  3. *The test* (10:31-35): God permits three men to pass his way, testing their compassion in helping one in need.
    a. The two who fail the test (10:31-32): Both the priest and Levite walk on, not wanting to get involved.
    b. The one who passes the test (10:33-35): The Samaritan stops, binds the wounds of the victim, carries him to an inn, and pays his room and board while he recovers.
C. The observance from the parable (10:36-37): Who is my neighbor? Anyone I can help!

III. Two Sisters (10:38-42): Jesus visits the home of Mary and Martha.
A. The complaint by Martha (10:38-40)
  1. *The diligent student* (10:38-39): Mary sits at Jesus' feet, listening to everything he says.
  2. *The dutiful servant* (10:40): Martha, busy in the kitchen, requests that Jesus instruct her sister to come and help her!
B. The counsel by Jesus (10:41-42): He tells Martha she must first be ministered to by the Savior before she can effectively minister for the Savior!

SECTION OUTLINE ELEVEN (LUKE 11)
Jesus teaches his disciples how to pray and explains why his power can't possibly come from Satan. He condemns those who ask him to perform a miraculous sign as proof of his divine identity.

I. Jesus Instructs His Friends (11:1-13, 27-28)
A. The disciples, on the subject of prayer (11:1-13)
  1. *The language of prayer* (11:1-4): In Luke's account, Jesus lists four elements in prayer.
    a. Worship (11:1-2): "May your name be honored."
    b. Petition (11:3): "Give us our food day by day."
    c. Confession (11:4a): "Forgive us our sins."
    d. Dependence (11:4b): "Don't let us yield to temptation."
  2. *The lessons from prayer* (11:5-13)
    a. Requirements (11:5-10): Successful prayer demands persistence. We need to ask, seek, and knock in prayer.
    b. Results (11:11-13): Successful prayer assures rewards!
      (1) Even sinful earthly fathers give good gifts to their children when they ask (11:11-12).
      (2) How much more will the heavenly Father give to his children when they ask (11:13)!

B. A woman, on the subject of blessedness (11:27-28)
1. *The woman to Jesus* (11:27): "God bless your mother—the womb from which you came, and the breasts that nursed you!"
2. *Jesus to the woman* (11:28): "More blessed are all who hear the word of God and put it into practice."

II. JESUS INDICTS HIS FOES (11:14-26, 29-54) This indictment is leveled against both Jewish laypeople and leaders alike.
A. Because of their accusations against God (11:14-26)
1. *The slander* (11:14-16): They say he is casting out demons by the power of Satan!
2. *The stupidity* (11:17-23): Jesus replies that if Satan is divided against himself, how can his kingdom stand?
3. *The sevenfold* (11:24-26): Jesus warns those who slander him that they are in danger of suffering a sevenfold demonic attack and possession!
B. Because of their actions against God (11:29-54)
1. *By the people in general* (11:29-36)
   a. What they have not done (11:29-32): They have refused to accept the ministry of Christ, while Old Testament Gentiles received the ministries of Solomon and Jonah!
   b. What they have done (11:33-36): They have substituted divine light for demonic darkness!
2. *By the Pharisees in particular* (11:37-54): Jesus pronounces six woes upon them.
   a. Because of their greed and wickedness (11:37-41): They make themselves clean on the outside but are filthy on the inside.
   b. Because they totally ignore love and justice (44:42)
   c. Because of their pride and self-promoting (11:43-44): They love the seats of honor and respectful greetings.
   d. Because they crush men with their heavy and godless traditions (11:45-46): They don't lift a finger to help them.
   e. Because of their history of bloodshed (11:47-51): They are murderers.
   f. Because they hide the truth from men (11:52-54): They keep men from entering the Kingdom and therefore won't enter themselves.

SECTION OUTLINE TWELVE (LUKE 12)

Jesus teaches on the ten topics of hypocrisy, fear, God's care for his children, acknowledging Christ, riches, worry, watchfulness, his own mission, perception, and reconciliation.

I. HYPOCRISY (12:1-3)
A. The example of hypocrisy (12:1): Jesus uses the wicked Pharisees to illustrate this topic.

B. The exposure of hypocrisy (12:2-3): At the judgment all hypocrites will be revealed!

II. TRUE FEAR (12:4-5)
  A. Don't fear people (12:4): They can only kill the body.
  B. Do fear God (12:5): He can destroy both body and soul!

III. GOD'S CARE (12:6-7)
  A. God provides for the sparrows, which are the least of his creatures (12:6).
  B. How much more will he provide for the saints, who are the greatest of his creatures (12:7)!

IV. ACKNOWLEDGING CHRIST (12:8-12)
  A. The believer and the Son (12:8-9): Acknowledge him, and be acknowledged by him before God.
  B. The believer and the Spirit (12:10-12): Depend on him, and be defended by him before people.

V. THE POVERTY OF RICHES (12:13-21): Jesus relates the parable of the rich fool.
  A. The dilemma (12:13-17): The harvest of a rich man is so great that he has no place to store his crops.
  B. The decision (12:18): He will solve his problem by building new and bigger barns.
  C. The delusion (12:19): The farmer now makes two fatal errors.
    1. *He assumes he has many years to live* (12:19a).
    2. *He assumes material goods can satisfy the soul* (12:19b).
  D. The destruction (12:20): God takes his life that very night.
  E. The definition (12:21): Don't store up earthly riches and ignore a relationship with God.

VI. WORRY (12:22-34)
  A. The two prohibitions (12:22-23)
    1. *Don't worry about the food you need to eat* (12:22a, 23a).
    2. *Don't worry about the clothes you need to wear* (12:22b, 23b).
  B. The two principles (12:24-31): Jesus gives two examples concerning why we should not worry about food or clothes.
    1. *The birds of the air* (12:24-26, 29-31)
      a. They neither sow nor reap, yet God feeds them (12:24).
      b. God views believers as more important than birds (12:25-26, 29-31).
    2. *The lilies of the field* (12:27-28)
      a. They are robed greater than was Solomon in all his glory (12:27).
      b. God views his friends as more important than flowers (12:28).

C. The two promises (12:32-34)
1. *Down here* (12:32): The Kingdom!
2. *Up there* (12:33-34): Treasures!

VII. WATCHFULNESS (12:35-48): Jesus emphasizes the importance of this virtue by relating a parable.
   A. The information in the parable (12:35-40)
   1. *The command* (12:35-36): Jesus instructs his people to be ready for his coming!
   2. *The celebration* (12:37-38): Those prepared ones will experience great joy when he returns.
   3. *The caution* (12:39-40): Constant watchfulness must be maintained, for he may return at any time!
   B. The application from the parable (12:41-48)
   1. *Faithfulness during his absence will result in rewards at his appearance* (12:41-44).
   2. *Faithlessness during his absence will result in severe rebuke at his appearance* (12:45-48).

VIII. JESUS' MISSION (12:49-53)
   A. The suffering (12:49-50): He will literally be baptized on the cross with God's wrath as he bears the world's sins.
   B. The separation (12:51-53): The gospel message will divide entire families, setting unbelieving members against believing members.

IX. PERCEPTION (12:54-56)
   A. What sinful Israel can do (12:54-55): They can discern the coming weather by examining the sky.
   B. What sinful Israel cannot do (12:56): They cannot discern the spiritual crisis all around them.

X. RECONCILIATION (12:57-59)
   A. The priority of attempting to settle with your adversary out of court (12:57-58a): Try to settle the matter before seeing the judge.
   B. The penalty for refusing to settle with your adversary out of court (12:58b-59): It may result in imprisonment.

SECTION OUTLINE THIRTEEN (LUKE 13)
Jesus teaches using several illustrations, shames his enemies when they question his healing on the Sabbath, and grieves over Jerusalem.

I. THE ILLUSTRATIONS (13:1-9, 18-30): Jesus offers various illustrations to emphasize certain topics.
   A. First two illustrations (13:1-5)
   1. *First illustration* (13:1-3): Jesus refers to some Jews who were murdered in the Jerusalem Temple.
   2. *Second illustration* (13:4-5): Jesus refers to some Jews who were crushed by the Tower of Siloam.

B. Third illustration (13:6-9)
  1. *A man plans to cut down a fig tree that has no fruit during the three years after its planting* (13:6-7).
  2. *The gardener suggests he wait one more year* (13:8-9).
C. Fourth and fifth illustrations (13:18-21)
  1. *Illustration of the mustard seed* (13:18-19): A tiny mustard seed grows, becomes a tree, and birds rest in its branches.
  2. *Illustration of the yeast* (13:20-21): A small amount of yeast permeates a large amount of dough.
D. Sixth illustration (13:22-30)
  1. *Jews who depend on their physical births will not be allowed into heaven* (13:22-28).
  2. *Gentiles who depend on their spiritual births will be allowed into heaven* (13:29-30).

II. THE CONFRONTATION (13:10-17)
  A. The reason for this confrontation (13:10-13): Jesus heals a crippled woman in a synagogue on the Sabbath.
  B. The responses during this confrontation (13:14-16)
    1. *The criticism of Jesus* (13:14): The synagogue ruler rebukes Jesus for healing on the Sabbath.
    2. *The condemnation by Jesus* (13:15-16): The Savior points out the sheer hypocrisy of the ruler and his friends.
      a. They would no doubt care for a needy animal on the Sabbath (13:15).
      b. How much more important to care for a needy person (13:16)!
  C. The results of this confrontation (13:17): Jesus' foes are shamed, and his followers are joyful because of his wonderful works.

III. THE DETERMINATION (13:31-33): In spite of Herod Antipas's threats against him, Jesus sets his face toward Jerusalem, that he might die there!

IV. THE LAMENTATION (13:34-35): The Savior weeps over Jerusalem.
  A. The pain he feels (13:34): He desires to gather Israel under his wings of protection, but they will not allow this.
  B. The prophecy he gives (13:35)
    1. *Israel's Temple will soon be destroyed* (13:35a).
    2. *Israel's people will remain in unbelief until the Millennium* (13:35b).

SECTION OUTLINE FOURTEEN (LUKE 14)
Dining rooms and discipleship: Jesus heals on the Sabbath, teaches about humility, and talks about the Kingdom of God; these involve dining rooms. He also teaches about the cost of being his disciple; this involves discipleship.

I. DINING ROOMS (14:1-24)
   A. **Scene 1—the power of Jesus is seen** (14:1-6).
      1. *The legalist and the Sabbath* (14:1-2): While attending a dinner on the Sabbath, Jesus is being carefully watched by some Pharisees to see if he will heal a man suffering with dropsy who is also present.
      2. *The Lord of the Sabbath* (14:3-6)
         a. What Jesus does (14:4): He heals the man.
         b. Why Jesus does it (14:5-6): He helps a human as the Pharisees would help an animal in need on the Sabbath!
   B. **Scene 2—the parables of Jesus are heard** (14:7-24): Jesus relates two parables set at banquets.
      1. *Parable of the ambitious guests* (14:7-14)
         a. How to be honored as a guest (14:7-11)
            (1) Negative (14:7-8): Don't sit at the head of the table, lest you be removed upon the arrival of someone more important!
            (2) Positive (14:9-11): Do sit at the lowest seat, where your host will no doubt invite you to move up!
         b. How to be honored as a host (14:12-14)
            (1) The rules (14:12-13): Don't invite friends, family, and rich neighbors! Do invite the poor, crippled, the lame and blind!
            (2) The reward (14:14): God himself will reward you!
      2. *Parable of the great banquet* (14:15-24)
         a. The invitation—first guest list (14:15-17): A man prepares a great feast and sends out many invitations.
         b. The invited (14:18-20): All the guests, however, make excuses why they cannot come.
            (1) First excuse (14:18): One person has just bought a field and must inspect it.
            (2) Second excuse (14:19): One person has just bought some oxen and must try them out.
            (3) Third excuse (14:20): One person has just been married.
         c. The invitation—second guest list (14:21-24)
            (1) The new guests (14:21-23): They consist of suffering and poor people everywhere, who gladly come.
            (2) The old guests (14:24): They don't even receive the smallest taste of what had been prepared for them!

II. DISCIPLESHIP (14:25-35)
  A. **Jesus instructs concerning discipleship** (14:25-27).
      1. *In regard to the candidate's family* (14:25-26): He or she must place Jesus above them.
      2. *In regard to the candidate* (14:27): He or she must carry his or her cross and follow Jesus.
  B. **Jesus illustrates concerning discipleship** (14:28-35).
      1. *Example of the unfinished building* (14:28-30): Make sure to count the cost, and make sure to have enough money before starting.
      2. *Example of the unsuccessful war* (14:31-33): Make sure your army is strong enough to defeat the enemy.
      3. *Example of the flavorless salt* (14:34-35): It is useless and will be thrown away.

SECTION OUTLINE FIFTEEN (LUKE 15)
Jesus offers three parables to illustrate the tragedy of lostness.

I. PARABLE OF THE LOST SHEEP (15:1-7)
  A. **The reason for this parable** (15:1-3): The Pharisees are faulting Jesus for associating with people they feel are notorious sinners.
  B. **The relating of this parable** (15:4-7)
      1. *The search* (15:4): A man who has a hundred sheep sets out to find one of them who has strayed away.
      2. *The sighting* (15:5): Having found it, he puts the sheep on his shoulders and returns home.
      3. *The singing* (15:6-7)
          a. On earth, because of a recovered sheep (15:6)
          b. In heaven, because of a repenting sinner (15:7)

II. PARABLE OF THE LOST COIN (15:8-10)
  A. **The search** (15:8): A woman who misplaces one of her ten valuable silver coins searches her house carefully for it.
  B. **The sighting** (15:9a): She finds it and calls in her friends.
  C. **The singing** (15:9b-10)
      1. *On earth, because of a recovered coin* (15:9b)
      2. *In heaven, because of a repenting sinner* (15:10)

III. PARABLE OF THE LOST SON (15:11-32): A father has two sons.
  A. **The rebellion of the younger son** (15:11-16)
      1. *The foolishness he exhibits* (15:11-13)
          a. In seeking his inheritance (15:11-12): The son demands his share of his father's estate.
          b. In squandering his inheritance (15:13): Soon he has wasted all his money in wild living and finds himself penniless in a foreign country.

2. *The famine he endures* (15:14-16): Eventually he is forced to eat the food of the pigs he feeds.

B. The return of the younger son (15:17-32)

1. *The realization* (15:17): He finally comes to his senses in regard to his terrible circumstances.
2. *The resolve* (15:18-19)
   a. To return (15:18a)
   b. To repent (15:18b-19)
3. *The reunion* (15:20-21): The father greets his son with open arms.
4. *The rejoicing* (15:22-24): The father plans a big celebration for the occasion.
5. *The resentment* (15:25-30): The older son is furious at the way his father has received the younger son.
6. *The reminder* (15:31-32): The father explains his actions to his older son.

SECTION OUTLINE SIXTEEN (LUKE 16)

Jesus tells the parables of the shrewd manager and of the rich man and Lazarus.

I. PARABLE OF THE SHREWD MANAGER (16:1-18)

A. The crisis (16:1-2)

1. *The dishonesty of a manager* (16:1): He is accused of wasting his master's possessions.
2. *The dismissal of the manager* (16:2): He is fired.

B. The concern (16:3): The dishonest manager is worried about the future.

C. The craftiness (16:4-7)

1. *The resolve of the manager* (16:4): He devises a plan to secure his future with some of his master's debtors.
2. *The reductions by the manager* (16:5-7): He reduces their debts by as much as 50 percent.

D. The commendation (16:8): His master grudgingly admits the shrewdness of the dishonest manager.

E. The caution (16:9-12): Jesus warns believers to be faithful even in little matters so that they can be trusted in larger matters.

F. The choice (16:13): One must choose between God and money!

G. The condemnation (16:14-18): Jesus condemns the Pharisees of being greedy, lawbreaking hypocrites!

II. PARABLE OF THE RICH MAN AND LAZARUS (16:19-31)

A. The two persons (16:19-21)

1. *The rich man* (16:19): He wears the best of clothes and lives in total luxury.
2. *The beggar* (16:20-21)
   a. His pain (16:20): He is covered with sores.

b. His poverty (16:21): He longs to eat what falls from the rich man's table.

B. The two places (16:22-23)

1. *Paradise* (16:22a): The beggar dies and is carried by angels to be with Abraham.
2. *Perdition* (16:22b-23): The rich man dies, and his soul goes to hell.

C. The two prayers (16:24-31)

1. *The rich man's prayer concerning relief for his body* (16:24-26)
   a. The request (16:24): He asks Abraham if Lazarus can come over and help ease his agony in the fires of hell.
   b. The refusal (16:25): This request is denied.
   c. The reason (16:26): A great chasm separates them.
2. *The rich man's prayer concerning redemption for his brothers* (16:27-31)
   a. The request (16:27-28): He begs Abraham to send Lazarus back to warn his five evil brothers about this terrible place.
   b. The reasons for the refusal (16:29-31)
      (1) "Moses and the prophets have warned them" (16:29-30).
      (2) "If they won't listen to Moses and the prophets, they won't listen even if someone rises from the dead" (16:31).

SECTION OUTLINE SEVENTEEN (LUKE 17)

Jesus talks about temptation, forgiveness, faith, duty, the Kingdom, and his second coming. He heals ten lepers, but only one of them, a Samaritan, thanks him.

I. THE MIRACLE (17:11-19)

A. The request of the ten (17:11-14)

1. *The circumstances* (17:11-12): Jesus is met by ten lepers.
2. *The cry* (17:13): They call out to him for help.
3. *The command* (17:14a): He tells them to present themselves to the Temple priests.
4. *The cleansing* (17:14b): Their leprosy disappears en route!

B. The return of the one (17:15-19)

1. *Who he is* (17:16b): He is a Samaritan.
2. *Why he comes* (17:15-16a)
   a. That he might give testimony to God the Father (17:15)
   b. That he might give thanks to God the Son (17:16a)
3. *What he finds* (17:17-19)
   a. The sadness of Jesus (17:17-18): The Savior expresses regret over the nine who do not return.
   b. The salvation from Jesus (17:19): Jesus tells the Samaritan that his faith has resulted in healing of both body and soul!

II. THE MESSAGES (17:1-10, 20-37): Jesus gives five "mini messages" and one major message.
  A. The five mini messages (17:1-10, 20-21)
    1. *On the penalty for tempting others* (17:1-2): Severe punishment awaits anyone who tempts a young child to sin!
    2. *On forgiveness* (17:3-4)
      a. Rebuke a sinning brother (17:3a).
      b. Forgive a repentant brother as often as needed (17:3b-4): Even if he does wrong seven times a day and repents, forgive him.
    3. *On faith* (17:5-6)
      a. The request by the disciples (17:5): "We need more faith; tell us how to get it."
      b. The reply by the Savior (17:6): Even a little faith can do great things!
    4. *On the duty of servants (17:7-10)*
      a. The required action (17:7-9): To serve their masters day and night.
      b. The required attitude (17:10): To realize that by serving Christ, we are merely doing our duty!
    5. *On the Kingdom of God* (17:20-21)
      a. Questions by the Pharisees (17:20): "When will the Kingdom of God come?"
      b. Answer by the Savior (17:21): "The Kingdom of God is among (or within) you."
  B. The major message (17:22-37): Here Jesus discusses his second coming.
    1. *The rumors about the Second Coming* (17:22-24)
      a. The fiction (17:22-23): False reports will say he had returned to this place or another place.
      b. The facts (17:24): His return will be as evident as flashing lightning across the skies!
    2. *The prerequisite before the Second Coming* (17:25): He will first be rejected and crucified.
    3. *The conditions prevailing at the Second Coming* (17:26-30)
      a. Similar to conditions in the days of Noah (17:26-27): People will ignore the warnings and will party up to the time of destruction.
      b. Similar to conditions in the days of Lot (17:28-30): People will go about their daily business.
    4. *The warning concerning the Second Coming* (17:31-33): Run for your life.
    5. *The judgment following the Second Coming* (17:34-37)
      a. The separation (17:34-36)
        (1) Two men in a bed—one will be taken; the other, left (17:34).

(2) Two women grinding grain—one will be taken; the other, left (17:35).

(3) Two men working in the field—one will be taken; the other, left (17:36).

b. The slaughter (17:37): People may know by these signs that the end is near.

SECTION OUTLINE EIGHTEEN (LUKE 18)
Jesus teaches using parables and blesses some children. He has a conversation with a rich man and describes the difficulty of a wealthy person entering the Kingdom. He again predicts his death and heals a blind beggar.

I. EVENTS BEFORE THE RICH-MAN EPISODE (18:1-17): Jesus gives two illustrations and one invitation.
   A. **The illustrations** (18:1-14): Jesus relates two parables, illustrating the subjects of persistency and humility.
      1. *Parable of the widow and the judge* (18:1-8)
         a. How persistence is rewarded by a sinful judge (18:1-5)
            (1) The reason for her persistence (18:1-3): A widow continually appeals to this godless judge for justice against a man who harmed her.
            (2) The rewards for her persistence (18:4-5): The uncaring judge finally grants her justice, though only to rid himself of her constant appeals!
         b. How persistence will be rewarded by the Sovereign Judge (18:6-8): God also rewards persistency by his children, not because of weariness but rather due to his faithfulness!
      2. *Parable of the Pharisee and publican* (18:9-14)
         a. Two men enter the Temple (18:9-13): Both come to pray. One is a Pharisee; the other, a tax collector.
            (1) The Pharisee's prayer (18:11-12): His prayer is arrogant and self-centered.
            (2) The publican's prayer (18:13): His prayer is humble and sorrowful, crying out to God for mercy.
         b. Two men exit the Temple (18:14).
            (1) The Publican is received and exalted by God (18:14a).
            (2) The Pharisee is rejected and excluded by God (18:14b).
   B. **The invitation** (18:15-17): Some parents approach Jesus to have him bless their children.
      1. *They are rebuked by the disciples* (18:15): They chide the parents for "bothering" Jesus.
      2. *They are received by the Savior* (18:16-17): He invites the children into his presence.

II. EVENTS DURING THE RICH-MAN EPISODE (18:18-30)
   A. **Jesus speaks concerning riches** (18:18-27).

1. *The Savior and the man* (18:18-23)
   a. The seeking (18:18-22)
      (1) The confusion (18:18): The ruler desires to know how he can inherit eternal life.
      (2) The clarification (18:19-20): Jesus says to keep the commandments.
      (3) The confirmation (18:21): The man says he has done this since boyhood.
      (4) The conclusion (18:22): Jesus tells the man to sell everything he has, give the money to the poor, and follow him!
   b. The sorrow (18:23): The man turns away with sadness, not willing to give up his wealth.
2. *The Savior and the disciples* (18:24-27)
   a. The allegory (18:24-25): Jesus says that it is easier for a camel to go through the eye of a needle than for a rich man to enter heaven.
   b. The amazement (18:26): The disciples ask who can possibly be saved.
   c. The assurance (18:27): Jesus says that with God all things are possible!
B. **Jesus speaks concerning rewards** (18:28-30).
   1. *What the disciples have renounced for Jesus* (18:28): They have left their homes to follow him.
   2. *What the disciples will receive from Jesus* (18:29-30): They will be repaid many times over in this life and will receive eternal life in heaven.

III. EVENTS AFTER THE RICH-MAN EPISODE (18:31-43)
A. **The hostility against Jesus** (18:31-34)
   1. *The Savior's prophecy* (18:31-33): Jesus predicts his future rejection, trials, scourging, crucifixion, and resurrection.
   2. *The disciples' perplexity* (18:34): They cannot understand what he is saying!
B. **The healing by Jesus** (18:35-43)
   1. *The sightless one* (18:35-39)
      a. The cry (18:35-38): A blind beggar near Jericho begs Jesus to heal him.
      b. The criticism (18:39): The crowd attempts to silence him, but he only shouts louder.
   2. *The Sovereign One (18:40-43)*
      a. The conversation (18:40-41)
         (1) Jesus (18:40): "What do you want me to do for you?"
         (2) The beggar (18:41): "Lord, I want to see!"
      b. The restoration (18:42): The beggar receives his sight.
      c. The celebration (18:43): Both beggar and crowd now praise and worship God!

I. THE PARDON BY JESUS (19:1-10): Jesus meets Zacchaeus.
   A. **Zacchaeus the sinner** (19:1-2): He is a wealthy tax collector.
   B. **Zacchaeus the seeker** (19:3-4): He desires to meet Jesus, but he has a problem!
      1. *The source of his problem* (19:3): He is too short to see Jesus over the crowds!
      2. *The solution to his problem* (19:4): He climbs up into a sycamore tree.
   C. **Zacchaeus the sought** (19:5-7): The seeker now becomes the sought.
      1. *The Savior's request* (19:5): Jesus sees him and says: "Quick, come down! For I must be a guest in your home today."
      2. *The tax collector's response* (19:6): He comes down and welcomes Jesus gladly!
      3. *The crowd's reaction* (19:7): They complain that Jesus is associating with this notorious sinner.
   D. **Zacchaeus the saved** (19:8-10)
      1. *As witnessed by his testimony* (19:8)
         a. He will give half of his wealth to the poor (19:8a).
         b. He will restore fourfold any money to any person he has cheated (19:8b).
      2. *As witnessed by Jesus' testimony* (19:9-10): He says that Zacchaeus is indeed a saved man!

II. THE PARABLE OF JESUS (19:11-27): In explaining the nature of God's Kingdom, Jesus compares it to a nobleman and his ten servants.
   A. **The assignment to the servants** (19:12-14)
      1. *Why the nobleman is leaving* (19:12): He is going to another country, where he will be crowned king.
      2. *What the nobleman is leaving* (19:13): He gives each servant a mina (about three months' wages) and orders each to wisely invest that money.
      2. *How the people feel* (19:14): They hate the nobleman and send a delegation to say they do not want him to be their king.
   B. **The accounting from the servants** (19:15-27): Upon his return, the nobleman requires a financial report from each servant, three of which are recorded.
      1. *First servant* (19:15-17)
         a. His report (19:16): His mina has earned ten more!
         b. His reward (19:17): He is given charge over ten cities.
      2. *Second servant* (19:18-19)
         a. His report (19:18): His mina has earned five more!

      b. His reward (19:19): He is given charge over five cities.

    3. *Third servant* (19:20-27)

      a. His report (19:20-21): He hid his mina and has no increase to report.

      b. His rebuke (19:22-27): His mina is taken, and the servant is sent away in disgrace!

III. THE PARADE FOR JESUS (19:28-40): Here is Luke's record of the Triumphal Entry.

  A. The preparation (19:28-34)

    1. *The men* (19:28-29): Jesus instructs two disciples.

    2. *The mission* (19:30-34)

      a. Their orders (19:30-31): They are to fetch a colt from a nearby village for the Savior to ride on.

      b. Their obedience (19:32-34): They do exactly as Jesus has instructed.

  B. The celebration (19:35-38)

    1. *The crowds prepare his path* (19:35-36): They spread their cloaks on the road.

    2. *The crowds proclaim his praise* (19:37-38).

  C. The denunciation (19:39-40)

    1. *The Pharisee's rebuke* (19:39): "Teacher, rebuke your followers for saying things like that!"

    2. *The Savior's reply* (19:40): "If they kept quiet, the stones along the road would burst into cheers!"

IV. THE PROPHECY OF JESUS (19:41-44)

  A. His pain (19:41): He weeps over Jerusalem's unbelief.

  B. His prediction (19:42-44): Jerusalem will be attacked and utterly destroyed by her enemies!

V. THE PURIFICATION BY JESUS (19:45-46)

    1. *What he does* (19:45): He enters the Temple and drives out the merchants from their stalls.

    2. *Why he does it* (19:46): They have turned this house of prayer into a den of thieves!

VI. THE PLOT AGAINST JESUS (19:47-48): His enemies discuss ways they might kill him!

SECTION OUTLINE TWENTY (LUKE 20)
The religious leaders question Jesus' authority, but he refuses to
answer to them. Jesus tells the story of some evil farmers and teaches
about paying taxes to Caesar, the resurrection of believers, and the
identity of the Messiah.

I. THE PARABLE BY JESUS (20:9-19)
   A. **The purpose for this parable** (20:17-19): Jesus tells it to illustrate
      two things:
      1. *The Jewish leaders' contempt for their Messiah* (20:17)
      2. *The Jewish leaders' crushing by their Messiah* (20:18-19): He
         is the cornerstone, and all who stumble over him are crushed.
   B. **The particulars in this parable** (20:9-16)
      1. *The work agreement* (20:9): A man plants a vineyard, rents it
         out to some farmers, and goes away to a distant land.
      2. *The wickedness* (20:10-15a): At harvesttime the landowner
         attempts to collect his share of the crop.
         a. The messengers he sends (20:10-15a)
            (1) First he sends three servants (20:10a, 11a, 12a).
            (2) Finally, he sends his son (20:13).
         b. The mistreatment they suffer (20:10b, 11b, 12b, 14-15a)
            (1) All three servants are mistreated (20:10b, 11b, 12b).
            (2) His son is murdered (20:14-15a)!
      3. *The wrath* (20:15b-16): The furious landowner then returns to
         kill the wicked farmers and rent the vineyard to others.
   C. **The prophecy pointing to this parable** (20:17-18): Jesus says all
      this is predicted in Psalm 118:22.
   D. **The plot following this parable** (20:19): Stung by Jesus' obvious
      indictment of them, the Jewish leaders look for a way to arrest
      Jesus.

II. THE PHARISEES AND JESUS (20:1-8, 20-47)
   A. **The confrontations:** (20:1-8, 20-44): Jesus is challenged by these
      wicked Jewish leaders on four occasions.
      1. *Concerning his authority* (20:1-8)
         a. Their demand (20:1-4): They want to know who gives him
            the authority to do what he does. He responds by asking
            them a question they cannot answer: Who gave John the
            Baptist his authority?
         b. Their dilemma (20:5-6)
            (1) If they say John's authority was "from heaven," then he
            will ask why they didn't believe him (20:5).
            (2) If they say John's authority was "merely human," the
            people will stone them (20:6).
         c. Their defeat (20:7-8): They refuse to answer him, so he
            refuses to answer them.
      2. *Concerning paying tribute to Caesar* (20:20-26)
         a. Their deceit (20:20-22): Pretending to recognize him as a

great teacher, they want to know if the Jews should pay
taxes to the Romans.
b. Their defeat (20:23-26): Again he silences them by his
wisdom, saying, "Give to Caesar what belongs to him. But
everything that belongs to God must be given to him."
3. *Concerning resurrection and marriage (20:27-40)*
a. The Sadducees' silly example (20:27-33): A woman marries
seven brothers and was left a widow after each marriage.
Finally, she dies. In the resurrection, whose wife will she be?
b. The Sadducees' serious errors (20:34-40)
(1) There are no marriages as such in heaven (20:34-36).
(2) There is a resurrection (20:37-40).
4. *Concerning the nature of the Messiah* (20:41-44)
a. He is David's son, thus affirming his humanity (20:41).
b. He is David's Lord, thus affirming his deity (20:42-44).
B. **The condemnation** (20:45-47): Jesus denounces the godless Jewish leaders.
1. *Their pride* (20:45-46): They love to walk around in flowing
robes and have everyone bow to them. They also love the
seats of honor at banquets.
2. *Their cruelty* (20:47a): They cheat widows out of their
property.
3. *Their hypocrisy* (20:47b): They make long prayers in public.
4. *Their punishment* (20:47c): Their punishment will be great.

SECTION OUTLINE TWENTY-ONE (LUKE 21)
Jesus compares the Temple offerings of the rich with that of a poor
widow. He then talks about the Great Tribulation.

I. THE PRAISE FROM JESUS, IN REGARD TO A WIDOW (21:1-4): Jesus
observes as people place their gifts into the Temple treasury.
A. **When much amounts to little** (21:1, 4a): He sees the rich give
money they probably won't even miss!
B. **When little amounts to much** (21:2-3, 4b): He sees a poor
widow give two small copper coins, all that she has.

II. THE PROPHECIES FROM JESUS, IN REGARD TO THE FUTURE (21:5-28)
A. **The immediate future** (21:5-7)
1. *The background* (21:5): The disciples are admiring their
beautiful Temple.
2. *The bombshell* (2:6-7): Jesus warns them concerning the
coming utter destruction of their Temple!
B. **The distant future** (21:8-28): These verses seem to describe
events occurring in the coming Great Tribulation.
1. *The first half of the Great Tribulation* (21:8-19)
a. Counterfeits (21:8): Many will come claiming to be the
Messiah.

     b. Combat (21:9-10): There will be wars and insurrections, but these will not be cause for panic.

     c. Calamity (21:11): Earthquakes, famines, epidemics, and great signs in the heavens will occur.

     d. Contempt (21:12, 16-17): Believers everywhere will be hated and persecuted because of their allegiance to Jesus.

        (1) Religious and political persecution (21:12): People will be dragged into synagogues and prisons and accused before kings and governors.

        (2) Family persecution (21:16): Close relatives will betray each other.

        (3) General persecution (21:12): Everyone will hate believers because of their allegiance to Jesus.

     e. Chances (21:13): There will be many opportunities for believers to witness.

     f. Conservation (21:14-15, 18-19): God himself will protect believers by giving the right words to say; not a hair of their heads shall perish.

  2. *The final half of the Great Tribulation* (21:20-28)

     a. Destruction (21:24b): Jerusalem will be destroyed and occupied by the Gentiles.

     b. Destitution (21:20-21): Survivors will flee the city.

     c. Disaster (21:22-23): God's vengeance will be fulfilled when his most severe judgment falls on Israel.

     d. Death (21:24a): The people will be killed or enslaved.

     e. Doom (21:25): Strange events and signs will occur in the heavens.

     f. Distress (21:26): The most courageous hearts will melt with fear.

     g. Delight (21:27-28): Christ will return on the clouds with power and glory.

III. THE PARABLE FROM JESUS, IN REGARD TO THE BEGINNING OF THE END (21:29-38)

  A. The symbol in the parable (21:29): "Notice the fig tree, or any other tree. When the leaves come out, you know without being told that summer is near."

  B. The significance of the parable (21:30-31): "Just so, when you see the events I've described taking place, you can be sure that the Kingdom of God is near."

  C. The stability from the parable (21:32-33)

    1. *God's nation will endure forever* (21:32): "This generation will not pass from the scene until all these things have taken place."

    2. *God's Word will endure forever* (21:33).

  D. The summary following the parable (21:34-38): Keep constant watch for these things to happen.

SECTION OUTLINE TWENTY-TWO (LUKE 22)

Jesus and the disciples celebrate the Passover supper in the upper room. Jesus predicts Peter's denial. He prays on the Mount of Olives. Judas leads a mob to arrest Jesus. Peter fulfills Jesus' prediction by denying him three times.

I. EVENTS TAKING PLACE AT PASSOVER (22:1-38)
   A. **The final plot** (22:1-6): Judas and the chief priests.
      1. *The attempts to kill Jesus* (22:1-2): The religious leaders are seeking a way to eliminate him without starting a riot.
      2. *The agreement to kill Jesus* (22:3-6): Judas volunteers to betray Jesus for two reasons.
         a. The diabolical reason (22:3): Satan enters Judas.
         b. The financial reason (22:4-6): The religious leaders promise Judas a reward.
   B. **The final Passover** (22:7-30): Jesus and the disciples.
      1. *The mission concerning the upper room* (22:7-13): Jesus sends Peter and John to prepare the upper room for the Passover.
      2. *The meal in the upper room* (22:14-30)
         a. The desire (22:14-16): Jesus tells the disciples how he has longed to eat the Passover with them before his suffering.
         b. The distribution (22:17-20)
            (1) Jesus takes the cup (22:17-18, 20): He says, "This wine is the token of God's new covenant to save you—an agreement sealed with the blood I will pour out for you."
            (2) Jesus takes the bread (22:19): He says, "This is my body, given for you."
         c. The disloyalty (22:21-23): He announces that one at the table will betray him!
         d. The dispute (22:24-27): The disciples now begin to argue over who is the greatest among them, and Jesus presents two definitions of greatness.
            (1) As viewed by the Gentiles (22:24-25): Greatness consists of the least serving the greatest!
            (2) As viewed by God (22:26-27): Greatness consists of the greatest serving the least!
         e. The domain (22:28-30): Jesus promises the disciples that they will assist him in ruling Israel during the Millennium.
   C. **The final predictions** (22:31-38)
      1. *The Savior's prophecy concerning Peter* (22:31-34)
         a. His prayer for Peter (22:31-32): He asks the Father to strengthen Peter's faith.
         b. His prediction about Peter (22:33-34): He says Peter will deny him three times.

2. *The Scripture's prophecy concerning Jesus* (22:35-38): Here the Savior reminds the disciples of the prophecy of Isaiah, who said that the Messiah would be condemned as a criminal (Isa. 53:12).

II. EVENTS TAKING PLACE ON THE MOUNT OF OLIVES (22:39-53)
   A. **Jesus and the disciples** (22:39-40, 45-46): Jesus asks that Peter, James, and John watch and pray with him. But they fall asleep!
   B. **Jesus and the Father** (22:41-44)
      1. *The agony* (22:41-42, 44): In great distress, Jesus prays to his Father.
         a. His heart's request (22:41-42a): "If you are willing, please take this cup of suffering away from me."
         b. His spirit's release (22:42b): "Yet I want your will, not mine."
         c. His body's resistance (22:44): He is in such agony that his sweat falls to the ground like great drops of blood.
      2. *The angel* (22:43): An angel strengthens him.
   C. **Jesus and the betrayer** (22:47-48): Judas betrays Jesus with a kiss!
   D. **Jesus and the high priest's servant** (22:49-51): When one of the disciples cuts off this man's ear, Jesus restores it.
   E. **Jesus and his arresters** (22:52-53): He rebukes them for treating him as a dangerous criminal!

III. EVENTS TAKING PLACE IN A COURTYARD (22:54-71)
   A. **Jesus' friend denies him** (22:54-62): Peter denies Jesus on three occasions.
      1. *The record* (22:54-60)
         a. First occasion (22:54-57): A servant girl recognizes Peter, but he says he doesn't know Jesus.
         b. Second occasion (22:58): Someone else, looking at Peter, says he was with Jesus, but Peter denies it.
         c. Third occasion (22:59-60): Another person says Peter was with Jesus because he is a Galilean. He denies it, and a rooster crows.
      2. *The remorse* (22:61-62): When he sees the Savior, who is being led from one trial to another, Peter leaves the area, crying bitterly!
   B. **Jesus' foes debase him** (22:63-71): He now stands before the Sanhedrin.
      1. *He is brutalized* (22:63-65): They mock, beat, hit, and insult him.
      2. *He is charged with blasphemy* (22:66-71): He says he is the Son of God.

SECTION OUTLINE TWENTY-THREE (LUKE 23)
Jesus stands trial before Pilate. Pilate finds Jesus innocent but gives in to the crowd and sentences him to death. Jesus dies on the cross, saving the world from sin. A man named Joseph asks for and receives permission to give Jesus a proper burial.

I. EVENTS PRECEDING THE CRUCIFIXION (23:1-25)
   A. Jesus stands before Pilate for the first time (23:1-5).
   1. *The charge* (23:1-2, 5): Jesus is accused of two crimes by the Pharisees.
      a. He is a political rebel (23:1-2a, 5): They say he causes riots and tells people not to pay taxes to Caesar.
      b. He is a religious blasphemer (23:2b): He claims to be the Messiah.
   2. *The cross-examination* (23:3): Jesus acknowledges to Pilate that he is indeed the Messiah!
   3. *The (initial) conclusion* (23:4): Pilate says he finds no fault with Jesus.
   B. Jesus stands before Herod Antipas (23:6-12).
   1. *The deference to Herod* (23:6-7): Upon learning of Jesus' Galilean background, Pilate sends him to Herod, for that territory is under Herod's jurisdiction.
   2. *The desire of Herod* (23:8-9): Herod is anxious to meet Jesus, but the Savior refuses to answer any of his questions.
   3. *The derision by Herod* (23:10-12)
      a. Jesus is ridiculed by Herod (23:10-11): Herod and his soldiers put a royal robe on Jesus.
      b. Herod is reconciled with Pilate (23:12): They become friends this day.
   C. Jesus stands before Pilate for the second time (23:13-25).
   1. *The conclusion* (23:13-15): Once again Pilate reminds the angry Jews of Jesus' innocence.
      a. Pilate has found him guiltless (23:13-14).
      b. Herod has found him guiltless (23:15).
   2. *The custom* (23:17): It is Pilate's custom to release a Jewish prisoner each year during the Passover feast.
   3. *The choice* (23:18-21): The Jewish leaders select a notorious criminal named Barabbas over Jesus.
      a. "Release Barabbas to us!" (23:18b-19).
      b. "Crucify him [Jesus]!" (23:18a, 20-21).
   4. *The capitulation* (23:16, 22-25): Pilate caves in to the pressure!
      a. He chastens and condemns Jesus (23:16, 22-24).
      b. He releases Barabbas (16:25).

II. EVENTS DURING THE CRUCIFIXION (23:26-44, 46)
   A. The carrier of the cross (23:26): Simon from Cyrene is forced to carry Jesus' cross for him.

B. The crying concerning the cross (23:27-31)
1. *The pain of the maidens* (23:27): A group of grief-stricken women follow Jesus, weeping for him.
2. *The prophecy of the Messiah* (23:28-31): He predicts the coming destruction of Jerusalem.
C. The criminals alongside the cross (23:32-33): Jesus is crucified between two thieves.
D. The calls from the cross (23:34a, 43, 46): Luke records three statements made by Jesus on the cross.
1. *The first and final ones are addressed to the Father in heaven* (23:34a, 46).
   a. "Father, forgive these people, because they don't know what they are doing" (23:34a).
   b. "Father, I entrust my spirit into your hands!" (23:46).
2. *The second one is addressed to one of the thieves, who begs Jesus to remember him in heaven* (23:43): "I assure you, today you will be with me in paradise."
E. The clothing beneath the cross (23:34b): The soldiers cast lots for his clothing.
F. The contempt for the cross (23:35-37, 39): It comes from various sources.
1. *From the watching crowd* (23:35): They say he saved others; he should be able to save himself.
2. *From the soldiers* (23:36-37): They offer him a drink of sour wine.
3. *From one of the thieves* (23:39): He wants Jesus to save himself and them, too.
G. The citation over the cross (23:38): The sign reads, "This is the King of the Jews."
H. The conversion on the cross (23:40-43): One of the thieves now both rebukes and requests.
1. *The rebuke* (23:40-41): He chastens the other thief for his insults against Jesus.
2. *The request* (23:42): He asks Jesus to remember him when he comes into his Kingdom.
3. *The reward* (23:43): Jesus assures the man that he will be with him today in paradise.
I. The cloud covering above the cross (23:44): Darkness settles over the area from noon till 3 P.M., at which time Jesus breathes his last.

III. EVENTS FOLLOWING THE CRUCIFIXION (23:45, 47-56)
A. The tearing of the veil (23:45): The Temple curtain is suddenly torn in two!
B. The tribute of the centurion (23:47): He praises God and says, "Surely this man was innocent."
C. The travail of the crowd (23:48): A number who watched him die now go home in deep sorrow.

D. The testimony of the women (23:49, 55-56)
1. *The Golgotha watch* (23:49): They stand at a distance, watching.
2. *The graveside watch* (23:55-56): They see where he is buried, go home to prepare spices, and wait till the Sabbath is over to embalm him.

E. The transaction of Joseph (23:50-54): This godly, rich believer receives permission from Pilate to bury Jesus' body.

SECTION OUTLINE TWENTY-FOUR (LUKE 24)
Luke describes four post-Resurrection appearances of Jesus.

I. FIRST APPEARANCE (24:1-12)
A. The anointing for the tomb (24:1): On Sunday morning the women carry spices to the tomb for the anointing of Jesus' body.
B. The arrival at the tomb (24:2-3)
1. *The women find an open tomb* (24:2): The stone has been rolled away.
2. *The women find an empty tomb* (24:3): Jesus is not there.
C. The angels beside the tomb (24:4-8)
1. *Their radiance* (24:4): They are arrayed in dazzling robes.
2. *Their reassurance* (24:5): They comfort the frightened women.
3. *Their reminder* (24:6-8): The women are reminded of Jesus' words:
   a. Concerning his crucifixion (24:6-7a): He would be betrayed and crucified.
   b. Concerning his resurrection (24:7b-8): He would rise again on the third day.
D. The account concerning the tomb (24:9-12)
1. *The messengers* (24:10): The women involved are Mary Magdalene, Joanna, Mary the mother of James, and others.
2. *The message* (24:9, 11-12): They tell the disciples what they saw.
   a. Most ignore their report (24:9, 11): The story sounds like nonsense.
   b. One investigates their report (24:12): Peter goes to the tomb to see for himself.

II. SECOND APPEARANCE (24:13-35) Jesus appears to two of his followers on the road to Emmaus.
A. The reunion with Jesus (24:13-16): These two believers are joined by the Savior.
1. *Their discussion* (23:13-14): They are talking about the Crucifixion.
2. *Their darkness* (24:15-16): Neither disciple recognizes the stranger who joins them.
B. The request from Jesus (24:17): He asks why they are so sad.

C. The reply to Jesus (24:18-24)
1. *They tell him their problem* (24:18-21): The Crucifixion has dashed their hopes that perhaps Jesus of Nazareth is indeed the Messiah!
2. *They tell him their puzzle* (24:22-24): Some women found his tomb empty and were told by two angels that he has risen!
D. The rebuke by Jesus (24:25-27)
1. *Their ignorance of the Scriptures* (24:25): He says they have forgotten the prophecies concerning his death and resurrection.
2. *His interpretation of the Scriptures* (24:26-27): He now reviews for them all the Old Testament passages which speak of him.
E. The recognition of Jesus (24:28-35)
1. *The meal* (24:28-31a)
   a. The invitation (24:28-29): The two disciples invite Jesus to join them for a meal.
   b. The revelation (24:30-31a): After he prays, Jesus distributes the bread. At that moment they recognize him!
2. *The miracle* (24:31b): He suddenly disappears out of sight!
3. *The meditation* (24:32): They reflect, "Didn't our hearts feel strangely warm as he talked with us on the road and explained the Scriptures to us?"
4. *The mission* (24:33-35): The two disciples now return to Jerusalem and report all this to the apostles!

III. THIRD APPEARANCE (24:36-49)
A. The reappearing of Jesus (24:36): He suddenly stands before the apostles!
B. The reassuring by Jesus (24:37-43)
1. *Their panic* (24:37): The apostles are terrified, believing he is a ghost!
2. *His proof* (24:38-43): He offers a twofold proof, showing that he is not a ghost but has a real body.
   a. First proof (24:38-40): He shows them the wounds in his hands and feet.
   b. Second proof (24:41-43): He eats a piece of fish as they watch.
C. The revealing by Jesus (24:44-49)
1. *He reviews his past ministry* (24:44-47): Jesus speaks of his crucifixion and resurrection.
2. *He previews their future ministry* (24:48-49): The apostles will be filled with the Holy Spirit, enabling them to become faithful witnesses!

IV. FOURTH APPEARANCE (24:50-53)
A. The place (24:50): It occurs near Bethany.
B. The particulars (24:51-53): After blessing the apostles, Jesus ascends into heaven!

John

SECTION OUTLINE ONE (JOHN 1)
John begins his Gospel by talking about the deity of Christ, then describes the ministry of John the Baptist. Jesus is baptized and calls his first disciples.

I. FACTS CONCERNING THE PREINCARNATE CHRIST (1:1-5)
   A. His relationship to the Father (1:1-2)
   1. *Christ's eternality is declared* (1:1a, 2): He already existed in the beginning.
   2. *Christ's deity is declared* (1:b): He is God.
   B. His relationship to the world (1:3-5)
   1. *He is the sole creator* (1:3): Nothing exists that he didn't make.
   2. *He is light and life* (1:4-5): His life gives light to everyone, and the darkness cannot extinguish it.

II. FACTS CONCERNING THE INCARNATE CHRIST (1:6-51)
   A. The miracle (1:14): God became human and lived on earth among us!
   B. The mission (1:10-13): He came to save sinners.
   1. *Some rejected him* (1:10-11): The world and even the people in his own country did not understand him.
   2. *Some received him* (1:12-13): Those who believed him became children of God.
   C. The men (1:6-9, 15-51)
   1. *Christ's faithful forerunner* (1:6-9, 15-34)
      a. John the Baptist and the crowds (1:6-9, 15-18): John makes three key statements to the people.
         (1) He is to serve as a witness to Christ (1:6-9).
         (2) Christ is greater than John or Moses (1:15-17).
      b. John the Baptist and the critics (1:19-28): John speaks to the Pharisees who are sent to cross-examine him.
         (1) John says that he is not the Messiah (1:19-20).
         (2) John says that he is not Elijah (1:21).
         (3) John says that he has been sent to prepare the way for the Lord (1:22-28).
      c. John the Baptist and the Christ (1:29-34)

(1) He introduces the Savior (1:29-31).
(2) He baptizes the Savior (1:32-34).
2. *Christ's first five followers (1:35-51)*
   a. Andrew and John the apostle (1:35-39)
   b. Peter (1:40-42)
   c. Philip (1:43)
   d. Nathanael (1:44-51)

SECTION OUTLINE TWO (JOHN 2)
Jesus performs his first miracle and drives the merchants and money changers out of the Temple. When the Jewish leaders challenge his authority, Jesus says he will restore the detroyed temple (his body) in three days.

I. JESUS' FIRST MIRACLE (2:1-11)
   A. **The occasion** (2:1-3)
      1. *The ceremony* (2:1-2): Jesus and his disciples are invited to a wedding in Cana.
      2. *The crisis* (2:3): The wine supply runs out, and Jesus' mother comes to him with the problem.
   B. **The observation** (2:4): Jesus reminds her his time has not yet come.
   C. **The orders** (2:5-7)
      1. *From the mother* (2:5): Mary instructs the servants to do whatever Jesus tells them to do.
      2. *From the Messiah* (2:6-7): He tells them to fill six huge jars with water.
   D. **The obedience** (2:8): They follow his instructions, and the water turns into wine!
   E. **The opinion** (2:9-10): Those at the wedding testify that the wine is the best they have ever consumed!
   F. **The outcome** (2:11): This miracle demonstrates Jesus' glory, causing the disciples to put their faith in him!

II. JESUS' FIRST TEMPLE CLEANSING (2:12-25): He later does this again at least once (see Matt. 21:12-13).
   A. **Purging in regard to his Father's Temple** (2:12-17)
      1. *The cleansing of the Temple* (2:12-15)
         a. The wickedness (2:12-14): Jesus finds dishonest merchants selling animals in the Temple.
         b. The whip (2:15): He makes a whip out of ropes and drives them out!
      2. *The condemning of the thieves* (2:16-17)
         a. The scoundrels he faces (2:16): Jesus accuses them of turning his Father's house into a market!
         b. The Scripture he fulfills (2:17): Psalm 69:9 predicts that the Messiah will do this!

B. Predicting in regard to his fleshly temple (2:18-25)
   1. *The ignorance of the Jewish leaders* (2:18-22)
      a. The sign demanded (2:18): They insist that Jesus work a miracle to validate his authority from God.
      b. The sign described (2:19): Jesus says, "Destroy this temple, and in three days I will raise it up."
      c. The sign distorted (2:20-21): They think he is referring to Herod's Temple and not his body.
      d. The sign discerned (2:22): After Jesus' death and resurrection, the disciples understand the full significance of his statement.
   2. *The insincerity of the Jewish laity* (2:23-25): Many in Jerusalem profess belief in Jesus, but for insincere motives!

SECTION OUTLINE THREE (JOHN 3)
Jesus meets with Nicodemus and tells him in order to be saved, all people must be born again. John the Baptist tells his disciples that Jesus is the Messiah.

I. JESUS EXPLAINS THE PLAN OF SALVATION (3:1-21): A man named Nicodemus visits Jesus by night.
   A. The credentials of Nicodemus (3:1): He is both a member of the Jewish Sanhedrin and a Pharisee.
   B. The confession of Nicodemus (3:2): He acknowledges that Jesus is from God because of his miracles.
   C. The command to Nicodemus (3:3): Jesus says he needs the new birth.
   D. The confusion of Nicodemus (3:4): He confuses spiritual birth with physical birth.
   E. The chastening of Nicodemus (3:9-13): Jesus chides him for not knowing these things even though he is a respected Jewish teacher.
   F. The clarification for Nicodemus (3:5-8, 14-15): Jesus employs three illustrations to explain the new birth to Nicodemus.
      1. *A physical illustration* (3:5-7): Unless one is born of water and the Spirit, he cannot enter into the Kingdom of God.
      2. *A natural illustration* (3:8): Just as you don't know where the wind comes from or where it is going, so it is impossible to explain being born of the Spirit.
      3. *A scriptural illustration* (3:14-15): As Moses lifted up the snake in the wilderness, so must the Son of Man be lifted up.
   G. The conclusion for Nicodemus (3:16-21): Jesus now summarizes both the subjects of salvation and condemnation!
      1. *The persons* (3:16)
         a. The Father gave his Son (3:16a).
         b. The Son will give his life (3:16b).

2. *The purpose* (3:17)
    a. It is not to condemn sinners (3:17a).
    b. It is to convert sinners (3:17b).
3. *The people* (3:18-21)
    a. Condemnation for those who reject Christ (3:18b-20)
    b. Salvation for those who receive Christ (3:18a, 21)

II. JOHN EXALTS THE PERSON OF SALVATION (3:22-36)
  A. The argument (3:22-26): A debate occurs among John's disciples concerning which baptism is valid—those performed by John or Jesus.
  B. The affirmation (3:27-36): John once again gives testimony concerning the greatness of Jesus.
    1. *Jesus is the bridegroom, while John is but a friend of the bridegroom* (3:27-29).
    2. *Jesus must become greater and greater, while John must become less and less* (3:30-36).

SECTION OUTLINE FOUR (JOHN 4)

Jesus meets a Samaritan woman at a well and offers her living water. Many Samaritans in the woman's village believe in him. He heals the son of a government official in Capernaum.

I. JESUS REDEEMS A SAMARITAN WOMAN (4:1-42).
  A. The Savior at Sychar (4:1-6): Jesus leaves Judea for Galilee.
    1. *Why he leaves* (4:1-3): He departs to avoid a popularity contest between himself and John.
    2. *Where he stops* (4:4-6): He rests beside Jacob's well at Sychar, a town in Samaria.
  B. The sinner at Sychar (4:7-27): A Samaritan woman comes to the well for water.
    1. *The contact* (4:7-9)
      a. Jesus' request (4:7-8): He asks her for a drink.
      b. Her response (4:9): She wants to know why he, a Jew, is even talking to her, a Samaritan!
    2. *The contrasts* (4:10-27)
      a. Jesus contrasts liquid water with living water (4:10-15).
        (1) Liquid water (4:11-14)
          (a) His revelation (4:13-14): Liquid water must be drunk often, but living water becomes an eternal perpetual spring from within!
          (b) Her response (4:11-12): First, how can he draw such water without a rope or bucket, and second, is he greater than the patriarch Jacob?
        (2) Living water (4:10, 15)
          (a) His revelation (4:10): He will give her living water if she but asks.

        (b) Her reaction (4:15): She desires this kind of water!
    b. Jesus contrasts real worship with ritual worship (4:16-27).
        (1) The command (4:16): "Go and get your husband."
        (2) The concealment (4:17a): "I don't have a husband."
        (3) The correction (4:17b-18): Jesus says he knows she has
           had five husbands and is now living with a man to
           whom she is not married.
        (4) The cleverness (4:19): Attempting to change the
           subject, she says, "You must be a prophet."
        (5) The confusion (4:20): She asks, "Why is it that you Jews
           insist that Jerusalem is the only place of worship, while
           we Samaritans claim it is here at Mount Gerizim?"
        (6) The clarification (4:21-24): Jesus says that true worship
           involves not the *where* but rather the *how;* that is, God
           must be worshiped in spirit and truth!
        (7) The conversion (4:25-26): She acknowledges Jesus as
           the Messiah!
        (8) The concern (4:27): The disciples arrive just as she
           departs and are amazed that he was talking to an
           immoral woman!
  C. The soul winner in Sychar (4:28-42)
    1. *The faithfulness of the Samaritan woman* (4:28-38)
      a. As seen by the message she proclaims (4:28-30): She
        returns to Sychar and witnesses to the entire city!
      b. As seen by the model she presents (4:31-38): Jesus uses her
        as a role model to his disciples on the subject of soul
        winning.
        (1) He talks about the real food (4:31-34): When urged to
           eat some food they have brought him, he says his food
           is to do God's will!
        (2) He talks about the ripe fields (4:35-38): He says that the
           fields of human souls are ripe for harvest!
    2. *The fruitfulness of the Samaritan woman* (4:39-42): At her
      urging, many townspeople agree to hear the Savior and
      believe in him!

II. JESUS RESTORES A GALILEAN BOY (4:43-54)
  A. The places (4:43-46): A father meets with Jesus in Cana concern-
    ing his son who lies sick in Capernaum.
  B. The plea (4:47): He begs Jesus to heal the boy.
  C. The problem (4:48): Jesus laments the fact that people demand
    he perform miracles before believing in him.
  D. The persistence (4:49): The father continues to seek help from
    Jesus.
  E. The promise (4:50): Jesus says the boy will live.
  F. The payoff (4:51-54)
    1. *The physical restoration of the boy* (4:51-53a)
    2. *The spiritual redemption of the household* (4:53b-54)

SECTION OUTLINE FIVE (JOHN 5)
Jesus heals a lame man at the pool of Bethesda. Responding to harassment by the Jewish leaders, Jesus affirms that he is the divine Son of God.

I. THE MIRACLE BESIDE THE POOL OF BETHSEDA (5:1-15)
   A. **The crippled man and the Messiah—their first meeting** (5:1-9)
      1. *The man is wallowing on his pallet* (5:1-8).
         a. The misery beside the waters (5:1-5): A man who has been an invalid for 38 years lies there on his bed.
         b. The moving of the waters (5:6-7): The man tells Jesus he believes that when the waters are supernaturally stirred, they will heal him, but his infirmity prevents him from entering.
         c. The miracle beside the waters (5:8): Jesus tells him to pick up his mat and walk!
      2. *The man is walking with his pallet* (5:9).
   B. **The crippled man and the critics** (5:10-13): He is now confronted by the wicked Jewish leaders.
      1. *Their denunciation* (5:10): "You can't work on the Sabbath! It's illegal to carry that sleeping mat!"
      2. *His defense* (5:11-13): "The man who healed me said to me, 'Pick up your sleeping mat and walk.'"
   C. **The crippled man and the Christ—their final meeting** (5:14-15): Jesus warns him not to keep on sinning, lest something worse happen to him!

II. THE MESSAGE BESIDE THE POOL OF BETHESDA (5:16-47)
   A. **The tirade against Jesus** (5:16-18): The godless Pharisees condemn Jesus on two counts.
      1. *He heals on the Sabbath* (5:16).
      2. *He makes himself equal with God* (5:17-18).
   B. **The Trinity and Jesus** (5:19-20, 23)
      1. *The Father loves the Son* (5:19-20).
      2. *The Father honors the Son* (5:23).
   C. **The tasks assigned to Jesus** (5:21-22, 24-29)
      1. *He imparts eternal life* (5:21, 24, 26).
      2. *He will raise the dead* (5:25, 28-29).
         a. Some to everlasting joy (5:25, 28-29a)
         b. Some to everlasting punishment (5:29b)
      3. *He judges all men* (5:22, 27).
   D. **The testimonies concerning Jesus** (5:30-47): Witness to the supernatural claims of Jesus comes from four sources.
      1. *From John the Baptist* (5:31-35): He preached the truth.
      2. *From his own works* (5:36): His teachings and miracles come from the Father.
      3. *From the Father* (5:30, 37-38): The Father has testified about him.

4. *From the Scriptures* (5:39-47): The Scriptures point to him, but though the people say they believe the Scriptures, they don't believe in him.

SECTION OUTLINE SIX (JOHN 6)
Jesus feeds the 5,000 and walks on water. He teaches that he is the "bread from heaven" and that all who wish to have eternal life must eat his flesh and drink his blood. Many of his followers, unable to accept this difficult symbolism, desert him.

I. TWO MIRACLES (6:1-24)
  A. First miracle (6:1-15): Jesus feeds the 5,000.
    1. *Events preceding this miracle* (6:1-9)
      a. The place (6:1-4): It occurs on the banks of the Galilean Sea.
      b. The problem (6:5-6): Jesus asks his disciples how they propose to feed the multitudes that surround him.
      c. The pessimism (6:7-9)
        (1) As demonstrated by Philip (6:7): He says it would take a small fortune to feed them.
        (2) As demonstrated by Andrew (6:8-9): He brings a boy with five barley loaves and two fish but doesn't believe that's enough for the crowd.
    2. *Events during this miracle* (6:10-13)
      a. The scarcity of food (6:10): Jesus takes the only available food—five barley loaves and two fish—gives thanks, and orders its distribution.
      b. The surplus of food (6:11-13): After all have eaten their fill, there are twelve baskets of leftover food!
    3. *Events following this miracle* (6:14-15)
      a. The determination of the people (6:14): Concluding that he is the Messiah, they plan to crown him as their king!
      b. The departure of the Savior (6:15): He quickly withdraws from them into the hills.
  B. Second miracle (6:16-24): Jesus walks on water.
    1. *The stormy sea* (6:16-18): The disciples' boat is threatened by a sudden squall.
    2. *The sovereign Savior* (6:19-21): A twofold miracle now occurs.
      a. He walks on the water (6:19-20).
      b. He brings the boat to land immediately (6:21).
    3. *The seeking sinners* (6:22-24): A large crowd assembles to meet him.
II. TWO MESSAGES (6:25-71)
  A. Public comments (6:25-66)
    1. *Christ and the curious* (6:25-40)

    a. He speaks concerning God's salvation (6:25-36).
      (1) Their confusion (6:25-26, 28, 30-31, 36)
        (a) They want to know how he got there (6:25).
        (a) They seek him only for physical bread (6:26).
        (b) They don't know how to please God (6:28).
        (c) They assume the Old Testament manna came from Moses (6:30-31).
        (d) They don't believe in him even though they have seen him (6:36).
      (2) His correction (6:27, 29, 32-35)
        (a) They are to seek him for spiritual bread (6:27, 33-35).
        (b) They will please God by believing in him (6:29).
        (c) He says the Old Testament manna came from God (6:32).
    b. He speaks concerning God's sovereignty (6:37-40).
      (1) Guaranteeing that all the elect will come to Christ (6:37): They will never be rejected.
      (2) Guaranteeing that all the elect will continue in Christ (6:38-40): All who believe in him will be raised at the last day.
  2. *Christ and the critical* (6:41-59)
    a. Their criticism (6:41-42, 52)
      (1) He is simply the son of Joseph (6:41-42).
      (2) No one can (physically) eat his flesh and drink his blood (6:52).
    b. His correction (6:43-51, 53-59)
      (1) Jesus says he is the bread of life (6:43-51).
      (2) Jesus says that anyone who wants eternal life must (spiritually) eat his flesh and drink his blood (6:53-59).
  3. *Christ and the carnal* (6:60-66)
    a. Many of his followers now decide against him (6:60-65).
    b. Many of his followers now depart from him (60:66).
B. Private comments (6:67-71): Jesus now addresses his chosen ones.
  1. *The Savior and all the apostles (6:67-69)*
    a. Jesus asks, "Are you going to leave, too?" (6:67).
    b. Peter answers, "Lord, to whom would we go? You alone have the words that give eternal life. We believe them, and we know you are the Holy One of God" (6:68-69).
  2. *The Savior and the evil apostle (6:70-71)*
    a. The nature of this apostle (6:70): He gave himself over to Satan.
    b. The name of this apostle (6:71): He is Judas Iscariot!

SECTION OUTLINE SEVEN (JOHN 7)
This chapter can be summarized by two words: *disbelief* and *division.*

I. THE DISBELIEF JESUS ENCOUNTERS IN NAZARETH (7:1-10)
   A. **The ridicule** (7:1-5): Jesus' half brothers and sisters laugh at the claims of their older half brother!
   B. **The response** (7:6-10): Jesus says that the world hates him for exposing its sin.

II. THE DIVISION JESUS ENCOUNTERS IN JERUSALEM (7:11-53): Jesus receives a mixed reception while attending the Festival of Shelters.
   A. **The reaction to the Savior** (7:11-13, 20, 25-27, 30-32, 40-42)
      1. *From the people* (7:11-13, 20, 25-27, 30-32, 40-53)
         a. Some feel he is a good man (7:11-12).
         b. Some feel he is a deceiver (7:13).
         c. Some feel he is demon-possessed (7:20).
         d. Some feel he is an ordinary man (7:25-27, 41b-42).
         e. Some feel he is a prophet (7:40).
         f. Some feel he is the Messiah (7:31, 41a).
      2. *From the Pharisees* (7:30, 32, 44-53)
         a. Their intentions to arrest him (7:30, 32, 44): It is not his time.
         b. Their inability to arrest him (7:45-53)
            (1) They are frustrated by the military (7:45-49): The guards sent out to seize him come back empty-handed, saying, "We have never heard anyone talk like this!"
            (2) They are frustrated by a member (7:50-53): One of their own members, Nicodemus, now stands up for Jesus.
   B. **The response from the Savior** (7:14-19, 21-24, 28-29, 33-39)
      1. *The overview* (7:16-19, 21-24, 28-29, 33-34)
         a. Jesus says that his mission and message originate from God (7:14-18, 28-29).
         b. Jesus says that the people in his audience do not keep the law of Moses and in fact want to kill him right now (7:19).
         c. Jesus asserts that both healing and circumcising are permitted by the law to be done on the Sabbath (7:21-24).
         d. Jesus tells them that he will soon leave but that they will be unable to find him (7:33-36).
      2. *The offer* (7:37-39)
         a. What (7:38): Jesus offers streams of living water to all those who are thirsty!
         b. When (7:37): Jesus makes the offer on the final day of the Festival of Shelters.
         c. Who (7:39): Jesus speaks of the Holy Spirit, who will soon indwell all believers!

I. A SINNER JESUS FORGIVES—THE SAVIOR AND THE PROSTITUTE (8:1-11)
  A. **The connivers** (8:1-4)
    1. *The accusers* (8:3a): A group of Jewish leaders approaches Jesus.
    2. *The accused* (8:3b-4): They put before him a woman caught in the act of adultery!
  B. **The conniving** (8:5-6a)
    1. *What they say* (8:5): "The law of Moses says to stone her. What do you say?"
    2. *Why they said it* (8:6a): They want him to say something they can use against him.
  C. **The challenge** (8:6b-8)
    1. *What Jesus does* (8:6b, 8): Twice he bends down and writes in the dust.
    2. *What Jesus says* (8:7): "Let those who have never sinned throw the first stones!"
  D. **The convicted** (8:9): They all walk away in shame.
  E. **The cleansed** (8:10-11): The woman now experiences:
    1. *No earthly condemnation* (8:10): Her accusers have disappeared.
    2. *No heavenly condemnation* (8:11): Jesus tells her to go and sin no more.

II. A SERMON JESUS GIVES—THE SAVIOR AND THE PHARISEES (8:12-59): Jesus and the Pharisees dialogue back and forth in four rounds of debate.
  A. **Round one** (8:12-21)
    1. *The Pharisees' criticism* (8:13, 19a)
      a. That Jesus serves as his own witness, thus making his testimony invalid (8:13)
      b. That he cannot show them his Father (8:19a)
    2. *Jesus' correction* (8:12, 14-18, 19b): He begins by saying that he is the light of the world, then answers their charges.
      a. Jesus says his claims are validated by two witnesses (8:14-17).
        (1) The testimony of the Son on earth (8:18a)
        (2) The testimony of the Father in heaven (8:18b)
      b. Jesus says his accusers cannot know the Father, because they refuse to know the Son (8:19b).
  B. **Round two** (8:21-30)
    1. *Jesus' claims* (8:21, 23-24, 25b-26, 28-29)
      a. That he will go away but that they will die in their sins, unable to follow where he goes (8:21)

    b. That he is from above while they are from below (8:23-24)

    c. That he is the Messiah sent from God (8:25b-26)

    d. That he will be crucified (8:28-29)

  2. *The confusion* (8:22, 25a, 27)

    a. The Pharisees wonder what Jesus means when he says they cannot follow where he is going (8:22).

    b. "Tell us who you are" (8:25a, 27).

  3. *The conversions* (8:30): Many now put their faith in him!

C. Round three (8:31-47)

  1. *The confusion* (8:33): The Jews feel they are free men because Abraham was their father.

  2. *The clarification* (8:32, 34-44)

    a. Jesus says all unsaved men are not free but are enslaved by sin (8:31-32, 34-36).

    b. Jesus says that Satan is their true father, not Abraham (8:37-44).

      (1) The Devil is a liar, and they are liars (8:44b).

      (2) Abraham is not their real father, so they don't follow Jesus (8:37-41).

      (3) The Devil is a murderer, and they are attempting to kill him (8:42-44a).

  3. *The claim* (8:45-47): Jesus claims to be sinless!

D. Round four (8:48-59)

  1. *The Jewish leaders try to slander Jesus* (8:48-58).

    a. Their accusation (8:48, 52): They accuse Jesus of being a demon-possessed Samaritan!

    b. His answer (8:49-51, 54-55)

      (1) "I honor my Father" (8:49-50).

      (2) "It is my Father who says these glorious things about me" (8:54-55).

      (3) "Anyone who obeys my teaching will never die!" (8:51).

    c. Their accusation (8:53): "Are you greater than our father Abraham?"

    d. His answer (8:56): "Abraham rejoiced as he looked forward to my coming!"

    e. Their accusation (8:57): "You aren't even fifty years old. How can you say you have seen Abraham?"

    f. His answer (8:58): "I existed before Abraham was even born!"

  2. *The Jewish leaders try to stone Jesus* (8:59): He hides himself and slips away from them.

SECTION OUTLINE NINE (JOHN 9)
Jesus heals a man who was born blind.

I. INCONSIDERATION! THE DISCIPLES AND THE BLIND MAN (9:1-5)
   A. They look upon the blind man (9:1): They see him sitting there, a helpless beggar.
   B. They look beyond the blind man (9:2-5): Out of curiosity and not compassion, they ask Jesus a question.
      1. *What they ask* (9:2): "Was [his blindness] a result of his own sins or those of his parents?"
      2. *How he answers* (9:3-5)
         a. "It was not because of his sins or his parents' sins" (9:3a).
         b. "He was born blind so the power of God could be seen in him" (9:3b-5).

II. DEMONSTRATION! THE SAVIOR AND THE BLIND MAN (9:6-7): Jesus demonstrates his awesome power.
   A. The mud (9:6): He spits on the ground, makes mud from the spittle, and puts it on the man's eyes.
   B. The miracle (9:7): Obeying Jesus, the man washes in the pool of Siloam and returns able to see!

III. SPECULATION! THE NEIGHBORS AND THE BLIND MAN (9:8-12)
   A. Their confusion (9:8-9a): They question whether he is the same man.
   B. His clarification (9:9b-12): He affirms that he is.

IV. INTERROGATION! THE PHARISEES AND THE BLIND MAN (9:13-23): These wicked religious leaders now investigate both the man and his parents.
   A. The man (9:13-17)
      1. *The day* (9:13-14): Jesus healed him on the Sabbath.
      2. *The demand* (9:15)
         a. The Pharisees ask the man what happened (9:15a).
         b. The man tells them how Jesus healed him (9:15b).
      3. *The division* (9:16-17)
         a. Some Pharisees say, "This man Jesus is not from God, for he is working on the Sabbath" (9:16a).
         b. Others say, "How could an ordinary sinner do such miraculous signs?" (9:16b).
         c. The healed man says, "I think he must be a prophet" (9:17).
   B. The parents (9:18-23)
      1. *The Pharisees* (9:18-19)
         a. "Is this your son?" (9:18-19a).
         b. "Was he born blind?" (9:19b).
         c. "How can he see?" (9:19c).
      2. *The parents* (9:20-23): They answer yes to the first two questions but decline to answer the third for fear of the Jews!

V. CASTIGATION! THE PHARISEES AND THE BLIND MAN (9:24-34): For the
second time, the former blind man is summoned to appear before
these godless men.
  A. **Jesus is denounced by the Pharisees** (9:24, 26, 28-29).
    1. *"We know Jesus is a sinner"* (9:24).
    2. *"We don't know anything about him"* (9:26, 28-29).
  B. **Jesus is defended by the blind man** (9:25, 27, 30-34).
    1. *"I don't know whether he is a sinner. But I know this: I was
      blind, and now I can see!"* (9:25, 27).
    2. *"Never since the world began has anyone been able to open
      the eyes of someone born blind. If this man were not from
      God, he couldn't do it"* (9:30-33).
  C. **The former blind man is thrown out of the synagogue** (9:34).

VI. SUMMATION! JESUS AND THE BLIND MAN (9:35-41): The Savior says he
has come into this world for two reasons.
  A. **That the blind might see** (9:39a): Spiritual sight will be given to
    all those who sincerely ask.
    1. *The witness by Jesus* (9:35-37): He informs the former blind
      man he is indeed the Messiah!
    2. *The worship of Jesus* (9:38): The man worships the Savior.
  B. **That those who think they can see might be blinded** (9:39b-41):
    Overhearing this, the Pharisees rightly conclude that Jesus is
    referring to them!

SECTION OUTLINE TEN (JOHN 10)
Jesus compares his followers to sheep and says that he is the Good
Shepherd. He also says that he is the Son of God and that his Father
and he are one.

  I. THE MESSAGE BY JESUS (10:1-21)
    A. **The metaphor** (10:1-6): Jesus illustrates his mission on earth by
      describing two different ways to enter a sheepfold.
      1. *The wrong way, climbing over a wall* (10:1): This is the
        method of thieves and robbers.
      2. *The right way, entering through the gate* (10:2-6): This is the
        method of a true shepherd.
    B. **The meaning** (10:7-18): He explains his illustration by giving the
      characteristics of three kinds of individuals.
      1. *Characteristics of the Good Shepherd* (10:7, 9, 10b-11,
        14-18): Here he describes himself.
        a. His relationship with the sheep (10:7, 9, 10b-11, 14-18)
          (1) He is the entrance to their salvation (10:7).
          (2) He allows them to go in and out, and find green
            pasture (10:9).
          (3) He gives them life in all its fullness (10:10b).

(4) He lays down his own life for them (10:11).

(5) He knows his sheep and they know him (10:14).

b. His relationship with the Father (10:15-18)

   (1) He knows his Father, and the Father knows him (10:15-16).

   (2) He is loved by His Father (10:17).

   (3) He is given power by the Father to lay down his life and take it up again (10:18).

2. *Characteristics of thieves and robbers* (10:8, 10a): Their purpose is to steal, kill, and destroy!

3. *Characteristics of a hired hand* (10:12-13)

   a. He forsakes the sheep in time of danger (10:12).

   b. He cares nothing for the sheep (10:13).

C. **The mixed views** (10:19-21): There is much confusion concerning Jesus after he speaks these words.

1. *Some say he is insane* (10:19, 20b).

2. *Some say he is demon-possessed* (10:20a).

3. *Some question whether he would be able to heal if he were in fact demon-possessed* (10:21).

II. THE MALICE AGAINST JESUS (10:22-39): The Jews now attempt to kill the Savior on two specific occasions because of his claims to be the Son of God.

A. **First attempt** (10:22-31)

1. *His words* (10:25-30)

   a. He says they are not his sheep (10:25-26).

   b. He says his sheep listen to him (10:27).

   c. He says his sheep will never perish and are eternally secure (10:28-29).

   d. He says he and the Father are one (10:30).

2. *Their wickedness* (10:22-24, 31): They ask Jesus if he is the Messiah. When he says he is, they become angry and pick up stones to hurl at him.

B. **Second attempt** (10:32-39)

1. *His words* (10:32-38)

   a. He says they refuse to believe in the Scriptures (10:32-36).

   b. He says they should believe in his miracles (10:37-38).

2. *Their wickedness* (10:39): Again they unsuccessfully attempt to seize him.

III. THE MEETING WITH JESUS (10:40-42): Jesus now leaves Jerusalem for awhile.

A. **The place** (10:40): He goes to where John once baptized.

B. **The people** (10:41-42): Many meet with him there and are saved.

SECTION OUTLINE ELEVEN (JOHN 11)
Jesus raises his friend Lazarus from the dead. The Jewish leaders plot Jesus' death.

I. THE WONDROUS WORK BY JESUS (11:1-44): Many believe this event is the greatest of all Jesus' miracles!
   A. **The sickness of Lazarus** (11:1-3)
      1. *The background* (11:1-2): Lazarus, beloved friend of Jesus and brother of Mary and Martha, lies sick in Bethany.
      2. *The beckoning* (11:3): The sisters notify Jesus of this sickness.
   B. **The summary concerning Lazarus** (11:4-16): Jesus uses this sad event to overview the purpose for his earthly ministry.
      1. *The declaration* (11:4): He says Lazarus's sickness and death are allowed to bring about God's glory!
      2. *The devotion* (11:5): Jesus loves Lazarus and his sisters.
      3. *The delay* (11:6): Jesus remains where he is for two days.
      4. *The decision* (11:7): He announces his plans to visit Bethany.
      5. *The dialogue* (11:8-15): Jesus and his disciples now discuss this issue.
         a. Their concern (11:8): The disciples protest that it's too dangerous for Jesus to go to Bethany.
         b. His commitment (11:9-11): They will, however, go there, for he intends to awake Lazarus from his sleep!
         c. Their confusion (11:12-13): They think Jesus is referring to natural sleep.
         d. His clarification (11:14-15): He tells them Lazarus has died!
      6. *The despair* (11:16): Thomas agrees to go but prepares for the worst!
   C. **The sorrow over Lazarus** (11:17-37)
      1. *The sorrow of the Jews* (11:17-19): Many come from Jerusalem to pay their respects.
      2. *The sorrow of Martha* (11:20-28)
         a. Martha's meeting with Jesus (11:20-27): She waits for him outside of Bethany.
            (1) Her frustration (11:20-21): "Lord, if you had been here, my brother would not have died."
            (2) Her faith (11:22-27)
               (a) In the word of God (11:22-24): She believes in the Old Testament promises regarding the resurrection.
               (b) In the Son of God (11:25-27): She accepts Jesus' statement that he is the resurrection!
         b. Martha's ministry for Jesus (11:28): She informs Mary of his presence.
      3. *The sorrow of Mary* (11:29-32): She knows if Jesus had been there, Lazarus wouldn't have died.
      4. *The sorrow of Jesus* (11:33-37)
         a. He weeps (11:33-35).

      b. They wonder (11:36-37): Those watching this ask why Jesus, who can heal the blind, couldn't keep his friend from dying.

  D. The summons to Lazarus (11:38-44)

    1. *The preparation by Jesus* (11:38-40)

      a. The Savior's request (11:38-39a): He tells some men to remove the stone covering the cave where Lazarus is buried.

      b. The sister's reluctance (11:39b): Martha is hesitant, telling Jesus her brother's body had been in there four days already!

      c. The Savior's reminder (11:40): "Didn't I tell you that you will see God's glory if you believe?"

    2. *The prayer of Jesus* (11:41-42): He thanks his Father for what is about to happen!

    3. *The power from Jesus* (11:43-44)

      a. The order (11:43): "Lazarus, come out!"

      b. The obedience (11:44): Lazarus comes out!

II. THE WICKEDNESS AGAINST JESUS (11:45-53)

  A. The problem (11:45-48)

    1. *The council* (11:45-47): The Pharisees call a meeting to discuss the attention Jesus is receiving because of his miracles.

    2. *The concern* (11:48): They are afraid this will bring the wrath of the Romans down upon them.

  B. The prophecy (11:49-52): The high priest Caiaphas says: "Why should the whole nation be destroyed? Let this one man die for the people."

  C. The plot (11:53): From that day on, they plot to kill Jesus!

III. THE WITHDRAWAL BY JESUS (11:54): He and his disciples leave Judea briefly and retire to a village called Ephraim.

IV. THE WATCH FOR JESUS (11:55-57): Many people at the Passover feast wonder if Jesus will attend.

SECTION OUTLINE TWELVE (JOHN 12)
Mary anoints Jesus' feet with an expensive bottle of perfume, and Jesus defends her action when Judas condemns it. Jesus fulfills prophecy by riding triumphantly into Jerusalem. He predicts his death.

I. JESUS IS ANOINTED IN BETHANY (12:1-11).

  A. The purpose (12:1-2a): A dinner is given to honor Jesus.

  B. The people (12:2b): Among those attending are Lazarus and his sisters.

  C. The perfume (12:3): Mary anoints Jesus with some expensive perfume.

  D. The protest (12:4-8)

1. *The denouncing of Mary* (12:4-6): Judas Iscariot rebukes Mary for this.
   a. What he says (12:4-5): "That perfume . . . should have been sold and the money given to the poor!"
   b. Why he says it (12:6): He wants to keep some of that money for himself.
2. *The defending of Mary* (12:7-8): Jesus says she has done this in preparation for his burial.

E. The popularity (12:9): Many Jews now come to see both Lazarus and Jesus.

F. The plot (12:10-11): The godless Jewish leaders lay plans to kill both Lazarus and Jesus!

II. JESUS IS ACCLAIMED IN JERUSALEM (12:12-50).

A. Events during the Triumphal Entry (12:12-19)
1. *The parade* (12:12): The people line the roadside to welcome Jesus.
2. *The praise* (12:13): "Hail to the King of Israel!"
3. *The prophecy* (12:14-16): This event was predicted by the Old Testament prophet Zechariah (Zech 9:9).
4. *The popularity* (12:17-18): Again, people flock to Jesus because of the Lazarus miracle.
5. *The protest* (12:19): The Pharisees are furious over Jesus' popularity.

B. Events following the Triumphal Entry (12:20-50)
1. *Jesus and the disciples* (12:20-26)
   a. The request (12:20-22): Philip and Andrew tell Jesus that some Greeks desire to see him.
   b. The response (12:23-26): The Savior speaks of his impending death.
2. *Jesus and the Father* (12:27-29)
   a. The request (12:27-28a): Jesus asks the Father to "bring glory to your name!"
   b. The response (12:28b-29): The Father reassures the Son with a loud voice from heaven that is heard by the crowd that this indeed will be done.
3. *Jesus and the Passover crowd* (12:30-50)
   a. The first session (12:30-36)
      (1) Jesus tells them both the world and Satan will soon be judged (12:30-31).
      (2) He will save men by way of the cross (12:32-34).
      (3) They need to accept him before it is too late (12:35-36).
   b. The second session (12:37-50)
      (1) The prophecy (12:37-41): Jesus tells the Jewish crowd their unbelief was predicted centuries before by Isaiah (Isa. 53:1; 6:10).

(2) The praise seekers (12:42-43): Some Jewish leaders
believe Jesus is the Messiah but will not confess him,
for they love men's praise more than God's praise.
(3) The promise (12:44-50): To accept Christ is to accept
the Father, which leads to life everlasting.

SECTION OUTLINE THIRTEEN (JOHN 13)

Jesus washes his disciples' feet and predicts both Judas's betrayal and
Peter's denial.

I. THE WASHING BY JESUS (13:1-17): He washes the feet of his disciples.
   A. The Passover feast (13:1)
   B. The plot (13:2): Satan influences Judas to betray Jesus.
   C. The particulars (13:3-5)
      1. *Jesus wraps a towel around his waist and pours water into a
         basin* (12:3-5a).
      2. *He begins washing their feet* (12:5b).
   D. The protest (13:6-11)
      1. *Peter* (13:6-8a): "You will never wash my feet!"
      2. *Jesus* (13:8b): "If I don't wash you, you won't belong to me!"
      3. *Peter* (13:9): "Then wash my hands and head as well, Lord,
         not just my feet!"
      4. *Jesus* (13:10-11): "A person who has bathed all over does not
         need to wash, except for the feet."
   E. The pattern (13:12-17): The disciples should do for others what
      he has just done for them.

II. THE WARNING BY JESUS (13:18-38): Jesus now makes three troubling
    predictions.
    A. In regard to Judas's defection (13:18-30)
       1. *The Scripture* (13:18-25): Jesus quotes from Psalm 41:9, which
          predicts his betrayal.
       2. *The sign* (13:26-30): Jesus says the one sharing the bread with
          him is the traitor.
    B. In regard to Jesus' departure (13:31-35)
       1. *He must leave* (13:31-33).
       2. *They must love* (13:34-35): He commands them to love one
          another as he has loved them.
    C. In regard to Peter's denials (13:36-38): Jesus says that before the
       rooster crows, Peter will deny him three times!

SECTION OUTLINE FOURTEEN (JOHN 14)
Jesus speaks to the disciples.

I. THE CONSOLATION HE GIVES TO HIS DISCIPLES (14:1-4)
   A. **"I am going to prepare a place for you"** (14:1-2).
   B. **"When everything is ready, I will come and get you, so that you will always be with me where I am"** (14:3-4).

II. THE CONVERSATION HE HAS WITH HIS DISCIPLES (14:5-31): Jesus answers three questions asked him by three disciples.
   A. **Thomas and Jesus** (14:5-7)
      1. *Thomas's question:* "We haven't any idea where you are going, so how can we know the way?" (14:5).
      2. *Jesus' answer* (14:6-7)
         a. "I am the way, the truth and the life" (14:6a).
         b. "No one can come to the Father except through me" (14:6b-7).
   B. **Philip and Jesus** (14:8-21)
      1. *Philip's question* (14:8): "Lord, show us the Father and we will be satisfied."
      2. *Jesus' answer* (14:9-21)
         a. He says anyone who has seen him has seen the Father (14:9).
         b. He says that he is in the Father and that the Father is in him (14:10).
         c. He says they will do greater things than he has done because he is going to the Father (14:11-14).
         d. He says he will ask the Father to send them the Holy Spirit (14:15-21).
   C. **Judas (not Judas Iscariot) and Jesus** (14:22-31)
      1. *Judas's question* (14:22): "Lord, why are you going to reveal yourself only to us and not to the world at large?"
      2. *Jesus' answer* (14:23-31)
         a. He says that he only reveals himself to those who love and obey him (14:23-24).
         b. He promises that the Holy Spirit will explain all this to them (14:25-26).
         c. He reminds them again of his departure and return (14:27-31).

SECTION OUTLINE FIFTEEN (JOHN 15)
Jesus speaks to his disciples about fruit bearing, loving, suffering, and witnessing.

I. FRUIT BEARING (15:1-8)
   A. **The symbols** (15:1, 5a-5b)
      1. *The Son is the true vine* (15:1a, 5a).

  2. *The Father is the gardener* (15:1b).
  3. *The believer is the branch* (15:5b).
 B. The steps (15:2-4, 5c-6)
  1. *We must submit to pruning by the Father* (15:2-3).
  2. *We must abide in the Son* (15:4, 5c-6).
 C. The success (15:7-8)
  1. *It results in bountiful fruit* (15:7-8a).
  2. *It results in glorifying the Father* (15:8b).

II. LOVING (15:9-17)
 A. The priority (15:9-12)
  1. *The Father loves the Son* (15:9b, 10b).
  2. *The Son loves the believer* (15:9a, 10a, 11).
  3. *The believer is to love other believers* (15:12).
 B. The proof (15:13-15)
  1. *What Jesus will do for his disciples* (15:13): He will lay down his life.
  2. *What Jesus now does for his disciples* (15:14-15): He calls them friends, not servants.
 C. The promises (15:16-17)
  1. *Our branches will bear permanent fruit* (15:16a).
  2. *Our prayers will be answered* (15:16b-17).

III. SUFFERING (15:18-25)
 A. The facts (15:18-24)
  1. *All Christians will be hated because Christ was hated* (15:18-19).
  2. *No servant is greater than his master* (15:20-21).
  3. *The reason for this hatred is Jesus' fearless preaching against sin* (15:22-24).
 B. The foretelling (15:25): All this is predicted in Psalms 35:19 and 69:4.

IV. WITNESSING (15:26-27): Jesus speaks of a twofold witness.
 A. The Holy Spirit will soon witness to the disciples concerning the Savior (15:26).
 B. The disciples should then witness to the world concerning the Savior (15:27).

SECTION OUTLINE SIXTEEN (JOHN 16)
This chapter records three rounds of conversation between Jesus and his disciples.

I. ROUND ONE (16:1-15)
 A. Jesus speaks of the conflict that will come to them from the world (16:1-4).
  1. *The review of this persecution* (16:1-2)
   a. They will be put out of the synagogue (16:1-2a).

      b. They will be killed (16:2b).

      c. They will be looked upon as enemies of God (16:2c).

    2. *The reason for this persecution* (16:3-4): Their persecutors do not love the Father or the Son.

  B. Jesus speaks of the Counselor (the Holy Spirit) that will come to them from the Father (16:5-15).

    1. *The prerequisite* (16:5-7): Jesus says unless he goes away, the Holy Spirit will not come.

    2. *The purpose* (16:8-15): He will come to accomplish a fourfold purpose.

      a. To convict sinners (16:8-10)

      b. To condemn Satan (16:11)

      c. To counsel saints (16:12-13)

      d. To champion the Savior (16:14-15)

II. ROUND TWO (16:16-28)

  A. The confusion (16:16-18): The disciples do not understand when Jesus says, "In just a little while I will be gone, and you won't see me anymore. Then, just a little while after that, you will see me again" (16:16).

  B. The clarification (16:19-22)

    1. *His explanation* (16:19)

      a. "You won't see me anymore" (16:19a): A reference to his death, which will bring about great grief.

      b. "You will see me again" (16:19b): A reference to his resurrection, which will bring about great joy!

    2. *His example* (16:20-22): To illustrate the way their sorrow will turn to joy, Jesus refers to a woman giving birth.

  C. The comfort (16:23-28)

    1. *Jesus says that the Father will give them all they need because of the Son* (16:23).

    2. *Jesus says the Father loves them dearly* (16:24-28).

III. ROUND THREE (16:29-33)

  A. The disciples speak (16:29-30).

    1. *"At last you are speaking plainly"* (16:29).

    2. *"We believe that you came from God"* (16:30).

  B. The Savior speaks (16:31-33).

    1. *The bad news* (16:31-33a): "You will have many trials and sorrows."

    2. *The glad news* (16:33b): "Take heart, because I have overcome the world."

SECTION OUTLINE SEVENTEEN (JOHN 17)
Jesus prays for his disciples and for all who will ever believe in him.

I. THE SAVIOR PRAYS FOR HIMSELF (17:1-5).
   A. **The faithful Son** (17:1, 5)
      1. *What he asks* (17:1a, 5): "Glorify your Son."
      2. *Why he asks* (17:1b): "So he can give glory back to you."
   B. **The fruitful Son** (17:2-4)
      1. *He has given eternal life to all the elect* (17:2-3).
      2. *He has completed his assignment* (17:4).

II. THE SAVIOR PRAYS FOR HIS DISCIPLES (17:6-19).
   A. **Jesus' report** (17:6-10, 12, 14, 18-19): He reviews his ministry
      for the disciples.
      1. *He has revealed the Father to them* (17:6-7).
      2. *He has given the Father's words to them* (17:8, 14).
      3. *He has prayed for them* (17:9-10).
      4. *He has kept them safe, with the exception of Judas* (17:12).
      5. *He has set himself apart for their sanctification* (17:19).
      6. *He has sent them into the world* (17:18).
   B. **Jesus' requests** (17:11, 13, 15-17): He previews the Father's
      future ministry for the disciples.
      1. *He asks that the Father unify them* (17:11).
      2. *He asks that the Father impart joy to them* (17:13).
      3. *He asks that the Father protect them* (17:15-16).
      4. *He asks that the Father sanctify them* (17:17).

III. THE SAVIOR PRAYS FOR HIS CHURCH (17:20-26).
   A. **He asks that the Father unify the church** (17:20-21a, 22).
   B. **He asks that the church honor the Son** (17:21b).
   C. **He asks that the church display God's love** (17:23).
   D. **He asks that the church experience God's love** (17:25-26).
   E. **He asks that the church enjoy Christ's glory in heaven forever**
      (17:24).

SECTION OUTLINE EIGHTEEN (JOHN 18)
Jesus is betrayed by Judas into the hands of a battalion of Roman
soldiers and Temple guards. The high priest questions Jesus. Peter
denies Jesus, as the Savior predicted. Jesus stands trial before Pilate.

I. EVENTS IN GETHSEMANE (18:1-11)
   A. **Jesus' confrontation with his foes** (18:1-7)
      1. *The traitor* (18:1-2): Judas arrives in Gethsemane, prepared to
         betray his master.
      2. *The Temple guard* (18:3-7)
         a. What they carry (18:3): Blazing torches, lanterns, and
            weapons.

b. Why they have come (18:4-7)
(1) The Savior (18:4): "Whom are you looking for?"
(2) The soldiers (18:5-7): "Jesus of Nazareth!"
B. Jesus' concern for his friends (18:8-11)
1. *The request* (18:8-9): He agrees to go with the soldiers and asks that they let the disciples leave.
2. *The rebuke* (18:10-11): He chastens Peter for cutting off the right ear of Malchus, the high priest's servant.

II. Events after Gethsemane (18:12-40): Two words aptly describe this passage: *denials* and *trials.*
A. The denials (18:15-18, 25-27): On three separate occasions, Peter denies his Lord.
1. *First denial* (18:15-18)
a. The accusation (18:15-17a): A servant girl asks if Peter is one of Jesus' disciples.
b. The answer (18:17b-18): Peter denies it.
2. *Second denial (18:25)*
a. The accusation (18:25a): An unnamed person asks Peter the same question.
b. The answer (18:25b): Again, Peter denies it.
3. *Third denial* (18:26-27)
a. The accusation (18:26): A relative of the man whose ear Peter cut off says they saw him in Gethsemane with Jesus!
b. The answer (18:27): For the third time, Peter denies this, and immediately a rooster crows!
B. The trials (18:12-14, 19-24, 28-40): Jesus endures three trials.
1. *First trial, before Annas, former high priest* (18:12-14, 19-23)
a. Jesus is bound (18:12-14).
b. Jesus is bullied (18:19-21).
(1) Annas (18:19): Annas asks Jesus about his followers and about his teachings.
(2) Jesus (18:20-21): Jesus replies that his teachings are widely known because he has always spoken openly in the Temple and synagogues.
c. Jesus is buffeted (18:22-23): An official now strikes him in the face.
2. *Second trial, before Caiaphas, current high priest* (18:24): The Gospel of John does not record what transpired at this trial.
3. *Third trial, before Pilate, the Roman governor* (18:28-40)
a. Pilate and the Jews—first encounter (18:28-32)
(1) Pilate (18:28-29): "What is your charge against this man?"
(2) The Jews (18:30): "We wouldn't have handed him over to you if he weren't a criminal!"
(3) Pilate (18:31a): "Then take him away and judge him by your own laws!"
(4) The Jews (18:31b-32): "Only the Romans are permitted to execute someone."

       b. Pilate and Jesus (18:33-38a)

         (1) Pilate (18:33): "Are you the King of the Jews?"

         (2) Jesus (18:34): "Is this your own question, or did others tell you about me?"

         (3) Pilate (18:35): "Am I a Jew? Your own people and their leading priests brought you here. Why? What have you done?"

         (4) Jesus (18:36): "My kingdom is not of this world."

         (5) Pilate (18:37a): "You are a king then?"

         (6) Jesus (18:37b): "You are right. I was born for that purpose. And I came to bring truth to the world."

         (7) Pilate (18:38a): "What is truth?"

       c. Pilate and the Jews—second encounter (18:38b-40)

         (1) Pilate (18:38b-39): "He is not guilty of any crime. . . . If you want me to, I'll release the King of the Jews."

         (2) The Jews (18:40): "No! Not this man, but Barabbas!"

SECTION OUTLINE NINETEEN (JOHN 19)

Pilate gives in to the crowd and sentences Jesus to death. Jesus dies on the cross, saving all the world from sin. Joseph of Arimathea asks Pilate for permission to bury Jesus' body and places it in a new, previously unused tomb.

I. EVENTS PRECEDING THE CRUCIFIXION (19:1-15)

   A. Jesus' final torment before the cross (19:1-3)

      1. *The scourging* (19:1): Pilate has him flogged.

      2. *The sarcasm* (19:2-3): The soldiers ridicule and mock him.

   B. Jesus' final trial before the cross (19:4-15)

      1. *Pilate and the Jews—first encounter* (19:4-7)

         a. Pilate (19:4-5, 6b): Twice he reminds the Jews, "I find him not guilty."

         b. The Jews (19:6a, 7): Twice the Jews respond, "He ought to die because he called himself the Son of God."

      2. *Pilate and Jesus* (19:8-11)

         a. Pilate (19:8-10): "Don't you realize that I have the power to release you or to crucify you?"

         b. Jesus (19:11): "You would have no power over me at all unless it were given to you from above."

      3. *Pilate and the Jews—final encounter* (19:12-15)

         a. The futility (19:12a, 13-14, 15b): Time and again Pilate attempts to release Jesus, but to no avail.

         b. The hostility (19:12b, 15a, 15c): The Jews continually scream out, "Crucify! Crucify! Crucify!"

II. EVENTS DURING THE CRUCIFIXION (19:16-30)

   A. The walk to the cross (19:16-17): Pilate releases Jesus to the

soldiers, who lead him (carrying his own cross) to a place known as "Skull Hill" *(Golgotha).*
B. The wrongdoers on the cross (19:18): Two thieves are crucified with Jesus, one on each side of him.
C. The writing above the cross (19:19-22)
1. *The record of the sign* (19:19-20): It says, "Jesus of Nazareth, the King of the Jews."
2. *The request to remove the sign* (19:21): The Pharisees demand that Pilate change it to read: "He said, I am the King of the Jews."
3. *The resolve to keep the sign* (19:22): Pilate says, "What I have written, I have written!"
D. The wardrobe below the cross (19:23-24)
1. *The soldiers* (19:23-24a): They divide Jesus' clothes into four parts, one for each of them, and cast lots for his seamless garment.
2. *The Scripture* (19:24b): This action was predicted by David in Psalm 22:18.
E. The women at the cross (19:25): Various women are there, including Jesus' mother, her sister, the wife of Clopas, and Mary Magdalene.
F. The words from the cross (19:26-30)
1. *Jesus speaks to Mary and John (19:26-27).*
   a. To Mary (19:26): "Woman, he is your son."
   b. To John (19:27): "She is your mother."
2. *Jesus speaks to the guards* (19:28-29): "I am thirsty."
3. *Jesus speaks to the Father* (19:30): "It is finished!"

III. EVENTS FOLLOWING THE CRUCIFIXION (19:31-42)
A. The piercing of Jesus' body (14:31-37)
1. *The request by the Jews* (19:31): They ask Pilate to remove the victims from the cross before the Sabbath.
2. *The response by the soldiers* (19:32-37)
   a. In regard to the robbers (19:32): They are not dead, so the soldiers break their legs.
   b. In regard to the Redeemer (19:33-37)
      (1) The spear (19:33-34): Finding him to be dead already, the soldiers pierce his side.
      (2) The spectator (19:35): John the apostle apparently witnesses all this.
      (3) The Scriptures (19:36-37): Two Old Testament prophecies are fulfilled at this time—Psalm 34:20 and Zechariah 12:10.
B. The preparing of Jesus' body (19:38-40)
1. *Who the preparers are* (19:38-39a): Joseph of Arimathea asks for and receives the body of Jesus from Pilate; then Nicodemus helps prepare the body.
2. *What the preparers do* (19:39b-40): They anoint his body with myrrh and aloes and wrap it in a long linen cloth.

C. The placing of Jesus' body (19:41-42): Jesus' body is now placed in a new garden tomb where no one has ever been laid before.

SECTION OUTLINE TWENTY (JOHN 20)

Jesus rises from the grave, defeating the power of death for all time, and appears to Mary Magdalene and the disciples, except for Thomas. When Thomas doubts the truth of the Resurrection, Jesus appears specially to him.

I. THE MESSAGE OF MARY MAGDALENE (20:1-2)
   A. What she sees (20:1): She finds the stone that had blocked the entrance of Jesus' tomb rolled away.
   B. What she says (20:2): She reports to Peter and John, "They have taken the Lord's body!"

II. THE MISSION OF TWO DISCIPLES (20:3-10)
   A. Who they are (20:3a): Peter and John.
   B. What they do (20:3b): They visit the empty tomb.
   C. What they see (20:4-9)
      1. *John (20:4-5, 8-9)*
         a. At first he looks inside and sees the burial cloth that covered Jesus' body, but he does not go in (20:4-5).
         b. Finally, he goes in and believes (20:8-9).
      2. *Peter* (20:6-7): He goes in and sees both the body cloth and head cloth of Jesus.
   D. Where they go (20:10): After they see that Jesus is no longer in the tomb, they both go home.

III. THE MANIFESTATIONS OF JESUS CHRIST (20:11-29): John describes three post-Resurrection appearances of Jesus.
   A. The appearance before Mary Magdalene (20:11-18)
      1. *The sorrowful one* (20:11): She goes back to the tomb and weeps.
      2. *The shining ones* (20:12-13): Two angels appear.
         a. Their question (20:12-13a): "Why are you crying?"
         b. Her answer (20:13b): "Because they have taken away my Lord, and I don't know where they have put him."
      3. *The sovereign one* (20:14-18)
         a. Mary's error (20:14-15): Jesus suddenly appears, but she mistakes him for the gardener.
         b. Mary's ecstasy (20:16-18): She recognizes Jesus and later shares the good news with the disciples.
   B. The appearance before the ten (20:19-23)
      1. *The fearful ones* (20:19a): The disciples are meeting behind locked doors for fear of the Jews.
      2. *The faithful one* (20:19b-23)

        a. He comforts them (20:19b-20): Suddenly Jesus appears, showing them his hands and side.

        b. He commissions them (20:21-23): They are to become his Spirit-filled witnesses.

C. The appearance before Thomas (20:24-29)

    1. *The reluctance by Thomas* (20:24-25)

        a. The reason (20:24): Thomas was absent when Jesus first appeared to the disciples and can't believe their wonderful report.

        b. The requirements (20:25): Thomas says he will not believe unless he sees and touches the wounds of Jesus.

    2. *The recognition by Thomas* (20:26-29)

        a. The manifestation (20:26): Jesus suddenly appears!

        b. The invitation (20:27): Thomas is invited to feel Jesus' wounds.

        c. The adoration (20:28): Thomas falls to his knees and worships.

        d. The observation (20:29): Jesus says:

           (1) "You believe because you have seen me" (20:29a).

           (2) "Blessed are those who haven't seen me and believe anyway" (20:29b).

IV. THE MISSION OF JOHN'S GOSPEL (20:30-31): "That you may believe that Jesus is the Messiah, the Son of God, and that by believing in him you will have life!"

SECTION OUTLINE TWENTY-ONE (JOHN 21)

The resurrected Christ meets with his disciples by the Sea of Galilee.

I. THE FISHERMEN ON THE SEA (21:1-3)

    A. The disciples (21:1-2): There are seven there, including Peter, Thomas, Nathanael, James, and John.

    B. The decision (21:3): They decide to go fishing but catch nothing all night.

II. THE FISHER OF MEN ON THE SHORE (21:4-25)

    A. The call (21:4-5): Standing there, unrecognized, Jesus calls out, asking if they have caught any fish. They reply that they have not.

    B. The command (21:6a): He tells them to throw their net on the right-hand side of the boat.

    C. The catch (21:6b): Immediately the net is filled with fish!

    D. The comprehension (21:7): Peter suddenly recognizes Jesus and begins swimming toward him.

    E. The coals (21:8-9): When all the disciples arrive, they find fish frying over a fire and some bread.

    F. The count (21:10-11): There are 153 large fish in the net!

G. The communion (21:12-14): Jesus now invites all seven to break-fast and personally serves them!

H. The confessions (21:15-17): After breakfast Jesus gives Peter the opportunity to confess his love for Jesus three times.

1. *Round one* (21:15)
   a. Jesus (21:15a):"Simon son of John, do you love me more than these?"
   b. Peter (21:15b):"Yes, Lord, you know I love you."
   c. Jesus (21:15c):"Then feed my lambs."

2. *Round two* (21:16)
   a. Jesus (21:16a): "Simon son of John, do you love me?"
   b. Peter (21:16b): "Yes, Lord, you know I love you."
   c. Jesus (21:16c): "Then take care of my sheep!"

3. *Round three* (21:17)
   a. Jesus (21:17a): "Simon son of John, do you love me?"
   b. Peter (21:17b): "Lord, you know everything. You know I love you."
   c. Jesus (21:17c): "Then feed my sheep."

I. The cross (21:18-19): Jesus predicts that Peter will someday die a martyr's death by crucifixion.

J. The concern (21:20-21): Peter asks Jesus what kind of death John will die.

K. The chiding (21:22): Jesus tells Peter, "If I want him to remain alive until I return, what is that to you?"

L. The confusion (21:23): A false rumor spreads among the believers that John will never die.

M. The confirmation (21:24-25)

1. *Concerning the witness for Jesus* (21:24): John testifies that all he has said about Jesus is true!

2. *Concerning the works by Jesus* (21:25): He says if everything that the Savior did while on earth was written down, the whole earth could not contain the books!

PART SIX

Acts

Acts

SECTION OUTLINE ONE (ACTS 1)
Luke opens Acts, his second book, with a review of the ascension of
Jesus. The twelve apostles choose Matthias to replace Judas Iscariot.

I. THE ACTION ON THE MOUNT OF OLIVES (1:1-11)
   A. **The assurance from Jesus** (1:1-8)
      1. *The confirmation* (1:1-3)
         a. The recorder (1:1b): Luke the physician wrote the book of
            Luke and is the author of the book of Acts.
         b. The recipient (1:1a): He writes to someone named
            Theophilus.
         c. The reason (1:2-3): He writes to confirm the resurrection of
            Jesus Christ!
      2. *The command* (1:4-5): The disciples (called "apostles" in Acts)
         are to remain in Jerusalem until they are baptized with the
         Holy Spirit.
      3. *The confusion* (1:6): The apostles want to know if Jesus will
         establish his kingdom at this time.
      4. *The clarification* (1:7): Jesus tells them that the Father will
         determine when that will occur.
      5. *The commission* (1:8): Meanwhile, they are to witness for
         Jesus in Jerusalem, Judea, Samaria, and throughout the whole
         world!
   B. **The ascension of Jesus** (1:9-11)
      1. *The action* (1:9): Jesus is taken up before their eyes.
      2. *The attendants* (1:10): Two white-robed men suddenly stand
         beside them.
      3. *The assurance* (1:11): The two men tell the amazed apostles
         that Jesus will return someday just as he left!
II. THE ACTION IN THE UPPER ROOM (1:12-26)
   A. **The prayer meeting** (1:12-15): Those present are:
      1. *The eleven apostles* (1:12-13)
      2. *Mary the mother of Jesus and other godly women* (1:14a)
      3. *The half brothers of Jesus* (1:14b)
      4. *In all, 120 people* (1:15)

B. The business meeting (1:16-26)
   1. *In regard to the defection of Judas* (1:16-20)
      a. The suicide (1:18-19): Luke records graphically how Judas died.
      b. The Scriptures (1:16-17, 20): Peter quotes from Psalms 69:25 and 109:8, which predicted Judas's death and replacement.
   2. *In regard to the election of Matthias* (1:21-26)
      a. The conditions (1:21-22): The new apostle has to be a long-time believer and one who saw the resurrected Christ.
      b. The candidates (1:23): Two men are nominated—Barsabbas and Matthias.
      c. The counsel (1:24-25): The disciples seek God's will in prayer and by casting lots.
      d. The choice (1:26): The lot falls on Matthias.

SECTION OUTLINE TWO (ACTS 2)
The Holy Spirit comes at Pentecost and fills the believers. Peter, who once denied the Savior out of fear, now preaches boldly to a huge crowd, sharing the gospel. Many respond to his message by believing in Christ, and the new church begins to grow.

I. THE CLOVEN TONGUES (2:1-4)
  A. The sounds at Pentecost (2:1-2): Sound like a mighty wind from heaven fills the upper room.
  B. The sights at Pentecost (2:3): Tongues of fire appear and settle on the heads of the believers.
  C. The speeches at Pentecost (2:4): They all begin to speak in other languages.

II. THE CROWD (2:5-11)
  A. The men in this crowd (2:5): Jews have come from over a dozen foreign countries to attend the Feast of Pentecost.
  B. The marvel by this crowd (2:6-11): They are amazed to hear their own languages being spoken by the apostles!

III. THE CONFUSION (2:12-13)
  A. The people in the crowd ask each other, "What can this mean?" (2:12).
  B. Some of them say, "They're drunk, that's all!" (2:13).

IV. THE CLARIFICATION (2:14-21)
  A. The speaker (2:14): Peter addresses the crowd.
  B. The statement (2:15): "Some of you are saying these people are drunk. It isn't true!"
  C. The Scriptures (2:16-21): Peter tells the crowd that the prophet Joel foretold all this (see Joel 2:28-32).

      1. *Joel wrote concerning the Spirit of God* (2:16-18): The Spirit would be poured out on all people.

      2. *Joel wrote concerning the signs of God* (2:19-20).

        a. Blood, fire, and smoke on earth (2:19)

        b. The darkening of the sun and moon in the heavens (2:20)

      3. *Joel wrote concerning the salvation of God* (2:21): Anyone who calls on the name of the Lord will be saved!

V. THE CONDEMNATION (2:22-28): Peter now stresses two points:

    A. The Messiah was crucified by his foes (2:22-23): Both the Jewish nation and the Roman government are guilty of this crime.

    B. The Messiah was resurrected by his Father (2:24-28).

      1. *The significance* (2:24): It is impossible for death to keep Jesus in its grip!

      2. *The Scriptures* (2:25-28): Centuries ago David predicted this (see Ps. 16:8-11).

VI. THE TWOFOLD CONCLUSION (2:29-36)

    A. Concerning Jesus' resurrection (2:29-32): David must have had the Messiah's resurrection in mind, for he himself died and was buried.

    B. Concerning Jesus' exaltation (2:33-36): Inasmuch as David never ascended into heaven to sit on his throne, he is referring to Jesus in Psalm 110:1.

VII. THE CONVICTION (2:37): God's Spirit now stirs the people's sinful hearts.

VIII. THE COMMANDS (2:38-39): Peter tells the crowd that they must do two things.

    A. "Each of you must turn from your sins and turn to God" (2:38a).

    B. "Be baptized in the name of Jesus Christ for the forgiveness of your sins" (2:38b-39).

IX. THE CHALLENGE (2:40): Peter urges his listeners to accept Christ.

X. THE CONVERSIONS (2:41): Three thousand people believe and are baptized!

XI. THE COMMUNION (2:42-47): The newly formed church now involves itself in several activities.

    A. Bible study (2:42a)

    B. Prayer and worship (2:42d, 45-46a, 47a)

    C. Fellowship (2:42b)

    D. Sharing and caring (2:44, 46c, 47b)

    E. The Lord's Supper (2:42c, 46b)

    F. Signs and wonders (2:43)

SECTION OUTLINE THREE (ACTS 3)
Peter, filled with the Holy Spirit, heals a crippled beggar and
preaches in the Temple.

I. THE MIRACLE (3:1-11)
   A. **Two consecrated men** (3:1): Peter and John go to the Temple to
      pray.
   B. **One crippled man** (3:2-11)
      1. *The money he requests* (3:2-3): This man, lame from birth,
         asks Peter and John for money.
      2. *The miracle he receives* (3:4-11)
         a. The witness of the apostle (3:4-6): Peter commands the
            cripple in the name of Jesus to walk.
         b. The worship of the cripple (3:7-8): Walking and leaping, he
            enters the Temple, praising God.
         c. The wonder of the crowd (3:9-11): The people are amazed
            at this.

II. THE MESSAGE (3:12-26)
   A. **Peter's explanation** (3:12-16)
      1. *He speaks of restoration* (3:12-13a, 16): The apostle says that
         God healed this man to bring glory to his Son, Jesus.
      2. *He speaks of rejection* (3:13b-15a): Israel, however, crucified
         its own Messiah!
      3. *He speaks of the Resurrection* (3:15b): God brought his Son
         back from the dead!
   B. **Peter's exhortation** (3:17-26)
      1. *The divine plea* (3:17, 19)
         a. Why Israel rejected Jesus (3:17): This was done out of igno-
            rance!
         b. Why Israel should now receive Jesus (3:19): So that they
            might experience redemption and cleansing.
      2. *The divine program* (3:18, 20-26)
         a. The prophets (3:22-25): God spoke through Moses, Samuel,
            and all the Old Testament prophets in regard to this plan of
            the ages.
         b. The prophecies involved (3:18, 20-21, 26)
            (1) Jesus' crucifixion (3:18)
            (2) Jesus' resurrection (3:26)
            (3) Jesus' present ministry (3:21)
            (4) Jesus' second coming (3:20)

SECTION OUTLINE FOUR (ACTS 4)
The religious leaders arrest Peter and John and demand to know
by what power they healed the cripple. Peter says it was Jesus'
power! Ordered never again to preach about Jesus, the believers
pray for courage, and still more people believe.

I. FRUSTRATION (4:1-3)
   A. **The anger of the Jewish leaders** (4:1-2): They are disturbed
   because Peter and John are proclaiming that there is a resurrection from the dead.
   B. **The arrest by the Jewish leaders** (4:3): Peter and John are seized
   and jailed overnight.

II. MULTIPLICATION (4:4): In spite of persecution, the number of
    believers now reaches a new high of 5,000 men!

III. INTERROGATION (4:5-22): Peter and John are questioned by the high
     priest.
   A. **First ordeal** (4:5-12)
      1. *Question* (4:5-7): "By what power, or in whose name, have
      you [healed this cripple]?"
      2. *Answer* (4:8-11): "He was healed in the name and power of
      Jesus Christ."
         a. The power (4:8-10): Invoking the name of Jesus alone is
         sufficient.
         b. The prophecy (4:11): David predicted this (see Ps. 118:22).
         c. The pardon (4:12): His name and his name alone results in
         redemption.
   B. **Private meeting** (4:13-17)
      1. *The dismissal* (4:13-15): The two apostles are sent out of the
      room for a while so the religious leaders can confer together.
      2. *The dilemma* (4:16): The leaders agree that they cannot deny
      the healing of the cripple, because everyone in Jerusalem is
      aware of it.
      3. *The decision* (4:17): They decide to call the apostles back in
      and threaten them.
   C. **Second ordeal** (4:18-22)
      1. *The threats* (4:18, 21-22): The religious leaders warn Peter and
      John never again to speak about Jesus.
      2. *The testimony* (4:19-20): The apostles respond, "We cannot
      stop telling about the wonderful things we have seen and
      heard."

IV. SUPPLICATION (4:23-30)
   A. **The believers acknowledge God's sovereignty in dealing with
   his enemies** (4:25-28).
      1. *David wrote of it* (4:25-26): See Psalm 2:1-2.

2. *The disciples witnessed it* (4:27-28): They saw Pilate, Herod, and the Jewish leaders conspire against Jesus.
B. **The believers ask for God's strength in dealing with their enemies** (4:23-24, 29-30).

V. DEMONSTRATION (4:31): God's mighty power shakes the building!

VI. COOPERATION (4:32-35): The believers sell their possessions and freely share with each other.

VII. EXEMPLIFICATION (4:36-37): A godly believer named Barnabas is singled out as an example of this sacrificial sharing.

SECTION OUTLINE FIVE (ACTS 5)
Ananias and Sapphira lie, and God kills them. The apostles heal many people. They are arrested, but an angel frees them. Again they are arrested and ordered not to speak about Jesus. But they keep preaching, and the church keeps growing.

I. THE PURITY IN THE EARLY CHURCH (5:1-11): Ananias and Sapphira are judged for their sin.
A. **The deception by Ananias and Sapphira** (5:1-2): This couple lies about the amount of a gift they donate to the church.
B. **The discovery of Ananias and Sapphira** (5:3-4): Peter finds out what they did and severely rebukes them.
C. **The deaths of Ananias and Sapphira** (5:5-11)
1. *Ananias's death* (5:5-6): He falls to the floor dead and is carried out.
2. *Sapphira's death* (5:7-11): She dies the same way as her husband.

II. THE POWER BY THE EARLY CHURCH (5:12-16)
A. **As seen by the signs the apostles do** (5:12-14): They do miraculous signs and wonders.
B. **As seen by the sick the apostles deliver** (5:15-16): Many sick and demon-possessed people are healed.

III. THE PERSECUTION AGAINST THE EARLY CHURCH (5:17-42)
A. **The anger of the Sadducees** (5:17-18): Filled with envy, they order the arrest of the apostles.
B. **The angel of the Lord** (5:19-21): A heavenly messenger appears and releases the apostles.
C. **The astonishment of the jailers** (5:22-26)
1. *The prisoners are gone* (5:22-24): The gates are still locked and guarded, but the prisoners are gone.
2. *The preachers are back* (5:25-26): They find the apostles in the Temple courtyard proclaiming Jesus.

D. The accusation by the Sanhedrin (5:27-28): "Didn't we tell you never again to teach in this man's name?"
E. The answer by the apostles (5:29-32)
1. *They explain their mission* (5:29, 32): "We must obey God rather than human authority."
2. *They explain their Messiah* (5:30-31).
   a. "You killed him" (5:30b).
   b. "God . . . raised Jesus from the dead" (5:30a, 31).
F. The advice of a lawyer (5:33-42)
1. *The counsel* (5:33-37)
   a. The identity of the lawyer (5:33-34): He is a highly respected Pharisee named Gamaliel.
   b. The illustrations by this lawyer (5:35-37): He offers examples of two unsuccessful spiritual revolts in past days.
      (1) That of Theudas (5:35-36): Theudas pretended to be great, and 400 people followed him. After he was killed, his followers scattered.
      (2) That of Judas of Galilee (5:37): He was killed, and his followers also scattered.
2. *The conclusion* (5:38-39): Gamaliel says, "Leave these men alone. If they are teaching and doing these things merely on their own, it will soon be overthrown. But if it is of God, you will not be able to stop them."
3. *The consensus* (5:40): Gamaliel's advice is accepted. The apostles are flogged, warned, and set free.
4. *The commitment* (5:41-42): The apostles rejoice that God has counted them worthy to suffer for Jesus, and they continue their witness for him!

SECTION OUTLINE SIX (ACTS 6)
The twelve apostles call a meeting of all the believers and choose seven men to administer a food program for the rapidly multiplying church. One of them, Stephen, is arrested and put on trial.

I. THE SELECTION OF THE SEVEN DEACONS (6:1-7)
A. The complaint to the church leaders (6:1): The Greek-speaking widows feel that the Hebrew-speaking widows are being favored in the daily distribution of food.
B. The conference of the church leaders (6:2-4)
1. *Their dilemma* (6:2): They want to help but feel they have no time.
2. *Their decision* (6:3): They determine to select seven men and assign them this task.
3. *Their duties* (6:4): The leaders believe their ministry should consist of praying, teaching, and preaching.

C. The choice by the church leaders (6:5-7)
1. *The individuals* (6:5): The men chosen for this task are Stephen, Philip, Procorus, Nicanor, Timon, Parmenas, and Nicolas.
2. *The installation* (6:6): The apostles lay hands on the seven and pray for them.
3. *The increase* (6:7): Soon the number of believers increases, including the conversion of many Jewish priests!

II. THE SLANDER AGAINST THE ONE DEACON (6:8-15)
   A. The miracles by Stephen (6:8): He performs great wonders among the people through the power of God.
   B. The malice against Stephen (6:9-14)
   1. *Who* (6:9): A group of Jews from the Synagogue of Freed Slaves begins debating with Stephen.
   2. *Why* (6:10): They hate Stephen because they are unable to stand against his Spirit-anointed wisdom.
   3. *What* (6:11-14): They charge Stephen with teaching a twofold blasphemy.
      a. That Jesus will destroy the Temple of God (6:13a)
      b. That Jesus will destroy the law of God (6:11-12, 13b-14)
   C. The meekness of Stephen (6:15): The council members see that Stephen's face has become as bright as an angel's!

SECTION OUTLINE SEVEN (ACTS 7)
Stephen addresses the council. Jesus appears to Stephen while he is testifying, and the enraged Jewish leaders drag Stephen out of the city and stone him to death. A young man named Saul is one of the official witnesses at the stoning.

I. THE MESSAGE OF STEPHEN TO THE SANHEDRIN (7:1-53): Stephen has been falsely accused of speaking against the Temple. Now he says that the Temple is not necessary for worshiping the true God!
   A. Israel was favored by God before possessing either its Tabernacle or two Temples (7:1-38).
   1. *As illustrated by the life of Abraham* (7:1-8)
      a. God led him into Canaan (7:1-4).
      b. God promised him that his seed would possess Canaan (7:5-7).
      c. God gave him the seal of circumcision (7:8a).
      d. God gave him Isaac, the heir of the covenant (7:8b).
   2. *As illustrated by the life of Joseph* (7:9-16)
      a. God protected Joseph the prisoner in Egypt (7:9): God was always with him.
      b. God promoted Joseph to prime minister over Egypt (7:10-16): God gave him favor with Pharaoh.
   3. *As illustrated by the life of Moses* (7:17-38)

a. His first 40 years, in Egypt (7:17-28): God promoted him.
   b. His second 40 years, in the Sinai desert (7:29): God
      prepared him.
   c. His final 40 years, en route to Canaan (7:30-38): God
      empowered him.
B. **Israel was faithless to God after possessing both its Tabernacle
   and two Temples** (7:39-53).
   1. *They rebelled during the Tabernacle period* (7:39-43a, 44-45).
   2. *They rebelled during the first Temple period* (7:43b, 46-50).
   3. *They are rebelling during the second Temple period* (7:51-53):
      Stephen now utterly condemns his audience with a threefold
      indictment:
      a. They are heathens at heart and deaf to the truth (7:51).
      b. They betrayed and murdered their own Messiah (7:52).
      c. They are deliberately disobeying God's laws (7:53).

II. THE MARTYRDOM OF STEPHEN BY THE SANHEDRIN (7:54-60)
   A. **His persecutors** (7:54, 57-58)
      1. *The ones playing an active role* (7:54, 57-58a): Some
         members of the Sanhedrin mob Stephen and drag him out of
         the city to stone him.
      2. *The one playing an inactive role* (7:58b): Saul of Tarsus
         watches the coats of the killers.
   B. **His preview of glory** (7:55-56): Stephen sees the glory of God
      and Jesus standing at God's right hand!
   C. **His prayers** (7:59-60)
      1. *Stephen prays for himself* (7:59): "Lord Jesus, receive my
         spirit!"
      2. *Stephen prays for his foes* (7:60a): "Don't charge them with
         this sin!"
   D. **His passing** (7:60b): After he says this, he dies.

SECTION OUTLINE EIGHT (ACTS 8)

After Stephen's death, most of the believers flee, still preaching
the gospel. Philip preaches in Samaria and witnesses to an
Ethiopian eunuch in Gaza. Simon the sorcerer tries to purchase
the Holy Spirit's power and is rebuked by the apostles.

I. SAUL THE PERSECUTOR (8:1-3)
   A. **He approves the death of Stephen** (8:1).
   B. **He attempts the destruction of the church** (8:2-3).

II. PHILIP THE PREACHER (8:4-8, 26-40)
   A. **His public ministry in Samaria** (8:4-8)
      1. *The person of Philip's message* (8:4-5): Philip tells the
         Samaritans about the Messiah.
      2. *The power of Philip's message* (8:6-8)

a. The sick are restored (8:7b).

b. The possessed are released (8:6-7a).

c. The people rejoice (8:8).

B. His private ministry in Gaza (8:26-40)

1. *His message from an angel* (8:26): Philip is instructed to go to the Gaza desert.

2. *His meeting with a eunuch* (8:27-40)

a. The charge given to the eunuch (8:27): Candace, Queen of Ethiopia, has entrusted all her riches to him.

b. The confusion of the eunuch (8:28-34): Philip finds this man reading from the Scriptures.

(1) The passage (8:28): He is reading from Isaiah 53:7-8 and cannot understand what he is reading.

(2) The problem (8:29-34): The eunuch asks Philip if the prophet is speaking of himself or someone else.

c. The clarification to the eunuch (8:35): Philip preaches the gospel to him!

d. The conversion of the eunuch (8:36-37): He confesses that Jesus Christ is the Son of God, and Philip baptizes him.

3. *His ministry at Azotus* (8:38-40): After the eunuch is baptized, the Holy Spirit immediately catches Philip away and brings him to the city of Azotus, where Philip resumes his teaching as he travels to Caesarea.

III. SIMON THE PRETENDER (8:9-25)

A. The circumstances (8:14-17): The Jerusalem church sends two men to help Philip during his Samaritan crusade.

1. *Who they are* (8:14): Peter and John.

2. *What they do* (8:15-17): They lay hands on new converts so they may receive the Holy Spirit.

B. The confrontation (8:9-13, 18-25): Peter and John meet Simon the sorcerer.

1. *The pride of Simon* (8:9): He is a sorcerer, arrogant and boastful, claiming to be great.

2. *The popularity of Simon* (8:10-11): Many people in Samaria believe his claims because of his magic.

3. *The profession of Simon* (8:12-13): Amazed by Philip's miracles, Simon accepts Christ and is baptized!

4. *The perversion of Simon* (8:18-19): He attempts to purchase the power to bestow the Holy Spirit to new converts from Peter and John.

5. *The punishment of Simon* (8:20-23): Peter warns Simon that he is being controlled by Satan!

6. *The plea of Simon* (8:24-25): He begs Peter to pray for him.

I. ACTIVITIES IN THE LIFE OF SAUL (9:1-31)
   A. **Saul's vendetta against the saints of God** (9:1-2)
      1. *His hatred for the Jerusalem Christians* (9:1)
      2. *His hatred for the Damascus Christians* (9:2): Saul sets out to
         persecute believers in Damascus.
   B. **Saul's vision of the Son of God** (9:3-9)
      1. *The revelation* (9:3-6)
         a. What he sees (9:3): He sees a brilliant and blinding light
            from heaven.
         b. What he hears (9:4-6): Jesus says to him, "Why are you
            persecuting me?"
      2. *The results* (9:7-9): Saul's traveling companions lead him into
         Damascus blind, and he consumes neither food nor water for
         the next three days.
   C. **Saul's visitation by the servant of God** (9:10-25)
      1. *Events preceding this visit* (9:10-16): God appears to a believer
         in Damascus named Ananias.
         a. The revelation (9:10-12): God instructs Ananias to go and
            minister to Saul.
         b. The reluctance (9:13-14): Knowing Saul's evil past, Ananias
            is afraid to go.
         c. The reassurance (9:15-16): God assures Ananias that Saul is
            now a believer.
      2. *Events during this visit* (9:17-19): Ananias lays hands on Saul,
         with a twofold result.
         a. Saul is healed of his blindness (9:17a, 18a).
         b. Saul is filled with the Spirit (9:17b, 18b-19).
      3. *Events following this visit* (9:20-25)
         a. Saul's evangelism in Damascus (9:20-22): He preaches
            Christ in all the synagogues.
         b. Saul's escape from Damascus (9:23-25): Upon hearing of a
            plot against him, Saul leaves for Jerusalem.
   D. **Saul's validation by the statesman of God** (9:26-31)
      1. *The person* (9:26-27): The highly respected Barnabas reassures
         some fearful Jerusalem believers of Saul's sincerity.
      2. *The preaching* (9:28): Saul preaches the gospel in Jerusalem as
         he did in Damascus.
      3. *The plot* (9:29-31): After an attempt is made on Saul's life, he
         departs for his hometown of Tarsus.

II. ACTIVITIES IN THE LIFE OF PETER (9:32-43)
  A. **He restores a cripple at Lydda** (9:32-35).
    1. *Aeneas the helpless* (9:32-33): He is a paralytic who has been bedridden for eight years.
    2. *Aeneas the healed* (9:34-35): Peter raises him from his mat!
  B. **He raises a corpse at Joppa** (9:36-43).
    1. *The deeds of Dorcas* (9:36): This godly woman performed many wonderful works during her life.
    2. *The death of Dorcas* (9:37): She becomes ill and dies.
    3. *The deliverance of Dorcas* (9:38-43): Peter raises her up during her own funeral!

SECTION OUTLINE TEN (ACTS 10)

Peter receives a vision from God, telling him that the Good News is for Gentiles as well as Jews. He goes to the home of Cornelius, a Roman officer, and tells him about Christ. Cornelius and his family believe and are filled with the Holy Spirit.

I. CORNELIUS, RELIGIOUS SINNER IN CAESAREA (10:1-8)
  A. **His veneration for God** (10:1-2): Though unsaved, Cornelius does good works and seeks after God.
  B. **His visitation from God** (10:3-8)
    1. *The messenger* (10:3-4): God sends an angel to him.
    2. *The message* (10:5-8): Cornelius is told to send men to Joppa and fetch Simon Peter.

II. PETER, RELUCTANT SOULWINNER IN JOPPA (10:9-23)
  A. **The three visions upstairs** (10:9-17a): Peter receives a vision that is repeated three times.
    1. *The contents* (10:9-12): He sees a great canvas sheet descending from heaven, filled with all kinds of unclean animals.
    2. *The command* (10:13-16)
      a. God's order (10:13): "Kill and eat them."
      b. Peter's objection (10:14): "Never, Lord, I have never in all my life eaten anything forbidden by our Jewish laws."
      c. God's overrule (10:15-16): "If God says something is acceptable, don't say it isn't."
    3. *The confusion* (10:17a): Peter wonders what all this means.
  B. **The three visitors downstairs** (10:17b-23): Just then the men from Cornelius arrive and request that Peter accompany them to Caesarea.

III. CORNELIUS AND PETER, REDEEMED SAINTS IN CHRIST (10:24-48)
  A. **The conversation with Cornelius** (10:24-35)
    1. *The reception* (10:24-26): Cornelius attempts to worship Peter but is prohibited from doing so.

2. *The review* (10:27-33): Peter reviews the circumstances that have brought him to Caesarea.

3. *The realization* (10:34-35): Peter now understands the meaning of his vision—namely, that God doesn't show partiality.

B. **The clarification to Cornelius** (10:36-43): Peter preaches a sermon.

1. *He talks about the message of the gospel* (10:36-37): It is the good news of peace through Jesus Christ.

2. *He talks about the Messiah of the gospel* (10:38, 43).

3. *He talks about the ministers of the gospel* (10:39-42): Peter says he and the other apostles are eyewitnesses of Jesus' crucifixion and resurrection!

C. **The conversion of Cornelius** (10:44-48)

1. *The heavenly baptizer* (10:44-45): Upon Cornelius's belief in Jesus, the Holy Spirit falls upon him.

2. *The earthly baptizer* (10:46-48): Convinced that Cornelius and his family have received the Holy Spirit, Peter has them baptized.

SECTION OUTLINE ELEVEN (ACTS 11)

Some of the Jewish Christians in Jerusalem criticize Peter for associating with Gentiles. Peter explains that the Holy Spirit has come upon the Gentiles as well as the Jews. Saul and Barnabas preach in Antioch of Syria, with huge results.

I. PETER AND THE CRITICS AT JERUSALEM (11:1-18)

A. **The accusation** (11:1-3): Peter is criticized by some legalistic Jewish believers for fellowshipping with Cornelius and other Gentiles at Caesarea.

B. **The argument** (11:4-17)

1. *Peter reviews his case* (11:4-16): He tells them about his vision from God and his visit to Caesarea.

2. *Peter rests his case* (11:17): He says God has given the same Holy Spirit to those Gentiles as the Jewish believers had previously received.

C. **The acceptance** (11:18): Peter's critics believe him and offer praises to God for saving the Gentiles also.

II. BARNABAS AND THE CONVERTS AT ANTIOCH (11:19-30)

A. **The Christian assembly at Antioch** (11:19-21): A church begins to flourish in the city of Antioch.

B. **The Christian associates at Antioch** (11:22-30)

1. *Barnabas* (11:22-24): He is sent by the Jerusalem church to help the new church.

2. *Saul* (11:25-26): Barnabas brings Saul to Antioch from Tarsus to assist him.

3. *Agabus* (11:27-30): He is a prophet who issues a warning.
   a. The revelation (11:27-28): Agabus predicts that a great famine will soon strike the land of Israel.
   b. The response (11:29-30): Believers in Antioch decide to send relief to those Christians living in Judea.

SECTION OUTLINE TWELVE (ACTS 12)

King Herod Agrippa has the apostle James killed and Peter put in prison. The night before Peter's trial, an angel comes to the jail and frees him! Herod accepts worship from the people of Tyre and Sidon; God strikes him with a sickness, and he dies.

I. PETER'S DELIVERANCE (12:1-19a)
   A. The death of James (12:1-2): King Herod Agrippa has James killed with a sword.
   B. The deliverance of Peter (12:3-19a)
      1. *His success in escaping a prison* (12:3-11)
         a. Why his escape takes place (12:3-5): It is because the church of Jerusalem is praying that God will deliver him!
         b. When his escape takes place (12:6): It is on the eve of his trial.
         c. How his escape takes place (12:7-11): God sends an angel to loosen his chains and open the prison door.
      2. *His struggle in entering a house* (12:12-19a): Peter arrives at the home of John Mark's mother and knocks on the door.
         a. The problem (12:12-15)
            (1) The recognition by Rhoda (12:12-14): A servant girl recognizes Peter's voice and reports the news to the others.
            (2) The ridicule of Rhoda (12:15): She is accused of being out of her mind and then of having seen Peter's angel rather than Peter himself.
         b. The persistence (12:16-17): Peter continues to knock and finally is allowed entrance, to the utter astonishment of all.
         c. The punishment (12:18-19a): Herod Agrippa orders the execution of the soldiers who were guarding Peter.

II. HEROD AGRIPPA'S DEATH (12:19b-23): The people of Tyre and Sidon seek and receive an audience with Herod Agrippa.
   A. The reason for their meeting (12:19b-20): It is to resolve their differences with him for economic purposes.
   B. The results of this meeting (12:21-25)
      1. *The king's pride* (12:21-22): The arrogant ruler accepts the flattery of the crowd when they shout that he is a god and not a man.

2. *The king's punishment* (12:23): God's angel strikes Herod with a fatal sickness for his blasphemy.

III. THE GOSPEL'S DISPERSION (12:24-25): The Good News spreads rapidly, and many more become believers.

SECTION OUTLINE THIRTEEN (ACTS 13)

Saul sets out on the first great missionary journey, taking Barnabas with him to Antioch of Syria, Cyprus, Perga, and Antioch of Pisidia. Along the way, John Mark joins the team but later abandons the others. Saul changes his name to Paul.

I. PAUL AND BARNABAS IN ANTIOCH OF SYRIA (13:1-3)
   A. **They are chosen by the Spirit of God** (13:1-2): The Holy Spirit tells the Antioch leaders to set these men apart for special service.
   B. **They are commissioned by the church of God** (13:3): The prophets and teachers in the assembly lay hands on the two and send them on their way.

II. PAUL AND BARNABAS IN CYPRUS (13:4-12): John Mark joins the team.
   A. **The openness to God's Word** (13:4-7): Their message is well received throughout the island, especially by the governor, Sergius Paulus.
   B. **The opposition to God's Word** (13:8-11)
      1. *Elymas's blasphemy* (13:8): This false prophet and sorcerer (also called Bar-Jesus) attempts to prevent the governor from accepting Christ.
      2. *Elymas's blindness* (13:9-11): He is blinded by the judgment of God at the hand of Paul.
   C. **The obedience to God's Word** (13:12): The governor becomes a believer.

III. PAUL AND BARNABAS IN PERGA (13:13): John Mark abandons the team.

IV. PAUL AND BARNABAS IN ANTIOCH OF PISIDIA (13:14-52): Here Paul delivers two sermons.
   A. **First sermon** (13:14-43): It is a message concerning the Jewish Messiah.
      1. *The overview of the Messiah* (13:14-37)
         a. Historical preparation for his coming (13:14-23): Paul shows from the Old Testament how God prepared the nation from which Christ would come.
            (1) The selection of Israel (13:14-17a)
            (2) The deliverance from Egypt (13:17b)
            (3) The wilderness experience (13:18)
            (4) The conquest of Canaan (13:19)
            (5) The rule of the judges and kings (13:20-23)

      b. Homiletical preparation for his coming (13:24-25): John the Baptist served as Jesus' forerunner.

      c. Prophetical preparation for his coming (13:26-37)

        (1) Psalm 2:6-9 predicts God will honor the Messiah (13:26-33).

        (2) Isaiah 55:3 predicts God will fulfill in the Messiah the promises given to David (13:34).

        (3) Psalm 16:10 predicts God will not allow the body of the Messiah to see corruption (13:35-37).

  2. *The offer by this Messiah* (13:38-41)

      a. The repenting sinner is forgiven of sin (13:37-38a).

      b. The repenting sinner is declared righteous (13:38b-41).

  3. *The obedience to the Messiah* (13:42-43): Many of Paul's audience respond favorably to his message.

B. Second sermon (13:44-52)

  1. *Unbelieving Jews* (13:44-46, 50-52)

      a. They reject God (13:44-45, 50-52).

      b. God rejects them (13:46).

  2. *Believing Gentiles* (13:47-49)

      a. The foretelling (13:47): Paul says Isaiah predicted this (Isa. 49:6).

      b. The fulfilling (13:48-49): Many Gentiles accept Jesus.

SECTION OUTLINE FOURTEEN (ACTS 14)

Paul and Barnabas continue on their missionary journey.

I. PAUL AND BARNABAS IN ICONIUM (14:1-7)

  A. The conversions (14:1): A great number of both Jews and Gentiles respond to the gospel message.

  B. The confirmation (14:3): Paul and Barnabas spend considerable time here, discipling the new converts.

  C. The contrast (14:4): Paul's message divides the city in half, some receiving and others rejecting.

  D. The conspiracy (14:2, 5-7): The two apostles leave after discovering a plot by their enemies to stone them.

II. PAUL AND BARNABAS IN LYSTRA (14:8-20)

  A. The cripple (14:8): There is a man in Lystra who has never walked.

  B. The command (14:9-10): Paul orders him to stand up and walk, and he does.

  C. The confusion (14:11-14)

    1. *What the people assume* (14:11-12): The amazed crowd mistakes the two disciples for gods.

      a. They think Barnabas is Zeus (14:11-12a).

      b. They think Paul is Hermes (14:12b).

    2. *What the people attempt* (14:13-14): They prepare to offer sacrifices and worship the disciples.

D. The correction (14:15-18): A horrified Paul quickly stops this, pointing out the identity of the true God, for whom they are witnesses.

E. The conspiracy (14:19-20)

1. *The slander against Paul* (14:19a): Some Jews from Antioch and Iconium turn the crowds against the apostles.
2. *The stoning of Paul* (14:19b-20): Paul is dragged out of the city, stoned, and left for dead, but he gets up and actually walks back into the city!

III. PAUL AND BARNABAS IN DERBE (14:21): Again a large number respond to the gospel message.

IV. PAUL AND BARNABAS BACK IN LYSTRA, ICONIUM, AND ANTIOCH OF PISIDIA (14:22-25): The apostles now minister in a twofold way to the new converts in these cities.

A. They strengthen everyone in the churches (14:22).

B. They select elders for the churches (14:23-25).

V. PAUL AND BARNABAS BACK IN ANTIOCH OF SYRIA (14:26-28)

A. They report to their home church (14:26-27).

B. They remain (for a long time) in their home church (14:28).

SECTION OUTLINE FIFTEEN (ACTS 15)

A council is held in Jerusalem to determine whether Gentiles who become Christians must adhere to the old Jewish customs.

I. THE DEBATE IN JERUSALEM (15:1-34): A special council is called by the Jerusalem church.

A. The reason for this council meeting (15:1, 6): There is a disagreement concerning whether saved Gentile believers should be circumcised.

B. The reports during this council meeting (15:2-5, 7-18)

1. *The pro-circumcision advocates* (15:5): These men were Pharisees before they became Christians.
2. *The anti-circumcision advocates* (15:2-4, 7-18)
   a. Paul and Barnabas's defense (15:2-4, 12): They review how God saved many Gentiles apart from circumcision during their recent missionary journey.
   b. Peter's defense (15:7-11): He speaks of Cornelius's conversion and that of his Gentile household.
   c. James's defense (15:13-18): He reminds all present that the conversion of Gentiles was predicted by the Old Testament prophet Amos (Amos 9:11-12).

C. The resolution from this council (15:19-34)

1. *The decision* (15:19-21): James announces that saved Gentiles will not be forced into circumcision and will be encouraged to abstain only from a few activities.

a. Eating meat sacrificed to idols (15:20a)
b. Engaging in sexual immorality (15:20b)
c. Consuming blood (15:20c)
d. Eating the meat of strangled animals (15:20d)
2. *The delegates* (15:22-34): Godly representatives such as Silas and Barsabbas are commissioned to carry letters announcing the council's decision to the various churches.

II. THE DISAGREEMENT IN ANTIOCH (15:35-41): Paul and Barnabas have a sharp disagreement.
   A. **The reason for this disagreement** (15:35-38): Should John Mark accompany the team during the second missionary journey?
      1. *Barnabas says yes* (15:35-37).
      2. *Paul says no* (15:38).
   B. **The results of this disagreement** (15:39-41)
      1. *Barnabas and John Mark set sail for Cyprus* (15:39).
      2. *Paul and Silas leave for Asia Minor* (15:40-41).

SECTION OUTLINE SIXTEEN (ACTS 16)
Paul sets off on his second missionary journey, taking with him Silas and Timothy. Paul and Silas are imprisoned, but God sends an earthquake to loose their chains and open the prison door!

I. THE CIRCUMCISION AT LYSTRA (16:1-5)
   A. **The recipient** (16:3b): Paul circumcises Timothy, who now joins the team.
   B. **The reason** (16:1-3a): Paul does this so as not to offend the Jews, for Timothy's mother is a Jewess, but his father is a Gentile.
   C. **The results** (16:4-5): The expanded team preaches the gospel in surrounding areas with much success.

II. THE CALL AT TROAS (16:6-10)
   A. **The Spirit tells Paul not to go north or south** (16:6-8).
   B. **The Spirit tells Paul to go west** (16:9-10): Paul has a vision of a man from Macedonia pleading with him to come and help the Macedonians.

III. THE CONVERSIONS AT PHILIPPI (16:11-34): The gospel team wins two key people to Jesus and frees one person from a demon.
   A. **A businesswoman** (16:11-15)
      1. *The place* (16:11-13): It occurs at a prayer meeting beside a river.
      2. *The person* (16:14): She is Lydia, a merchant of expensive purple cloth.
      3. *The proof* (16:15): Lydia is baptized as a testimony of her newfound faith.

B. A slave girl (16:16-21)
   1. *The demon in this girl* (16:16-17)
      a. The money it produces through her (16:16): The demon enables the girl to tell fortunes, earning much money for the girl's masters.
      b. The message it proclaims through her (16:17): The demon pretends to agree with the message preached by Paul.
   2. *The deliverance of this girl* (16:18-23)
      a. The girl is set free (16:18): Paul commands the demon to leave her.
      b. The apostles are set upon (16:19-23): Paul and Silas are arrested, beaten, and imprisoned.
C. A prison guard (16:24-34)
   1. *His command* (16:24): He is ordered to secure the two prisoners or (most likely) forfeit his life.
   2. *His confusion* (16:25-26)
      a. Because of the singing of the prisoners (16:25): He hears Paul and Silas praising God.
      b. Because of the shaking of the prison (16:26): God sends an earthquake that frees all the inmates.
   3. *His consternation* (16:27-31)
      a. What he assumes (16:27): Believing the prisoners have escaped, he prepares to kill himself.
      b. What he asks (16:28-31): Being assured by Paul that no one has left the prison, he asks how to be saved!
   4. *His conversion* (16:32-33): Responding to Paul's answer, the jailer and his family are saved and baptized.
   5. *His celebration* (16:34): With great joy the new convert washes the wounds of the disciples and feeds them.

IV. THE CONSTERNATION AT THE JAILER'S HOUSE (16:35-40)
   A. The authorities' fear (16:35-39): Upon learning that the men they have beaten and imprisoned are Roman citizens, the city officials apologize to Paul and Silas and beg them to leave the city.
   B. The apostles' freedom (16:40): Paul and Silas return to the home of Lydia to meet with other believers before leaving town.

SECTION OUTLINE SEVENTEEN (ACTS 17)
Paul and Silas continue on their missionary journey. Paul preaches a sermon in Athens.

I. PAUL AND SILAS IN THESSALONICA (17:1-9)
   A. The faithfulness of the missionaries (17:1-3): For three Sabbaths in a row, Paul preaches the crucifixion and resurrection of Christ in the Jewish synagogues.
   B. The fruits of the missionaries (17:4): Some Jews and many Gentile men and women are saved.

C. The foes of the missionaries (17:5-9)
  1. *The assault* (17:5): A mob rushes into Jason's house, where Paul and Silas are staying, in search of the missionaries.
  2. *The arrest* (17:6a): Unable to find Paul and Silas, the mob drags Jason before the city council.
  3. *The accusations* (17:6b-9)
    a. Paul and Silas are charged with troublemaking, and Jason is charged with allowing them to stay in his home (17:6b-7a).
    b. Paul and Silas are charged with treason (17:7b-9): "They profess allegiance to another king, Jesus."

II. PAUL AND SILAS IN BEREA (17:10-15)
  A. The openness to God's Word (17:10-12)
    1. *The Bereans research it* (17:10-11): They listen eagerly and check the Scriptures.
    2. *The Bereans receive it* (17:12): Many Jews believe, as do some of the Greek men and women.
  B. The opposition to God's Word (17:13-15)
    1. *The demonstration against Paul* (17:13): Some Jews from Thessalonica come to Berea and instigate a riot.
    2. *The departure of Paul* (17:14-15): He leaves for Athens.

III. PAUL (ONLY) IN ATHENS (17:16-34): On Mars Hill, Paul preaches his most famous sermon, identifying the Lord as the "unknown God" the Atheneans have been worshiping.
  A. The need for this sermon (17:16-17): The entire city is filled with idols.
  B. The audience for this sermon (17:18-21)
    1. *Their identity* (17:18a): The crowd consists of two philosophical groups, the Epicureans and the Stoics.
    2. *Their insults* (17:18b): They accuse Paul of babbling or advocating some strange foreign religion when he speaks of Jesus' resurrection.
    3. *Their idleness* (17:21): They spend all their time in useless discussion about the latest ideas.
    4. *Their invitation* (17:19-20): To their credit, however, Paul is invited to address them.
  C. The introduction to this sermon (17:22-23)
    1. *Paul's observation* (17:22-23a): "I notice that you are very religious, for as I was walking along I saw your many altars. And one of them had this inscription on it—'To an Unknown God.'"
    2. *Paul's revelation* (17:23b): "You have been worshiping him without knowing who he is, and now I wish to tell you about him."
  D. The points in this sermon (17:24-31): Paul reviews the works of the true God in the past, present, and future.
    1. *Regarding the past* (17:24-26, 28-29): He created all things, as testified by:

a. The Hebrew account (17:24-26): He is the maker of everything.
b. Their own account (17:28-29): One of their own poets said,
"We are his offspring."
2. *Regarding the present* (17:27, 30): He desires to save people if
they will do two things:
a. Reach out (17:27): He wants people to seek after him.
b. Repent (17:30): They are to turn from idols and turn to him.
3. *Regarding the future* (17:31): God will someday judge the
world through Jesus Christ, whom he raised from the dead.
E. **The reaction to this sermon** (17:32-34)
1. *Some mock* (17:32a).
2. *Some delay* (17:32b): They want to hear more later.
3. *Some believe* (17:33-34).

SECTION OUTLINE EIGHTEEN (ACTS 18)

Paul meets Priscilla and Aquila in Corinth and receives a vision in
which God tells him not to be afraid of his enemies. Priscilla and
Aquila instruct Apollos at Ephesus.

I. THE ACTIVITIES OF PAUL (18:1-23)
A. **Paul in Corinth** (18:1-17)
1. *The apostle's friends in this city* (18:1-3): Paul meets Aquila
and Priscilla, who are tentmakers like he is.
2. *The apostle's faithfulness in this city* (18:4-5): He continually
preaches the gospel to Jews and Gentiles.
3. *The apostle's foes in this city* (18:6, 12-17)
a. The unbelieving Jews abuse him (18:6).
b. The unbelieving Jews arrest him (18:12).
c. The unbelieving Jews accuse him (18:13-17): They bring
him before the Roman governor Gallio and charge Paul
with blasphemy, but Gallio refuses to try the case.
4. *The apostle's fruit in this city* (18:7-8): Many are saved,
including Crispus, the leader of the Jewish synagogue.
5. *The apostle's heavenly Father in this city* (18:9-11): God
himself reassures Paul in a vision: "Don't be afraid! Keep
preaching, for I have many people in this city!"
B. **Paul in Cenchrea** (18:18): Here he shaves his head and takes a
vow.
C. **Paul in Ephesus** (18:19-21): The apostle's stay here is short, for
he plans to observe a special feast soon to be celebrated in Jerusalem.
D. **Paul in Antioch of Syria** (18:22): No doubt he gives a report here
at his home church.
E. **Paul in Galatia** (18:23): He begins his third missionary journey.

II. THE ACTIVITIES OF APOLLOS (18:24-28)
  A. **Apollos in Ephesus** (18:24-26)
    1. *Who he is* (18:24): Apollos is an anointed Bible preacher from Alexandria in Egypt.
    2. *What he knows* (18:25-26)
      a. The incomplete account (18:25): He knows only what John the Baptist said about Jesus.
      b. The complete account (18:26): After hearing Apollos's preaching, Aquila and Priscilla fill him in with all the facts.
  B. **Apollos in Greece** (18:27-28): Here he is greatly used by God in strengthening the churches.

SECTION OUTLINE NINETEEN (ACTS 19)

Paul's third missionary journey takes him to Ephesus, where he preaches and performs many miracles. A riot develops in the city when Paul crosses some idol makers, but the mayor is able to quell the uproar.

I. THE DISCIPLES OF JOHN (19:1-7): Paul meets twelve former disciples of John the Baptist.
  A. **What he asks them** (19:1-2a): "Did you receive the Holy Spirit when you believed?"
  B. **How they answer him** (19:2b-7)
    1. *The confusion* (19:2b): They have never heard of the Holy Spirit.
    2. *The clarification* (19:3-4): Paul brings them up to date concerning Jesus' ministry.
    3. *The conversions* (19:5-7): When they are baptized in the name of Jesus, they receive the Holy Spirit.

II. THE DECLARATION OF THE GOSPEL (19:8-10)
  A. **The first three months** (19:8): Paul preaches the Good News boldly each Sabbath in the synagogue.
  B. **The final two years** (19:9-10): Due to open hostility, he moves to the public hall of Tyrannus and preaches daily.

III. THE DISTRIBUTION OF PRAYER CLOTHS (19:11-12): God so anoints Paul that even a handkerchief of cloth that has touched Paul's skin brings about healing when placed on the sick.

IV. THE DIVINATIONS OF SCEVA'S SONS (19:13-17)
  A. **The presumption** (19:13-14): Seven brothers attempt to cast out a demon, using the name of Jesus as a magical incantation.
  B. **The penalty** (19:15-17): The demon comes out but then jumps on them, beating them severely.

V. THE DEDICATION OF NEW CONVERTS (19:18-20)
   A. Who they are (19:18): These new believers have been brought
   out of the occult through Paul's preaching.
   B. What they do (19:19-20): They burn their books on black magic.

VI. THE DECISION OF PAUL (19:21-22): The apostle vows to visit Rome in
the near future.

VII. THE DEFENDERS OF ARTEMIS (19:23-41): A riot breaks out in Ephesus.
   A. The lecture of Demetrius (19:23-27)
      1. *Demetrius the tradesman* (19:23-24): He employs many
         craftsmen to make silver shrines of the Greek goddess Artemis.
      2. *Demetrius the troublemaker* (19:25-27): He calls his associates
         together and lectures them concerning how Paul's preaching
         is harming to their business.
   B. The lunacy of the crowd (19:28-34): Demetrius's fiery speech
   incites mob action against Paul and his associates.
      1. *The cry of the mob* (19:28-31): They meet in the city
         amphitheater and for two hours cry out, "Great is Artemis of
         the Ephesians!"
      2. *The confusion of the mob* (19:32-34): Many simply rush there
         without even knowing why.
   C. The logic of the mayor (19:35-41): This intelligent Greek official
   calms down the mob through four logical arguments.
      1. *The divinity of the statue* (19:35-36): All the world knows that
         Ephesus is the official guardian of the image of the goddess
         Artemis, which he says fell down to them from heaven.
      2. *The honesty of the opponents* (19:37): The apostles have
         neither said nor done any punishable thing.
      3. *The legality of the matter* (19:38-39): Demetrius should pursue
         any and all grievances through the court system.
      4. *The (possible) penalty of the uprising* (19:40-41): Unless the
         mob disperses, the Roman officials may well intervene.

SECTION OUTLINE TWENTY (ACTS 20)
Paul travels to Troas, where a young man named Eutychus falls
asleep during one of Paul's sermons and tumbles out of a third-
story window to his death, but Paul brings him back to life
and then continues his sermon!

I. PAUL IN GREECE (20:1-3)
   A. The time (20:1-3a): He spends three months there.
   B. The treachery (20:3b): There is a plot by the Jews against his life.

II. PAUL EN ROUTE TO TROAS (20:4-6): He is accompanied by seven
associates, including Timothy.

III. PAUL IN TROAS (20:7-12)
   A. **The midnight message** (20:7): Paul preaches until midnight.
   B. **The mishap** (20:8-9): A young man in attendance named
      Eutychus accidentally falls to his death from an upper window.
   C. **The miracle** (20:10-12): Paul raises him from the dead.

IV. PAUL EN ROUTE TO MILETUS (20:13-16): The apostle is hurrying to
   Jerusalem for the celebration of Pentecost.

V. PAUL IN MILETUS (20:17-38): The apostle shares his heart with a
   group of select men.
   A. **The participants** (20:17): Paul sends for the Ephesian elders to
      join him at Miletus.
   B. **The perspective** (20:18-35): Paul summarizes the gospel ministry
      in a threefold manner.
      1. *He reviews the past* (20:18-21, 26-27, 31, 33-35)
         a. Paul reminds them of his uncompromising ministry
            (20:18-21, 31): For three years he fearlessly, faithfully, and
            tearfully preached Christ among them.
         b. Paul reminds them of his faithful ministry (26:26-27): He
            has always been faithful in declaring God's Word, so no
            one's damnation can be blamed on him.
         c. Paul reminds them of his unselfish ministry (20:33-35).
            (1) What he does (20:33-35a): He fully supports himself,
               taking money from no one.
            (2) Why he does it (20:35b): He remembers—and
               challenges them to remember—Jesus' words: "It is
               more blessed to give than to receive!"
      2. *He overviews the present* (20:22-25, 28, 32)
         a. Paul explains (20:22-25): This will be their final meeting,
            for he will face difficult times ahead.
         b. Paul exhorts (20:28, 32)
            (1) "Feed and shepherd God's flock" (20:28).
            (2) "I entrust to you God and the word of his grace" (20:32).
      3. *He previews the future* (20:29-30): Paul warns them to watch
         out for false teachers in the church.
         a. The iniquity of these men (20:29): They will be like vicious
            wolves, not sparing the flock.
         b. The identity of these men (20:30): They will come from the
            leadership of the church itself.
   C. **The prayer** (20:36-38): When Paul finishes speaking, he kneels
      and prays for them. After a tearful farewell, he departs for Jerusa-
      lem.

SECTION OUTLINE TWENTY-ONE (ACTS 21)
Paul travels to Jerusalem despite prophecies that he will be
imprisoned and despite his friends' pleading with him not to
endanger his life by going. Sure enough, in Jerusalem Paul is
arrested and brought before the city's Roman commander.

I. PAUL EN ROUTE TO TYRE (21:1-3)

II. PAUL IN TYRE (21:4-6)
   A. **The week** (21:4a): He stays seven days with some believers.
   B. **The warning** (21:4b-6): The Holy Spirit warns Paul through these
      believers that trouble awaits him in Jerusalem.

III. PAUL IN PTOLEMAIS (21:7): He is here for one day only.

IV. PAUL IN CAESAREA (21:8-15)
   A. **The warrior of God** (21:8): Paul visits with Philip the evangelist,
      one of the seven deacons.
   B. **The women of God** (21:9): Philip has four unmarried daughters
      who have the gift of prophecy.
   C. **The warning from God** (21:10-12)
      1. *The prophet* (21:10-11): God speaks though Agabus, warning
         Paul of his arrest and imprisonment in Jerusalem.
      2. *The plea* (21:12): Paul's traveling companions and the
         believers at Caesarea beg him not to go to Jerusalem.
   D. **The will of God** (21:13-15): Realizing Paul is determined to
      visit Jerusalem, the believers declare: "The will of the Lord be
      done!"

V. PAUL IN JERUSALEM (21:16-40)
   A. **The report** (21:16-19): Upon arriving Paul reviews for James and
      the Jerusalem elders the many things God has done among the
      Gentiles through his work.
   B. **The rumor** (21:20-26)
      1. *The slander* (21:20-22): Paul learns he is being accused of
         being against the laws of Moses and forbidding the ceremony
         of circumcision.
      2. *The suggestion* (21:23-26): To counteract this, Paul is advised to
         shave his head and take a vow in the Temple, and he agrees.
   C. **The reprobation** (21:27-29): An angry Jewish mob attacks Paul
      in the Temple, believing that he is guilty of two blasphemous
      acts:
      1. *That he advocated disobedience to the law of God* (21:27)
      2. *That he brought a Gentile into the Temple of God* (21:28-29)
   D. **The riot** (21:30-31): They take Paul outside the city gate and try
      to kill him.
   E. **The rescue** (21:32-36): Paul is saved from certain death by the
      commander of the Roman garrison stationed in Jerusalem.

F. The request (21:37-40): After correcting the Roman commander's mistaken notion that Paul is a former Egyptian rebel, Paul
asks and receives permission to address the angry crowd.

SECTION OUTLINE TWENTY-TWO (ACTS 22)

Paul addresses the angry crowd but fails to placate them. The
Roman commander gives orders to have Paul whipped but with-
draws the order when he learns that Paul is a Roman citizen.

I. PAUL STANDS BEFORE AN ANGRY MOB (22:1-21)
   A. He speaks concerning his pre-conversion (22:1-5, 20).
      1. *His background* (22:1-3)
         a. He was born in Tarsus (22:1-3a).
         b. He was trained by Gamaliel (22:3b).
         c. He was zealous for God (22:3c).
      2. *His bias* (22:4-5, 20): He hated and hounded Jerusalem
         Christians (including agreeing with the stoning of Stephen) and
         was en route to Damascus for the same purpose!
   B. He speaks concerning his conversion (22:6-16).
      1. *His vision of the Son of God (22:6-11)*
         a. The revelation (22:6-10)
            (1) What he saw (22:6): Near Damascus he saw a blinding
               light from heaven.
            (2) What he heard (22:7-10): Jesus gave him a twofold
               message.
               (a) "Why are you persecuting me?" (22:7).
               (b) "Go into Damascus, and there you will be told all
                  that you are to do" (22:8-10).
         b. The results (22:11): He was led into the city blind.
      2. *His visit by the servant of God* (22:12-16): A godly believer
         named Ananias ministered to the sightless Paul.
   C. He speaks concerning his post-conversion (22:17-19, 21).
      1. *How God saved him from the Jews* (22:17-19)
      2. *How God sent him to the Gentiles* (22:21)

II. PAUL STANDS BEFORE THE ROMAN MILITARY (22:22-29)
   A. The anarchy of the crowd (22:22-23): Again the mob turns violent and attempts to kill Paul, forcing the soldiers to secure him
   in their barracks.
   B. The action of the commander (22:24-29)
      1. *The command* (22:24): He orders the apostle whipped, hoping
         Paul will reveal why the crowd hates him so much.
      2. *The countermand* (22:25-29): He quickly repeals the order
         upon learning of Paul's Roman citizenship.

III. PAUL STANDS BEFORE THE JEWISH SANHEDRIN (22:30): The apostle is
   given the opportunity to testify before these leaders.

SECTION OUTLINE TWENTY-THREE (ACTS 23)
Paul speaks to the high council. He wisely turns their attention away from him by referring to the resurrection, which the Pharisees espouse and the Sadducees deny. The Lord appears to Paul and tells him to go to Rome. A plot against Paul's life is thwarted by his nephew.

I. THE COUNCIL (23:1-10): Paul stands before the Jewish Sanhedrin.
   A. **The assault** (23:1-2): After greeting the council members, Paul is struck on the mouth by order of the high priest.
   B. **The anger** (23:3): Not knowing his tormentor's identity, Paul says, "God will slap you, you whitewashed wall!"
   C. **The apology** (23:4-5): Upon learning it is the high priest, Paul apologizes.
   D. **The argument** (23:6-10): A dispute breaks out between the Sadducees and Pharisees.
      1. *The reason for this argument* (23:6-8): Paul boasts of being a Pharisee, knowing this group disagrees with the Sadducees over three issues—the fact of the resurrection, the existence of angels, and the existence of spirits.
         a. The Pharisees believe all three (23:6-7, 8b).
         b. The Sadducees deny all three (23:8a).
      2. *The results of this argument* (23:9-10): It becomes so violent that Paul has to be removed by the soldiers for his own protection.

II. THE COMFORT (23:11)
   A. **The Lord appears to Paul that night** (23:11a).
   B. **The Lord speaks to Paul that night** (23:11b): "Be encouraged, Paul. Just as you have told the people about me here in Jerusalem, you must preach the Good News in Rome."

III. THE CONSPIRACY (23:12-24)
   A. **The reprisal against Paul** (23:12-15): More than 40 men vow not to eat or drink until they kill Paul.
   B. **The relative of Paul** (23:16-22): The son of Paul's sister hears of the plot and reports it to the apostle and the Roman commander.
   C. **The removal of Paul** (23:23-24): A detachment of 470 soldiers prepares to transport Paul from Jerusalem to Caesarea.

IV. THE COMMUNICATION (23:25-30): Claudius Lysias, the Roman commander, writes a letter to Governor Felix in Caesarea, explaining why Paul is being sent.

V. THE CONFINEMENT (23:31-35): In Caesarea Paul is kept in the prison at Herod's palace.

SECTION OUTLINE TWENTY-FOUR (ACTS 24)
The Roman governor Felix interrogates Paul, then keeps him in prison for two years.

I. FELIX REVIEWS THE CHARGES AGAINST PAUL (24:1-23)
   A. **The defamation by the prosecution** (24:1-9): The Jewish high priest comes to Caesarea from Jerusalem accompanied by a Jewish lawyer named Tertullus, who levels three charges against Paul:
      1. *He is a political rebel* (24:1-5a).
      2. *He is a ringleader of the Nazarene sect* (24:5b).
      3. *He is a Temple defiler* (24:6-9).
   B. **The defense by the prisoner** (24:10-21): Paul responds:
      1. *He denies charges one and three* (24:10-13, 15-20).
      2. *He affirms charge number two* (24:14, 21).
   C. **The deference by the politician** (24:22-23): Not willing to offend the high priest, Felix promises to render a verdict at a later date.

II. FELIX REFUSES THE CHRIST OF PAUL (24:24-25): Both the governor and his wife, Drusilla, hear Paul in a private meeting.
   A. **Paul's theme** (24:24-25a): He speaks on righteousness and future judgment.
   B. **Felix's terror** (24:25b): The fearful governor responds, "Go away for now. When it is more convenient I'll call for you again."

III. FELIX REQUESTS SOME CASH FROM PAUL (24:26-27): For the next two years, Felix continually visits the imprisoned Paul, hoping (in vain) to receive bribe money.

SECTION OUTLINE TWENTY-FIVE (ACTS 25)
Paul testifies before Porcius Festus, who is Governor Felix's replacement, and Herod Agrippa.

I. FESTUS AND PAUL (25:1-12)
   A. **The governor and the plotters** (25:1-5)
      1. *Their request* (25:1-3): Jewish leaders ask Festus to bring Paul on his visit to Jerusalem, for they plan to kill him en route.
      2. *His refusal* (25:4-5): Festus declines, saying Paul will remain in Caesarea for his trial.
   B. **The governor and the prisoner** (25:6-12)
      1. *The accusations* (25:6-7): The Jewish leaders bring many charges against Paul but can't prove any of them.
      2. *The answer* (25:8): Paul pleads innocent to all these charges.
      3. *The appeasement* (25:9): Anxious to please the Jews, Festus asks Paul to continue his trial in Jerusalem.
      4. *The appeal* (25:10-12): Paul refuses and appeals to Caesar, and his request is granted.

II. FESTUS AND AGRIPPA (25:13-27)
A. **The information about Paul** (25:13-22): Festus tells the visiting monarch about this famous political prisoner.
1. *The review by Festus* (25:13-21)
    a. He talks about Paul's accusers (25:13-19).
    b. He talks about Paul's appeal (25:20-21).
2. *The request by Agrippa* (25:22): The king desires to meet Paul.
B. **The introduction of Paul** (25:23-27): Festus has Paul brought in to stand before the king.

SECTION OUTLINE TWENTY-SIX (ACTS 26)
Paul speaks to King Agrippa.

I. THE PERMISSION (26:1): Agrippa invites Paul to tell his story.

II. THE PERSONAL TESTIMONY (26:2-23)
A. **Paul reviews his life as a religious man** (26:2-11).
1. *His activities as a Pharisee* (26:2-8): From birth he was very zealous in this strict Jewish sect.
2. *His activities as a persecutor* (26:9-11): He hated and hounded Christians.
B. **Paul reviews his life as a redeemed man** (26:12-23).
1. *He speaks of his conversion* (26:12-14): It occurred on the road to Damascus when Jesus himself appeared.
2. *He speaks of his commission* (26:15-18): God appointed him to preach repentance and forgiveness of sin to the Gentiles.
3. *He speaks of his consistency* (26:19-23): In spite of terrible persecution, Paul faithfully obeyed the message of his heavenly vision.

III. THE PROTEST (26:24-25)
A. **Festus's accusation** (26:24): The governor interrupts Paul, accusing him of insanity.
B. **Paul's answer** (26:25): The apostle assures Festus he is speaking only the "sober truth."

IV. THE PERSUASION (26:26-29)
A. **Paul to Agrippa** (26:26-27): "Do you believe the prophets? I know you do."
B. **Agrippa to Paul** (26:28): "Do you think you can make me a Christian so quickly?"
C. **Paul to Agrippa** (26:29): "I pray to God that both you and everyone here in this audience might become as I am, except for these chains."

V. THE POSTSCRIPT (26:30-32): After the meeting Agrippa and Festus agree that Paul could be set free had he not appealed to Caesar.

SECTION OUTLINE TWENTY-SEVEN (ACTS 27)
Paul is shipwrecked en route to Rome.

I. PHASE ONE: FROM CAESAREA TO SIDON (27:1-3)
  A. **The command given to Julius the centurion** (27:1-2): Paul and some other prisoners are handed over to him.
  B. **The compassion shown by Julius the centurion** (27:3): Paul is treated very kindly by Julius and is allowed to visit his friends at Sidon.

II. PHASE TWO: FROM SIDON TO MYRA (27:4-6): The prisoners are transferred to an Egyptian ship headed for Italy.

III. PHASE THREE: FROM MYRA TO FAIR HAVENS (27:7-12): Paul warns the centurion not to continue the voyage.
  A. **The reason for Paul's warning** (27:7-10): He knows it is the season for storms on the Mediterranean.
  B. **The rejection of Paul's warning** (27:11-12): The ship's captain and owner determine that the voyage will continue.

IV. PHASE FOUR: FROM FAIR HAVENS TO MALTA (27:13-44)
  A. **The fearful storm** (27:13-20)
    1. *The name for this storm* (27:13-14): It is called a "northeaster" and refers to a treacherous wind of typhoon strength.
    2. *The nature of this storm* (27:15-20): The wind is so strong and the waves so high that eventually all hope for survival is gone.
  B. **The cheerful saint** (27:21-44): Paul stands before the terrified passengers, assuring them concerning what God had told him on the previous night:
    1. *The foretelling* (27:21-38)
      a. God says they will all be shipwrecked on an island (27:21-32).
      b. God says not one person will lose his life, so all should eat and take courage (27:33-38).
    2. *The fulfilling* (27:39-44)
      a. Shipwreck (27:39-44a)
        (1) The ship runs aground and begins to fall apart (27:39-41).
        (2) The soldiers want to kill the prisoners to make sure none of them escape, but the commanding officer forbids it in order to save Paul's life (27:42-44a).
      b. Safety (27:44b): All make it safely to shore.

I. PAUL AT MALTA (28:1-10)
  A. **The apostle and the people on the island** (28:1-6)
    1. *They first look on him as a murderer* (28:1-4).
      a. The crisis (28:1-3): Paul is bitten by a poisonous snake.
      b. The conclusion (28:4): The people say, "A murderer, no
         doubt! Though he escaped the sea, justice will not permit
         him to live."
    2. *They finally look on him as a god* (28:5-6): When nothing
       happens to the apostle, they conclude that he is a god of some
       sort.
  B. **The apostle and the politician on the island** (28:7-10): Paul
     meets the governor, Publius.
    1. *Paul heals Publius's father* (28:7-8): He is delivered from fever
       and dysentery.
    2. *Paul heals Publius's people* (28:9-10): Soon the other sick
       people on the island come and are also healed.

II. PAUL EN ROUTE TO ROME (28:11-14): Paul's ship makes three brief
    stops on the way to Rome. Paul is encouraged when some fellow
    believers meet him at one of the ports.

III. PAUL IN ROME (28:15-31)
  A. **Where** (28:15-16): Paul is allowed to live by himself with a sol-
     dier to guard him.
  B. **Who** (28:17-29): Paul schedules two separate meetings with the
     Jewish leaders living in Rome.
    1. *First meeting* (28:17-22)
      a. His review (28:17-20): Paul introduces himself and the
         message of the Cross.
      b. Their reaction (28:21-22): They have never heard of the
         messenger or his message but want to hear more.
    2. *Second meeting* (28:23-29)
      a. The revelation (28:23): Many people come to hear Paul
         speak about Jesus from the Old Testament Scriptures, and
         Paul teaches from morning till evening.
      b. The responses (28:24): Some believe, and some do not.
      c. The reminder (28:25-29): Paul reminds them that their
         unbelief was predicted by the Old Testament prophet
         Isaiah (Isa. 6:9-10).
  C. **When** (28:30-31): For the next two years, Paul remains in his
     rented house, under guard, witnessing to all who visit him.

PART SEVEN

Letters

Romans

SECTION OUTLINE ONE (ROMANS 1)

Paul opens his letter to the Roman church by talking about God's anger with sin. The opening chapter may be thought of as a trial, where God is the judge and sinful humans are the accused.

I. THE COURT RECORDER (1:1-17): Here Paul, author of Romans, provides his readers with some pretrial introductory material.
   A. **His credentials** (1:1, 5): Paul relates four facts about himself.
      1. *He is a servant of Jesus* (1:1a).
      2. *He is an apostle* (1:1b).
      3. *He has been set apart to preach the gospel* (1:1c).
      4. *He is a missionary to the Gentiles* (1:5).
   B. **His Christ** (1:2-4)
      1. *The Messiah was prophesied in the Old Testament* (1:2).
      2. *The Messiah is now proclaimed in the New Testament* (1:3-4).
         a. In regard to his human nature (1:3): He is a descendant of David.
         b. In regard to his divine nature (1:4): His resurrection proves his deity.
   C. **His congregation** (1:6-15): Paul writes this epistle to a local church assembly.
      1. *The identity of this church* (1:6-7): It is the congregation in Rome.
      2. *The intercession for this church* (1:8-10)
         a. His praise of them (1:8): Paul praises them for their universally known faith.
         b. His prayers for them (1:9-10): He prays for the church and asks God that he be allowed to visit them.
      3. *The interest in this church* (1:11-13)
         a. Paul desires to see them (1:11-12).
         b. Paul desires to serve them (1:13): He desires to sow seed among them.
      4. *The indebtedness to the church* (1:14-15): Paul feels an obligation to minister to them.

D. His confidence (1:16-17): Paul expresses his full assurance in the power of the gospel to accomplish two things.

1. *To bring about saving faith for sinners* (1:16): Through faith a sinner may be saved.
2. *To bring about sanctifying faith for saints* (1:17): Through faith a righteous person may have life.

II. THE COURT RECORD (1:18-32): Paul records the evidence presented at this trial.

A. The general charge (1:18-19): "God shows his anger from heaven against all sinful, wicked people who push the truth away from themselves. For the truth about God is known to them instinctively."

B. The specific charges (1:20-32)

1. *First indictment—inexcusable ignorance* (1:20): God has always revealed his existence and power to mankind.
2. *Second indictment—ingratitude* (1:21): People are thankless, refusing to worship their Creator.
3. *Third indictment—insolence* (1:22): Claiming themselves to be wise without God, they become fools instead.
4. *Fourth indictment—idolatry* (1:23): They exchange God's glory for idols resembling mere people, birds, animals, and snakes.
5. *Fifth indictment—immorality* (1:24-27): They are guilty of lesbianism and homosexuality.
6. *Sixth indictment—incorrigibility* (1:28-32)
   a. They embrace their wicked deeds (1:28-31).
   b. They endorse their wicked deeds (1:32).

SECTION OUTLINE TWO (ROMANS 2)

Paul describes God's dealings with three kinds of people. Each is charged with high treason against God.

I. THE MORAL PERSON AND GOD (2:1-11)

A. The plea rendered (2:1a): The moral person says, "I should be acquitted on grounds that I am not as bad as some pagans are."

B. The plea refuted (2:1b-11)

1. *The reason for this* (2:1b-4): God says, "You do the same basic things, only in a more refined way!"
2. *The results of this* (2:5-11)
   a. To be the object of God's terrible wrath (2:5-8)
   b. To experience sorrow and suffering (2:9-11)

II. THE PAGAN PERSON AND GOD (2:12-16)

A. The plea rendered (2:12-13): The pagan person says, "I should be acquitted on the grounds of ignorance!"

B. The plea refuted (2:14-16): God says, "You have the twin witnesses of conscience and nature (see also 1:19-20). Therefore, you will be judged by these and not by the written law."

III. THE RELIGIOUS PERSON AND GOD (2:17-29)
   A. **The plea rendered** (2:17-20): The religious man says, "I should be acquitted on the grounds that I know the law of God and teach courses in religion!"
   B. **The plea refuted** (2:21-29): God says, "You don't practice what you preach!"
       1. *The marks of religious Jews* (2:21-24): Because of their hypocrisy, they dishonor God's holy name among the Gentiles.
       2. *The marks of redeemed Jews* (2:25-29): Their hearts are right with God.

SECTION OUTLINE THREE (ROMANS 3)
Paul presents six questions and answers them for his readers.

   I. FIRST QUESTION AND ANSWER (3:1-2)
   A. **Question** (3:1): What are the advantages of being a Jew or of being circumcised?
   B. **Answer** (3:2): The most important advantage is that Israel has been entrusted with the Word of God.

   II. SECOND QUESTION AND ANSWER (3:3-4)
   A. **Question** (3:3): Will Israel's unfaithfulness nullify God's promises?
   B. **Answer** (3:4)
       1. *Paul's testimony* (3:4a): "Of course not! Though everyone else in the world is a liar, God is true."
       2. *David's testimony* (3:4b): Paul quotes from Psalm 51:4 to prove his point.

   III. THIRD QUESTION AND ANSWER (3:5-8)
   A. **Question** (3:5): If our unrighteousness brings out God's righteousness, isn't he unfair to punish us?
   B. **Answer** (3:6-8)
       1. *The reprobation* (3:8b): Paul has been falsely accused of teaching this very thing—that is, do evil that good may result.
       2. *The reply* (3:6-8a): Paul responds, "If you follow that kind of thinking . . . you might as well say that the more we sin the better it is! Those who say such things deserve to be condemned."

   IV. FOURTH QUESTION AND ANSWER (3:9-20)
   A. **Question** (3:9a): Are the Jews better than all other people?
   B. **Answer** (3:9b-20)
       1. *The corruption* (3:10-18): Paul describes the cancer of sin that has infected the human race.

a. Human conscience is depraved (3:10-11): No one even desires to know and follow God.
b. Human character is depraved (3:12): All have left the path of good and have became worthless.
c. Human conversation is depraved (3:13-14): People's talk is foul and filthy, resembling:
   (1) The stench from an open grave (3:13a)
   (2) The poison from a deadly snake (3:13b-14)
d. Human conduct is depraved (3:15-18).
   (1) "They are quick to commit murder" (3:15-17).
   (2) "They have no fear of God" (3:18).
2. *The conclusion* (3:9, 19-20): After presenting all the terrible facts, Paul reaches this twofold conclusion:
   a. Both Jew and Gentile have sinned against God (3:9).
   b. Both Jew and Gentile stand accused before God (3:19-20).

V. FIFTH QUESTION AND ANSWER (3:21-30)
   A. Question (3:21a): How then does God save people?
   B. Answer (3:21b-30)
   1. *The need for salvation* (3:23): It is desperately needed, for all have sinned and fallen short of God's glory.
   2. *The Old Testament witness to salvation* (3:21b): The Scriptures promise salvation apart from the law.
   3. *The method of salvation* (3:22, 24-25, 27-28)
      a. Negative (3:27-28): It is not accomplished by good works.
      b. Positive (3:22, 24-25): It comes about by grace through faith in the sacrifice of Christ.
   4. *The legal accomplishment of salvation* (3:26): It permits a just and holy God to declare repenting sinners righteous.
   5. *The scope of salvation* (3:29-30): It is available for both Jews and Gentiles alike.

VI. SIXTH QUESTION AND ANSWER (3:31)
    A. Question (3:31a): Does faith nullify the law?
    B. Answer (3:31b): To the contrary, faith fulfills the law!

SECTION OUTLINE FOUR (ROMANS 4)
Paul employs two of the most famous Old Testament men to illustrate the doctrine of justification by faith.

I. THE ILLUSTRATION FROM THE LIFE OF ABRAHAM, ISRAEL'S RACIAL FATHER (4:1-5, 9-25)
   A. Abraham and his salvation (4:1-5, 9-15)
   1. *What Abraham received* (4:1-5): God himself canceled Abraham's sins and declared him righteous.
   2. *How Abraham received it* (4:1-5)
      a. It did not come about by his works (4:1-2, 4).

     b. It did come about by his faith (4:3, 5).
    3. *When Abraham received it* (4:9-15)
      a. He received it before he was circumcised (4:9-12).
      b. He received it before the giving of the law (4:13-15).
  B. Abraham and his seed (4:16-25): Paul shows the results of Abraham's faith following his salvation.
    1. *Abraham's physical seed* (4:18-22)
      a. The promise (4:18): God told Abraham he would bear a son through Sarah.
      b. The problem (4:19): Abraham and his barren wife were too old for this.
      c. The perseverance (4:20-22): Abraham continued to believe God for the impossible, and Isaac was born!
    2. *Abraham's spiritual seed* (4:16-17, 23-25): All Jews and Gentiles who exercise the kind of faith Abraham had are, spiritually speaking, related to Abraham, who is called the "father of all who believe."

II. THE ILLUSTRATION FROM THE LIFE OF DAVID, ISRAEL'S ROYAL FATHER (4:6-8)
  A. The transgressions of David (4:6): He was guilty of adultery and murder (see 2 Sam. 11:1-24).
  B. The testimony of David (4:7-8): The repentant king was forgiven, cleansed, and justified by faith.

SECTION OUTLINE FIVE (ROMANS 5)
Paul talks about the joy that comes from faith. He contrasts the sinful Adam with the sinless Christ.

I. A SUMMARY OF JUSTIFICATION (5:1-11): Paul lists five results of divine justification.
  A. The believer has peace with God (5:1): This is accomplished through the work done by Jesus Christ.
  B. The believer has access to God (5:2): This high privilege brings about great confidence and joy concerning the future.
  C. The believer has assurance from God (5:3-4).
    1. *The fact of this assurance* (5:3): It helps us in time of suffering.
    2. *The fruit of the assurance* (5:4): Suffering produces perseverance, which produces character, which produces hope.
  D. The believer is indwelt by God (5:5): The Holy Spirit lives in the hearts of believers.
  E. The believer is preserved in God (5:6-11): A believer's salvation is secure, guaranteed by:
    1. *Christ's past work on Calvary's cross* (5:6-8)
      a. What he did (5:6): He died on the cross for us.
      b. Why he did it (5:7-8a): He died because he loves us.

      c. When he did it (5:8b): He did it when we were still helpless and hostile sinners.

    2. *Christ's present work at God's right hand* (5:9-11): Paul says Christ died to save us and now lives to keep us saved.

II. A Summary of Condemnation (5:12-21): Paul contrasts the work of Adam (the sinful father of all people) with the work of Christ (the sinless Savior of all people).

  A. The work of Adam (5:12-15, 16a, 17a, 18a, 19a, 20a, 21a)

    1. *The reality of his act* (5:12a): "When Adam sinned, sin entered the entire human race."

    2. *The scope of his act* (5:12b-13): "So death spread to everyone, for everyone sinned."

    3. *The nature of his act* (5:19a): "Because one person disobeyed God, many people became sinners."

    4. *The results of his act* (5:14-15a, 16a, 17a, 18a, 21a)

      a. Imputed judgment on Adam's posterity (5:14): "They all died anyway—even though they did not disobey an explicit commandment of God, as Adam did."

      b. Eternal judgment on all unsaved (5:15a, 16a, 17a, 18a, 21a): Adam's sin brought death and condemnation upon all people.

    5. *The relationship of the law to his act* (5:20a): "God's law was given so that all people could see how sinful they were."

  B. The work of Christ (5:15b, 16b, 17b, 18b, 19b, 20b, 21b): Because of Christ's death, people can be saved in spite of their sin.

    1. *The scope of his act (5:15b, 18b)*

      a. "Jesus Christ . . . brought forgiveness to many through God's bountiful gift" (5:15b).

      b. "Christ's one act of righteousness makes all people right in God's sight and gives them life" (5:18b).

    2. *The nature of his act* (5:19b): "Because one other person obeyed God, many people will be made right in God's sight."

    3. *The results of his act* (5:16b, 17b, 21b)

      a. Justification (5:16b): All people can now be accepted by God.

      b. Sanctification (5:17b): All people can now be made righteous in God's eyes.

      c. Glorification (5:21b): All people can now have eternal life.

    4. *The relationship of sin to his act* (5:20b): "As people sinned more and more, God's wonderful kindness became more abundant."

SECTION OUTLINE SIX (ROMANS 6)
Paul introduces God's threefold method leading to sanctification.

I. STEP 1—KNOW (6:1-10): Believers must be aware of three facts.
   A. **They have been crucified with Christ** (6:1-3).
   B. **They have been resurrected with Christ** (6:4-5).
   C. **They are now both dead and alive** (6:6-10).
      1. *Dead to their sin* (6:6-7): We should no longer be slaves to sin, for we have been crucified with Christ.
      2. *Alive in the Savior* (6:8-10): We are now to live in the resurrection power of the one who rose from the dead and is forever alive.

II. STEP 2—RECKON (6:11): We are to count our crucifixion and resurrection as accomplished events.

III. STEP 3—YIELD (6:12-23): Paul describes two kinds of yielding.
   A. **The wrong kind** (6:12-13a): We are not to yield the members of our body as tools of wickedness.
   B. **The right kind** (6:13b-23)
      1. *The confusion* (6:15a): "Since God's grace has set us free from the law, does this mean we can go on sinning?"
      2. *The correction* (6:15b-18): "Of course not! Don't you realize that whatever you choose to obey becomes your master? You can choose sin, which leads to death, or you can choose to obey God and receive his approval."
      3. *The challenge* (6:13b-14, 19-22): We are to yield the members of our body as tools of righteousness.
      4. *The conclusion* (6:23)
         a. "The wages of sin is death" (6:23a).
         b. "The free gift of God is eternal life through Christ Jesus our Lord" (6:23b).

SECTION OUTLINE SEVEN (ROMANS 7)
Paul discusses how the law of God applies to and affects three kinds of people.

I. SPIRITUAL PEOPLE AND THE LAW (7:1-6)
   A. **Their relationship to the law** (7:1-3, 5)
      1. *They are like widows freed from their husbands* (7:1-3).
      2. *They are like dead men freed from their lusts* (7:5).
   B. **Their relationship to the Savior** (7:4, 6)
      1. *They have been raised by Christ* (7:4a, 6): They are released from the law.
      2. *They are now to produce fruit through Christ* (7:4b): Thus spiritual people are delivered from the law.

II. NATURAL PEOPLE AND THE LAW (7:7-13): The law is used in a twofold manner.
   A. **The illustration usage** (7:7, 10): God used the law to reveal the sinfulness of the flesh.
   B. **The condemnation usage** (7:8-9, 11-13): Sin used the law to rekindle the sinfulness of the flesh. Thus natural people are doomed by the law.

III. CARNAL PEOPLE AND THE LAW (7:14-26)
   A. **Paul has learned that any attempt to keep the law leads to carnality** (7:14-23).
      1. *The confusion* (7:14-16): Paul's frustration is twofold.
         a. He doesn't do the things he wants to do (7:14-15a, 16a).
         b. He does the things he doesn't want to do (7:15b, 16b).
      2. *The corruption* (7:17-20): He realizes the total corruption of his old sinful nature.
      3. *The conclusion* (7:21-23): He understands the daily struggle within him.
         a. The old nature, always attempting to do wrong (7:21a, 23)
         b. The new nature, always attempting to do right (7:21b-22)
   B. **Paul has learned that no attempt to keep the law can lead to spirituality** (7:24-25).
      1. *The agony of Paul's problem* (7:24): "What a miserable person I am! Who will free me from this life that is dominated by sin?"
      2. *The answer to Paul's problem* (7:25): "Thank God! The answer is in Jesus Christ our Lord."

SECTION OUTLINE EIGHT (ROMANS 8)
Paul outlines seven new assurances accompanying salvation.

I. THE BELIEVER HAS A NEW POSITION (8:1-8).
   A. **Our position in regard to the Son of God** (8:1-3): The believer is in Christ.
      1. *The miracle involved* (8:1, 3a): Believers receive no condemnation and are freed from sin and death.
      2. *The means involved* (8:2, 3b): This was accomplished not through the law of Moses but by the death of Christ.
   B. **Our position in regard to the law of God** (8:4-8): We are now able to fulfill the righteous requirements of the law in and through Christ.

II. THE BELIEVER HAS A NEW GUEST (8:9-14).
   A. **Who he is** (8:9): He is the blessed Holy Spirit himself.
   B. **What he does** (8:10-14)
      1. *He once strengthened Christ and raised him from the dead* (8:11).

2. *He now lives within us and controls us* (8:9).
3. *He now strengthens us and will someday raise us from the dead* (8:10, 12-14).

III. THE BELIEVER HAS A NEW ADOPTION (8:15-17): We are now members of God's family.
   A. **Giving us an intimacy with the Father** (8:15-16)
   B. **Giving us an inheritance from the Father** (8:17)

IV. THE BELIEVER HAS A NEW HOPE (8:18-25): The nature of this hope is the full and final redemption of all things, including:
   A. **Christians** (8:18, 23-25)
      1. *The present grief* (8:18a, 23): Believers groan to be released from pain and suffering.
      2. *The future glory* (8:18b, 24-25)
         a. The comparison (8:18b): Today's grief is nothing when compared with tomorrow's glory.
         b. The command (8:24-25): Until then, however, we are to wait patiently and confidently.
   B. **Creation** (8:19-22)
      1. *Nature, the victim* (8:20, 21b-22): The natural world of plants and animals groans in pain because of the fall.
      2. *Nature, the victor* (8:19, 21a): Nature, too, will be liberated from decay and death to freedom and fruitfulness.

V. THE BELIEVER HAS A NEW PRAYER HELPER (8:26-27).
   A. **The identity of this helper** (8:26a): He is the Holy Spirit.
   B. **The indispensability of this helper** (8:26b): His prayers are vital, because we don't even know what we should pray for.
   C. **The intensity of this helper** (8:26c-27)
      1. *How he prays* (8:26c): He prays for us with groanings that cannot be expressed in words.
      2. *What he prays* (8:27): He pleads for us in harmony with God's own will.

VI. THE BELIEVER HAS A NEW CONFIDENCE (8:28).
   A. **What it involves** (8:28a): God causes everything to work together for good.
   B. **Whom it involves** (8:28b): Those who love God and are called according to his purpose for them.

VII. THE BELIEVER HAS A NEW DESTINY (8:29-39).
   A. **The summary** (8:29): The Father himself has decreed that all believers should become like his dear Son!
   B. **The steps** (8:30)
      1. *We were foreknown by the Father* (8:30a).
      2. *We were predestined by the Father* (8:30b).
      3. *We were called by the Father* (8:30c).

4. *We were justified by the Father* (8:30d).
5. *We were glorified by the Father* (8:30e).
C. **The security** (8:31-39)
   1. *There exists no possible accusation against believers* (8:31-34).
     a. The Father will not allow this (8:31-33).
       (1) He once gave us his Son (8:31-32a).
       (2) He now gives us all things (8:32b-33).
     b. The Son will not allow this (8:34).
       (1) He died for us (8:34a).
       (2) He was resurrected for us (8:34b).
       (3) He now prays for us (8:34c).
   2. *There exists no possible separation from the Savior* (8:35-39): This includes:
     a. Both life and death (8:35-38a)
     b. Both angels and demons (8:38b)
     c. Both present and future (8:38c)
     d. Both height and depth (8:39)

SECTION OUTLINE NINE (ROMANS 9)

In the next three chapters, Paul overviews God's threefold dealings with Israel. Here, he overviews the sovereignty of God and Israel's selection in the past.

I. THE NINE SPIRITUAL ADVANTAGES OF THIS SOVEREIGN SELECTION (9:1-5)
  A. **Paul's grief over Israel** (9:1-3): The apostle is so burdened over Israel's unbelief that he is willing to suffer eternal damnation if that would help them come to Christ.
  B. **God's gifts to Israel** (9:4-5)
    1. *They are a special nation* (9:4a).
    2. *They have been adopted by God* (9:4b, 5).
    3. *They have had God's glory revealed to them* (9:4c).
    4. *They have been given the covenants* (9:4d).
    5. *They have been given the law* (9:4e).
    6. *They have the privilege of worshiping him (9:4f).*
    7. *They have the messianic promises* (9:4g).
    8. *They have a godly ancestry* (9:5a).
    9. *They are the people from which Christ came* (9:5b).

II. THE FIVE PERSONAL EXAMPLES OF THIS SOVEREIGN SELECTION (9:6-29)
  A. **The example of Ishmael and Isaac** (9:6-10): God chose Isaac (Abraham's son through Sarah) over Ishmael (Abraham's son through Hagar).
  B. **The example of Esau and Jacob** (9:11-13)
    1. *What God did* (9:12b-13): He chose Jacob (the second-born twin son of Isaac) over Esau (the firstborn twin).

2. *When God did it* (9:11a, 12a): He made this choice long before they were even born.
3. *Why God did it* (9:11b): He did it to show that his sovereign decrees are not based on what yet-unborn human beings might or might not do.

C. **The example of Pharaoh** (9:14-24)
  1. *The facts involved* (9:15-18)
    a. God determined to pardon sinful Israel with undeserved grace (9:15-16).
    b. God determined to punish sinful Pharaoh with deserved judgment (9:17-18).
  2. *The fairness involved* (9:14, 19-24)
    a. In light of this, is God righteous? *Yes!* (9:14, 21-24).
      (1) As a potter creates vessels, God creates nations (9:14, 21-22).
      (2) As a potter controls those vessels, God controls nations (9:23-24).
    b. In light of this, is man responsible? *Yes!* (9:19-20): As the vessels have no right to criticize the potter, the nations have no right to criticize the Lord.

D. **The example from Hosea** (9:25-26): This Old Testament prophet predicted that God would not limit his grace to Israel but would save repenting Gentile peoples; Hosea called these Gentiles "children of the living God" (Hos. 2:23; 1:10).

E. **The example from Isaiah** (9:27-29): Paul quotes from Isaiah to demonstrate God's sovereignty concerning Israel.
  1. *Out of the millions of Israelites, only a small remnant will be saved* (Isa. 10:22-23) (9:27-28).
  2. *Even the remnant would perish apart from the grace of God* (Isa. 1:9) (9:29).

III. THE TWO GRAND CONCLUSIONS CONCERNING THIS SOVEREIGN SELECTION (9:30-33)
  A. **Through faith the Gentiles have found righteousness without even seeking it** (9:30).
  B. **Through the law Israel has not found righteousness even after seeking it** (9:31-33).
    1. *The seeking* (9:31-32): They tried to be saved by works.
    2. *The stumbling* (9:33): They have stumbled over Christ the rock, as predicted by Isaiah (Isa. 8:14; 28:16).

SECTION OUTLINE TEN (ROMANS 10)
Paul overviews God's righteousness and Israel's present rejection.

I. THE PRAYER CONCERNING GOD'S RIGHTEOUSNESS (10:1-3)
  A. The prayer (10:1): Paul prays for Israel's salvation.
  B. The problem (10:2-3): Israel possesses:
    1. *Zeal without knowledge* (10:2-3a)
    2. *Works without faith* (10:3b)

II. THE SOURCE OF GOD'S RIGHTEOUSNESS (10:4-5)
  A. It is found in Christ (10:4).
  B. It was foretold by Moses (Lev. 18:5) (10:5).

III. THE AVAILABILITY OF GOD'S RIGHTEOUSNESS (10:6-8)
  A. Negative (10:6-7): One need not search the heavens or descend into the deep to find it.
  B. Positive (10:8): It is, through Christ, as near as one's mouth and heart! Moses predicted this in Deuteronomy 30:12-14.

IV. THE RECEPTION OF GOD'S RIGHTEOUSNESS (10:9-10): Both one's heart and mouth are involved.
  A. It is conceived in the heart (10:9b-10a).
  B. It is confirmed by the mouth (10:9a, 10b).

V. THE SCOPE OF GOD'S RIGHTEOUSNESS (10:11-13)
  A. It is impartial (10:11-12): It does not distinguish between Jews and Gentiles.
  B. It is universal (10:13): Anyone calling on the name of the Lord will be saved.

VI. THE PRESENTATION OF GOD'S RIGHTEOUSNESS (10:14-15): Paul presents a compelling case for faithful witnessing.
  A. A sinner must call on the Lord to be saved (10:14a).
  B. A sinner must believe in order to call (10:14b).
  C. A sinner must hear in order to believe (10:14c-15): Isaiah described the results: "How beautiful . . . are the feet of those who bring good news" (Isa. 52:7).

VII. THE REJECTION OF GOD'S RIGHTEOUSNESS (10:16-21)
  A. Israel has heard the Good News (10:18): Paul proves this by quoting from Psalm 19:4.
  B. Israel has refused to heed the Good News (10:16-17, 19-21).
    1. *Isaiah predicted this* (10:16-17, 20-21): See Isaiah 53:1; 65:1-2.
    2. *Moses predicted this* (10:19): See Deuteronomy 32:21.

SECTION OUTLINE ELEVEN (ROMANS 11)
Paul overviews the wisdom of God and Israel's future restoration.

I. THIS FUTURE RESTORATION IS ASSURED BECAUSE ISRAEL'S PRESENT
   REJECTION IS NOT TOTAL (11:1-10, 11b-24).
   A. The factions of Israel (11:1-10): Paul divides Israel into two
   groups.
   1. *The minority group* (11:1-6)
      a. As represented by Paul in the New Testament (11:1):
         His own conversion shows that God has not rejected all
         Israelites.
      b. As represented by Elijah in the Old Testament (11:2-6): This
         powerful prophet, along with 7,000 other Israelites, did not
         bow to Baal (see also 1 Kings 19:18).
   2. *The majority group* (11:7-10): Three Old Testament men
      predicted that God would harden the hearts of unbelieving
      Israel.
      a. Moses (Deut. 29:4) (11:7-8a)
      b. David (Ps. 69:22-23) (11:9-10)
      c. Isaiah (Isa. 29:10) (11:8b)
   B. The fullness of the Gentiles (11:11b-25): This phrase refers to a
   specific period of time.
   1. *The definition of this period* (11:25): It is the time span
      involved in the completion of the body of Christ, consisting of
      both Jews and Gentiles, beginning at Pentecost and ending at
      the Rapture.
   2. *The details concerning this period* (11:11b-24)
      a. The purpose (11:11b-12): One purpose is to make Israel
         jealous to be in God's favor again.
      b. The preacher (11:13-15): Paul has been appointed by God
         himself to help make this a reality.
      c. The parable (11:16-24): Paul employs an olive tree to illus-
         trate all this.
         (1) The roots of the tree are made up of Abraham and
             other godly Old Testament men (11:16).
         (2) Some of the original branches have been broken off,
             referring to unbelieving Jews (11:17a).
         (3) Now some branches from a wild olive tree have been
             grafted in, referring to believing Gentiles (11:17b-23).
         (4) The once-removed original branches will someday be
             grafted back in, referring to the future repentant Israel
             (11:24).

II. THIS FUTURE RESTORATION IS ASSURED BECAUSE ISRAEL'S PRESENT
    REJECTION IS NOT FINAL (11:11a, 26-36).
    A. The Israel of God (11:11a, 26-32)
    1. *The foretelling* (11:11a, 26-27)
       a. Israel restored through the promised Christ (11:26): Isaiah

predicted that the Deliverer would accomplish this (Isa.
59:20).

   b. Israel restored through the promised covenant (11:27):
      Isaiah predicted that God would keep his covenant with
      Israel (Isa. 59:21).

 2. *The faithfulness* (11:28-32): All the above will come to pass,
    for God's gifts and calling are irrevocable.

B. The God of Israel (11:33-36): Paul praises God by uttering one
of Scripture's greatest doxologies.

SECTION OUTLINE TWELVE (ROMANS 12)
Paul urges his readers to make their bodies living sacrifices for the
glory of God.

I. THE BELIEVER AND SELF (12:1-2)

 A. What we are to offer (12:1): Bodily dedication.

  1. *The reason for this* (12:1b): It is to be done because we have
     experienced God's mercy.

  2. *The results of this* (12:1a): God is pleased if we offer a living
     and holy sacrifice.

 B. What we are to avoid (12:2a): Worldly contamination.

 C. What we are to achieve (12:2b): Godly transformation.

II. THE BELIEVER AND SERVICE (12:3-21)

 A. The grace (12:3): Be honest in your estimate of yourselves.

 B. The gifts (12:4-8)

  1. *The illustration concerning these gifts* (12:4-5): Paul likens
     spiritual gifts to members of the human body.

  2. *The identification of these gifts* (12:6-8): Seven spiritual gifts
     are listed.

   a. Prophesying (12:6)
   b. Serving (12:7a)
   c. Teaching (12:7b)
   d. Encouraging (12:8a)
   e. Giving (12:8b)
   f. Leading (12:8c)
   g. Showing kindness (12:8d)

 C. The guidelines (12:9-21)

  1. *How to deal with one's friends* (12:9-13, 15-16)
   a. Love and honor them (12:9-10).
   b. Show them your zeal and joy (12:11-12).
   c. Share with them (12:13).
   d. Mourn and weep with them (12:15).
   e. Live in harmony with them (12:16).

  2. *How to deal with one's foes* (12:14, 17-21)
   a. Bless them when they persecute you (12:14).

b. Let God repay them for the evil done to you (12:17-19).
c. Give them food when they are hungry and water when they are thirsty (12:20-21).

SECTION OUTLINE THIRTEEN (ROMANS 13)
Paul discusses the believer's responsibilities toward society.

I. DUTIES TOWARD THE RULERS OF THE STATE (13:1-7)
  A. **What we are to do** (13:1, 6-7)
    1. *We are to submit ourselves to governing authorities* (13:1).
    2. *We are to pay our taxes* (13:6).
    3. *We are to give honor and respect to all those to whom it is due* (13:7).
  B. **Why we are to do it** (13:2-5)
    1. *Because of the power behind the throne* (13:2): God has established human governments, so to disobey human laws is to disobey God.
    2. *Because of the punishment from the throne* (13:3-5): God has also decreed that lawbreakers should be punished by those representing human government.

II. DUTIES TOWARD THE REST OF THE STATE (13:8-14)
  A. **Continue to love** (13:8-10): God's love seeks and satisfies.
    1. *Love seeks the best for one's neighbor* (13:9-10).
    2. *Love satisfies the law of God* (13:8).
  B. **Continue to look** (13:11-14).
    1. *The realization* (13:11-12a): We need to know the Lord's coming is near.
      a. Time is running out (13:11a, 12a).
      b. The time of salvation is near (13:11b).
    2. *The response* (13:12b-14)
      a. What we are to put off (13:12b, 13b): Works of darkness.
      b. What we are to put on (13:13a, 14): Deeds of light.

SECTION OUTLINE FOURTEEN (ROMANS 14)
Paul discusses the believer's responsibilities toward those Christians who are weak in the faith.

I. NO BELIEVER SHOULD BE JUDGED BY ANOTHER BELIEVER DOWN HERE (14:1-8, 13-23).
  A. **We are not to criticize others' legalism** (14:1-8).
    1. *The rules* (14:1-6)
      a. Don't judge in matters of diet (14:1-4, 6b): Some feel it is wrong to eat meat or any food that has been sacrificed to an idol.

b. Don't judge in matters of days (14:5-6a): Some feel certain days are more sacred than others.

2. *The reason* (14:7-8): Both the weaker and stronger believer belong to the Lord and must love each other.

B. We are not to corrupt our liberty (14:13-23).

1. *The mature Christian is not to become a stumbling block* (14:13-18).

a. He is not to permit good and lawful things to be viewed as evil and lawless (14:13-16).

b. He is not to forget that love is more important than personal liberties (14:17-18).

2. *The mature Christian is to become a stepping-stone* (14:19-23).

II. EVERY BELIEVER WILL BE JUDGED BY THE SAVIOR UP THERE (14:9-12).

A. The foundation of this judgment (14:9): It is based on the death, resurrection, and ascension of Christ.

B. The forbearance in light of this judgment (14:10): Don't compound your problems up there by judging your brother down here.

C. The features of this judgment (14:11-12)

1. *Every knee will bow (14:11a).*

2. *Every tongue will confess* (14:11b).

3. *Everyone will give an account to the Lord (14:12).*

SECTION OUTLINE FIFTEEN (ROMANS 15)
Paul talks about how Christians should live in relation to others. He writes about his travel plans and prayers for his Roman audience.

I. THE PROMPTING OF PAUL (15:1-4, 8-12)

A. His exhortation (15:1-2): Paul urges the mature believer not to please himself but to build up the faith of weaker Christians.

B. His example (15:3-4, 8-12)

1. *He points to the Scriptures* (15:4): Its pages are full of examples where many endured and encouraged others.

2. *He points to the Savior* (15:3, 8-12).

a. Jesus came not to gratify himself but to give himself (15:3).

b. Jesus came to guarantee God's salvation to Jews and Gentiles (15:8-12).

(1) To the Jews (15:8): He came to show that God keeps his promises to the Jews.

(2) To the Gentiles (15:9-12): See also Deuteronomy 32:43; Psalm 18:49; and Isaiah 11:10.

II. THE PRAYER OF PAUL (15:5-7, 13)
   A. He prays that God would favor the Roman church with endurance, encouragement, and unity (15:5-7).
   B. He prays that God will fill the Roman church with joy, peace, and hope (15:13).

III. THE PLANS OF PAUL (15:14-29)
   A. The apostle reviews his past activities (15:14-22).
      1. *He writes concerning his main ministry* (15:14-18): Paul reminds his readers of his special calling to the Gentiles.
      2. *He writes concerning his miracles* (15:19a): God has empowered him to perform signs and wonders.
      3. *He writes concerning his mission field* (15:19b): Paul has preached Christ from Jerusalem to Illyricum.
      4. *He writes concerning his methodology* (15:20-22).
         a. As practiced by Paul (15:20): He preached the gospel where Christ was not known in order to avoid building on another's foundation.
         b. As predicted by Isaiah (15:21-22): This Old Testament prophet wrote concerning this seven centuries earlier (Isa. 52:15).
   B. The apostle previews his future activities (15:23-29).
      1. *Eventual future plans* (15:23-24)
         a. To visit Spain (15:23-24a)
         b. To visit Rome (15:24b)
      2. *Immediate future plans* (15:25-29)
         a. The place (15:25a): Jerusalem
         b. The purpose (15:25b-29): To present a financial gift for needy believers there, which Paul has collected during his missionary journeys

IV. THE PLEA OF PAUL (15:30-33): The apostle requests the church's prayers concerning two matters.
   A. That he be protected in Jerusalem from unbelievers (15:30-31a)
   B. That he be accepted in Jerusalem by believers (15:31b-33)

SECTION OUTLINE SIXTEEN (ROMANS 16)

In closing, Paul greets a few specific friends and gives some final instructions.

I. PAUL AND THE PEOPLE OF THE GOSPEL (16:1-16, 21-24)
   A. He is sending a special woman to the church in Rome (16:1-2).
      1. *Who she is* (16:1a): She is Phoebe, a godly servant of Christ.
      2. *Where she is coming from* (16:1b): She is from the church in Cenchrea.
      3. *Why she is coming* (16:2): She will minister to the Roman church as she has done for many others.

B. He sends a special welcome to the church in Rome (16:3-16, 21-24).
   1. *Paul sends greetings to 26 individuals* (16:3-16).
      a. His friends Aquila and Priscilla (16:3-5a)
      b. His friend Epenetus, who was the first Christian in Asia (16:5b)
      c. Mary, who has worked hard for the Roman church (16:6)
      d. His relatives Andronicus, Junias, and Herodion (16:7, 11a)
      e. Other friends and coworkers: Ampliatus, Urbanus, Stachys, Apelles, the household of Aristobulus, the Christians in the household of Narcissus, Tryphena, Tryphosa, Persis, Rufus, his mother, Asyncritus, Phlegon, Hermes, Patrobas, Hermas, Philologus, Julia, Nereus and his sister, and Olympas (16:8-10, 11b-16)
   2. *Paul sends greetings from eight individuals* (16:21-24).
      a. Timothy (16:21a)
      b. Paul's relatives Lucius, Jason, and Sosipater (16:21b)
      c. Tertius, the scribe who is writing Romans as Paul dictates it (16:22)
      d. Gaius and Quartus (16:23-24)

II. PAUL AND THE PERVERSION OF THE GOSPEL (16:17-19): Paul warns of some troublemakers in the Roman church.
   A. What they are doing (16:17)
      1. *Causing divisions* (16:17a)
      2. *Teaching false doctrine* (16:17b)
      3. *Upsetting people's faith* (16:17c)
   B. Why they are doing it (16:18-19): To gain money and power for themselves.

III. PAUL AND THE PROMISE OF THE GOSPEL (16:20): God will someday crush Satan under our feet.

IV. PAUL AND THE POWER OF THE GOSPEL (16:25-27)
   A. It has the power to strengthen saints (16:25a).
   B. It has the power to save sinners (16:25b-27).

1 Corinthians

SECTION OUTLINE ONE (1 CORINTHIANS 1)
Paul begins his first letter to the Corinthian church by giving thanks
to God for the many gifts this church has received from the Lord. He
then addresses two problems facing the Corinthian church.

I. THE PERSONAL GREETINGS FROM PAUL (1:1-3)
   A. **The recipients** (1:1-2)
      1. *Paul writes to the Corinthian believers* (1:1-2a).
      2. *Paul writes to all believers* (1:2b).
   B. **The blessing** (1:3): Paul wishes them grace and peace.

II. THE PRAYER OF PAUL (1:4-9)
   A. **Paul thanks God for the gifts God has given the Corinthian
      believers** (1:4-7): They received all the spiritual gifts.
   B. **Paul thanks God for the guarantee God gave the Corinthian
      believers** (1:8-9): This guarantee refers to their eternal security.

III. THE PROBLEMS ADDRESSED BY PAUL (1:10-31): Paul discusses two of
   the numerous problems confronting the Corinthian church.
   A. **They are elevating human leaders** (1:10-17).
      1. *The individuals* (1:10-12): Some are fans of Paul; some, of
         Apollos; and others, of Simon Peter.
      2. *The issue* (1:14-16): Apparently the argument consists mainly
         of who baptized them.
      3. *The insanity* (1:13, 17): Paul rebukes them, hitting his own
         "fan club" the hardest.
         a. "Was I, Paul, crucified for you?" (1:13a).
         b. "Were any of you baptized in the name of Paul?" (1:13b).
         c. "Christ didn't send me to baptize, but to preach the Good
            News" (1:17).
   B. **They are exalting human wisdom** (1:18-31): Paul contrasts and
      compares the egocentric wisdom of people with the eternal wis-
      dom of God.
      1. *The response to God's wisdom* (1:18, 22-23)
         a. In regard to unbelieving Jews and Gentiles (1:18, 22-23)

(1) To the Jews who demand supernatural signs, it becomes a stumbling block (1:18a, 22a, 23a).
(2) To the Gentiles who depend upon vain philosophy, it becomes foolishness (1:18b, 22b, 23b).
b. In regard to believing Jews and Gentiles (1:18c, 24-25): It represents both the power and wisdom of God.
2. *The results of God's wisdom* (1:19-21)
a. It is used to destroy worldly wisdom (1:19-20).
b. It is used to deliver repenting sinners (1:21).
3. *The reason for God's wisdom* (1:26-31): Why did God choose the Cross to save people?
a. Paul's overview (1:27-31): God delights in using foolish, weak, lowly, and despised things to nullify the wise, strong, exalted, and respected things.
b. Paul's observation (1:26): He tactfully reminds the arrogant Corinthians of their own lack of worldly influence and academic wisdom!

SECTION OUTLINE TWO (1 CORINTHIANS 2)
Paul reflects on his founding of the church in Corinth and reminds the Corinthian believers of several facts in regard to the Cross.

I. THE MESSAGE OF THE CROSS IS NOT OF THIS WORLD (2:1-6).
A. The apostle's resolve (2:1-4)
1. *What he determines not to do* (2:1): He will not depend on eloquence or education in his preaching.
2. *What he determines to do* (2:2-4): He will depend completely on the power of the Holy Spirit.
B. The apostle's reason (2:5-6): He will do this so their faith will rest on God's Word and not on his wisdom.

II. THE MESSAGE OF THE CROSS WAS ORDAINED BEFORE THIS WORLD (2:7-8).
A. Handcrafted for the saved (2:7): This involves God's wise plan to bring believers into the glories of heaven.
B. Hidden from the unsaved (2:8): Had they known the truth, they would not have crucified the Lord of glory.

III. THE MESSAGE OF THE CROSS WAS RESERVED FOR THE HEIRS OF THIS WORLD (2:9-16).
A. Concealed from the human spirit (2:9): No mortal can ever see, hear, or even imagine what wonderful things God has prepared for those who love him.
B. Revealed by the Holy Spirit (2:10-16)
1. *What he does* (2:10-12): He reveals to us God's deepest secrets.
2. *How he does it* (2:13-16): This is accomplished through the Scriptures.

SECTION OUTLINE THREE (1 CORINTHIANS 3)

Paul again reminds the Corinthians not to elevate teachers of the
Word of God over the Word itself.

I. THE "BABY" CHRISTIANS IN THE CORINTHIAN CHURCH (3:1-10): Paul
   addresses some squabbling believers in this assembly.
   A. **Paul's criticism** (3:1-2)
      1. *What he hopes to do* (3:1): The apostle wants to give them the
         solid meat of the Word.
      2. *What he has to do* (3:2): Because of their carnality and
         immaturity, he can only feed them milk.
   B. **Paul's correction** (3:3-10)
      1. *Their sinful view of Christian leaders* (3:3-4): They are looking
         to men (like Paul and Apollos) instead of to Christ.
      2. *His scriptural view of Christian leaders* (3:5-10)
         a. What the leaders do (3:5a, 6a, 7a, 8-10): They can only
            sow and water the spiritual seed.
         b. What the Lord does (3:5b, 6b, 7b): God alone can cause
            the crop to grow.

II. THE BEMA JUDGMENT AND THE CORINTHIAN CHURCH (3:11-23)
   A. **The works** (3:11-15): Paul says all believers will someday stand
      before an elevated platform (called a "bema") to be tested in
      regard to their service for Christ.
      1. *The objects in this test* (3:11-13): Our works here are classified
         as gold, silver, jewels, wood, hay, and straw.
      2. *The outcome of this test* (3:14-15)
         a. The owner of the gold, silver, and jeweled works will
            receive a reward (3:14).
         b. The owner of the wood, hay, and straw works will receive
            no reward (3:15).
   B. **The warning** (3:16-23)
      1. *Don't defile your temple* (3:16-17): God regards our bodies as
         temples.
      2. *Don't deceive yourselves* (3:18-21): Paul warns not to depend
         on earthly wisdom or human leaders but on God himself.
      3. *You belong to Christ as Christ belongs to God* (3:22-23).

SECTION OUTLINE FOUR (1 CORINTHIANS 4)

Paul writes about the office and duties of a steward. A steward is a
trusted servant whom the master has appointed to conduct his business
matters in his absence.

I. THE CONTRASTS BETWEEN FAITHFUL AND FAITHLESS STEWARDS (4:1-13)
   A. **The faithless steward** (4:6-8, 10b, 10d-10e)
      1. *This person is filled with pride* (4:6-7).

2. *This person is presumptuous* (4:8).
3. *This person is wise in his own eyes* (4:10b).
4. *This person is physically strong* (4:10d).
5. *This person is well thought of by the world* (4:10e).
   B. The faithful steward (4:1-5, 9-10a, 10c, 10f-13)
1. *This person possesses a clear conscience* (4:1-4).
2. *This person does not judge others* (4:5).
3. *This person becomes a spectacle* (4:9).
4. *This person is written off as a fool* (4:10a).
5. *This person may be physically weak* (4:10c).
6. *This person is laughed at by the world* (4:10f).
7. *This person is often hungry, thirsty, and without warm clothes* (4:11a).
8. *This person is brutally treated and homeless* (4:11b).
9. *This person is acquainted with backbreaking labor* (4:12a).
10. *This person blesses his or her enemies* (4:12b, 13a).
11. *This person is looked upon as the world's garbage* (4:13b).

II. THE COUNSEL TO THE FAITHFUL AND FAITHLESS STEWARDS (4:14-21)
   A. Paul's appeal (4:14-16)
1. *His reminder* (4:14-15): The apostle reminds the Corinthian believers that he led them to Christ.
2. *His request* (4:16): "Follow my example and do as I do."
   B. Paul's ambassador (4:17): He will soon be sending Timothy their way to assist them.
   C. Paul's appearance (4:18-21): The apostle plans to visit them personally in the near future.

SECTION OUTLINE FIVE (1 CORINTHIANS 5)
Paul writes about church discipline.

I. THE NEED FOR DISCIPLINE (5:1): There is a terrible sin prevalent in the Corinthian church.
   A. The notoriousness of their sin (5:1a): It is something so evil that even the heathen won't permit it.
   B. The nature of their sin (5:1b): A member is living in immorality with his own mother (or possibly stepmother).

II. THE REFUSAL TO DISCIPLINE (5:2): Due to pride and indifference, the church has not removed this man.

III. THE COMMAND TO DISCIPLINE (5:3-5): Paul orders the church to call a special meeting to resolve this issue.
   A. The authority (5:3-4): He reminds them that the Savior has given authority to the local church.

B. The action (5:5)
1. *What the church is to do* (5:5a): They must hand this guilty man over to Satan.
2. *Why the church is to do it* (5:5b): This will hopefully bring him to repentance so that his spirit might be saved.

IV. THE REASONS FOR DISCIPLINE (5:5-8)
A. To bring the offender back to God (This has already been seen—5:5.)
B. To keep the offense from spreading in the church (5:6-7): Thus, the church is to:
1. *Cut out the cancer* (5:6-7a)
2. *Continue in the Savior* (5:7b)
C. To keep the celebration of Christ, the Passover Lamb, pure and true (5:8)

V. THE EXTENT OF DISCIPLINE (5:9-13)
A. This discipline involves only church members (5:9-11).
1. *The church has no right to judge godless outsiders* (5:9-10).
2. *The church has the responsibility to avoid godless outsiders* (5:11).
B. The discipline involves all church members (5:12-13).

SECTION OUTLINE SIX (1 CORINTHIANS 6)
Paul deals with two sins plaguing the Corinthian church.

I. LAWSUITS (6:1-11)
A. The facts (6:1, 6): Some Christians in Corinth are taking fellow believers to court before pagan judges to settle petty matters.
B. The folly (6:2-5, 7-11): Paul condemns this action on three accounts.
1. *It is illogical* (6:2-5): Inasmuch as believers will someday judge angels, can they not be expected to settle their differences down here with the help of other Christians?
2. *It is illegal* (6:7-8): Apparently they are using the court system to defraud each other.
3. *It is inexcusable* (6:9-11).
a. God has forgiven them of so many horrible sins (6:11).
b. Could they not forgive one another of a few lesser sins (6:9-10)?

II. LASCIVIOUSNESS (6:12-20): Paul warns them to control their bodies in all areas.
A. The realms (6:12-18)
1. *In regard to food* (6:12-13a): In a nutshell, don't let food master you.

2. *In regard to sexual matters* (6:13b-18): We are to flee from sexual immorality.
   B. **The rationale** (6:19-20): Our body is God's temple, paid for by the blood of Jesus.

SECTION OUTLINE SEVEN (1 CORINTHIANS 7)
Paul talks about marriage.

I. MARRIAGE—SOME GENERAL INSTRUCTIONS (7:1-2, 7-9, 17-24, 29-35)
   A. **The argument** (7:1-2, 7-9, 32-35): Is it better to be married than not to be married?
      1. *The advantages of marriage* (7:2, 7, 9)
         a. It helps prevent immoral actions and attitudes (7:2, 9).
         b. It is God's will for many people to marry (7:7).
      2. *The advantages of remaining single* (7:1, 8, 32-35): For the most part, a single person is free to devote all his or her attention to the work of the Lord, having no need to share time with a spouse or children.
   B. **The answer** (7:17-24, 29-31): Which course is the best? It depends totally on God's perfect plan for each believer.
      1. *God's will must govern any decisions concerning marriage* (7:17).
      2. *Pleasing God is the supreme objective* (7:18-19).
      3. *We are not our own but have been bought and paid for by Christ* (7:20-24).
      4. *Even if married, Christ must occupy first place in our life* (7:29-31).

II. MARRIAGE—SOME SPECIFIC INDIVIDUALS: (7:3-6, 10-16, 25-28, 36-40): Paul now addresses four groups.
   A. **Saved couples** (7:3-6, 10-11)
      1. *Both are to submit their bodies to each other* (7:3-4).
      2. *Both must agree if physical intimacy is set aside for a while to facilitate prayer and fasting* (7:5-6).
      3. *Both must strive to stay together and not divorce* (7:10-11).
   B. **Spiritually mixed couples** (7:12-16)
      1. *The saved spouse should continue living with the unsaved spouse if possible* (7:12-13).
      2. *This action may result in the salvation of the unsaved spouse* (7:14).
      3. *The saved spouse should allow the unsaved spouse to depart if he or she insists on it* (7:15-16).
   C. **Virgins** (7:25-28, 36-38): Paul advises the unmarried not to rush into marriage.
   D. **A widow** (7:39-40): She is free to marry another believer.

SECTION OUTLINE EIGHT (1 CORINTHIANS 8)
In the next three chapters, Paul deals with the subject of Christian liberty. Here Paul answers a question the Corinthian church asked him concerning food.

 I. THE CONFUSION (8:4a): Is it right for a Christian to eat meat that has been sacrificed to idols?

 II. THE CLARIFICATION (8:4b-6, 8)
   A. **There are many idols, all of which represent gods who do not exist** (8:4b-5).
   B. **There is only one true God, the creator of all things and the giver of life** (8:6).
   C. **In light of the above, there is no connection between food and spirituality** (8:8).

 III. THE CONCERN (8:7): Paul warns, however, that not all Christians fully realize this, and some are upset when other believers eat such meat.

 IV. THE CHALLENGE (8:1-3, 9-12)
   A. **Don't become a stumbling block to other Christians** (8:9-12).
     1. *To do so is to sin against your weaker brother* (8:9-11).
     2. *To do so is to sin against your Savior* (8:12).
   B. **Do become a stepping-stone** (8:1-3): Knowledge puffs up, but love builds up.

 V. THE CONCLUSION (8:13): Paul says, "If what I eat is going to make another Christian sin, I will never eat meat again as long as I love—for I don't want to make another Christian stumble."

SECTION OUTLINE NINE (1 CORINTHIANS 9)
Paul offers himself as a proper role model.

 I. CHRISTIAN LIBERTY—PAUL'S APPROACH (9:1-23): How the apostle views his liberty in Christ and his rights as a believer.
   A. **The basis of his rights** (9:1-3)
     1. *He is an apostle of Christ* (9:1a).
     2. *He has seen Christ* (9:1b).
     3. *He has led many to Christ* (9:1c-3).
   B. **The extent of his rights** (9:4-12a, 13-14): Paul's rights include:
     1. *The right of hospitality* (9:4): Paul has earned the right to be entertained by other believers.
     2. *The right to travel with his family* (9:5-6)
     3. *The right to enjoy financial support* (9:7-12a, 13-14)
       a. A soldier is paid for his services (9:7a).
       b. A vineyard owner eats from the grapes he harvests (9:7b).
       c. A shepherd drinks from the milk of his flock (9:7c).

    d. A farmer shares in the fruit of his crops (9:8-12a).

    e. A priest partakes from the animal sacrifices he offers
       (9:13-14).

  C. The use of his rights (9:12b, 15-18, 20-22): How Paul employs
    his rights.

    1. *What he does not do* (9:12b, 15-18): Paul chooses not to use
       his rights but supplies his own needs.

    2. *What he does* (9:19-22a): He becomes a servant to everyone.

      a. To the Jews he becomes like a Jew (9:19-20).

      b. To the Gentiles he becomes like a Gentile (9:21).

      c. To the weak he becomes weak (9:22a).

    3. *Why he does it* (9:22b-23): He becomes all things to all
       people so that he might save some.

II. CHRISTIAN LIBERTY (9:24-27): Paul makes an appeal.

  A. The apostle's challenge (9:24-26)

    1. *Run to win the race* (9:24-25).

    2. *Fight to win the battle* (9:26).

  B. The apostle's concern (9:27)

    1. *What he does* (9:27a): He keeps his body in subjection by
       punishing it like an athlete would do.

    2. *Why he does it* (9:27b): He does not want sin to creep in and
       disqualify him from the battle.

SECTION OUTLINE TEN (1 CORINTHIANS 10)
Paul writes concerning Israel's tragic failure in the past and provides
both examples and exhortations.

I. EXAMPLES (10:1-10): The factors that led to Israel's destruction.

  A. The advantages enjoyed by Israel (10:1-4)

    1. *They were led by the cloud of God's glory* (10:1).

    2. *The waters of the Red Sea parted for them* (10:2).

    3. *They were supernaturally provided with food and water*
       (10:3-4a).

    4. *Christ himself accompanied them* (10:4b).

  B. The apostasy committed by Israel (10:5-10)

    1. *They displeased God, and many were killed* (10:5-6).

    2. *They were guilty of idolatry* (10:7): They engaged in pagan
       revelry.

    3. *They were guilty of immorality* (10:8): Twenty-three thousand
       of them died in one day.

    4. *They were guilty of impunity* (10:9): They died of snakebites.

    5. *They were guilty of ingratitude* (10:10): They grumbled, and
       God sent the angel of death.

II. EXHORTATIONS (10:11-33): The factors that lead to our deliverance.
  A. **The faithfulness of God** (10:11-13): Paul speaks of God's faithful-
    ness in the hour of temptation.
    1. *God has not promised to shield us from temptation* (10:11-12).
    2. *God has promised to see us through temptation* (10:13).
  B. **The fellowship with God** (10:14-22): Among all of Israel's sins,
    idolatry was apparently the most serious. Paul explains and con-
    trasts divine fellowship with devilish fellowship.
    1. *Divine fellowship* (10:14-18): This fellowship is especially
      seen through the Lord's Supper, which expresses the unity
      among the members and their participation in the blood and
      body of Christ.
    2. *Devilish fellowship* (10:19-22): The same is true in pagan
      worship, where sacrifices are actually offered up to demons.
  C. **Freedom in God** (10:23-33): Paul addresses two issues.
    1. *What believers can do* (10:23): They can partake, for this
      practice is permissible.
    2. *What believers should do* (10:24-33): Since some weaker
      Christians might be offended by certain actions, mature
      believers should:
      a. Do what they do for the good of all (10:24-30, 32-33)
      b. Do what they do for the glory of God (10:31)

SECTION OUTLINE ELEVEN (1 CORINTHIANS 11)
Paul describes just how children of God should conduct themselves
in the house of God.

I. GUIDANCE CONCERNING CLOTHING (11:1-16): The desired proper
  appearance.
  A. **The pattern** (11:1-3)
    1. *The role model* (11:1-2): Paul instructs believers to follow his
      examples just as he follows Christ's.
    2. *The relationships* (11:3)
      a. The head of the woman is man (11:3b).
      b. The head of the man is the Savior (11:3a).
      c. The head of the Savior is the Father (11:3c).
  B. **The parties** (11:4-16)
    1. *Rules concerning the man* (11:4, 7-9, 14)
      a. His head is to be uncovered (11:4, 7-9).
        (1) Demonstrating his relationship to his Savior (11:4, 7)
        (2) Demonstrating his relationship to his spouse (11:8-9)
      b. His hair is to be cut (11:14).
    2. *Rules concerning the woman* (11:5-6, 10, 13, 15-16)
      a. Her head is to be covered (11:5, 10, 13).
        (1) Demonstrating her submission to her Savior (11:13)
        (2) Demonstrating her submission to her spouse (11:5)

(3) Demonstrating her submission to the angels (11:10)
b. Her hair is not to be cut (11:6, 15-16): It should not be shorn or shaved.
3. *Rules concerning both* (11:11-12)
a. The woman is not to be independent of the man (11:11).
b. The man is not to be independent of the woman (11:12).

II. GUIDANCE CONCERNING COMMUNION (11:17-34): The Corinthian believers are not observing the Lord's Table as they should.
   A. The perversion (11:17-22)
   1. *They separate into their own little groups* (11:17-20).
   2. *They share with no one else* (11:21-22).
   B. The pattern (11:23-25): Paul describes the original Lord's Supper as conducted by Jesus in the upper room.
   1. *What the Savior did* (11:23, 25a)
   a. He held up the bread (11:23).
   b. He held up the cup (11:25a).
   2. *What the Savior said* (11:24, 25b)
   a. Concerning the bread (11:24): "This is my body, which is given for you."
   b. Concerning the cup (11:25b): "This cup is the new covenant between God and you, sealed by the shedding of my blood."
   C. The purpose (11:26, 28): Any Lord's Table involves a threefold look.
   1. *It serves as a backward look to the cross* (11:26a).
   2. *It serves as an inward look to the conscience* (11:28).
   3. *It serves as a forward look to the crown* (11:26b).
   D. The penalty (11:27, 29-30): Any believer who partakes in an unworthy manner is guilty and risks punishment.
   1. *To eat and drink God's judgment on oneself* (11:27-29)
   2. *To be divinely judged with physical sickness* (11:30a)
   3. *To be divinely judged with physical death* (11:30b)
   E. The profit (11:31-34)
   1. *It can be used for judging ourselves* (11:31-32).
   2. *It can be used for giving ourselves* (11:33-34).

SECTION OUTLINE TWELVE (1 CORINTHIANS 12)
Paul discusses spiritual gifts.

I. THE COMMAND TO KNOW THE GIFTS (12:1-3): This knowledge will help dispel any ignorance concerning the giver of the gifts.

II. THE SOURCE OF THE GIFTS (12:4-6, 11): They are imparted by the Holy Spirit.

III. THE EXTENT OF THE GIFTS (12:7, 29-30)
   A. **Each believer is given at least one gift** (12:7).
   B. **No believer is given all the gifts** (12:29-30).

IV. THE DIVERSITY OF THE GIFTS (12:8-10, 28)
   A. **Wisdom** (12:8a)
   B. **Knowledge** (12:8b)
   C. **Faith** (12:9a)
   D. **Healing** (12:9b, 28e)
   E. **Miracles** (12:10a, 28d)
   F. **Prophecy** (12:10b, 28b)
   G. **Discernment** (12:10c)
   H. **Tongues** (12:10d, 28h)
   I. **Interpretation of Tongues** (12:10e)
   J. **Apostleship** (12:28a)
   K. **Teaching** (12:28c)
   L. **Helping** (12:28f)
   M. **Administration** (12:28g)

V. THE ANALOGY OF THE GIFTS (12:12-27): Paul compares the body of Christ and its many spiritually gifted members to the human body with its many physical members.
   A. **Each member in both bodies performs a vital task** (12:12-13, 18).
   B. **No member in either body can be independent of the other members** (12:14-17, 19-24).
      1. *The foot and the ear are not to show envy toward the hand and the eye* (12:14-17).
      2. *The eye and the head are not to show pride toward the hands and the feet* (12:21).
   C. **Each member in both bodies is to rejoice and suffer with the other members** (12:19-20, 22-27).

VI. THE GREATEST OF THE GIFTS (12:31): Paul ends this chapter by promising to show "the most excellent way," which he does in chapter 13.

SECTION OUTLINE THIRTEEN (1 CORINTHIANS 13)
This is the famous love chapter.

I. THE IMPORTANCE OF LOVE (13:1-3)
   A. **The gift of tongues is useless without it** (13:1).
   B. **The gift of prophecy is useless without it** (13:2a).
   C. **The gift of knowledge is useless without it** (13:2b).
   D. **The gift of faith is useless without it** (13:2c).
   E. **The gift of giving is useless without it** (13:3).

II. THE IMPECCABILITY OF LOVE (13:4-7)
   A. **In relation to saints** (13:4a): It is patient and kind, not jealous.

B. **In relation to self** (13:4b-5a): It is not boastful, proud, or rude, and it never seeks its own way.

C. **In relation to sin** (13:5b-6): It is not irritable, nor does it keep a record of wrongs; it is never glad about injustice or unrighteousness but rejoices with the truth.

D. **In relation to situations** (13:7): It never gives up, never loses faith, is always hopeful, and endures through every circumstance.

III. THE INDESTRUCTIBILITY OF LOVE (13:8-12)

A. **Unlike the other gifts, love is permanent** (13:8).

1. *Prophecy will cease* (13:8a).
2. *Tongues will cease* (13:8b).
3. *Knowledge will cease* (13:8c).

B. **Unlike other gifts, love is complete** (13:9-12): Paul offers two illustrations.

1. *The child/adult illustration* (13:9-11)
   a. The gifts, if used without love, may be likened to the attitudes and actions of an immature child (13:9-11a).
   b. Love may be likened to the attitudes and actions of a mature adult (13:11b).
2. *The mirror/face-to-face illustration* (13:12)
   a. In the present, through the gifts, we see but a mirrorlike reflection of God (13:12a).
   b. In the future, through love, we will see God face-to-face (13:12b).

IV. THE INVINCIBILITY OF LOVE (13:13)

A. **Faith and hope are among God's greatest gifts** (13:13a).

B. **Love is God's greatest gift** (13:13b).

SECTION OUTLINE FOURTEEN (1 CORINTHIANS 14)
Paul contrasts and compares the gifts of tongues and prophecy.

I. THE GIFT OF PROPHECY (14:1, 3, 4b-12, 18-19, 29-33)

A. **The admonition to seek this gift** (14:1): Love should be the highest goal, but prophecy should be sought after as well.

B. **The advantages of this gift** (14:3, 4b-6, 18-19)

1. *It strengthens, encourages, and comforts believers* (14:3).
2. *It edifies the entire church* (14:4b).
3. *It is Paul's personal choice for the Corinthian church* (14:5).
4. *It is Paul's most effective way to help all the churches* (14:6).
5. *In fact, he feels this gift is 2,000 times more effective than the gift of tongues* (14:18-19).

C. **The analogies concerning this gift** (14:7-12): Paul offers three analogies, each proving the superiority of prophecy over tongues.

1. *From the music world* (14:7): No one recognizes the melody unless each note is sounded clearly.
2. *From the military world* (14:8): An unclear call to battle is useless.
3. *From the daily world* (14:9-12): Unclear language is useless language.

D. The admonitions concerning this gift (14:29-33)
1. *Only two or three people should prophesy in a service, and the others should evaluate what is said* (14:29).
2. *If one person is prophesying and another receives a divine revelation, the first person should allow the second to speak* (14:30-31).
3. *Those who prophesy must remain in control of their spirit so that they can wait their turn to speak* (4:32-33).

II. THE GIFT OF TONGUES (14:2, 4a, 13-17, 21-25, 27-35)
A. The reasons for this gift (14:2, 4a, 21-25)
1. *In regard to believers* (14:2, 4a)
   a. The speaker utters mysteries to God that are unknown to man (14:2).
   b. The speaker edifies himself (14:4a).
2. *In regard to unbelievers* (14:21-25)
   a. The prediction (14:21): Paul quotes from Isaiah, where the prophet warned that God would allow foreign-speaking nations (Assyria, Babylon, etc.) to punish his sinful people (Isa. 28:11-12).
   b. The purpose (14:22): The gift of tongues is thus a sign of judgment for unbelieving Israel.
   c. The problem (14:23): Paul warns against the entire church's exercising the gift of tongues, lest an unsaved person come in and conclude that all are out of their minds.
   d. The persuasion (14:24-25): However, if the gift of prophecy (preaching) is in effect, that unsaved person might be convinced to accept Christ.

B. The rules governing this gift (14:13-17, 27-32, 34-35)
1. *Those speaking in tongues should pray that what is said might be correctly interpreted* (14:13-14).
2. *The one praying and singing with his spirit is also to do both with his mind* (14:15-17).
3. *No more than two or three should speak in tongues at any service* (14:27a).
4. *They should speak one at a time* (14:27b).
5. *Someone must be present to interpret, or they should keep quiet* (14:27c-28).
6. *Women are not to speak in tongues or prophesy in the church meetings* (14:34-35).

IV. THE GUIDELINES FOR BOTH GIFTS (14:20, 33, 36-40): Paul offers a fourfold conclusion covering both gifts.
  A. **Be as innocent as infants and as intelligent as adults in exercising these gifts** (14:20).
  B. **These gifts and all others should be used solely for the edification of others** (14:26).
  C. **Be eager to prophesy, and don't forbid tongues** (14:39).
  D. **Do everything in a fitting and orderly way** (14:33, 40).
  E. **Obey what Paul has written, for these are God's commands** (14:36-38).

SECTION OUTLINE FIFTEEN (1 CORINTHIANS 15)
Paul writes about the resurrection of Christ and the resurrection of believers.

I. THE PROMINENCE OF THE RESURRECTION (15:1-4)
  A. **The resurrection of Christ is the focal point in reference to salvation** (15:1-2).
  B. **The resurrection of Christ is the focal point in reference to the Scriptures** (15:3-4).

II. THE PROOFS OF THE RESURRECTION (15:5-11): The various appearances of the risen Christ are offered as proof.
  A. **His appearance to Peter** (15:5a)
  B. **His appearance to the apostles with Thomas absent** (15:5b)
  C. **His appearance to 500 disciples** (15:6)
  D. **His appearance to James, the half brother of Christ** (15:7a)
  E. **His appearance to the apostles with Thomas present** (15:7b)
  F. **His appearance to Paul** (15:8-11)
    1. *The unworthiness of Paul* (15:8-9): Paul once persecuted the church.
    2. *The unmerited favor of God* (15:10-11): Grace made Paul what he is.

III. THE PROTEST AGAINST THE RESURRECTION (15:12-19, 29-34): The doctrine of the resurrection is under attack.
  A. **The charge** (15:12): The enemies of the gospel deny it.
  B. **The conclusion** (15:13-19, 29-32): If there is no resurrection, one must be forced to accept the following horrible conclusions:
    1. *In regard to Christ* (15:13, 16): The Easter story is a lie.
    2. *In regard to gospel preaching* (15:14a): It is useless.
    3. *In regard to gospel preachers* (15:15): They are all liars.
    4. *In regard to living believers* (15:14b, 17, 19, 29-31)
      a. Our trust in God is empty, worthless, and hopeless (15:14b).
      b. We are still in our sin (15:17).

    c. We are the most miserable of all creatures (15:19).
    d. Those who live, suffer, and die for Christ are fools
       (15:29-31).
  5. *In regard to departed believers* (15:18): They are forever dead,
    never to rise again.
  6. *In regard to this present life* (15:32): We should live it up, for
    tomorrow we may die!
C. The chastening (15:33-34): Paul rebukes Christians who have
been listening to the lies of unbelievers about the resurrection.

IV. THE PROGRAM OF THE RESURRECTION (15:20-28)
  A. The two representatives (15:21-22)
    1. *The first Adam brought about ruin and death* (15:21a, 22a).
    2. *The second Adam (Christ) brings about resurrection and
      deliverance* (15:21b, 22b).
  B. The three resurrections (15:20, 23-24a)
    1. *The resurrection of Christ* (15:20, 23a): Christ was raised first.
    2. *The Rapture resurrection* (15:23b): When Christ returns, all his
      people will be raised.
    3. *The resurrection of Old Testament and Tribulation saints*
      (15:24a)
  C. The 1,000-year reign (15:24b-28)
    1. *The final enemy will be destroyed* (15:24b, 26): This terrible
      foe is physical death.
    2. *The future Kingdom will be established* (15:25-27).

V. THE PATTERN OF THE RESURRECTION (15:35-41): Paul illustrates the
difference between the earthly and heavenly bodies through
analogies.
  A. The difference between a planted seed and a harvested seed
  (15:35-38): A planted seed is dead, but a harvested seed is alive.
  B. The difference between animal flesh and human flesh (15:39)
  C. The difference between the moon and the sun (15:40-41): They
  differ from each other in their beauty and brightness.

VI. THE PERFECTION OF THE RESURRECTION (15:42-9): Paul describes the
new body as superior to the old.
  A. The old body (15:42a, 43a, 43c, 44a, 45a, 46a, 47a, 48a, 49a)
    1. *It is sown a perishable body* (15:42a, 45a, 47a).
    2. *It is sown in dishonor* (15:43a).
    3. *It is sown in weakness* (15:43c).
    4. *It is sown a natural body* (15:44a, 46a, 48a).
    5. *It is sown bearing the likeness of the first Adam* (15:49a).
  B. The new body (15:42b, 43b, 43d, 44b, 45b, 46b, 47b, 48b, 49b)
    1. *It will be raised imperishable* (15:42b).
    2. *It will be raised in glory* (15:43b).
    3. *It will be raised in power* (15:43d).
    4. *It will be raised a spiritual body* (15:44b, 46b, 48b).
    5. *It will be raised giving life* (15:45b).

6. *It will come from heaven* (15:47b).

7. *It will be raised bearing the likeness of Christ* (15:49b).

VII. THE PROMISE OF THE RESURRECTION (15:50-58)

    A. The situation requiring this promise (15:50): Flesh and blood cannot inherit God's Kingdom.

    B. The secret associated with this promise (15:51): All believers alive at Christ's coming will go to heaven without dying.

    C. The suddenness of this promise (15:52a): This will occur in the amount of time it takes to blink an eye.

    D. The signal introducing this promise (15:52b): The last trumpet will signify the fulfillment of this promise.

    E. The schedule of this promise (15:52c, 53)

        1. *Departed believers will exchange their corrupted bodies for incorruptible ones* (15:52c).

        2. *Living believers will exchange their mortal bodies for immortal ones* (15:53).

    F. The Scriptures predicting this promise (15:54-57): Old Testament prophets Isaiah and Hosea wrote of this (Isa. 25:8; Hos. 13:14).

    G. The strength derived from this promise (15:58): Because of the resurrection, no labor done for the Lord is in vain.

SECTION OUTLINE SIXTEEN (1 CORINTHIANS 16)

Paul concludes with instructions about the offering for the Christians in Jerusalem and about his future visit to them. He conveys greetings from several people and ends with a curse on unbelievers and a plea for Christ's return.

I. PAUL'S COLLECTION (16:1-4): The apostle gives directions concerning an offering the Corinthian church is taking.

    A. Why it is being received (16:1): It is for the needy believers in Jerusalem.

    B. When it is to be taken (16:2a): On the first day of every week.

    C. What amount is expected from each person (16:2b): The amount will depend on each person's income.

    D. Who will deliver the money to Jerusalem (16:3-4): The Corinthian church will choose these individuals.

II. PAUL'S COMMITMENT (16:5-9)

    A. He promises to visit them in Corinth in the near future (16:5-7).

    B. He plans to stay in Ephesus for the present (16:8-9).

        1. *When he will leave* (16:8): He plans to stay until Pentecost.

        2. *Why he will stay* (16:9): God has opened up a great preaching opportunity for him.

III. PAUL'S COWORKERS (16:10-12, 15-20): He mentions seven of his companions.
   A. **Timothy** (16:10-11): Paul requests two things in regard to Timothy.
      1. *"Treat him with respect"* (16:10): When he comes, they are to warmly welcome this servant of the Lord.
      2. *"Send him on his way with your blessings when he returns to me"* (16:11).
   B. **Apollos** (16:12): Paul has begged Apollos to visit the Corinthians, but the latter feels the timing is not right.
   C. **Stephanas** (16:15-16): This godly man and his family, Paul's first converts in Greece, will soon visit the Corinthians.
   D. **Fortunatus and Achaicus** (16:17-18): These fellow believers have just arrived to encourage and assist Paul.
   E. **Aquila and Priscilla** (16:19-20): They and the church that meets in their house send greetings.

IV. PAUL'S CHALLENGES (16:13-14)
   A. **"Stand true to what you believe"** (16:13).
   B. **"Everything you do must be done with love"** (16:14).

V. PAUL'S CLOSING WORDS (16:21-24)
   A. *Anathema* (16:22a): "If anyone does not love the Lord, that person is cursed."
   B. *Maranatha* (16:22b-24): "Our Lord, come! May the grace of the Lord Jesus be with you. My love to all of you in Christ Jesus."

2 Corinthians

SECTION OUTLINE ONE (2 CORINTHIANS 1)

Paul opens his second letter to the Corinthian church with consolation in the face of suffering and an explanation of his recent experiences.

I. CONSOLATION (1:1-7)
   A. **The person of consolation and comfort** (1:1-3): Paul describes the Father of our Lord Jesus Christ as "the source of every mercy and the God who comforts us."
   B. **The purpose of consolation and comfort** (1:4-5)
      1. *The root* (1:5): The more we suffer, the more God comforts us.
      2. *The fruit* (1:4): The more he comforts us, the more we can comfort others.
   C. **The pattern of consolation and comfort** (1:6-7): Paul offers his own experiences as an example of this tremendous principle.

II. EXPLANATION (1:8-24)
   A. **Paul writes about his recent trip to Asia** (1:8-14).
      1. *The apostle's trials in Asia* (1:8): He suffered much hardship.
      2. *The apostle's testimony in the hour of death* (1:9-11)
         a. He depended upon the God of life (1:9).
         b. He was delivered by the God of life (1:10-11).
   B. **Paul speaks of his planned trip to Macedonia** (1:12-24): Apparently the Corinthians accused Paul of lying when he did not visit them as promised. Paul declares both his and the Savior's truthfulness.
      1. *Paul's truthfulness* (1:12-18): Paul has always been straightforward with them.
      2. *Jesus' truthfulness* (1:19-24): Jesus is always truthful.

SECTION OUTLINE TWO (2 CORINTHIANS 2)

Paul writes about forgiveness and about the effect the gospel is having on those he witnesses to.

I. THE TEARS (2:1-4): Paul refers to his previous letter to the believers in Corinth—namely, 1 Corinthians.

A. The purpose for this letter (2:1-3): He wrote hoping the church would get some matters straightened out before he visited them.

B. The pain behind this letter (2:4): He penned it in great distress and anguish.

II. THE TRANSGRESSOR (2:5-11)

A. The individual (2:5-6): The church previously ousted an immoral and unrepentant believer (see 1 Corinthians 5).

B. The instructions (2:7-11): The man repented, and Paul commands the church to restore him, lest Satan take advantage of their unforgiving spirit.

III. THE TRIUMPH (2:12-17)

A. Paul's concern (2:12-13): He experiences some initial unrest when he does not find Titus in Troas.

B. Paul's confidence (2:14-17): Whatever his lot, Paul has the assurance of ultimate victory.

1. *The fragrance of the gospel message* (2:14-16)
    a. To the saved, it has the smell of life (2:14-15, 16b).
    b. To the lost, it has the smell of death (2:16a).
2. *The faithfulness of the gospel messenger* (2:17): Paul does not preach the gospel for profit but in the power of God.

SECTION OUTLINE THREE (2 CORINTHIANS 3)
Paul writes about the grace of God and the glory of the new covenant.

I. THE UNWRITTEN GRACE OF GOD (3:1-6)

A. The Pharisees' written letters of recommendation (3:1): Boastful Jewish leaders carry about with them long letters of recommendation.

B. The apostle's living letters of recommendation (3:2-6): Paul has no such need for dead and formal letters, as the transformed lives of his converts literally shout about his effectiveness and God's grace.

II. THE UNVEILED GLORY OF GOD (3:7-18): Paul contrasts the law of Moses with the gospel of grace, showing the superiority of the latter over the former.

A. The law of Moses (3:7, 9a, 10a, 11a, 13-15)

1. *It was accompanied by a fading glory* (3:7, 10a).
2. *It was temporary* (3:11a).
3. *It led to death* (3:9a).
4. *It functioned as a veil, restricting God's glory* (3:13-14a, 15).
5. *It prevented Christlikeness in the lives of unsaved Jews and Gentiles* (3:14b).

B. The gospel of grace (3:8, 9b, 10b, 11b-12, 16-18)
1. *It is accompanied by an unfading glory* (3:10b).
2. *It is eternal* (3:11b).
3. *It leads to life* (3:8).
4. *It functions as a mirror, reflecting God's glory* (3:16-18).
5. *It produces Christlikeness in the lives of saved Jews and Gentiles* (3:9b).
6. *It produces boldness* (3:12).

SECTION OUTLINE FOUR (2 CORINTHIANS 4)
Paul writes about appropriate attitudes toward the Scriptures and toward suffering.

I. HOW TO HANDLE THE SCRIPTURES (4:1-7)
   A. As practiced by Paul the apostle (4:1-2, 5-7)
   1. *His approach in regard to the divine message* (4:1-2, 5)
      a. He does not use secret and shameful methods (4:1-2a).
      b. He does not distort the Word of God (4:2b).
      c. He preaches Jesus and not himself (4:5).
   2. *His attitude in regard to the human messenger* (4:6-7)
      a. The illustration (4:6-7a): Paul pictures our body as a jar of clay, into which God has placed the treasure of the gospel.
      b. The implication (4:7b): This is done "so everyone can see that our glorious power is from God and is not our own."
   B. As practiced by Satan, the adversary (4:3-4): He blinds the minds of unbelievers, preventing them from seeing the light of the gospel.

II. HOW TO HANDLE SUFFERING (4:8-18): Paul discusses the reality of suffering and the desired reaction to it in the lives of believers.
   A. The reality of suffering (4:8-9): Paul says he is:
   1. *Pressed on every side by troubles* (4:8a)
   2. *Perplexed but not giving up* (4:8b)
   3. *Hunted down but not abandoned* (4:9a)
   4. *Knocked down but able to keep going* (4:9b)
   B. The (desired) reaction to suffering (4:10-13)
   1. *Paul shares in the death of Jesus so that the life of Jesus may be seen* (4:10).
   2. *He lives under constant danger so that Jesus will be obvious to them* (4:11-12).
   3. *He continues to preach* (4:13).
   C. The rewards of suffering (4:14-18)
   1. *Concerning the future* (4:14): A resurrected body.
   2. *Concerning the present* (4:16-18): A renewed body.

SECTION OUTLINE FIVE (2 CORINTHIANS 5)
Paul writes about the new bodies believers will one day receive and about the duty of believers as ambassadors for Christ.

I. THE REASSURANCE (5:1-8): Paul speaks concerning our new bodies.
   A. **The old body** (5:1a, 2a, 3-4a, 6-8)
      1. *Referred to as an earthly tent* (5:1a)
      2. *Filled with groans and sighs* (5:2a)
      3. *Dying* (3-4a)
      4. *Unable to see Jesus face-to-face* (5:6-8)
   B. **The new body** (5:1b, 2b, 4b-5)
      1. *Referred to as a home in heaven* (5:1b)
      2. *Without groans or sighs* (5:4b)
      3. *Eternal* (5:2b)
      4. *Able to see Jesus face-to-face* (5:5)

II. THE RESOLVE (5:9): Paul determines to please God in both bodies.

III. THE RECKONING (5:10): The apostle reminds his readers of a sober truth.
   A. **The place** (5:10a): It is the judgment seat of Christ.
   B. **The purpose** (5:10b): Here the quality (or lack of quality) of our life will be tested.

IV. THE RECONCILING (5:11-21)
   A. **God's special ministry** (5:14-15, 18-19, 21a)
      1. *He has reconciled all sinners* (5:14-15): This he has accomplished by the death of Christ on the cross.
      2. *He has regenerated all repenting sinners* (5:18-19, 21a): Each new believer receives a new nature.
   B. **Our special ministry** (5:11-13, 16-17, 20, 21b)
      1. *The task* (5:11-13, 21b): We have been given the ministry of reconciliation.
      2. *The title* (5:16-17, 20): God looks upon us as his earthly ambassadors!

SECTION OUTLINE SIX (2 CORINTHIANS 6)
Paul writes about the hardships he has endured and warns the Corinthians not to marry, or "team up with," unbelievers.

I. THE PLEA (6:1-2): Both Paul and Isaiah implore us not to receive God's grace in vain.
   A. **Paul's pleading** (6:1): We are not to reject God's kindness.
   B. **Isaiah's pleading** (6:2): See Isaiah 49:8.

II. THE PRIORITY (6:3): Paul feels that it is all-important not to put a stumbling block in anyone's way.

III. THE PAIN (6:4-5): Paul reviews his sufferings.
   A. **He has been beaten and imprisoned** (6:4-5a).
   B. **He has faced angry mobs** (6:5b).
   C. **He was worked to exhaustion** (6:5c).
   D. **He has endured sleepless nights and hunger** (6:5d).

IV. THE PATIENCE (6:6-7): He has endured all these things through God's love and power.

V. THE PARADOX (6:8-10): A paradox is an apparent but not real contradiction.
   A. **Paul is honest yet has been called a liar** (6:8).
   B. **He is known yet unknown** (6:9a).
   C. **He is dying, yet he lives** (6:9b).
   D. **He is sorrowful yet always rejoices** (6:10a).
   E. **He is poor yet makes many rich** (6:10b).
   F. **He has nothing yet possesses everything** (6:10c).

VI. THE PARENT (6:11-13): Paul speaks to the Corinthians as a loving father would address his children.

VII. THE PROHIBITION (6:14-18)
   A. **The restriction** (6:14a): Don't be yoked with unbelievers.
   B. **The reasons** (6:14b-16a): Paul asks what possible fellowship could exist between three groups:
      1. *Light and darkness* (6:14b)
      2. *Christ and Satan* (6:15)
      3. *The true God and a false idol* (6:16a)
   C. **The rewards** (6:16b-18): Three rewards are promised to all who obey and who separate themselves from the unclean.
      1. *God will live in them* (6:16b).
      2. *God will walk among them* (6:16c-17).
      3. *God will be a Father to them* (6:18).

SECTION OUTLINE SEVEN   (2 CORINTHIANS 7)
Paul expresses his joy over the Corinthian church's repentance.

I. THE RESOLUTION (7:1): Paul urges the Corinthians to turn from the unclean and to seek God's holiness.

II. THE REQUEST (7:2-4)
   A. **What the apostle asks** (7:2a): He asks that they make room for him in their hearts.
   B. **Why the apostle asks** (7:2b-4)
      1. *He has never wronged them* (7:2b).
      2. *He has them in his heart* (7:3-4).

III. THE RELIEF (7:5-7): Paul expresses a twofold relief.
   A. **Upon seeing Titus the man** (6:5-6): Paul has been beside himself worrying about Titus's safety.
   B. **Upon hearing Titus the messenger** (6:7): Paul is overjoyed to hear from Titus that the Corinthians warmly received both Titus himself and Paul's rebuke, which resulted in their repentance.

IV. THE REPENTANCE (7:8-11): Paul contrasts godly repentance with worldly repentance.
   A. **The first is brought about by genuine sorrow over one's sin and leads to salvation** (7:8-10a, 11).
   B. **The second is false and leads to death** (7:10b).

V. THE REAFFIRMATION (7:12-16): Paul's faith in the Corinthian church is reaffirmed by two factors.
   A. **They received Titus** (7:13b-16).
   B. **They repented of their sin** (7:12-13a).

SECTION OUTLINE EIGHT   (2 CORINTHIANS 8)
Paul writes concerning the financial offering the Corinthian church is taking for the destitute believers in Jerusalem.

I. GODLY GIVING—ILLUSTRATIONS (8:1-5, 9): Paul offers two examples of sacrificial giving.
   A. **The Macedonian believers** (8:1-5)
      1. *First they surrendered their will to the Savior* (8:5).
      2. *Then they sacrificially shared their wealth with the saints* (8:1-4).
   B. **The Lord Jesus Christ** (8:9)
      1. *What he was* (8:9a): Very rich.
      2. *What he became* (8:9b): Very poor.
      3. *Why he did it* (8:9c): So he could make spiritually poor people rich.

II. GODLY GIVING—INSTRUCTIONS (8:6-8, 10-15)
   A. **Give knowingly** (8:6-8): Paul says financial giving is related to the other spiritual gifts.
   B. **Give willingly** (8:10-11).
   C. **Give realistically** (8:12).
   D. **Give confidently** (8:13-15).

III. GODLY GIVING—INDIVIDUALS (8:16-24): Paul promises to send three men who will receive the offering at Corinth.
   A. **The names of these three men** (8:16-19): One is Titus; the other two are not named.
   B. **The need for these three men** (8:20-24): This will guard against any suspicion.

SECTION OUTLINE NINE (2 CORINTHIANS 9)
Paul completes a subject he began in the previous chapter—namely, the grace of giving.

I. THE MONETARY GIFT BY THE CORINTHIANS (9:1-14)
  A. **The review** (9:1-5)
    1. *Paul's confidence in the church at Corinth* (9:1-2): He brags about their past enthusiasm to collect an offering for the saints at Jerusalem.
    2. *Paul's charge to the church at Corinth* (9:3-5): He urges them to complete this task, for he is sending some men to receive the offering.
  B. **The reminder** (9:6-9)
    1. *The principle* (9:6, 8-9)
      a. To sow little is to reap little (9:6a).
      b. To sow much is to reap much (9:6b, 8-9).
    2. *The participant* (9:7): Each person should determine the amount of his or her gift freely, not in response to pressure.
  C. **The rewards** (9:10-14)
    1. *The giver will be blessed by the Lord* (9:10, 13).
    2. *The giver will be blessed by the recipient* (9:11-12, 14).

II. THE MAGNIFICENT GIFT BY THE FATHER (9:15): He gave us his own Son, Jesus Christ!

SECTION OUTLINE TEN (2 CORINTHIANS 10)
Paul defends his apostleship against the lies of the wicked Judaizers.

I. THE APOSTLE'S DEFENSE (10:1-13)
  A. **His meekness** (10:1): He appeals with the meekness and gentleness of Christ to the Corinthian believers.
  B. **His methodology** (10:2-6)
    1. *What Paul does not do* (10:2-3): He does not depend upon the tactics of this world.
    2. *What Paul does* (10:4-6): He uses God's mighty weapons to knock down Satan's strongholds.
  C. **His militancy** (10:7-11)
    1. *The ridicule* (10:7a, 10): What Paul's enemies say about him.
      a. He possesses no power or authority (10:7a).
      b. He writes like a lion but in person is weak as a lamb (10:10).
    2. *The response* (10:7b-9, 11): What Paul says about himself.
      a. He possesses the power and authority of Christ himself (10:7b).
      b. They will soon discover he is as a lion both in pen and in person (10:9, 11).

D. His measure (10:12-13)
　　1. *He does not compare himself to other men* (10:12).
　　2. *He does conform himself to Jesus Christ* (10:13).

II. THE APOSTLE'S DESIRE (10:14-18)
　A. His desire for them (10:14-15): Paul prays that their faith will grow.
　B. His desire for himself (10:16-18)
　　1. *That he be allowed to preach the gospel to the regions beyond* (10:16-17)
　　2. *That he be approved by God himself* (10:18)

SECTION OUTLINE ELEVEN (2 CORINTHIANS 11)
Paul warns against false apostles and talks more about the many trials he has endured for the gospel.

I. PAUL'S JEALOUSY OVER THE CHURCH (11:1-2)
　A. It is a godly jealousy (11:1-2a).
　B. It is a goal-oriented jealousy (11:2b): He desires to present the church as a pure virgin bride to Christ.

II. PAUL'S CONCERN REGARDING THE CHURCH (11:3-4)
　A. What he fears (11:3): He is concerned lest Satan deceive the Corinthian church as he once deceived Eve.
　B. Why he fears (11:4) They are so gullible, ready to believe anything they hear about Jesus and the gospel.

III. PAUL'S SERVICE TO THE CHURCH (11:5-12)
　A. He is not a "super" apostle, but knows what he is talking about (11:5-6).
　B. He "robbed" other churches, receiving their support so he could minister in Corinth at no cost (11:7-8).
　C. He earned his own keep, receiving nothing from the Corinthians when he ministered there (11:9-12).

IV. PAUL'S WARNING TO THE CHURCH (11:13-15): Paul describes their enemies—namely, the Judaizers.
　A. What they are able to do (11:13): The Judaizers deceive the church into accepting them as true apostles of Christ.
　B. How they are able to do it (11:14-15)
　　1. *The root of this ability* (11:14): Satan himself masquerades as an angel of light.
　　2. *The fruit of this ability* (11:15): Satan is then able to transform his followers in similar fashion.

V. PAUL'S CREDENTIALS AND THE CHURCH (11:16-22)
   A. **The Judaizers and their false credentials** (11:16-21a): These foes
      of the church use their credentials to harm believers.
   B. **The apostle and his valid credentials** (11:21b-22): This friend of
      the church uses his credentials to help believers.

VI. PAUL'S SUFFERINGS FOR THE CHURCH (11:23-33): The pain and
    persecution Paul endured are almost inconceivable.
    A. **He was imprisoned often** (11:23a).
    B. **He was whipped times without number** (11:23b).
       1. *He received 39 lashes from the Jews on five occasions* (11:24).
       2. *He was beaten with rods on three occasions* (11:25a).
    C. **He faced death time and again** (11:23c).
       1. *He faced danger from flooded rivers* (11:26b).
       2. *He faced danger from robbers* (11:26c).
       3. *He faced danger from both Jewish and Gentile mobs*
          (11:26d).
    D. **He was stoned once** (11:25b).
    E. **He was shipwrecked three times** (11:25c).
    F. **He spent a terror-filled night and day on the open sea** (11:25d).
    G. **He traveled many weary miles** (11:26a).
    H. **He spent sleepless nights** (11:27a).
    I. **He knew constant hunger and thirst** (11:27b).
    J. **He was often cold and ill-clothed** (11:27c).
    K. **He experienced harrowing escapes** (11:32-33).
    L. **He bore daily the burden for the many churches he had started**
       (11:28-31).

SECTION OUTLINE TWELVE (2 CORINTHIANS 12)
Paul describes his experience of being "caught up into the third
heaven" and talks about his thorn in the flesh God allowed to keep
him humble. He writes about some of his concerns for the Corinthians.

I. PAUL AND THE THIRD HEAVEN (12:1-10)
   A. **The vision of the apostle** (12:1-6)
      1. *Where he went* (12:1-3): He was suddenly transported to
         paradise.
      2. *What he heard* (12:4-6): He heard things so astounding that he
         cannot describe them in earthly language.
   B. **The vexation of the apostle** (12:7)
      1. *What he received* (12:7a): Satan inflicted Paul with a thorn in
         the flesh to torment him.
      2. *Why he received it* (12:7b): God permitted the Devil to do this
         to keep Paul from pride.

C. The victory of the apostle (12:8-10)
  1. *Paul's request* (12:8): Three times he begged the Lord to take the thorn in his flesh away.
  2. *God's refusal* (12:9): Each time the Lord responded, "My gracious favor is all you need."
  3. *Paul's realization* (12:10): "When I am weak, then I am strong."

II. PAUL AND THE THIRD TRIP (12:11-21): Paul talks about his planned third visit to the Corinthian church.
  A. His reminder (12:11-13): Contrary to what his enemies say, Paul reminds the Corinthians that his previous miracles performed among them demonstrate that he is a true apostle.
  B. His relationship (12:14-19): Paul likens himself to a loving father and the Corinthian believers to unloving children.
  C. His regret (12:20-21): Paul is apprehensive that he will find the church still filled with pride, gossip, division, and disorder upon his arrival.

SECTION OUTLINE THIRTEEN (2 CORINTHIANS 13)
Paul talks about his coming visit to Corinth and gives a few closing words.

I. PAUL'S COMING VISIT (13:1-10)
  A. The number (13:1a): This will be his third visit.
  B. The need (13:1b-10): The apostle feels this trip is necessary for several reasons.
    1. *Paul's witness against them* (13:1b-4): He reminds the church of Deuteronomy 19:15, which says that every truth must be established by the testimony of two or three witnesses; thus, Paul's third trip.
    2. *Paul's warning to them* (13:5-6): He urges the Corinthians to examine themselves to determine whether they are actually saved.
    3. *Paul's wish for them* (13:7-10): He hopes to find them mature, having no need for further chastisement.

II. PAUL'S CLOSING WORDS (13:11-13)
  A. His fourfold admonition (13:11)
    1. *Rejoice* (13:11a).
    2. *Change your ways* (13:11b).
    3. *Encourage each other* (13:11c).
    4. *Live in harmony and peace* (13:11d).
  B. His threefold benediction (13:12-13)
    1. *"May the love of the Father be with you"* (13:12, 13b).
    2. *"May the grace of our Lord Jesus Christ be with you"* (13:13a).
    3. *"May the fellowship of the Holy Spirit be with you"* (13:13c).

Galatians

SECTION OUTLINE ONE (GALATIANS 1)
Paul opens his letter to the Galatian church with an affirmation of his identity as an apostle of Christ. He expresses grief that the Galatians have turned from the gospel, and he talks briefly about his own conversion experience.

I. PAUL'S GREETINGS (1:2-5)
   A. **To the saints in Galatia** (1:2): Paul sends greetings from himself and the Christians he is with.
   B. **From the Savior in glory** (1:3-5)
      1. *Who died to save us* (1:3-4a)
      2. *Who lives to sanctify us* (1:4b-5)

II. PAUL'S GRIEF (1:6-10)
   A. **The apostle's concern** (1:6-7): He grieves that the Galatians have turned from the gospel of grace to the bondage of the law.
   B. **The apostle's curse** (1:8-10): He pronounces God's severe judgment on those who dare pervert the gospel message.

III. PAUL'S GOSPEL CALL (1:1, 11-24)
   A. **The revelation** (1:11-12)
      1. *It is not of man* (1:1, 11): The gospel was not compiled by any human authority, reasoning, or logic.
      2. *It is not from man* (1:12): The gospel was communicated to Paul by none other than Jesus Christ.
   B. **The review** (1:13-24)
      1. *Paul speaks of his pre-conversion activities* (1:13-14).
         a. His cruelty toward Christianity (1:13): He persecuted Christians.
         b. His commitment to Judaism (1:14): As a very religious Jew he followed all the laws and customs.
      2. *Paul speaks of his post-conversion activities* (1:15-24).
         a. His choosing by God (1:15-16): He was chosen before he was born, and the Son was revealed to him.
         b. His travels from Arabia to Damascus (1:17)
         c. His travels from Damascus to Jerusalem (1:18-20): Three

years after his conversion, he went to Jerusalem and met with Peter and James, the Lord's brother, for 15 days.

   d. His travels from Jerusalem to Syria and Cilicia (1:21-24)

SECTION OUTLINE TWO (GALATIANS 2)

Paul writes about his second trip to Jerusalem and about his rebuke of Peter.

I. THE RECEPTION OF PAUL IN JERUSALEM (2:1-10): Paul, accompanied by Barnabas and Titus, visited Jerusalem for a second time 14 years after his first visit.

   A. The reason for the visit (2:1-2): It was to confer with the Christian leaders there concerning Paul's ministry to the Gentiles.

   B. The results of their visit (2:3-10)

      1. *Paul and the leaders* (2:3, 6-10)

         a. The leaders agreed with Paul that Titus should not be circumcised (2:3).

         b. The leaders accepted Paul as a coworker (2:6-10).

      2. *Paul and the legalizers* (2:4-5): They made an unsuccessful attempt to push their legalism upon him.

II. THE REBUKE BY PAUL IN ANTIOCH (2:11-21)

   A. The need for Paul's rebuke (2:11-13): Peter was refusing to fellowship with saved but uncircumcised Gentiles.

   B. The nature of Paul's rebuke (2:14-21)

      1. *The contents* (2:14-18): He reminded Peter that it is faith, not circumcision, that saves both Jews and Gentiles.

      2. *The conclusion* (2:19-21)

         a. All believers have been crucified with Christ (2:19-20a).

         b. All believers are to live by the faith of the indwelling Christ (2:20b-21).

SECTION OUTLINE THREE (GALATIANS 3)

Paul offers five arguments, all demonstrating the sufficiency of justification by faith alone.

I. THE ARGUMENT FROM THE GALATIANS THEMSELVES (3:1-5)

   A. They became believers by turning to the gospel (3:1-2).

   B. They are becoming bewitched by turning from the gospel (3:3-5).

II. THE ARGUMENT FROM ABRAHAM (3:6-9, 15-18)

   A. How Abraham was saved (3:6-9)

      1. *His salvation* (3:6): He was justified by faith.

      2. *Our salvation* (3:7-9): Both Jews and Gentiles are justified by faith.

B. Who saved Abraham (3:15-16): It was Christ, who came from the line of Abraham.

C. When Abraham was saved (3:17-18): The promise was given to him 430 years before the law was introduced.

III. THE ARGUMENT FROM THE LAW (3:10-12, 19-25)
   A. The problem of the law (3:10-12): Those under the law who do not obey all of it are cursed by the law.
   B. The purpose of the law (3:19-25)
      1. *It helps to point out our sin* (3:19-20).
      2. *It helps to prepare for our Savior* (3:21-25): The law serves as teacher and guide to bring us to Christ.

IV. THE ARGUMENT FROM THE WORK OF THE SON OF GOD (3:13-14)
   A. What he did (3:13a): He redeemed us from the curse of the law.
   B. How he did it (3:13b): He became a curse for us on the cross.
   C. Why he did it (3:14): He did it to fulfill the promise God gave Abraham.

V. THE ARGUMENT FROM THE WORK OF THE SPIRIT OF GOD (3:26-29)
   A. What he does (3:26-27): He baptizes repenting Jews and Gentiles into the body of Christ.
   B. Why he does it (3:28-29): This assures that all may share in the promise once given to Abraham.

SECTION OUTLINE FOUR (GALATIANS 4)
In an attempt to free the Galatians from the terrible yoke of legalism, Paul appeals to their heads and their hearts.

I. PAUL'S "HEAD" WORDS (4:1-7, 21-31): He offers two illustrations.
   A. A legal illustration (4:1-7)
      1. *The Roman father and his son* (4:1-2)
         a. The frustration (4:1): Until he comes of age, the son can enjoy very little of his father's estate.
         b. The freedom (4:2): Upon coming of age, the son can enjoy all of his father's estate.
      2. *The redeemer's Father and the Father's children* (4:3-7)
         a. The frustration (4:3): While under the law, they enjoyed very little of the Father's estate.
         b. The freedom (4:4-7): Upon coming of age (effected by Christ's death), they can enjoy all of their Father's estate.
   B. An Old Testament illustration (4:21-31): Paul uses the example of Hagar and Sarah, two Old Testament women, to allegorize the law of Moses and the grace of God.
      1. *Hagar* (an allegory of the law) (4:21-22a, 23a, 24-25, 29a, 30-31a)
         a. She was a slave (4:21-22a).
         b. Her marriage to Abraham was fleshly directed (4:23a).

      c. Her son, Ishmael, was naturally born (4:24).

      d. Their son persecuted Abraham's second son, Isaac (4:29a).

      e. Her child was not considered Abraham's rightful heir (4:30-31a).

      f. She corresponds to earthly Jerusalem (4:25).

    2. *Sarah* (an allegory of grace) (4:22b, 23b, 26-28, 29b, 31b)

      a. She was a free woman (4:22b).

      b. Her marriage to Abraham was spirit directed (4:23b).

      c. Her son, Isaac, was supernaturally born (4:27).

      d. This son was persecuted by Ishmael (4:29b).

      e. Her child was considered Abraham's rightful heir (4:28).

      f. Sarah represents the new covenant (4:27).

      g. She corresponds to the heavenly Jerusalem (4:26).

II. PAUL'S "HEART" WORDS (4:8-20)

  A. The rebuke (4:8-11): Again he faults them for their return to legalism.

  B. The review (4:12-18)

    1. *Paul reminds them that they once were his friends* (4:12-15).

    2. *Paul wants to know if they are now his foes* (4:16-18).

  C. The rebirth (4:19-20): Paul will again suffer the pains of childbirth until Christ is fully developed in them.

SECTION OUTLINE FIVE (GALATIANS 5)

Paul shows how the miracle of justification by faith brings about both freedom and fruit.

I. THE FREEDOM IN THE SON (5:1-15)

  A. Protection from the legalism of the legalizers (5:1-12)

    1. *The work of Christ has freed us from the bondage of the law* (5:1-4, 6-12).

    2. *The work of Christ will (someday) free us from the bondage of our body* (5:5).

  B. Protection from the license of the libertines (5:13-15): Paul warns against using freedom to indulge the sinful nature.

II. THE FRUIT OF THE SPIRIT (5:16-26)

  A. The conflict (5:16-18): Paul describes the fierce struggle within the believer.

    1. *The contenders* (5:17-18)

      a. The evil nature (5:17a)

      b. The Holy Spirit (5:17b-18)

    2. *The council* (5:16)

      a. "Live according to your new life in the Holy Spirit" (5:16a).

      b. "Then you won't be doing what your sinful nature craves" (5:16b).

B. The children (5:19-26)
    1. *The fruit of the flesh* (5:19-21): Immorality, idolatry, hatred, discord, selfish ambition, envy, drunkenness, etc.
    2. *The fruit of the Spirit* (5:22-26): Love, joy, peace, patience, kindness, goodness, faithfulness, gentleness, and self-control.

SECTION OUTLINE SIX (GALATIANS 6)
Paul closes his letter with some final instructions.

I. PAUL AND THE SAINTS (6:1-10): Paul writes his final instructions to the Galatian believers, reminding them of three laws.
  A. The law of sharing and caring (6:1-5)
    1. *The name of this law* (6:1-2): Paul calls it the law of Christ.
    2. *The nature of this law* (6:3-5): Spiritual believers are to gently restore fallen believers back to fellowship.
  B. The law of receiving and giving (6:6): Those who are taught the Word of God should help their teachers by paying them.
  C. The law of sowing and reaping (6:7-10)
    1. *Those who sow only sinful desires will reap everlasting death* (6:7-8a).
    2. *Those who sow what is good will reap everlasting life* (6-8b-10).

II. PAUL AND THE SAVIOR (6:11-18)
  A. Paul testifies concerning his submission to Christ (6:11-16).
    1. *The legalizers boast in the ceremony of circumcision* (6:11-13).
    2. *The apostle boasts in the cross of Christ* (6:14-16).
  B. Paul testifies concerning his sufferings for Christ (6:17-18): He bears on his body the marks of his suffering for Jesus.

Ephesians

Paul opens his letter to the church in Ephesus by likening the church to a body.

I. THE CREATION OF THIS BODY (1:1-14): The entire Trinity was involved.
   A. **It was planned by the Father** (1:1-6).
      1. *He blessed us* (1:1-3).
      2. *He selected us* (1:4).
         a. When this occurred (1:4a): "Before he made the world."
         b. Why this occurred (1:4b): That we might be "holy and without fault in his eyes."
      3. *He adopted us* (1:5-6).
   B. **It was purchased by the Son** (1:7-12).
      1. *What Jesus did* (1:7-10)
         a. He redeemed us by his blood (1:7-8).
         b. He will someday gather us in his name (1:9-10).
      2. *Why Jesus did it* (1:11-12): That we might give praise to God.
   C. **It is preserved by the Spirit** (1:13-14).
      1. *What the Holy Spirit does* (1:13): His presence serves as a special seal on our heart.
      2. *Why the Holy Spirit does it* (1:14): His presence guarantees our eternal security.

II. THE CONSECRATION OF THIS BODY (1:15-23): Paul prays that God will allow his church to understand four things about himself.
   A. **Concerning his person** (1:15-17): "So that you might grow in your knowledge of God."
   B. **Concerning his promise** (1:18): "So that you can understand the wonderful future he has promised to those he called."
   C. **Concerning his power** (1:19-20a): "That you will begin to understand the incredible greatness of his power. . . . This is the same mighty power that raised Christ from the dead."

D. Concerning his position (1:20b-23)
1. *Christ's position in heaven* (1:20b-21): He occupies the exalted place at the right hand of the Father himself.
2. *Christ's position on earth* (1:22-23): He has been appointed head of the church.

SECTION OUTLINE TWO (EPHESIANS 2)

Paul likens the church to a temple. He reviews the what, why, and how concerning this spiritual temple of salvation.

I. WHAT WE ONCE WERE (2:1-3, 11-12)
   A. Dead in sin (2:1)
   B. Influenced by Satan (2:2)
   C. Controlled by lust (2:3a)
   D. Under God's wrath (2:3b)
   E. Pagans without God (2:11)
   F. Separated from Christ (2:12a)
   G. Without hope in this present world (2:12b)

II. WHAT GOD DID (2:4-6)
   A. He loved us (2:4).
   B. He liberated us (2:5).
   C. He lifted us (2:6).

III. WHY GOD DID IT (2:7): He did it so that he might display us as trophies of his grace.

IV. HOW GOD DID IT (2:8-9, 13)
   A. Through his special favor (2:8a)
   B. Through faith (2:8b-9)
   C. Through blood (2:13)

V. WHAT WE ARE NOW (2:10, 14-22)
   A. We are the products of grace (2:10).
      1. *The task* (2:10a): We have been created in Christ to do good works!
      2. *The time* (2:10b): This was planned before the foundation of the world.
   B. We are the partners of Israel (2:14-18).
      1. *The reconciler* (2:14): Christ has destroyed the barrier separating Jews from Gentiles.
      2. *The results* (2:15-18): He has joined into one body, a new person, both Jews and Gentiles.
   C. We are the people of God (2:19).
   D. We are the pillars of the temple (2:20-22).
      1. *The foundation* (2:20a): It is the apostles and prophets.
      2. *The cornerstone* (2:20b-22): It is Jesus Christ himself.

SECTION OUTLINE THREE (EPHESIANS 3)
Paul likens the church to a mystery.

I. PAUL'S EXPLANATION TO THE EPHESIANS (3:1-13): Paul talks about a special mystery.
   A. **The recipient of this mystery** (3:1-4, 7-9, 13): Paul has been given the details of this mystery.
      1. *The mistreatment of the apostle* (3:1a, 13): Even though guilty of no crime, Paul is in prison.
      2. *The mission of the apostle (3:1b-4, 9)*
         a. In regard to the divine Scriptures (3:1b-4): He is to preach God's Word to the Gentiles.
         b. In regard to the divine secret (3:9): He is to explain it to all people.
      3. *The meekness of the apostle* (3:7-8): He looks upon himself as "the least deserving Christian there is."
   B. **The time of this mystery** (3:5)
      1. *This mystery was once concealed in the Old Testament* (3:5a).
      2. *This mystery is now revealed in the New Testament* (3:5b).
   C. **The nature of this mystery** (3:6): The secret is that both Jews and Gentiles have been joined to the body of Christ.
   D. **The reasons for this mystery** (3:10-12)
      1. *That God's wisdom be experienced by the church* (3:10b-12)
      2. *That God's wisdom be exhibited to the angels* (3:10a)

II. PAUL'S SUPPLICATION FOR THE EPHESIANS (3:14-21): The apostle offers a threefold prayer for these believers.
   A. **In regard to the Spirit of God** (3:14-16): He prays that the Spirit will strengthen their inner beings.
   B. **In regard to the Son of God** (3:17): He prays that Christ might be more and more at home in their hearts.
   C. **In regard to the love of God** (3:18-21): He prays that they might be able to grasp the full dimensions of God's love.

SECTION OUTLINE FOUR (EPHESIANS 4)
Paul likens the church to a new creation.

I. THE POSITION OF THIS NEW CREATION (4:1-16)
   A. **The unity** (4:1-6): Paul appeals for Christian unity based on seven wonderful scriptural facts.
      1. *There is one body* (4:1-4a): Christ's body.
      2. *There is one Spirit* (4:4b): The Holy Spirit.
      3. *There is one hope* (4:4c): Eternal life.
      4. *There is one Lord* (4:5a): The triune God.
      5. *There is one faith* (4:5b): The Christian faith.

6. *There is one baptism* (4:5c): The baptism of the Spirit into Christ's body.
7. *There is one God and Father* (4:6): The heavenly Father.
B. **The Unifier** (4:7-16): The work of Christ brings all these things together.
1. *His gifts to believers* (4:7-11)
 a. When these gifts were given (4:7-10): It was after his ascension.
 b. What these gifts were (4:11)
  (1) Apostleship (4:11a)
  (2) Prophets (4:11b)
  (3) Evangelists (4:11c)
  (4) Pastors and teachers (4:11d)
2. *His goal for believers* (4:12-16)
 a. That they be equipped (4:12)
 b. That they be mature (4:13)
 c. That they be settled (4:14-16)

II. THE DISPOSITION OF THIS NEW CREATION (4:17-32): A new life demands a new lifestyle.
A. **Believers are to avoid immoral lifestyles** (4:17-19): Paul describes the unsaved as having:
1. *Confused thoughts* (4:17)
2. *Hardened hearts* (4:18b)
3. *Closed minds* (4:18a)
4. *Impure and greedy thoughts* (4:19)
B. **Believers are to adopt a spiritual lifestyle** (4:20-32).
1. *They are to have a renewal of spiritual thoughts and attitudes* (4:20-23).
3. *They are to put off the old self, including* (4:24, 26-28a, 29a, 30-32):
 a. Lying (4:24)
 b. Uncontrolled anger (4:26-27)
 c. Stealing (4:28a)
 d. Corrupt longings (4:29a, 31)
 e. Grieving the Holy Spirit (4:30)
2. *They are to put on the new self, including* (4:25, 28b-29, 32):
 a. Truthfulness (4:25)
 b. Honest labor (4:28b)
 c. Helping those in need (4:28c)
 d. Building one another up (4:29b)
 e. Kindness and compassion (4:32a)
 f. Forgiveness (4:32b)

SECTION OUTLINE FIVE (EPHESIANS 5)
Paul likens the church to obedient children, husbands, and wives.

I. OBEDIENT CHILDREN (5:1-21): Twelve rules for the Father's household:
   A. **Follow Christ in love** (5:1-2).
   B. **Avoid all immorality** (5:3).
   C. **Refrain from obscene language** (5:4-5).
   D. **Don't allow others to deceive you** (5:6-7).
   E. **Walk in the light** (5:8-9, 11-14).
   F. **Seek God's will and do it** (5:10, 17).
   G. **Use every opportunity for doing good** (5:15-16).
   H. **Don't get drunk on wine** (5:18a).
   I. **Be filled with the Spirit** (5:18b).
   J. **Use music to encourage each other and to worship God** (5:19).
   K. **Be thankful for all things** (5:20).
   L. **Submit to one another** (5:21).

II. OBEDIENT HUSBANDS AND WIVES (5:22-33)
   A. **Wives are to submit to their husbands as the church submits to Christ** (5:22-24).
   B. **Husbands are to love their wives as Christ loves the church** (5:25-33).
      1. *Christ died for the church* (5:25).
      2. *Christ lives to make the church holy and clean* (5:26).
      3. *Christ will someday present the church to himself as a glorious church without stain or wrinkle* (5:27).
   C. **Husbands are to love their wives as they love their own bodies** (5:28-33).

SECTION OUTLINE SIX (EPHESIANS 6)
Paul likens the church to a soldier.

I. BOOT-CAMP TRAINING (6:1-9)
   A. **The example of children and parents** (6:1-4)
      1. *As soldiers, children are to honor and obey their parents* (6:1-3).
      2. *As commanders, parents are to discipline and instruct their children* (6:4).
   B. **The example of servants and masters** (6:5-9)
      1. *Servants are to serve their masters as they would serve Christ* (6:5-8).
      2. *Masters are to treat their servants as they would treat Christ* (6:9).

II. FRONTLINE FIGHTING (6:10-24)
   A. **The exhortation** (6:10-11a, 13, 18-20): Paul issues a fourfold exhortation.
      1. *Be strong* (6:10): Find your strength in God's mighty power.
      2. *Prepare yourself* (6:11a): Put on the full armor of God.
      3. *Stand firm* (6:13).
      4. *Pray always* (6:18-20).
         a. For yourselves (6:18a)
         b. For others (6:18b)
         c. For Paul himself (6:19-20)
   B. **The enemy** (6:11b-12): Satan.
      1. *His craftiness* (6:11b)
      2. *His cohorts* (6:12): The wicked demons of Satan's kingdom.
   C. **The equipment** (6:14-17)
      1. *The belt of truth* (6:14a)
      2. *The body armor of God's righteousness* (6:14b)
      3. *The sandals of the Good News* (6:15)
      4. *The shield of faith* (6:16)
      5. *The helmet of salvation* (6:17a)
      6. *The sword of the Spirit* (6:17b): The Word of God
   D. **The envoy** (6:21-22): Paul is sending Tychicus, a faithful helper in the Lord's work, to encourage and inform the Ephesians concerning Paul's welfare.
   E. **The benediction** (6:23-24): "May God give you peace, dear friends, and love with faith, from God the Father and the Lord Jesus Christ. May God's grace be upon all who love our Lord Jesus Christ with an undying love."

Philippians

SECTION OUTLINE ONE (PHILIPPIANS 1)

Paul opens his letter to the church in Philippi with a presentation of Christ as the believer's life purpose.

I. PAUL'S SUPPLICATION FOR THE PHILIPPIAN BELIEVERS (1:1-11)
   A. **For whom he prays** (1:1-2): Pastors, deacons, and all Christians in Philippi.
   B. **When he prays** (1:3): "Every time I think of you."
   C. **How he prays** (1:4): He prays with his heart filled with joy.
   D. **Why he prays** (1:5, 7-8): The Philippian believers have rendered great assistance to Paul, both in prison and out of prison.
   E. **What he prays** (1:6, 9-11)
      1. *That God's Word be carried to its completion in every believer until the return of Christ* (1:6)
      2. *That they might be filled with love* (1:9)
      3. *That they might have the spirit of discernment* (1:10)
      4. *That they be filled with the fruits of righteousness (or of salvation)* (1:11)

II. PAUL'S EXPLANATION TO THE PHILIPPIAN BELIEVERS (1:12-30)
   A. **The report** (1:12-13): Paul's imprisonment has served to advance the gospel, starting with the palace guard and spreading from there.
   B. **The reaction** (1:14-17)
      1. *Concerning his friends* (1:14, 16): Paul's chains encourage them to increase their efforts in proclaiming the gospel.
      2. *Concerning his foes* (1:15, 17): They, too, are spreading the gospel, hoping to make the apostle jealous.
   C. **The rejoicing** (1:18): Whatever the motive, Paul rejoices that the gospel is being preached.
   D. **The resolve** (1:19-26)
      1. *Paul's dilemma* (1:19-23)
         a. To remain in this life would result in additional fruit (1:19-21a, 22).
         b. To depart this life would mean being with Christ (1:21b, 23).

2. *Paul's decision* (1:24-26): He will remain.
E. **The request** (1:27-28): Whatever happens to him, the Philippians are to continue conducting themselves in a manner worthy of the gospel.
F. **The reminder** (1:29-30): They have been granted two wonderful privileges.
    1. *To trust in Christ* (1:29a)
    2. *To suffer for Christ* (1:29b-30)

SECTION OUTLINE TWO (PHILIPPIANS 2)
Paul presents Christ as the believer's life pattern.

I. THE CHALLENGE FROM PAUL (2:1-18): He desires that the church strive for humility.
  A. **The essentials in humility** (2:1-4)
    1. *Unity in love* (2:1-2a)
    2. *Unity in spirit and purpose* (2:2b-4)
  B. **The example of humility** (2:5-11): Paul holds up the earthly ministry of Christ.
    1. *The pain* (2:5-8b)
      a. Even though he was God, he did not cling to his rights as God (2:5-6).
      b. He laid aside his glory (2:7a).
      c. He took upon himself the nature of a human servant (2:7b).
      d. He humbled himself (2:8a).
      e. He became obedient and died on the cross (2:8b).
    2. *The gain* (2:9-11)
      a. God has exalted him to the highest place (2:9a).
      b. He has been given a name above all other names (2:9b).
      c. Someday all people will acknowledge that he is Lord (2:10-11).
  C. **The exhortation to humility** (2:12-18)
    1. *Let God perfect in you his salvation* (2:12-13).
    2. *Don't complain* (2:14).
    3. *Shine as beacons of light in a dark world* (2:15).
    4. *Hold to the Word of life* (2:16).
    5. *Rejoice with Paul in his sacrifice* (2:17-18).

III. THE COWORKERS FROM PAUL (2:19-30): Paul promises to send two special messengers to the Philippian church.
  A. **Timothy** (2:19-24)
    1. *Timothy, messenger of God* (2:19): Paul says Timothy will minister to them.
    2. *Timothy, man of God* (2:20-23): Paul describes Timothy as a spiritual giant.
    3. *Paul, too, hopes to come visit them soon* (2:24).
  B. **Epaphroditus** (2:25-30)

1. *The soldier* (2:25): The Philippians sent this faithful spiritual warrior to help Paul.
2. *The stricken* (2:26-30)
   a. Epaphroditus was desperately ill (2:26b-27a, 30).
   b. God healed him (2:27b).
   c. Paul is sending him back home (2:26a, 28-29).

SECTION OUTLINE THREE (PHILIPPIANS 3)
Paul presents Christ as the believer's life prize.

I. THE CORRUPTION (3:1-3, 18-19): The Philippian church is facing deadly foes.
   A. **Who these foes are** (3:1-3): They are the Judaizers, whom Paul calls dogs because they say circumcision is necessary for salvation.
      1. *The true circumcision* (3:3a): "We who worship God in the Spirit . . . are truly circumcised."
      2. *The false circumcision* (3:3b) "We put no confidence in human effort."
   B. **What these foes are** (3:18, 19b)
      1. *They are enemies of the cross* (3:18).
      2. *They are proud and sensual materialists* (3:19b).
   C. **Where these foes are headed** (3:19a): "Their future is eternal destruction."

II. THE COST (3:4-8): Paul has given up two things to become a child of God.
   A. **His prestige among the Jews** (3:4-5)
   B. **His persecution against the church** (3:6)

III. THE CATCH (3:7-8): Paul gave up what he thought was important and gained the priceless knowledge of Christ.

IV. THE CROWN (3:9-14, 20-21): Paul has gained four things from becoming a child of God.
   A. **A new righteousness** (3:9-12)
   B. **A new goal** (3:13-14)
   C. **A new home** (3:20)
   D. **A new body** (3:21)

V. THE COMMAND (3:15-17): Paul says, "Pattern your lives after mine."

SECTION OUTLINE FOUR (PHILIPPIANS 4)
Paul concludes his letter with a presentation of Christ as the believer's life power.

I. UNIFYING POWER (4:1-3)
   A. **The contenders** (4:1-2): Two women in the church, Euodia and Syntyche, are arguing with each other.
   B. **The counselor** (4:3): Paul asks a godly man in the church to help reconcile these women.

II. FORTIFYING POWER (4:4-7)
   A. **The prayer** (4:4-6): Two rules must be observed for this power to function.
      1. *We must never be stressful in anything* (4:4-6a).
      2. *We must always be thankful in everything* (4:6b).
   B. **The peace** (4:7): If we obey these rules, God's peace will fortify and guard our heart.

III. PURIFYING POWER (4:8): We are to fix our thoughts on what is true, good, and right.

IV. EXEMPLIFYING POWER (4:9): Paul offers himself as a spiritual role model.

V. SATISFYING POWER (4:10-13)
   A. **The satisfaction** (4:10-12)
      1. *Paul is content even when hungry and in need of many things* (4:10, 11b-12a, 12d, 12f).
      2. *Paul is content when filled and in need of nothing* (4:11a, 12b-12c, 12e).
   B. **The satisfier** (4:13): Jesus himself is the source of Paul's strength.

VI. SANCTIFYING POWER (4:14-18, 21-23): Paul thanks the Philippians for their gifts to him, which are a "sweet-smelling sacrifice that is acceptable to God and pleases him." He sends greetings to all the Philippians.

VII. MULTIPLYING POWER (4:19): God will meet the needs of the Philippians as he has met the needs of Paul.

VIII. GLORIFYING POWER (4:20): God uses his power to glorify himself.

Colossians

SECTION OUTLINE ONE (COLOSSIANS 1)
Paul opens his letter to the Colossian church with thanksgiving and prayer and a discussion about Christ.

I. PAUL AND THE CHURCH AT COLOSSE (1:1-14, 24-29)
   A. The apostle's praise of this church (1:1-8)
      1. *How they received the gospel* (1:1-6): Paul commends them in regard to three things.
         a. Their faith toward the Lord (1:1-4a)
         b. Their love toward each other (1:4b)
         c. Their hope toward the future (1:5-6): They are looking forward to the joys of heaven.
      2. *From whom they received the gospel* (1:7-8): Epaphras shared Christ with them and is now ministering with Paul.
   B. The apostle's prayer for this church (1:9-14)
      1. *That they will grow in the knowledge of God* (1:9)
      2. *That they will please God* (1:10a)
      3. *That they will bear fruit for God* (1:10b)
      4. *That they will be strengthened by God* (1:11)
      5. *That they will be thankful to God* (1:12-14)
         a. For what the Father did (1:12-13)
         b. For what the Son did (1:14)
   C. The apostle's proclamation to the church (1:24-29): He has been chosen to reveal God's secret plan to them.
      1. *The particulars* (1:24-27): The secret is this: "Christ lives in you, and this is your assurance that you will share in his glory."
      2. *The purpose* (1:28-29): "We want to present them to God, perfect in their relationship to Christ."

II. CHRIST AND THE CHURCH AT COLOSSE (1:15-23)
   A. Who Christ is (1:15): He is the visible image of the invisible God.
   B. What Christ has done (1:16-23)
      1. *In regard to creation* (1:16-17, 20)
         a. He created all things (1:16).

b. He sustains all things (1:17).

c. He will reconcile all things (1:20).

2. *In regard to the church* (1:18-19, 21-23): He has been appointed head of the church.

SECTION OUTLINE TWO (COLOSSIANS 2)

Paul refers to two churches, one in Colosse and one in Laodicea.

I. PAUL'S WISHES FOR THESE TWO CHURCHES (2:1-7)

   A. That both be encouraged and knit together by strong ties of love (2:1-2a)

   B. That both understand God's secret plan (2:2b-3)

   C. That both guard against theological deception (2:4-5)

   D. That both continue growing in Christ (2:6-7a)

   E. That both rejoice and be thankful (2:7b)

II. PAUL'S WARNINGS TO THESE TWO CHURCHES (2:8-23): The apostle warns against four dangerous and destructive philosophies.

   A. Gnosticism (2:8-10)

   1. *The fiction* (2:8): The Gnostics diminish Christ to an angel.

   2. *The facts* (2:9-10): Paul says Christ was God incarnate in bodily form.

   B. Legalism (2:11-17)

   1. *Paul describes the love of Christ* (2:11-15).

   a. We have been crucified and raised to new life with him (2:11-12).

   b. He has forgiven our sins (2:13).

   c. He has blotted out the charges against us (2:14-15).

   2. *Paul describes the liberty in Christ* (2:16-17): Because of this, believers should not criticize each other.

   a. In matters of diet (2:16a): No one should condemn another believer for what he or she eats or drinks.

   b. In matters of days (2:16b-17): No one should condemn another believer for not celebrating certain holy days, for these old rules were only shadows.

   C. Mysticism (2:18-19)

   1. *The fiction* (2:18): Mysticism teaches that God can be known through two methods:

   a. Through the worship of angels (2:18a)

   b. Through the seeing of visions (2:18b)

   2. *The facts* (2:19): One can only know God through Christ, who is the head of the body, the church.

   D. Asceticism (2:20-23)

   1. *The fiction* (2:21-22): Asceticism teaches that one can purify the spirit by punishing the body.

2. *The facts* (2:20, 23)
   a. The spirit cannot be purified by punishing the body (2:23).
   b. The believer's body and spirit have been crucified with Christ (2:20).

SECTION OUTLINE THREE (COLOSSIANS 3–4:1)

Paul writes about the principles of holy living and addresses six types of individuals in regard to this matter.

I. HOLY LIVING: THE PRINCIPLES (3:1-17)
   A. **In regard to the believer's affection** (3:1-4)
      1. *The place of our affection* (3:1-3): We must transfer our affection from earth to heaven.
      2. *The person of our affection* (1:4): We must direct our affection toward Jesus.
   B. **In regard to the believer's spiritual apparel** (3:5-17)
      1. *What to put off* (3:5-9): God's anger comes on those who practice:
         a. Immorality and idolatry (3:5)
         b. Anger, malice, slander, and filthy language (3:8)
         c. Lying (3:9)
      2. *What to put on* (3:10-17)
         a. A new nature (3:10-11)
         b. Compassion, kindness, humility, gentleness, and patience (3:12)
         c. Forgiveness and love (3:13-14)
         d. God's peace and thankfulness (3:15)
         e. The words of Christ (3:16-17)

II. HOLY LIVING: THE PEOPLE (3:18-25; 4:1): Paul addresses six types of individuals.
   A. **Wives** (3:18): Submit to your husbands.
   B. **Husbands** (3:19): Love your wives, and never treat them harshly.
   C. **Children** (3:20): Obey your parents.
   D. **Fathers** (3:21): Don't aggravate your children.
   E. **Servants** (3:22-25): Serve your master as you would serve the Lord.
   F. **Masters** (4:1): Treat your servants as you would have your heavenly Master treat you.

SECTION OUTLINE FOUR (COLOSSIANS 4:2-18)
Paul closes his letter with a challenge to the Colossians, greetings sent from eight fellow believers, and Paul's own special greetings and encouragements.

I. PAUL'S CHALLENGE (4:2-6)
   A. **The Colossians are to be prayerful** (4:2a, 3-4, 18).
      1. *For themselves* (4:2a)
      2. *For the apostle himself* (4:3-4, 18)
   B. **The Colossians are to be watchful** (4:2b).
   C. **The Colossians are to be thankful** (4:2c).
   D. **The Colossians are to be fruitful** (4:5-6).

II. PAUL'S COWORKERS (4:7-14): Eight fellow believers send their greetings to the Colossians.
   A. **Tychicus** (4:7-8)
   B. **Onesimus** (4:9)
   C. **Aristarchus and Mark** (4:10)
   D. **Justus** (4:11)
   E. **Epaphras** (4:12-13)
   F. **Luke and Demas** (4:14)

III. PAUL'S GREETINGS (4:15): Paul sends greetings to the Christian brothers and sisters.

IV. PAUL'S COMMANDS (4:16-17)
   A. **To the church at Colosse** (4:16)
      1. *They are to read this letter* (4:16a).
      2. *They are to give this letter to the Laodicean church to read* (4:16b).
      3. *They are to read the letter Paul wrote to the Laodicean church* (4:16c).
   B. **To Archippus, a church member at Colosse** (4:17): "Be sure to carry out the work the Lord gave you."

V. PAUL'S BENEDICTION (4:18): Paul urges the Colossians to "remember my chains" and says, "May the grace of God be with you."

1 Thessalonians

SECTION OUTLINE ONE (1 THESSALONIANS 1)
Paul opens his first letter to the Thessalonians by listing five
characteristics of the church in Thessalonica.

I. IT IS AN ENERGETIC CHURCH (1:1-3): Paul gives thanks to God.
   A. For their strong faith (1:1-3a)
   B. For their labor of love (1:3b)

II. IT IS AN ELECT CHURCH (1:4): They have been chosen by God
    himself.

III. IT IS AN EXEMPLARY CHURCH (1:5-7)
   A. Paul's example to the church (1:5-6)
      1. *His preaching is anointed by the Holy Spirit* (1:5).
      2. *His personal lifestyle is anointed by the Holy Spirit* (1:6).
   B. Their example to the world (1:7): They are a model to all the
   believers in Greece.

IV. IT IS AN EVANGELISTIC CHURCH (1:8): Their faith in God has become
    known everywhere.

V. IT IS AN EXPECTANT CHURCH (1:9-10): They are looking forward to
   the return of Jesus from heaven.

SECTION OUTLINE TWO (1 THESSALONIANS 2)
Paul talks about the trip he took to visit Thessalonica and about his
desire to go again.

I. PAUL'S PAST TRIP TO THESSALONICA (2:1-16): The apostle overviews
   two factors concerning his visit to Thessalonica.
   A. How the gospel was relayed to the believers there (2:1-12): The
   preacher in the pulpit.
      1. *Paul the persecuted* (2:1-2): He speaks of his sufferings at
      Philippi just prior to coming to Thessalonica.

2. *Paul the pattern* (2:3-6, 9-10): The apostle served as a positive role model to the church.
  a. Concerning his words (2:3-6, 10): Paul's preaching was bold, truthful, straightforward, and sincere.
  b. Concerning his works (2:9): Paul labored long, weary hours so that he would not be a burden to the church.
3. *Paul the parent* (2:7-8, 11-12)
  a. He fed and cared for them as would a loving mother (2:7-8).
  b. He encouraged and comforted them as would a loving father (2:11-12).
- **B. How the gospel was received by the believers there** (2:13-16): The people in the pews.
  1. *The enthusiasm* (2:13): They accepted Paul's words as being from God.
  2. *The enemies* (2:14-16): They persevered through suffering and persecution.

II. PAUL'S PLANNED TRIP TO THESSALONICA (2:17-20)
- **A. Why the apostle is anxious to revisit them** (2:17, 19-20)
  1. *They are his reward and crown* (2:17, 19b).
  2. *They are his pride and joy* (2:19a, 20).
- **B. Why the apostle has been unable to revisit them** (2:18): He has been hindered by Satan.

SECTION OUTLINE THREE (1 THESSALONIANS 3)
Paul talks more about his visit to the Thessalonians and rejoices over the good news Timothy has brought back to him about them.

I. PAUL'S REVIEW (3:1-5): The apostle calls to remembrance events both during and after his previous visit to Thessalonica.
- **A. The action during his visit** (3:4): While he was with them, Paul warned the church that they could expect future persecution because of their faith in Christ; this soon came to pass.
- **B. The action after his visit** (3:1-3, 5)
  1. *Where he was* (3:1): He was in Athens, experiencing great concerns over the spiritual welfare of the church in Thessalonica.
  2. *What he did* (1:2-3, 5): He sent Timothy to minister to them.

II. PAUL'S REPORT (3:6-9)
- **A. The return of Timothy** (3:6): Paul informs them that Timothy has brought back the joyous news that they are growing in faith and love.
- **B. The rejoicing of Paul** (3:7-9): The apostle is greatly comforted by this news.

III. **PAUL'S REQUEST** (3:10-13): Paul now lifts up a twofold prayer request.
   A. For himself (3:10-11): Paul asks God to permit him to visit the church again.
   B. For the church (3:12-13)
      1. *That their love will both increase and overflow* (3:12)
      2. *That their hearts will be strengthened in matters of holiness* (3:13)

SECTION OUTLINE FOUR (1 THESSALONIANS 4)
Paul discusses the glorious rapture of the church.

I. THE CHALLENGES IN VIEW OF THE RAPTURE (4:1-12)
   A. What we are to do (4:1-2): Believers are to live their lives in a way that is pleasing to God.
   B. How we are to do it (4:3-12)
      1. *Be holy and pure* (4:3-5, 7-8).
      2. *Don't defraud another believer* (4:6).
      3. *Love all believers* (4:9-10).
      4. *Take care of your own business* (4:11).
      5. *Earn your own living* (4:12).

II. THE CHRONOLOGY OF THE RAPTURE (4:13-18)
   A. The purpose (4:13, 18): Paul explains the Rapture for two reasons:
      1. *To clarify* (4:13): He does not want them to be ignorant of God's prophetic plan.
      2. *To comfort* (4:18): This glorious event may be used to encourage each other.
   B. The particulars (4:14-17)
      1. *The return of the Lord* (4:14, 16a-c)
         a. The saints (4:14): All believers currently in heaven will accompany him.
         b. The sound (4:16a-c)
            (1) A loud command (4:16a)
            (2) The voice of the archangel (4:16b)
            (3) The trumpet call of God (4:16c)
      2. *The resurrection of the dead* (4:16d): The bodies of dead believers will rise first.
      3. *The rapture of the living* (4:15, 17): The believers on earth will be caught up to meet the Lord in the air.

SECTION OUTLINE FIVE (1 THESSALONIANS 5)

Paul sets forth several rules for the church in light of the coming Rapture, then ends his letter with three requests.

I. THE RULES (5:1-22)
   A. **Be watchful** (5:1-10).
      1. *The action* (5:1-2): The event Paul describes here is the Day of the Lord.
      2. *The reaction* (5:3-10): There has been, is, and will be a twofold response to this terrible time of judgment.
         a. The response by the children of darkness (5:3, 7): In their drunken unbelief, the unsaved will believe all is quiet and peaceful until sudden destruction falls on them.
         b. The response by the children of light (5:4-6, 8-10): We are to put on the full armor of God, for God has saved us.
   B. **Be helpful** (5:11, 14).
      1. *Build one another up* (5:11).
      2. *Warn, encourage, be compassionate, and show patience with one another* (5:14).
   C. **Be respectful** (5:12-13): Honor and love your spiritual leaders.
   D. **Be merciful** (5:15): Do not return evil for evil.
   E. **Be joyful** (5:16): At all times.
   F. **Be prayerful** (5:17): In all things.
   G. **Be thankful** (5:18): No matter what happens.
   H. **Be careful** (5:19-22)
      1. *What not to do* (5:19-20)
         a. Don't quench the Spirit (5:19).
         b. Don't despise prophecy (5:20).
      2. *What to do* (5:21-22)
         a. Do test everything (5:21).
         b. Do avoid every kind of evil (5:22).

II. THE REASSURANCES (5:23-24)
   A. **What God will do** (5:23)
      1. *At the present* (5:23a): He will sanctify us through and through.
      2. *In the future* (5:23b): He will present us blameless at Christ's coming.
   B. **Why God will do it** (5:24): Because he is faithful.

III. THE REQUESTS (5:25-28)
   A. **Pray for me** (5:25).
   B. **Greet everyone for me** (5:26).
   C. **Read this letter to all the Christians** (5:27-28).

2 Thessalonians

SECTION OUTLINE ONE (2 THESSALONIANS 1)

Paul opens his second letter to the Thessalonians by praising them for faith in Christ and for their love for others. He encourages them, saying that the persecution they are enduring will prepare them for the Kingdom.

I. PAUL'S PRAISE OF THE CHURCH AT THESSALONICA (1:1-4)
   A. **The church's testimony** (1:1-3)
      1. *Their faith in the Savior has grown more and more* (1:1-3a).
      2. *Their love for the saints has grown more and more* (1:3b).
   B. **The church's trials** (1:4): They have grown spiritually in spite of troubles and trials.

II. PAUL'S PROMISE TO THE CHURCH AT THESSALONICA (1:5-10): The apostle says their trials will be used to accomplish a twofold purpose.
   A. **What (1:5-6)**
      1. *Concerning the persecuted* (1:5): Their hardships will be used to prepare believers for the Kingdom of God.
      2. *Concerning the persecutors* (1:6): God is already preparing judgment and punishment for those who harm believers.
   B. **When** (1:7-10): Both purposes will be accomplished at Christ's second coming.

III. PAUL'S PRAYER FOR THE CHURCH AT THESSALONICA (1:11-12)
   A. **Concerning God's power** (1:11a): That it might strengthen them.
   B. **Concerning God's purpose** (1:11b): That it might be fulfilled in them.
   C. **Concerning God's person** (1:12): That he might be glorified by them.

Paul writes about the Great Tribulation and gives thanks to God for
the faithful believers at Thessalonica.

I. THE DAY OF THE LORD (2:1-12): This is a reference to the coming
   Great Tribulation.
   A. The day of the Lord and the church (2:1-3)
      1. *The confusion* (2:1-2): The church at Thessalonica has been
         falsely taught they are currently going through the Great
         Tribulation.
      2. *The clarification* (2:3b, 3c): Paul reassures them this is not the
         case, for two events must occur prior to that terrible time.
         a. A worldwide religious apostasy (2:3b)
         b. The appearance of a satanic superman (2:3c)
   B. The day of the Lord and the Antichrist (2:3a-4, 8-9)
      1. *His titles* (2:3a, 8a, 9a)
         a. "The man of lawlessness" (2:3a, 8a)
         b. "This evil man" (2:9a)
      2. *His travesty* (2:4): He will sit in the Temple of God and claim
         that he is God.
      3. *His trickery* (2:9b): He will deceive the world by his miracles,
         signs, and wonders.
      4. *His trampling* (2:8b): He will be utterly crushed and consumed
         by Jesus at the Second Coming.
   C. The day of the Lord and the restrainer (2:5-7): The Holy Spirit
      will hold the Antichrist back until the appointed time.
   D. The day of the Lord and the unsaved (2:10-12): God will allow
      the unsaved to be totally deceived by the Antichrist for their sin
      of rejecting the truth.

II. THE DISCIPLES OF THE LORD (2:13-17): Paul gives thanks for the
    believers at Thessalonica.
   A. Their election by the Lord (2:13-14): God chose them from the
      very beginning.
   B. Their exhortation by the apostle (2:15-17): Paul tells them to
      stand firm and to keep a strong grip on the truth.

Paul closes his letter with a request for prayer and an exhortation to
godly living.

I. PAUL'S REQUEST (3:1-2): He asks for prayer for two things from the
   believers in Thessalonica.
   A. That they pray for God's messenger (3:2): He asks for prayer that
      he would be delivered from wicked and evil men.

B. That they pray for God's message (3:1): Paul desires that the gospel message be allowed to spread rapidly everywhere.

II. PAUL'S REASSURANCE (3:3-5)
   A. He reassures them concerning God's faithfulness (3:3-4).
   B. He reassures them concerning God's love and patience (3:5).

III. PAUL'S REPRIMAND (3:6-18)
   A. The recipients (3:6-11, 13, 14b): Paul lists three kinds of individuals needing to be rebuked.
      1. *The lazy* (3:6-10): They should work hard.
      2. *The gossipers* (3:11, 13): They should mind their own business and do good.
      3. *The disobedient* (3:14b): Stay away from them.
   B. The rules (3:12, 14a, 15): Paul gives three steps to be taken in dealing with these individuals.
      1. *Step 1—identify them* (3:14a)
      2. *Step 2—admonish them* (3:12, 15a)
      3. *Step 3—love them* (3:15b): Look upon the person not as an enemy but as an erring brother or sister.

IV. PAUL'S FINAL REMARKS (3:16-18)
   A. The apostle's heart (3:16, 18)
      1. *He prays that they will experience God's peace* (3:16).
      2. *He prays that they will experience God's grace* (3:18).
   B. The apostle's hand (3:17): He pens the closing words with his own hand.

1 Timothy

SECTION OUTLINE ONE (1 TIMOTHY 1)
Paul opens his first letter to Timothy with a warning against false
teaching and a set of instructions for Timothy.

I. THE WELL-BELOVED OF PAUL (1:1-2): Timothy is Paul's beloved
spiritual son in the faith.

II. THE WARNING BY PAUL (1:3-11): The apostle urges Timothy to
remain in Ephesus so that he might counteract some false teachings
in regard to the law of Moses.
  A. **The perverting of the law of Moses** (3:1-7)
    1. *The perverters* (1:3a): They are self-appointed "experts" of the
       law, going about spreading their poison.
    2. *The perversion* (1:3b-7): These men have added a grievous
       mixture of myths, fables, and endless genealogies to the law.
  B. **The purpose of the law of Moses** (3:8-11)
    1. *It was not made to control saved people* (1:8a).
    2. *It was made to control unsaved people* (1:8b-11).

III. THE WITNESS BY PAUL (1:12-17): Here the apostle expresses his
profound thanksgiving for God's faithfulness.
  A. **What God did** (1:12, 14-15)
    1. *He saved Paul (1:14-15).*
    2. *He selected Paul (1:12).*
  B. **When God did it** (1:13): At the time, the apostle was a blas-
    phemer and violent persecutor of Christians.
  C. **Why God did it** (1:16-17): He did it to demonstrate his amazing
    grace to even the worst of sinners.

IV. THE WISDOM BY PAUL (1:18-20)
  A. **What Timothy is to do** (1:18-19b)
    1. *Fight the good fight (1:18).*
    2. *Keep the faith (1:19a).*
    3. *Maintain a clear conscience (1:19b).*

B. What Hymenaeus and Alexander have done (1:19c-20)
   1. *Their perversion* (1:19c): They have made a shipwreck of their faith, bringing shame to the name of Christ.
   2. *Their punishment* (1:20): Paul has delivered them over to Satan.

SECTION OUTLINE TWO (1 TIMOTHY 2)
Paul writes about proper worship of God.

I. THE WORSHIP OF GOD (2:1-2, 8): Paul discusses the subject of prayer.
   A. For whom we should pray (2:1-2a)
      1. *For those in authority (2:2a)*
      2. *For everyone (2:1)*
   B. Why we should pray (2:2b): "So that we can live in peace and quietness."
   C. How we should pray (2:8): "With holy hands lifted up to God, free from anger and controversy."

II. THE WILL OF GOD (2:3-7)
   A. The mission (2:3-4): "God . . . wants everyone to be saved."
   B. The mediator (2:5): Jesus Christ stands between God and people.
   C. The method (2:6): Salvation was effected by the death of Christ.
   D. The messenger (2:7): Paul has been chosen by God to serve as a missionary to the Gentiles.

III. THE WOMAN OF GOD (2:9-15)
   A. Her responsibilities (2:9-11)
      1. *In matters of apparel* (2:9-10): She should dress modestly as one who professes to worship God.
      2. *In matters of attitude* (2:11): She should listen and learn quietly and humbly.
   B. Her restrictions (2:12-14)
      1. *The rule* (2:12): The woman is not permitted to teach or have authority over a man.
      2. *The reason* (2:13-14): Two factors are given.
         a. The factor of the original creation (2:13): Adam was created before Eve.
         b. The factor of the original corruption (2:14): Adam was not deceived by Satan as was the woman.
   C. Her redemption (2:15): She will be "saved" through childbearing and by living in faith, love, holiness, and modesty.

SECTION OUTLINE THREE (1 TIMOTHY 3)
Paul gives qualifications for pastors and deacons in the church and
gives a sixfold summary of Jesus' earthly ministry.

I. THE SHEPHERDS FOR THE CHURCH (3:1-13)
   A. **Qualifications for a pastor** (3:1-7)
      1. *Positive qualifications* (3:1-2, 3c-5, 7)
         a. He must be above reproach (3:1-2a).
         b. He must have only one wife and be faithful to her (3:2b).
         c. He must be temperate, self-controlled, respectable, hospitable, and able to teach (3:2c).
         d. He must be gentle and have a well-behaved family (3:3c-5).
         e. He must be respected by those outside the church (3:7).
      2. *Negative qualifications* (3:3a-3b, 3d, 6)
         a. He must not be a heavy drinker (3:3a).
         b. He must not be violent (3:3b).
         c. He must not be proud (3:6b).
         d. He must not be greedy (3:3d).
         e. He must not be a new Christian (3:6a).
   B. **Qualifications for a deacon** (3:8-13)
      1. *Positive qualifications* (3:8a, 9-13)
         a. He must be sincere and worthy of respect (3:8a).
         b. He must be a man of spiritual depth (3:9).
         c. He must be a man of proven character and ability (3:10).
         d. He must be faithful to his wife, and his wife must be a woman of good character (3:11-13).
      2. *Negative qualifications* (3:8b-8c)
         a. He must not be a heavy drinker (3:8b).
         b. He must not be greedy (3:8c).

II. THE SHEEP IN THE CHURCH (3:14-15): Paul tells Timothy to instruct the congregation concerning how they should behave themselves in the house of God.

III. THE SAVIOR OF THE CHURCH (3:16): In this single and supreme verse, Paul gives a sixfold summary of Jesus' earthly ministry.
   A. **He appeared in a body** (3:16a).
   B. **He was vindicated by the Spirit** (3:16b).
   C. **He was seen by angels** (3:16c).
   D. **He was announced to the nations** (3:16d).
   E. **He was believed on in the world** (3:16e).
   F. **He was taken up into heaven** (3:16f).

SECTION OUTLINE FOUR (1 TIMOTHY 4)
Paul contrasts two kinds of shepherds.

I. GODLESS SHEPHERDS (4:1-5): Paul warns Timothy against false teachers.
   A. **Who they are** (4:2): Hypocritical and lying religious leaders.
   B. **What they will do** (4:1b-1c, 3)
      1. *Abandon the faith* (4:1b)
      2. *Follow teachings that come from lying spirits and demons* (4:1c)
      3. *Forbid marriage and the eating of certain foods* (4:3)
   C. **When they will do it** (4:1a): In the "last times" before Jesus' coming.
   D. **Why they are wrong** (4:4-5)
      1. *Everything God created is good and thus should not be rejected* (4:4).
      2. *Everything God created is made holy by God's Word and by prayer* (4:5).

II. GODLY SHEPHERDS (4:6-16): Paul lists some dos and don'ts concerning Christian ministry.
   A. **The don'ts** (4:7a, 12a, 14)
      1. *Don't waste time arguing over foolish ideas and silly myths* (4:7a).
      2. *Don't be intimidated because of your youth* (4:12a).
      3. *Don't neglect your spiritual gift* (4:14).
   B. **The dos** (4:6, 7b-11, 12b-13, 15-16)
      1. *Warn the church members concerning apostasy* (4:6).
      2. *Keep spiritually fit* (4:7b-11).
      3. *Be a godly role model in all you do* (4:12b).
      4. *Continue to publicly read, teach, and preach the Word of God (4:13).*
      5. *Give yourself wholly to the ministry* (4:15).
      6. *Keep close check on your own life* (4:16).

SECTION OUTLINE FIVE (1 TIMOTHY 5)
Paul gives advice concerning older and younger men, older and younger women, widows, and church elders.

I. THE PEOPLE (5:1-16): Paul gives advice concerning church members.
   A. **In regard to older men** (5:1a): Treat them as respected fathers.
   B. **In regard to younger men** (5:1b): Treat them as brothers.
   C. **In regard to older women** (5:2a): Treat them as mothers.
   D. **In regard to younger women** (5:2b): Treat them as sisters.
   E. **In regard to widows** (5:3-16)

     1. *Older widows* (5:3-10, 16)
       a. Widows who are over sixty, godly, and have no living children (5:3, 5, 9-10, 16): These are to be honored and provided for.
       b. Widows who have living children and grandchildren (5:4, 8, 16): They are to be cared for by their families.
       c. Widows who are carnal and live only for pleasure (5:6-7): They are to receive no help.
     2. *Younger widows* (5:11-15)
       a. The rule (5:11-12, 14): Let them remarry and raise children.
       b. The reason (5:13, 15): This will keep them from immorality and idle talk.

II. THE PREACHERS (5:17-25): Paul's advice concerning church elders.
  A. Elders in general (5:17-22, 24-25)
    1. *They are worthy of double honor* (5:17-18).
    2. *They must never be unjustly accused* (5:19-20, 24-25).
    3. *They must be impartial* (5:21).
    4. *They must be proven before being ordained* (5:22a).
    5. *They must keep themselves pure* (5:22b).
  B. Timothy in particular (5:23): "Drink a little wine for the sake of your stomach because you are sick so often."

SECTION OUTLINE SIX (1 TIMOTHY 6)
Paul addresses the workers, the wicked, the wise, and the wealthy. He closes his letter with some final instructions for Timothy.

I. PAUL'S WORDS TO THE PEOPLE (6:1-10): Paul addresses four types of individuals.
  A. The workers (6:1-2): Paul urges Christian servants to render faithful service to their masters, lest the name of God be slandered.
  B. The wicked (6:3-5)
    1. *They deny the faith* (6:3-4a).
    2. *They are conceited and argumentative (6:4b).*
    3. *They cause confusion, envy, and friction (6:4c).*
    4. *They use spiritual things for financial gain (6:5).*
  C. The wise (6:6-8): They realize that godliness with contentment is great gain.
  D. The wealthy (6:9-10)
    1. *The desire* (6:10): "The love of money is at the root of all kinds of evil."
    2. *The destruction* (6:9): This kind of greed, if unchecked, will result in ruin and destruction.

II. PAUL'S WORDS TO THE PASTOR (6:11-21)
  A. What Timothy is to do (6:11-14, 17-21)
    1. *Flee from evil, and follow after good* (6:11).

2. *Fight the good fight of faith* (6:12).
3. *Faithfully fulfill your ministry* (6:13-14, 20a).
4. *Warn the rich* (6:17-19).
   a. What they should do (6:17-18)
      (1) Don't trust in your money (6:17).
      (2) Use it to help others (6:18).
   b. Why they should do it (6:19): God will reward them both on earth and in heaven.
5. *Reject godless philosophies* (6:20b-21).
B. **For whom Timothy is to do it** (6:15-16): God.
   1. *The blessed and only Almighty God* (6:15a)
   2. *The King of Kings* (6:15b)
   3. *The Lord of Lords* (6:15c)
   4. *The immortal and invisible God* (6:16a)
   6. *The One dwelling in unapproachable light* (6:16b)

2 Timothy

SECTION OUTLINE ONE (2 TIMOTHY 1)
Paul opens his second letter to Timothy with encouragement and some news.

I. PAUL SPEAKS CONCERNING HIS SON (1:1-8, 13-14): The apostle regards Timothy as his spiritual son.
   A. **The reassurance by Paul** (1:1-3): He tells Timothy that he is praying for him night and day.
   B. **The remembrance by Paul** (1:4-5)
      1. *He is aware of Timothy's tears* (1:4).
      2. *He is aware of Timothy's testimony* (1:5).
         a. The faith of Timothy (1:5a)
         b. The faith of Timothy's family (1:5b)
   C. **The requests by Paul** (1:6-8, 13-14): The apostle urges Timothy to:
      1. *Stir up his gift* (1:6)
      2. *Be fearless, strong, and loving* (1:7)
      3. *Be unashamed of Jesus or of Paul* (1:8a)
      4. *Be ready to suffer for Jesus* (1:8b)
      5. *Guard the great body of scriptural truth that has been given him* (1:13-14)

II. PAUL SPEAKS CONCERNING HIS SAVIOR (1:9-10)
   A. **He has redeemed and called us to a holy life** (1:9a).
   B. **He did this by his grace before the world began** (1:9b).
   C. **He has destroyed death and has introduced eternal life** (1:10).

III. PAUL SPEAKS CONCERNING HIMSELF (1:11-12, 15-18)
   A. **The apostle's calling** (1:11): His calling from God is twofold:
      1. *To be an apostle and preacher* (1:11a)
      2. *To be a teacher of the Gentiles* (1:11b)
   B. **The apostle's confinement** (1:12a): Because of his calling, he is suffering as a prisoner.
   C. **The apostle's confidence** (1:12b): In spite of everything, Paul is not ashamed, for he knows the one in whom he trusts.
   D. **The apostle's companions** (1:15-18)

1. *His deserting friends* (1:15): Most of Paul's coworkers in Asia have abandoned him.
2. *His devoted friend* (1:16-18): Onesiphorus has remained a faithful and helpful friend.

SECTION OUTLINE TWO (2 TIMOTHY 2)
Paul describes the duties assigned to a pastor.

I. THE ROLE MODEL (2:1-7): Paul likens the ministry to four secular occupations.
  A. A teacher (2:1-2)
    1. *As a student Timothy was taught many things by Paul* (2:1-2a).
    2. *As a pastor Timothy must now teach those things to other godly people* (2:2b).
  B. A soldier (2:3-4)
    1. *Give all of your energies to the warfare* (2:3).
    2. *Give none of your energies to worldly affairs* (2:4).
  C. An athlete (2:5): Strive for the victor's crown.
  D. A farmer (2:6-7): Work hard to harvest a large crop.

II. THE REMINDERS (2:8-10): A prisoner in Rome, Paul asks Timothy to reflect on two things.
  A. God's messenger is chained (2:8-9a).
  B. God's message cannot be chained (2:9b-10).

III. THE RESULTS (2:11-13)
  A. If we die for Christ, we will live with Christ (2:11).
  B. If we endure hardship for Christ, we will reign with Christ (2:12a).
  C. If we deny Christ, he will deny us (2:12b).
  D. If we are unfaithful, Christ remains faithful (2:13).

IV. THE RESPONSIBILITIES (2:14-26): Paul lists some of Timothy's duties as a pastor.
  A. Remind your people of the great scriptural truths (2:14a).
  B. Warn them against petty arguments (2:14b).
  C. Strive to become an approved workman before God (2:15).
  D. Avoid godless controversies (2:16-19, 23-26).
    1. *The examples* (2:16-17): Paul points out two men, Hymenaeus and Philetus, who have involved themselves in these controversies.
    2. *The error* (2:18-19): They are claiming that the resurrection from the dead has already occurred.
    3. *The endeavor* (2:23-26): Timothy must gently instruct those who would oppose him with the goal of leading them to repentance.

E. **Present your body as a clean vessel to God** (2:20-21).
F. **Avoid evil, and pursue good** (2:22).

SECTION OUTLINE THREE (2 TIMOTHY 3)
Paul warns of the coming great apostasy.

I. THE PERVERSIONS (3:1-9)
  A. **The evil** (3:1-5)
    1. *People will love only themselves and their money* (3:1-2a).
    2. *They will be proud, abusive, disobedient to their parents, ungrateful, and unholy* (3:2b).
    3. *They will be without love, unforgiving, slanderous, without self-control, and brutal* (3:3).
    4. *They will be treacherous and will be lovers of pleasure rather than lovers of God* (3:4).
    5. *They will have a form of godliness but will deny its power* (3:5).
  B. **The examples** (3:6-8): Paul lists two types of people involved in apostasy.
    1. *Sexually weak-willed, sin-burdened women* (3:6-7)
    2. *Depraved men who will oppose God as Jannes and Jambres once opposed Moses* (3:8-9)

II. The Prescription (3:10-17): Having diagnosed the disease, Paul now proposes a twofold preventative against it.
  A. **Timothy is to continue in the work of God** (3:10-13): Paul offers his own ministry as a pattern.
  B. **Timothy is to continue in the Word of God** (3:14-17).
    1. *What the Scriptures did for Timothy the lad* (3:14-15): God's Word gave him the wisdom to accept God's salvation.
    2. *What the Scriptures will do for Timothy the leader* (3:16-17)
      a. The guidelines (3:16): Timothy will find the divinely inspired book useful.
        (1) For doctrine and reproof (3:16a)
        (2) For correction and instruction in righteousness (3:16b)
      b. The goal (3:17): To equip Timothy for every good work.

SECTION OUTLINE FOUR (2 TIMOTHY 4)
Paul closes his letter (which is most likely his last letter before being executed) with six "finals."

 I. PAUL'S FINAL CHARGE (4:1-2, 5)
   A. Timothy is to preach the Word of God (4:1-2).
      1. *How he is to preach it* (4:1, 2b): He is to use it for correction, rebuke, and encouragement.
      2. *When he is to preach it* (4:2a): Urgently, at all times.
   B. Timothy is to reach his world for God (4:5).

 II. PAUL'S FINAL WARNING (4:3-4, 14-15): The apostle issues a twofold warning.
   A. In regard to apostasy (4:3-4)
      1. *Men will someday turn from sound doctrine* (4:3).
      2. *Men will someday turn to satanic doctrine* (4:4).
   B. In regard to Alexander (4:14-15): Paul warns Timothy to beware of this godless coppersmith who has caused Paul so much grief.

 III. PAUL'S FINAL TESTIMONY (4:6-8)
   A. What he has done (4:6-7)
      1. *He has fought a good fight* (4:6-7a).
      2. *He has finished his cause* (4:7b).
      3. *He has kept the faith* (4:7c).
   B. What God will do (4:8): He will reward the apostle with a crown of righteousness.

 IV. PAUL'S FINAL REQUEST (4:9, 11-13)
   A. The individuals (4:9, 11-12)
      1. *He asks that Timothy come as soon as possible* (4:9).
      2. *He asks that Timothy bring Mark with him* (4:11).
      3. *He has sent Tychicus to Ephesus* (4:12).
   B. The items (4:13): Paul requests three things.
      1. *His cloak* (4:13a).
      2. *His study books* (4:13b).
      3. *His Old Testament scrolls* (4:13c).

 V. PAUL'S FINAL SORROW (4:10, 16)
   A. Demas has forsaken him (4:10).
   B. His Roman friends have forsaken him (4:16).

 VI. PAUL'S FINAL SONG OF PRAISE (4:17-18)
   A. God has delivered him from the mouth of the lion (4:17-18a).
   B. God will deliver him to the Kingdom of Heaven (4:18b).

 VII. PAUL SENDS HIS FINAL GREETINGS (4:19-22).

Titus

SECTION OUTLINE ONE (TITUS 1)

Paul greets Titus and talks about the role of elders in the church. He warns Titus against legalists.

I. PAUL'S INTRODUCTION (1:1-4)
   A. **The apostle's assignment from God** (1:1-3): He has been sent to reach and teach the elect of the Lord.
   B. **The apostle's affection for Titus** (1:4): Titus is his true child in the faith.

II. PAUL'S INSTRUCTIONS (1:5-16): Titus is advised on how to deal with two categories of people.
   A. **The leaders in his church** (1:5-9)
      1. *Their appointments* (1:5): Titus is to select a group of men who will function as elders.
      2. *Their assignments* (1:6-9)
         a. An elder must be blameless and above reproach (1:6a, 7a).
         b. An elder must have only one wife and be faithful to her; he must be the head of a godly family (1:6b).
         c. An elder must not be overbearing or quick-tempered (1:7b).
         d. An elder must not be a heavy drinker, violent, or greedy (1:7c).
         e. An elder must be hospitable and must love what is good (1:8a).
         f. An elder must be self-controlled, upright, and holy (1:8b).
         g. An elder must be able to use doctrine to encourage the sincere and reject the insincere (1:9).
   B. **The legalists in his church** (1:10-16)
      1. *The apostasy of these men* (1:10, 11b-12, 15-16)
         a. They are rebellious and deceptive (1:10).
         b. They are ruining entire households (1:11b).
         c. They are greedy (1:11c).
         d. They are lying and lazy gluttons (1:12).
         e. Their walk totally contradicts their talk (1:16).
         f. They view everything through evil eyes (1:15).

2. *The actions against these men* (1:11a, 13-14)
   a. They are to be totally silenced (1:11a).
   b. They are to be soundly rebuked (1:13-14).

SECTION OUTLINE TWO (TITUS 2)
Paul addresses both people and pastor.

I. THE PEOPLE IN THE PEWS (2:2-6, 9-14)
   A. **The apostle gives instructions concerning groups of people in the church** (2:2-6, 9-10).
      1. *Older men* (2:2): They should be temperate, worthy of respect, self-controlled, and sound in the faith.
      2. *Older women* (2:3-5)
         a. What they are to be (2:3): Respectful, positive toward others, and not inclined toward heavy drinking.
         b. What they are to do (2:4-5): They are to teach godliness to the younger women.
      3. *Young men* (2:6): They should be self-controlled.
      4. *Servants* (2:9-10): They should serve their masters faithfully.
   B. **The apostle gives instructions concerning everyone in the church** (2:11-14).
      1. *What God has done for them* (2:11, 14): He has redeemed them by his grace.
      2. *What they should do for God* (2:12-13)
         a. They should live for him (2:12).
         b. They should look for him (2:13).

II. THE PASTOR IN THE PULPIT (2:1, 7-8, 15)
   A. **Titus is to teach sound doctrine** (2:1).
   B. **Titus is to be a positive role model** (2:7-8).
   C. **Titus is to encourage and rebuke with authority** (2:15).

SECTION OUTLINE THREE (TITUS 3)
Paul closes his letter to Titus with a discussion of the will of God, the work of God, a warning from God, and the workers for God.

I. THE WILL OF GOD (3:1-2): Paul summarizes the divine will for believers.
   A. **In regard to rulers** (3:1): We are to obey them.
   B. **In regard to the rest** (3:2): We are to be gentle and courteous.

II. THE WORK OF GOD (3:3-7)
   A. **Our godlessness** (3:3): We were once deceived, disobedient, depraved sinners.
   B. **His graciousness** (3:4-7)
      1. *Christ came to earth* (3:4).
      2. *He washes away our sins* (3:5a).
      3. *He gives us the indwelling Spirit* (3:5b-6).

4. *He fully justifies us* (3:7a).

5. *He assures us of eternal life* (3:7b).

III. THE WARNING FROM GOD (3:8-11)

   A. Concerning controversial issues (3:8-9): Titus must not involve himself in arguing over foolish and unanswerable questions.

   B. Concerning controversial individuals (3:10-11)

      1. *They are to be warned twice* (3:10a).

      2. *They are (if unrepentant) to be excommunicated* (3:10b-11).

IV. THE WORKERS FOR GOD (3:12-15): Paul closes by referring to four of his co-laborers and sends his greetings.

   A. He will soon send either Artemas or Tychicus to Crete (3:12).

   B. Titus is to help Zenas and Apollos with their trip (3:13-14).

   C. Paul sends greetings to all the believers (3:15).

Philemon

SECTION OUTLINE ONE (PHILEMON 1)

Paul's short letter to Philemon consists mainly of a plea for this godly man to graciously receive his runaway slave Onesimus, who has become a Christian and whom Paul is now sending back to his master.

I. THE APPRECIATION AND PRAISE FOR PHILEMON (1:1-7)
  - **A. Philemon is a family man** (1:1-3): His wife's name is Apphia, and his son's name is Archippus.
  - **B. Philemon is a faithful man** (1:4-5): Paul gives thanks for Philemon's faith.
  - **C. Philemon is a fruitful man** (1:6-7): He befriended and encouraged both Paul and many other believers.

II. THE APPEAL AND PLEA FOR ONESIMUS (1:8-17)
  - **A. Forgive him for your own sake** (1:8-15).
    1. *"Show kindness to Onesimus"* (1:8-10).
    2. *"Onesimus hasn't been of much use to you in the past, but now he is very useful to both of us"* (1:11).
    3. *"I really wanted to keep him here with me while I am in these chains for preaching the Good News. . . . But I didn't want to do anything without your consent"* (1:12-14).
    4. *"Onesimus ran away for a little while so you could have him back forever"* (1:15).
  - **B. Forgive him for his sake** (1:16): He is now your brother in Christ.
  - **C. Forgive him for my sake** (1:17): Paul asks Philemon to receive Onesimus as he would receive the apostle himself.

III. THE ASSURANCE AND PLEDGE FROM PAUL (1:18-25)
  - **A. The guarantee** (1:18-19a): Paul promises to pay Philemon any debt owed by Onesimus.
  - **B. The gentle reminder** (1:19b): Paul reminds Philemon of the great spiritual debt Philemon himself owes the apostle.
  - **C. The guest room** (1:22): Paul asks Philemon to keep a room available for when he is next able to visit.

D. The greetings (1:23-25): Epaphras, Mark, Aristarchus, Demas, and Luke, Paul's co-laborers, send their greetings to Philemon from Rome.

Hebrews

SECTION OUTLINE ONE (HEBREWS 1)

Hebrews opens with a discussion of Christ as the selected one and the superior one.

I. CHRIST, THE SELECTED ONE (1:1-3): The Father has chosen his Son to minister in four all-important areas.
   A. **Revelation** (1:1-2a)
      1. *In the Old Testament, God revealed himself through his messengers* (1:1).
      2. *In the New Testament, God revealed himself through his Messiah* (1:2a).
   B. **Creation** (1:2b-3)
      1. *The Son made the universe* (1:2b).
      2. *The Son maintains the universe* (1:3b).
   C. **Representation** (1:3a): Jesus is the radiance of God's glory and the exact representation of God's being.
   D. **Purification** (1:3c): Jesus died to cleanse us from our sins.

II. CHRIST, THE SUPERIOR ONE (1:4-14): Christ is superior to the angels in three important ways.
   A. **In regard to his relationship** (1:4-7): The Father has declared Jesus to be his unique Son.
   B. **In regard to his reign** (1:8-12)
      1. *It will be a righteous reign* (1:8-9).
      2. *It will be an eternal reign* (1:10-12).
   C. **In regard to his reward** (1:13-14): The Father has promised to make Jesus' enemies his footstool.

SECTION OUTLINE TWO (HEBREWS 2)
This chapter contains a warning from Christ against drifting away from the faith and a discussion of the work of Christ.

I. THE WARNING FROM CHRIST (2:1-4): This warning has to do with God's salvation.
   A. **The command** (2:1-2)
      1. *Don't drift from God's message of truth* (2:1).
      2. *Don't disobey God's message of truth* (2:2).
   B. **The communicators** (2:3): This salvation was preached by both Jesus and his apostles.
   C. **The confirmation** (2:4): The gospel message was confirmed by signs and wonders.

II. THE WORK OF CHRIST (2:5-18)
   A. **His sovereign ministry** (2:5-8a)
      1. *Christ created all people* (2:5-6a).
      2. *Christ cares for all people* (2:6b-7).
      3. *Christ commissioned all people* (2:8a): Adam was put in charge of God's original creation.
   B. **His submissive ministry** (2:9a): Christ agreed to come to earth and become "lower than the angels."
   C. **His saving ministry** (2:8b-10)
      1. *The rebellion* (2:8b): Sin caused people to forfeit their control over nature.
      2. *The redemption* (2:9b-10): Christ died on the cross for everyone.
   D. **His sanctifying ministry** (2:11-13): Christ now lives to make us holy.
   E. **His subduing ministry** (2:14-15): By his death Jesus broke the power of Satan, who once held the power of death.
   F. **His sympathizing ministry** (2:16-18): Having once suffered, Jesus is now able and willing to help those who are suffering.

SECTION OUTLINE THREE (HEBREWS 3)
Jesus is compared to Moses and is declared to be greater than Moses. A warning is given from the Holy Spirit against the sin of unbelief.

I. THE WORTHINESS OF THE SAVIOR (3:1-6): Jesus is compared and contrasted to Moses.
   A. **The comparison** (3:2)
      1. *Jesus was faithful to God* (3:2a).
      2. *Moses was faithful to God* (3:2b).
   B. **The contrast** (3:3-6)
      1. *Moses was a faithful servant in God's house* (3:5).
      2. *Jesus is the faithful son over God's house* (3:3-4, 6).
   C. **The conclusion** (3:1): Jesus is greater, so fix your eyes on him.

II. THE WARNING BY THE SPIRIT (3:7-19): This warning has to do with the terrible sin of unbelief.
  A. **The example of unfaithfulness** (3:9-11, 16-19)
    1. *Israel's sin in the wilderness* (3:9-10): They allowed unbelief to turn their hearts against God.
    2. *Israel's sentence in the wilderness* (3:11, 16-19): An entire generation died in the desert and did not enter the Promised Land.
  B. **The exhortation to faithfulness** (3:7-8, 12-15)
    1. *When you hear God's Word, heed God's Word* (3:7-8, 15).
    2. *Encourage one another daily* (3:12-14).

SECTION OUTLINE FOUR (HEBREWS 4)
God promises rest for his people.

I. THE PROMISE OF GOD (4:1-11): This promise involves the rest that God has prepared for his people.
  A. **The whereabouts** (4:3b, 5-6, 8-10)
    1. *God's Old Testament rest* (4:3b, 5-6): This was the Promised Land, which Israel failed to enter due to unbelief.
    2. *God's New Testament rest* (4:8-10): This is the place of his perfect will, which is available for all believers.
  B. **The way** (4:2-3a): "Only we who believe can enter his place of rest."
  C. **The witnesses** (4:4, 7)
    1. *Moses spoke of these rests (Gen. 2:2)* (4:4).
    2. *David spoke of these rests (Ps. 95:11)* (4:7).
  D. **The wisdom** (4:1, 11): Guided by godly fear, we are to do our utmost to enter into this rest.

II. THE POWER OF GOD (4:12-13)
  A. **What it is** (4:12a-b)
    1. *Its definition* (4:12a): It is the spoken and written Word of God.
    2. *Its description* (4:12b): It is living, active, and sharper than any double-edged sword.
  B. **What it does** (4:12c-13)
    1. *It exposes all thoughts and desires* (4:12c).
    2. *It exposes all humankind* (4:13).

III. THE PRIEST OF GOD (4:14-16)
  A. **Who he is** (4:14a): He is Jesus, the Son of God.
  B. **What he is** (4:14b-15): He is our great High Priest.
    1. *He once was tempted in all areas* (4:15).
    2. *He now can help us in any area* (4:14b).
  C. **Where he is** (4:16): At the very throne of grace.

SECTION OUTLINE FIVE (HEBREWS 5)

Christ, the great High Priest, is compared to Aaron, the first high priest.

I. THE REQUIREMENTS IN REGARD TO THE PRIESTS (5:1-10): The author of Hebrews compares and contrasts the high priestly ministries of both Aaron and Christ.
   A. **Comparisons** (5:1-4)
      1. *Both were selected by God from among men* (5:1a, 4).
      2. *Both were appointed to represent people before God* (5:1b).
      3. *Both were to pray and offer up sacrifices* (5:1c).
      4. *Both were to demonstrate compassion* (5:2a).
      5. *Both experienced infirmities of the flesh* (5:2b-3).
   B. **Contrasts** (5:5-10)
      1. *Only Christ is called God's Son* (5:5).
      2. *Only Christ was given an everlasting priesthood* (5:6a).
      3. *Only Christ was made a priest after the order of Melchizedek* (5:6b, 9-10).
      4. *Only Christ cried out to God in Gethsemane "with a loud cry and tears, to the one who could deliver him out of death"* (5:7-8).

II. THE REBUKE IN REGARD TO THE PEOPLE (5:11-14)
   A. **The frustration** (5:11-12a)
      1. *The author has much to say, but his readers are slow to learn* (5:11).
      2. *They should be teachers but instead need to be taught* (5:12a).
   B. **The food** (5:12b-14)
      1. *Baby believers can be fed only milk* (5:12b-13).
      2. *Mature believers can easily digest solid food* (5:14).

SECTION OUTLINE SIX (HEBREWS 6)

The author of Hebrews challenges his readers to strive for spiritual maturity and writes about how such maturity may be obtained.

I. THE APPEAL FOR SPIRITUAL MATURITY (6:1-12)
   A. **The author's challenge** (6:1-3): The writer of Hebrews issues a twofold challenge to his readers.
      1. *Don't go backward* (6:1-2): He urges them to stop going over the same old ground again and again.
         a. In the importance of turning from sin and toward God (6:1)
         b. In the importance of baptism, the laying on of hands, the resurrection, and judgment (6:2)
      2. *Do go forward* (6:3): Push on to maturity in Christ.
   B. **The author's concern** (6:4-8): He warns in regard to a dreadful situation.
      1. *The impossibility in this situation* (6:4-6)

      a. The who (6:4b-5): Those who have tasted the heavenly gift, who have shared in the Holy Spirit and have tasted of God's Word.

      b. The what (6:6a): After experiencing this, they turn from God.

      c. The why (6:4a, 6b): These people cannot be brought back to repentance, for they crucify the Son of God all over again.

    2. *The illustration for this situation* (6:7-8): The author refers to a piece of land to illustrate his point.

      a. When the land is fruitful, it is blessed (6:7).

      b. When the land is fruitless, it is cursed (6:8).

  C. The author's confidence (6:9-12): He is confident his warning does not apply to his readers.

II. THE ANCHOR FOR SPIRITUAL MATURITY (6:13-20): This desired maturity is assured.

  A. Because of the Father's promise (6:13-18)

    1. *God promised to bless Abraham, and he did* (6:13-15).

    2. *God promised to bless us, and he will* (6:16-18).

  B. Because of the Savior's priesthood (6:19-20)

SECTION OUTLINE SEVEN (HEBREWS 7)
The author identifies and equates the priesthood of Jesus with that of Melchizedek.

I. A HISTORICAL PERSPECTIVE (7:1-3)

  A. The person of Melchizedek (7:1a, 2b-3)

    1. *Who he was* (7:2b): His name means "king of justice," and he was also the "king of peace."

    2. *What he did* (7:1a): He was both priest and king over the city of Salem.

    3. *Where he came from* (7:3): There is no record of either his birth or his death.

  B. The preeminence of Melchizedek (7:1b-2a)

    1. *The battle* (7:2a): Following the defeat of his enemies, Abraham met Melchizedek and paid tithes to him.

    2. *The blessing* (7:1b): Melchizedek blessed Abraham.

II. A THEOLOGICAL PERSPECTIVE (7:4-28): The author lists the various characteristics of Jesus, who, according to the Father's decree, is to be a priest after the order of Melchizedek (see Ps. 110:4). Thus, his priesthood would be:

  A. Royal (as was that of Melchizedek) (see 7:1)

  B. Superior (7:4-10)

    1. *To whom?* (7:5-7): To Levi, founder of the levitical priesthood.

    2. *Why? (7:4, 8-10)*

a. Abraham was the ancestor of Levi (7:9).
b. The yet unborn Levi thus tithed to Melchizedek while still in the loins of Abraham (7:4, 8, 10).
C. **Independent** (7:11-15)
1. *Independent of the law* (7:11-12).
2. *Independent of the tribe of Levi* (7:13-15): Christ came from the tribe of Judah.
D. **Everlasting** (7:16-17)
E. **Guaranteed** (7:20-22): The Father himself took an oath concerning this.
F. **Continuous** (7:23)
G. **Permanent** (7:24)
H. **Holy** (7:26)
I. **All-sufficient** (7:18-19, 25, 27)
J. **Flawless (7:28)**

SECTION OUTLINE EIGHT (HEBREWS 8)
The author discusses the threefold security of the New Covenant over the Old Covenant.

I. ITS SANCTUARY IS SUPERIOR (8:1-2).
A. **The place is better** (8:1): It is located in the heavenly sanctuary.
B. **The priest is better** (8:2): Jesus himself ministers in this sanctuary.

II. ITS SACRIFICE IS SUPERIOR (8:3-4).
A. **The levitical priests offered up animals in the earthly sanctuary** (8:4).
B. **The Lamb of God offers up himself in the heavenly sanctuary** (8:3).

III. ITS SECURITY IS SUPERIOR (8:5-13).
A. **The old agreement was mediated by Moses** (8:5, 7-8a).
1. *It was ruined by Israel's sin* (8:7-8a).
2. *It was written on dead stones* (see Ex. 32:15).
B. **The new agreement is mediated by Christ** (8:6, 8b-13).
1. *It is restored by Jesus' sacrifice* (8:6, 8b-9).
2. *It is written on living hearts* (8:10-13).

SECTION OUTLINE NINE (HEBREWS 9)
The features that relate to both the earthly and heavenly sanctuaries are discussed in this chapter.

I. THE REVIEW OF EACH SANCTUARY (9:1-15)
A. **The earthly sanctuary** (9:1-10)
1. *The information* (9:1-7)

      a. The objects in the Tabernacle (9:1-5): The author describes the location of the gold lampstands, the incense altar, etc.

      b. The overseers of the Tabernacle (9:6-7): The duties of both priests and the high priest are listed.

    2. *The illustration* (9:8-10): The Holy Spirit used the many regulations surrounding the use of the Tabernacle to illustrate the fatal weakness of the earthly Tabernacle—namely, its sacrifices could not cleanse the hearts of the people.

  B. The heavenly sanctuary (9:11-15): This sanctuary is superior to the earthly one in four areas.

    1. *The person offering the sacrifice* (9:11): It is Jesus Christ himself.

    2. *The preciousness of the sacrifice* (9:12b): He offered his own blood.

    3. *The permanence of the sacrifice* (9:12a): It was done only once and will last for all time.

    4. *The power of the sacrifice* (9:12c-15): It brings about eternal redemption.

II. THE RATIFICATION OF EACH SANCTUARY (9:16-28): Both sanctuaries had to be purified and ratified by the blood of a sacrifice.

  A. The earthly sanctuary (9:16-22)

    1. *The sprinkler of this blood* (9:16-19a): Moses.

    2. *The source of this blood* (9:19b): An animal.

    3. *The summary of this blood* (9:20-22): It could never take away sins.

  B. The heavenly sanctuary (9:23-28)

    1. *The sprinkler of this blood* (9:23): Christ.

    2. *The source of this blood* (9:25-26a): Himself.

    3. *The summary of this blood* (9:24, 26b-28): Here the author gives us a threefold summary of the Savior's work.

      a. He once appeared to die for us (9:26b-28a).

      b. He now appears to pray for us (9:24).

      c. He will appear to rule over us (9:28b).

SECTION OUTLINE TEN (HEBREWS 10)

This chapter begins with a comparison and concludes with a challenge.

I. THE COMPARISON (10:1-18): Here the blood of earthly lambs is compared with the blood of the heavenly Lamb.

  A. The inferiority of earthly lambs (10:1-4, 11)

    1. *The frequency of these sacrifices* (10:1-3, 11a): The priest had to offer up animals again and again.

    2. *The failure of these sacrifices* (10:4, 11b): They could never take away sin.

B. The superiority of the heavenly Lamb (10:5-10, 12-18)
1. *The purpose* (10:5-10): Jesus came for one purpose—namely, to offer up himself.
2. *The permanence* (10:12, 14): His offering was once for all time, never to be repeated.
3. *The patience* (10:13): "He waits until his enemies are humbled as a footstool under his feet."
4. *The purification* (10:15-18): Someday he will purify the hearts of unbelieving Israel.

II. THE CHALLENGE (10:19-39): This challenge is in the form of a fourfold exhortation.
A. Approach the throne of God (10:19-22): Christ's sacrifice allows us to boldly petition God's throne.
B. Advance the people of God (10:23-25): Believers are to be kind and helpful to each other.
C. Avoid the judgment of God (10:26-31).
1. *The contrast* (10:26-29)
   a. A reminder of how God once punished those who rejected the law of Moses (10:26-28)
   b. A reminder of how God will punish those who reject the Lamb of God (10:29)
2. *The certainty* (10:30-31): We are assured God will judge his people.
D. Acknowledge the faithfulness of God (10:32-39).
1. *His past faithfulness* (10:32-34): The author urges believers not to forget God's care for them during a former period of suffering.
2. *His permanent faithfulness* (10:35-39): Whatever the present and future holds, they can depend on his continuous care.

SECTION OUTLINE ELEVEN (HEBREWS 11)
This is the famous faith chapter.

I. THE EXPLANATION OF FAITH (11:1-3, 6)
A. Its nature (11:1-2)
1. *"It is the confident assurance that what we hope for is going to happen"* (11:1a).
2. *"It is the evidence of things we cannot yet see"* (11:1b).
B. Its necessity (11: 3, 6)
1. *With it people in the Old Testament were approved by God* (11:2).
2. *With it we are able to believe the power of God* (11:3): This is especially true in regard to his creative power.
3. *Without it we are unable to please the person of God* (11:6).

II. THE EXAMPLES OF FAITH (11:4-5, 7-40)

   A. **Who they were** (11:4a, 5a, 7a, 8a-11a, 12, 17-18, 20a, 21a, 22a, 23a, 24, 27a, 28a, 31a, 32): Sixteen people of faith are named, and many others are referred to as well.

      1. *Abel* (11:4a)
      2. *Enoch* (11:5a)
      3. *Noah* (11:7a)
      4. *Abraham* (11:8a, 9, 12, 17-18)
      5. *Sarah* (11:11a)
      6. *Isaac* (11:20a)
      7. *Jacob* (11:21a)
      8. *Joseph* (11:22a)
      9. *Moses' parents* (11:23a)
    10. *Moses* (11:24, 27a, 28a)
    11. *The people of Israel* (11:29a, 30a)
    12. *Rahab* (11:31a)
    13. *Gideon* (11:32a)
    14. *Barak* (11:32b)
    15. *Samson* (11:32c)
    16. *Jephthah* (11:32d)
    17. *David* (11:32e)
    18. Samuel (11:32f)
    19. *All the prophets* (11:32g)

   B. **What they did** (11:4b, 5b, 7b, 8b, 11b, 19, 20b, 21b, 22b, 23b, 25, 27b, 28b-30, 31b, 33-35a)

      1. *Abel gave the Lord an acceptable offering* (11:4b).
      2. *Enoch left the earth without dying* (11:5b).
      3. *Noah survived the great Flood* (11:7b).
      4. *Abraham inherited a land* (11:8b).
      5. *Sarah bore a son through a barren womb and began a nation* (11:11b).
      6. *Abraham believed that God could raise the dead* (11:19).
      7. *Isaac and Jacob both predicted the future* (11:20b, 21b).
      8. *Joseph anticipated the Exodus long before it happened* (11:22b).
      9. *Moses' parents defied the king of Egypt* (11:23b).
    10. *Moses forsook the pleasures of sin* (11:25).
    11. *Moses left the land of Egypt and was not afraid of the king* (11:27b).
    12. *The people of Israel kept the Passover* (11:28b).
    13. *The people of Israel crossed the Red Sea* (11:29).
    14. *The people of Israel shouted down a city* (11:30).
    15. *Rahab protected some Hebrew spies* (11:31b).
    16. *The prophets and judges subdued kingdoms, shut the mouths of lions, quenched flames, escaped the sword, exchanged weakness for strength, put enemy armies to flight, and a few even raised the dead* (11:33-35a).

    C. What they endured (11:35b-38)
       1. *Terrible torture* (11:35b)
       2. *Ridicule* (11:36a)
       3. *Cruel flogging* (11:36b)
       4. *Imprisonment* (11:36c)
       5. *Stoning* (11:37a)
       6. *Being sawn in two* (11:37b)
       7. *Death by the sword* (11:37c)
       8. *Extreme poverty* (11:37d-38)
    D. Why they endured (11:10, 13-15, 16b, 26, 35c)
       1. *They saw the invisible City of God* (11:10, 13-15, 16b).
       2. *They believed that suffering for the sake of Christ was better than having all the riches of this world* (11:26).
       3. *They looked forward to their own resurrection* (11:35c).
    E. What they received (11:16a, 39-40)
       1. *In the past* (11:16a, 39): The earthly and temporary approval of God.
       2. *In the future* (11:40): The heavenly and eternal approval of God.

SECTION OUTLINE TWELVE (HEBREWS 12)

The author compares a godly life to a great race and explains to his readers the reasons behind God's discipline. He again warns against the sin of unbelief.

  I. THE CONTEST (12:1-4)
    A. The race (12:1): We are to faithfully run the spiritual race God has marked out for each of us.
    B. The role model (12:2-3)
       1. *Who he is* (12:2a): We are to fix our eyes on Jesus, the start and finish of our faith.
       2. *What he did* (12:2b-3): He endured the opposition of sinners and died on the cross.
       3. *Why he did it* (12:2c): Because of the joy he knew would be his.
       4. *Where he is now* (12:2d): At God's right hand.
    C. The reassurance (12:4): The readers are informed they have not suffered as Christ suffered.

  II. THE CHASTENING (12:5-13): Divine discipline is the theme of this passage.
    A. The relationship (12:7b-10)
       1. *The disciplinarian* (12:9-10): The heavenly Father himself.
       2. *The disciplined* (12:7b-8): All believers. As earthly fathers discipline their children, so the heavenly Father disciplines his children.

B. The reminder (12:5a): The readers have forgotten Solomon's words concerning this in Proverbs 3:11-12.

C. The reaction (12:5b-5c, 7a): Believers are urged to respond positively to discipline.

1. *Negative reactions* (12:5b-5c)
   a. "Don't ignore it when the Lord disciplines you" (12:5b).
   b. "Don't be discouraged when he corrects you" (12:5c).
2. *Positive reaction* (12:7a): "Remember that God is treating you as his own children."

D. The reasons (12:6)

1. *To prove we are his children* (12:6b)
2. *To prove his love* (12:6a)

E. The rewards (12:11)

1. *Discipline produces righteousness* (12:11b).
2. *Discipline produces peace* (12:11a).

F. The renewal (12:12-13)

1. *"Take a new grip with your tired hands and stand firm on your shaky legs"* (12:12).
2. *"Mark out a straight path for your feet"* (12:13).

III. THE CHALLENGES (12:14-17)

A. The author's exhortation (12:14-15)

1. *"Try to live in peace with everyone"* (12:14a).
2. *"Seek to live a clean and holy life"* (12:14b).
3. *"Watch out that no bitter root of unbelief rises up among you"* (12:15).

B. The author's example (12:16-17): Esau is held up as a tragic example of what not to do.

1. *He was immoral* (12:16a).
2. *He was godless* (12:16b).
3. *He despised his birthright* (12:16c-17).

IV. THE CONTRASTS (12:18-24): Two mountains are contrasted.

A. Mount Sinai (12:18-21)

1. *The person* (12:21): Moses.
2. *The principle* (12:18-20): The law of God.

B. Mount Zion (12:22-24)

1. *The person* (12:24a): Christ.
2. *The principle* (12:22-23, 24b): The grace of God.

V. THE CAUTION (12:25-27): The author solemnly warns his readers about the terrible results of unbelief.

VI. THE CONSUMING FIRE (12:28-29)

A. Our God is a coming King (12:28).

B. Our God is a consuming fire (12:29).

SECTION OUTLINE THIRTEEN (HEBREWS 13)
The writer of Hebrews concludes with words about love, leaders, legalism, and lordship.

I. A WORD ABOUT LOVE (13:1-6)
  A. Positive (13:1-4): Whom we are to love.
    1. *Each other* (13:1)
    2. *Strangers* (13:2)
    3. *Prisoners* (13:3)
    4. *Our spouse* (13:4)
  B. Negative (13:5-6)
    1. *What we are not to love* (13:5a): Money.
    2. *Why we are not to love it* (13:5b-6): We are to be satisfied with what we have.
      a. God has promised never to forsake us (13:5b).
      b. God has promised to be our helper (13:6).

II. A WORD ABOUT LEADERS (13:7, 17-19, 22-25)
  A. The author tells his readers to honor and obey the spiritual leaders of their church (13:7, 17).
    1. *Let them serve as role models* (13:7).
    2. *Submit to their authority* (13:17).
  B. The author tells his readers to pray for the spiritual leaders outside their church (13:18-19, 22-25).
    1. *He refers to himself* (13:18-19, 22).
    2. *He refers to Timothy* (13:23-25).

III. A WORD ABOUT LEGALISM (13:9-11): What altar and sacrifice should the believer be associated with?
  A. Negative (13:11): Not the altar in the Tabernacle.
  B. Positive (13:9-10): The altar at Calvary.

IV. A WORD ABOUT LORDSHIP (13:8, 12-16, 20-21)
  A. The Shepherd of the fold (13:8, 12, 20-21)
    1. *Who he is* (13:8): He is Jesus Christ, who is the same yesterday, today, and forever.
    2. *What he has done* (13:12, 20-21)
      a. He once redeemed us (13:12, 20).
      b. He now equips us (13:21).
  B. The sheep in the fold (13:13-16)
    1. *We are to live for him down here* (13:13, 15-16).
      a. We are to suffer for him (13:13).
      b. We are to sacrifice to him (13:15-16).
        (1) The sacrifice of our words (13:15)
        (2) The sacrifice of our works (13:16)
    2. *We are to look forward to living with him up there* (13:14): This world is not our home.

James

SECTION OUTLINE ONE (JAMES 1)
James opens with a greeting and short discussions on trials and
temptations, trusting, transition, treasure, and true religion.

I. JAMES'S GREETING (1:1): James addresses his book to the twelve
Israelite tribes scattered among the nations.

II. JAMES SPEAKS OF TRIALS AND TEMPTATIONS (1:2-4, 12-16): Here he
pictures these experiences in a twofold light.
   A. Positive (1:2-4, 12): As seen from God's perspective.
      1. *The purpose* (1:2-3): To purify and strengthen us.
      2. *The products* (1:4)
         a. Perseverance (1:4a)
         b. Maturity (1:4b)
      3. *The promise* (1:12): God will someday give the crown of life
      to those who successfully endure.
   B. Negative (1:13-16): As seen from Satan's perspective.
      1. *The purpose* (1:13-14): To pervert and weaken us.
      2. *The products* (1:15-16)
         a. Evil actions (1:15a)
         b. Possible death (1:15b-16)

III. JAMES SPEAKS OF TRUSTING (1:5-8)
   A. When to trust God (1:5): When we need wisdom.
   B. How to trust God (1:6b-8)
      1. *Positive* (1: 6a): We need only to ask him in faith.
      2. *Negative* (1:6b-8): Wisdom will not be given to a faithless
      person.

IV. JAMES SPEAKS OF TRANSITION (1:9-11): James touches on the shortness
of life.
   A. The example (1:9a, 10a, 11): Human glory is like a beautiful
   flower that blossoms and soon fades away.
   B. The exhortation (1:9b, 10b): Only God's glory is eternal.

V. JAMES SPEAKS OF TREASURE (1:17-25): The treasure here is the Bible itself.
  A. **The source of this treasure** (1:17): It came as a perfect gift from the unchanging God, who "created all heaven's lights."
  B. **The salvation in this treasure** (1:18): We have become his children through this priceless gift.
  C. **The symbol for this treasure** (1:19-25): James compares the Bible to a mirror.

VI. JAMES SPEAKS OF TRUE RELIGION (1:26-27)
  A. **The fiction** (1:26): Some believe they can claim the name of Christ and continue to slander other Christians.
  B. **The facts** (1:27): James lists two (of many) signs indicating true religion.
    1. *Having compassion upon orphans and widows* (1:27a)
    2. *Keeping from the pollution of the world* (1:27b)

SECTION OUTLINE TWO (JAMES 2)
James discusses the subjects of godless favoritism and godly faith.

I. GODLESS FAVORITISM (2:1-13)
  A. **The command against favoritism** (2:1-8)
    1. *The examples* (2:1-4): His readers are guilty of the following sins:
      a. Treating rich visitors with great respect (2:1-2a, 3a)
      b. Treating poor visitors with no respect (2:2b, 3b-4)
    2. *The enigma* (2:5-7): James cannot understand this, for often it was the rich who persecuted them and ridiculed their Savior.
    3. *The exhortation* (2:8): James says, "Obey our Lord's royal command found in the Scriptures."
  B. **The consequences of favoritism** (2:9-13)
    1. *To break this law is to break all laws* (2:9-12).
    2. *To show no mercy is to receive no mercy* (2:13).

II. GODLY FAITH (2:14-26): James contrasts having only head faith with having head, heart, and hand faith.
  A. **Two examples of having only head faith** (2:14-20)
    1. *In regard to the destitute* (2:14-18): Head faith by itself is empty faith and attempts to minister to the poor by pious words not accompanied by works.
    2. *In regard to the demons* (2:19-20)
      a. The fiction (2:19a): "Do you still think it's enough just to believe that there is one God?"
      b. The facts (2:19b-20): "Well, even the demons believe this, and they tremble in terror!"

B. Two examples of having head, heart, and hand faith (2:21-26)
1. *Abraham* (2:21-24): He proved his faith by his willingness to offer up his son Isaac.
2. *Rahab* (2:25-26): She proved her faith by protecting the two Israelite spies.

SECTION OUTLINE THREE (JAMES 3)
James talks about the tongue.

I. IMPORTANCE OF THE TONGUE (3:1-2): Anyone who can control his or her tongue is a perfect (totally mature) person, able to keep the entire body in check.

II. ILLUSTRATIONS OF THE TONGUE (3:3-5)
   A. How it can control (3:3-4)
   1. *It is as a bridle to a horse* (3:3).
   2. *It is as a rudder to a ship* (3:4).
   B. How it can consume (3:5): It is like a spark, which, though small, can destroy a great forest.

III. INIQUITY OF THE TONGUE (3:6): It can be set on fire by hell itself, utterly corrupting and destroying its owner.

IV. INCORRIGIBILITY OF THE TONGUE (3:7-8)
   A. People have been able to train the brute creatures (3:7).
   B. No person has been able to train the tongue (3:8).

V. INCONSISTENCY OF THE TONGUE (3:9-12)
   A. The contradiction (3:9-10): It tries to do two things simultaneously.
   1. *It tries to praise God* (3:9a, 10a).
   2. *It tries to curse people* (3:9b, 10b).
   B. The conclusion (3:11-12): It cannot do these two things simultaneously.
   1. *Fresh water and salt water cannot flow from the same spring* (3:11, 12c).
   2. *A fig tree cannot bear olives* (3:12a).
   3. *A grapevine cannot produce figs* (3:12b).

VI. INSTRUCTIONS FOR THE TONGUE (3:13-18)
   A. The path it should follow (3:13, 17-18): In order to control the tongue, the owner should always allow God's wisdom.
   B. The path it should flee (3:14-16): The owner should never allow his or her tongue to be influenced by Satan.

SECTION OUTLINE FOUR (JAMES 4)

James discusses the pollution of the human heart and the solution to this problem.

I. THE POLLUTION IN THE HUMAN HEART (4:1-5, 11-13, 16-17)
   A. **The root of the problem** (4:1a): Envy and wicked desires.
   B. **The fruit of the problem** (4:1b-5, 11-13, 16-17)
      1. *Constant fighting and quarreling* (4:1)
      2. *Killings* (4:2a)
      3. *Total breakdown in prayer* (4:2b-3)
         a. Not asking God for spiritual things (4:2b)
         b. Asking God for sinful things (4:3)
      4. *World lovers* (4:4)
      5. *Grieving the Holy Spirit* (4:5)
      6. *Slandering* (4:11-12)
      7. *Boasting about the future* (4:13, 16-17)

II. THE SOLUTION FOR THE HUMAN HEART (4:6-10, 14-15)
   A. **Humble yourself** (4:6, 10): This act alone results in a twofold blessing.
      1. *God will give you grace* (4:6).
      2. *God will lift you up* (4:10).
   B. **Submit to God** (4:7a).
   C. **Resist the Devil** (4:7b).
   D. **Repent** (4:8-9).
   E. **Depend on God for the future** (4:14-15).
      1. *The wrong action* (4:14): James reminds his readers that no one knows what tomorrow will bring.
      2. *The right action* (4:15): James urges his readers to simply preface their plans by the following words: *"If the Lord wants us to."*

SECTION OUTLINE FIVE (JAMES 5)

James discusses the topics of the selfish rich, suffering, swearing, supplication, and soul winning.

I. THE SELFISH RICH (5:1-6)
   A. **The consternation of the selfish rich** (5:1-3a): James warns the rich of the future misery awaiting them.
      1. *Their very clothes will rot* (5:1-2).
      2. *Their gold and silver will corrode* (5:3a).
   B. **The cruelty of the selfish rich** (5:4-6)
      1. *They cheat their workers* (5:4).
      2. *They live in sinful luxury and self-indulgence* (5:5).
      3. *They condemn and murder innocent people* (5:6).
   C. **The condemnation of the selfish rich** (5:3b): Their greed stores up for them the fires of hell.

II. SUFFERING (5:7-11): James gives three examples of steadfastness in suffering.
   A. **From the soil** (5:7): "Be patient as you wait for the Lord's return. Consider the farmers who eagerly look for the rains in the fall and in the spring."
   B. **From the Scriptures** (5:10-11): "Job is an example of a man who endured patiently."
   C. **From the Second Coming** (5:8-9): "You, too, must be patient. And take courage, for the coming of the Lord is near."

III. SWEARING (5:12)
   A. **Negative** (5:12a): Don't swear by heaven or earth or anything else.
   B. **Positive** (5:12b): Let your answer be a simple yes or no.

IV. SUPPLICATION (5:13-18)
   A. **The exhortation to prayer** (5:13-16a)
      1. *Seasons of prayer* (5:13): When should we pray?
         a. In times of trouble (5:13a)
         b. In times of triumph (5:13b)
      2. *Reasons for prayer* (5:14-16a)
         a. Prayer will raise up the sick (5:14-15a).
         b. Prayer will restore the sinner (5:15b-16a).
   B. **The example of prayer** (5:16b-18)
      1. *The power* (5:16b): A righteous person's prayer is both powerful and effective.
      2. *The person* (5:17-18): James selects Elijah as his role model here.
         a. "Elijah was as human as we are, and yet when he prayed earnestly that no rain would fall, none fell for the next three and a half years!" (5:17).
         b. "Then he prayed for rain, and down it poured" (5:18).

V. SOUL WINNING (5:19-20)
   A. **The faithfulness of a soul winner** (5:19)
   B. **The fruits of a soul winner** (5:20): The person who turns another from sin has saved that sinner from death.

1 Peter

SECTION OUTLINE ONE (1 PETER 1)

Peter opens his first letter with an overview of some glorious facts concerning salvation.

I. THE SOURCE OF OUR SALVATION (1:1-2)
   A. **We have been chosen by the Father** (1:1-2a).
   B. **We have been made holy by the Spirit** (1:2b).
   C. **We are cleansed by the blood of the Son** (1:2c).

II. THE GUARANTEE OF OUR SALVATION (1:3-5)
   A. **The proof** (1:3): It is guaranteed by the resurrection of Christ.
   B. **The permanence** (1:4): It is kept in heaven for us.
   C. **The power** (1:5): God's mighty power assures us that we will safely arrive in heaven.

III. THE JOY OF OUR SALVATION (1:6-9)
   A. **The promise** (1:6): This joy can be ours even in the midst of trials.
   B. **The products** (1:7-9): Our trials produce a twofold fruit.
      1. *They increase our faith in God* (1:7).
      2. *They increase our love for God* (1:8-9).

IV. THE OLD TESTAMENT PROPHETS AND OUR SALVATION (1:10-12a)
   A. **What they did not understand** (1:10-11): They could not fully comprehend all their prophecies concerning the future work of the Messiah.
      1. *In regard to his grief* (1:10-11a)
      2. *In regard to his glory* (1:11b)
   B. **What they did understand** (1:12a): They knew that their prophecies would not be fulfilled until after their deaths.

V. THE ANGELS AND OUR SALVATION (1:12b): They long to know more about this wonderful subject.

VI. THE RESPONSE TO OUR SALVATION (1:13-17)
   A. **In regard to ourselves** (1:13): We are to be self-controlled.
   B. **In regard to our Savior** (1:14-17)
      1. *We are to be holy before God* (1:14-16).
      2. *We are to be respectful toward God* (1:17).

VII. THE COST OF OUR SALVATION (1:18-21)
  A. The price (1:18-19)
    1. *Negative* (1:18): It was not purchased with silver or gold.
    2. *Positive* (1:19): It was bought by the precious blood of Jesus.
  B. The planning (1:20-21): Christ was chosen before the foundation of the world to do this.

VIII. THE VEHICLE OF OUR SALVATION (1:22-25)
  A. The new birth (1:22-23a): One must experience regeneration to be saved.
  B. The old book (1:23b-25): It is God's Word that brings this about.

SECTION OUTLINE TWO (1 PETER 2)
Peter speaks of renouncing, relationships, respect, and a role model.

I. THE RENOUNCING (2:1-3, 11)
  A. What we are to renounce (2:1, 11b): We are to rid ourselves of deceit, hypocrisy, envy, slander, and worldliness.
  B. What we are to receive (2:2-3): We are to crave pure spiritual milk.

II. THE RELATIONSHIPS (2:4-12)
  A. What Christians are (2:5, 9a, 10-11a)
    1. *We are living stones* (2:5a).
    2. *We are royal priests* (2:5b).
    3. *We are a chosen people* (2:9a, 10).
    4. *We are strangers on earth* (2:11a).
  B. What Christ is (2:4, 6-8, 9b, 12)
    1. *He is the living foundation* (2:4a).
      a. He is a precious foundation for believers (2:4b, 7a).
      b. He is a stumbling block for unbelievers (2:8).
    2. *He is the cornerstone* (2:6, 7b).
    3. *He is the chosen one* (2:4c).
    4. *He is the judge* (2:12).
    5. *He is the light* (2:9b).

III. THE RESPECT (2:13-20): For the Lord's sake, we are to show respect (and submission) to the following parties:
  A. Civil authorities (2:13-16)
  B. Employers (2:18-20)
  C. Everyone (2:17)

IV. THE ROLE MODEL (2:21-25)
  A. Who he is (2:21-22): He is our sinless Savior, Jesus Christ.
  B. What he did (2:23-24a): He died on Calvary's cross.
  C. Why he did it (2:24b-25)
    1. *That his wounds might heal ours* (2:24b)
    2. *That we might turn to the Shepherd* (2:25)

SECTION OUTLINE THREE (1 PETER 3)
Peter talks about appropriate conduct for believers in light of what Christ has done for us.

I. THE CONDUCT OF BELIEVERS (3:1-17)
   A. Responsibilities of wives (3:1-6)
      1. *Peter's exhortation* (3:1-5)
         a. Concerning their behavior (3:1-2): Wives should depend upon their lives more than their lips in witnessing to unsaved husbands.
         b. Concerning their beauty (3:3-5): Inner beauty is far more important than outer beauty.
      2. *Peter's example* (3:6): He uses Sarah of the Old Testament as a role model.
   B. Responsibilities of husbands (3:7)
      1. *What they are to do* (3:7a): Husbands must be considerate of their wives and respect them.
      2. *Why they are to do it* (3:7b): If they fail here, their prayers will not be answered.
   C. Responsibilities of all (3:8-17)
      1. *Live in loving harmony* (3:8).
      2. *Reward both good and evil with good* (3:9-14).
      3. *Worship Christ as Lord, and always be ready to explain your faith* (3:15).
      4. *Be ready to defend your faith* (3:16-17).

II. THE CHRIST OF BELIEVERS (3:18-22): Peter describes a fourfold ministry accomplished by the Savior.
   A. His death (3:18)
      1. *The permanence* (3:18a): He died for our sins once and for all.
      2. *The purpose* (3:18b): He died to reconcile sinners to God.
   B. His journey to the spirit world (3:19-20)
      1. *The transgression* (3:19): Jesus preached against the sins of these evil spirits.
      2. *The time* (3:20): They committed their wickedness in the days of Noah.
   C. His resurrection (3:21)
      1. *The salvation* (3:21a): Jesus' resurrection guarantees our redemption.
      2. *The symbol* (3:21b): Water baptism.
   D. His ascension and exaltation (3:22)

SECTION OUTLINE FOUR (1 PETER 4)

Peter writes about suffering.

I. THE PURPOSE OF SUFFERING (4:1-11, 15, 17-18)
   A. **To cleanse and purify the spiritual believer** (4:1-11)
      1. *The triumph* (4:1-3): Suffering causes sin to lose its power.
      2. *The testimony* (4:4-6): The unsaved friends of a new Christian marvel that he does not desire to share their wicked lifestyle as he once did.
      3. *The tenderness* (4:7-9): Suffering should develop our love for other believers.
      4. *The talents* (4:10-11): We should faithfully employ all of our God-given spiritual gifts.
   B. **To chasten and punish the carnal believer** (4:15, 17-18): God will judge his people.

II. THE PRIVILEGE OF SUFFERING (4:12-14, 16)
   A. **It is to be expected** (4:12): All believers will be allowed to suffer.
   B. **It is to be esteemed** (4:13-14, 16)
      1. *To suffer for Christ means to share his past grief* (4:13a, 14a, 16a).
      2. *To suffer for Christ means to share his future glory* (4:13b, 14b, 16b).

III. THE PATIENCE IN SUFFERING (4:19): We are to do two things in the hour of pain.
   A. **We are to commit ourselves to God** (4:19b).
   B. **We are to continue to do good** (4:19a).

SECTION OUTLINE FIVE (1 PETER 5)

Peter gives advice for elders and other church members and sends his final greetings.

I. THE APPEAL BY PETER (5:1-11)
   A. **He writes to the elders in the church** (5:1-4).
      1. *The role model* (5:1): Peter himself is an elder in his church.
      2. *The responsibilities* (5:2-3)
         a. Feed the flock of God (5:2).
         b. Lead the flock of God (5:3).
      3. *The reward* (5:4): To receive a crown of glory from the head Shepherd himself.
   B. **He writes to the other members of the church** (5:5-11).
      1. *Live as a servant* (5:5-7).
         a. Be in subjection to your superiors (5:5).
         b. Be in subjection to your Savior (5:6-7).
      2. *Live as a soldier* (5:8-9).
         a. Recognize the enemy (5:8).

      b. Resist the enemy (5:9).
    3. *Live as a sufferer* (5:10-11).
      a. The duration (5:10): It only lasts for a short time.
      b. The dynamics (5:11): It makes one strong, firm, and stead-
         fast.

II. THE ASSISTANCE TO PETER (5:12-14): Silas, whom Peter considers a
    faithful brother, has helped Peter write this letter.

2 Peter

SECTION OUTLINE ONE (2 PETER 1)
Peter opens his letter by exhorting his readers to grow in the
knowledge of God and the Scriptures.

I. THE PROCLAMATION OF THE RIGHTEOUSNESS OF GOD (1:1-4): Peter
writes concerning our Christian faith.
   A. **The preciousness** (1:1-2): Great value is attached to our faith.
   B. **The power** (1:3): God has given us everything we need for living
   a holy life.
   C. **The promises** (1:4)
      1. *Protection* (1:4a): We will be delivered from the corruption of
      this world.
      2. *Participation* (1:4b): We will actually share in the Lord's divine
      nature.

II. THE MULTIPLICATION OF THE VIRTUES OF GOD (1:5-11): We are to add
these virtues to our faith.
   A. **The command** (1:5-9)
      1. *Positive* (1:5-8): These virtues are goodness, knowledge,
      self-control, perseverance, godliness, kindness, and love.
      2. *Negative* (1:9): If these are not added, we will become
      spiritually blind.
   B. **The certainty** (1:10-11): By doing this, we validate our own
   salvation.

III. THE REVELATION TO THE APOSTLE OF GOD (1:12-15)
   A. **What God has revealed to Peter** (1:12-14): The apostle knows
   he will die a martyr's death for Christ.
   B. **What Peter requires from us** (1:15): He wants us to remember
   the great spiritual truths in his epistles.

IV. THE TRANSFIGURATION OF THE SON OF GOD (1:16-18): Here Peter
reviews that marvelous event.
   A. **The glorious sight** (1:16): He was an eyewitness of Christ's
   splendor.
   B. **The glorious sound** (1:17-18): He heard the Father giving full
   approval of his beloved Son.

V. THE INSPIRATION OF THE WORD OF GOD (1:19-21)
  A. **Its accomplishments** (1:19): God's Word shines as a light in dark places.
  B. **Its author** (1:20-21)
    1. *It did not come from the biblical writers* (1:20-21a).
    2. *It did come* the biblical writers by the power of the Holy Spirit (1:21b).

SECTION OUTLINE TWO (2 PETER 2)
Peter writes about false religious teachers.

I. THE CORRUPTION OF THESE FALSE TEACHERS (2:1, 3a, 4-10, 12, 13b-17b, 22)
  A. **Their identity** (2:1a, 2, 4-9, 15-16)
    1. *Prophets and teachers* (2:1a, 2)
    2. *Fallen angels* (2:4)
    3. *The pre-Flood world* (2:5)
    4. *Sodom and Gomorrah* (2:6-9)
    5. *Balaam* (2:15-16)
  B. **Their iniquity** (2:1b-1c, 3a, 10, 12, 13b-14, 17a-17b, 22)
    1. *The symbols for these men* (2:12b, 13b, 17a-17b, 22)
      a. Brute beasts (2:12b)
      b. Stains upon Christianity (2:13b)
      c. Dried-up springs of water (2:17a)
      d. Unstable, storm-driven clouds (2:17b)
      e. Dogs returning to their vomit (2:22a)
      f. Hogs wallowing in the mud (2:22b)
    2. *The sin of these men* (2:1b-1c, 3a, 10, 12a, 14, 18
      a. Propagating destructive heresies (2:1b)
      b. Denying Christ (2:1c)
      c. Materialism (2:3a, 14c)
      d. Lust and adultery (2:10a, 14a)
      e. Pride and arrogance (2:10b)
      f. Scoffing at the "glorious ones" (2:10c)
      g. Blasphemy (2:12a)
      h. Seducing the unstable (2:14b, 18b)
      i. Boasting (2:18a)
      j. Hypocritical lying (2:19-21)

II. THE CONDEMNATION OF THESE FALSE TEACHERS (2:1b, 1d, 3b, 11, 12c, 13a, 17c)
  A. **They will be judged not by angels** (2:11).
  B. **They will experience a swift and terrible end** (2:1d).
  C. **They will be caught and destroyed like wild beasts** (2:12c).
  D. **They will be destroyed** (2:3b).

E. They will reap all that they have sowed (2:13a).

F. They will be consigned to the blackest darkness (2:17c).

SECTION OUTLINE THREE (2 PETER 3)

Peter describes three "worlds."

I. THE ANCIENT WORLD (3:5b-6): This world was destroyed by the great Flood in the days of Noah.

II. THE PRESENT WORLD (3:1-5a, 7-12, 14-18)

A. The documents (3:1-2): Peter has written both his epistles admonishing his readers to remember the great truths.

1. *The truths spoken by the Old Testament prophets* (3:1-2a)

2. *The truths spoken by the New Testament apostles* (3:2c)

3. *The truths spoken by the Savior himself* (3:2b)

B. The derision (3:3-5a): Peter warns that scoffers will appear during the last days.

1. *They will falsify the facts concerning the future fire judgment* (3:3-4): They will say, "Jesus promised to come back, did he? Then where is he?"

2. *They will deliberately forget the facts concerning the past flood judgment* (3:5a).

C. The destruction (3:7, 10, 12b)

1. *The fact of this destruction* (3:7): The same God who once sent the flood will one day send fire.

2. *The fury of this destruction* (3:10, 12b): It will utterly consume both earthly and heavenly elements.

D. The delay (3:8-9)

1. *The timelessness of God* (3:8): A day to him is as a thousand years, and a thousand years is as a day.

2. *The tenderness of God* (3:9): He is patient, not wanting anyone to perish.

E. The dedication (3:11-12a, 14-18): In light of all this, two biblical writers admonish believers to live godly and holy lives.

1. *Peter's exhortation* (3:11-12a, 14, 17-18): Grow in favor with the Lord.

2. *Paul's exhortation* (3:15-16): The Lord is waiting to return so that more people will have time to be saved.

III. THE NEW WORLD (3:13): This future earth will become the home of universal righteousness.

1 John

SECTION OUTLINE ONE (1 JOHN 1)

John opens his first letter with a presentation of Christ as both the life and light of believers.

I. JESUS CHRIST, THE LIFE OF BELIEVERS (1:1-4)
   A. **John's proclamation** (1:1-2): The apostle offers a twofold description of this divine giver of life.
      1. *The eternal Christ* (1:1a): He existed before the world began.
      2. *The earthly Christ* (1:1b-2): John saw, heard, and touched the physical body of the Savior.
   B. **John's purpose** (1:3-4): He writes this that we might know the two reasons for Jesus' incarnation.
      1. *The vertical reason* (1:3): That we might experience fellowship with both the Father and Son.
      2. *The horizontal reason* (1:4): That we might share our joy with one another.

II. JESUS CHRIST, THE LIGHT OF BELIEVERS (1:5-10)
   A. **The fact** (1:5): "God is light and there is no darkness in him at all."
   B. **The fruits** (1:6-10)
      1. *Negative* (1:6, 8, 10): If we walk in darkness with unconfessed sin, we will remain barren.
      2. *Positive* (1:7-9): If we walk in the light and confess our sin, we will be cleansed and fruitful.

SECTION OUTLINE TWO (1 JOHN 2)

John writes about the Savior, surety, sinful society, and the satanic one.

I. JOHN WRITES ABOUT THE SAVIOR (2:1-2, 24-25)
   A. **He is the forgiver of every sin** (2:1-2).
      1. *He died for the sins of the saved* (2:1-2a).
      2. *He died for the sins of the unsaved* (2:2b).
   B. **He is the giver of eternal life** (2:24-25).

II. John Writes about Surety (2:3-14, 28-29): How can we be sure that Jesus is indeed our Savior?
   A. **The guidelines** (2:3-11, 28-29)
      1. *We must obey God* (2:3-6).
      2. *We must love God and God's people* (2:7-11).
      3. *We must live holy lives for God* (2:28-29).
   B. **The groups** (2:12-14)
      1. *John writes to little children* (2:12, 14a).
      2. *John writes to fathers* (2:13a, 14b).
      3. *John writes to young men* (2:13b, 14c).

III. John Writes about Sinful Society (2:15-17): The apostle has in mind here the systems of this world.
   A. **The warning against these worldly systems** (2:15)
   B. **The wickedness coming from these worldly systems** (2:16): This wickedness is threefold.
      1. *The lust of the flesh* (2:16a)
      2. *The lust of the eyes* (2:16b)
      3. *The pride of life* (2:16c)
   C. **The worthlessness of these worldly systems** (2:17): They will all soon fade away.

IV. John Writes about the Satanic One (2:18-19, 22-23, 26)
   A. **The arrival of the Antichrist** (2:18)
      1. *Many antichrists have come* (2:18a).
      2. *The real Antichrist will come* (2:18b).
   B. **The apostles of the Antichrist** (2:19): They show their loyalty to him by departing from the Christian faith.
   C. **The apostasy of the Antichrist** (2:22-23, 26)
      1. *He will deny the true Christ* (2:22-23).
      2. *He will attempt to deceive true believers* (2:26).

V. John Writes about the Spirit (2:20-21, 27).
   A. **He teaches and anoints believers** (2:27).
   B. **He indwells believers** (2:20-21).

SECTION OUTLINE THREE (1 John 3)
John writes about salvation.

I. The Part Played by the Trinity in Bringing About Our Salvation (3:1-5, 8, 24b)
   A. **The role of the Father** (3:1-3)
      1. *He bestows his love upon us* (3:1a).
      2. *He calls us his own children* (3:1b-2a).
      3. *He will someday make us like Jesus* (3:2b-3).
   B. **The role of the Son** (3:4-5, 8)
      1. *He died for our sins* (3:4-5).

2. *He destroyed the works of the Devil* (3:8).

C. The role of the Spirit (3:24b): He now indwells us.

II. THE PART PLAYED BY THE BELIEVER IN WORKING OUT OUR SALVATION (3:6-7, 9-24a)

    A. The confirmation (3:6-7, 9-10)

        1. *Question* (3:6a, 7, 9): How can we know we are truly saved?

        2. *Answer* (3:6b, 8, 10): The one who lives in continuous sin is not of God.

    B. The compassion (3:11-18)

        1. *The exhortation to love* (3:11-15): Unlike Cain, who killed his brother, we are to love our spiritual brothers and sisters.

        2. *The extent of our love* (3:16-18): If need be, we should be willing to lay down our life for others.

    C. The confidence (3:19-24a): This obedience will give us great assurance as we approach God.

SECTION OUTLINE FOUR (1 JOHN 4)

John writes about discerning false prophets and loving one another.

I. LOCATE THE SPIRITS (4:1-6): We are to test those who claim to speak by the Spirit by asking whether their message comes from a false prophet, a demon, or from God.

    A. The scriptural claim (4:1-2, 4, 6): All messages acknowledging that Jesus Christ has come in the flesh are of God.

    B. The satanic claim (4:3, 5): All messages that do not are not of God.

II. LOVE THE SAINTS (4:7-21).

    A. What love proves (4:7-11, 14, 19-21)

        1. *Our love for God is proven by our love for one another* (4:7-8, 11, 19-21).

        2. *God's love for us was proven by the sacrificial death of Christ* (4:9-10, 14).

    B. What love produces (4:12-13, 15-18)

        1. *God is joined to us* (4:12, 15-16).

        2. *We are joined to him* (4:13).

        3. *We are given confidence* (4:17).

        4. *We are protected from fear* (4:18).

SECTION OUTLINE FIVE (1 JOHN 5)

John talks about a test, a testimony, and two transgressions.

I. THE TEST (5:1-5, 13-15, 18-21)

    A. The Question (5:13): How do I know I am born of God?

    B. The Answers (5:1-5, 14-15, 18-21)

     1. *The saved person believes Jesus is the Christ* (5:1, 5).
     2. *The saved person loves and obeys God* (5:2-4).
     3. *The saved person has his prayers answered* (5:14-15).
     4. *The saved person does not live in continuous sin* (5:18-21).

II. THE TESTIMONIES (5:6-12)
  A. As given by the Father and Spirit (5:6-9, 11-12)
     1. *Regarding the Son of God* (5:6-9): Jesus is the second person
       in the Trinity.
     2. *Regarding the saints of God* (5:11-12): We have eternal life in
       Jesus.
  B. As given by all believers (5:10): We must believe that Jesus is the
    Son of God.

III. THE TWO TRANSGRESSIONS (5:16-17): John gives direction on how a
    believer should pray for another believer who has committed one of
    these transgressions.
  A. A transgression that does not lead to death (5:16a): Here prayer
    should be made.
  B. The transgression that does lead to death (5:16b-17): Here
    prayer need not be made.

2 John

3 John

SECTION OUTLINE ONE (3 JOHN 1)

John addresses this epistle to an exhorter concerning an egotist and an example.

I. THE PERSEVERANCE OF GAIUS THE EXHORTER (1:1-8, 13-14)
   A. **John's prayer for Gaius** (1:1-2): That his physical body will be as healthy as John knows his soul is.
   B. **John's praise of Gaius** (1:3-8)
      1. *He has been faithful to God's message* (1:3-4).
      2. *He has been faithful to God's messengers* (1:5-8): Gaius has rendered much loving help to traveling teachers and missionaries.
   C. **John's plans concerning Gaius** (1:13-14): He will visit him in the near future.

II. THE PRIDE OF DIOTREPHES THE EGOTIST (1:9-11)
   A. **The evil** (1:9-10): John indicts this church member on six counts.
      1. *His demand to occupy the leading place* (1:9a)
      2. *His refusal to receive John himself* (1:9b)
      3. *His slander of the other apostles* (1:10a)
      4. *His unwillingness to entertain missionaries* (1:10b)
      5. *His attempts to excommunicate other believers* (1:10c)
      6. *His utterly wicked character* (1:10d)
   B. **The exhortation** (1:11): "Don't let this bad example influence you."

III. THE PERSONAL TESTIMONY OF DEMETRIUS THE EXAMPLE (1:12)
   A. **His associates hold him in highest esteem** (1:12a).
   B. **The apostle holds him in highest esteem** (1:12b).

IV. JOHN'S BENEDICTION (1:15): "May God's peace be with you."

Jude

SECTION OUTLINE ONE (JUDE 1)

Jude writes about apostasy.

I. THE BURDEN TO WARN AGAINST APOSTASY (1:1-3)
   - **A. Jude's prayer** (1:1-2): He asks God to grant his readers mercy, peace, and love.
   - **B. Jude's plan** (1:3a): He originally planned to write concerning God's wonderful salvation.
   - **C. Jude's perception** (1:3b): He then realized that the Spirit wanted him to warn against apostasy.

II. THE NEED TO WARN AGAINST APOSTASY (1:4a): Wicked apostates have secretly slipped in among the believers.

III. THE HISTORICAL EXAMPLES OF APOSTASY (1:5-6, 7b, 11): Jude lists six such examples.
   - **A. The nation of Israel** (1:5): Apostasy caused by unbelief.
   - **B. Fallen angels** (1:6): Apostasy caused by rebellion.
   - **C. Sodom and Gomorrah** (1:7b): Apostasy caused by sexual immorality.
   - **D. Cain** (1:11a): Apostasy caused by religious perversion.
   - **E. Balaam** (1:11b): Apostasy caused by financial greed.
   - **F. Korah** (1:11c): Apostasy caused by rejection of divine authority.

IV. THE CHARACTERISTICS OF APOSTASY (1:4b-4c, 8-10, 16-19)
   - **A. Changing God's grace into a license for immorality** (1:4b)
   - **B. Denying the deity of Jesus Christ** (1:4c)
   - **C. Degrading the human body** (1:8a)
   - **D. Rejecting authority** (1:8b)
   - **E. Slandering celestial beings** (1:8c-9): Here Jude gives a classic example underlining the seriousness of this particular sin.
      1. *The background* (1:8c-9a): The archangel Michael was disputing with Satan about the body of Moses.
      2. *The back-down* (1:9b): Michael refused to level a slanderous accusation against the Devil, leaving that to God himself.
   - **F. Degenerating into brute unreasoning animals** (1:10)
   - **G. Faultfinding** (1:16a)

H. Flattering others only for their own advantage (1:16b)
I. Scoffing and divisive, following their own evil instincts, which are totally devoid of God (1:17-19)

V. THE METAPHORS FOR APOSTASY (1:12-13)
   A. Dangerous reefs that can cause shipwrecks (1:12a)
   B. Self-centered shepherds (1:12b)
   C. Waterless clouds (1:12c)
   D. Dead autumn trees (1:12d)
   E. Wild waves of the sea (1:13a)
   F. Wandering stars (1:13b)

VI. THE DIVINE JUDGMENT ON APOSTASY (1:7b, 14-15)
   A. Past judgment (1:7a): Jude reminds his readers of the fiery judgment rained down upon the wicked cities of Sodom and Gomorrah.
   B. Future judgment (1:7b, 14-15): Jude predicts God's fire judgment on apostasy and reminds his readers of Enoch's prophecy concerning Christ's second coming.

VII. THE SAFEGUARDS AGAINST APOSTASY (1:20-25)
   A. The believer and self (1:20-21)
      1. *Believers are to build on the Word of God* (1:20a).
      2. *Believers are to pray in the power of God* (1:20b).
      3. *Believers are to remain in the love of God* (1:21).
   B. The believer and sinners (1:22-23): Jude instructs on how to deal with three types of sinners.
      1. *Those who are in great doubt* (1:22)
      2. *Those who are in great danger* (1:23a)
      3. *Those who are in great depravity* (1:23b)
   C. The believer and the Savior (1:24-25)
      1. *Jesus' ministry* (1:24)
         a. His current ministry (1:24a): Preventing us from falling down here.
         b. His coming ministry (1:24b): Presenting us faultless up there.
      2. *Jesus' magnificence* (1:25): "Glory, majesty, power, and authority belong to him, in the beginning, now, and forevermore. Amen."

PART EIGHT

Revelation

Revelation

SECTION OUTLINE ONE (REVELATION 1)
The resurrected Christ appears to the apostle John and tells him to "write down what you see, and send it to the seven churches." John presents his outline for the book: "The things that are now happening and the things that will happen later."

I. THE SERVANT OF GOD (1:1-10): The apostle John receives an extended heavenly message.
   A. **The source of this message** (1:1-2)
      1. *From the Father to the Son* (1:1a)
      2. *From the Son to an angel* (1:1b)
      3. *From the angel to John the apostle* (1:1c-2)
   B. **The promise in this message** (1:3): A special blessing is promised.
      1. *To those who read and obey its contents* (1:3a)
      2. *To those who hear and obey its contents* (1:3b)
   C. **The recipients of this message** (1:4a): It is written to the seven churches in Asia.
   D. **The greetings in this message** (1:4b-5a)
      1. *From the Father* (1:4b)
      2. *From the sevenfold spirit* (1:4c)
      3. *From the Son* (1:5a)
   E. **The theme of this message** (1:5b-8): Jesus Christ is its grand and glorious theme.
      1. *Who he is* (1:5b-5e, 8)
         a. God's faithful witness (1:5b)
         b. The firstborn from the dead (1:5c)
         c. Ruler of the kings of this earth (1:5d)
         d. The Alpha and Omega (1:8a)
         e. The Eternal One (1:8b)
      2. *What he has done* (1:5e-6)
         a. Shed his blood to redeem us (1:5e)
         b. Made us a kingdom of priests (1:6)
      3. *What he will do* (1:7): He will come again in the clouds.
         a. Revealing himself to the Jews (1:7a)

b. Revealing himself to the Gentiles (1:7b)
F. The place of this message (1:9): John was on the Isle of Patmos.
G. The time of this message (1:10a): It was on the Lord's Day.
H. The sound of this message (1:10b): "A voice like a trumpet blast."

II. THE SON OF GOD (1:11-20)
  A. The appearance by Jesus (1:11-16)
    1. *His command* (1:11): Again John is instructed to send the message to the seven churches in Asia.
    2. *His countenance* (1:12-16)
      a. He appears standing among seven gold lampstands (1:12-13a).
      b. He is wearing a long robe with a golden band across the chest (1:13b).
      c. His hair is white like snow (1:14a).
      d. His eyes are like blazing fire (1:14b).
      e. His feet are as burnished bronze (1:15a).
      f. His voice thunders like mighty ocean waves (1:15b).
      g. His right hand holds seven stars (1:16a).
      h. Out of his mouth comes a double-edged sword (1:16b).
      i. His face shines as the noonday sun (1:16c).
  B. The reassurance by Jesus (1:17-20)
    1. *Comforting* (1:17-18): He reassures the fear-stricken John.
      a. "I was dead but am alive forever and ever" (1:17-18a).
      b. "I hold the keys of death and the grave" (1:18b).
    2. *Clarification* (1:19-20): He explains what the lampstands and stars represent.
      a. The seven lampstands are the seven churches (1:20b).
      b. The seven stars are the angels of the seven churches (1:19-20a).

SECTION OUTLINE TWO (REVELATION 2)
John writes Christ's words to the first four churches.

I. THE CHURCH IN EPHESUS (2:1-7)
  A. The Counselor (2:1): Jesus holds the seven stars and walks among the seven lampstands.
  B. The commendation (2:2-3, 6)
    1. *Through hard work and patience, the church has performed many righteous deeds* (2:2a).
    2. *They do not tolerate sin in the church* (2:2b).
    3. *They allow only sound doctrine to be taught* (2:2c).
    4. *They have suffered for Jesus* (2:3).
    5. *They hate the practices of the Nicolaitans* (2:6).
  C. The chastening (2:4): They have, however, left their first love.
  D. The counsel (2:5)

1. *The procedure involved* (2:5a-5c)
   a. They are to remember their first love (2:5a).
   b. They are to repent (2:5b).
   c. They are to return to their first love (2:5c).
2. *The penalty* (2:5d): If this does not happen, their lampstand will be removed.
   E. The challenge (2:7): Jesus promises all overcomers would receive fruit from the tree of life in paradise.

II. THE CHURCH IN SMYRNA (2:8-11)
   A. The Counselor (2:8): Jesus says he is the First and Last, who was dead and is alive forevermore.
   B. The commendation (2:9)
   1. *They are persecuted and poor, yet they are rich* (2:9a).
   2. *They have been slandered by those belonging to Satan himself* (2:9b).
   C. The chastening: None given.
   D. The counsel (2:10): They are to remain faithful unto death and will receive a crown of life.
   E. The challenge (2:11): They will not be hurt by the second death.

III. THE CHURCH IN PERGAMOS (2:12-17)
   A. The Counselor (2:12): Jesus still carries his two-edged sword.
   B. The commendation (2:13)
   1. *They remain faithful even though living in Satan's headquarters* (2:13a).
   2. *One of their members, Antipas, had become a martyr* (2:13b).
   C. The chastening (2:14-15)
   1. *They are tolerating the teachings of Balaam* (2:14).
   2. *They are tolerating the teachings of the Nicolaitans* (2:15).
   D. The counsel (2:16): Repent or be punished.
   E. The challenge (2:17)
   1. *To partake of the hidden manna* (2:17a)
   2. *To be given a white stone with a new name* (2:17b)

IV. THE CHURCH IN THYATIRA (2:18-29)
   A. The Counselor (2:18): Jesus' eyes are as blazing fire, and his feet are like polished bronze.
   B. The commendation (2:19): Their works, love, faith, and patience have greatly increased.
   C. The chastening (2:20-23)
   1. *The wickedness* (2:20): They are allowing a false prophetess named Jezebel to teach immorality and idolatry.
   2. *The warning* (2:21-23): Unless they repent, both she and her followers will suffer both sickness and death.
   D. The counsel (2:24-25): Jesus tells the faithful there to hold on to what they have.

E. The challenge (2:26-29)
1. *They will help rule over the nations* (2:26-28a).
2. *They will be given the morning star* (2:28b-29).

SECTION OUTLINE THREE (REVELATION 3)
Christ speaks to the final three churches.

I. THE CHURCH IN SARDIS (3:1-6)
A. The counselor (3:1a): Jesus holds the seven spirits of God and the seven stars.
B. The commendation (3:4): There are some in the church that have not soiled their garments with sin.
C. The chastening (3:1b-2)
1. *They have a reputation of being alive but are dead* (3:1b).
2. *Their deeds are far from right in God's sight* (3:2).
D. The counsel (3:3): They are to remember, repent, watch, and wait, lest Jesus come upon them as a thief in the night.
E. The challenge (3:5-6)
1. *They will be dressed in white* (3:5a).
2. *Their names will be announced before the Father and his angels* (3:5b-6).

II. THE CHURCH IN PHILADELPHIA (3:7-13)
A. The counselor (3:7)
1. *The holy and true Jesus holds the keys of David* (3:7a).
2. *He opens closed doors and closes open doors* (3:7b).
B. The commendation (3:8)
1. *Though weak, they have kept his Word* (3:8a).
2. *They have not denied his name* (3:8b).
C. The chastening: None given.
D. The counsel (3:11): Hold on to what you have so that no one will take your crown.
E. The challenge (3:9-10, 12-13)
1. *Their enemies will fall down before them* (3:9).
2. *They will be kept from the hour of trial* (3:10).
3. *They will become pillars in the Temple of God* (3:12a).
4. *They will be given new names* (3:12b-13).

III. THE CHURCH IN LAODICEA (3:14-22)
A. The counselor (3:14): Jesus is the faithful and true witness, the ruler of God's creation.
B. The commendation: None given.
C. The chastening (3:15-17)
1. *The fallacies* (3:17a): This church boasts of their riches and concludes they stand in need of nothing.
2. *The facts* (3:17b): In reality, God views them as wretched, pitiful, poor, blind, and naked.

3. *The fury* (3:15-16): Because the church is neither hot nor cold, God threatens to spit them out unless they repent.

D. The counsel (3:18)

1. *They are to seek spiritual clothing from God to cover their nakedness* (3:18a).
2. *They are to seek spiritual medicine from God to heal their blindness* (3:18b).

E. The challenge (3:19-22): After their severe rebuke, God reassures the Laodiceans.

1. *He rebukes them because he loves them* (3:19).
2. *He promises to enter into their hearts if they will allow him* (3:20).
3. *He will then prepare a place for them on his throne (3:21-22).*

SECTION OUTLINE FOUR (REVELATION 4)
John describes his vision of glory.

I. THE SUMMONS TO HEAVEN (4:1)

A. The vision (4:1a): John sees a door standing open in heaven.
B. The voice (4:1b): A voice says, "Come up here."

II. THE SIGHTS IN HEAVEN (4:2-8)

A. John sees someone seated on a throne (4:2-3a): He has the appearance of a jasper and cornelian stone.
B. John sees an emerald rainbow above the throne (4:3b).
C. John sees many creatures surrounding the throne (4:4, 5b, 6b-8).

1. *Twenty-four elders* (4:4): They are dressed in white and wear golden crowns.
2. *Seven spirits of God* (4:5b)
3. *Four living creatures* (4:6b-8)
   a. Their description (4:6b-8a)
      (1) They are covered with eyes (4:6b).
      (2) The first has the appearance of a lion; the second, an ox; the third, a man; and the fourth, a flying eagle (4:7).
      (3) Each has six wings (4:8a).
   b. Their duties (4:8b): Day and night they proclaim the holiness of God.

D. John sees a crystal sea of glass in front of the throne (4:6a).
E. John sees a storm developing from the throne (4:5a).

III. THE SONG OF HEAVEN (4:9-11)

A. The singers (4:9-10): All the inhabitants of heaven.
B. The song (4:11): They worship God for his great work in creating all things.

SECTION OUTLINE FIVE (REVELATION 5)

John continues his description of his heavenly vision. The Lamb is declared worthy to open the seven-sealed scroll.

I. THE OBSERVATION (5:1): John sees a seven-sealed scroll in the right hand of the one upon his throne.

II. THE PROCLAMATION (5:2): A mighty angel asks if anyone is able to break the seals and open the scroll.

III. THE INVESTIGATION (5:3): An unsuccessful threefold search is made.
   A. In heaven (5:3a)
   B. On earth (5:3b)
   C. Under the earth (5:3c)

IV. THE LAMENTATION (5:4): John weeps over this.

V. THE CONSOLATION (5:5c): He is told someone is indeed worthy to do this.

VI. THE MANIFESTATION (5:5a-5b, 6-7): This someone now steps forward.
   A. Who he is (5:5a-b, 6): Jesus Christ.
      1. *He is called the Lion of Judah* (5:5a-b).
      2. *He is called the Lamb of Jehovah* (5:6).
   B. What he does (5:7): He takes the scroll from the right hand of the enthroned one.

VII. THE SUPPLICATION (5:8): The twenty-four elders fall down before the Lamb, holding gold bowls filled with the prayers of God's people.

VIII. THE EXALTATION (5:9-14)
   A. The song (5:9-10, 12, 13d-14): The lyrics praise God for his wonderful work of redemption.
   B. The singers (5:11-14)
      1. *Their diversity* (5:11)
         a. All of heaven's elect angels (5:11a)
         b. All of heaven's redeemed sinners (5:11b)
      2. *Their universality* (5:13-14)
         a. Every creature in heaven (5:13a)
         b. Every creature on earth (5:13b)
         c. Every creature under the earth (5:13c)

SECTION OUTLINE SIX (REVELATION 6)

The Lamb breaks the first six seals, sending God's judgments upon the earth.

I. THE FIRST SEAL (6:1-2)
   A. The announcer (6:1): The first living creature announces this judgment.

B. The action (6:2)
1. *John sees a white horse* (6:2a).
2. *Its rider goes out to conquer with a bow in his hand and a crown on his head* (6:2b).

II. THE SECOND SEAL (6:3-4)
A. The announcer (6:3): The second living creature announces this judgment.
B. The action (6:4)
1. *John sees a red horse* (6:4a).
2. *Its rider is given power to take peace from the earth* (6:4b).

III. THE THIRD SEAL (6:5-6)
A. The announcer (6:5a): The third living creature announces this judgment.
B. The action (6:5b-6)
1. *John sees a black horse* (6:5b).
2. *Its rider is holding a pair of scales, indicating a great famine is at hand* (6:5c-6).

IV. THE FOURTH SEAL (6:7-8)
A. The announcer (6:7): The fourth living creature announces this judgment.
B. The action (6:8)
1. *John sees a pale green horse* (6:8a).
2. *Its rider is death and hell* (6:8b).
3. *Millions will now die by the sword, famine, plagues, and by wild beasts* (6:8c).

V. THE FIFTH SEAL (6:9-11)
A. What John sees (6:9): He sees the souls of the martyred under heaven's altar.
B. What John hears (6:10-11)
1. *The request of the martyrs* (6:10): "When will you avenge our blood?"
2. *The reply of the Messiah (6:11):* The martyrs are told to wait a little longer, until "the full number of the servants of Jesus had been martyred."

VI. THE SIXTH SEAL (6:12-17)
A. What John feels (6:12a): A great earthquake strikes.
B. What John sees (6:12b-14)
1. *The sun turns black, and the moon turns blood red* (6:12b).
2. *The stars fall* (6:13).
3. *The sky rolls up like a scroll* (6:14a).
4. *Every mountain and island is removed from its place* (6:14b).
C. What John hears (6:15-17)
1. *The place* (6:15b): The sound comes from the caves and among the rocks of the mountains.

2. *The persons* (6:15a): They include kings, warriors, rich and poor, slaves and free men.
3. *The prayer* (6:16-17): They all cry to be hidden from the wrath of the Lamb.

SECTION OUTLINE SEVEN (REVELATION 7)

John witnesses the sealing of God's 144,000 witnesses, and he hears the praise song of an unnumbered multitude of those who have been saved during the Great Tribulation.

I. THE SEALING OF GOD'S SERVANTS ON EARTH (7:1-8)
  A. The sealers (7:1-3)
    1. *What John sees* (7:1-2a)
      a. He sees four angels holding back the four winds of the earth (7:1).
      b. He sees another angel carrying the seal of God (7:2a).
    2. *What John hears* (7:2b-3): The fifth angel instructs the four not to harm the earth or sea until God's servants have been sealed.
  B. The sealed (7:4-8)
    1. *The total* (7:4): One hundred forty-four thousand are sealed.
    2. *The tribes* (7:5-8): Twelve thousand from each of Israel's twelve tribes are sealed.

II. THE SINGING OF GOD'S SERVANTS IN HEAVEN (7:9-17)
  A. Who they are (7:11, 13-17)
    1. *A great unnumbered multitude* (7:13-17)
      a. Their salvation (7:13-14): They are saved during the Great Tribulation.
      b. Their service (7:15a): They continually serve God in his Temple.
      c. Their Savior (7:15b-17): The Lamb himself will feed, lead, protect, and comfort them.
    2. *Angels, elders, and the four living creatures* (7:11): These join with the great multitude in the singing.
  B. What they sing (7:9-10, 12)
    1. *They praise God for his great salvation* (7:9-10).
    2. *They praise God for his glory, wisdom, and power* (7:12).

SECTION OUTLINE EIGHT (REVELATION 8)

The seventh seal consists of seven trumpets, four of which are sounded in this chapter.

I. EVENTS PRECEDING THE TRUMPET BLOWING (8:1-5)
  A. The pause (8:1): There is a 30-minute silence in heaven at the opening of the seventh seal.

B. The prayers (8:2-4): An angel offers up much incense on the golden altar to represent the prayers of the saints.

C. The preview (8:5): A sample of the frightful punishment to come is seen as the angel casts fire from his censer upon the earth.

II. EVENTS ACCOMPANYING THE TRUMPET BLOWING (8:6-13)

A. First trumpet (8:6-7): One-third of the trees and grass are burned by hail and fire mixed with blood.

B. Second trumpet (8:8-9): One-third of the marine life and ships are destroyed by a burning object that falls into the waters.

C. Third trumpet (8:10-11): One-third of the fresh waters are poisoned, killing many people by a falling object known as Bitterness.

D. Fourth trumpet (8:12-13)

1. *The action* (8:12): One third of the sun, moon, and stars are darkened.

2. *The aftermath* (8:13): A flying eagle now warns the earth in regard to the final three trumpet judgments.

SECTION OUTLINE NINE (REVELATION 9)

The fifth and sixth trumpets are sounded, bringing two demonic invasions on the earth.

I. THE FIFTH TRUMPET, RESULTING IN THE FIRST DEMONIC INVASION (9:1-12)

A. The home of these demons (9:1-2): Their abode is in the smoke-filled bottomless pit.

B. The horror of these demons (9:3-12)

1. *Their appearance* (9:3, 7-10a)
   a. They look like locusts and horses armored for battle (9:3a).
   b. They wear golden crowns, and they have men's faces, women's hair, and lions' teeth (9:7-8).
   c. They are protected by iron breastplates (9:9).
   d. They have stinging tails like scorpions (9:3b, 10a).

2. *Their administrator* (9:11-12): Their king is named Abaddon (in the Hebrew) and Apollyon (in the Greek), meaning "destroyer."

3. *Their assignment* (9:4-6, 10b)
   a. Negative (9:4a): They are not to harm the grass or trees.
   b. Positive (9:4b-6, 10b): They are to torture (but not kill) the unsaved for five months.

II. THE SIXTH TRUMPET, RESULTING IN THE SECOND DEMONIC INVASION (9:13-21)

A. The action (9:13-19)

1. *The home of these demons* (9:13-14)
   a. Their location (9:13, 14b): They are now bound in an area near the Euphrates River.

b. Their leaders (9:14a): They are led by four special demons.
   2. *The hostility of these demons* (9:15)
      a. Their preparation (9:15a): They have been kept in readiness for a particular year, month, day, and hour.
      b. Their purpose (9:15b): Upon being released, they kill a third of all mankind.
   B. **The horror of these demons** (9:16-19)
      1. *Their number* (9:16): The army numbers 200 million warriors.
      2. *Their nature* (9:17-19): They have the appearance of horses and riders.
         a. The horses have heads like lions and tails like deadly serpents, and they breathe out smoke and flaming sulphur (9:17b-19).
         b. The riders wear brightly colored breastplates (9:17a).
   B. **The reaction** (9:20-21): How do the survivors of this horrible invasion respond after witnessing the death of untold millions?
      1. *They refuse to repent* (9:20a).
      2. *They continue to rebel* (9:20b-21).

SECTION OUTLINE TEN (REVELATION 10)

John is given a small scroll and is told to eat it. He does, and as predicted, it tastes sweet in his mouth but makes his stomach sour.

I. THE MESSAGES GIVEN BY THE ANGEL OF GOD (10:1-7)
   A. **The appearance of this angel** (10:1)
      1. *He is robed in a cloud with a rainbow over his head* (10:1a).
      2. *His face is as the sun and his legs as fiery pillars* (10:1b).
   B. **The actions by this angel** (10:2-7)
      1. *What he holds* (10:2a): He holds an open scroll in his hand.
      2. *What he does* (10:2b): He stands on the land and sea.
      3. *What he says* (10:3-7)
         a. First message (10:3-4): John hears what is said but is forbidden to write it down.
         b. Second message (10:5-7): The angel says God's message will be revealed at the sound of the seventh trumpet.

II. THE MISSION GIVEN TO THE APSOTLE OF GOD (10:8-11)
   A. **To partake** (10:8-9a): He is to eat the scroll held by the angel.
      1. *It will taste like honey in his mouth* (10:9b, 10a).
      2. *It will turn sour in his stomach* (10:9c, 10b).
   B. **To prophesy** (10:11): He is to write concerning nations, tribes, and kings.

SECTION OUTLINE ELEVEN (REVELATION 11)
John sees the two witnesses of God carrying out their 1,260-day
ministry before being murdered by the Antichrist. The seventh
trumpet is blown.

I. THE TEMPLE OF GOD (11:1-2)
   A. **The command** (11:1a): John is told to measure the Tribulation
      Temple.
   B. **The count** (11:1b): He is to number the worshipers.
   C. **The court** (11:2a): He is to exclude the outer court, which has
      been given to the Gentiles.
   D. **The contempt** (11:2b): The Gentiles will trample the Holy City
      for forty-two months.

II. THE TWO WITNESSES OF GOD (11:3-14)
   A. **The ministry of these two witnesses** (11:3-6)
      1. *The duration of their ministry* (11:3): They will prophesy for
         1,260 days.
      2. *The dedication of their ministry* (11:4): They function as God's
         two olive trees and lampstands.
      3. *The devastation caused by their ministry* (11:5-6)
         a. They devour their enemies by supernatural fire (11:5).
         b. They cause a three-and-one-half-year drought (11:6a).
         c. They turn waters into blood (11:6b).
         d. They strike the earth with plagues (11:6c).
   B. **The martyrdom of the two witnesses** (11:7-10)
      1. *The corrupt one causing their deaths* (11:7-9)
         a. Who he is (11:7a): He is the Antichrist himself.
         b. Where he comes from (11:7b): The bottomless pit.
         c. What he does (11:9b): He refuses to permit anyone to bury
            the witnesses' bodies.
         d. Where he does it (11:8): They lie in the streets of Jerusalem.
         e. Why he does it (11:9a): To show his utter contempt for the
            two witnesses.
      2. *The celebration following their deaths* (11:10): The entire
         world rejoices over their deaths.
   C. **The metamorphosis of the two witnesses** (11:11-14)
      1. *Resurrection* (11:11-12): They are raptured up into heaven.
      2. *Destruction* (11:13-14): An earthquake destroys one-tenth of
         Jerusalem, leaving seven thousand dead.

III. THE TRUMPET OF GOD (11:15-19)
   A. **The testimony of heaven** (11:15-18): All heaven praises and wor-
      ships God at the sounding of the seventh trumpet.
      1. *For his universal reign* (11:15-16)
      2. *Thanking him for his great power* (11:17)
      3. *For his righteous judgments* (11:18)
         a. In rewarding the saints (11:18b)

        b. In punishing sinners (11:18a, c)
  B. The Temple in heaven (11:19): John sees the Temple and the Ark of the covenant.

SECTION OUTLINE TWELVE (REVELATION 12)
John sees an interplay between a woman and a dragon, symbolizing the nation of Israel and Satan.

I. SATAN'S FORMER HATRED FOR GOD AND HIS PEOPLE (12:1-5)
  A. His sin at the beginning (12:3-4): This seems to refer to his original fall.
  B. His sin at Bethlehem (12;1-2, 4-5)
    1. *Satan's persecution of God's nation* (12:1-2)
    2. *Satan's persecution of God's Son* (12:4b, 5b)
      a. The birth of Jesus (12:4a, 5a)
      b. The ascension of Jesus (12:5c)

II. SATAN'S FUTURE HATRED FOR GOD AND HIS PEOPLE (12:6-18)
  A. The woman in the wilderness (12:6, 13-18): The woman here is the nation of Israel.
    1. *Israel will be persecuted by Satan during the Great Tribulation* (12:13, 15, 17-18).
    2. *Israel will be protected by God during the Great Tribulation* (12:6, 14, 16).
  B. The war in the heavens (12:7-12): Some believe this will occur in the middle of the Great Tribulation.
    1. *The results* (12:7-9)
      a. The defeat of Satan (12:7-8): Michael the archangel will defeat him.
      b. The dismissal of Satan (12:9): He will be cast down to earth.
    2. *The reaction* (12:10-12)
      a. Satan will be filled with wrath (12:10b, 12c).
      b. Saints will be filled with joy (12:10a, 11-12a).
      c. Sinners will be filled with fear (12:12b).

SECTION OUTLINE THIRTEEN (REVELATION 13)
John sees two beasts, one from the sea and one from the earth, symbolizing the Antichrist and his false prophet.

I. THE BEAST OUT OF THE SEA (13:1-10): This is the Antichrist.
  A. His appearance (13:1-2)
    1. *He has ten horns (each with a crown) and seven heads (each with a blasphemous name)* (13:1).
    2. *He looks like a leopard with feet like a bear and a mouth like a lion* (13:2a).

B. His authority (13:2b): It comes from Satan himself.

C. His (possible) assassination (13:3a): Some believe he will be killed and then rise from the dead.

D. His adulation (13:3b-4, 8): Following this the entire world is astonished and worships him.

E. His arrogance (13:5-6): For a period of forty-two months, he blasphemes God.

F. His activities (13:7, 9-10)

    1. *In regard to God's people* (13:7a, 9-10)

      a. The cruelty (13:7a, 9-10a): He persecutes and conquers them.

      b. The challenge (13:10b): They are exhorted to display endurance and faithfulness.

    2. *In regard to all people* (13:7b): He rules over them.

II. THE BEAST OUT OF THE EARTH (13:11-18): This is the false prophet.

A. His mission (13:11-12): With the appearance of a lamb but the voice of a dragon, he forces the world to worship the Antichrist.

B. His miracles (13:13, 15): He performs great miracles.

    1. *He calls down fire from heaven* (13:13).

    2. *He gives life to a statue* (13:14-15): This statue bears the image of the Antichrist.

C. His mark (13:16-18)

    1. *What it is* (13:18): It is the number 666.

    2. *Where it is applied* (13:16): Either on the right hand or forehead.

    3. *Why it is applied* (13:17): No one is able to buy, sell, etc., without it.

SECTION OUTLINE FOURTEEN (REVELATION 14)

The 144,000 sing a song of praise to God. John is given a preview of Armageddon, when Christ will return triumphantly to the earth and will wipe out his enemies.

I. THE SONG OF THE REDEEMED OF GOD (14:1-5)

A. What John sees (14:1)

    1. *The Lamb standing on Mount Zion* (14:1a)

    2. *The 144,000 standing with him* (14:1b)

B. What John hears (14:2-5)

    1. *Heavenly harps* (14:2)

    2. *Heavenly hosannas* (14:3-5): The 144,000 now sing a song no one else can sing.

II. THE MESSAGE OF THE ANGELS OF GOD (14:6-12)

A. The first angel's message (14:6-7): "Fear God. Give glory to him when he will sit as judge. Worship him."

B. The second angel's message (14:8): "Babylon is fallen."

C. The third angel's message (14:9-12)
1. *The plea* (14:9): "Don't receive the mark of the Antichrist."
2. *The penalty* (14:10-11): "Eternal torment in the lake of fire awaits those who do."
3. *The perseverance* (14:12): The angel urges God's people to remain faithful.

III. THE ASSURANCE OF THE SPIRIT OF GOD (14:13): "Blessed are the martyrs, for they will soon be rewarded."

IV. THE REAPING OF THE HARVEST OF GOD (14:14-20)
A. The Judge (14:14-15, 17-18a): Jesus himself is the reaper, accompanied by three angels.
B. The judged (14:18b): The unsaved and unrepentant of the earth.
C. The judgment (14:19-20)
1. *Sinners will be crushed as overripe grapes in a winepress* (14:19).
2. *Their blood will flow out in a stream 180 miles long and as high as a horse's bridle* (14:20).

SECTION OUTLINE FIFTEEN (REVELATION 15)
Seven angels prepare to pour out seven more judgments upon the earth. John hears the victors over the Antichrist singing a song of praise to God.

I. WHAT JOHN SEES (15:1-2a, 5-8)
A. He sees seven angels (15:1-2a, 6-7)
1. *Their assignment* (15:1, 7): They are to pour out God's final judgment, consisting of seven wrath-filled bowls.
2. *Their appearance* (15:6): They are dressed in clean, shining linen and wear golden sashes around their chests.
B. He sees a sea of fire and glass, upon which stand those who have been victorious over the Antichrist (15:2a)
C. He sees a smoke-filled Temple (15:5, 8)
1. *The entrance to the Holy of Holies is opened* (15:5).
2. *The Temple itself is closed to all until the bowl judgments are completed* (15:8).

II. WHAT JOHN HEARS (15:2b-4): He hears singing.
A. The singers (15:2b): Those who have been victorious over the Antichrist.
B. The song (15:3-4): It is the song of Moses, praising God for his justice, eternality, holiness, and righteousness.

SECTION OUTLINE SIXTEEN (REVELATION 16)
The seven angels pour out their seven judgment bowls.

I. FIRST JUDGMENT BOWL (16:1-2)
   A. The place (16:1-2a): It is poured out on the earth.
   B. The punishment (16:2b): Horrible malignant sores break out on those who have received the mark of the beast.

II. SECOND JUDGMENT BOWL (16:3)
   A. The place (16:3a): It is poured out upon the seas.
   B. The punishment (16:3b): The waters become as blood, killing all life in them.

III. THIRD JUDGMENT BOWL (16:4-7)
   A. The place (16:4a): It is poured out on the rivers and springs.
   B. The punishment (16:4b): These fresh water sources also become as blood.
   C. The proclamation (16:5-7): The angel now announces the reason for this, namely to avenge the blood of the martyrs.

IV. FOURTH JUDGMENT BOWL (16:8-9)
   A. The place (16:8a): It is poured out on the sun.
   B. The punishment (16:8b): The sun now scorches all people with its fire.
   C. The perversion (16:9): Everyone responds to this plague by cursing God and refusing to repent.

V. FIFTH JUDGMENT BOWL (16:10-11)
   A. The place (16:10a): It is poured out upon the throne of the beast.
   B. The punishment (16:10b): His entire kingdom is plunged into darkness.
   C. The perversion (16:11): Once again people refuse to repent.

VI. SIXTH JUDGMENT BOWL (16:12-16)
   A. The place (16:12a): It is poured out upon the great river Euphrates, and its waters dry up.
   B. The punishment (16:12b-14, 16): Demons deceive the kings of the east to march their armies westward across the Euphrates to prepare for Armageddon.
   C. The promise (16:15): A blessing is promised to those who prepare their hearts for Christ's return.

VII. SEVENTH JUDGMENT BOWL (16:17-21)
   A. The place (16:17a): It is poured out into the air.
   B. The proclamation (16:17b): There comes a voice from the Temple, saying, "It is finished!"
   C. The punishment (16:18-21a)
      1. *History's greatest earthquake now occurs* (16:18).
      2. *It splits Babylon into three parts* (16:19a).
      3. *The great cities of the world collapse* (16:19b).

4. *Islands vanish, and mountains are flattened* (16:20).
5. *Hailstones weighing seventy-five pounds fall from the sky* (16:21a).
   D. **The perversion** (16:21b): Unrepentant people continue to curse God.

SECTION OUTLINE SEVENTEEN (REVELATION 17)
John describes in highly metaphorical language a filthy religious prostitute.

I. THE INFORMATION IN REGARD TO THIS PROSTITUTE (17:1-6)
   A. **Her corruption** (17:1-2, 4)
      1. *She commits adultery with both potentates and people of this earth* (17:2).
      2. *She says blasphemous things about God* (17:4b).
      3. *She is utterly materialistic* (17:4a).
   B. **Her compromise** (17:3): She has aligned herself with the godless political systems of this world.
   C. **Her caption** (17:5): On her forehead is written, "Babylon the Great, Mother of All Prostitutes and Obscenities in the World."
   D. **Her cruelty** (17:6): She is drunk with the blood of martyrs she has murdered.

II. THE INTERPRETATION IN REGARD TO THIS PROSTITUTE (17:7-18)
   A. **What John sees** (17:7): He sees a woman riding a beast with seven heads and ten horns.
   B. **What John is told** (17:8-18)
      1. *The woman represents a corrupt religious system depicted by the city of Babylon* (17:8).
      2. *The beast represents various kings* (17:9).
         a. Some have already ruled (17:10-11).
         b. One king will be the most powerful (17:13).
         c. Ten kings are yet to rule (17:12).
         d. These kings will destroy the woman but will themselves be destroyed by the Lamb (17:14-18).

SECTION OUTLINE EIGHTEEN (REVELATION 18)
John witnesses the destruction of the city of Babylon.

I. THE REVELATION (18:1): An angel with great authority and splendor announces Babylon's destruction.

II. THE REASONS (18:2-3, 5, 7, 13b, 23c-24): The city is destroyed for its many sins.
   A. **It has become a den of demons** (18:2).
   B. **It is filled with immorality** (18:3a).

C. **It is materialistic to the core** (18:3b).
D. **Its sins are as high as the heavens** (18:5).
E. **It is totally proud and arrogant** (18:7).
F. **It has deceived the nations and killed the saints** (18:23c-24).
G. **It is buying and selling human slaves** (18:13b).

III. THE REMOVAL (18:4): God orders his people to leave this corrupt city.

IV. THE RETRIBUTION (18:6, 8, 10b, 17a, 19b): The city is destroyed by God himself.
   A. **The severity of the destruction** (18:6): She is given double punishment for all her evil deeds.
   B. **The suddenness of the destruction** (18:8, 10b, 17a, 19b): Fire from heaven consumes the city in a single moment.

V. THE REACTION (18:9, 10a, 11-16, 17b-19a, 20)
   A. **Great remorse by the unsaved** (18:9-10a, 11-19a)
      1. *What the merchants of the world cry out* (18:10a, 16, 19a): "How terrible, how terrible for Babylon, that great city!"
      2. *Why they cry out* (18:9, 11-15, 17b-18): Because there is no one left to buy their cargoes of precious metals, clothing, wood, ivory, brass, iron, marble, perfume, food, cattle, and even human slaves.
   B. **Great rejoicing by the saved** (18:20)

VI. THE RESULTS (18:21-23b): The city disappears from the face of the earth, resulting in:
   A. **No sound of music in Babylon** (18:21-22a)
   B. **No industry in Babylon** (18:22b)
   C. **No light in Babylon** (18:23a)
   D. **No joyous weddings in Babylon** (18:23b)

SECTION OUTLINE NINETEEN (REVELATION 19)
The Second Coming! Christ returns to earth and destroys his enemies. A vast crowd in heaven praises the Lamb.

I. THE CELEBRATION IN HEAVEN (19:1-10)
   A. **Praising the Lamb for his wrath on a corrupt whore** (19:1-5)
      1. *The reasons for this judgment* (19:2): This false religious system is condemned on two counts.
         a. Corrupting the earth with immorality (19:2a)
         b. Murdering the saints of God (19:2b)
      2. *The rejoicing over this judgment* (19:1, 3-5)
         a. The song (19:1b, 3, 4b-5): It consists of one great, grand, and glorious word: *"Halleujah!"*

b. The singers (19:1a, 4a)
   (1) A vast multitude (19:1a)
   (2) The twenty-four elders (19:4a)
B. Praising the Lamb for his wedding to a chaste wife (19:6-10)
   1. *The clothing of the bride* (19:6-9): She wears the cleanest, whitest, and finest of linens.
   2. *The chastening of the apostle* (19:10): John is rebuked for attempting to worship the angel who is revealing these things to him.

II. THE CONFRONTATION ON EARTH (19:11-21)
   A. The appearance of heaven's King (19:11): John sees Jesus, who is called Faithful and True, seated on a white horse, coming from heaven.
   B. The apparel of heaven's King (19:12-13, 15-16)
      1. *His eyes are like flaming fire* (19:12a).
      2. *He is wearing many crowns* (19:12b).
      3. *His robe is dipped in blood* (19:13a).
      4. *His titles* (19:13b, 16)
         a. The Word of God (19:13b)
         b. King of Kings and Lord of Lords (19:16)
      5. *He holds a sword in his mouth* (19:15)
   C. The armies accompanying heaven's King (19:14): They are dressed in finest linen and follow him on white horses.
   D. The avenging by heaven's King (19:17-21)
      1. *Jesus defeats the Antichrist and false prophet* (19:17-19, 21): Their armies are utterly routed.
      2. *Jesus destroys the Antichrist and false prophet* (19:20): Both are thrown into the lake of fire.

SECTION OUTLINE TWENTY (REVELATION 20)
Christ rules on earth for one thousand years. After the Millennium, Satan is finally defeated once and for all and is thrown into hell. The Great White Throne Judgment occurs.

I. THE GREAT CHAIN (20:1-3)
   A. The prisoner (20:1-2): An angel captures and chains Satan.
   B. The prison (20:3): The devil is confined to the bottomless pit for one thousand years.

II. THE GREAT REIGN (20:4-6)
   A. The resurrection of the just (20:4a): All those who were martyred during the Great Tribulation are now raised from the dead.
   B. The rule of the just (20:4b-6): They now reign with Christ for one thousand years.

III. THE GREAT REVOLT (20:7-10)
   A. The adversary (20:7): After the one thousand years, Satan is released from his prison.

B. The apostasy (20:8): He then goes out and deceives the nations.
C. The attack (20:9a): He and his armies attack Jerusalem.
D. The annihilation (20:9b-10)
   1. *Satan's henchmen are consumed by the fires of heaven* (20:9b).
   2. *Satan himself is consumed by the fires of hell* (20:10).

IV. THE GREAT THRONE (20:11-15)
   A. The Judge (20:11): The Savior is seen sitting on his throne.
   B. The judged (20:12-13): All the unsaved throughout human history are now judged.
      1. *The books in this judgment* (20:12a-12b)
         a. Various books (20:12a)
         b. The Book of Life (20:12b)
      2. *The basis of this judgment* (20:12c-13): Their deeds done while on this earth.
   C. The judgment (20:14-15): To be thrown into the lake of fire forever.

SECTION OUTLINE TWENTY-ONE (REVELATION 21)
John describes the new Jerusalem.

I. JOHN'S VISION OF THE NEW JERUSALEM (21:1-8)
   A. What he sees (21:1-2)
      1. *A new heaven and earth* (20:1)
      2. *The Holy City descending from heaven* (20:2)
   B. What he hears (21:3-8)
      1. *The words of the angel* (21:3-4)
         a. He says God himself will mingle among his people (21:3).
         b. He says God himself will minister to his people (21:4).
      2. *The words of the Almighty* (21:5-8)
         a. He will be the Father to all the saved (21:5-7).
         b. He will be the foe to all the unsaved (21:8): They will be cast into the lake of fire.

II. JOHN'S VISIT TO THE NEW JERUSALEM (21:9-27): The apostle records the following facts.
   A. John describes what he sees (21:9-18, 19-21, 26).
      1. *The city itself* (21:9-11, 18b): It is filled with God's glory and shines like a precious jewel and pure gold.
      2. *The gates and walls* (21:12-14, 18a, 21a)
         a. The gates (21:12b-13, 21a): There are twelve gates, each made of solid pearl, guarded by twelve angels. The names of the twelve tribes of Israel are written on the gates.
         b. The walls (21:12a, 14, 18a): The walls are made of jasper, supported by twelve foundations, on which are written the names of the twelve apostles.

   2. *The size and dimensions* (21:15-17)
      a. The city measures 1,400 miles long by 1,400 miles wide by
         1,400 miles high (21:15-16).
      b. The walls are two hundred feet thick (21:17).
   3. *The foundations* (21:19-20): Each of the twelve foundations is
      inlaid with a different precious jewel.
   4. *The street* (21:21b): It is made of pure gold, like transparent
      glass.
   5. *The worship* (21:26): All nations bring their glory and honor to
      the temple.
B. **John describes what he does not see** (21:22-25, 27).
   1. *There is no Temple there* (21:22).
   2. *There is no need of the sun* (21:23-24).
   3. *There are no closed gates* (21:25).
   4. *There is no impurity or evil* (21:27).

SECTION OUTLINE TWENTY-TWO (REVELATION 22)
John continues his description of the Holy City, New Jerusalem,
in this final chapter.

I. FACTS ABOUT THE CITY (22:1-2, 3a-3b, 5a, 14, 17)
   A. **Its river of life** (22:1-2a)
   B. **Its tree of life** (22:2b, 14)
   C. **Its throne** (22:3b)
   D. **Its purity** (22:3a)
   E. **Its divine light** (22:5a)
   F. **Its invitation to enter** (22:17)

II. FACTS ABOUT THE CITIZENS (22:3c-4, 5b)
   A. **We will see Jesus** (22:4).
   B. **We will serve Jesus** (22:3c).
   C. **We will reign with Jesus** (22:5b).

III. FACTS ABOUT THE CHRIST (22:6-7, 12-13, 16, 20)
   A. **His description of himself** (22:13, 16): Jesus refers to himself as
      follows:
      1. *The Alpha and the Omega* (22:13a)
      2. *The First and Last* (22:13b)
      3. *The Beginning and the End* (22:13c)
      4. *The root and offspring of David* (22:16a)
      5. *The bright morning star* (22:16b)
   B. **His provision for his saints** (22:6-7, 12, 20)
      1. *He will come for us* (22:6-7, 12a, 20).
      2. *He will reward us* (22:12b).

IV. FACTS ABOUT THE CORRESPONDENT (22:8-11, 18-19): What the
    author, John, says concerning himself.
   A. **In regard to his worship** (22:8-9)

    1. *He tries to worship the creature* (22:8): John falls down and attempts to worship the angel who is showing him the New Jerusalem.

    2. *He is told to worship the Creator* (22:9): The angel tells him to worship God alone.

B. In regard to his writings (22:10-11, 18-19)

    1. *He is told not to seal up the writings* (22:10).

    2. *All will continue to do as they have been* (22:11).

    3. *We are warned not to add to it* (22:18).

    4. *We are warned not to take from it* (22:19).